Dictionary of International Business Terms

Third Edition

John J. Capela, MBA
Assistant Professor of Business
St. Joseph's College
Brooklyn, New York

President, CADE International
East Northport, New York

Stephen W. Hartman, Ph.D.
Professor, School of Management
New York Institute of Technology
Old Westbury, New York

D0815145

BARRON'S

All inquiries should be addressed to:
Barron's Educational Series, Inc.
250 Wireless Boulevard
Hauppauge, NY 11788
http://www.barronseduc.com

Library of Congress Catalog Card No. 2003060505

International Standard Book No. 0-7641-2445-5

Library of Congress Cataloging-in-Publication Data
Capela, John J.
    Dictionary of international business terms / John J. Capela, Stephen
W. Hartman.— 3rd ed.
        p.   cm.
    ISBN 0-7641-2445-5
    1. International business enterprises—Management—Dictionaries.
2. International trade—Dictionaries. I. Hartman, Stephen. II. Title.
HD62.4C36 2004
382'.03—dc22   2003060505

PRINTED IN THE UNITED STATES OF AMERICA

9 8 7 6 5 4 3 2 1

CONTENTS

DEDICATION

Alan G. Hartman
The world is your oyster

Stephanie R. Hartman
The apple of my eye

My sons, John and Christopher Capela
Their never ending support is the reason this book has been
completed, with a special thanks to Christopher who assisted
in the identification of new terms for this third edition.

My mother and father, Caroline and John Capela
Two very important people who are greatly missed

My "Cioci" Mary who has always been there to provide
support in times of need, with a special thanks to my
Uncle Johnnie who will be missed.

Fred Schnaittacher and Gregory Marames
Two mentors who inspired my interest and career in
International Business

PREFACE

The global marketplace is a fast growing and rapidly changing field. What occurs in one part of the world immediately impacts the rest of the world. International business is exploding as a direct result of technological advancements, rapidly advancing economies, and international trade agreements. This reference book will provide individuals with the requisite knowledge and up-to-date information for entering or advancing in this challenging and highly rewarding global marketplace.

This book will serve as a comprehensive dictionary of more than 4,500 international business, trade and Internet terms. Terms found in the dictionary include the international dimensions of accounting, business policy and strategy, information systems and technology, marketing, management, finance, and trade. In addition, the third Edition has incorporated about 200 terms related to the topic of international terrorism.

This book will be an aid to anyone interested in international business, irrespective of their level of experience, including those involved in international trade, entrepreneurs, government administrators, and students.

As the result of telecommunications, we live and do business in a real-time environment. What occurs in one part of the world immediately impacts the rest of the world. International business is exploding as a direct result of technological advancements, rapidly advancing economies, and international trade agreements, including the North American Free Trade Agreement (NAFTA) and the General Agreement on Tariff and Trade (GATT). This book is directed at fulfilling a tremendous need for a reference resource to assist all those involved in this international business environment.

The terms are brief, concise, and understandable for those both experienced and inexperienced in international business. In addition, the book includes appendices containing a comprehensive listing of international information sources as well as samples of international trade sources. A partial listing of material contained in the appendices includes U.S. government trade-related offices, American and foreign Chambers of Commerce, international organizations, a multilingual reference table, a table of measurement conversions, and a listing of international business resources available on the World Wide Web.

The terms are succinctly defined, enabling the reader to quickly grasp their meaning and content. All entries are listed alphabetically, enabling the reader to quickly locate a particular definition. Terms defined in other parts of the dictionary are shown in SMALL CAPITALS.

The size and style of this book is meant to be user-friendly.

The authors of this book would like to thank Ms. Wendy Sleppin, Editor, and the entire editorial staff at Barron's Educational Series, Inc. for their consistently professional and enthusiastic support and guidance.

JJC and SWH

HOW TO USE THIS BOOK EFFECTIVELY

Alphabetization: All entries are alphabetized by word rather than by letter. For example, *advance payment* precedes *advanced technology codes*. When abbreviations or acronyms appear in the main text, they are used as cross-references to the actual term while also appearing in the list of international abbreviations and acronyms in Appendix A.

Where a term has several meanings, they are listed numerically by order of common usage.

Abbreviations: There is a separate list of international abbreviations and acronyms in Appendix A. It contains abbreviations found in the text referring to common international business and trading terms, business organizations, and government agencies.

Cross-References: Where applicable, other related terms in the context of the definition are referred to using SMALL CAPITALS. Normally, they are printed in small capitals only the first time they are referred to. Terms printed at the end of the definition may be similar or opposite to the defined term and are preceded by the words *see also*. For example, the definition for SOFT CURRENCY is followed by *see also* HARD CURRENCY. Where an entry is fully defined at another entry, a reference rather than a definition is provided: for example, FIAS *see* FOREIGN INVESTMENT ADVISORY SERVICE.

Parentheses: Parentheses are used for three purposes:
1. in entry titles to indicate that an abbreviation is commonly used with the same frequency. For example, FINES, PENALTIES, AND FORFEITURES SYSTEM (FPFS).
2. to add understanding to a term. For example, household effects (including personal computers), vehicles, and tools of the trade (including highly technical ones).
3. to clarify which definition is being referred to. For example, *see* GENERAL LICENSE (GTF–U.S.).

Examples: The examples are designed to illustrate international business concepts in a manner that is helpful to the reader.

Organizations and Associations: Those organizations and associations that play an active role in international business are included in the dictionary, along with a brief discussion of their mission and location. They are also listed by initials in the list of abbreviations and acronyms in Appendix A.

A

AADFI *see* ASSOCIATION OF AFRICAN DEVELOPMENT FINANCE INSTITUTIONS.

AAEI *see* AMERICAN ASSOCIATION OF EXPORTERS AND IMPORTERS.

AAIB *see* ARAB–AFRICAN INTERNATIONAL BANK.

AAR *see* AGAINST ALL RISKS.

AATPO *see* ASSOCIATION OF AFRICAN TRADE PROMOTION ORGANIZATIONS.

A.B. or **AKTB** *see* AKTIEBOLAGER.

ABANDONMENT the act of refusing delivery of a SHIPMENT so badly damaged in transit that it is worthless; damage to a vessel that is so severe that it is considered a CONSTRUCTIVE TOTAL LOSS. *see also* INSURED VALUE.

ABBROCHMENT the wholesale purchase of all merchandise intended to be sold in a particular retail market for the purpose of controlling that market.

ABC *see* AMERICAN BUSINESS CENTER.

ABEDA *see* ARAB BANK FOR ECONOMIC DEVELOPMENT IN AFRICA.

ABI *see* AMERICAN BUSINESS INITIATIVE; AUTOMATED BROKER INTERFACE.

ABOUT term used in a LETTER OF CREDIT construed to allow a difference not to exceed 10% more or 10% less than the monetary amount, or the quantity, or the unit price stipulated in the letter of credit. *see also* APPROX, CIRCA.

ABOVE THE LINE ITEMS *see* AUTONOMOUS TRANSACTIONS.

ABRAZO a term used in Mexico meaning to embrace. In Mexico and other Latin American countries, there is a greater degree of physical contact between members of the same sex. It is common for men to greet each other with an abrazo (embrace), whereas women may kiss. Hugs, pats on the back, and general physical contact are a part of communication in the Latin CULTURE.

ABROGATION a term meaning to nullify, suppress, or negate. The OVERSEAS PRIVATE INVESTMENT CORPORATION (OPIC) provides EXPROPRIATION insurance coverage, which protects against any abrogation, REPUDIATION, or BREACH OF CONCESSIONAL AGREEMENTS between the U.S. company and the foreign government.

ABSOLUTE ADVANTAGE a theory initially presented by Adam Smith stating that, because different countries can produce goods more efficiently than other countries, they should specialize and EXPORT those items that they produce more efficiently and IMPORT those items that they cannot produce or produce less efficiently. *see also* COMPARATIVE ADVANTAGE; NATURAL ADVANTAGE; ACQUIRED ADVANTAGE.

ABSOLUTE CONTRABAND *see* CONTRABAND.

ABSOLUTE QUOTAS a governmental limit on the quantity of goods that may enter into the commerce of a country within a specified period of time. When an absolute quota is filled, no further goods are allowed in during the specified time period. *see also* ESCAPE CLAUSE; GENERAL AGREEMENT ON TARIFFS AND TRADE (GATT); IMPORT QUOTA; TARIFF RATE QUOTAS.

ABSORPTION investment and consumption purchases by households, businesses, and governments, both domestic and imported. When absorption exceeds production, the excess is the country's CURRENT ACCOUNT DEFICIT.

ABTA *see* ASSOCIATION OF BRITISH TRAVEL AGENTS.

ABU DHABI FUND FOR ARAB ECONOMIC DEVELOPMENT (ADFAED) fund promoting economic and social development in African, Arab, and Asian developing countries. Created in July 1971 and beginning operations in September 1974, ADFAED headquarters is in Abu Dhabi, United Arab Emirates.

ABU SAYYAF a small Philippine Islamic group fighting to establish an Iranian-style Islamic state in Mindanao.

ACAB *see* ASSOCIATION OF CENTRAL AFRICAN BANKS.

ACC *see* ADMINISTRATIVE COMMITTEE ON COORDINATION; ARAB COOPERATION COUNCIL.

ACCELERATED TARIFF ELIMINATION a term used when countries agree to speed up TARIFF reductions in accordance with international trade agreements. The ultimate goal of any FREE-TRADE AGREEMENT is the total elimination of TRADE BARRIERS between countries by a certain date. At times, countries will submit requests to accelerate tariff elimination under the free-trade agreement. *see also* CANADA–U.S. FREE TRADE AGREEMENT; FREE TRADE AGREEMENT OF 1989; NORTH AMERICAN FREE TRADE AGREEMENT (NAFTA); TARIFF BARRIER; U.S.–ISRAELI FREE TRADE AGREEMENT.

ACCEPTABLE USE POLICY (AUP) many computer NETWORKS have policies that restrict the use to which the network may be put. An AUP of some networks does not allow commercial use. Enforcement of AUPs varies with the network. *see also* NATIONAL SCIENCE FOUNDATION.

ACCEPTANCE
1. a TIME DRAFT or bill of exchange that the DRAWEE has accepted and is unconditionally obligated to pay at maturity. The draft must be presented first for acceptance and then for payment.

2. drawee's act in receiving a DRAFT and entering into the obligation to pay its value at maturity.

3. an agreement to purchase goods under specified terms.

ACCEPTANCE FINANCING a method used by exporters to obtain financing on EXPORT transactions. An EXPORTER may need
- preshipment financing to produce or purchase the product or to provide a service or
- postshipment financing.

Banks or other lenders may be willing to buy TIME DRAFTS that a creditworthy FOREIGN BUYER has accepted or agreed to pay at a specified future date. Banks agree to accept the obligations of paying a DRAFT, for a fee; this is called a BANKER'S ACCEPTANCE. *see also* ACCEPTING BANK; DISCOUNTING; DISCOUNTING OF ACCEPTED BILLS OF EXCHANGE; DISCOUNTING OF DRAWING UNDER A LETTER OF CREDIT.

ACCEPTED BILL OF EXCHANGE *see* TRADE ACCEPTANCE.

ACCEPTED DRAFT a BILL OF EXCHANGE accepted by the DRAWEE (ACCEPTOR) by putting his or her signature (ACCEPTANCE) on its face. In doing so, the individual commits to pay the bill upon presentation at maturity. *see also* D/A SIGHT DRAFT; DRAFT; LETTER OF CREDIT.

ACCEPTING BANK a financial institution that endorses a SIGHT or TIME DRAFT for immediate payment. The accepting bank agrees to pay the value of the draft upon maturity or to discount it in favor of the beneficiary prior to maturity. *see also* ACCEPTANCE FINANCING; DRAFT; TRADE ACCEPTANCE.

ACCEPTOR a party that signs a DRAFT or obligation, thereby agreeing to pay the stated sum at maturity.

ACCESSION process by which a country becomes a member of an international agreement, such as the GENERAL AGREEMENT ON TRADE AND TARIFFS (GATT) or the EUROPEAN COMMUNITY. Accession to the GATT involves negotiations to determine the specific obligations a nonmember country must undertake before it is entitled to full GATT membership benefits.

ACCESSIONS goods affixed to and part of other goods.

ACCESSORIAL CHARGES charges made for additional, special, or supplemental services, normally over and above the LINE HAUL services.

ACCESSORIAL SERVICES services performed by a shipping line or airline in addition to the normal transportation service.

ACCOMMODATION
1. arrangement or engagement made as a favor to another, not dependent upon a consideration received.
2. note or BILL OF EXCHANGE or BANKER'S ACCEPTANCE that is endorsed, accepted, or drawn by one party (the accommodating party) to

benefit another party. The accommodating party generally does not charge or seek compensation for this act.

ACCOMMODATING TRANSACTIONS below the line items used in international transactions to offset imbalances experienced in international TRADE. For example, if a country has a TRADE DEFICIT in a given quarter, then gold, official foreign currency reserves, and/or official debt are used as the accommodating transaction to balance international cash flows. *see also* AUTONOMOUS TRANSACTIONS; BALANCE OF PAYMENTS.

ACCORD *see* INTERNATIONAL AGREEMENTS.

ACCORD-CADRE (French) *see* FRAMEWORK AGREEMENT.

ACCORD-CADRE FRAMEWORK AGREEMENT (French) a type of collective agreement, otherwise known as a FRAMEWORK AGREEMENT, establishing the goals, patterns, and matters of future collective bargaining between the parties negotiating the agreement and for other secondary levels of collective bargaining. In France these agreements are typically reached both at the level of the overall economy and at individual sectorial levels. The terms *accord d'orientation* and *accord de mithode* have the same meaning. The first framework agreements occurred in the 1970s in order to foster collective bargaining and to organize and coordinate the various bargaining levels. More recently there has been a proliferation of framework agreements where collective bargaining is not considered to be sufficient in the areas of technological change, duration and organization of working time, and vocational training.

ACCORD AND SATISFACTION means of discharging a CONTRACT or cause of action by which the parties agree (the accord) to alter their obligations and then perform (the satisfaction) the new obligations.

ACCORD DE PARTICIPATION (French) *see* PROFIT SHARING.

ACCOUNT NUMBER identifying number issued by a CARRIER'S accounting office to identify a SHIPPER and/or CONSIGNEE.

ACCOUNT PARTY APPLICANT at whose request a bank issues a LETTER OF CREDIT (L/C).

ACCOUNTING EXPOSURE a risk of depreciation or appreciation of entries appearing on an accounting statement due to FOREIGN EXCHANGE fluctuations. *see also* ECONOMIC EXPOSURE; EXCHANGE RATE; FLOATING EXCHANGE RATE; TRANSACTION EXPOSURE; TRANSLATION EXPOSURE.

ACCREDITIEF (Dutch) *see* LETTER OF CREDIT.

ACCREDITIF (French) *see* LETTER OF CREDIT.

ACCRUAL OF OBLIGATION maturing of an obligation to the date when the obligated party must perform (e.g., as a time draft which must be paid by the drawee on the date stated).

ACCULTURATION a process of adapting to the cultural differences of a HOST COUNTRY. *see also* CULTURE; ETHNOCENTRISM; POLYCENTRISM.

ACCT *see* AGENCE DE COOPERATION CULTERELLE ET TECHNIQUE.

ACDA *see* ARMS CONTROL AND DISARMAMENT AGENCY.

ACE *see* AUTOMATED COMMERCIAL ENVIRONMENT.

ACEP *see* ADVISORY COMMITTEE ON EXPORT POLICY.

ACM *see* ARAB COMMON MARKET.

ACQUIRED ADVANTAGE a trade theory that states that a country acquires an advantage in the production of goods through technology rather than available resources. *see also* ABSOLUTE ADVANTAGE; COMPARATIVE ADVANTAGE; NATURAL ADVANTAGE.

ACQUIRED GROUP MEMBERSHIP cultural affiliations not determined by birth: examples include religious, political affiliation, professional and other membership associations. *see also* ASCRIBED GROUP MEMBERSHIP; CULTURE.

ACQUISITION the taking over of one company by another company.

ACROSS THE BOARD TARIFF REDUCTIONS an agreement between GATT members to reduce all TARIFFS by a fixed percentage in all member countries. *see also* GENERAL AGREEMENT ON TARIFF AND TRADE (GATT); ITEM-BY-ITEM TARIFF REDUCTIONS; LINEAR REDUCTION IN TARIFFS.

ACT *see* AMAZONIAN COOPERATION TREATY.

ACT OF GOD an act of nature beyond man's control such as lightning, flood, earthquake, or hurricane. Many SHIPPING and other performance CONTRACTS include a FORCE MAJEURE clause that excuses a party who breaches the CONTRACT due to acts of God. *see also* CASUS MAJOR.

ACT OF STATE DOCTRINE international law that states that a sovereign country can legally do what it likes within its own borders. *see also* SOVEREIGN.

ACTION EX CONTRACTU legal action for breach of a promise stated in an express or implied CONTRACT.

ACTION EX DELICTO
1. a legal action for a breach of a DUTY that is not stated in a CONTRACT but arises from the contract.
2. a legal action that arises from a wrongful act, such as fraud.

ACTIVE INCOME income derived from the ongoing activity of trade or business. *see also* PASSIVE INCOME.

ACTPN *see* ADVISORY COMMITTEE ON TRADE POLICY AND NEGOTIATIONS.

ACTUAL VALUE the value for CUSTOMS purposes of imported goods based on similar or like values of goods offered for sale in competitive situations.

ACU *see* ASIAN CLEARING UNION.

AD VALOREM according to value. Any charge, tax, or DUTY that is applied as a percentage of value. Example: a 10% ad valorem tax applied to an item valued at $100.00 (10% × 100) would equal $10.00.

AD VALOREM DUTY (AD VAL) *see* AD VALOREM; DUTY.

AD VALOREM EQUIVALENT (AVE) rate of DUTY that would have been required on dutiable IMPORTS if the U.S. CUSTOMS value of such imports were based on the U.S. PORT OF ENTRY value.

ADAPTATION a global marketing strategy wherein the producer adapts products or services to the needs of foreign consumers. Adaptation can occur in areas such as packaging, pricing, sales promotion, advertising, distribution, and sales service. *see also* STANDARDIZE.

ADB *see* ASIAN DEVELOPMENT BANK.

ADDRESS three types of INTERNET common addresses:
- E-MAIL ADDRESS.
- IP, INTERNET, OR INTERNET ADDRESS.
- hardware or MAC ADDRESS.

ADDRESS OF RECORD official or primary location for an individual, company, or other organization.

ADELA GROUP (ADELA) Atlantic Community Development Group for Latin America (Fondo De Desarollo De La Comunidad Atlantica Para America Latina).

ADF *see* AFRICAN DEVELOPMENT FOUNDATION; ASIAN DEVELOPMENT FUND.

ADFAED *see* ABU DHABI FUND FOR ARAB ECONOMIC DEVELOPMENT.

ADHESION CONTRACT CONTRACT with standard, often printed, terms for sale of goods and services offered to consumers who usually cannot negotiate any of the terms and cannot acquire the product unless they agree to the terms.

ADJUDICATION a process of settling disputes through a recognized court. *see also* ARBITRATION, INTERNATIONAL COURT OF JUSTICE (ICJ).

ADJUSTABLE PEG a system of FIXED EXCHANGE RATES with occasional DEVALUATION when situations warrant.

ADJUSTMENT *see* ADJUSTMENT POLICIES.

ADJUSTMENT ASSISTANCE financial training and reemployment technical assistance to workers, including technical assistance to firms and industries, to help them cope with adjustment difficulties arising from increased IMPORT competition; *see also* TRADE ACT OF 1974; TRADE ADJUSTMENT ASSISTANCE (TAA).

ADJUSTMENT POLICIES measures taken by governments to correct a BALANCE OF PAYMENT disequilibrium. *see also* EXCHANGE CONTROLS; FISCAL POLICY; MONETARY POLICY; NONTARIFF BARRIERS (NTBS); TARIFF BARRIERS; VOLUNTARY EXPORT RESTRAINTS (VER).

ADMINISTRACION NACIONAL DE TELECOMUNICATIONES (ANTEL) a company that supplies telephone and telecommunications in Uruguay. ANTEL operates a network of domestic and international direct dialing telephone, TELEX, telefax, and data transmission services.

ADMINISTRATIVE AGENCY government unit accountable and responsible for the implementation of legislation. For example, the U.S. INTERNATIONAL TRADE COMMISSION (ITC) is an administrative agency responsible for the investigation of DUMPING complaints brought to its attention by industries in the United States. *see also* ADMINISTRATIVE LAW; TRADE ACT OF 1974.

ADMINISTRATIVE COMMITTEE ON COORDINATION (ACC) the ACC was established by the UNITED NATIONS in 1946 and is composed of the Secretary-General of the United Nations and the executive heads of the specialized agencies and the INTERNATIONAL ATOMIC ENERGY AGENCY (IAEA). Its purpose is to supervise the implementation of the agreements between the United Nations and the specialized agencies as well as to ensure the full coordination of activities of these bodies. The ACC carries out its work through its set of committees, sub-committees, and ad hoc bodies to perform particular tasks.

ADMINISTRATIVE EXCEPTION NOTES description of COMMODITIES that can be approved solely at a nation's discretion. Using national discretion (also called administrative exception), a member nation of the COORDINATING COMMITTEE FOR MULTILATERAL EXPORT CONTROLS (COCOM) may approve COMMODITY exports on its own, but COCOM must be notified after the fact.

ADMINISTRATIVE LAW legislation governing the actions of administrative agencies. *see also* ADMINISTRATIVE AGENCY.

ADMINISTRATIVE LAW JUDGE a jurist responsible for overseeing civil matters in the United States. *see also* DETERMINATION.

ADMINISTRATIVE NOTES *see* ADMINISTRATIVE EXCEPTION NOTES.

ADMINISTRATIVE PROTECTIVE ORDER (APO) protective order issued by an American federal administrative agency to protect proprietary data obtained during an administrative proceeding. Within the U.S. DEPARTMENT OF COMMERCE, APO is most frequently used in connection with the ANTIDUMPING/COUNTERVAILING DUTY SYSTEM and COUNTERVAILING DUTY investigations to prohibit opposing counsel from releasing data. The term is also applied in connection with the civil enforcement of EXPORT control laws to protect against the disclosure of sensitive national security information and information provided by companies being investigated for violations.

ADMINISTRATIVE REVIEW annual review and determination by the U.S. DEPARTMENT OF COMMERCE'S INTERNATIONAL TRADE ADMINISTRATION of the amount of any ANTIDUMPING DUTY, beginning on the anniversary of the date of publication of an ANTIDUMPING DUTY ORDER, if an interested party requests such a review. The results of this review are published in the U.S. FEDERAL REGISTER noting any antidumping duty to be assessed, estimated DUTY to be deposited, or a suspended investigation to be resumed. *see also* TARIFF ACT OF 1930.

ADMIRALTY any civil or criminal matter having to do with maritime law.

ADMIRALTY COURT court of law that has jurisdiction over maritime legal issues.

ADMISSION TEMPORAIRE free entry of normally DUTIABLE goods. *see also* AD VALOREM DUTY; COMPOUND DUTY; DUTY; SPECIFIC DUTY.

ADRs *see* ADVANCE DETERMINATION RULINGS; AMERICAN DEPOSITORY RECEIPTS.

ADS *see* AGENT/DISTRIBUTOR SERVICE.

ADUANA Spanish term for customs. Aduana is also used when referring to CUSTOMS DUTY.

ADVANCE AGAINST COLLECTION short-term loan or credit extended to a seller (usually the exporter) by the seller's bank after the buyer (generally the importer) has accepted a DRAFT.

ADVANCE ARRANGEMENTS transportation arrangements for CARGO that requires special handling (e.g., hazardous cargo, overweight, oversized, over normal quantity, time sensitive, shipped unpacked, live animals). Not every carrier can or will transport every kind of cargo.

ADVANCE DEPOSIT ACCOUNT/EXPRESS MAIL a centralized advance deposit account at the U.S. Postal Service for International Express Mail.

ADVANCE DETERMINATION RULINGS (ADRs) an application to the U.S. Internal Revenue Service to determine whether or not the TRANSFER PRICE policy of a MULTINATIONAL CORPORATION is appropriate.

ADVANCE IMPORT DEPOSITS a form of FOREIGN EXCHANGE control requiring importers to deposit a percentage of the value of the product being imported for a required period of time. This method is used in countries that have limited amounts of FOREIGN EXCHANGE. *see also* CONVERTIBLE CURRENCY; HARD CURRENCY; IMPORT LICENSE; SOFT CURRENCY.

ADVANCE PAYMENT *see* PAYMENT IN ADVANCE.

ADVANCED TECHNOLOGY CODES *see* ADVANCED TECHNOLOGY PRODUCTS.

ADVANCED TECHNOLOGY PRODUCTS 500 of some 22,000 COMMODITY classification codes used in reporting U.S. merchandise TRADE are identified with advanced technology codes if they meet the following criteria:
- The code contains products whose technology is from a recognized high-technology field (e.g., biotechnology);
- These products represent leading edge technology in that field; and
- Such products constitute a significant part of all items covered in the selected classification code.

ADVICE
1. report from one party informing another party of an occurrence of some business transaction (e.g., shipment, collection, or manufacture).
2. notification by an advising bank on behalf of the issuing bank informing a beneficiary of the terms of a LETTER OF CREDIT (L/C).

ADVICE OF ACCEPTANCE statement from the collecting BANK to the bank from which the COLLECTION ORDER was received confirming the amount, amounts collected, charges, disbursements, expenses, and disposal of funds. *see also* ADVICE OF FATE.

ADVICE OF FATE statement from the collecting BANK to the bank from which the COLLECTION ORDER was received confirming the status of the collection. *see also* ADVICE OF ACCEPTANCE; ADVICE OF NONACCEPTANCE.

ADVICE OF NONACCEPTANCE statement sent by the collecting BANK to the bank from which the COLLECTION ORDER was received advising nonpayment or nonacceptance. *see also* ADVICE OF FATE.

ADVICE OF NONPAYMENT *see* ADVICE OF NONACCEPTANCE.

ADVISED CREDIT LETTER OF CREDIT whose terms and conditions have been confirmed by a BANK.

ADVISING BANK a BANK, operating in the EXPORTER's country, that handles LETTERS OF CREDIT for a foreign bank by notifying the exporter firm that the credit has been opened in its favor. The advising bank fully informs the exporter of the conditions of the letter of credit without necessarily bearing responsibility. *see also* BENEFICIARY.

ADVISORY COMMITTEE FOR THE CO-ORDINATION OF INFORMATION SYSTEMS (ACCIS) a UNITED NATIONS subcommittee of the UN ADMINISTRATIVE COMMITTEE ON COORDINATION (ACC) and composed of representatives of all participating United Nations organizations. Established in 1983, ACCIS works to facilitate access by member states to United Nations' information and to promote the improvement of the information infrastructure within the United

Nations system. Its mandate includes an advisory service to United Nations system organizations on proposals for the creation of new information systems, seeking to avoid unnecessary duplication within the current United Nations system. Working through temporary technical panels, ACCIS promotes the use of common standards to enhance compatibility of information systems.

ADVISORY COMMITTEE ON EXPORT POLICY (ACEP) U.S. federal interagency dispute resolution body that operates at the Assistant Secretary level. ACEP is chaired by the U.S. DEPARTMENT OF COMMERCE. Its membership includes the U.S. Departments of Defense, Energy, and State; the Arms Control and Disarmament Agency; and the intelligence community. Disputes not resolved by the ACEP must be addressed by the EXPORT ADMINISTRATION REVIEW BOARD within specific time frames set forth under a U.S. National Security Directive.

ADVISORY COMMITTEE ON TRADE POLICY AND NEGOTIATIONS (ACTPN) committee (membership of 45; 2-year terms) appointed by the President of the United States to provide advice on matters of TRADE policy and related issues, including TRADE AGREEMENTS. The TRADE ACT OF 1974 requires the ACTPN's establishment and broad representation of key economic sectors affected by trade. Below the ACTPN are seven policy committees: SPAC (Services Policy Advisory Committee), INPAC (Investment Policy Advisory Committee), IGPAC (Intergovernmental Policy Advisory Committee), IPAC (Industry Policy Advisory Committee), APAC (Agriculture Policy Advisory Committee), LAC (Labor Advisory Committee), and DPAC (Defense Policy Advisory Committee). Below the policy committees are sectoral, technical, and functional advisory committees. *see also* INDUSTRY CONSULTATIONS PROGRAM.

ADVISORY NOTES *see* ADMINISTRATIVE EXCEPTION NOTES.

ADVOCACY CENTER center, established in November 1993, facilitating high-level U.S. official advocacy to assist U.S. firms competing for major projects and procurements worldwide. Located in the U.S. Commerce Department, the Advocacy Center is directed by the Trade Promotion Coordinating Committee, Washington, DC. *see also* TRADE PROMOTION COORDINATING COMMITTEE.

AEF *see* AFRICA ENTERPRISE FUND.

AEROMEXICO Mexican airline serving international travelers. They also offer charter and CARGO service through subsidiaries Mextur and Mexpress.

AERP *see* AUTOMATED EXPORT REPORTING PROGRAM.

AESTHETICS that part of a country's CULTURE concerned with beauty and good taste. Aesthetics has implications in international business in areas such as the design of the manufacturing facility, product, and package design.

AFC *see* AFRICAN GROUNDNUT COUNCIL.

AFDB *see* AFRICAN DEVELOPMENT BANK.

AFESD *see* ARAB FUND FOR ECONOMIC AND SOCIAL DEVELOPMENT.

AFFILIATE business enterprise located in one country directly or indirectly owned or controlled by a person or company of another country having 10% or more of its voting securities for an incorporated business enterprise or an equivalent interest for an unincorporated business enterprise, including a branch. The affiliate for foreign investment is referred to as a FOREIGN AFFILIATE. A domestic investment affiliate in the United States is referred to as a U.S. AFFILIATE.

AFFILIATED COMPANY *see* SUBSIDIARY.

AFFILIATED FOREIGN GROUP group that is either the foreign parent organization or is controlled by any foreign person or persons having more than 50% ownership.

AFFIRMATIVE ACTION policies used in recruitment and promotion of employees that are designed for the purpose of eliminating the effects of past discrimination. The policies started in 1964 with the passage of the U.S. Civil Rights Act. *see also* EQUAL OPPORTUNITY; PAY EQUITY.

AFFIRMATIVE DUMPING DETERMINATION a decision that a country has engaged in the sale of a COMMODITY in a foreign market at less than fair value and is subject to various penalties. *see also* DOWNSTREAM DUMPING; DUMPING; DUMPING MARGIN.

AFFREIGHTMENT *see* CONTRACT OF AFFREIGHTMENT.

AFFREIGHTMENT CONTRACT CONTRACT with a shipowner to hire all or part of a ship for transporting goods.

AFGHANI unit of currency, Afghanistan (100 puis equal 1 afghani).

AFIANZADORAS Mexican bonding companies that enable the IMPORTER in Mexico to guarantee payment to the foreign EXPORTER. In the event that the Mexican importer fails to make payment on a debt to a foreign exporter, these bonding companies will make the payment on behalf of the exporter and then pursue the Mexican importer for payment.

AFKN *see* ARMED FORCES KOREA NETWORK.

AFLOAT CARGO shipment on board a vessel between ports.

AFREXIMBANK *see* AFRICAN EXPORT-IMPORT BANK.

AFRICA ENTERPRISE FUND (AEF) fund operating under the INTERNATIONAL FINANCE CORPORATION (IFC), which began operations in late 1989. The AEF assists small and medium-size enterprises in sub-Saharan Africa, supports investment projects, and promotes development of private enterprises in Africa to stimulate economic growth and productive employment.

AFRICA PROJECT DEVELOPMENT FACILITY (APDF) United Nations Development Program project established in 1986 with the INTERNATIONAL FINANCE CORPORATION (IFC) as the administrative agency and the African Development Bank as the regional sponsor. The APDF seeks to accelerate development of productive enterprises sponsored by private African entrepreneurs as a means of generating self-sustained economic growth and productive employment in sub-Saharan Africa. The facility provides advisory services to private African entrepreneurs in preparing viable projects, works with the entrepreneurs to secure financing, and helps them obtain technical and managerial assistance to start their projects. The facility maintains offices in Nairobi (Kenya), Harare (Zimbabwe), and Abidjan (Côte d'Ivoire).

AFRICAN, CARIBBEAN, AND PACIFIC (ACP) COUNTRIES developing countries that are designated beneficiaries under the Lomé Convention.

AFRICAN DEVELOPMENT BANK (AFDB) (French: Banque Africaine Developpement) bank providing financing through direct loans to African member states to cover the FOREIGN EXCHANGE costs incurred in bank-approved development projects in those countries. Fifty-one African countries are members and ordinarily receive loans. The Republic of South Africa is the only African country that is not a member. The African Development Bank is composed of the AFDB as well as the African Development Fund and the Nigeria Trust Fund. The bank was established in August 1963 and began operations in July 1966. The AFDB headquarters is in Abidjan, Côte d'Ivoire. *see also* AFRICAN DEVELOPMENT FOUNDATION; AFRICAN EXPORT-IMPORT BANK; DEVELOPMENT FUND FOR AFRICA; NIGERIA TRUST FUND.

AFRICAN DEVELOPMENT FOUNDATION (ADF) U.S. public corporation that was established by Congress in 1980 and became operational in 1984. The ADF provides economic assistance to groups and institutions involved in development projects at the local level. The foundation's assistance, designed as a complement to the U.S. foreign aid program, is awarded only to native African organizations and individuals. The ADF headquarters is in Washington, DC. *see also* AFRICAN DEVELOPMENT FUND; DEVELOPMENT FUND FOR AFRICA.

AFRICAN DEVELOPMENT FUND (ADF OR AFDF) (French: Fonds Africain de Developpement, FAD) AFFILIATE of the AFRICAN DEVELOPMENT BANK (AFDB) providing interest-free loans to African countries for projects that promote economic and social development and improve international TRADE among members of the AFDB. ADF was established in July 1972 and commenced operations in 1973.

AFRICAN EXPORT–IMPORT BANK (AFREXIMBANK) African bank offering short-term EXPORT TRADE financing to African exporters designed to enhance intra-African TRADE and Africa's exports. The agreement to create AFREXIMBANK was based on a January 1993 agreement reached in Cairo, Egypt, among African governments, central banks, regional and subregional financial institutions and other organizations. The bank is based on an idea from the AFRICAN DEVELOPMENT BANK and is owned by 23 African states, 16 African central banks, and 86 financial institutions in Africa and elsewhere. It has authorized capital of $750 million. Its objective is to extend credit to African exporters, importers of African goods, and African businesses that want to IMPORT goods for conversion into exports. AFREXIMBANK headquarters is located in Cairo, Egypt.

AFRICAN GROUNDNUT COUNCIL (AFC) (French: Conseil Africain de l'Arachide) COMMODITY group formed in 1964 to promote consumption of the product. Member countries are Gambia, Mali, Niger, Nigeria, Senegal, Sudan, and Burkina Faso. The AFC is headquartered in Nigeria.

AFRICAN MANAGEMENT SERVICES COMPANY (AMSCO) company established in 1989 by the INTERNATIONAL FINANCE CORPORATION. AMSCO provides temporary managers and management training to support the development of African companies. AMSCO works through a network of representatives in Africa. Its clients include privately owned companies, public-sector companies, and subsidiaries of international companies. AMSCO is funded by the UNITED NATIONS DEVELOPMENT PROGRAM (UNDP), INTERNATIONAL FINANCE CORPORATION (IFC), AFRICAN DEVELOPMENT FUND (ADF), AFRICAN DEVELOPMENT BANK (ADB), development institutions in several European countries, and private-sector investors. AMSCO's headquarters is in Amsterdam, Netherlands.

AFRICAN REGIONAL ORGANIZATION FOR STANDARDIZATION (ARSO) (French: Organisation Régionale Africaine de Normalisation, ORAN) African organization promoting and coordinating standardization, quality control, certification, and meteorology practices in Africa. The organization has been developing African Regional Standards (ARS) in nine areas:
• general standards,
• agricultural and food products,
• building and civil engineering,
• mechanical engineering and metallurgy,
• chemistry and chemical engineering,
• electrotechnology,
• textiles,
• transport and communications, and
• environmental products and pollution control.

ARSO is also seeking adoption of a regional certification marking scheme and establishment of a laboratory accreditation program. ARSO was established in 1977, and its membership is restricted to official representatives of member governments. ARSO's headquarters is in Nairobi, Kenya.

AFRICAN TIMBER ORGANIZATION (ATO) COMMODITY group formed in 1975 to coordinate the sale and influence the price of wood in the world marketplace. The ATO is headquartered in Libreville, Gabon, and the member nations are Cameroon, Central African Republic, Congo, Côte d'Ivoire, Equatorial Guinea, Gabon, Ghana, Liberia, Malagasy Republic, Tanzania, and Zaire.

AFT at or toward a ship's stern or aircraft tail.

AFTA *see* ASEAN FREE-TRADE AREA.

AFTER DATE a phrase indicating that the date of maturity of a DRAFT or other negotiable instrument is fixed by the date on which it was drawn a specified number of days after presentation of the draft to the DRAWEE or PAYEE. *see also* AFTER SIGHT; AT SIGHT.

AFTER SIGHT a phrase indicating that the date of maturity of a DRAFT or other negotiable instrument is fixed by the date on which it was drawn a specified number of days after presentation of the draft to the DRAWEE or PAYEE. *see also* AFTER DATE; AT SIGHT.

AG *see* AUSTRALIA GROUP; AKTIENGESELLSCHAFT.

A.G. *see* AKTIENGESELLSCHAFT.

AGAINST ALL RISK (AAR) an international business term for discounting standard business risks.

AGENCE CANADIENNE DE DEVELOPPEMENT INTERNA-TIONAL *see* CANADIAN INTERNATIONAL DEVELOPMENT AGENCY.

AGENCE DE COOPERATION CULTERELLE ET TECHNIQUE (ACCT) (English: Agency for Cultural and Technical Cooperation) French agency created in 1970 to promote cultural and technical cooperation among French-speaking countries. Members include Belgium, Benin, Burkina, Burundi, Canada, Central African Republic, Chad, Comoros, Congo, Côte d'Ivoire, Djibouti, Dominica, France, Gabon, Guinea, Haiti, Lebanon, Luxembourg, Mali, Mauritius, Monaco, Niger, Rwanda, Senegal, Seychelles, Togo, Tunisia, Vanuatu, Vietnam, and Zaire. ACCT also includes seven associate members: Cameroon, Egypt, Guinea-Bissau, Laos, Mauritania, Morocco, and Saint Lucia. ACCT's agency headquarters is in Paris, France.

AGENCJA ROZWOJU PRZEMYSLU S.A. the Industrial Development Agency (IDA) of Poland established on January 25, 1991. The IDA was formed to support the transformations of the Polish economy on the basis of the act of December 14, 1990.

AGENCY FOR CULTURAL AND TECHNICAL COOPERA-TION *see* AGENCE DE COOPÉRATION CULTERELLE ET TECHNIQUE.

AGENCY FOR INTERNATIONAL DEVELOPMENT (AID) U.S. agency created in 1961 to administer foreign economic assistance programs. AID has field missions and representatives in approximately 70 developing countries in Africa, Latin America, the Caribbean, and the Near East. In 1992 AID administered over $14.75 billion in foreign aid throughout the world.

AGENT in the client-server computer NETWORK, the system element that prepares information and exchanges it to a CLIENT or SERVER application.

AGENT/DISTRIBUTOR SERVICE (ADS) an INTERNATIONAL TRADE ADMINISTRATION (ITA) fee-based service that locates foreign IMPORT agents and distributors. ADS provides a custom search overseas for interested and qualified foreign representatives on behalf of a U.S. EXPORTER. Officers abroad conduct the search and prepare a report identifying up to six foreign prospects that have examined the U.S. company's product literature and have expressed interest in representing the U.S. company's products.

AGENT FOR EXPORTER the duly authorized FORWARDING AGENT of the EXPORTER.

AGENTIA ROMANA DE DEZVOLTARE the Romanian Development Agency responsible for providing information to foreign investors interested in doing business with Romania.

AGGREGATED SHIPMENTS several SHIPMENTS from various SHIPPERS that are consolidated and treated as a single CONSIGNMENT.

AGREED VALUATION set value of a shipping load that is agreed upon by both the SHIPPER and the CARRIER to define rate and/or liability.

AGREEMENT CORPORATION *see* EDGE ACT CORPORATIONS.

AGREEMENT OF THE INTERPRETATION AND APPLICATION OF ARTICLES VI, XVI, AND XXII OF THE GENERAL AGREEMENT OF TARIFFS AND TRADE (GATT) *see* STANDARDS CODE.

AGREEMENT OF TWO INSTRUMENTS *see* INTERNATIONAL AGREEMENT.

AGREEMENT ON ANTIDUMPING PRACTICES an agreement resulting from the TOKYO ROUND of multilateral negotiations. It confirmed the definitions of dumped goods and established a procedure for the imposition of penalties and a process by which claims can be investigated and actions taken. *see also* ANTIDUMPING; ANTIDUMPING DUTY; ANTIDUMPING INVESTIGATION NOTICE; ANTIDUMPING DUTY ORDER; ANTIDUMPING PETITION; DUMPING; DUMPING MARGIN.

AGREEMENT ON CUSTOMS VALUATION an agreement resulting from the TOKYO ROUND of multilateral negotiations. The agreement created a uniform system of CUSTOMS VALUATION. *see also* HARMONIZED COMMODITY DESCRIPTION AND CODING SYSTEM.

AGREEMENT ON GOVERNMENT PROCUREMENT an agreement resulting from the TOKYO ROUND of multilateral negotiations. The agreement signed by 12 countries created a uniform set of guidelines pertaining to government procurement.

AGREEMENT ON IMPORT LICENSING an agreement resulting from the TOKYO ROUND of multilateral negotiations. The agreement was signed by 27 countries at the end of 1988 and was intended to ensure that IMPORT licensing requirements were not to be used as TRADE BARRIERS.

AGREEMENT ON TECHNICAL BARRIERS TO TRADE *see* STANDARDS CODE.

AGREEMENT ON TRADE IN CIVIL AIRCRAFT an agreement resulting from the TOKYO ROUND of multilateral negotiations. The agreement became effective on January 1, 1988, and was signed by 22 countries. The objective of the agreement was to
- eliminate duties on aircraft and aircraft parts
- liberalize government procurement procedures in the purchase of civil aircraft, and
- establish guidelines for the production of civil aircraft.

AGREMENT agreement by one government to accept the accreditation of an ambassador from another government.

AGRICULTURAL MARKETING SERVICE (AMS) service provided by the U.S. Department of Agriculture (USDA) to foreign buyers providing assurance that any product shipped overseas meets contract specifications. The service is operated on a user-fee basis. AMS works with the buyers to write a specification that can be certified. The requirements for USDA certification can be made a part of the purchase contract.

AGRICULTURAL OFFICERS U.S. embassy officials who are responsible for addressing agricultural TRADE policy issues and preparing reports on agricultural COMMODITIES such as rice, wheat, and dairy products. These officers promote U.S. exports by providing market information, one-on-one consultations, and facilitative contacts with foreign buyers and by sponsoring trade events, such as shows, trade missions, and seminars.

AGRICULTURAL ON-LINE ACCESS (AGRICOLA) *see* NATIONAL AGRICULTURAL LIBRARY.

AGRICULTURAL TRADE AND MARKETING INFORMATION CENTER *see* NATIONAL AGRICULTURAL LIBRARY.

AGRICULTURAL TRADE LEADS a report appearing on Tuesdays, Thursdays, and Fridays in the second section of the JOURNAL OF COMMERCE. It lists the description of the agricultural product desired, the name and address of the overseas buyer, and the address of the FOREIGN COMMERCIAL OFFICER at the U.S. EMBASSY. These leads are provided by the Department of Agriculture, and are for both fresh and processed agricultural products.

AGRICULTURAL TRADE OFFICES (ATOs) *see* FOREIGN AGRICULTURAL SERVICE.

AGRICULTURE INFORMATION SYSTEM (AGRIS) an international cooperative bibliographic database on agricultural research, production, science, and technology coordinated under the auspices of the Food and Agricultural Organization. Participating countries contribute information for inclusion in AGRIS. *see also* NATIONAL AGRICULTURAL LIBRARY.

AGROTERRORISM terrorist attacks that affect the food supply by destroying crops.

AGUINALDO a mandatory bonus given to Mexican employees of 15–30 days' pay normally presented at Christmas time.

AIAFD *see* ASSOCIATION OF AFRICAN DEVELOPMENT FINANCE INSTITUTIONS.

AIB *see* ARAB INTERNATIONAL BANK.

AIBD *see* ASSOCIATION OF INTERNATIONAL BOND DEALERS.

AID *see* AGENCY FOR INTERNATIONAL DEVELOPMENT.

AIDE-MEMOIRE short written summary of oral remarks made to a foreign government representative and left with that individual.

AIES *see* AUTOMATED INFORMATION EXCHANGE SYSTEM.

AIG *see* AIRBUS INDUSTRIES GROUP.

AIOEC *see* ASSOCIATION OF IRON ORE EXPORTING COUNTRIES.

AIRBUS INDUSTRIES GROUP (AIG) supranational management organization responsible for design, development, manufacture, marketing, sales, and support of selected commercial aircraft. Member countries are France, Germany, Spain, and the United Kingdom. Airbus Industrie, G.I.E. is a consortium of four West European producers—Aérospatiale (France), Deutsche Aerospace Airbus GmbH (Germany), British Aerospace Airbus Ltd. (United Kingdom), and Construcciones Aeronáuticas S.A. (Spain)—established as a groupement d'intérêt économique (G.I.E.) under French law.

AIR CARGO property of any kind that is transported by aircraft (excluding passenger baggage).

AIR MARSHAL a federal marshal whose purpose is to ride commercial flights, dressed in plain clothes and armed to prevent hijackings.

AIR PARCEL POST term used to describe priority mail, consisting of first-class mail that weighs more than 13 ounces.

AIR WAYBILL (AWB) BILL OF LADING (B/L) that covers both domestic and international flights transporting goods to a specified destination.

Technically, it is a nonnegotiable instrument of air transport that serves as a receipt for the shipper, indicating that the CARRIER has accepted the goods listed therein and obligates itself to carry the consignment to the airport of destination according to specified conditions.

AIT *see* AMERICAN INSTITUTE IN TAIWAN.

AITS *see* AUTOMATED INFORMATION TRANSFER SYSTEM.

AJUSTABONOS bonds sold on the Mexican Stock Exchange with a 3- or 5-year maturity that pay a fixed real yield above consumer price inflation.

AKKREDITIV (German) *see* LETTER OF CREDIT.

AKTIEBOLAGER (A.B. or **AKTB)** a Swedish joint stock company.

AKTIENGESELLSCHAFT AG (German, meaning stock company) German corporation with a separate legal personality having at least five partners. The company name usually reflects the activities of the company and must include AG.

AKTIESELSKABET (A.S. or **AKTS)** a Danish or Norwegian joint stock company.

AL JAZEERA satellite television station based in Qatar and broadcast throughout the Middle East.

AL QAEDA an international terrorist group founded around 1989 and dedicated to opposing non-Islamic governments with force and violence.

ALIEN a person living in one country although a citizen of another. *see also* FOREIGNER; RESIDENT ALIEN.

ALIENABLE ability to be transferred or conveyed.

ALIGNED EXPORT DOCUMENTATION SYSTEM method of entering information onto a master document, enabling it to be electronically reproduced on individual forms of similar design.

ALJ *see* ADMINISTRATIVE LAW JUDGE.

ALL-CARGO AIRCRAFT any aircraft that is used for the sole purpose of transporting CARGO.

ALL OTHER PERILS & MISFORTUNE *see* PERILS OF THE SEA.

ALL RISK CLAUSE *see* ALL RISK COVERAGE.

ALL RISK COVERAGE
1. type of MARINE INSURANCE. It includes the broadest kind of standard coverage, but excludes damage caused by war, strikes, and riots.
2. insurance provision against all risks of physical loss or damage from any external clause, excepting those losses that are self caused. *see also* INHERENT VICE.

ALLOCATION UNDER LINES OF CREDIT medium- and long-term financing to FOREIGN BUYERS of Canadian capital goods and services by foreign banks and private agencies under lines of credit established by Canada's EXPORT DEVELOPMENT CORPORATION.

ALLOWANCE deduction or discount from the seller's price.

ALMA a Spanish term used by Mexicans referring to a person's inner qualities with regard to the person's soul or spirit. *see also* ESPIRITU.

ALONGSIDE phrase referring to the side of a ship. Goods to be delivered "alongside" are to be placed on the dock or lighter within reach of the transport ship's tackle so that they can be loaded aboard the ship. Goods are delivered to the port of embarkation, but without loading fees.

ALTERNATIVE TARIFF TARIFF with two or more rates for the same goods, to and from the same points, with the discretion to use the lowest of the charges.

AMAZON PACT *see* AMAZONIAN COOPERATION TREATY.

AMAZONIAN COOPERATION TREATY an agreement among the Amazon Basin countries to cooperate in the economic development of the region. The agreement was signed in 1978 by Bolivia, Brazil, Colombia, Ecuador, Guyana, Peru, Suriname, and Venezuela.

AMBASSADOR *see* TITLE AND RANK.

AMENDMENT any change made to a LETTER OF CREDIT after it has been issued. The fees charged by the banks involved in amending the letter of credit may be paid by either the EXPORTER or the FOREIGN BUYER, but who is to pay which charges should be specified in the letter of credit. *see also* ADVISING BANK; APPLICANT; BENEFICIARY; IRREVOCABLE LETTER OF CREDIT.

AMERICAN ASSOCIATION OF EXPORTERS AND IMPORTERS (AAEI) a lobbying and informational association formed in 1921 with regard to federal regulations concerning international trade. The AAEI is located at 11 West 42nd Street, New York, NY 10036.

AMERICAN BUSINESS CENTER (ABC) a U.S. DEPARTMENT OF COMMERCE program providing assistance to U.S. companies in exploring or establishing commercial opportunities in the independent states of the former Soviet Union with business services such as telephone and fax, temporary office space, market information, and assistance in making business contacts. An ABC has operated in Bratislava, Slovakia, under the direction of the U.S. Department of Commerce's INTERNATIONAL TRADE ADMINISTRATION in cooperation with the U.S. AGENCY FOR INTERNATIONAL DEVELOPMENT (AID). Additional centers are in Russia, the Ukraine, Kazakhstan, Uzbekistan.

AMERICAN BUSINESS INITIATIVE (ABI) (or AMERICAN BUSINESS AND PRIVATE SECTOR DEVELOPMENT INITIATIVE FOR EASTERN EUROPE) an INITIATIVE of several U.S. governmental agencies including the AGENCY FOR INTERNATIONAL DEVELOPMENT (AID), DEPARTMENT OF COMMERCE, EXIMBANK, OVERSEAS PRIVATE INVESTMENT CORPORATION (OPIC), and the TRADE DEVELOPMENT AGENCY (TDA). The ABI emphasizes the EXPORT of American telecommunications, energy, environment, housing, and agriculture products and services to Eastern European countries.

AMERICAN DEPOSITORY RECEIPTS (ADRs) negotiable receipts for the securities of a foreign company, which are kept in the vaults of an American bank, allowing Americans to TRADE the foreign securities in the United States while accruing any dividends and capital gains.

AMERICAN INSTITUTE IN TAIWAN (AIT) a nonprofit corporation that represents U.S. commercial, cultural, and other interests in Taiwan in lieu of an embassy. In 1979 the United States terminated formal diplomatic relations with Taiwan when it recognized the People's Republic of China as the sole legal government of China. AIT was authorized to continue commercial, cultural, and other relations between the United States and Taiwan. AIT headquarters is located in Arlington, Virginia; constituent offices are in Taipei and Kaohsiung, Taiwan. *see also* COORDINATION COUNCIL FOR NORTH AMERICAN AFFAIRS.

AMERICAN NATIONAL STANDARDS INSTITUTE (ANSI) organization responsible for approving U.S. standards in many areas, including computers and communications. ANSI standards are crucial in the area of international telecommunications. ANSI standards apply to equipment and other communication procedures. ANSI is a member of the INTERNATIONAL ORGANIZATION FOR STANDARDIZATION. *see also* COMMITTEE ON INTERNATIONAL TELEPHONE AND TELEGRAPH (CCITT); INTERNATIONAL STANDARDS ORGANIZATION (ISO); INTERNATIONAL TELECOMMUNICATIONS UNION (ITU); INTERNATIONAL RADIO CONSULTATIVE COMMITTEE (CCIR); EUROPEAN TELECOMMUNICATIONS STANDARDS INSTITUTE (ETSI).

AMERICAN PETROLEUM INSTITUTE (API) *see* API WEEKLY REPORT.

AMERICAN SELLING PRICE discontinued method of calculating duties on goods being imported into the United States.

AMERICAN TRADERS INDEX (ATI) the U.S. AND FOREIGN COMMERCIAL SERVICE headquarters compilation of individual U.S. and foreign commercial service domestic client files, for use by overseas American embassies to generate mailing lists.

AMF *see* ARAB MONETARY FUND.

AMIDSHIPS in the middle of the vessel; often preferred by SHIPPERS because of the minimal motion and the benefits to fragile FREIGHT. *see also* AFT; ATHWARTSHIPS; BALLAST; BATTENS.

AMORTIZATION gradual diminishment of any amount over a period of time. *see also* DEPRECIATION.

AMS *see* AGRICULTURAL MARKETING SERVICE; AUTOMATED MANIFEST SYSTEMS.

AMSCO *see* AFRICAN MANAGEMENT SERVICES COMPANY.

AMU *see* ARAB MAGHREB UNION.

ANDEAN DEVELOPMENT CORPORATION *see* ANDEAN GROUP.

ANDEAN GROUP (Spanish: Grupo Andino; sometimes referred to as Pacto Andino or Córporation Andino de Fomento; formal reference is Acuerdo de Cartegena in recognition of the group's establishment in Cartegena, Spain, in October 1969) an association of Latin American countries that promotes regional economic integration and political cooperation among themselves. Members include Bolivia, Colombia, Ecuador, Peru, and Venezuela; Chile withdrew in January 1976. The Andean Group's headquarters is in Lima, Peru.

ANDEAN RESERVE FUND (Spanish: Fondo Andina de Reservas) fund associated with the ANDEAN GROUP established to strengthen the BALANCE OF PAYMENTS positions of member countries by offering credit, guaranteeing loans, and promoting compatibility among members' monetary policies. Its headquarters is in Bogota, Colombia.

ANDEAN TRADE INITIATIVE (ATI) the TRADE element in U.S. drug policy. *see also* ANDEAN TRADE PREFERENCE ACT (ATPA).

ANDEAN TRADE PREFERENCE ACT (ATPA) a unilateral TRADE benefit program designed to promote economic development through private sector initiative in the four Andean countries of Bolivia, Colombia, Ecuador, and Peru. The ATPA encourages alternatives to coca cultivation and production by offering broader access to the U.S. market. The act also seeks to stimulate investment in nontraditional sectors and to diversify the Andean countries' EXPORT base. The primary provision of the program is expanded duty-free entry into the United States. Each country's eligibility is based on criteria set forth in the act. Bolivia, Colombia, Ecuador, and Peru have been designated as beneficiaries. The ATPA became effective in December 1991 and is due to expire in December 2001. The act requires periodic assessments of the impact of the trade preferences by the U.S. INTERNATIONAL TRADE COMMISSION and the U.S. Department of Labor.

AND/OR (CUSTOMS VALUATION) an expression that allows for the flexibility in making the necessary adjustments in valuing items for CUSTOMS purposes.

ANGLOPHONE a national of a country whose predominant language is English.

ANNEX *see* INTERNATIONAL AGREEMENTS.

ANONYMIZING a process by which something is deprived of its identity.

ANRPC *see* ASSOCIATION OF NATURAL RUBBER PRODUCING COUNTRIES.

ANS *see* ANSVARLIG SELSKAP.

ANSI *see* AMERICAN NATIONAL STANDARDS INSTITUTE.

ANSVARLIG SELSKAP a Norwegian unlimited general partnership.

ANTEL *see* ADMINISTRACION NACIONAL DE TELECOMUNICACIONES.

ANTIBOYCOTT LAW an amendment to the U.S. EXPORT ADMINISTRATION ACT, which prohibits compliance by American firms with the ARAB BOYCOTT OF ISRAEL. *see also* BOYCOTT.

ANTIDIVERSION CLAUSE *see* DESTINATION CONTROL STATEMENT.

ANTIDUMPING a reference to the system of laws to remedy DUMPING. Antidumping is the converse of dumping.

ANTIDUMPING CLAUSE a TARIFF imposed to discourage sale of foreign goods in the U.S. market at very low prices (below foreign country's domestic market), which might hurt U.S. manufacturers. *see also* ANTIDUMPING/COUNTERVAILING DUTY SYSTEM; ANTIDUMPING DUTY; ANTIDUMPING INVESTIGATION NOTICE; ANTIDUMPING DUTY ORDER; ANTIDUMPING PETITION.

ANTIDUMPING CODE negotiated under GATT during KENNEDY ROUND and TOKYO ROUND negotiations establishing standards for ANTIDUMPING activities. *see also* ANTIDUMPING DUTY; ANTIDUMPING INVESTIGATION NOTICE; ANTIDUMPING DUTY ORDER; ANTIDUMPING PETITION; DUMPING.

ANTIDUMPING/COUNTERVAILING DUTY SYSTEM a part of the U.S. CUSTOMS SERVICE'S AUTOMATED COMMERCIAL SYSTEM (ACS). It contains a case reference database and a statistical reporting system to capture data for INTERNATIONAL TRADE COMMISSION reports on antidumping and countervailing duties assessed and paid.

ANTIDUMPING DUTY a DUTY assessed on imported merchandise that is subject to an antidumping duty order. The antidumping duty is assessed on an entry-by-entry basis in an amount equal to the difference between the U.S. price of that entry and the foreign market value of such or similar merchandise at the time the merchandise was sold to the United States. *see also* TARIFF ACT OF 1930.

ANTIDUMPING DUTY ORDER a notice issued following final determination of sales at less than FAIR VALUE and material injury, or threat of material injury, providing for the imposition of antidumping duties. *see also* TARIFF ACT OF 1930.

ANTIDUMPING INVESTIGATION NOTICE the notice published in the FEDERAL REGISTER announcing the initiation of an antidumping investigation. An investigation must be initiated within 20 days of the filing of a valid petition. *see also* TARIFF ACT OF 1930.

ANTIDUMPING PETITION a petition filed on behalf of an affected U.S. industry, alleging that foreign merchandise is being sold in the United States at "less than FAIR VALUE" and that such sales are causing or threatening material injury to, or materially retarding the establishment of, a U.S. industry. U.S. DEPARTMENT OF COMMERCE regulations and INTERNATIONAL TRADE COMMISSION regulations specify the information a petition should contain. *see also* TARIFF ACT OF 1930.

ANTIDUMPING SUIT a complaint by a domestic producer that IMPORTS are being dumped, the resulting investigation, and any ANTIDUMPING DUTY, if DUMPING and injury are found.

ANTIQUIDATES a service indemnity bonus for Venezuelan workers equal to a half a month pay.

ANY QUANTITY CARGO rating that applies to an article without consideration of weight.

ANZUS PACT *see* AUSTRALIA–NEW ZEALAND–U.S. SECURITY PACT.

AO MAIL (Autres Objets, meaning other articles) includes printed matter of all kinds, matter for the blind and all packets. AO does not mean airmail. It consists of preferential (periodicals) and nonpreferential items (advertisements, catalogs, directories, books, sheet music and matter for the blind).

APCC *see* ASIAN AND PACIFIC COCONUT COMMUNITY.

APDF *see* AFRICA PROJECT DEVELOPMENT FACILITY.

APEC *see* ASIA–PACIFIC ECONOMIC COOPERATION.

API *see* APPLICATION PROGRAM INTERFACE.

API WEEKLY REPORT weekly report of the American Petroleum Institute production, imports, and refinery utilization for principal refined products and fuel oil. This report appears every Thursday in the JOURNAL OF COMMERCE.

APO form used in addressing mail to a FOREIGN SERVICE POST. Example: Commercial Section, American Embassy Manama, APO New York 09526. *see also* ASIAN PRODUCTIVITY ORGANIZATION; ADMINISTRATIVE PROTECTIVE ORDER; FPO.

APPLICANT the foreign buyer who applies to the BANK for the issuance of a LETTER OF CREDIT to the EXPORTER. *see also* BENEFICIARY.

APPLICATION a computer program that performs a function directly for a user. FTP, E-MAIL, and TELNET CLIENTS are examples of NETWORK applications.

APPLIED TARIFF the actual TARIFF RATE in effect at a country's border. *see also* MARKUP.

APPRECIATION a term used to indicate the direction of a movement in the EXCHANGE RATE. Appreciation of a country's currency occurs when the value of its currency increases in relation to the currency of another country. *see also* DEPRECIATION; DEVALUATION; REVALUATION.

APPROPRIABILITY THEORY a theory explaining that firms will favor an equity form of investment in a foreign country over such nonequity forms as LICENSING, because competitors will be less likely to have access to proprietary information.

APPROX term used in a LETTER OF CREDIT (L/C) permitting a difference not to exceed 10% more or less than the monetary amount, or the quantity or the unit price stipulated in the L/C. *see also* ABOUT, CIRCA.

APRON area of the airport where planes are parked for loading and unloading.

ARAB-AFRICAN INTERNATIONAL BANK (AAIB) a pan-Arab CONSORTIUM incorporated in 1964 as a self-governing autonomous entity between the Ministry of Finance of Kuwait and the CENTRAL BANK of Egypt; each of which as cofounders hold 49.37% of the bank's shares. A New York branch of the AAIB was established in 1981 to facilitate the financing of TRADE between North America and the Middle East. AAIB headquarters is in Cairo.

ARAB BANK FOR ECONOMIC DEVELOPMENT IN AFRICA (ABEDA) (French: BANQUE ARABE POUR LE DÉVELOPPEMENT ECONOMIQUE EN AFRIQUE—BADEA) bank created by the LEAGUE OF ARAB STATES in November 1973 and began operations in March 1975. ABEDA promotes economic and technical cooperation between Arab and African states. Members include Algeria, Bahrain, Egypt, Iraq, Jordan, Kuwait, Lebanon, Libya, Mauritania, Morocco, Oman, Qatar, Saudi Arabia, Sudan, Syria, Tunisia, the United Arab Emirates, and the Palestine Liberation Organization. ABEDA headquarters is in Khartoum, Sudan.

ARAB BOYCOTT OF ISRAEL an EMBARGO by Arab states against firms investing in or doing business with Israel. *see also* ANTIBOYCOTT LAW; BLACKLIST; BOYCOTT.

ARAB COMMON MARKET (ACM) a union between Egypt, Iraq, Sudan, Syria, the United Arab Emirates, and Yemen to remove TRADE BARRIERS and to establish common TARIFF and NONTARIFF policies with respect to IMPORTS from countries outside the agreement. *see also* CUSTOMS UNION.

ARAB COOPERATION COUNCIL (ACC) Arab group created in 1989 to promote economic cooperation and integration. Members include Egypt, Iraq, Jordan, and North Yemen. The ACC, partly intended as a counterpart to the GULF COOPERATION COUNCIL (GCC), was created one day subsequent to the establishment of the ARAB MAGHREB UNION.

ARAB FUND FOR ECONOMIC AND SOCIAL DEVELOPMENT (AFESD) Arab fund promoting regional economic integration and social development in Arab states. Members include Algeria, Bahrain, Djibouti, Egypt, Iraq, Jordan, Kuwait, Lebanon, Libya, Mauritania, Morocco, Oman, Qatar, Saudi Arabia, Somalia, Sudan, Syria, Tunisia, the United Arab Emirates, Yemen, and the Palestine Liberation Organization. AFESD, associated with the LEAGUE OF ARAB STATES, started operations in February 1972. Its headquarters is in Safat, Kuwait.

ARAB INTERNATIONAL BANK (AIB) Arab bank providing financing to support development of foreign TRADE among member nations and other Arab states. The bank was established in October 1971. Its headquarters is in Cairo, Egypt. AIB members include the governments of Oman, Qatar, and the United Arab Emirates; the CENTRAL BANK of Egypt; and the Libyan Arab Foreign Bank.

ARAB LEAGUE *see* LEAGUE OF ARAB STATES.

ARAB MAGHREB UNION (AMU) (French: Union du Maghreb Arabe, UMA) Arab union that includes Algeria, Libya, Mauritania, Morocco, and Tunisia. The union was established in February 1989 to foster integration of the Maghreb economy. The union also seeks to combine with the GULF COOPERATION COUNCIL (GCC) states in a common market.

ARAB MONETARY FUND (AMF) Arab fund originally aimed at correcting chronic deficits in the BALANCE OF PAYMENTS in most of its member states. AMF promotes Arab integration in monetary and economic affairs. The fund's priorities have included:
- addressing payments imbalances,
- creating capital markets,
- stabilizing exchange rates, and
- eliminating payments and trade restrictions.

Members include Algeria, Bahrain, Egypt, Iraq, Jordan, Kuwait, Lebanon, Libya, Mauritania, Morocco, Oman, Qatar, Saudi Arabia, Somalia, Sudan, Syria, Tunisia, the United Arab Emirates, Yemen, and the Palestine Liberation Organization. The fund was created in 1976 and began operating in April 1977. AMF headquarters is in Abu Dhabi, United Arab Emirates. *see also* ARAB TRADE FINANCING PROGRAM.

ARAB TRADE FINANCING PROGRAM (ATFP) Arab funding program designed to promote TRADE among Arab countries and EXPORTS from Arab countries. The program was established in 1989 by the ARAB MONETARY FUND. Its headquarters is in Abu Dhabi, United Arab Emirates.

ARAB UNION a now defunct political agreement establishing a mutual defense pact between Jordan and Iraq.

ARBEIDSMILJOLOVEN the Norwegian Workers' Protection Act of 1974 containing employment regulations for private sector wage earners.

ARBITRAGE simultaneous buying and selling of the same COMMODITY or foreign exchange in two or more markets in order to take advantage of market price differentials.

ARBITRARY VALUE *see* FICTITIOUS VALUE.

ARBITRATION process whereby parties involved in a dispute present their cases to an impartial third party for the purposes of rendering a binding decision. *see also* ADJUDICATION; ARBITRATION CLAUSE; DISPUTE SETTLEMENT SYSTEM.

ARBITRATION CLAUSE that part of a contract between an EXPORTER and IMPORTER that specifies a procedure for the settlement of disputes. *see also* ARBITRATION; COMPORMIS.

ARIADNE NETWORK (Greece) an INTERNET network in Greece dedicated to giving the user basic assistance, examples, etc., in doing research. The server currently contains general information about the ARIADNE network, other networks, key network terms, contacts, etc.

ARMED FORCES KOREA NETWORK television network operated by and for the U.S. military in Korea.

ARMED ISLAMIC GROUP Algerian Islamic extremist group that aims to overthrow the secular regime in Algeria and replace it with an Islamic state.

ARMS CONTROL AND DISARMAMENT AGENCY (ACDA) independent U.S. agency within the U.S. Department of State. ACDA participates in interagency working groups that discuss EXPORT license applications requiring dispute resolution. ACDA is interested in dual-use license applications from a nonproliferation perspective—anything that could have an impact on the proliferation of missiles, chemical and biological weapons, and nuclear weapons. ACDA's positions need not be consonant with those of the U.S. State Department. The agency was created in 1961, and has about 200 to 250 staff. It has a fairly substantial and growing technology transfer and export control function. The director is the principal arms control adviser to the U.S. Secretary of State, the president, and the U.S. NATIONAL SECURITY COUNCIL (NSC) in the areas of conventional arms transfer; commercial sales of munitions, nuclear missiles, and chemical and biological warfare; East–West military munitions issues; and COCOM.

ARM'S LENGTH TRANSACTION/AGREEMENT
  1. a contract between two or more related parties to which they would have agreed had they been unrelated.

2. a contract between two or more parties with common interests, while the activities between the parties are carried out by some non-related third party.

ARNES NETWORK (Slovenia) an INTERNET network in Slovenia. The main user group is librarians. Courses in networking and on-line information retrieval are available several times a year for students and researchers. It has a remote data base for journals, library catalogues, journal catalogues, bibliographies, and the like.

ARNET NETWORK (Argentina) a NETWORK connected to the INTERNET. ARNET is a major science research network of Argentina. It connects approximately 300 sites, mainly universities and research organizations. As in other cooperative networks, ARNET has no central planning or central authority. The current international link and the top-level AR domain are managed by the UNITED NATIONS DEVELOPMENT PROGRAM (UNDP) at the Argentine Ministry of Foreign Affairs and Secretariat of Science and Technology.

ARNET is a store-and-forward message network based on the Unix communications facilities. The network is connected to the Internet through a satellite link at the University of Maryland.

ARP *see* ADDRESS RESOLUTION PROTOCOL.

ARPA *see* DEFENSE ADVANCED RESEARCH PROJECTS AGENCY.

ARRANGEMENT ON GUIDELINES FOR OFFICIALLY SUPPORTED EXPORT CREDITS an international agreement under ORGANIZATION FOR ECONOMIC COOPERATION AND DEVELOPMENT (OECD) auspices governing the conditions—such as interest rates, repayment terms, and cash down payments—of medium-and long-term official EXPORT credit. It does not apply to strictly private credit. For example, the arrangement specifies how governments relate the interest rate on their export credits to market levels. Although informal and nonenforceable, arrangement guidelines are regularly observed by the 22 OECD member governments that are "participants" to the agreement.

ARRANGEMENT REGARDING BOVINE MEAT an INTERNATIONAL AGREEMENT arrived at during the TOKYO ROUND of MULTILATERAL TRADE NEGOTIATIONS. It was signed by 25 nations and the objectives of the agreement are
- to promote world trade in beef
- discourage VOLUNTARY RESTRAINT AGREEMENTS, and
- to monitor the use of restrictive trade practices by producer-exporters.

ARRIVALS imported goods that have been placed in a BONDED WAREHOUSE for which DUTY has not been paid.

ARSO *see* AFRICAN REGIONAL ORGANIZATION FOR STANDARDIZATION.

AS *see* AUTONOMOUS SYSTEM.

A.S. or AKTS *see* AKTIESELSKABET.

ASCII *see* AMERICAN STANDARD CODE FOR INFORMATION INTERCHANGE.

ASCRIBED GROUP MEMBERSHIP cultural affiliations determined by birth such as sex, age, caste, and ethnic or national origin. *see also* ACQUIRED GROUP MEMBERSHIP; CULTURE.

ASEAN *see* ASSOCIATION OF SOUTHEAST ASIAN NATIONS.

ASEAN FREE-TRADE AREA (AFTA) FREE-TRADE AREA created in January 1992 by the ASSOCIATION OF SOUTHEAST ASIAN NATIONS (ASEAN). AFTA has a common effective preferential TARIFF. Under the agreement ASEAN members will cut tariff rates within 15 years of its start date of January 1994. Manufactured goods from 15 sectors designated as FAST TRACK are subject to a tariff reduction of 0–5% within 10 years, and 7 years if the starting rates were already below 20%. Fast track sectors include vegetable oils, cement, chemicals, pharmaceuticals, fertilizer, plastics, rubber products, leather products, pulp, textiles, ceramic and glass products, gems and jewelry, copper cathodes, electronics, and wooden and tartan furniture.

ASEGURADORA MEXICANA term used when referring to insurance companies in Mexico.

ASIA AND PACIFIC COUNCIL a regional group established in 1966 and consisting of Australia, Japan, New Zealand, the Philippines, Republic of Korea (South Korea), Republic of China (Taiwan), and Thailand. The purpose of the council is to discuss economic, social, and cultural matters of interest to the members.

ASIA PACIFIC ECONOMIC COOPERATION (APEC) an informal grouping of Asia Pacific countries established in November 1989, providing a forum for ministerial level discussion of a broad range of economic issues. APEC includes the six ASEAN countries (Brunei, Indonesia, Malaysia, Philippines, Singapore, and Thailand), plus Australia, Canada, China, Hong Kong, Japan, New Zealand, South Korea, Taiwan, and the United States.

ASIAN CLEARING UNION (ACU) Asian trading agreement established in 1974 to promote regional TRADE and economic cooperation, including arrangements to conserve foreign exchange and encourage domestic currencies in trade. Members include Bangladesh, India, Iran, Myanmar, Nepal, Pakistan, and Sri Lanka. Bhutan, Malaysia, the Peoples' Republic of China, the Philippines, Thailand, and Vietnam have expressed interest in membership. ACU's headquarters is in Tehran, Iran.

ASIAN DEVELOPMENT BANK (ADB) Asian bank established in 1965 and began operations in December 1966. ADB helps finance economic development in developing countries in the Asian and Pacific area through the provision of loans on near-market terms, with its Ordinary Capital Resources (OCR), and on concessional terms, through the ASIAN DEVELOPMENT FUND (ADF). ADB's headquarters is in Manila, Philippines.

ASIAN DEVELOPMENT FUND (ADF or ASDF) an affiliate of the ASIAN DEVELOPMENT BANK (ADB), it lends funds on concessionary terms to the bank's least-developed member countries.

ASIAN DOLLARS *see* EURODOLLARS.

ASIAN FUTURES a table appearing daily in the JOURNAL OF COMMERCE that includes financial futures from Japan, precious metal prices from the Tokyo Commodity Exchange, and currency quotes from the Singapore International Monetary Exchange.

ASIAN PACIFIC COCONUT COMMUNITY (APCC) an INTERNATIONAL COMMODITY GROUP established in 1969. Its membership consists of India, Indonesia, Malaysia, Papua New Guinea, the Philippines, Solomon Islands, Sri Lanka, Thailand, Vanuata, and Western Samoa with its headquarters in Jakarta, Indonesia. The purpose of the group is to coordinate information on the production, processing, and marketing of coconuts among the members.

ASIAN PRODUCTIVITY ORGANIZATION (APO) an organization established in 1971 and headquartered in Tokyo. Its purpose is to improve the productivity of industry in the Asian economic region.

AS IS indicates goods for sale but does not include a warranty or guarantee.

ASOCIACION LATINOAMERICANA DE INSTITUTIONES FINANCIERAS DE DESARROLLO (ALIDF) *see* LATIN AMERICAN ASSOCIATION OF DEVELOPMENT FINANCING INSTITUTIONS (ABCA).

ASOCIACIÓN LATINOAMERICANA DE INTEGRACION (ALADI) *see* LATIN AMERICAN INTEGRATION ASSOCIATION.

ASP *see* AMERICAN SELLING PRICE.

ASSAILING THIEVES a term used in marine insurance making reference to the forcible taking of property, but not sneak thievery or theft by any of the ship's crew.

ASSEMBLY SERVICE a service under which an airline combines multiple SHIPMENTS from multiple SHIPPERS into one shipment to one receiver.

ASSESSMENT ANTIDUMPING DUTIES imposed on imported merchandise. *see also* TARIFF ACT OF 1930.

ASSIGNMENT OF LETTER OF CREDIT the BENEFICIARY of a LETTER OF CREDIT advises the bank of his/her desires to forward the proceeds or a portion of them to another individual (assignee). Upon receipt of these instructions, the bank promises the assignee that he/she will receive stated share of the proceeds before the bank pays the balance to the beneficiary.

ASSIGNMENT STATUS refers to who will be accompanying an EXPATRIATE employee on an international assignment. Example: Bachelor Status, Married Status, Family Status, Single Status.

ASSOCIATED FINANCING managed financing available through the DEVELOPMENT ASSISTANCE COMMITTEE of the ORGANIZATION OF ECONOMIC COOPERATION AND DEVELOPMENT (OECD). EXPORT CREDITS are issued in the form of official development assistance. *see also* CONCESSIONAL FINANCING.

ASSOCIATION DES BANQUES CENTRALES AFRICAINES *see* ASSOCIATION OF CENTRAL AFRICAN BANKS.

ASSOCIATION DES INSTITUTIONS AFRICAINES DE FINANCEMENT DU DEVELOPPEMENT *see* ASSOCIATION OF AFRICAN DEVELOPMENT FINANCE INSTITUTIONS (AIAFD).

ASSOCIATION OF AFRICAN DEVELOPMENT FINANCE INSTITUTIONS (AADFI) (French: Association des Institutions Africaines de Financement du Développement, AIAFD) African association promoting cooperative financing for social development in Africa and economic integration. Established in March 1975, AADFI's headquarters is in Abidjan, Côte d'Ivoire.

ASSOCIATION OF AFRICAN TRADE PROMOTION ORGANIZATIONS (AATPO) African TRADE organization promoting inter-African trade, harmonization of commercial policies, communication among African states in trade matters, and research and training. With about 26 members AATPO was established in 1975 under the auspices of the Organization for African Unity and the AFRICAN DEVELOPMENT BANK. AATPO's headquarters is in Tangier, Morocco.

ASSOCIATION OF BRITISH TRAVEL AGENTS (ABTA) a British association of travel agents and tour operators working to create an advantageous business environment by maintaining high standards of service and accountability for the traveling public. Founded in 1950, the ABTA currently has 7,427 travel-agent members. The group requires the use of exact financial statements for travel and tour services, and it has established a continuing liaison with trade and governmental regulatory bodies concerning travel issues.

ASSOCIATION OF CENTRAL AFRICAN BANKS (ACAB) (French: Association des Banques Centrales Africaines, ABCA) Central African banking association promoting cooperation among monetary, banking, and financial institutions in Africa. Members include two African regional banks and about 32 national banks. The association was created in 1968. ACAB headquarters is in Dakar, Senegal.

ASSOCIATION OF COFFEE PRODUCING COUNTRIES (ACPC) a pact comprising 28 members of the INTERNATIONAL COFFEE AGREEMENT, which account for 85% of world coffee exports, has been seeking to strengthen world coffee prices through an EXPORT retention plan.

ASSOCIATION OF INTERNATIONAL BOND DEALERS (AIBD) a forum for over 500 members from 30 countries to review international securities market matters. The primary objectives of the AIBD are to provide a basis for examination and discussion of questions relating to the secondary market in Eurosecurities and rules governing their functions. AIBD maintains a close liaison between the primary and secondary markets in Eurosecurities. AIBD was established in 1969; it is headquartered in Zurich, Switzerland.

ASSOCIATION OF IRON ORE EXPORT PRODUCING COUNTRIES (ANIOEC) an INTERNATIONAL COMMODITY GROUP formed in 1970. The headquarters is located in Geneva, Switzerland, and its members are Algeria, Australia, India, Liberia, Mauritania, Peru, Sierra Leone, Sweden, and Venezuela. The purpose of the organization is to coordinate efforts on exploration, processing, and marketing of the COMMODITY.

ASSOCIATION OF NATURAL RUBBER PRODUCING COUNTRIES (ANRPC) an INTERNATIONAL COMMODITY GROUP formed in 1970. The headquarters is located in Kuala Lumpur, Malaysia and its members are India, Indonesia, Malaysia, Papua New Guinea, Singapore, Sri Lanka, and Thailand. The association serves as a means of collaboration among members to stabilize prices and ensure fair and profitable returns.

ASSOCIATION OF SOUTHEAST ASIAN NATIONS (ASEAN) Southeast Asian association established in 1967 to promote political, economic, and social cooperation among the six member countries: Indonesia, Malaysia, Philippines, Singapore, Thailand, and Brunei. ASEAN headquarters is in Jakarta, Indonesia. In January 1992, ASEAN agreed to create a FREE-TRADE AREA, ASEAN FREE TRADE AREA (AFTA).

ASSUMED SHELTER COST a hypothetical cost of housing in HOME or HOST country used in computing a COST DIFFERENTIAL allowance.

ASSURED the individual who has insured a shipment and has title to the goods.

ASYCUDA *see* AUTOMATED SYSTEM FOR CUSTOMS DATA.

ASYMMETRIC THREAT the use of crude or low-tech methods to attack a superior or more high-tech enemy.

ASYNCHRONOUS TRANSFER MODE (ATM) a method for the dynamic allocation of BANDWIDTH using a fixed-size packet (called a cell). ATM is also known as a "fast packet."

AT POST EDUCATION location at the site of the assignment where dependent children attend educational facilities. *see also* AWAY FROM POST EDUCATION.

AT SIGHT a phrase indicating that payment of the DRAFT or other negotiable instrument is payable upon presentation. *see also* AFTER DATE; AFTER SIGHT; LETTER OF CREDIT.

ATA (A TEMPORARY ADMISSION) CARNET standardized international CUSTOMS document used to obtain a DUTY-FREE temporary admission of certain goods into the countries that are signatories to the ATA CONVENTION. This is particularly applicable to commercial and professional travelers who may take commercial samples, tools of the trade, advertising material, cinematographic, audiovisual, medical, scientific, or other professional equipment into member countries temporarily without paying CUSTOMS DUTIES and taxes or posting a BOND at the border of each country visited. The CARNETS are generally valid for 12 months.

ATA CONVENTION international agreement whereby commercial and professional travelers may take commercial samples, tools of the trade, advertising material, and cinematographic, audiovisual, medical, scientific, or other professional equipment into member countries temporarily. Under the terms of the ATA Convention signatory countries are not required to pay customs duties and taxes or post a bond at the border of each country visited. *see also* ATA CARNET.

ATB TARIFF REDUCTION *see* ACROSS THE BOARD TARIFF REDUCTIONS.

ATFP *see* ARAB TRADE FINANCING PROGRAM.

ATHWARTSHIPS across a vessel from side to side. *see also* AFT; AMIDSHIPS.

ATI *see* AMERICAN TRADERS INDEX; ANDEAN TRADE INITIATIVE.

ATLAS *see* AUTOMATED TRADE LOCATOR ASSISTANCE NETWORK.

ATM *see* ASYNCHRONOUS TRANSFER MODE.

ATO *see* AFRICAN TIMBER ORGANIZATION.

ATPA *see* ANDEAN TRADE PREFERENCE ACT.

ATTACHE *see* TITLE AND RANK.

AUP *see* ACCEPTABLE USE POLICY.

AUSFUHRKREDIT-GESELLSCHAFT (AKA) (English: Export Credit Establishment) an association of German banks providing medium- and long-term funding for exports.

(DIE) AUSSTELLUNGS-UND MESSE-AUSSCHUSS DER DEUTSCHEN WIRTSCHAFT (AUMA) (English: The German Industry Council for Exhibitions and Trade Fairs) a private German organization receiving no government funds to support its general operations. AUMA promotes exports by bringing together government, semiprivate, and private organizations in the coordination of domestic and overseas TRADE EVENTS. The government may provide funds for special projects, such as research. AUMA also collects and distributes information to German firms on TRADE FAIRS worldwide.

AUSTRAL unit of currency, Argentina (100 centavos equal 1 austral).

AUSTRALIA GROUP (AG) an informal forum through which 22 industrialized nations cooperate to curb proliferation of chemical and biological weapons through a supply approach. The AG's first meeting, held at the Australian Embassy in Paris in June 1986, was attended by Australia, Canada, Japan, New Zealand, the United States, and those nations that were then members of the EUROPEAN COMMUNITY (EC). Membership has expanded to include Norway, Portugal, Spain, Switzerland, Austria, Argentina, Finland, Hungary, Iceland, and representatives of the European Commission, the European Community's executive arm.

AUSTRALIA–NEW ZEALAND–U.S. SECURITY PACT (ANZUS) mutual defense treaty established in 1951 among Australia, New Zealand, and the United States.

AUSTRALIAN DOLLAR unit of currency for Australia, Kiribati, Nauro, and Tuvalu (100 cents equal 1 Australian dollar).

AUSTRALIAN DOLLAR AREA *see* CURRENCY AREA.

AUSTRIAN ACADEMIC COMPUTER NETWORK (ACONET) Austrian private INTERNET network originally established in 1981 by the Austrian Federal Ministry of Science and Research. It connects all Austrian universities and public research institutions according to the rules of INTERNATIONAL STANDARDS ORGANIZATION'S (ISO) Open Systems Interconnection. The ACOnet Association was founded in 1986, and ACOnet was established in 1990.

    The University of Vienna provides access to the Internet. The main focus of the ACOnet is telecommunications traffic between the Austrian cities of Vienna and Linz. There are international connections in these cities giving access to worldwide services.

AUSTRIAN SHILLING unit of currency, Austria (100 groschen equal 1 Austrian shilling).

AUTARKY a country that has chosen to refrain from trade and diplomatic relations with other governments and international organizations. *see also* ECONOMIC NATIONALISM; OPEN ECONOMY.

AUTHENTICATION the validation of the identity of a person or process using a NETWORK on the INTERNET.

AUTHORITY TO PAY a letter mostly used in Far Eastern TRADE, addressed by a BANK to a seller of merchandise. The letter notifies the seller that the bank is authorized to purchase, with or without recourse, DRAFTS up to a stated amount drawn on a certain FOREIGN BUYER to cover certain shipments of merchandise.

AUTOMATED BROKER INTERFACE (ABI) a part of the U.S. CUSTOMS SERVICE AUTOMATED COMMERCIAL SYSTEM. ABI permits transmission of data pertaining to merchandise being imported into the United States. Qualified participants include brokers, importers, carriers, port authorities, and independent data processing companies referred to as service centers.

AUTOMATED CLEARINGHOUSE (ACH) a feature of the AUTOMATED BROKER INTERFACE (ABI), which is a part of the U.S. CUSTOMS SERVICE AUTOMATED COMMERCIAL SYSTEM. ACH combines elements of bank lock box arrangements with electronic funds transfer services to replace cash or check for payment of estimated duties, taxes, and fees on imported merchandise.

AUTOMATED COMMERCIAL ENVIRONMENT U.S. CUSTOMS electronic data system, which provides support for enforcing trade and CONTRABAND laws, ensuring trade compliance, and providing service and information to the international trade community.

AUTOMATED COMMERCIAL SYSTEM (ACS) a joint public–private sector computerized data processing and telecommunications system linking custom houses, members of the IMPORT TRADE community, and other government agencies with the U.S. CUSTOMS SERVICE computer.

Trade users file IMPORT data electronically, receive needed information on CARGO status, and query CUSTOMS' files to prepare submissions. Duties, taxes, and fees may be paid by electronic statement, through a U.S. Department of Treasury-approved clearinghouse bank. ACS contains the import data used by the U.S. Bureau of the Census to prepare U.S. foreign TRADE statistics. ACS began operating in February 1984 and includes:

- the AUTOMATED BROKER INTERFACE,
- the CENSUS INTERFACE SYSTEM,
- the Automated Manifest Systems (AMS),
- the BOND SYSTEM,
- the IN-BOND SYSTEM,
- the CARGO SELECTIVITY SYSTEM,
- the LINE RELEASE SYSTEM,
- the Collections System,
- the Security System,
- the Quota System,
- the Entry Summary Selectivity System,
- the ENTRY SUMMARY SYSTEM,
- the Automated Information Exchange,
- the ANTIDUMPING/COUNTERVAILING DUTY SYSTEM,
- the Firms System,
- the LIQUIDATION SYSTEM,
- the DRAWBACK SYSTEM,
- the FINES, PENALTIES, AND FORFEITURES SYSTEM, and
- the PROTEST SYSTEM.

AUTOMATED EXPORT REPORTING PROGRAM (AERP) telecommunications system providing for electronic submission of most information required on the SHIPPER'S EXPORT DECLARATION. The program was initiated in 1969 with the intent of enabling large-volume exporters to submit electronically and facilitating the U.S. Bureau of the Census's data entry and analysis. AERP was expanded in 1982 to allow freight forwarders, and again in 1985 to allow ocean carriers, to file electronically. At the beginning of fiscal year 1994, about 220 firms—accounting for 350,000 to 400,000 records a month—were participating in AERP. The program is administered by the Automated Data Reporting Branch, Foreign Trade Division, U.S. Bureau of the Census.

AUTOMATED INFORMATION EXCHANGE SYSTEM (AIES) a part of the U.S. CUSTOMS SERVICE'S AUTOMATED COMMERCIAL SYSTEM (ACS) that allows for exchange of classification and value information between field units and headquarters.

AUTOMATED INFORMATION TRANSFER SYSTEM a computerized EXPORT marketing information system of the U.S. DEPARTMENT OF COMMERCE.

AUTOMATED MANIFEST SYSTEMS (AMS) a part of the U.S. CUSTOMS SERVICE'S AUTOMATED COMMERCIAL SYSTEM (ACS) that controls imported merchandise from the time a CARRIER'S CARGO MANIFEST is electronically transmitted to the Customs Service until control is relinquished to another segment of the ACS.

AUTOMATED TRADE LOCATOR ASSISTANCE NETWORK (ATLAS) a U.S. Small Business Administration (SBA) sponsored, contractor-operated, automated system that provides market research on world markets by SIC code (and possibly HARMONIZED SYSTEM). Indirect access is available for businesses, with arrangements through the local SBA district office. ATLAS, which became operational in Spring 1993, replaced SBA's EXPORT INFORMATION SYSTEM (XIS).

AUTOMOTIVE PRODUCTS TRADE AGREEMENT an agreement between the United States and Canada signed in 1965 providing for DUTY-FREE ENTRY for new cars and original equipment automotive parts. *see also* SECTORAL TRADE AGREEMENT; U.S.–CANADA FREE TRADE AGREEMENT of 1989.

AUTONOMOUS SYSTEM (AS) a collection of ROUTERS under a single administrative authority using a common INTERIOR GATEWAY PROTOCOL for routing PACKETS.

AUTORITE DU BASSIN DU NEIGER *see* NIGER BASIN AUTHORITY.

AVE *see* AD VALOREM EQUIVALENT.

AVERAGE a term used in MARINE INSURANCE referring to any partial loss due to insured risks.

AVERAGE AGREEMENT document signed by the owners of CARGO wherein they agree to pay to the carrier any GENERAL AVERAGE contribution due so that the cargo may be released after a general average loss has occurred.

AVERAGE CLAUSES a clause in a CARGO insurance policy that determines the amount of recovery for a PARTICULAR AVERAGE loss.

AVERAGE IRRESPECTIVE OF PERCENTAGE broadest WITH AVERAGE clause appearing in a CARGO insurance policy. Losses by insured risks are paid regardless of percentage.

AVOIDANCE OF CONTRACT the legal cancellation of a CONTRACT because of an event that makes performance of the contract terms impossible or inequitable and releases the parties from their obligations.

AWARD a final judgment rendered by an independent third-party arbitrator. *see also* ARBITRATION; COMPROMISE.

AWAY FROM POST EDUCATION term used to describe dependents attending boarding schools in another country when adequate facilities are not available in the assigned location. *see also* AT POST EDUCATION.

AWB *see* AIR WAYBILL.

AXIS OF EVIL Iran, Iraq, and North Korea, as mentioned by President G.W. Bush during his State of the Union speech in 2002, as nations that were a threat to U.S. security because they harbored terrorism.

B

B1-VISA a specialized term used by U.S. immigration to describe a visitor on a business VISA. The visa is a stamp on the foreign national's passport issued by a U.S. consular officer, which allows the individual to enter the United States and conduct business.

BAATH PARTY The official political party in Iraq until the United States invaded Iraq in March 2003.

BACCONE (Italian, meaning little bite) *see* BRIBERY.

BACEN *see* CENTRAL BANK OF BRAZIL.

BACK HAUL to haul a SHIPMENT back over part of a route it has traveled.

BACK ORDER that portion of an order that cannot be delivered at the scheduled time, but will be delivered at a later date when available.

BACK-TO-BACK BORROWING process whereby a BANK brings together a borrower and a lender so that they agree on a loan CONTRACT. *see also* BACK-TO-BACK LETTER OF CREDIT; IMPORT CREDIT.

BACK-TO-BACK LETTER OF CREDIT a method of financing used when an EXPORTER is not supplying the goods directly. The goods instead are being supplied by another domestic supplier. The exporter upon receipt of the IRREVOCABLE LETTER OF CREDIT drawn in his/her favor arranges to have the ADVISING BANK issue a second irrevocable letter of credit in favor of the supplier from whom he/she is purchasing the goods. The exporter assigns a portion of the proceeds due him/her from the letter of credit, using his letter of credit as collateral for the second letter of credit. *see also* IRREVOCABLE TRANSFERABLE LETTER OF CREDIT.

BACK-TO-BACK LOAN a loan involving a firm in Country X with a subsidiary in Country Y, and a BANK in Country Y with a BRANCH in Country X. A firm will use back-to-back loans during periods of high interest rates or when there is a lack of available credit in the overseas country. An example of a back-to-back loan would be the following: The firm in Country X makes a U.S. dollar deposit with the branch of a foreign bank in the United States. At the same time the foreign bank will make an equivalent loan in foreign currency to the subsidiary in Country Y. The loan will be repaid at maturity. Once the loan has been repaid, the parent company withdraws its deposit plus accrued interest.

BACK TRANSLATION the process of retranslating promotional literature, catalogues, labels, instructional manuals, etc. back to their original form by an individual other than the one who provided the initial translation.

BACKBONE the top level in a hierarchical computer NETWORK. Other networks, which connect to the same backbone, are guaranteed to be interconnected as in the INTERNET.

BACKGROUND NOTES a Department of State publication that provides economic and trade information on major trading partners. Available by set or by subscription from the Superintendent of Documents, U.S. Government Printing Office, Washington, DC 20402.

BACKWARD INTEGRATION type of marketing strategy that occurs when a manufacturer of a product used in the manufacture of another product decides to expand to the next level, by producing the complete product as compared to just the components.

BAD FAITH intent to mislead or deceive; does not include misleading by an honest, inadvertent, or uncalled-for misstatement.

BAGGED CARGO refers to goods loaded in shipping sacks and then loaded into a container for shipment. The bags are normally made of jute, canvas, or various synthetic materials.

BAGHDAD PACT *see* CENTRAL TREATY ORGANIZATION (CENTO).

BAHAMAS DOLLAR unit of currency, Bahamas (100 cents equal 1 Bahamas dollar).

BAHRAINI DINAR unit of currency, Bahrain (1000 fils equal 1 Bahraini dinar).

BAHT unit of currency, Thailand (100 satang equal 1 baht).

BAILMENT DELIVERY of goods or personal property by one person (the bailer) to another (the bailee) on an express or implied CONTRACT and for a particular purpose related to the goods while in possession of the bailee, who has a DUTY to redeliver them to the bailer.

BAKSHEESH *see* BRIBERY.

BALANCED ECONOMY condition of national finances in which IMPORTS and EXPORTS are equal.

BALANCE OF CONCESSIONS *see* RECIPROCITY.

BALANCE OF INDEBTEDNESS *see* NET FOREIGN ASSET POSITION.

BALANCE OF PAYMENTS (BOP) a statistical summary of international transactions. These transactions are defined as the transfer of ownership of something that has an economic value measurable in monetary terms from residents of one country to residents of another. The transfer may involve

- goods, which consist of tangible and visible COMMODITIES or products;
- services, which consist of intangible economic outputs that usually must be produced, transferred, and consumed at the same time and in the same place;
- income on investments; and
- financial claims on, and liabilities to, the rest of the world, including changes in a country's reserve assets held by the central monetary authorities.

Generally, a transaction is the exchange of one asset for another—or one asset for several assets—but it may also involve a gift, which is the provision by one party of something of economic value to another party without something of economic value being received in return.

International transactions are recorded in the balance of payments on the basis of the double-entry principle used in business accounting, in which each transaction gives rise to two offsetting entries of equal value so that, in principle, the resulting credit and debit entries always balance. Transactions are generally valued at market prices and are, to the extent possible, recorded when a change of ownership occurs. Transactions in goods, services, income, and unilateral transfers constitute the current account, and transactions in financial assets and liabilities constitute the capital account.

The INTERNATIONAL MONETARY FUND (IMF), which strives for international comparability, defines the balance of payments as "a statistical statement for a given period showing

- transactions in goods, services, and income between an economy and the rest of the world;
- changes of ownership and other changes in that economy's monetary gold, special drawing rights SDRs, and claims on and liabilities to the rest of the world;
- unrequited transfers and counterpart entries that are needed to balance, in the accounting sense, any entries for the foregoing transactions and changes which are not mutually offsetting."

BALANCE OF TRADE (BOT) the difference between a country's total IMPORTS and EXPORTS. If exports exceed imports, a favorable balance of trade exists; if not, a TRADE DEFICIT is said to exist. *see also* BALANCE OF PAYMENTS.

BALBOA unit of currency, Panama (100 centisimos equal 1 balboa).

BALE large bundle of compressed and bound goods, such as cotton. *see also* BALE CARGO.

BALE CARGO bulky CARGO shipped in bales, usually of burlap. *see also* BALE.

BALLAST heavy material placed on a ship to improve its stability. *see also* AMIDSHIPS; BATTENS.

BALTIC FREIGHT INDEX a daily feature in the JOURNAL OF COMMERCE providing primary information for pricing trends in the CHARTER ocean freight business.

BANAMEX *see* BANCO NATIONAL DE MEXICO.

BANANA REPUBLIC a derogatory term used when making reference to Central American countries. The origin of the term comes from the fact that many Central American countries' economies relied on the EXPORT of bananas to the United States. *see also* BRANCH PLANT ECONOMY; DEPENDENT DEVELOPMENT.

BANCO CENTROAMERICANO DE INTEGRACIÓN ECONÓMICO (BCIE) *see* CENTRAL AMERICAN BANK FOR ECONOMIC INTEGRATION.

BANCO DE LA REPUBLICA ORIENTAL DEL URUGUAY (BROU) the IMPORT/EXPORT state BANK of Uruguay. To operate internationally, any new firm in Uruguay must register at the Banco de la Republica Oriental del Uruguay.

BANCO INTERAMERICANO DE DESAROLLO *see* INTER-AMERICAN DEVELOPMENT BANK.

BANCO LATINOAMERICANO DE EXPORTACIONES (BLADEX) (English: Latin American Export Bank) a multinational bank that provides short- (over 95% of its business) and medium-term years of financing. Operations are conducted in U.S. dollars. Borrowers are primarily Latin American commercial banks of member countries that finance specific trade transactions for their customers. The bank was incorporated in 1978 (began operations in January 1979); its headquarters is in Panama City, Panama. Shareholders include Latin American central and commercial banks, international commercial banks, and the International Finance Corporation.

BANCO NACIONAL DE COMERCIO EXTERIOR (BANCOMEXT) Mexico's national foreign TRADE bank. BANCOMEXT provides credits, guarantees, and promotion services to support Mexico's foreign trade. BANCOMEXT also assists Mexican importers by providing short-term loans to support importation of selected COMMODITIES and medium-term credits (up to 5 years) for importation of capital goods. Its headquarters is in Mexico City, Mexico.

BANCO NATIONAL DE MEXICO (BANAMEX) the largest private bank in Mexico. When President De La Madrid privatized the banking system in Mexico, BANAMEX, the largest, was sold $3.2 billion.

BANCOMEXT *see* BANCO NACIONAL DE COMERCIO EXTERIOR.

BANGLA the official language of Bangladesh. English is the second language and is widely used in education, business, and commerce.

Arabic is also learned and understood by the Muslim community as the religious language.

BANGLADESH BANK the CENTRAL BANK of Bangladesh is the EXCHANGE CONTROL AUTHORITY. Commercial banks in Bangladesh deal in FOREIGN EXCHANGE as per the norms issued by the Central Bank.

BANK a business entity formed to maintain checking and saving accounts, issue loans, and provide credit to businesses. Every country has a CENTRAL BANK that is responsible for the issuance of currency and the development of MONETARY POLICY. *see also* CURRENCY EXCHANGE CONTROLS; EXCHANGE CONTROL AUTHORITY; EXCHANGE CONTROLS; GLOBAL MONETARISM; MONETARISM.

BANK ADVISORY COMMITTEE an informal organization consisting mostly of lead bankers in an individual debtor country. The lead bankers, representing the interests of the debtor country's banking industry, develop restructuring plans that the committee proposes to its government. The debtor country government, in turn, proposes the plan to foreign lending governments. The Bank Advisory Committee, which in some respects has replaced the LONDON CLUB, is not a structured or formal organization.

BANK AFFILIATE ETC an EXPORT TRADING COMPANY (ETC) partially or wholly owned by a banking institution as provided under the EXPORT TRADING COMPANY ACT of 1982.

BANK AFFILIATE EXPORT TRADING COMPANY an EXPORT TRADING COMPANY partially or wholly owned by a banking institution as provided under the EXPORT TRADING COMPANY ACT.

BANK DELIVERY ORDER TO AN AIRLINE letter addressed to an air carrier from a CONSIGNEE bank designated on an AIR WAYBILL instructing the carrier to release a shipment. Although airlines will often accept as a delivery order a bank's endorsement on the AIR WAYBILL, it is a nonnegotiable document.

BANK DRAFT check drawn by one BANK against funds deposited into an account in another bank.

BANK FOR INTERNATIONAL SETTLEMENTS (BIS) financial institution established in 1930 by bankers and diplomats of Europe and the U.S. as a meeting place for the governors of West European central banks. The BIS serves to promote international financial cooperation among central banks in international financial settlements. It is the representative of several important West European financial enterprises and holds the accounts of the European Coal and Steel Community. The BIS is run by a board composed of eight West European CENTRAL BANK governors and five other financiers. Officials of the U.S. Federal Reserve System attend BIS meetings. BIS members include Australia, Austria, Belgium, Bulgaria, Canada, Czechoslovakia, Denmark, Finland, France, Germany, Greece, Hungary, Iceland, Ireland, Italy, Japan, Netherlands, Norway, Poland,

Portugal, Romania, South Africa, Spain, Sweden, Switzerland, Turkey, the United Kingdom, the United States, and the former Yugoslavia. The bank's headquarters is in Basel, Switzerland. *see also* EUROPEAN COMMUNITY (EC).

BANK GUARANTEE an assurance, obtained from a BANK by a foreign purchaser, that the bank will pay an EXPORTER up to a given amount for goods shipped if the foreign purchaser defaults. *see also* LETTER OF CREDIT.

BANK HOLDING COMPANY any company that directly or indirectly owns or controls, with power to vote, more than 5% of the voting shares of each of one or more BANKS.

BANK HOLIDAY day when BANKS are closed.

BANK NOTES an alternative term used when referring to the actual paper currency of a country.

BANK OF CENTRAL AFRICAN STATES (French: Banque des États de L'Afrique Central, BEAC) Central African bank that issues a common currency unit, the Central African franc. Members include Cameroon, Central African Republic, Chad, People's Republic of Congo, Gabon, and Equitorial Guinea. France participates in management of the bank and provides guarantees for the currency. The bank was established in April 1973, and its headquarters is in Yaoundé, Cameroon.

BANK OF DOCUMENTARY CREDIT INSURANCE (BDCI) the portion of the Canadian EXPORT DEVELOPMENT CORPORATION that provides guarantees to Canadian BANKS financing the exports of Canadian businesses. BDCI insures the bank against all losses on the covered transaction.

BANK RELEASE negotiable TIME DRAFT drawn on and accepted by a BANK, which adds its credit to that of an IMPORTER of merchandise. It allows the purchaser of items to take delivery. Demands from others may also need to be satisfied before the items can be released. Customs clearance must also be obtained. *see also* DRAFT BILL OF EXCHANGE.

BANK SWAPS *see* SWAP; SWAP ARRANGEMENTS.

BANKER'S ACCEPTANCE a DRAFT BILL OF EXCHANGE drawn on and accepted by a BANK. Depending on the bank's creditworthiness, the acceptance becomes a financial instrument that can be included in the FACTORING process.

BANKER'S BANK a BANK that is established by mutual consent by independent and unaffiliated banks to provide a clearinghouse for financial transactions.

BANKER'S DRAFT a DRAFT BILL OF EXCHANGE payable on demand and drawn by or on behalf of the BANK itself. It is regarded as cash and cannot be returned unpaid.

BANKRUPTCY a state of insolvency by an individual or organization that is not able to pay its debts.

BANQUE ARABE POUR LE DEVELOPPEMENT ECONOMIQUE EN AFRIQUE (BADEA) *see* ARAB BANK FOR ECONOMIC DEVELOPMENT IN AFRICA (ABEDA).

BANQUE CENTRALE DES ETATS DE L'AFRIQUE DE L'OUEST (BCEAO) BANK that operates as a CENTRAL BANK under authority of the WEST AFRICAN MONETARY UNION and issues the common currency for member states: Benin, Burkina Faso, Côte d'Ivoire, Mali, Niger, Senegal, and Togo.

BANQUE DE DEVELOPPEMENT DES ETATS DE L'AFRIQUE CENTRALE (BDEAC) *see* CENTRAL AFRICAN STATES DEVELOPMENT BANK.

BANQUE DE DEVELOPPEMENT DES ETATS DU GRAND LAC (BDEGL) *see* DEVELOPMENT BANK OF THE GREAT LAKES STATES.

BANQUE DES ETATS DE L'AFRIQUE CENTRALE (BEAC) *see* BANK OF CENTRAL AFRICAN STATES.

BANQUE FRANÇAISE DU COMMERCE EXTERIEUR (BFCE) a French government-owned agency that is the lender for officially supported EXPORT credits at preferential interest rates. The BFCE, which provides financing for international TRADE, plays a coordinating role between exporters and the French government. BFCE services include
- offering fixed-rate interim credit and payment plans during the manufacture of goods or performance of services;
- providing endorsements to gain access to refinancing and special low-interest loans and rediscounting the available portion of such credit with the Banque du France; and
- using funds borrowed in France and overseas under state guarantees to finance buyer credits running more than 7 years as well as refinancing supplier credits for the same term.

BFCE also manages Treasury guarantees on French overseas investment. *see also* COMPAGNIE FRANÇAISE D'ASSURANCE POUR LE COMMERCE EXTERIEUR.

BANQUE OUEST-AFRICAINE DE DEVELOPPEMENT *see* WEST AFRICAN DEVELOPMENT BANK.

BAREBOAT CHARTER charter of a vessel where the character party has the right to use his own master and crew on the vessel. *see also* CHARTER; CHARTER PARTY; CHARTER VESSEL; CHARTERER; DEMISE.

BARRATRY fraudulent, criminal, or wrongful act by ship's captain or crew that causes loss or damage to the ship or CARGO. Barratry includes purposefully running a ship aground and destroying or stealing a ship's cargo.

BARs *see* BUY AMERICAN RESTRICTIONS.

BARTER TRADE in which merchandise is exchanged directly for other merchandise or services without use of money.

BAS *see* CARIBBEAN/CENTRAL AMERICA BUSINESS ADVISORY SERVICE.

BASE CURRENCY the currency whose value is one when a quote is made between two currencies. Example: If the Japanese yen were trading at 100 yen to the U.S. dollar, the U.S. dollar would be the base currency, whereas the yen would be the QUOTED CURRENCY.

BASE MONEY the percentage of deposits that a BANK must hold on reserve, as required by the U.S. Federal Reserve System.

BASE PRODUCE a COMMODITY classification term used to describe bulk unprocessed agricultural goods. *see also* BULK CARGO.

BASEL CONVENTION multilateral treaty restricting TRADE in hazardous waste, some nonhazardous wastes, solid wastes, and incinerator ash. It was adopted in 1989 by a United Nations-sponsored conference of 116 nations in Basel, Switzerland. Twenty nations must ratify the treaty before it goes into effect.

BASELINE specification of a product or service that has been formally reviewed and agreed upon and that thereafter serves as the basis for further development.

BASIC BALANCE a term used in BALANCE OF PAYMENT analysis referring to the sum of the balances on the CURRENT ACCOUNT and the balances on the long-term capital account.

BASING POINT location used to determine rates between other points.

BASING RATE rate used for the sole purpose of determining other rates.

BASIS POINT one-hundredth of a percent, or 0.0001 (1% equals 100 basis points).

BASKET OF CURRENCIES means of establishing value for a composite unit consisting of the currencies of designated nations.

BASKET PEGGER a country that maintains a fixed exchange rate using an average of a combination of foreign currencies rather than a single currency.

BATTENS the protruding fixtures of the inside walls of a vessel's hold that keep CARGO away from the walls of the vessel. *see also* BALLAST.

BCIU *see* BUSINESS COUNCIL FOR INTERNATIONAL UNDERSTANDING.

BCP *see* BUYER CREDIT PROTOCOL.

BCS *see* BORDER CARGO SELECTIVITY.

BDCI *see* BANK OF DOCUMENTARY CREDIT INSURANCE.

BDEGL *see* DEVELOPMENT BANK OF THE GREAT LAKES STATES.

BEAC *see* BANK OF CENTRAL AFRICAN STATES.

BEARER person in possession of a negotiable instrument, document of title, or security marked "payable to bearer" or person in possession of one of these documents endorsed in blank.

BECAO *see* BANQUE CENTRALE DES ÉTATS DE L'AFRIQUE DE L'OUEST.

BECC *see* BORDER ENVIRONMENT COOPERATION COMMISSION.

BEET *see* BUSINESS EXECUTIVE ENFORCEMENT TEAM.

BEGGAR THY NEIGHBOR POLICY those actions to reduce imports and increase domestic production. Examples: the imposition of TARIFFS, QUOTAS, RESTRICTIVE STANDARDS, and BUY LOCAL programs. *see also* PROTECTIONISM; NONTARIFF BARRIERS; TARIFF ACT OF 1930; TARIFF BARRIERS.

BEIRUT AGREEMENT also known as the Agreement for Facilitating the International Circulation of Visual and Auditory Materials of an Educational, Scientific, and Cultural Character. The purpose of the agreement was to make provisions in the countries' customs laws to facilitate the importation of visual and auditory materials certified for educational purposes. The United States became a party to the agreement on January 12, 1967.

BELGIAN FRANC unit of currency, Belgium (100 centimes equal 1 Belgian franc).

BELGIUM-LUXEMBOURG ECONOMIC UNION (BLEU) (French: Union Economique Belgo-Luxembourgeoise, UEBL) a system of monetary association between Belgium and Luxembourg. The BLEU was established in July 1921.

BELGIUM-NETHERLANDS-LUXEMBOURG CUSTOMS UNION *see* BENELUX ECONOMIC UNION; CUSTOMS UNION.

BELLY CARGO CARGO loaded within the shipping carrier, either an airplane or vessel. *see* DECK CARGO.

BELLY PITS OR HOLDS compartments beneath the cabin of an aircraft used for the transport of CARGO or baggage. *see also* LOWER DECK CONTAINERS.

BELOW THE LINE ITEMS *see* ACCOMMODATING TRANSACTIONS.

BENCHMARK COUNTRY an approach used by the EXPORTER in determining the level of STANDARDIZATION in a marketing program. The exporter usually selects a country or market as a benchmark country. The exporter then evaluates all other markets in relation to the benchmark country. The benchmark country will usually be the HOME COUNTRY where the exporter is located, or the country in which the exporter has had the greatest level of success.

BENEFICIARY
1. individual or company entitled to draw or demand payment under the terms of a LETTER OF CREDIT (L/C).
2. person entitled to take insurance proceeds.
3. person for whose benefit a contract, trust, or will is executed or enforced.

BENEFIT ALLOWANCE any incentive to an individual to accept an international assignment. *see also* COMPLETION ALLOWANCE; CORRESPONDENCE ALLOWANCE; EDUCATION ALLOWANCE; EXPATRIATE PREMIUM; FURNISHING ALLOWANCE; HARDSHIP ALLOWANCE; HOME LEAVE ALLOWANCE; HOUSING ALLOWANCE; NEGATIVE DIFFERENTIALS; RELOCATION ALLOWANCE; SETTLING-IN ALLOWANCE.

BENEFIT DIFFERENTIAL the specific incentive offered to an individual to accept an international assignment. *see* BENEFIT ALLOWANCE.

BENEFIT GRATUITY *see* FOREIGN SERVICE PREMIUM.

BENEFITS FOR INTERNATIONAL SERVICE *see* BENEFIT ALLOWANCE; BENEFIT DIFFERENTIAL; FOREIGN SERVICE PREMIUM.

BENELUX *see* BENELUX ECONOMIC UNION.

BENELUX ECONOMIC UNION (BENELUX) (acronym for Belgium, Netherlands, and Luxembourg) an economic union originally established in January 1948 and revised in January 1960. Benelux continues as an internal regional association within the EUROPEAN COMMUNITY (EC) because the association's aims do not conflict with EC goals.

BERI *see* BUSINESS ENVIRONMENT RISK INDEX.

BERMUDA DOLLAR unit of currency, Bermuda (100 cents equal 1 Bermuda dollar).

BERNE CONVENTION an international agreement signed in 1886 providing for the protection of literary and artistic works. The Berne Convention of 1886 established procedures for international copyright protection. The Berne Convention required that all countries signing the agreement provide the same protection to authors and artists from other countries signatory that it would allow to its own nationals. *see also* UNIVERSAL COPYRIGHT CONVENTION.

BERNE UNION an organization of governmental agencies providing EXPORT CREDIT insurance such as the Export–Import Bank of the United States (EXIMBANK) and the Canadian Export Development Corporation (EDC). *see also* EXPORT CREDIT ENHANCED LEVERAGE; EXPORT CREDIT GUARANTEES PROGRAMS; EXPORT CREDIT GUARANTEES DEPARTMENT.

BERTH place beside a docking area where a ship is secured and CARGO can be loaded or unloaded.

BEST INFORMATION AVAILABLE process pursued under GATT rules when a respondent in an ANTIDUMPING/COUNTERVAILING DUTY SYSTEM case either declines to provide information or provides inadequate information. The investigating authority has the right to resort to other information. This practice is known as best information available. Determinations of BIA may be made on a case-by-case basis. In some cases, it may be information submitted by petitioners.

BHC *see* BRITISH HIGH COMMISSION.

BIC *see* BUSINESS INCOME COVERAGE.

BID (BUY) the amount that a FOREIGN EXCHANGE trader is willing to buy foreign exchange for. The bid is what the trader is willing to buy and the offer is what the trader is willing to sell foreign exchange for.

BID BOND guarantee established in connection with international tenders; guarantees fulfillment of the offer. *see also* STANDBY LETTER OF CREDIT.

BID GUARANTY COVERAGE guaranties issued by the OVERSEAS PRIVATE INVESTMENT CORPORATION (OPIC) on behalf of the U.S. EXPORTER of goods and services in favor of a foreign government buyer. The guaranties are usually in the form of IRREVOCABLE, on-demand STANDBY LETTERS OF CREDIT.

BIE *see* BUREAU OF INTERNATIONAL EXPOSITIONS.

BILATERAL AGREEMENT an agreement between two countries.

BILATERAL CLEARING AGREEMENT a government-to-government reciprocal trade arrangement whereby two nations agree to a trade turnover of specified value over one or more years. The value of the products traded under the agreement is denominated in accounting units expressed in major currencies (e.g., clearing U.S. dollars, clearing Swiss francs). EXPORTERS in each country are paid by designated local banks in domestic currencies.

BILATERAL INVESTMENT TREATY (BIT) agreement that ensures U.S. investments abroad of national or most favored nation treatment, prohibits the imposition of performance requirements, and allows the American investor to engage top management in a foreign country without regard to nationality. BITs ensure the right to make investment-related transfers and guarantee that expropriation takes place only in accordance with accepted international law. BITs also guarantee access by an investing party to impartial and binding international arbitration for dispute settlement.

BILATERAL STEEL AGREEMENTS (BSAs) U.S. bilateral agreements with ten major steel-trading partners. As a result of the BSAs, the governments agreed to reduce or eliminate state market intervention and domestic subsidies for their steel industries which acted as TRADE barriers with the United States.

BILATERAL TAX AGREEMENT an agreement between a foreign government and the United States establishing the personal tax liability of a U.S. CITIZEN assigned to a foreign country.

BILATERAL TRADE the movement of goods and services between any two countries. *see also* MULTILATERAL TRADE; TRILATERAL TRADE.

BILATERAL TRADE AGREEMENT an enforceable agreement achieved between two nations for the purposes of improved trade relations.

BILATERAL TREATIES a legally binding arrangement between two countries in written form and governed by international law. *see also* CONVENTION; INTERNATIONAL AGREEMENTS.

BILINGUALISM the ability to speak two languages equally well.

BILL
1. DRAFT.
2. written statement of contract terms.

BILL OF CREDIT written statement that authorizes the recipient to receive or collect money from a FOREIGN correspondent. *see also* CORRESPONDENT BANK.

BILL OF EXCHANGE *see* DRAFT.

BILL OF HEALTH certificate issued by Customs declaring the proper health of the crew or passengers of a vessel or airplane upon arrival or departure from port.

BILL OF LADING (BIL) contracts between the owner of the goods and the CARRIER. There are two types: a STRAIGHT BILL OF LADING is nonnegotiable, and a negotiable or shipper's order bill of lading can be bought, sold, or traded while goods are in transit and is used for many types of financing transactions. The customer usually needs the original or a copy as proof of ownership to take possession of the goods.

BILL OF PARCELS statement sent with a SHIPMENT that gives descriptions and prices for included items; often referred to as a packing slip. *see also* BILL OF SALE.

BILL OF SALE written document by which a party legally transfers ownership of goods to another party. *see also* BILL OF PARCELS.

BILL OF SIGHT Customs document that allows a party to see the goods before they pay DUTIES on them.

BILL-TO PARTY party designated on a BILL OF LADING as the one responsible for payment of the FREIGHT charges.

BILLED WEIGHT designated weight shown on the FREIGHT bill.

BILLING THIRD PARTY transference of transportation charges to a party other than the SHIPPER or CONSIGNEE.

BIMETALLISM a monetary system that uses two metals such as gold and silver to serve as backing for a country's MONEY SUPPLY. Bimetallism was a system designed to provide more economic stability than a system based on only one metal. It was a system practiced in the United States and other countries with the exception of England in the eighteenth and nineteenth centuries.

BINATIONAL DISPUTE-SETTLEMENT MECHANISM that part of the CANADA–U.S. FREE TRADE AGREEMENT that allows for an orderly settlement of disputes between parties to the agreement. These disputes can occur from differences in interpretation of the agreement.

BINATIONAL (BINDING) DISPUTE SETTLEMENT PANEL that part of the CANADA–U.S. FREE TRADE AGREEMENT to settle any ANTIDUMPING COUNTERVAILING DUTY disputes. The panel consists of five members chosen by the Canadian Minister of International Trade and the U.S. TRADE REPRESENTATIVE (USTR).

BINATIONAL SECRETARIAT (FTA BINATIONAL SECRE-TARIAT) an office founded under the CANADA–U.S. FREE TRADE AGREEMENT. The office maintains records for any actions involving the BINATIONAL DISPUTE MECHANISM of the free-trade agreement.

BINDER temporary insurance coverage awaiting the issuance of a formal insurance policy or certificate.

BINDING A TARIFF a country agreeing to maintain TARIFFS at a particular level.

BINDING AGREEMENT a formal agreement between two or more countries requiring each to comply with its terms and conditions.

BINDING ARBITRATION *see* ARBITRATION.

BINDING DECISIONS normal rulings as to the TARIFF classification of an item by the District or the Area Director of U.S. Customs. *see also* BINDING TARIFF CLASSIFICATION RULINGS.

BINDING RULINGS *see* BINDING TARIFF CLASSIFICATION RULING.

BINDING TARIFF CLASSIFICATION RULING a formal ruling as to the classification of an item being imported into the United States. The IMPORTER may obtain a binding tariff classification ruling, which can be relied upon when placing orders and for making other business determinations by writing to the U.S. Customs Service district director or to the Area Director of Customs. These rulings will be binding at all ports of entry unless revoked by the Customs Service's Office of Regulations and Rulings.

The following information is required in ruling requests:
- the names, addresses, and other identifying information of all interested parties.
- the name(s) of the port(s) in which the merchandise will be entered.

- a description of the transaction, for example, a prospective importation of (merchandise) from (country).
- a statement that there are, to the importer's knowledge, no issues on the COMMODITY pending before the Customs Service or any court.
- a statement as to whether classification advice had previously been sought from a Customs officer, and if so, from whom, and what advice was rendered, if any.

A request for a TARIFF classification ruling should include the following information:

- a complete description of the goods. Send samples (if practical), sketches, diagrams, or other illustrative material that will be useful in supplementing the written description.
- cost breakdowns of component materials and their respective quantities shown in percentages (if possible).
- a description of the principal use of the goods as a class or kind of merchandise in the United States.
- information as to commercial, scientific, or common designations as may be applicable.
- any other information that may be pertinent or required for the purpose of tariff classification.

BIOCHEMICAL WARFARE collective term for use of both chemical and biological warfare weapons.

BIOCHEMTERRORISM terrorism using as weapons biological or chemical agents.

BIOLOGICAL AGENTS several classes of biological agents identified according to their degree of pathogenic hazard that are controlled by the United States in accord with provisions of the AUSTRALIA GROUP (AG). Applications submitted to the U.S. DEPARTMENT OF COMMERCE for the EXPORT of certain biological agents are generally referred to the U.S. Department of State and the intelligence community on a case-by-case basis.

BIOLOGICAL AMMUNITION ammunition designed specifically to release a biological agent used as the warhead for biological weapons.

BIOLOGICAL WEAPONS CONVENTION (BWC) officially known as the "Convention on the Prohibition of Development, Production, and Stockpiling of Bacteriological (Biological) and Toxin Weapons and Destruction." The BWC works toward general and complete disarmament, including the prohibition and elimination of all types of weapons of mass destruction.

BIOTERRORISM the use of biological agents in a terrorist operation. Biological toxins include anthrax, ricin, botulism, the plague, smallpox, and tularemia.

BIOWARFARE the use of biological agents to harm targeted people either directly, by bringing the people into contact with the agents, or indirectly, by infecting other animals and plants, which would in turn harm the people.

BIRR unit of currency, Ethiopia (100 cents equal 1 birr).

BIS *see* BANK FOR INTERNATIONAL SETTLEMENTS.

BISNIS *see* BUSINESS INFORMATION SERVICE FOR THE NEWLY INDEPENDENT STATES.

BITNET an INTERNET academic computer network that provides interactive electronic mail and file transfer services, using a store-and-forward protocol, based on IBM Network Job Entry protocols.

BLACK MARKET a secondary currency market with rates different from those in the official market. The black market operates outside the control of government and appears in those countries with FOREIGN EXCHANGE CONTROLS. *see also* CONVERTIBLE CURRENCY; HARD CURRENCY; NONCONVERTIBLE CURRENCY; PARALLEL MARKET; SOFT CURRENCY.

BLACK MONEY illegal money earned through the international drug trade. *see also* DIRTY MONEY; GRAY MONEY.

BLACKLIST
1. (n.) a list of individuals or companies who have been punished as a result of some specific action. Example: Company X is one of many companies that appear on the Arab Boycott Blacklist.
2. (v.) to create a list of individuals or companies that have earned punishment as a result of some specific action. Example: If Syria were to blacklist Company X for violating the ARAB BOYCOTT OF ISRAEL, Company X would lose significant sales.

BLADEX *see* BANCO LATINOAMERICANO DE EXPORTACIONES.

BLANKET CERTIFICATE OF ORIGIN a signed statement as to the origin of the EXPORT item covering continuous shipments to the same IMPORTER by the same EXPORTER. *see also* CERTIFICATE OF ORIGIN.

BLANKET RATE special single rate applied to multiple articles in a single SHIPMENT.

BLEU *see* BELGIUM-LUXEMBOURG ECONOMIC UNION.

BLISTER AGENTS agents that cause pain and incapacitation instead of death and might be used to injure many people at once.

BLOCKADE prevention of commercial exchange by physically preventing CARRIERS from entering a specific port or nation. In international law a military blockade is considered an act of war. *see also* EMBARGO.

BLOCKED ACCOUNT an account in which the funds are not readily transferable. A government might decide to block or freeze the assets of a foreign government in an attempt to have them comply with certain political objectives.

BLOCKED CURRENCY a currency whose transfer is restricted. The blocked currency is one that cannot be freely converted to the currency of another country nor can it be physically transferred to another country.

BLOCKED EXCHANGE *see* BLOCKED CURRENCY.

BLOCKING LAWS laws prohibiting the release of confidential facts by financial organizations to anyone but the proper authorities.

BLOOD AGENTS agents based on cyanide compounds.

BLUE LANTERN a procedure pertaining to U.S. MUNITIONS LIST items. It is intended to verify that information stated on EXPORT license applications is valid and that the use of the COMMODITY or service exported is consistent with the terms of the license. It includes prelicense and postshipment checks of export applications conducted by designated officials at U.S. embassies. Blue Lantern was initiated in September 1990 by the U.S. State Department's Office of Defense Trade Controls.

BMWi *see* BUNDESMINISTERIUM FÜR WIRTSCHAFT.

BOARD OF INVESTMENTS (BOI) a special department in the Thai government. The BOI oversees the facilitation of FOREIGN INVESTMENT. It offers special tax incentives and other privileges particularly to companies engaged in EXPORT-ORIENTED, LABOR-INTENSIVE, and agro-based projects.

BODY LANGUAGE a nonverbal form of communication. Through nonverbal communication, individuals can use facial expression, gestures, etc., to convey messages. The meaning of a gesture in one country may have an entirely different meaning in another. Example: the O.K. hand sign commonly used in the United States means zero in France; signifies money in Japan, and is a vulgar gesture in South America.

BOLIVAR unit of currency, Venezuela (100 centimos equal 1 bolivar).

BOLIVIANO unit of currency, Bolivia (100 centavos equal 1 boliviano).

BOLSA MEXICANA DE VALORES the Mexican Stock Market. The Bolsa is located in Mexico City and is owned and operated by 25 Mexican brokerage houses. Approximately 210 companies are listed on the Bolsa, with capitalization of about U.S. $100 billion.

BONA FIDE a term meaning genuine or authentic. It is referred to in computing values for customs purposes.

BONA-FIDE FOREIGN RESIDENT a term used in the Internal Revenue Service Tax Code. It relates to Section 911 and the requirements for excluding foreign-earned income.

BOND *see* BOND SYSTEM.

BOND OF INDEMNITY agreement made with a CARRIER that relieves that carrier of any liability incurred under stated conditions.

BOND SYSTEM a part of the U.S. CUSTOMS SERVICE AUTOMATED COMMERCIAL SYSTEM (ACS) that provides information on bond coverage. A CUSTOMS BOND is a contract between a principal, usually an importer, and the U.S. Customs Service. A SURETY is obtained to ensure the performance of an obligation imposed by law or regulation. The bond covers potential loss of duties, taxes, and penalties for specific types of transactions. The U.S. Customs Service is the contract beneficiary.

BONDED describing goods stored by Customs until the IMPORT DUTIES are paid or the goods are exported. *see also* BONDED TERMINAL; BONDED WAREHOUSE.

BONDED EXCHANGE exchange that cannot be freely converted into other currencies.

BONDED GOODS goods placed in a BONDED WAREHOUSE. The payment of duties on these goods has been deferred until the goods have been removed from the bonded warehouse.

BONDED STORAGE *see* BONDED WAREHOUSE.

BONDED STORAGE EXEMPTIONS special considerations, including a possible rebate of duties, when the imported materials are used in products that are REEXPORTED. *see also* FREE-TRADE ZONE, SPECIAL CUSTOMS PRIVILEGED FACILITIES.

BONDED TERMINAL airline terminal approved by the U.S. Treasury Department for storage of goods until Customs DUTIES are paid or released. *see also* BONDED; BONDED TERMINAL; BONDED WAREHOUSES.

BONDED WAREHOUSES warehouses authorized by the U.S. CUSTOMS SERVICE for storage or the manufacture of goods on which payment of duties is deferred until the goods enter the Customs Territory. The goods are not subject to duties if they are reshipped to foreign points.

BOOK VALUE the original cost of an asset minus any accumulated depreciation.

BOOKING an arrangement with a steamship company for the acceptance and carriage of freight.

BOOKING CENTER any financial organization with headquarters outside the country. Transactions are recorded in these locations to take advantage of lower tax rates. *see also* OFFSHORE BANKING; OFFSHORE BANKING CENTERS.

BOOKING NUMBER an identifying number assigned to a contract of carriage. *see also* AIR WAYBILL; BILL OF LADING; CONTRACT OF AFFREIGHTMENT.

BORDER the line that separates one country from another.

BORDER CARGO SELECTIVITY (BCS) an automated CARGO selectivity system based on historical and other information. The system is designed to facilitate cargo processing and to improve U.S. CUSTOMS SERVICE enforcement capabilities by providing targeting information to border locations. The system is used for the land-border environment.

BORDER ENVIRONMENT COOPERATION COMMISSION (BECC) a U.S.–Mexican binational commission intended to facilitate border environmental clean-up and to provide additional support for community adjustment and investment related to the NORTH AMERICAN FREE TRADE AGREEMENT (NAFTA). The BECC will assist border states and local communities in coordinating, designing, and financing environmental infrastructure projects with cross-border impact. To be eligible, projects must observe the environmental laws for the place where the project is located or carried out. The BECC will certify projects to the NORTH AMERICAN DEVELOPMENT BANK (NADBANK) and will seek to mobilize financing from the NADBank; federal, state, and local grants; loans and guarantees; and the private sector.

BORDER OPERATIONS functions related to the processing of EXPORT and IMPORT declarations, collecting DUTIES, taxes, and fees, and determining admissibility or exportability of international CARGO.

BORDER TAX ADJUSTMENTS pertains to the return of duties collected on goods exported from a country so as not to hinder imports. *see also* DUTY; EXPORT DUTY.

BOTB *see* BRITISH OVERSEAS TRADE BOARD.

BOTH TO BLAME COLLISION COURSE *see* MARINE INSURANCE.

BOUNCE the turning back of an INTERNET mail message because of either an error in its addressing or technical difficulties.

BOUND RATE *see* TARIFF BINDING.

BOUNTIES
1. compensation paid to persons to induce certain actions.
2. government payments made to producers or EXPORTERS to strengthen their competitive position.

BOUNTY *see* SUBSIDY.

BOX
1. term referring to a trailer, semitrailer, or container used in transportation.
2. type of package of wood, cardboard, metal, plastic, or other material.

BOX CAR closed FREIGHT car.

BOYCOTT to decline to do business with a country, business, or individual. *see also* ARAB BOYCOTT OF ISRAEL; EMBARGO; TRADE BARRIER.

BPI *see* BUSINESS PROPRIETARY INFORMATION.

BRACERO a Mexican term used when referring to migrant farmer.

BRANCH *see* SUBSIDIARY.

BRANCH OFFICE a foreign operation not separate from the parent that owns it.

BRAZILIAN FEDERAL BOARD OF ACCOUNTANCY (CONSELHO FEDERAL DE CONTABILIDADE) *see* BRAZILIAN INSTITUTE OF ACCOUNTANTS (IBRACON).

BRAZILIAN FEDERAL LAND TAX (IPTR) an annual tax levied on the ownership or possession of real estate in rural areas. Tax rates vary on the land value and the buildings on the property.

BRAZILIAN IDENTIFICATION CARD *see* CARTEIRA DE IDENTIDADE DE ESTRANGEIRO.

BRAZILIAN INSTITUTE OF ACCOUNTANTS (IBRACON) together with the BRAZILIAN FEDERAL BOARD OF ACCOUNTANCY (CONSELHO FEDERAL DE CONTABILIDADE, CFC) are responsible for the establishment of accounting principles and standards used in Brazil.

BRAZILIAN SECURITIES COMMISSION (CVM) Brazilian commission responsible for regulating all publicly traded companies in Brazil. State-owned companies are regulated by the Ministry of Economy and the Ministry of Infrastructure as well as by the governing regulatory authorities.

BRAZILIAN WORK CARD *see* CARTEIRA DE TRABALHO; CARTEIRA PROFESSIONAL.

BREACH OF CONCESSIONAL AGREEMENTS an example of a material change unilaterally imposed by a HOST GOVERNMENT on project agreements. The OVERSEAS PRIVATE INVESTMENT CORPORATION (OPIC) provides EXPROPRIATION insurance coverage that protects against any ABROGATION, REPUDIATION, or breach of concessional agreements between the U.S. company and the foreign government.

BREACH OF SPECIFIED GOVERNMENTAL OBLIGATIONS a violation of a specific HOST GOVERNMENT obligation identified by a U.S. investor at the outset as vital to the successful operation of the project. The OVERSEAS PRIVATE INVESTMENT CORPORATION (OPIC) can provide insurance to protect against such losses.

BREAKAGE in marine insurance, referring to breakage of fragile goods such as glass and china; excluded from coverage, unless the policy specifically covers breakage.

BREAK BULK the process of reducing a large shipment into several smaller shipments each to be delivered to a specific customer. *see also* MAKE BULK.

BRETTON WOODS CONFERENCE a United Nations Monetary and Financial Conference that convened in July 1944 at Bretton Woods, NH. As a proactive measure to manage post World War II economic challenges, the WORLD BANK and the INTERNATIONAL MONETARY FUND (IMF) were created. The Bretton Woods monetary system required the participating countries to maintain currencies within a percentage point or two of an agreed dollar value. The IMF maintained the international monetary system through careful guidance as well as the use of credit. The system was operative until March 1973 when the Bretton Woods rules were disregarded following a 1971 U.S. action unlinking the dollar from gold valuation.

BRIBE payment that results in a benefit that would not have been received except for receipt of that money; a bribe is a criminal offense. *see also* BACCONE; BAKSHEESH; BUSTARELLA; DASH; KUROI KIRI.

BRIBERY anything, such as money or property, offered or given to a government official to make him/her act dishonestly or to influence or persuade the official to grant some specific privilege. *see also* BACCONE; BAKSHEESH; BUSTARELLA; DASH; KUROI KIRI.

BRITISH HIGH COMMISSION (BHC) (also called High Commission, HC, or Her Majesty's High Commission, HMHC) term used in lieu of EMBASSY in the COMMONWEALTH countries.

BRITISH KNOW HOW FUND a fund established in June 1989 for the purpose of supporting the development of a MARKET ECONOMY and democracy in Poland. This is to be accomplished through technology and skills transferred from Britain to Poland.

BRITISH OVERSEAS TRADE BOARD (BOTB) British TRADE board located in the British Department of Trade and Industry (DTI). The BOTB advises on international trade and guides the government's export promotion program, including policy, financing, and overseas projects. The board is composed of industry and government representatives. The chairman of the BOTB is an industrialist, and the Chief Executive is a member of DTI. The export departments of the BOTB's regional offices work together with commercial staff from the Foreign and Commonwealth Office (FCO) to provide commercial assistance through the UK's overseas offices.

BRITISH POUND unit of currency, United Kingdom (100 pence equal 1 British pound).

BROADBAND a signal transmission medium capable of supporting a wide range of frequencies. It can carry multiple signals by dividing the total capacity of the medium into multiple, independent BAND-WIDTH channels, where each channel operates only on a specific range of frequencies. *see also* BASEBAND.

BROKER a term often used when referring to a FREIGHT FORWARDER or CUSTOMS BROKER. *see also* EXPORT BROKER.

BROKERAGE FEE a charge paid to a FREIGHT FORWARDER or CUSTOMS BROKER for services rendered.

BROU *see* BANCO DE LA REPUBLICA ORIENTAL DEL URUGUAY.

BROWN GOODS an English term pertaining to furniture, also used in the United States and Canada when referring to durable goods. *see also* SOFT GOODS.

BRUNEI DOLLAR unit of currency, Brunei (100 cents equal 1 Brunei dollar).

BRUSSELS PRINCIPLES OF VALUATION the Brussels CONVENTION on the valuation of goods for CUSTOMS purposes, as amended, created the CUSTOMS COOPERATION COUNCIL. The council established a valuation committee that furnished information on the valuation of goods for customs purposes. *see also* BRUSSELS TARIFF NOMENCLATURE.

BRUSSELS TARIFF NOMENCLATURE (BTN) a formerly widely used international TARIFF classification system that preceded the CUSTOMS COOPERATION COUNCIL NOMENCLATURE (CCCN) and the Harmonized System Nomenclature (HS). The BTN was changed in name only to the CCCN in 1976 to avoid confusion with the tariff of the EUROPEAN COMMUNITY.

BSAS *see* BILATERAL STEEL AGREEMENTS.

BSD *see* BERKELEY SOFTWARE DISTRIBUTION.

BULK CARGO unbound CARGO as loaded and carried aboard ship. It is without mark or count, in a loose unpackaged form, and has homogeneous characteristics.

BULK CARRIER vessel designed for the SHIPMENT of bulk CARGO.

BULK FREIGHT FREIGHT not in packages or containers. *see also* BULK CARGO; CELL.

BULK SALE single transaction transfer of a large amount of inventory not in the usual course of business.

BULK SHIPPING a term used when referring to shipments made in a loose or unpackaged form.

BULK SOLIDS dry CARGO shipped loose in CONTAINERS.

BULLETIN BOARD SYSTEM (BBS) an on-line computer system, which provides a medium for electronic messaging services, archives of files, and any other services or activities of interest to the bulletin board system's operator. Originally started by hobbyists, increasingly BBSs are connected to the INTERNET, and many other BBSs are managed by government, educational, commercial, and research institutions. *see also* ELECTRONIC MAIL; USENET.

BUNDESBANK the German CENTRAL BANK. The main functions of the Bundesbank are to regulate the money supply, support the general economic policy of the German federal government, and issue banknotes. It sets the key discount rate, the LOMBARD RATE, and minimum reserve requirements. Bank headquarters is in Frankfurt, Germany.

BUNDESMINISTERIUM FÜR WIRTSCHAFT (BMWi) (English: Ministry for Economic Affairs) German government ministry that gathers and distributes market information and supports semiprivate and private organizations, such as overseas chambers of commerce. Within the BMWi is the Federal Office for Foreign Trade (Bundesstelle für Aussenhandelsinformation, BfAi), the German government's primary agency for gathering and disseminating information. BfAi collects and distributes market information through a worldwide network.

BUNDESSTELLE FÜR AUSSENHANDELSINFORMATION *see* BUNDESMINISTERIUM FÜR WIRTSCHAFT.

BUNKER compartment on a ship used for storage or fuel.

BUNKER ADJUSTMENT FACTOR adjustment in shipping charges to offset price fluctuations in the cost of BUNKER FUEL.

BUNKER FUEL the fuel used to power a ship.

BUREAU OF EXPORT ADMINISTRATION (BXA) an agency of the U.S. DEPARTMENT OF COMMERCE responsible for the administration and enforcement of EXPORT CONTROLS. *see also* EXPORT ADMINISTRATION REGULATIONS (EAR); EXPORT LICENSE; GENERAL LICENSE; INDIVIDUALLY VALIDATED LICENSE.

BUREAU OF INTERNATIONAL EXPOSITIONS (BIE) an international organization established by the PARIS CONVENTION of 1928 to regulate the conduct and scheduling of international expositions in which foreign nations are officially invited to participate. The BIE divides international expositions into different categories and types and requires each member nation to observe specified minimum time intervals in scheduling each of these categories and types of operations. Under BIE rules, member nations may not ordinarily participate in an international exposition unless the exposition has been approved by the BIE. The United States became a member of the BIE in April 1968. Participation by the United States in a recognized international exposition requires specific authorization by the U.S. Congress, based on the president's finding that participation is in the national interest.

BURUNDI FRANC unit of currency, Burundi (100 centimes equal 1 Burundi franc).

BUSH DOCTRINE the policy that holds nations that harbor or support terrorist organizations responsible and says that such countries are considered hostile to the United States.

BUSINESS AMERICA a biweekly publication of the U.S. DEPARTMENT OF COMMERCE. *Business America* provides current trade information, marketing advice, and trade leads. It is available from the Superintendent of Documents, U.S. Government Printing Office, Washington, DC 20402.

BUSINESS COUNCIL FOR INTERNATIONAL UNDERSTANDING (BCIU) an independent, nonpartisan, business association formed at the initiative of U.S. President Eisenhower. BCIU operates the U.S. Ambassadorial and Senior Diplomat Industry Program in which most U.S. ambassadors come to BCIU after appointment and again in midtour for briefings with top management of companies active or interested in the diplomat's country of assignment. While originally focused exclusively on U.S. diplomats, BCIU now also sponsors discussions with visiting Chiefs of Government, Ministers of Finance and Industry, CENTRAL BANK governors, and other foreign officials.

BUSINESS ENVIRONMENT RISK INDEX (BERI) an index that measures the general quality of a country's business climate. It is published quarterly and provides data about 40 countries.

BUSINESS EXECUTIVE ENFORCEMENT TEAM (BEET) informal group providing a channel for private-sector executives to discuss EXPORT control enforcement matters with the U.S. Bureau of Export Administration.

BUSINESS FACILITATION OFFICE (BFC) usually a booth with a reference desk showing product catalogs manned by the COMMERCIAL SECTION or a qualified contractor to assist fair visitors or buyers searching for U.S. products or services at an international trade fair.

BUSINESS FUNCTION group of business activities that together completely support one aspect of furthering the mission of the organization, describing what is done within the organization independently from the organization's structure.

BUSINESS INCOME COVERAGE (BIC) covers income losses resulting from damage to the investor's property caused by political violence. Compensation is based on expected net income plus continuing, normal operating expenses. Overseas Private Investment Corporation (OPIC) also will pay for expenses that will reduce the business income loss, such as renting a temporary facility. Compensation is paid until productive capacity is restored, not to exceed 1 year. *see also* POLITICAL RISK.

BUSINESS INFORMATION OFFICE (BIO) a post or contract-staffed commercial reference facility usually at a scheduled international trade exhibition.

BUSINESS INFORMATION SERVICE FOR THE NEWLY INDEPENDENT STATES (BISNIS) a one-stop shop for U.S. firms interested in obtaining assistance on selling in the markets of the NEWLY INDEPENDENT STATES (NIS) of the former Soviet Union (Armenia, Azerbaijan, Belarus, Georgia, Kazakhstan, Kyrgyzstan, Moldova, Russia, Tajikistan, Turkmenistan, Ukraine, and Uzbekistan). BISNIS provides information on trade regulations and legislation, defense conversion opportunities, commercial opportunities, market data, sources of financing, government and industry contacts, and U.S. government programs supporting TRADE and investment in the region. The BISNIS was established in June 1992 and maintains a 24-hour automated flashfax system through which U.S. companies can receive information on doing business in the NIS via fax.

BUSINESS PROCESS a specific business pursuit, executed through specific types of actions; an ordering of work activities across time and place, with a beginning, an end, and clearly identified inputs and outputs.

BUSINESS PROPRIETARY INFORMATION pertains to property in the form of documents used by firms and individuals who represent them.

BUSTARELLA (Italian, meaning small envelope). *see also* BRIBERY.

BUY AMERICAN ACTS U.S. federal and state government statutes that give a preference to U.S. produced goods in government CONTRACTS. *see also* BUY AMERICAN RESTRICTIONS (BAR); BUY NATIONAL (BUY LOCAL).

BUY AMERICAN RESTRICTIONS (BARS) restrictions derived from the U.S. Buy American Act (BAA) of March 1933 as amended by the Buy American Act of 1988. Restrictions may take several forms including:
- straightforward prohibition of public sector bodies from purchasing goods from foreign suppliers,
- establishing local content requirements of anything up to 100% of the value of the product,
- extending preferential terms to domestic suppliers, and
- setting up of manufacturing or assembly facilities in the United States.

The BAA contains four exceptions that permit an executive agency to procure foreign materials when:
- items are for use outside the United States,
- domestic items are not available,
- procurement of domestic items is determined to be inconsistent with the public interest, and
- the cost of domestic items is determined to be unreasonable.

The Trade Act of 1979 (which addressed implementation of the Tokyo Round) waives the BAA for certain designated countries that grant reciprocal access to U.S. Suppliers.

BUY NATIONAL (BUY LOCAL) pertains to the government programs supporting the purchase of items produced domestically versus the purchase of imported goods.

BUYBACK *see* COUNTERTRADE.

BUYER ALERT a program of the Department of Agriculture's FOREIGN AGRICULTURAL SERVICE (FAS). The FAS communicates sales offers of agricultural products by U.S. firms to buyers in foreign countries. To participate in the Buyer Alert Program, the U.S. Suppliers must provide product information, references, and contact information.

BUYER CREDIT PROTOCOL a program of the Canadian EXPORT DEVELOPMENT CORPORATION (EDC) to promote the purchase of Canadian manufactured goods or services by foreign buyers on credit. Under the program, there is an agreement signed between the EDC and a foreign BANK. The foreign bank provides guarantees for the EDC loans to foreign buyers. In the event that the foreign buyer defaults on the loan, the foreign bank will honor the commitment. *see also* EXPORT FINANCING; SUPPLIER CREDIT PROTOCOL.

BUYER CREDITS *see* LOAN (TO FOREIGN IMPORTERS).

BUYER'S MARKET situation that exists when goods can easily be secured and when the economic forces of business tend to cause goods to be priced below the vendor's estimate of value. *see also* SELLER'S MARKET.

BWC see BIOLOGICAL WEAPONS CONVENTION.

C

C & F *see* COST AND FREIGHT.

CABEE *see* CONSORTIA OF AMERICAN BUSINESSES IN EASTERN EUROPE.

CABEI *see* CENTRAL AMERICAN BANK FOR ECONOMIC INTEGRATION.

CABLE ADDRESS a code word of less than ten letters, registered annually with the U.S. Central Bureau of Registered Addresses, used in lieu of the entire name and address of a company receiving or sending cablegrams in order to reduce the number of words required in a cablegram.

CABLEGRAM a telegraphic message sent overseas via underwater cables. *see also* FAX; TELEX.

CABNIS *see* CONSORTIA OF AMERICAN BUSINESSES IN THE NEWLY INDEPENDENT STATES.

CABOTAGE
1. national law that requires coastal and intercoastal traffic to be carried by vessels belonging to the country owning the coast.
2. exclusive national right to operate air traffic within a nation's territory.
3. the right for a commercial air CARRIER to engage in the transportation of passengers, CARGO, and mail between two points within a country other than the country in which it is registered.

CABOTAGE RULES *see* CABOTAGE.

CAC *see* CODEX ALIMENTARIUS COMMISSION.

CACABATRO the Algerian word for a vacation accrual plan. Cacabatro is a form of indirect employee compensation.

CACM *see* CENTRAL AMERICAN COMMON MARKET.

C.A.D. *see* CASH AGAINST DOCUMENTS.

CADRE (French) a categorization approach (comparable to exempt versus nonexempt in the United States) that acts as a major determinant in employees' compensation and benefit programs in France.

CAF *see* CORPORACIÓN ANDINA DE FOMENTÓ.

CAIRNS GROUP an informal association of agricultural exporting countries established in August 1986 in Cairns, Australia. Members include Argentina, Australia, Brazil, Canada, Chile, Colombia, Fiji, Hungary, Indonesia, Malaysia, New Zealand, Philippines, Thailand, and Uruguay. The group seeks to reduce EXPORT subsidies and internal support measures and to bring about other reforms to international agricultural TRADE. The Cairns Group countries account for one-third of world farm exports.

CAISSE CENTRALE DE COOPÉRATION ECONOMIQUE (CCCE) a specialized financial institution that is the lead agency in the French Ministry of Cooperation and Development in providing funds for aid and cooperation. CCCE provides support for development and technical assistance in developing countries. This applies particularly in supporting economic and social development in Africa and in various countries on the Indian Ocean, the Caribbean, and the South Pacific and in overseas French departments and territories where it supports productive private and public investment. The Caisse was created in December 1941, and its headquarters is in Paris, France.

CALL
1. demand for early repayment of an obligation or for the performance of a specific act under a contract.
2. demand for the payment of money.
3. act of redeeming a bond earlier than the full term.
see CALL OPTION, MARGIN CALL.

CALL MONEY currency lent by BANKS on a very short-term basis, which can be called the same day, at one day's notice, or at two days' notice.

CALL OPTION contract guaranteeing the holder the right to receive from the issuer specified amount of a security at a specified price on or before a certain date. *see* CALL.

CALVO CLAUSE *see* CALVO DOCTRINE.

CALVO DOCTRINE legal principle holding that jurisdiction in international investment disputes lies with the country in which the investment is located; thus, the investor has no recourse but to use the local courts. The principle, named after an Argentinean jurist, has been applied throughout Latin America and other areas of the world.

CAMARA DE COMERCIO E INDUSTRIA the CHAMBER OF COMMERCE in Portugal. *see also* INSTITUTO DO COMERCIO EXTERNO DE PORTUGAL (ICEP).

CAMP X-RAY the detention facility in Guantanamo Bay, Cuba, that houses al Qaeda and Taliban prisoners.

CANADA EXPORT AWARDS a program of the Department of External Affairs and International Trade of Canada to acknowledge the accomplishments of firms in the EXPORT of Canadian goods. The program is directed at the promotion of international trade activities and advising the Canadian exporters regarding the types of available government programs available to support their export efforts. *see also* EXPORT SUPPORT PROGRAMS.

CANADA–U.S. FREE TRADE AGREEMENT OF 1989 an agreement between the United States and Canada that establishes a program leading to the unimpeded exchange and flow of goods and services between the two countries. *see also* FREE-TRADE AGREEMENT (FTA); NORTH AMERICAN FREE TRADE AGREEMENT (NAFTA).

CANADIAN COMMERCIAL CORPORATION (CCC) prime Canadian contractor in government-to-government sales transactions. The CCC facilitates exports of a wide range of Canadian goods and services. In response to requests from foreign governments and international agencies for individual products or services, the CCC identifies Canadian firms capable of meeting the customer's requirements, executes prime as well as back-to-back contracts, and follows through with contract management, inspection, acceptance, and payment.

CANADIAN DOLLAR unit of currency, Canada (100 cents equal 1 Canadian dollar).

CANADIAN EXPORT ASSOCIATION (CEA) a private organization established in 1943, headquartered in Ottawa, and established for the purpose of supporting the efforts of Canadian EXPORTERS.

CANADIAN IMPORT TRIBUNAL (defunct) *see* CANADIAN INTERNATIONAL TRADE TRIBUNAL.

CANADIAN INTERNATIONAL DEVELOPMENT AGENCY (CIDA) (French: Agence Canadienne de Développement International) official Canadian agency responsible for supporting sustainable development in developing countries. The agency was established in 1968, and its headquarters is in Hull, Quebec.

CANADIAN INTERNATIONAL TRADE TRIBUNAL a Canadian government agency concerned with IMPORTS, IMPORT DUTIES, and the effect of imports on Canadian industry. The agency reviews and makes recommendations concerning COUNTERVAILING DUTY and ANTIDUMPING PETITIONS submitted by Canadian industries seeking relief from imports that benefit unfair trade practices. *see also* SPECIAL IMPORT MEASURES TAX; INTERNATIONAL TRADE COMMISSION (ITC).

CAPACITY TO CONTRACT legal competency to make a CONTRACT.

CAPITAL ACCOUNT *see* BALANCE OF PAYMENTS.

CAPITAL CONTROLS any restriction which limits the flow of international capital such as TARIFFS, DUTIES, and QUOTAS. *see also* TARIFF BARRIER; TRADE BARRIER.

CAPITAL DEVELOPMENT INITIATIVE (CDI) an initiative administered by the U.S. AGENCY FOR INTERNATIONAL DEVELOPMENT (AID). The CDI encourages infrastructure investment in countries in central and eastern Europe. The CDI provides financial and technical services and assists U.S. businesses by providing up to 50% of estimated development work and feasibility study costs for proposed projects in energy, telecommunications, and the environment.

CAPITAL GOODS expensive, long-lasting industrial goods that are not purchased on a regular basis such as equipment used to produce products. These are goods that are used to produce other goods and are not consumer goods.

CAPITAL INFLOW an increase in a country's foreign assets located in that country or a reduction in a country's assets outside the country. *see also* BALANCE OF PAYMENTS; CASH OUTFLOW.

CAPITAL INTENSIVE an activity requiring a greater investment in capital goods as compared to an activity such as labor costs. *see also* LABOR INTENSIVE.

CAPITAL LEASES or **FINANCIAL LEASES** those where ownership of the asset is expected to be transferred to the foreign enterprise at the end of the lease. The OVERSEAS PRIVATE INVESTMENT CORPORATION (OPIC) provides INCONVERTIBILITY COVERAGE, which compensates the investor for lease payments that cannot be converted from local currency to dollars or cannot be transferred outside the HOST COUNTRY.

CAPITAL MARKET market for buying and selling long-term loans, in the form of bonds, mortgages, etc.

CAPITAL MOVEMENTS CODE *see* CODE OF LIBERALIZATION OF CAPITAL MOVEMENTS.

CAPITAL OUTFLOW a reduction of a country's foreign assets located in the country or an increase in that country's assets outside the country. *see also* CAPITAL INFLOW.

CAPITALISM an economic system that provides for private ownership of property; offers profits as an incentive to the individual or firm that accumulates it, and allows competition. *see also* COMMAND ECONOMY; COMMUNISM; MIXED ECONOMY; NONMARKET ECONOMY; SOCIALISM.

CAPTAIN'S PROTEST document prepared by the captain of a vessel upon arrival in port that notes any unusual conditions encountered during the voyage; relieves the shipowner of liability.

CAR *see* commercial activity report.

CAR BOMB an automobile used as a weapon by detonation of a bomb.

CARGO merchandise hauled by transportation lines.

CARGO AGENT agent appointed by an airline shipping line to solicit and process international air and ocean FREIGHT for SHIPMENTS.

CARGO CARRIER the freight company transporting the CARGO/FREIGHT, via air, ocean, truck, or rail.

CARGO CONSOLIDATION *see* CONSOLIDATION.

CARGO MANIFEST list of a ship's merchandise or passengers but without a listing of charges.

CARGO SELECTIVITY SYSTEM a part of the U.S. CUSTOMS SERVICE'S AUTOMATED COMMERCIAL SYSTEM. It specifies the type of examination (intensive or general) to be conducted for imported merchandise. The type of examination is based on database selectivity criteria such as assessments of risk by filer, CONSIGNEE, TARIFF number, country of origin, and manufacturer/shipper. A first-time consignee is always selected for an intensive examination. An alert is also generated in cargo selectivity the first time a consignee files an entry in a port with a particular tariff number, country of origin, or manufacturer/shipper.

CARGO TONNAGE weight of a SHIPMENT or of a ship's total CARGO expressed in tons.

CARGO WAR RISK POLICY a separate CARGO policy that indemnifies goods only while they are waterborne or airborne in a war zone. The insurance against war risks starts from the time the insured goods are loaded on board the ocean vessel or aircraft and ceases after being discharged at the ocean port of discharge or airport. *see also* MARINE INSURANCE; WAR RATES.

CARIBBEAN BASIN ECONOMIC RECOVERY ACT (CBERA) a TARIFF preference program affording nonreciprocal tariff preferences to developing countries in the Caribbean Basin area to aid their economic development and to diversify and expand their production and EXPORTS. The CBERA applies to merchandise entered or withdrawn from warehouse for consumption, on or after January 1, 1984. CBERA has no expiration date.

CARIBBEAN BASIN INITIATIVE (CBI) an inter-American program to increase economic aid and TRADE preferences for 28 states of the Caribbean region. The CARIBBEAN BASIN ECONOMIC RECOVERY ACT of 1983 provided for 12 years of duty-free treatment of most goods produced in the Caribbean region. The initiative was extended permanently (CBI II), by the Customs and Trade Act of August 1990. The 23 countries that are currently eligible for CBI benefits include Antigua and Barbuda, the Bahamas, Barbados, Belize, the British Virgin Islands, Costa Rica, Dominica, the Dominican Republic, El Salvador, Grenada, Guatemala, Guyana, Honduras, Jamaica, Montserrat, the Netherlands Antilles, Nicaragua, Panama, Saint Kitts-Nevis, Saint Lucia, Saint Vincent and the Grenadines, and Trinidad and Tobago. The following countries may be eligible for CBI benefits but have not formally requested designation: Anguilla, Cayman Islands, Suriname, and the Turks and Caicos Islands.

CARIBBEAN-CANADIAN ECONOMIC TRADE DEVELOPMENT ASSISTANCE PROGRAM (CARIBCAN) a program initiated in 1986 granting DUTY-FREE status on imports from the Commonwealth Caribbean. These are Caribbean countries that were previously British colonies.

CARIBBEAN/CENTRAL AMERICA BUSINESS ADVISORY SERVICE (BAS) service operating under the auspices of the United Nations Development Program and managed by the World Bank's International Finance Corporation. It helps entrepreneurs in the Caribbean and in Central America to develop project ideas into investment proposals and to obtain long-term finance for them. The service does not lend or invest, but it does provide advice and assistance in project structuring, identification of technical and marketing partners, project appraisal, and identification of financing resources. The BAS was established in 1981 as the Caribbean Business Advisory Service (CBAS). The BAS 1989 expansion to Central America extended its operations to all CBI beneficiary countries. *see also* CARIBBEAN BASIN INITIATIVE.

CARIBBEAN COMMON MARKET (CARICOM) trading agreement with 13 English-speaking Caribbean nations: Antigua and Barbuda, the Bahamas, Barbados, Belize, Dominica, Grenada, Guyana, Jamaica, Montserrat, Saint Kitts-Nevis, Saint Lucia, Saint Vincent and the Grenadines, and Trinidad and Tobago. CARICOM was established in 1973 and its headquarters is in Georgetown, Guyana.

CARIBBEAN DEVELOPMENT BANK (CDB) Caribbean bank promoting economic development and cooperation by providing long-term financing for productive projects in Caribbean Common Market (CARICOM) member countries and U.K.-dependent territories in the Caribbean. Members include Anguilla, Antigua and Barbuda, the Bahamas, Barbados, Belize, British Virgin Islands, Canada, Cayman Islands, Dominica, France, Grenada, Guyana, Jamaica, Mexico, Montserrat, Saint Kitts-Nevis, Saint Lucia, Saint Vincent and the Grenadines, Trinidad and Tobago, the Turks and Caicos Islands, the United Kingdom, and Venezuela. The bank was established in 1969. Its headquarters is in Saint Michael, Barbados, West Indies. Since 1977 the INTER-AMERICAN DEVELOPMENT BANK (IADB) has been able to make loans through the CDB to its members, whether or not those countries are members of the IADB.

CARIBBEAN FREE TRADE ASSOCIATION (CARIFTA) the former free trade area of the Caribbean. Its membership consisted of Antigua, Barbados, Belize, Dominica, Grenada, Guyana, Jamaica, Montserrat, Saint Kitts-Nevis, Saint Lucia, Saint Vincent and the Grenadines, and Trinidad and Tobago. CARIFTA was suspended in 1973 and replaced by the CARIBBEAN COMMON MARKET (CARICOM).

CARIBBEAN GROUP FOR COOPERATION IN ECONOMIC DEVELOPMENT (CGCED) a regional working group of the CARIBBEAN COMMON MARKET (CARICOM), the purpose of which is to promote economic growth in the region.

CARIBCAN *see* CARIBBEAN–CANADIAN ECONOMIC TRADE DEVELOPMENT ASSISTANCE PROGRAM.

CARICOM *see* CARIBBEAN COMMON MARKET.

CARIFTA *see* CARIBBEAN FREE TRADE ASSOCIATION.

CARNET customs documents permitting the holder to carry or send sample merchandise temporarily into certain foreign countries without paying duties or posting bonds. Foreign customs regulations vary widely; in some countries, duties and extensive customs procedures on sample products may be avoided by obtaining an ATA CARNET. The carnets are generally valid for 12 months.

CARRIAGE AND INSURANCE PAID TO (CIP) a TERM OF SALE indicating that carriage and insurance is paid to the named place of destination. The term applies in place of COST, INSURANCE, and FREIGHT (CIF), for shipment by mode other than water.

CARRIAGE OF GOODS BY SEA ACT OF 1936 a U.S. Statute that regulates ocean shipping in the United States. It establishes limits for the carrier's liability resulting from loss or damage to CARGO.

CARRIAGE PAID TO (CPT) a pricing term indicating that carriage is paid to the named place of destination. The term applies in place of C&F OR CFR (COST AND FREIGHT), for shipment by a mode other than water. *see also* TERMS OF SALE.

CARRIAGE TRADE a term formerly used when referring to wealthy individuals accorded special privileges.

CARRIER in PIGGYBACK EXPORTING, the carrier is the firm that is actually doing the exporting. It is usually the larger firm with an established export organization and a network of international distributors. *see also* CARGO CARRIER; RIDER.

CARRIER'S CERTIFICATE document issued by the shipping company that certifies the ownership of the goods to a named individual. *see also* BILL OF LADING.

CARTA DE CREDITO (Portuguese) *see* LETTER OF CREDIT.

CARTAGE AGENT ground service that provides transport and DELIVERY of FREIGHT in areas not directly served by air or ocean.

CARTAGENA AGREEMENT *see* ANDEAN PACT.

CARTAGENA GROUP *see* GROUP OF ELEVEN (G-11).

CARTEIRA DE IDENTIDADE DE ESTRANGEIRO Brazilian identification card.

CARTEIRA DE TRABALHO Brazilian Ministry of Labor work card.

CARTEL an organization of independent producers formed to regulate the production, pricing, or marketing practices of its members in order to limit competition and maximize their market power. *see also* ORGANIZATION OF PETROLEUM EXPORTING COUNTRIES (OPEC).

CASE OF NEED (PRINCIPAL'S REPRESENTATIVE) an individual nominated by a person who has entrusted the handling of his/her collection to a bank to act as his/her representative in the event of nonacceptance and/or nonpayment of the COLLECTION ORDER. *see also* DOCUMENTS AGAINST ACCEPTANCE; DOCUMENTS AGAINST PAYMENT; DRAFT; SIGHT DRAFT.

CASH AGAINST DOCUMENTS term denoting that payment is made when the BILL OF LADING is presented.

CASH IN ADVANCE (CIA) a means of payment where the buyer pays cash prior to delivery of the order.

CASH POSITION a situation when a FOREIGN EXCHANGE trader has cash available for current use in making trades.

CASH WITH ORDER (CWO) a means of payment where the buyer pays cash when ordering. The order is binding on both the seller and buyer.

CASTE SYSTEM very strict occupational and social system found most extensively in Hindu India. It consists of an extensive hierarchy of distinct jatis, or castes, which manifest religious traditions, occupation, locale, culture status, or tribal affiliation. Furthermore, society is divided into four varna, or social classes—the Brahmans, priests and scholars; Kshatriyas, the military and rulers; Vaisyas, farmers and merchants; and Sudras, peasants and laborers. Below the Sudras were the untouchables, who performed the most menial tasks. Untouchability was legally abolished by India in 1949, and some occupational barriers are breaking down, but strong social distinctions remain resistant to change, especially in rural areas.

CASUS MAJOR major casualty that is usually accidental, such as flood or shipwreck. *see also* ACT OF GOD; FORCE MAJEURE.

CATALOG EXHIBITIONS low-cost promotional exhibits of U.S. firms' catalogs and videos offering small, less-experienced companies an opportunity to test overseas markets for their products without travel. The INTERNATIONAL TRADE ADMINISTRATION promotes exhibitions, provides staff fluent in the local language to answer questions, and forwards all trade leads to participating firms.

CATEGORY GROUPS Groupings of controlled products. *see also* EXPORT CONTROL CLASSIFICATION NUMBER.

CAVAL the first securities rating agency established in Mexico and responsible for securities investments and credit risks. It began operation in May 1990. In December 1991 the MEXICAN NATIONAL SECURITIES COMMISSION (CMV) authorized the establishment of two new rating agencies for Mexican securities, bringing the total number of rating agencies in Mexico to three. *see also* AJUSTABONOS; BONDES; CETES; PAGAFES; TESOBONOS.

CAVEAT EMPTOR let the buyer beware. Purchaser buys with the understanding that certain risks may be involved.

CBD *see* CASH BEFORE DELIVERY; COMMERCE BUSINESS DAILY.

CBERA *see* CARIBBEAN BASIN ECONOMIC RECOVERY ACT.

CBI *see* CARIBBEAN BASIN INITIATIVE.

CCC *see* CANADIAN COMMERCIAL CORPORATION; COMMODITY CREDIT CORPORATION; CUSTOMS COOPERATION COUNCIL.

CCCE *see* CAISSE CENTRALE DE COOPÉRATION ECONOMIQUE.

CCF *see* COCOM COOPERATION FORUM

CCFF *see* COMPENSATORY AND CONTINGENCY FINANCING FACILITY.

CCIRN *see* COORDINATING COMMITTEE FOR INTERCONTINENTAL RESEARCH NETWORKS.

CCITT *see* CONSULTATIVE COMMITTEE FOR INTERNATIONAL TELEPHONE AND TELEGRAPHY (French: Comité Consultatif International Télégraphique et Téléphonique).

CCL *see* COMMERCE CONTROL LIST.

CCNAA *see* COORDINATION COUNCIL FOR NORTH AMERICAN AFFAIRS.

CDB *see* CARIBBEAN DEVELOPMENT BANK.

CDC *see* COMMONWEALTH DEVELOPMENT CORPORATION.

CDI *see* CAPITAL DEVELOPMENT INITIATIVE.

CDT *see* CENTER FOR DEFENSE TRADE.

CE *see* COMMITTEE OF EXPERTS; COMMUNAUTÉS EUROPÉENES; CONFORMITÉ EUROPÉENE.

CEA *see* CHINESE ECONOMIC AREA.

CEAO *see* WEST AFRICA ECONOMIC COMMUNITY.

CEAU *see* COUNCIL OF ECONOMIC ARAB UNITY.

CECA (French: Communauté Européenne du Charbon et de L'Acier) *see* EUROPEAN COAL AND STEEL COMMUNITY.

CEEAC (French: Communauté Economique des États de l'Afrique Centrale) *see* ECONOMIC COMMUNITY OF CENTRAL AFRICAN STATES; ECONOMIC COMMUNITY OF CENTRAL AFRICAN STATES.

CEEB *see* CUSTOMS ELECTRONIC BULLETIN BOARD.

CEENET *see* CENTRAL AND EAST EUROPEAN NETWORKING ASSOCIATION.

CEFTA *see* CENTRAL EUROPE FREE TRADE ASSOCIATION.

CELL on-board storage space for one shipping CONTAINER on a ship. *see also* BUNKER FREIGHT.

CELL
1. the smallest unit within a guerrilla or terrorist group.
2. a cell generally consists of two to five people dedicated to a terrorist cause.

CEN *see* EUROPEAN COMMITTEE FOR STANDARDIZATION.

CENELEC *see* EUROPEAN COMMITTEE FOR ELECTROTECHNICAL STANDARDIZATION.

CENSUS INTERFACE SYSTEM a part of the United States Customs' AUTOMATED COMMERCIAL SYSTEM, the Census Interface System includes edits and validations provided by the U.S. Bureau of the Census to allow for the accurate and timely collection and submission of summary data of merchandise entering the United States. The census interface is accomplished through AUTOMATED BROKER INTERFACE entry summary transmissions.

CENTER FOR DEFENSE TRADE (CDT) a center created in 1990 within the Bureau of Politico-Military Affairs (PM) at the U.S. Department of State. The CDT was established with the purpose of improving the U.S. Department of State's export licensing services. The CDT is also responsible for clarifying all defense trade policy guidelines. The center includes two offices:

- The Office of DEFENSE TRADE CONTROLS (DTC), which administers controls on permanent exports and temporary imports of defense articles and technology covered by the U.S. MUNITIONS LIST (USML) and performs USML export license review and compliance functions.

- The OFFICE OF DEFENSE TRADE POLICY (DTP), which seeks to support the efforts of the U.S. defense industry to sell products overseas. DTP provides policy guidance to licensing officers in support of their efforts to implement the INTERNATIONAL TRAFFIC IN ARMS REGULATIONS (ITAR) and provides advice on technology transfer and strategic trade issues.

CENTER FOR FOREIGN INVESTMENT SERVICES (CFIS) a government office in Korea providing current information on investment opportunities and an appraisal of the Korean business environment to firms interested in doing business with Korea. It obtains and consolidates information from a variety of sources including governmental agencies, private firms, tips, and insights.

CENTER FOR INTERNATIONAL RESEARCH (CIR) a component of the U.S. Commerce Department's Bureau of the Census. CIR conducts research with funds from government and private business sponsors. It provides analyses and forecasts of world demographic trends and economic developments in selected countries, based on current statistics obtained through international agreements. *see also* INTERNATIONAL DATA BASE.

CENTER FOR TRADE AND INVESTMENT SERVICES (CTIS) an information center sponsored by the Agency for International Development for businesses interested in doing business abroad. CTIS was established in September 1992 and promotes increased participation of U.S. businesses in generating economic development in less-developed countries that receive assistance from AID.

CENTO *see* CENTRAL TREATY ORGANIZATION.

CENTRAL AFRICAN CUSTOMS AND ECONOMIC UNION (French: Union Douanière et Economique de l'Afrique Centrale, UDEAC) Central African organization created in 1966 (revised 1974) to promote the establishment of a Central African Common Market with a common external tariff. The union's members include Cameroon, Central African Republic, Chad, Congo, Equatorial Guinea, and Gabon, and its headquarters is in Bangui, Central African Republic.

CENTRAL AFRICAN STATES DEVELOPMENT BANK (French: Banque de Développement des tats de l'Afrique Centrale, BDEAC) Central African bank created in December 1975 (began operations in January 1977) to provide loans for economic development and to support integration projects. The bank's members include Cameroon, Central African Republic, Chad, Congo, Equatorial Guinea, and Gabon, and its headquarters is in Brazzaville, Congo.

CENTRAL AMERICAN BANK FOR ECONOMIC INTEGRATION (CABEI) (Spanish: Banco Centroamericano de Integración Económico, BCIE) an institution of the central AMERICAN COMMON MARKET established in 1960 (began operations in September 1961) to promote economic integration and development. Bank members include Costa Rica, El Salvador, Guatemala, Honduras, and Nicaragua, and its headquarters is in Tegucigalpa, Honduras.

CENTRAL AMERICAN COMMON MARKET (CACM) (Spanish: Mercado Común Centroamericano, MCCA) common market of Central American nations. Originally established in 1960 under the auspices of the ORGANIZATION OF AMERICAN STATES (OAS). A restructuring was started in 1973. Members include Honduras, Guatemala, El Salvador, Nicaragua, and Costa Rica. The common market covers all products traded within the region. A second step toward regional integration will be the establishment of a common external tariff. CACM is associated with the CENTRAL AMERICAN BANK FOR ECONOMIC INTEGRATION, and its headquarters is in Guatemala City, Guatemala.

CENTRAL AND EAST EUROPEAN NETWORKING ASSOCIATION (CEENET) a telecommunications network for countries that choose to connect to Vienna, Austria, by leased lines. This set of connections is referred to as CEENet.

CENTRAL BANK the principal financial institution of a country responsible for the administration and control of that country's MON-

ETARY POLICY. This includes the issuance of currency, the control of foreign exchange reserves, and the issuance of IMPORT LICENSES.

CENTRAL BANK OF BRAZIL (BACEN) the principal financial institution in Brazil responsible for the administration and control of MONETARY POLICY. In Brazil the EXCHANGE CONTROL POLICY has been established by the Minister of Finance. It is the responsibility of BACEN to administer this policy. BACEN controls the exclusive rights in Brazil to operate in FOREIGN EXCHANGE. It can, however, assign these rights to a commercial bank, which must operate in accordance with the rules established and administered by BACEN. *see also* CONSELHO MONETARIO NACIONAL.

CENTRAL BANK OF THE PHILIPPINES responsible for maintaining domestic monetary stability and preserving the international value of the PHILIPPINE PESO. The Central Bank of the Philippines attempts to promote development, contain inflation, and maintain debt levels at reasonable levels. *see also* CENTRAL BANK; MONETARY POLICY.

CENTRAL BANK OF WEST AFRICAN STATES (CBWAS) *see* BANQUE CENTRALE DES ETATS DE L'AFRIQUE DE L'OUEST (BCEAO).

CENTRAL BANK SWAPS an exchange of currencies between the CENTRAL BANKS of different countries to maintain transferability of the currencies and to provide protection from future changes in FOREIGN EXCHANGE rates. Also referred to as SWAP ARRANGEMENTS.

CENTRAL EUROPE FREE TRADE ASSOCIATION (CEFTA) a TRADE agreement among the "VISEGRAD" countries—Poland, the Czech Republic, Slovakia, and Hungary—that is somewhat parallel to the EUROPEAN FREE TRADE ASSOCIATION.

CENTRAL GERAL DOS TRABALHADORES (CGT) and **CENTRAL UNICA DOS TRABALHADORES (CUT)** the most powerful labor unions in Brazil. Union organization is the strongest in Brazil's steel, car, and transport industries. All workers are required to make an annual contribution equal to one day's pay, whether or not they are members of the union. Payment is automatically deducted by the employer.

CENTRAL INTELLIGENCE AGENCY (CIA) the federal agency responsible for gathering foreign intelligence.

CENTRAL TREATY ORGANIZATION (CENTO) a mutual defense treaty formed in 1959 to replace the BAGHDAD PACT. Its members are Iraq, Iran, Pakistan, Turkey, and Britain. After the revolution in Iran, Iran removed itself from CENTO, and today the organization ceases to exist as a mutual defense treaty.

CENTRALIZED (CENTRALIZATION) an organizational concept when decision making is done at the HOME COUNTRY level rather than at the local level. A firm will have to determine where decisions on such topics as product policy, marketing programs, and acquisitions are to be made. The higher the level in the organization at which decisions are made, the more centralized the organization is said to be. *see also* DECENTRALIZED.

CENTRALLY PLANNED ECONOMY (CPE) a national economic system in which production and distribution are primarily controlled by the central government. The concept is normally associated with a socialist or communist form of government. The former Soviet Union first implemented a planned economy in 1928, using Lenin's New Economic Plan.

CENTRALLY PLANNED MARKETS market management and planning associated with socialist countries. Centrally planned markets occur as the result of a socialist country planning the national economy including what products should be produced and in what quantities.

CENTRE EUROPEEN DE RECHERCHE NUCLEAIRE (CERN) (English: European Center for Nuclear Research) a huge lab located outside Geneva, partly in Switzerland and partly in France, that is used by international collaborators to do frontier work in nuclear and particle physics. The center, created after World War II and open to physicists from all countries, is funded by countries according to their abilities.

CENTRE FRANÇAIS DU COMMERCE EXTERIEUR *see* DIRECTION DES RELATIONS ECONOMIQUES EXTERIEURES.

CENTRO INTERNACIONAL DE AGRICULTURA TROPICAL (CIAT) *see* CONSULTATIVE GROUP ON INTERNATIONAL AGRICULTURAL RESEARCH.

CEPGL (COMMUNAUTÉ ECONOMIQUE DES PAYS DES GRANDS LACS) *see* ECONOMIC COMMUNITY OF THE GREAT LAKES COUNTRIES.

CEPT *see* CONFERENCE EUROPÉENNE DES ADMINISTRATIONS DES POSTES ET DES TÉLÉCOMMUNICATIONS.

CERN *see* CENTRE EUROPÉEN DE RECHERCHE NUCLEAIRE.

CERTIFICATE OF DELIVERY *see* DELIVERY VERIFICATION CERTIFICATE.

CERTIFICATE OF HEALTH (FUMIGATION/INSPECTION) a sanitary certificate issued for a ship indicating the vessel is approved for the transport of goods as well as carrying passengers. The certificate of health is also referred to as a boatmaster's certificate, vessel's certificate of approval, clearance certificate, or a deratting certificate.

CERTIFICATE OF INSPECTION (or SPECIAL POLICY)

1. a document prepared by the insured or the insurance company serving as evidence of insurance to the buyer or BANK for an EXPORT/IMPORT shipment. The certificate lists the terms and conditions of the policy. *see also* MARINE INSURANCE.
2. a document certifying that merchandise (such as perishable goods) was in good condition immediately prior to shipment. Preshipment inspection is a requirement for importation of goods into many developing countries.

CERTIFICATE OF MANUFACTURE a document (often notarized) in which a goods producer certifies that product manufacturing has been completed and the goods are now at the disposal of the buyer.

CERTIFICATE OF ORIGIN a signed statement required by certain nations as to the origin of an EXPORT item. Such certificates are usually obtained through a semiofficial organization such as a local chamber of commerce. A certificate may be required even though the commercial invoice contains the information.

CERTIFICATE OF WEIGHT document stating the weight of a SHIPMENT.

CERTIFIED TRADE FAIR (CTF) PROGRAM a U.S. Department of Commerce program designed to encourage private organizations to recruit U.S. firms NEW-TO-MARKET and NEW-TO-EXPORT to exhibit in overseas TRADE FAIRS. To receive certification, the organization must demonstrate that
- the fair is a leading international TRADE event for an industry;
- the fair organizer is capable of recruiting U.S. exhibitors and assisting them with freight forwarding, customs clearance, exhibit design and setup, public relations, and overall show promotion. The show organizer must agree to assist new-to-export exhibitors as well as small businesses interested in exporting.

  In addition to the services the organizer provides, the U.S. Department of Commerce will:
- assign a Washington coordinator;
- operate a business information office, which provides meeting space;
- provide translators, hospitality, and assistance from U.S. exhibitors and foreign customers;
- help to contact buyers, agents, distributors, and other business leads and provide marketing assistance; and
- provide a press release on certification.

CERTIFIED TRADE MISSIONS TRADE MISSIONS planned and organized by state development agencies, trade associations, chambers of commerce, and other EXPORT-oriented groups. To qualify for U.S. government sponsorship, organizers of this type of trade mission must agree to follow INTERNATIONAL TRADE ADMINISTRATION (ITA) criteria in planning and recruiting the mission. ITA offers guidance and assistance from planning through completion of the mission and coordinates the support of all relevant offices and the assistance of overseas commercial officers in each foreign city on the itinerary. The missions are normally led by a representative of the sponsoring organization. Organizers of certified TRADE missions recruit for the event and cover the expenses of the event incurred by ITA's overseas post. Certified trade missions may use the seminar format, the exhibit format, the traditional trade mission format, or a combination, such as a seminar/mission or exhibit/mission.

CES *see* COMPREHENSIVE EXPORT SCHEDULE.

CESANTIA (Venezuela) a term referring to the half-month bonus to which employees in Venezuela are entitled upon termination.

CESSION OF GOODS surrender of goods.

CET *see* COMMON EXTERNAL TARIFF.

CETES short-term Treasury Bills that are issued by the Mexican government in four maturities: 28 day, 91 day, 182 day, and 364 day. *see also* AJUSTABONOS; BONDES; PAGAFES; TESOBONOS.

CFA FRANC unit of currency for the French African Community, Benin, Burkina Faso, Central African Republic, Chad, Côte d'Ivoire (Ivory Coast), Equatorial Guinea, Gabon, Mali, Niger, Senegal, and Togo (100 centimes equal 1 CFA franc).

CFC *see* COMMON FUND FOR COMMODITIES.

CFIS *see* CENTER FOR FOREIGN INVESTOR SERVICES.

CFIUS *see* COMMITTEE ON FOREIGN INVESTMENT IN THE UNITED STATES.

CFP FRANC unit of currency for present and former French Colonies and Territories in the Pacific Ocean, French Polynesia, New Caledonia, and the Wallis and Futuna Islands (100 centimes equal 1 CFP franc).

CFR *see* COST AND FREIGHT; CODE OF FEDERAL REGULATIONS.

CGIAR *see* CONSULTATIVE GROUP ON INTERNATIONAL AGRICULTURAL RESEARCH.

CGT *see* CENTRAL GERAL DOS TRABALHADORES.

CHAEBOL Korean conglomerates, characterized by strong family control, authoritarian management, and centralized decision making. Chaebol dominates the Korean economy, growing out of the takeover of the Japanese monopoly of the Korean economy following World War II. Korean government tax breaks, financial incentives emphasizing industrial reconstruction, and EXPORTS provided continuing support to the growth of chaebols during the 1970s and 1980s. In 1988, the output of the 30 largest chaebols represented almost 95% of Korea's gross national product.

CHAMBER OF COMMERCE an association of business people organized to promote local business interests. *see also* INTERNATIONAL CHAMBER OF COMMERCE.

CHAMBRE DE COOPERATION DE L'AFRIQUE DE L'OUEST (CCAO) *see* WEST AFRICAN CLEARING HOUSE.

CHANNEL MANAGER the international marketing manager whose task it is to minimize price increases in a competitive market situation. *see also* PRICE ESCALATION.

CHARGEABLE WEIGHT weight of a SHIPMENT used in determining FREIGHT charges.

CHARGE D'AFFAIRES (CHG) *see* TITLE AND RANK.

CHARGES FORWARD charges associated with EXPORTING materials into a country. The charges consist of trade commission and brokerage fees, legal charges and fees; and pilotage dues and charges.

CHARGES HERE *see* CHARGES FORWARD.

CHARTER to rent a vessel or a portion of its cargo space for a period of time or trip. *see also* CHARTER PARTY; CHARTER VESSEL; CHARTERER.

CHARTER PARTY
1. the individual renting the vessel or CARGO space.
2. a written contract between the owner of a vessel and an individual who rents the vessel or a part of its cargo space. The contract usually includes the freight rates and the ports involved in the transportation. *see also* CHARTER; CHARTER VESSEL.

CHARTER SERVICE temporary hiring of an aircraft for the transportation of CARGO or passengers. *see also* BAREBOAT CHARTER; CHARTER; CHARTER PARTY; CHARTER VESSEL; CHARTERER.

CHARTER VESSEL the vessel that is being rented by the CHARTER PARTY. *see also* CHARTER; CHARTER PARTY.

CHARTERED SHIP ship leased by its owner for a stated time, voyage, or voyages. *see also* BAREBOAT CHARTER; CHARTER; CHARTER PARTY; CHARTER VESSEL; CHARTERER.

CHARTERER a term used to refer to the individual who rents the use of the vessel or part of its freight space. *see also* CHARTER; CHARTER PARTY; CHARTER VESSEL.

CHASSIS
1. special trailer or undercarriage on which containers are moved over the road.
2. vehicle undercarriage.

CHB *see* CUSTOMSHOUSE BROKER.

CHECKSUM a method of verifying telecommunications data between a sending and receiving computer. Essentially the methodology is a method of comparing received PACKETS of data with sent data packets. If the comparison is the same, there is a high degree of reliability in the received data; however, if the data comparison is not identical, the received data packet is not reliable. In the latter case, a checksum error will be generated.

CHEMICAL AGENT toxic substances used for operations to debilitate, immobilize, or kill military or civilian personnel.

CHEMICAL AMMUNITION commonly a missile, bomb, rocket, or artillery shell, designed to deliver chemical agents.

CHEMICAL ATTACK the intentional release of toxic liquid, gas, or solid to poison the environment or people.

CHEMICAL WARFARE the use of toxic chemicals as weapons, not including herbicides used to defoliate battlegrounds or riot-control agents, such as tear gas or mace.

CHEMICAL/BIOLOGICAL WEAPONS (CBW) foreign policy export controls on certain chemical precursors, equipment and biological agents useful in chemical warfare maintained by the U.S. DEPARTMENT OF COMMERCE. The United States cooperates with other nations through the AUSTRALIA GROUP (AG) in controlling chemical and biological weapons proliferation. The AG developed a list of 54 precursors useful for chemical weapons development, along with control on certain biological organisms and on equipment useful in producing CBW agents. The AG also provides the forum in which the member countries share information concerning the activities of nonmember countries where the proliferation of these weapons is of concern, including entities that are seeking chemical precursors and related items.

CHEMICAL WEAPONS CONVENTION (CWC) an international agreement prohibiting the development, production, stockpiling, and use of chemical weapons. The convention permits monitoring, collection and review of data and on-site inspections that involve questions of protection of proprietary rights and confidentiality. The convention was signed by over 160 nations and became effective in 1995.

CHEMTERRORISM the use of chemical agents in a terrorist operation. Well-known chemical agents include sarin and VX nerve gas.

CHIEF OF MISSION (COM) person designated to manage a diplomatic post. The CHARGE D'AFFAIRS is the Chief of Mission when an AMBASSADOR is not appointed.

CHILEAN PESO unit of currency, Chile (100 centisimos equal 1 Chilean peso).

CHINESE ECONOMIC AREA (CEA) an informal reference to the economic integration of Southern China with Hong Kong and Taiwan, which has proceeded without any "arrangement."

CHIPS *see* CLEARINGHOUSE INTERBANK PAYMENT SYSTEM.

CHOKING AGENT compounds that primarily injure the respiratory tract (i.e., nose, throat, and lungs).

CIA *see* CASH IN ADVANCE, CENTRAL INTELLIGENCE AGENCY.

CICA *see* CONFEDERATION INTERNATIONALE DU CREDIT AGRICOLE.

CIDA *see* CANADIAN INTERNATIONAL DEVELOPMENT AGENCY.

CIF *see* COST, INSURANCE, AND FREIGHT.

CIFRA one of the largest retailers in Mexico with sales exceeding U.S. $2 billion. CIFRA has also entered into a JOINT VENTURE with the Wal-Mart corporation and the Club Aurrera, which is comparable to merchandise warehouse clubs found in the United States.

CIMS *see* COMMERCIAL INFORMATION MANAGEMENT SYSTEM.

CIPRO an antibiotic that combats inhalation anthrax. Cipro (ciprofloxacin) is a trademark of Bayer Corporation.

CIPs *see* COMMODITY IMPORT PROGRAMS.

CIR *see* CENTER FOR INTERNATIONAL RESEARCH.

CIRCA term used in a LETTER OF CREDIT (L/C) understood as a difference not to exceed 10% more or 10% less than the monetary amount, or the quantity or unit price stipulated in the L/C. *see also* APPROX, CIRCA.

CIS *see* COMMONWEALTH OF INDEPENDENT STATES.

CISG *see* CONVENTION ON CONTRACTS FOR THE INTERNATIONAL SALE OF GOODS.

CIT *see* COURT OF INTERNATIONAL TRADE.

CITA *see* COMMITTEE FOR THE IMPLEMENTATION OF TEXTILE AGREEMENTS.

CITIZEN a person owing loyalty to and entitled to the protection of a specific country. Citizenship may be acquired by birth or by the process of NATURALIZATION.

CITY TERMINAL SERVICE service provided by some airlines that involves transporting CARGO to in-town terminals at lower rates than charged for door-to-door DELIVERY.

CJ *see* COMMODITY JURISDICTION.

CLAIM
1. payment demand.
2. an insured's demand for payment of money or property as the result of a loss.

3. in transportation, a demand for return of overpaid charges.
4. demand for reimbursement of losses due to loss or casualty to CARGO or failure to deliver.

"CLASS OR KIND" OF MERCHANDISE term used in defining the scope of an ANTIDUMPING INVESTIGATION notice. Included in the "class or kind" of merchandise is merchandise sold in the home market that is "such or similar" to the petitioned product. "Such or similar" merchandise is merchandise that is identical to or like the petitioned product in physical characteristics. *see also* TARIFF ACT OF 1930.

CLASSIFICATION
1. merchandise categorization.
2. transportation determination of freight rates within a TARIFF.
3. determination of CUSTOMS duty status within the HARMONIZED TARIFF SCHEDULE.

CLAUSED BILL OF LADING notation on the BILL OF LADING that denotes a deficient condition of the goods or packaging. *see also* CLEAN BILL OF LADING.

CLAYTON ACT a major U.S. antitrust law passed in 1914 to supplement the SHERMAN ACT. The Clayton Act deals primarily with the prohibition of price discrimination among buyers and sellers in the sale of commodities and certain corporate mergers where the effect may be to substantially lessen competition or tend to create a monopoly.

CLDP *see* COMMERCIAL LAW DEVELOPMENT PROGRAM.

CLEAN AIR ACT a series of American legislative acts setting standards for fuel economy and emissions of automobiles. The Clean Air Act has been amended several times in order to decrease the amount of permissable emissions.

CLEAN BILL OF LADING a receipt for goods issued by a CARRIER with an indication that the goods were received in "apparent good order and condition," without damages or other irregularities. If damaged or a shortage is noted, a clean bill of lading will not be issued.

CLEAN COLLECTION a method of financing an EXPORT sale that requires the EXPORTER to submit only the DRAFT to the BANK with instructions to collect payment from the IMPORTER. The original documents have already been forwarded in advance to the importer, and in some instances the documents are traveling with the CARGO. *see also* BILL OF LADING; COLLECTING BANK; COLLECTION ORDER; COLLECTION PAPERS; COLLECTIONS.

CLEAN DRAFT a DRAFT to which no documents have been attached.

CLEAN FLOAT a system in which exchange rates are determined by market forces rather than government intervention or restrictions. *see also* DIRTY FLOAT.

CLEAR CUSTOMS a term used to describe the process of entering imported goods into the commerce of the country. The process consists of preparing and submitting the appropriate documentation, arranging to have the goods inspected, having CUSTOMS determine the dutiable value of the goods, and securing the appropriate customs clearance documents. An individual may make his/her own customs clearance of goods for personal or business use, or he/she may use the services of a licensed CUSTOMS BROKER. *see also* CUSTOMS; DUTY.

CLEARANCE completion of CUSTOMS ENTRY requirements that results in the release of goods to the IMPORTER.

CLEARING ARRANGEMENTS a system of BARTER where two countries agree to exchange a number of products, during a specified period of time. The products being exchanged are not often easily sold on the open market. If the agreed-upon goods are not exchanged within the specified time period, outstanding balances must be resolved either by accepting additional goods or paying a penalty. *see also* BUYBACK; COUNTERPURCHASE; COUNTERTRADE; SWITCH ARRANGEMENTS.

CLEARINGHOUSE a facility that reconciles the movement of funds between BANKS.

CLEARINGHOUSE INTERBANK PAYMENT SYSTEM (CHIPS) an international check-clearing mechanism for foreign currency transactions in the United States. CHIPS coordinates the transfer of funds among U.S. BANKS, branches of foreign banks, and EDGE ACT subsidiaries of out-of-state banks.

CLIENT a computer that is connected to and dependent on another computer system or process. An example is a workstation connected as a client of a server.

CLOSED ECONOMY a planned economic system that does not engage in international trade. *see also* AUTARKY; OPEN ECONOMY.

CLOSED-END TRANSACTION credit transaction with a fixed amount of time for repayment. *see also* OPEN-END CONTRACT.

CLOSING DATE *see* EXPIRATION DATE.

CLUB DU SAHEL an informal coalition that seeks to reverse the effects of drought and the desertification in the eight Sahelian zone countries: Burkina Faso, Chad, the Gambia, Mali, Mauritania, Niger, Senegal, and the Cape Verde Islands. The club coordinates plans and arranges the financing of aid and sustained economic development in the region. The club (sometimes called Club des Amis du Sahel), formed in December 1975, comprises both donor countries (Austria, Belgium, Canada, France, the Netherlands, Switzerland, the United Kingdom, and the United States) and Sahelian zone countries. Its headquarters is in Ouagadougou, Burkina Faso.

CMA *see* COMMON MONETARY AGREEMENT.

CMEA *see* COUNCIL FOR MUTUAL ECONOMIC ASSISTANCE.

CNI *see* COALITION FOR NETWORKED INFORMATION.

CNUSA *see* COMMERCIAL NEWS USA.

COAL TERMINAL REPORT a table appearing every Tuesday in the JOURNAL OF COMMERCE that identifies the vessels transporting coal scheduled to call at U.S. and Canadian ports and the estimated tonnage of coal being transported by those ships.

COALITION FOR NETWORKED INFORMATION (CNI) a consortium formed by American Research Libraries, Cause, and Educom to promote the creation of, and access to, information resources in networked environments in order to enrich scholarship and enhance intellectual productivity.

COAP *see* COTTONSEED OIL ASSISTANCE PROGRAM.

COASTAL TRADE trade conducted between the ports of one nation.

COCOA PRODUCERS' ALLIANCE (COPAL) COMMODITY group formed in 1962 to promote the consumption and to coordinate production and prices among its members. COPAL is headquartered in Lagos, Nigeria, and its member countries consist of Brazil, Cameroon, Côte d'Ivoire, Ecuador, Gabon, Ghana, Mexico, Nigeria, São Tomé and Principe, Toga, and Trinidad and Tobago.

COCOM *see* COORDINATING COMMITTEE ON MULTILATERAL EXPORT CONTROLS.

COCOM COOPERATION FORUM (CCF) a venue for emerging democracies in Central and Eastern Europe and the former Soviet Union to discuss international EXPORT CONTROLS and to help coordinate technical assistance efforts. The forum, established in June 1992, held its first meeting in November 1992. At the close of 1992, 42 nations were CCF participants, including most states of the former Soviet Union (except Georgia, Tajikistan, and Turkmenistan) and all the former Soviet satellites of Eastern and Central Europe (except the former Yugoslav republics).

CODE LAW SYSTEM a systematic set of laws organized by subject matter into a code. This system attempts to explain the law with regard to all possible legal questions rather than to rely on precedent or an interpretation of the court. *see also* COMMON LAW SYSTEM; INTERNATIONAL LAW; ISLAMIC LAW.

CODE OF CONDUCT a norm of behavior considered to be acceptable by members of the international community. *see also* VALDEZ PRINCIPLES.

CODE OF CONDUCT FOR LINER CONFERENCES a norm of behavior initiated in 1974 under the sponsorship of the UNITED NATIONS CONFERENCE ON TRADE AND DEVELOPMENT (UNCTAD) that affirmed the right of developing countries to have an allocation within a CONFERENCE in the ocean transportation of goods with other countries.

CODE OF FEDERAL REGULATIONS (CFR) the classification of the rules published in the FEDERAL REGISTER by the executive departments and agencies of the U.S. federal government. The EXPORT ADMINISTRATION REGULATIONS (EAR) can be found in 15 CFR (Chapter VII), Parts 730–799.

CODE OF LIBERALIZATION OF CAPITAL MOVEMENTS a norm of behavior agreed to by members of the ORGANIZATION OF ECONOMIC COOPERATION AND DEVELOPMENT (OECD). The code obligates those countries signing the agreement to promote the free movement of capital among them and to avoid any activities that would limit DIRECT INVESTMENT. The code does, however, allow for limited protection for those industries critical to national security.

CODETERMINATION *see* MITBESTIMMUNG.

CODEX ALIMENTARIUS COMMISSION (CAC or CODEX) a subsidiary body of the United Nations Food and Agricultural Organization (FAO) and the World Health Organization that develops food standards and Recommended International Codes of Hygienic and/or Technological Practices. Commission standards are voluntary, becoming enforceable only if accepted as national standards. The commission also works in cooperation with regional coordinating committees (Africa, Europe, Latin America, and the Caribbean) in promoting regional standards activities. The commission was established in 1962 and its headquarters is in Rome, Italy.

CODING STANDARD format in which a specified data element is reported.

CODING STANDARD SOURCE documentation of a coding standard.

COE *see* COUNCIL OF EUROPE.

COFACE *see* COMPAGNIE FRANÇAISE D'ASSURANCE POUR LE COMMERCE EXTÉRIEUR.

COFC *see* CONTAINER ON FLAT CAR.

COLLAR agreement that puts upper and lower limits on the interest rate of an agreement that is binding even if the market rate falls outside of this range.

COLLECT CHARGES
1. transportation practice where the freight and other charges are paid to the carrier.
2. collection practice where the buyer is expected to pay the bank charges for handling the collection.

COLLECT ON DELIVERY (COD) service where the purchase price of a shipment is collected by the carrier upon delivery of the shipment and subsequently paid to the shipper.

COLLECTING BANK any BANK, other than the REMITTING BANK, involved in the handling of a COLLECTION ORDER.

COLLECTION BY DRAFT *see* DRAFT.

COLLECTION LETTER customer's written instructions to a bank on how to handle a collection. Many banks have an instruction form for use instead of a letter.

COLLECTION ORDER document that, together with commercial and financial documents, provides the COLLECTING BANK with a precise and complete set of instructions pertaining to the collection. Instructions would advise the collecting bank under what conditions they should release the documents. *see also* BILL OF EXCHANGE; DOCUMENTS AGAINST ACCEPTANCE; DOCUMENTS AGAINST PAYMENT; DRAFT; METHOD OF PAYMENT; SIGHT DRAFT.

COLLECTION PAPERS all documents (INVOICES, BILLS OF LADING, etc.) submitted to a buyer for the purpose of receiving payment for a shipment.

COLLECTIONS a method of payment where the EXPORTER and IMPORTER agree to use the services of the exporter's bank to process the payment for the goods. *see also* CLEAN COLLECTION; DOCUMENTARY COLLECTION; DRAFT.

COLLECTIONS SYSTEM a part of the U.S. CUSTOMS SERVICE'S AUTOMATED COMMERCIAL SYSTEM that controls and accounts for the billions of dollars in payments collected by the Customs Service each year and the millions in refunds processed each year. Daily statements are prepared for the automated brokers who select this service. The collections system permits electronic payments of the related duties and taxes through the AUTOMATED CLEARINGHOUSE capability. Automated collections also meet the needs of the importing community through acceptance of electronic funds transfers for deferred tax bills and receipt of electronic payments from lockbox operations for Customs bills and fees.

COLLECTIVITE (French) *see* CORPORATION.

COLOMBIAN PESO unit of currency, Colombia (100 centavos equal 1 Colombian peso).

COLOMBO PLAN an economic development agreement established in 1951 to promote economic and social development among members in Asia and the Pacific. Members include Afghanistan, Australia, Bangladesh, Bhutan, Burma, Cambodia, Canada, Fiji, India, Indonesia, Iran, Japan, South Korea, Laos, Malaysia, Maldives, Nepal, New Zealand, Pakistan, Papua New Guinea, Philippines, Singapore, Sri Lanka, Thailand, the United Kingdom, and the United States. The plan's formal name is the Colombo Plan for Cooperative Economic Development in South and Southeast Asia, and its headquarters is in Colombo, Sri Lanka.

COLON
1. unit of currency, Costa Rica (100 centimos equal 1 Costa Rican colon).
2. unit of currency, El Salvador (100 centavos equal 1 El Salvadoran colon).

COLONIA one of two 100-hectare public FREE ZONES in Uruguay. The other is located next to the city of Nueva Palmira. These ports have been designated by Uruguay for DUTY-FREE entry of any nonprohibited goods. Merchandise may be stored, displayed, used for manufacturing, etc., within the zone and REEXPORTED without duties being paid. Duties are imposed on the merchandise (or items manufactured from the merchandise) only when the goods pass from the free zone into an area of the country subject to the customs authority. *see also* FREE PORT; FREE-TRADE ZONE.

COM *see* COSTS OF MANUFACTURE.

COMBI AIRCRAFT a specially designed aircraft that carries unitized cargo on the upper deck of the airplane forward of the passenger section.

COMBINATION AIRCRAFT aircraft capable of transporting both CARGO and passengers on the same flight. *see also* COMBI AIRCRAFT.

COMBINED BILL OF LADING BILL OF LADING covering a SHIPMENT of goods by more than one mode of transportation. *see also* ORDER BILL OF LADING; STRAIGHT BILL OF LADING.

COMBINED TRANSPORT CONSIGNMENT sent by various modes of transport.

COMECON *see* COUNCIL FOR MUTUAL ECONOMIC ASSISTANCE.

COMISION ECONOMICA PARA AMERICA LATIANA Y EL CARIBE (CEPAL) *see* UNITED NATIONS REGIONAL COMMISSIONS.

COMISION NACIONAL DE VALORES the organization responsible for the regulation of the BOLSA MEXICANA DE VALORES, the Mexican Stock Market. It would be the equivalent of the Securities and Exchange Commission in the United States. The Comisión Nacional de Valores establishes regulation for those firms selling stock on the exchange and also rules for trading of shares by individuals.

COMISION PANAMERICANA DE NORMAS TECNICAS (COPANT) (English: PAN AMERICAN STANDARDS COMMISSION) a commission coordinating the activities of all institutes of standardization in the Latin American countries. The commission develops all types of product standards, standardized test methods, terminology, and related matters. COPANT headquarters is in Buenos Aires, Argentina. U.S. contact with COPANT is maintained through the AMERICAN NATIONAL STANDARDS INSTITUTE.

COMITE CONSULTATIF INTERNATIONAL DES RADIO-COMMUNICATIONS *see* INTERNATIONAL RADIO CONSULTATIVE COMMITTEE.

COMITE CONSULTATIF INTERNATIONAL TELEGRAPHIQUE ET TELEPHONIQUE (CCITT) *see* CONSULTATIVE COMMITTEE FOR INTERNATIONAL TELEPHONE AND TELEGRAPHY.

COMITE PERMANENT CONSULTATIF DU MAGHREB (CPCM) (English: MAGHREB PERMANENT CONSULTATIVE COMMITTEE) committee seeking to improve economic coordination among Maghreb countries with the eventual expectation of establishing a Maghreb economic community. Originally established in October 1964, the committee began operations in February 1966, and its headquarters is in Tunis, Tunisia. *see also* MAGHREB STATES.

COMITE PERMANENT INTERETATS DE LUTTE CONTRE LA SÉCHERESSE DAN LE SAHEL *see* PERMANENT INTERSTATE COMMITTEE FOR DROUGHT CONTROL IN THE SAHEL.

COMITY a principle of international law that provides that there be a mutual respect for the laws of each country. *see also* ACT OF STATE DOCTRINE; CONFLICT OF LAWS; SOVEREIGN.

COMMAND ECONOMY a planned NONMARKET ECONOMY directed by the government. The best example of a command economy is the former Soviet Union and other communist states. A command economy has a central bureaucracy that plans and directs the manufacture and supply of goods within the economy according to political directives of the central government. Communist nations having a command economy belonged to the former COUNCIL FOR MUTUAL ASSISTANCE (CMEA).

COMMANDITAIRE VENOOTSCHAP (CV) (Dutch) *see* PARTNERSHIP.

COMMERCE BUSINESS DAILY (CBD) the U.S. Department of Commerce's daily newspaper, which lists government procurement invitations and contract awards, including foreign business opportunities and foreign government procurements.

COMMERCE CONTROL LIST (CCL) a list maintained by the U.S. DEPARTMENT OF COMMERCE that includes all items—COMMODITIES, software, and technical data—subject to the U.S. BUREAU OF EXPORT ADMINISTRATION (BXA) EXPORT controls and incorporates not only the national security controlled items agreed to by COCOM (the "core" list) but also items controlled for foreign policy (i.e., biological warfare, nuclear proliferation, missile technology, regional stability, and crime control) and short supply. The list is divided into ten general categories:

- materials,
- materials processing,
- electronics,
- computers,
- telecommunications and cryptography,
- sensors,
- avionics and navigation,
- marine technology,
- propulsion systems and transportation equipment, and
- miscellaneous.

COMMERCIAL ACTIVITY REPORT (CAR) annual report prepared by the economic and commercial sections of the U.S. embassies covering over 100 countries where the U.S. DEPARTMENT OF COMMERCE is not represented. The CAR assesses the country's political, economic, and business activities and its market potential and strategies for increasing U.S. sales.

COMMERCIAL ATTACHE the commerce expert on the diplomatic staff of his/her country's embassy or large consulate.

COMMERCIAL BANK GUARANTEE PROGRAMS of the EXPORT–IMPORT BANK OF THE UNITED STATES (EXIMBANK). The EXIMBANK has numerous programs to assist firms in the financing of U.S. exports. The Commercial Bank Guarantee Programs provide repayment guarantees to eligible lenders for secured loans that would not be made without the EXIMBANK guarantee. It is envisioned that these guaranteed loans will promote exports by small, medium-sized, and minority-owned businesses and agricultural concerns. *see also* DIRECT LOAN PROGRAM; INTERMEDIARY LOAN PROGRAM; LEASE GUARANTEES; WORKING CAPITAL GUARANTEE PROGRAM.

COMMERCIAL INFORMATION MANAGEMENT SYSTEM (CIMS) a PC-based system used by the INTERNATIONAL TRADE ADMINISTRATION staff in export counseling. CIMS is a trade-related application using NATIONAL TRADE DATA BANK CD-ROMS to disseminate market research and international economics data to U.S. AND FOREIGN COMMERCIAL SERVICE domestic offices and overseas posts. The system includes data on foreign traders and supports local collection and update of information on business contacts.

COMMERCIAL INVOICE a bill for the goods from the seller to the buyer. These INVOICES are often used by governments to determine the true value of goods for the assessment of CUSTOMS DUTIES and are also used to prepare consular documentation. Governments using the commercial invoice to control IMPORTS often specify its form, content, number of copies, language to be used, and other characteristics.

COMMERCIAL LAW the body of jurisprudence exclusively concerned with the rights, actions, and relations of persons engaged in commerce, TRADE, or mercantile activities. *see also* ANTIDUMPING CODE; CAPITAL MOVEMENTS CODE; CUSTOMS VALUATION CODE; GATT

CUSTOMS VALUATION CODE; GATT LICENSING CODE; OMNIBUS INVESTMENTS CODE OF 1987; STANDARDS CODE; SUBSIDIES (AND COUNTERVAILING MEASURES) CODE.

COMMERCIAL LAW DEVELOPMENT PROGRAM (CLDP) a legal development program designed to help Central and Eastern Europe and the Baltic States develop a commercial infrastructure consistent with free-market principles. The program, operated through the U.S. DEPARTMENT OF COMMERCE'S INTERNATIONAL TRADE ADMINISTRATION (ITA), is part of the U.S. government's efforts to assist the region. The CLDP is also compiling a Language Resources List of U.S. commercial law experts with strong language capabilities.

COMMERCIAL MEXICANA one of the principal retail department store and supermarket chains of Mexico. The others are CIFRA, GRUPO GIGANTE, and Soriana. Commercial Mexicana operates over 155 outlets, and has established a JOINT VENTURE relationship with the Price Club of the United States.

COMMERCIAL NEWS USA (CNUSA) an INTERNATIONAL TRADE ADMINISTRATION (ITA) fee-based magazine, published ten times per year. CNUSA provides exposure for U.S. products and services through an illustrated catalog and electronic bulletin boards. The catalog is distributed through U.S. embassies and consulates to business readers in 155 countries. Copies are provided to international visitors at trade events around the world.

The CNUSA program covers more than 30 industry categories. To be eligible, products must be at least 51% U.S. parts and 51% U.S. labor. The service helps U.S. firms identify potential EXPORT markets and make contacts leading to representation, distributorships, joint venture or licensing agreements, or direct sales.

COMMERCIAL OFFICERS embassy officials who assist U.S. business through arranging appointments with local business and government officials, providing counsel on local trade regulations, laws, and customs. They also identify importers, buyers, agents, distributors, and joint venture partners for U.S. firms and provide other business assistance. At larger posts, INTERNATIONAL TRADE ADMINISTRATION (ITA) staff perform these functions. At smaller posts, commercial interests are represented by the U.S. Department of State's economic officers. *see also* ECONOMIC OFFICERS; FOREIGN SERVICE POSTS.

COMMERCIAL POLICIES official or unofficial rules directing a nation's international trade. Example: the COURT OF INTERNATIONAL TRADE hears ANTIDUMPING, product classification, and COUNTERVAILING DUTY matters as well as appeals of UNFAIR TRADE practice cases from the INTERNATIONAL TRADE COMMISSION brought against the United States.

COMMERCIAL PRESENCE the existence of an enterprise seeking to do business in a particular market. *see also* CONSORTIA OF AMERICAN BUSINESSES IN EASTERN EUROPE (CABEE); CONSORTIA OF AMERICAN BUSINESSES IN THE NEWLY INDEPENDENT STATES (CABNIS).

COMMERCIAL REGISTER (BRAZIL) a publication in which subsidiaries of foreign firms in Brazil must register in order to operate in Brazil. These subsidiaries may not operate unless they have made an application to the Minister of Industry and Commerce and are granted special authorization. Once authorization is granted, the firms must be registered in the Commercial Register and use the same name at the home office.

COMMERCIAL RISKS an EXIMBANK guarantee covering nonpayment for reasons other than specified political risks. Examples of commercial risks include insolvency or protracted default. *see also* POLITICAL RISKS.

COMMERCIAL SECTION that section of an EMBASSY, CONSULATE, or other delegation in a foreign city responsible for commercial matters such as the issuance of visas or the legalization of documents.

COMMERCIAL SET primary documents required to ship goods; usually includes an INVOICE, BILL OF LADING, BILL OF EXCHANGE, and INSURANCE CERTIFICATE.

COMMERCIAL TRADE SCHOOL PROGRAM (SENAC) a Brazilian training program to improve the quality of the unskilled work force from regions other than the principal metropolitan areas. Brazil also operates an industrial training school program (SENAI).

COMMERCIAL TREATY an agreement between two or more countries setting forth the conditions under which business between the countries may be transacted. A commercial treaty may outline TARIFF privileges, terms on which property may be owned, the manner in which claims may be settled, etc.

COMMINGLING
1. the combining of articles subject to different rates of DUTY in the same shipment or package such that the quantity or value of each kind of product cannot be readily ascertained by a CUSTOMS officer (without the physical segregation of the shipment or package). In such a case, the commingled articles will be subject to the highest rate of duty applicable to any part of the commingled lot, unless the CONSIGNEE or his/her agent segregates the shipment under Customs supervision.
2. the illegal combination of funds or properties into one common fund.

COMMISSION AGENT an agent who purchases goods in his or her own country on behalf of foreign importers such as government agencies or large private business.

COMMISSION ECONOMIQUE POUR L'EUROPE *see* UNITED NATIONS REGIONAL ECONOMIC COMMISSIONS; ECONOMIC COMMISSION FOR EUROPE.

COMMITTEE a group of people selected to perform a particular task.

COMMITTEE FOR THE IMPLEMENTATION OF TEXTILE AGREEMENTS (CITA) an interagency committee chaired by the U.S. DEPARTMENT OF COMMERCE that exercises the rights of the United States under the MULTIFIBER ARRANGEMENT. CITA initiates "calls" for consultation when imports of a particular textile product from a particular country disrupt the U.S. domestic market for that product. Other member agencies include the U.S. Departments of Labor, State, and Treasury and the U.S. TRADE REPRESENTATIVE (USTR).

COMMITTEE OF EXPERTS (CE) an autonomous body of 20 independent legal experts appointed by the INTERNATIONAL LABOR ORGANIZATION'S (ILO) governing body. The CE meets annually prior to the June conference to examine reports of governments on ILO conventions and information provided by governments on what they have done with newly adopted conventions. The CE submits its report and findings to the International Labor Conference Committee on the Application of Conventions and Recommendations.

COMMITTEE ON FOREIGN INVESTMENT IN THE UNITED STATES (CFIUS) committee created in 1975 of the Omnibus Trade and Competitiveness Act of 1988 (Section 721 of the Defense Production Act). This gives the President of the United States authority to review mergers, acquisitions, and takeovers of U.S. companies by foreign interests and to prohibit, suspend, or seek divestiture in the courts of investments that may lead to actions that threaten to impair the national security. CFIUS provides guidance on arrangements with foreign governments for advance consultations on prospective major foreign governmental investments in the United States and considers proposals for new legislation or regulation relating to foreign investment.

CFIUS has 11 members: the Secretaries of the U.S. Departments of Treasury (the chair), State, Defense, and Commerce; the chairperson of the COUNCIL OF ECONOMIC ADVISORS; the U.S. TRADE REPRESENTATIVE (USTR); the Attorney General; the Director of the Office of Management and Budget; the Director of the Office of Science and Technology Policy; the Assistant to the President for National Security Affairs; and the Assistant to the President for Economic Policy. *see also* EXON–FLORIO.

COMMITTEE ON RENEWABLE ENERGY, COMMERCE, AND TRADE (CORECT) a committee composed of 14 U.S. federal agencies: the Departments of Commerce, Defense, Energy, Interior, State, and Treasury; the Agency for International Development; Environmental Protection Agency; EXPORT–Import Bank; Overseas Private Investment Corporation; Small Business Administration; Trade and Development Agency; United States Information Agency; and U.S. TRADE REPRESENTATIVE (USTR). CORECT facilitates the cost-effective use of U.S. renewable energy products and services around the world. The committee, chaired by the U.S. Department of Energy, was established by legislation in 1984.

COMMITTEE ON TRADE AND DEVELOPMENT (CTD) committee established in 1965 as a part of the GENERAL AGREEMENT ON TARIFFS AND TRADE (GATT) to consider how the economic development of LESS-DEVELOPED COUNTRY (LDC) contracting parties (that is, LDC members) can be assisted.

COMMODITY a wide range of products used in TRADE or commerce, especially an agricultural, financial, mining or petroleum product, that can be transported or transacted. A commodity is classified according to the grade of production it has undergone (e.g., crude oil or heating oil) or the modality in which it is transported (e.g., BULK CARGO or BAGGED CARGO). Commodities are traded in a commodity market, which includes grains and oilseeds, livestock and meat, food and fiber, metals, petroleum, and lumber and financial futures, such as Treasury bonds, stocks, and currencies.

COMMODITY AGREEMENT *see* INTERNATIONAL COMMODITY AGREEMENT.

COMMODITY CODE system of identifying a COMMODITY by a certain number to determine its COMMODITY RATE for transport. *see also* COMMODITY RATE.

COMMODITY CONTROL LIST *see* COMMERCE CONTROL LIST.

COMMODITY CREDIT CORPORATION (CCC) a government-owned and -operated corporation within the U.S. Department of Agriculture (USDA). The CCC finances a variety of U.S. government domestic and international farm programs, including Title I, Title II, and Title III of Public Law 480 (Food for Peace). The CCC is managed by a board of directors headed by the U.S. Secretary of Agriculture. All members of the board and the corporation's officers and staff are officials of USDA. The CCC provides financing and stability to the marketing and exporting of agricultural COMMODITIES.

COMMODITY ELIGIBILITY products that qualify for participation in AGENCY FOR INTERNATIONAL DEVELOPMENT (AID). Eligible products are those that make a positive contribution to the development of the beneficiary country. Items not eligible for AID financing are unsafe or ineffective products, luxury goods, surplus or used items, items for military use, weather modification equipment, and commodities for support of police or other law enforcement agencies.

COMMODITY GROUPINGS a numerical system used by the U.S. Bureau of the Census to group IMPORTS and EXPORTS in broader categories than those provided by the TARIFF SCHEDULES. *see also* CUSTOMS COOPERATION COUNCIL NOMENCLATURE; HARMONIZED TARIFF SCHEDULE; STANDARD INDUSTRIAL CLASSIFICATION.

COMMODITY IMPORT PROGRAMS (CIPS) a U.S. government program designed to finance the EXPORT of U.S. goods to U.S.-aid recipient countries. Under CIPs, the AGENCY FOR INTERNATIONAL DEVELOPMENT (AID) makes dollars available to the assisted country on a loan or grant basis to pay for essential commodity imports. In nearly all cases, these IMPORTS come from the United States. CIPs are used to provide relatively fast disbursement of BALANCE OF PAYMENTS support or to generate local currency for budget support for project goals, particularly in efforts designed to encourage private-sector development.

CIP agreements usually provide for AID's financing of a wide variety of basic items including agricultural goods, construction and transportation equipment, fertilizer, chemicals, raw materials, semi-finished products, and foodstuffs. CIPs do not finance military or police equipment, luxury items, or items of questionable safety or efficacy. In some cases, the range of allowable commodities is narrowed in order to tailor them to the development needs of particular sectors in the assisted country or to accomplish other, specific development goals.

COMMODITY JURISDICTION (CJ) EXPORT jurisdiction of products administered by the U.S. State Department's OFFICE OF DEFENSE TRADE CONTROLS (DTC) if the commodities are defense articles, technical data, and services or by the U.S. DEPARTMENT OF COMMERCE'S BUREAU OF EXPORT ADMINISTRATION if the commodities are dual-use items. An exporter may request DTC to conduct a commodity jurisdiction review if the exporter is uncertain as to whether an item is covered by the U.S. MUNITIONS LIST (USML) or believes it has been inappropriately placed on the list. CJ procedures include deadlines for making a determination and the use of criteria assessing performance, significant military or intelligence applicability, and significant civilian applicability.

COMMODITY PRICE AGREEMENT *see* INTERNATIONAL PRICE AGREEMENT.

COMMODITY PRICE LIMITATIONS a regulation in AGENCY FOR INTERNATIONAL DEVELOPMENT (AID) governing eligibility and certain price restrictions in procurement programs. The basic price condition is that the price may not exceed the current EXPORT market price for the item being procured.

COMMODITY RATE rate applicable for shipping a given COMMODITY between points. *see also* COMMODITY CODE.

COMMODITY TERMS OF TRADE the relationship between a nation's EXPORT price index and its IMPORT price index (times 100). This permits a country to establish TRADE advantages with foreign nations. *see also* TERMS OF TRADE.

COMMON AGRICULTURAL POLICY (CAP) a set of regulations by which member states of the EUROPEAN COMMUNITY (EC) seek to merge their individual agricultural programs into a unified effort to promote regional agricultural development, fair and rising standards of living for the farm population, stable agricultural markets, increased agricultural productivity, and methods of dealing with food supply security. Two of the principal elements of the CAP are the variable levy (an IMPORT duty amounting to the difference between EC target farm prices and the lowest available market prices of imported agricultural COMMODITIES) and export restitutions, or subsidies, to promote EXPORTS of farm goods that cannot be sold within the EC at the target prices.

COMMON DATA ELEMENTS basic requirements that are normally occurring and routinely used, commonly found in commercial level data, for IMPORT and EXPORT transactions.

COMMON EXTERNAL TARIFF (CET or CXT) a uniform TARIFF adopted by a customs union to be assessed on IMPORTS entering the union territory from countries outside the union.

COMMON FUND FOR COMMODITIES (CFC) a funding source for INTERNATIONAL COMMODITY GROUP, constituted by the United National Conference on Trade and Development (UNCTAD). The common fund proposal is the core of the UNCTAD's plan to regulate prices and ensure supplies of COMMODITIES through an integrated program instead of a case-by-case approach. Ratified in 1989, the fund has a governing council, an executive board, and a consultative committee located at UNCTAD headquarters in Geneva, Switzerland.

COMMON LAW SYSTEM a system of law founded on custom and judicial precedent. Originating in the Royal Court of medieval England and so called because it represents common, rather than local, custom, the common law prevails in most English-speaking nations, including the United States (except Louisiana, which adheres to Code Law from the Napoleonic Code). Early common law often proved to be inflexible, often leading to allegations of injustice, and in 15th century England the first of many decrees were published to restore equity (fairness). This, in turn, led to equity law, which was often merged with the common law in many jurisdictions. In most jurisdictions, common law has been replaced by statutory law where the respective legislatures pass laws superseding the common law.

COMMON MARKET an international market organization having a common external tariff (as opposed to a FREE-TRADE AREA), which may allow for labor mobility and common economic policies among the participating nations. The EUROPEAN COMMUNITY is the most notable example of a common market.

COMMON MONETARY AGREEMENT (CMA) a monetary agreement between South Africa, Lesotho, and Swaziland under which they apply uniform exchange control regulations to ensure monetary order in the region. Funds are freely transferable among the three countries, and Lesotho and Swaziland have free access to South African capital markets. Lesotho also uses the South African currency, the RAND. The CMA was formed in 1986 as a result of the renegotiation of the Rand Monetary Agreement (RMA), which was originally formed in 1974 by the same member countries.

COMMON POINT location serviced by two or more transportation lines.

COMMON STANDARD LEVEL OF EFFECTIVE PROTECTION (CSP) the minimum shared standards between the United States and COCOM members for implementing an effective export control system, including licensing and enforcement elements.

COMMONWEALTH a free association of sovereign independent states that has no CHARTER, treaty, or constitution. The association promotes cooperation, consultation, and mutual assistance among members. The British Commonwealth (with headquarters in London, England) is the most notable example. It included 50 states at the beginning of 1991.

COMMONWEALTH DEVELOPMENT CORPORATION (CDC) a British public corporation that provides medium- and long-term loans and equity financing for development-related private- and public-sector projects in selected countries. CDC financing is available for projects in the following sectors: agriculture (livestock, horticulture, and aquaculture), forestry, fishing, mineral extraction, industry, public utilities, transport, telecommunications, low-cost housing, hotels, construction and civil engineering, financial management and consulting services, and leasing of assets. The corporation does not invest in schools, colleges, hospitals, public service works, or broadcasting. Since 1969, CDC has been able to invest in non-Commonwealth countries with ministerial agreement. The CDC was established in 1948, and its headquarters is in London, England.

COMMONWEALTH OF INDEPENDENT STATES (CIS) an association of 11 republics of the former Soviet Union established in December 1991. The members include Russia, Ukraine, Belarus (formerly Byelorussia), Moldova (formerly Moldavia), Armenia, Azerbaijan, Uzbekistan, Turkmenistan, Tajikistan, Kazakhstan, and Kirgizstan (formerly Kirghizia). The Baltic States did not join. Georgia maintained observer status, before joining the CIS in November 1993. Until that time, the NEWLY INDEPENDENT STATES (NIS) differed from the CIS in that the NIS is a collective reference to 12 Soviet republics, including Georgia.

COMMUNAUTE ECONOMIQUE DE L'AFRIQUE DE L'OUEST *see* WEST AFRICAN ECONOMIC COMMUNITY.

COMMUNAUTE ECONOMIQUE DES ETATS DE L'AFRIQUE CENTRALE *see* ECONOMIC COMMUNITY OF CENTRAL AFRICAN STATES.

COMMUNAUTE ECONOMIQUE DES PAYS DES GRANDS LACS *see* ECONOMIC COMMUNITY OF THE GREAT LAKES COUNTRIES.

COMMUNAUTES EUROPEENES (CE) a mark applied to products, their packaging, or their paperwork as a declaration of conformity, third-party testing and/or certification, quality assurance audit, and/or full type approval by a body authorized by a EUROPEAN ECONOMIC COMMUNITY member state and recognized by the European Commission. Effective January 1, 1993, the CE mark on a product attests that it complies with all in-force directives pertinent to it. The CE mark preempts all other EUROPEAN COMMUNITY national safety marks. If it is discovered that the CE mark has been improperly affixed, the product in question will be prohibited and no longer marketed. Legal penalties are at the discretion of each member state.

COMMUNICATIONS SATELLITE CORPORATION (COMSAT) organization established in 1963 under provision of the Communications Satellite Act of 1962 representing the United States in the International Telecommunications Satellite Organization. U.S. legislation directed that COMSAT establish the world's first commercial international satellite communications system. The act also stipulated that the company operate as a shareholder-owned, "for-profit" corporation.

COMMUNICATIONS SOFTWARE programs that enable a computer to communicate with another computer, typically through a MODEM or NETWORK.

COMMUNISM a social and political system where property, particularly real property and the means of production, is owned by the state. Communism advocates the violent overthrow of CAPITALISM through revolution. In 1848 Karl Marx and Friedrich Engels published the *Communist Manifesto* in Germany. It advocated what came to be known as Marxism, premising the inevitability of communism arising from class warfare, the overthrow of capitalism, and the creation of a classless society. The modern communist political movement began when V.I. Lenin led a successful armed revolution in Russia. With their triumph in the 1917 Russian Revolution, the Bolsheviks formed the Communist Party in 1918 and established a party dictatorship. Subsequently, communism was established through Eastern and Central Europe, Southeast Asia, China, and Cuba. However, popular uprisings, economic collapse, and free elections led to the collapse of Eastern European communist governments in 1989 and 1990. By the early 1990s traditional communist party dictatorships held power only in China, Cuba, Laos, North Korea, and Vietnam. Additionally, China, Laos, and Vietnam have reduced state control of the economy in order to stimulate growth.

COMPAGNIE FRANCAISE D'ASSURANCE POUR LE COMMERCE EXTERIEUR (COFACE) a French company acting as a commercial EXPORT finance agency by insuring short-term political and commercial risk and by facilitating the financing for export credit. Any French EXPORTER (manufacturers, intermediaries, confirmers, and merchants) of French goods and services can be insured for sales abroad. In conjunction with the Banque Française du Commerce Extérieur and other banks and institutions, COFACE provides services similar to the EXIMBANK. COFACE was established in 1946, and its headquarters is in Paris, France. *see also* BANQUE FRANCAISE DU COMMERCE EXTERIUR.

COMPANY organization of people developed for the purpose of carrying out commerce or TRADE. Company forms include partnerships, corporations, associations, and stock companies.

COMPARABLE UNCONTROLLED PRICE METHOD one of three methods allowed by the United States Internal Revenue Service in reviewing TRANSFER PRICES that appear to reflect ARM'S LENGTH TRANSACTIONS. This method is also referred to as the market price. The other methods are the RESALE PRICE METHOD and the COST-PLUS METHOD.

COMPARATIVE ADVANTAGE economic theory used in international trade originally developed by David Ricardo. Ricardo noted that some nations lack an ABSOLUTE ADVANTAGE in certain product or commodity areas. However, these nations could gain from FREE TRADE if they concentrated on those products or commodities where they had a relative advantage in production. This principle is the theoretical basis of the free-trade argument. A country can benefit from trading certain goods even though its trading partners can produce those goods more cheaply. The comparative advantage is achieved when the production costs and price received for each trading partner's product realizes a better price in another country than it will at home. If each country concentrates on producing the goods in which it has a comparative advantage, more goods are produced, and the wealth of both the buying and the selling nations increases.

COMPARISON SHOPPING SERVICE a customized service provided by the U.S. DEPARTMENT OF COMMERCE, INTERNATIONAL TRADE ADMINISTRATION (ITA) providing U.S. firms with specific information on marketing and representation for a specific product in a foreign country. Fees for such surveys can range from $500 to $4000. *see also* AGENT/DISTRIBUTOR SERVICE (ADS); ECONOMIC BULLETIN BOARD; GOLD KEY SERVICES; MATCHMAKER TRADE DELEGATIONS; NATIONAL TRADE DATA BANK; TRADE OPPORTUNITIES PROGRAM; WORLD TRADE DATA REPORT.

COMPENSATION a concession granted in the process of negotiation when a previously agreed to concession is subsequently nullified. The concept of compensation is frequently used in bilateral TRADE negotiations where one side will request a quid pro quo concession as compensation for the granting of concession to the other trading partner.

COMPENSATION TRADE
1. an understanding developed whereby an EXPORTER of heavy equipment, technology, or even entire facilities agrees to pur-

chase a certain percentage of the output of the resulting product or facility.

2. an offsetting compensation in international politics when one nation demands a concession from another. Example: Jay's Treaty, negotiated in 1794 to settle the outstanding differences between the United States and Great Britain, provided for a commission requiring Great Britain to pay compensation for the illegal seizure of American ships and for the Americans to make payment of prewar debts owed to British merchants. The treaty seriously restricted American TRADE with the British West Indies, and the British were allowed to trade with the United States on a most-favored-nation basis.

COMPENSATORY AND CONTINGENCY FINANCING FACILITY (CCFF) an INTERNATIONAL MONETARY FUND (IMF) facility that provides resources to an IMF member for a shortfall in EXPORT earnings or an excess in cereal IMPORT costs that is due to factors largely beyond the member's control and is temporary. Compensatory financing, introduced in 1963 and broadened several times, provides aid to members experiencing BALANCE OF PAYMENTS problems as a result of fluctuations in COMMODITY prices and shortfalls of receipts in tourism, "workers' remittances," and most services. Contingency financing helps members with IMF-supported adjustment programs to maintain the momentum of adjustment efforts in the face of a broad range of unanticipated, adverse external shocks. Example: changes in international interest rates or prices or primary imports or exports.

COMPENSATORY TRADE a number of alternative methods of trade whereby goods and services are traded for each other. Compensatory trade is used primarily when dealing with firms being unable to access hard or convertible currency. *see also* BARTER; COUNTERTRADE; OFFSET TRADE.

COMPETITION process where buyers and sellers interact to establish prices and exchange goods and services in an open market. In a competitive market, the self-interest of buyers and sellers acts to serve the needs of society as well as those of individual market participants. Society benefits when the maximum number of goods is produced at the lowest possible prices.

Perfect competition exists when

- there is a large number of businesses as well as purchasers;
- individual firms do not constitute a major proportion of the market share; and
- all transactions are open and known within the market.

Perfect competition produces the lowest cost, optimum supply, and satisfied consumers. However, perfect competition rarely exists. *see also* FREE TRADE; PROTECTIONISM.

COMPETITIVE RATE rate determined by one transportation line to compete with the rate of another transportation line.

COMPLEMENTARY IMPORTS IMPORTS of raw materials or products that a country does not internally possess or produce.

COMPLETELY KNOCKED DOWN (CKD) goods being shipped completely unassembled.

COMPLETION AGREEMENT an agreement required by the OVERSEAS PRIVATE INVESTMENT CORPORATION that INVESTMENT FINANCE PROGRAM participants are obligated to provide any additional financing necessary to complete a project and to have adequate working capital to perform their obligation under the agreement.

COMPLETION ALLOWANCE added compensation provided annually or at the end of an assignment. A form of direct compensation used to provide incentives to employees to remain at a hardship assignment for the agreed to time period.

COMPOSITE CURRENCY PEG *see* EXCHANGE RATE(S) CLASSIFICATIONS.

COMPOSITE THEORETICAL PERFORMANCE (CTP) computer hardware EXPORT license requirements are evaluated according to Composite Theoretical Performance, which replaced the former Processing Data Rate (PDR) parameter. CTP is measured in Million Theoretical Operations Per Second (MTOPS). CTP was developed by the United States as a new parameter and was adopted by COCOM during the CORE LIST negotiations, because PDR was not applicable to certain modern computer architectures such as vector processors, massively parallel processors, and array processors. CTP is designed to measure all these architectures, as well as signal-processing equipment.

COMPOUND DUTY *see* MIXED TARIFF; DUTY.

COMPRADORE agent in a FOREIGN country employed by a domestic businessperson to facilitate transactions with local businesses within the FOREIGN country. *see also* COMMISSION.

COMPREHENSIVE EXPORT SCHEDULE (CES) a list developed by the U.S. DEPARTMENT OF COMMERCE detailing goods for which foreign buyers are required to have an EXPORT PERMIT.

COMPRO an on-line TRADE data retrieval system maintained by the INTERNATIONAL TRADE ADMINISTRATION within the U.S. DEPARTMENT OF COMMERCE. The system is exclusively for use within the federal government trade community (ITA, USTR, ITC, and other executive branch agencies). It is also the oldest and best-known component of the TRADE POLICY INFORMATION SYSTEM (TPIS). COMPRO was replaced in September 1997 by TPIS.

COMPROMIS (French) *see* ARBITRATION; AWARD.

COMPUTED VALUE an alternative method of computing the value of merchandise for customs purposes when the TRANSACTION VALUE method cannot be used. The computed value consists of the sum of the following items:

- materials, fabrication, and other processing used in producing the imported merchandise;
- profit and general expenses;
- any assist, if not included in the first two items, and
- packing costs. *see also* DEDUCTIVE VALUE.

COMSAT *see* COMMUNICATIONS SATELLITE CORPORATION.

CONCEALED DAMAGE damage to the contents of a package that is not apparent from the condition of the exterior. *see also* CONCEALED LOSS.

CONCEALED LOSS damage, loss, or shortage of goods within a package that is not apparent from its exterior condition. *see also* CONCEALED DAMAGE.

CONCENTRATION STRATEGY a strategy used when a multinational firm develops a program for evaluating and selecting countries to enter and commit resources. A concentration strategy involves entering one or a select few markets initially, and then building and developing the selected markets before moving on to other markets. *see also* DIRECT INVESTMENT; DIVERSIFICATION STRATEGY.

CONCERNVERSLAGLEGGING (Dutch) *see* CORPORATION.

CONCESSIONAL FINANCING credit consisting of low interest rate loans with extended payment terms often having lengthy grace periods intended for LESS DEVELOPED COUNTRIES (LDC). These SOFT LOANS are sponsored by several different international agencies including the ASIAN DEVELOPMENT FUND (ADF), ENHANCED STRUCTURAL ADJUSTMENT FACILITY sponsored by the INTERNATIONAL MONETARY FUND, THE KUWAIT FUND FOR ARAB ECONOMIC DEVELOPMENT, NORWEGIAN AGENCY FOR DEVELOPMENT COOPERATION'S Mixed Credit Tied Aid Credit, and the U.S. Department of Agriculture's FOOD FOR PEACE PROGRAM.

CONCILIATION a settlement of dispute by a means other than arbitration. Conciliation is less formal that arbitration and usually involves the appointment of an independent third party acting as a mediator. *see also* ARBITRATION.

CONDITIONAL CONTRABAND *see* CONTRABAND.

CONDITIONAL DATA ELEMENT specific data element that must be reported only under those conditions specified by an agency or trade entity.

CONDITIONAL EXEMPTIONS a special category of exemption from the requirements for the filing of a SHIPPER'S EXPORT DECLARATION. Shipper's Export Declarations are not required for the following classes of COMMODITIES when they are not shipped as CARGO under a BILL OF LADING or an AIRWAY BILL and do not require an INDIVIDUALLY VALIDATED EXPORT LICENSE:

- Baggage or personal effects of individuals leaving the country;
- Usual and reasonable amounts of furniture and household effect;
- Usual and reasonable kind and quantities of vehicles.

CONDITIONALITY the conditions a nation must meet before the INTERNATIONAL MONETARY FUND will extend credit. These may include certain national economic policy requirements such as reducing the rate of inflation by raising interest rates.

CONFEDERATION INTERNATIONALE DU CREDIT AGRICOLE (CICA) (English: International Confederation of Agricultural Credit, ICAC) agricultural credit banks and other institutions that provide or study agricultural credits. ICAC coordinates documentation and information improvements pertaining to agricultural credit. The confederation was established in 1932, and its headquarters is in Zurich, Switzerland.

CONFERENCE agreements between international ocean shipping companies or lines on freight rates and the development of international sailing schedules. The net effect of a conference is to establish a CARTEL of shipping companies carrying certain types of CARGO between certain destinations.

CONFERENCE EUROPEENNE DES ADMINISTRATIONS DES POSTES ET DES TELECOMMUNICATIONS (CEPT) (English: EUROPEAN CONFERENCE OF POSTAL AND TELECOMMUNICATIONS ADMINISTRATION) European conference that harmonizes, simplifies, and improves postal and telecommunications services. Many CEPT standards-creating activities have been assumed by the EUROPEAN TELECOMMUNICATIONS STANDARDS INSTITUTE. CEPT maintains offices in Paris, France, and Bern, Switzerland.

CONFERENCE LINE agreements, known as conferences, regulating competition among ship owners providing liner service. The conferences establish passenger fares and freight rates for all the respective members. In the United States, these conferences are administered by the FEDERAL MARITIME COMMISSION in accordance with the Shipping Act of 1916. Rate changes, modifications of agreements, and other joint activities must be approved by the commission before they are effective. However, it is illegal for conferences to be collusive and prevent free and open competition. *see also* CONFERENCE.

CONFERENCE ON SECURITY AND COOPERATION IN EUROPE (CSCE) the successor to the Eastern bloc's COUNCIL FOR MUTUAL ECONOMIC ASSISTANCE (CMEA OR COMECON). Established in 1991 the CSCE administers residual tariffs and quotas and relations with other organizations.

CONFERENCE PRICING a unit price set or fixed according to a conference agreement. For example, the price of shipping CARGO is determined by a SHIPPING CONFERENCE agreement.

CONFIRMED LETTER OF CREDIT a LETTER OF CREDIT, issued by the importer's bank, whose validity has been confirmed by a bank in the EXPORTER'S country. An exporter is assured of payment even if the foreign buyer or the foreign bank defaults. From the seller's viewpoint, foreign political risk is eliminated and replaces the commercial risk of the buyer's bank with that of a confirmed letter of credit. As soon as the documents are presented to the bank, the seller receives payment. *see also* IRREVOCABLE LETTER OF CREDIT.

CONFIRMING a financial service in which an independent company confirms an EXPORT order in the seller's country and makes payment for the goods in the currency of that country. Among the items eligible for confirmation are the goods; inland, air, and ocean transportation costs; forwarding fees; custom brokerage fees; and duties. Confirming permits the entire export transaction from plant to end user to be fully coordinated and paid for over time. It is mainly a European practice.

CONFISCATION foreign property seized or NATIONALIZED by another nation without compensation. CARGO seized on the high seas may be covered under MARINE INSURANCE. Under wartime conditions cargo can be indemnified through a CARGO WAR RISK POLICY, which is a form of WAR RISK INSURANCE. During wartime international law allows belligerents to stop and search neutral vessels for CONTRABAND. The penalty traditionally imposed by belligerents on neutral carriers engaged in commercial traffic with the enemy consists of confiscation of cargos. By international agreement this includes confiscation of the carrying vessel, if more than half the cargo is contraband. Confiscation of a neutral vessel or cargo, however, must always be adjudicated in a prize court, which may award damages to the owner if the evidence is insufficient to show "probable cause" for capture.

CONFLICT OF LAWS a philosophy whereby there is a dispute between the local laws of different countries. These conflicts usually occur when the countries have different legal systems such as a code law system, a common law system, or Islamic law.

CONFORMITE EUROPEENE (CE) a mark signifying that a product meets specific EC-wide conformity assessment requirements. The mark does not endorse the quality or durability of a product but only that it satisfies mandatory technical requirements. The designation is needed for sale of products that become subject to community-wide "new-approach" directives. *see also* COMMUNAUTÉS EUROPÉENES; EUROPEAN NORM.

CONGESTION flood of data that occurs when the capacity of a data communication path is equaled or exceeded. This can lead to transmission delays as well as transmission errors.

CONNECTING CARRIER CARRIER that has direct physical connection with another carrier or forms a connecting link between two or more carriers.

CONNECTION-ORIENTED the data communication method in which communication proceeds through three well-defined phases: connection establishment, data transfer, connection release. TCP is a connection-oriented protocol. *see also* CONNECTIONLESS.

CONNECTIONLESS the data communication method in which communication occurs between HOSTS with no previous setup. Packets between two hosts may take different routes, because each is independent of the other. UDP is a connectionless protocol. *see also* CONNECTION-ORIENTED.

CONSEIL DE COOPERATION DOUANIÉRE (CCD) *see* CUSTOMS COOPERATION COUNCIL.

CONSEIL DE L'ENTENTE (Entente Council) an alliance of Benin, Burkina Faso, Côte d'Ivoire, Niger (all formerly part of French West Africa), and Togo (which joined in 1966). The council was established in 1959, and its headquarters is in Abidjan, Côte d'Ivoire.

CONSEIL DE L'EUROPE *see* COUNCIL OF EUROPE.

CONSELHO FEDERAL DE CONTABILIDADE (CFC) *see* BRAZILIAN FEDERAL BOARD OF ACCOUNTANCY; BRAZILIAN INSTITUTE OF ACCOUNTANTS (IBRACON).

CONSELHO MONETARIO NACIONAL (CMN) the National Monetary Council in Brazil. The President of the CMN is the Minister of Finance, and the council consists of representatives from both the government and the private sector. The CMN is responsible for the formulation of monetary and credit policy. *see also* CENTRAL BANK OF BRAZIL (BACEN); NATIONAL MONETARY COUNCIL.

CONSENSUS RATES export credits provided for private sector borrowers in highly indebted countries, which would previously have been too great a risk for most agencies to cover. Consensus rates are achieved through international governmental cooperation allowing for lower rates of interest. *see also* EXPORT CREDIT ENHANCED LEVERAGE.

CONSIGNEE the person or company named in a freight contract to whom goods have been consigned or turned over. For EXPORT control purposes, the documentation differentiates between an "intermediate" consignee and an "ultimate" consignee. *see also* CONSIGNOR.

CONSIGNOR the person or firm named in a freight contract who has shipped the merchandise. It also can be used when referring to the person or firm selling the goods. *see also* CONSIGNEE.

CONSIGNMENT merchandise delivered from an EXPORTER (the CONSIGNOR) to an agent (the CONSIGNEE) under agreement that the agent sell the merchandise for the account of the exporter. The consignor retains title to the goods until sold. The consignee sells the goods for commission and remits the net proceeds to the consignor.

CONSOLIDATED CARRIER freight company carrying cargo or freight via air, ocean, truck, or rail, and providing consolidation services for customers. *see also* CARGO CARRIER; CONSOLIDATED SHIPMENT; CONSOLIDATOR.

CONSOLIDATED CONTAINER shipping CONTAINER that contains CARGO from numerous shippers for DELIVERY to numerous CONSIGNEES.

CONSOLIDATED SHIPMENT a situation occurring when different shippers combine their goods in the same shipment sharing the shipping charges. This enables each shipper to reduce shipping costs, taking advantage of volume discounts offered by the carriers.

CONSOLIDATION *see* CONSOLIDATED SHIPMENT.

CONSOLIDATOR company that provides consolidation services.

CONSORTIA OF AMERICAN BUSINESSES IN EASTERN EUROPE (CABEE) a program, administered by the U.S. DEPARTMENT OF COMMERCE, providing grants of up to $500,000 to each of five nonprofit consortia of for-profit companies to cover up to one-half of costs of starting-up commercial operations in Eastern Europe. Launched under the American Business and Private-Sector Development Initiative for Eastern Europe, CABEE is intended to help overcome difficulties faced by small and medium-sized firms in entering Eastern Europe markets. CABEE was established in June 1991.

CONSORTIA OF AMERICAN BUSINESSES IN THE NEWLY INDEPENDENT STATES (CABNIS) a cooperative, cost-sharing program of government and the private sector that helps nonprofit business consortia establish a commercial presence and pursue business in the Newly Independent States on behalf of profit-making U.S. corporations and associations. The program provides matching government grants of up to $500,000 to each consortium. CABNIS was established in July 1992 and is administered by the U.S. DEPARTMENT OF COMMERCE INTERNATIONAL TRADE ADMINISTRATION (ITA).

CONSORTIUM the process of combining separate entities for the purpose of forming a stronger unit striving for common objectives. These entities could be individual firms or governments. An example of a consortium is the Organization of Petroleum Exporting Countries (OPEC). These governments formed OPEC to strengthen their bargaining position in the marketing of oil.

CONSORTIUM INSURANCE method of indemnifying very large risks through a syndicate of insurance companies. This a method of sharing the risk among a group of insurance companies as opposed to reinsurance, where an insurance company actually buys insurance from another insurance company to provide coverage for a particular risk.

CONSTANTA SUD and **SALINA** the two major FREE PORTS operating in Romania. Storage and transshipment of merchandise in the free-port zone will be without the collection of CUSTOMS DUTIES.

CONSTRUCTED VALUE (CV) a means of determining fair or foreign market value when sales of such or similar merchandise do not exist or, for various reasons, cannot be used for comparison purposes. The constructed value consists of the cost of materials and fabrication or other processing employed in producing the merchandise, general expenses of not less than 10% of material and fabrication costs, and profit of not less than 8% of the sum of the production costs and general expenses. To this amount is added the cost of packing for exportation to the United States. *see also* TARIFF ACT OF 1930.

CONSTRUCTIVE TOTAL LOSS (CTL) a term used in MARINE INSURANCE referring to a situation when the cost of recovering or repairing damaged goods, when recovered or repaired, exceeds the value for which the goods were insured. *see also* INSURED VALUE.

CONSUL GENERAL (CG); CONSULATE GENERALE *see also* TITLE AND RANK.

CONSULAR DECLARATION a formal statement, made to the CONSUL of a foreign country, describing goods to be shipped.

CONSULAR DUTIES refers to the responsibilities of a foreign government official sent to another country to represent the interests and nationals of his/her country. *see also* TITLE AND RANK.

CONSULAR INFORMATION SHEET *see* TRAVEL ADVISORY PROGRAM.

CONSULAR INVOICE a document, required by some foreign countries, describing a shipment of goods and showing information such as the CONSIGNOR, CONSIGNEE, and value of the shipment. Certified by a consular official of the foreign country, it is used by the country's customs officials to verify the value, quantity, and nature of the shipment.

CONSULAR MISSION *see* TITLE AND RANK.

CONSULATE a place where representatives of the foreign government represent legal interests of their nationals. Consular establishments are usually located in an area of the host country outside the seat of government. A consulate is headed by a Principal Officer; a Consulate General is headed by a Principal Officer who is also a Consul General. The distinction between Consulates and Consulates General is often (but not necessarily) one of size of the establishment. Status is another factor. A consular section is always attached to an EMBASSY (even though it may be located in a separate facility). The section is headed by a Counsular Chief who oversees that section and any other consular establishments in the country. Consular Officers extend the protection of the government to its citizens and their property abroad. Their responsibilities include adjudicating VISAS and PASSPORTS and providing assistance to its citizens (birth and death certificates, notarizing documents, maintaining lists of attorneys, and acting as liaison with police and other officials). *see also* TITLE AND RANK.

CONSULTATION OFFICE FOR OVERSEAS COMPANIES (COOC) a department within the Korean Ministry of Trade and Industry headquartered in Seoul, Korea, that is responsible for providing information and advice to firms interested in doing business with Korea. These services include providing information of trade and investment procedures and problems, offering general advice on the relevant regulation on doing business with Korea, and acting as a liaison for issues with the government.

CONSULTATIVE COMMITTEE FOR INTERNATIONAL TELEPHONE AND TELEGRAPHY (CCITT) (French: Comité Consultatif International Télégraphique et Téléphonique) organization part of the United National INTERNATIONAL TELECOMMUNICATIONS UNION (ITU), which is an international treaty organization. The CCITT is responsible for making technical recommendations about telephone and data communications systems. Every 4 years CCITT holds plenary sessions where they adopt new standards. *see also* INTERNATIONAL TELEGRAPHIC AND TELEPHONE CONSULTATIVE COMMITTEE.

CONSULTATIVE COMMITTEE ON INTERNATIONAL RADIO (CCIR) together with the CONSULTATIVE COMMITTEE FOR INTERNATIONAL TELEPHONE AND TELEGRAPHY (CCITT) facilitates United States coordination of communication standards issues.

CONSULTATIVE GROUP ON INTERNATIONAL AGRICULTURAL RESEARCH (CGIAR) an informal association of public- and private-sector donors that supports international agricultural research centers (IARCs) around the world. The centers develop new ways to increase sustainable food production and improve the nutritional and economic well-being of low-income people. CGIAR is sponsored by the World Bank and other international organizations, and its Secretariat is in Washington, DC. CGIAR has research centers in 15 countries.

CONSUMER GOODS goods purchased for personal or household use, as compared to CAPITAL GOODS, which are used in the production of other goods.

CONSUMER MOVEMENT a MODE OF SUPPLY under the GENERAL AGREEMENT ON TRADE-IN SERVICES, this one entails the buyer moving (temporarily) to the foreign location of the seller, as in the case of tourism. *see also* CROSS-BORDER SUPPLY; MOVEMENT OF NATURAL PERSONS; PRODUCER PRESENCE; TEMPORARY PORDUCER MOVEMENT.

CONSUMPTION EFFECT OF A TARIFF reduced consumer demand for imported products as a result of a TARIFF imposed by the importing country. Tariffs increase the cost to the consumer of the imported product. Tariffs also protect domestic industries from international competition resulting in increased prices for domestically produced goods. The reduction in international trade creates a less-competitive domestic market with the consumer being forced to pay higher prices. The net result is that domestic consumption is reduced for protected items.

CONSUMPTION ENTRY CUSTOMS ENTRY where the IMPORTER pays the applicable dues and the goods are released from Customs custody. *see also* IMPORTS FOR CONSUMPTION.

CONTADORA GROUP a group that first met on the Panamanian island of Contadora in January 1983 and seeks solutions to conflict in Central America. Members include the foreign ministers of Colombia, Mexico, Panama, and Venezuela. Group headquarters is in Mexico City, Mexico.

CONTAINER a uniform, sealed, reusable metal box in which merchandise is shipped by vessel, truck, or rail. Standard lengths include 10, 20, 30, and 40 feet (40-foot lengths are generally able to hold about 40,000 pounds). Containers of 45 and 48 feet long are also used, as are containers for shipment by air.

CONTAINER FREIGHT CHARGE charge made for the packing or unpacking of CARGO from ocean FREIGHT CONTAINERS.

CONTAINER LOAD SHIPMENT of CARGO that, according to weight or volume, will fit any number of standard CONTAINERS.

CONTAINER ON FLATCAR CONTAINER without wheels that is put on railcars for transport.

CONTAINER PART LOAD shipment of CARGO that, according to weight or volume, will not fit into any number of standard CONTAINERS.

CONTAINER SHIP ships carrying large truck bodies that can be discharged and loaded in 1 day as compared to the 10 days required by conventional ships of the same size. The development of container ships began in 1956, when Sea–Land Service commenced operations between New York City and Houston, Texas. Container ships formed a symbiotic relationship with the trucking industry.

A container ship can discharge and load CARGO in approximately 13 hours, compared with 84 hours for a conventional ship, thus affording faster turnaround time. Damage claims on container cargo are much lower, they are weatherproof, theft has become insignificant, and gang labor costs are 1/20 of a similar sized conventional ship. *see also* LASH (LIGHTER ABOARD SHIP).

CONTAINERIZATION the use of CONTAINERS for shipping merchandise in the airline, railroad, and shipping industries. Containerization of CARGO has many advantages over conventional methods.
- It sharply reduces theft and shrinkage.
- It is much less labor-intensive.

- It reduces damage claims.
- It expedites the loading and unloading processes.

CONTAS DE GRUPO (Portuguese) *see* CORPORATION.

CONTENT ANALYSIS a practice of comparing the advertising messages among countries. Messages can be compared by counting the number of times a particular phrase, word, or picture appears in an advertisement. This enables the marketer to search for differences in advertising messages among competitive countries facilitating the identification of the most appropriate message for the targeted market.

CONTI DI GRUPPO (Italian) *see* CORPORATION.

CONTINGENCY PROTECTION protection and indemnity insurance for CARGO carried on board a ship.

CONTRABAND merchandise carried by neutral vessels under wartime conditions that may be confiscated by a belligerent power in order to prevent delivery to the enemy.

There are two contraband categories:

- absolute contraband: various resources that may be directly used for war or converted into the means of war including munitions, chemicals and certain types of technology.
- conditional contraband: food and livestock feed. These items can be seized by belligerents if it is believed they are intended to aid the enemy's armed forces rather than being intended for civilian use and consumption.

Because modern warfare increasingly has become an urban-based phenomenon, belligerents often consider all COMMODITIES to be absolute contraband. Although numerous international treaties have been concluded defining contraband, almost all treaties have been systematically violated and ignored during periods of war. In addition, while international law permits neutral nations to TRADE, at their own risk, with any or all nations engaged in warfare, belligerents can and do CONFISCATE the cargoes intended for the enemy. This can be extended to seizing the entire ship if more than half the CARGO is considered contraband.

CONTRACT an agreement between two or more individuals who agree or not agree to do something.

CONTRACT CARRIER excluding common CARRIERS, any person or company who under special CONTRACT will transport passengers or goods for agreed-upon compensation.

CONTRACT MANUFACTURING
1. a method of using a lower-cost international manufacturer to produce goods for a domestic corporation at a lower cost. A contract manufacturer will manufacture any product within its capabilities for any producer willing to contract for their services.
2. a method used to lower overhead costs and increase the volume of production by distributing materials to workers in their residences

and paying for work piecemeal. This led to the creation of the sweatshop where employees work long hours under substandard conditions for low wages.

CONTRACT OF AFFREIGHTMENT a contract by a ship owner to transport goods by sea or to put a vessel at the disposal of charterers for the purpose of chartering the ship to carry goods.

CONTRACT OF EMPLOYMENT a written agreement clarifying the employee/employer relationship. This agreement includes such issues as the duties and responsibilities of the position, together with information on compensation.

CONTRACTING PARTIES signatory countries to the GENERAL AGREEMENT ON TARIFFS AND TRADE (GATT). These countries have accepted the specified obligations and privileges of the GATT agreement.

CONTRACTOR'S INDEX a listing of all firms interested in taking part in AGENCY FOR INTERNATIONAL DEVELOPMENT (AID) financed projects. All firms with expertise in areas such as consulting research, architect engineering, and construction are recommended to register. The index is maintained by the Small and Disadvantaged Business Utilization division of the Agency for International Development and serves as a comprehensive listing of firms available to participate in projects by areas of expertise.

CONTRAT (French) *see* CONTRACT.

CONTRAT DE TRAVAIL (French) *see* CONTRACT OF EMPLOYMENT.

CONTRATO (Portuguese) *see* CONTRACT.

CONTRATO (Spanish) *see* CONTRACT.

CONTRIBUICAO SOCIAL PARA FINANCIAMENTO DE SEGURIDADE SOCIAL an employer-financed social security tax in Brazil, based on 2% of all sales.

CONTROLLED FACILITY a facility in a FREE PORT that is a portion of the national territory. For example, a free port can cover an entire region such as Hong Kong or may be confined to a special portion of a country as in the free port of Manaus in Brazil. If the free port is a part of national territory, goods held in the controlled facility are exempt from the payment of duties. As the goods leave the facility and pass into other areas of the country, customs duties are then assessed.

CONTROLLED IN FACT term that applies to any U.S. domestic company's foreign subsidiary, partnership, affiliate, branch office, or other permanent foreign establishment that is "controlled in fact" by such domestic company. Controlled in fact refers to the authority of the domestic company to establish general policy or to control day-to-day operations over the foreign subsidiary, partnership, affiliate, branch office, or other permanent foreign establishment.

CONVENIENCE STATEMENTS financial statements translated into the language of the foreign country where the monetary amounts are expressed in the foreign country's currency. However, the accounting principles and standards used in the preparation of these financial statements continue to be those of the HOME COUNTRY.

CONVENIOS term used when referring to annual salary increases awarded to employees in Spain.

CONVENTION *see* INTERNATIONAL AGREEMENTS.

CONVENTION ON CONTRACTS FOR THE INTERNATIONAL SALE OF GOODS (CISG) the United Nations Convention on Contracts for the International Sale of Goods became the law of the United States in January 1988. CISG establishes uniform legal rules governing the formation of international sales contracts and the rights and obligations of the buyer and seller. CISG applies automatically to all contracts for the sale of goods between traders from two different countries that have both ratified the CISG, unless the parties to the contract expressly exclude all or part of the CISG or expressly stipulate a law other than the CISG.

CONVENTIONAL ARMS TRANSFER the transferal of nonnuclear weapons, aircraft, equipment, and military services from supplier states to recipient states. U.S. arms are transferred by grants as in the MILITARY ASSISTANCE PROGRAM (MAP), by private commercial sales, and by government-to-government sales under FOREIGN MILITARY SALES (FMS). MAP provides defense articles and defense services to eligible foreign governments on a grant basis.

CONVERGENCE CRITERIA the macroeconomic requirements for membership in the EUROPEAN MONETARY UNION, which govern three basic issues: government spending, interest rates, and inflation. The specific criteria, per Article 104c of the MAASTRICHT TREATY, are summarized below.
1. The candidate nation has to participate in the EUROPEAN EXCHANGE RATE MECHANISM for two years.
2. Long-term interest rates cannot exceed a certain average (set at 7.8%).
3. Inflation cannot exceed a certain average (set at 2.7%).
4. Outstanding official debt has to be less than 60% of GDP or, if not, the percentage must be lower than the year before.
5. The national budget deficit cannot exceed 3% of GDP, except under unusual circumstances.

CONVERSION EXPOSURE the risk to be anticipated in converting the currency of one country into the currency of another country. *see also* CONVERSION RESTRICTIONS; CURRENCY CONTRACT PERIOD; CURRENCY CONVERTIBILITY; CURRENCY EXCHANGE CONTROLS; CURRENCY FORECAST; CURRENCY GYRATIONS; CURRENCY INCONVERTIBILITY; CURRENCY OPTION CONTRACT; CURRENCY SWAP; FOREIGN EXCHANGE.

CONVERSION RATE the rate of exchange used to determine the value of goods for customs purposes when the invoices presented are stated in a foreign currency. The U.S. CUSTOMS SERVICE uses rates of exchange determined and certified by the Federal Reserve Bank of New York and based on the New York market buying rates for the foreign currencies involved. For U.S. Customs purposes, the date of exportation of the goods is the date used to determine the applicable certified rate of exchange.

CONVERSION RESTRICTIONS limits placed on foreign investors by foreign governments in the conversion of remittances from local currency to U.S. dollars and the transfer of these remittances outside the host country. *see also* CURRENCY INCONVERTIBILITY.

CONVERTIBILITY attribute of being exchangeable, such as a currency freely able to be exchanged for another or as preferred stock or bonds to be exchanged for common stock.

CONVERTIBLE CURRENCY a national currency that may be readily exchanged for another nation's currency without restriction. A convertible currency is also one that is readily accepted by non-residents for the payment of goods and services. *see also* HARD CURRENCY; SOFT CURRENCY.

CONVEYANCE term used to refer to the means by which the CARGO has been transported such as the vessel or airplane. In MARINE CARGO INSURANCE the insurance does not go into effect until the goods are placed on the conveyance and ceases when the goods are discharged from the conveyance or when the conveyance arrives at the port.

COOPERATIVE EXPORT ORGANIZATION an independent firm that serves as the EXPORT department for a manufacturer, soliciting and transacting export business on behalf of the firm. *see also* EXPORT MANAGEMENT COMPANY (EMC); INDIRECT EXPORT; PIGGYBACK EXPORTING.

COOPERATOR PROGRAM *see* FOREIGN MARKET DEVELOPMENT PROGRAM.

COORDINATING COMMITTEE FOR INTERCONTINENTAL RESEARCH NETWORKS (CCIRN) an INTERNET committee that includes the United States FEDERAL NETWORKING COUNCIL (FNC) and its counterparts in North America and Europe. Co-chaired by the executive directors of the FNC and the EUROPEAN ASSOCIATION OF RESEARCH NETWORKS (RARE), the CCIRN provides a forum for cooperative planning among the principal North American and European research networking bodies.

COORDINATING COMMITTEE ON MULTILATERAL EXPORT CONTROLS (COCOM) an informal organization that cooperatively restricted strategic EXPORTS to controlled countries. COCOM controlled three lists:
- the INTERNATIONAL INDUSTRIAL LIST synonymous with the "dual-use" or "core" list,

- the INTERNATIONAL MUNITIONS LIST, and
- the INTERNATIONAL ATOMIC ENERGY LIST.

The 17 COCOM members were Australia, Belgium, Canada, Denmark, France, the Federal Republic of Germany, Greece, Italy, Japan, Luxembourg, the Netherlands, Norway, Portugal, Spain, Turkey, the United Kingdom, and the United States. Other countries, including Austria, Finland, Hong Kong, Ireland, New Zealand, Sweden, and Switzerland, were designated as cooperating countries. These countries received many of the benefits ascribed to COCOM member countries.

COCOM terminated on March 31, 1994.

COORDINATION COUNCIL FOR NORTH AMERICAN AFFAIRS (CCNAA) the counterpart to the AMERICAN INSTITUTE IN TAIWAN. It unofficially represents Taiwan's interests in the United States. The council provides information on trade, business, and investment opportunities to the American business community. Council headquarters is in Washington, DC.

COP *see* COST OF PRODUCTION.

COPAL *see* COCOA PRODUCERS ALLIANCE.

COPANT *see* COMISION PANAMERICANA DE NORMAS TECNICAS.

COPRODUCTION a U.S. government program implemented either by a government-to-government arrangement or through specific licensing arrangements by designated commercial firms. These programs enable foreign entities to acquire the know-how to manufacture or assemble, repair, maintain, and operate all or part of a specific defense item or weapon, communication, or support system.

CORE GATEWAY one of a group of GATEWAYS (ROUTERS) managed by the INTERNET Network Operations Center at Bolt, Beranek and Newman (BBN). The core gateway system acts as a main part of Internet routing since all groups must display paths to their networks using a core gateway.

CORE INFLATION basic level of inflation over a period of time as opposed to temporary fluctuations.

CORE LIST national security controls based largely on COCOM'S INTERNATIONAL INDUSTRIAL LIST (known generally as the core list), which replaced the old industrial list effective September 1991. The core list includes items in ten categories:
- materials,
- materials processing,
- electronics,
- computers,
- telecommunications and cryptography,
- sensors,
- avionics and navigation,
- marine technology,

- propulsion systems and transportation equipment, and
- miscellaneous.

CORECT *see* COMMITTEE ON RENEWABLE ENERGY, COMMERCE, AND TRADE.

CORPORACION ANDINA DE FOMENTO (CAF) Venezuelan organization supporting economic integration among members of the ANDEAN GROUP by encouraging specialization, distribution of investments and by providing financial and technical help. The CAF was founded in 1968 and began operations in 1970. Its headquarters is in Caracas, Venezuela.

CORPORATE DUMPING practice of EXPORTING banned or out-of-date goods to a FOREIGN market where restrictions on that product are not as severe. *see also* DUMPING.

CORPORATION a legal entity chartered by the state or federal government, separate from the persons owning it. A corporation has the rights of a person. It has the ability to own property, assume debts, and sue and be sued. The principal features of the corporate form of ownership are
- limited liability (an owner's liability is limited to the amount of their investment);
- ease in transfer of ownership, through the sale of stock; and
- continuity of existence.

CORPORATION FOR RESEARCH AND EDUCATIONAL NETWORKING (CREN) organization that was formed in October 1989, when BITNET and CSNET (Computer + Science NETwork) were combined under one administrative authority. CSNET is no longer operational, but CREN still runs BITNET.

CORRESPONDENCE ALLOWANCE the reimbursement for the use of correspondence courses by a dependent child during an assignment in a foreign country. Such courses may be required when acceptable schooling is not available at an assigned location, or should the dependent child have any special education requirements.

CORRESPONDENT (CORRESPONDENT RELATIONSHIP) *see* CORRESPONDENT BANK.

CORRESPONDENT BANK a bank that, in its own country, handles the business of a foreign bank.

COST AND FREIGHT (C & F) a seller's price quote for goods to a named overseas port of IMPORT that includes the cost of transportation to the named point of debarkation. The cost of insurance is left to the buyer's account. (Typically used for ocean shipments only, CPT, or CARRIAGE PAID TO, is a term used for shipment by modes other than water.) Also, a method of import valuation that includes insurance and freight charges with the merchandise values.

COST-BASED TRANSFER PRICES the price at which the parent firm sells products to its foreign affiliates or the price at which the foreign affiliate sells products to its parent based on the actual cost of goods for firm supplying the goods. *see also* COMPARABLE UNCONTROLLED PRICE METHOD; RESALE PRICE METHOD; COST-PLUS METHOD.

COST DIFFERENTIAL an additional payment provided by the company to reimburse the employee for the difference in cost of living expenses between the HOST and HOME COUNTRIES. *see also* ASSUMED SHELTER COST; AWAY FROM POST EDUCATION; CORRESPONDENCE ALLOWANCE; EDUCATION ALLOWANCE; FURNISHING ALLOWANCE; HOUSING ALLOWANCE; UTILITIES ALLOWANCE.

COST, INSURANCE, AND FREIGHT (CIF) a seller's price quote for goods to a named overseas port of IMPORT. Typically used only for ocean shipments, a CIF quote is comprehensive including all insurance, transportation, and miscellaneous charges to the point of debarkation for the vessel. (CIP, or CARRIAGE AND INSURANCE PAID TO, is a term used for shipment by modes other than water.)

COST OF COVERAGE premiums charged for investment insurance supplied by the OVERSEAS PRIVATE INVESTMENT CORPORATION (OPIC). The premium rates depend on the risk profile of the project, but once established, the rates are fixed for the life of the contract.

COST OF CREDIT a column appearing daily in the JOURNAL OF COMMERCE providing the journal's analysis of worldwide lending rates.

COST OF LIVING ALLOWANCE *see* COST DIFFERENTIAL.

COST OF PRODUCTION (COP) a term used to refer to the sum of the cost of materials, fabrication, and/or other processing employed in producing the merchandise sold in a home market or to a third country together with appropriate allocations of general administrative and selling expenses. COP is based on the producer's actual experience and does not include any mandatory minimum general expense or profit as in constructed value. *see also* TARIFF ACT OF 1930.

COST PLUS METHOD similar to the COST-BASED METHOD OF TRANSFER PRICE; however, in this case goods are transferred at cost plus a reasonable markup to cover the expenses for the firm supplying the goods to the foreign affiliate. *see also* COMPARABLE UNCONTROLLED PRICE METHOD; COST-BASED TRANSFER PRICE SYSTEMS; RESALE PRICE METHOD; TRANSFER PRICE.

COSTS OF MANUFACTURE (COM) the costs of manufacture equal to the sum of the materials, labor, and both direct and indirect factory overhead expenses required to produce merchandise undergoing a dumping investigation.

COTTONSEED OIL ASSISTANCE PROGRAM (COAP) one of four EXPORT subsidy programs operated by the U.S. Department of Agriculture (USDA). COAP helps U.S. exporters meet prevailing world prices for cottonseed oil in targeted markets. The USDA pays cash to U.S. exporters as bonuses, making up the difference between the higher U.S. cost of acquiring cottonseed oil and the lower world price at which it is sold.

COUNCIL FOR INVESTMENTS IN TRADE, TOURISM, AGRICULTURE, NATURAL RESOURCES, TRANSPORTATION, COMMUNICATION, AND SERVICES (PHILIPPINES) council created in the Philippines by the Omnibus Investments Code of 1987. The council serves the following functions:

- coordinate investment development programs,
- provide information to local and foreign investors concerning the establishment of operations or investments,
- to promote the Philippines as a prime area for foreign investment, and
- to make recommendation to the authorities concerning modification to existing investment laws and procedures.

COUNCIL FOR MUTUAL ECONOMIC ASSISTANCE (CMEA or COMECON) CMEA was a Soviet initiative with Bulgaria, Czechoslovakia, Hungary, Poland, and Romania as founder members. The council was later joined by the German Democratic Republic, Mongolia, Cuba, and Vietnam. Yugoslavia held associate status. Members normally received some products, particularly oil and gas, from the former Soviet Union at below-market prices. Established in 1949 ostensibly to create a common market, CMEA was succeeded in 1991 by the Organization for Economic Cooperation (OIEC).

COUNCIL OF AMERICAN STATES IN EUROPE (CASE) council that is composed of state representatives resident in Europe and supportive of official U.S. commercial trade promotions.

COUNCIL OF CANADIAN TRADING HOUSES (CCTH) an association organized by the CANADIAN EXPORT ASSOCIATION (CEA) for the purpose of coordinating and administering the accreditation process of trading houses in Canada, and the promotion and the providing of information on the use of trading houses in Canada to interested parties.

COUNCIL OF ECONOMIC ARAB UNITY (CEAU) Arab organization that fosters economic integration among Arab nations. The council's activities include compiling statistics, conducting research, and promoting a customs union. The council oversees the Arab Common Market, which comprises Egypt, Iraq, Jordan, Libya, Mauritania, Syria, and Yemen. The council was established in 1964, and its headquarters is in Amman, Jordan.

COUNCIL OF EUROPE (COE) (also CE; French: Conseil de l'Europe) European organization established in May 1949 to encourage unity and social and economic growth among members, which currently include Austria, Belgium, Cyprus, Denmark,

Finland, France, Germany, Greece, Hungary, Iceland, Ireland, Italy, Liechtenstein, Luxembourg, Malta, the Netherlands, Norway, Portugal, San Marino, Spain, Sweden, Switzerland, Turkey, and the United Kingdom. COE headquarters is in Strasbourg, France.

COUNTERPURCHASE *see* COUNTERTRADE.

COUNTERTERRORISM measures used to prevent, preempt, or retaliate against terrorist attacks.

COUNTERTRADE an umbrella term for several sorts of TRADE in which the seller is required to accept goods, services, or other instruments or trade, in partial or whole payment for its products. Forms include BARTER, buy-back or COMPENSATION, offset requirements, SWAP, SWITCH or triangular trade, and evidence or BILATERAL CLEARING AGREEMENTS. Some include offset deals as a form of countertrade; others make a distinction based on the view that countertrade is a reciprocal exchange of goods and services used to alleviate foreign exchange shortages of importers and that offsets are used as a means for advancing industrial development objectives and may include equity investments. *see also* OFFSETS.

COUNTERVAILING DUTY (CVD) an extra charge that a country places on imported goods to counter the subsidies or bounties granted to the EXPORTERS of the goods by their home governments. The duty is allowed by the ANTIDUMPING/COUNTERVAILING DUTY SYSTEM negotiated at the TOKYO ROUND, if the importing country can prove that the subsidy would cause injury to domestic industry. U.S. countervailing duties can be imposed only after the INTERNATIONAL TRADE COMMISSION has determined that the imports are causing or threatening to cause material injury to a U.S. industry.

COUNTRY COUNSELING term that refers to various programs offered by the U.S. DEPARTMENT OF COMMERCE, which provide assistance to firms interested in doing business in foreign countries. *see also* AGENT/DISTRIBUTOR SERVICE (ADS); CUSTOMIZED SALES SURVEY (CSS); ECONOMIC BULLETIN BOARD (EBB); GOLD KEY SERVICE; NATIONAL TRADE DATA BANK (NTDB); WORLD TRADERS DATA REPORT (WTDR); TRADE OPPORTUNITIES PROGRAM (TOP).

COUNTRY OF DEPARTURE country from which a ship or SHIPMENT has or is scheduled to depart. *see also* COUNTRY OF DESTINATION; COUNTRY OF DISPATCH; COUNTRY OF EXPORT DESTINATION; COUNTRY OF ORIGIN.

COUNTRY OF DESTINATION *see* COUNTRY OF EXPORT DESTINATION.

COUNTRY OF DISPATCH the country from which the seller has to send the goods to the named place of destination. *see also* COUNTRY OF EXPORT DESTINATION.

COUNTRY OF EXPORTATION usually, the country in which the merchandise was manufactured and produced and from where it was first EXPORTED. *see also* COUNTRY OF DESTINATION; COUNTRY OF DISPATCH; COUNTRY OF EXPORT DESTINATION; COUNTRY OF ORIGIN.

COUNTRY OF EXPORT DESTINATION the country where the goods are to be consumed, further processed, or manufactured, as known to the shipper at the time of EXPORTATION. If the shipper does not know the country of ultimate destination, the shipment is credited to the last country to which the shipper knows that the merchandise will be shipped in the same form as exported.

COUNTRY OF ORIGIN the country where an article was wholly grown, manufactured, or produced, or, if not wholly grown, cultivated or produced in one country, the last country in which the article underwent a substantial transformation. DUTY rates vary according to the country of origin.

COUNTRY GROUPS seven country groups designated by the symbols Q, S, T, V, W, Y, Z by the BUREAU OF EXPORT ADMINISTRATION of the U.S. DEPARTMENT OF COMMERCE for EXPORT control purposes. Canada and Antarctica are not included in any country group. Canada is referred to by name throughout the export Administration Regulations. Antarctica is controlled according to the country that occupies the area in Antarctica where the items proposed for export or reexport will be used. *see also* EXPORT CONTROL CLASSIFICATION NUMBER.

COUNTRY RISK financial risk of a transaction that relates to the political, economic, or social instability of a country. *see also* COUNTRY RISK ANALYSIS; DEL CREDERE RISK; RISK AVERSION; RISK POSITION; WAR RISK INSURANCE.

COUNTRY RISK ANALYSIS the evaluation of the political and financial situation in a country and the degree to which these factors affect the ability of a country to honor its financial obligations as they become due.

COUNTRY SIMILARITY THEORY theory that states that when a firm develops a new product in response to a perceived need in its home market, it will then look to foreign markets that are viewed to be similar to those in the home market.

COUNTRY SIZE THEORY *see* THEORY OF COUNTRY SIZE.

COURIER operation characterized by small package DELIVERY or express mail service of a large number of SHIPMENTS to a variety of deliveries to parties on a single CONVEYANCE.

COURT OF ARBITRATION an independent panel chosen by the disputing parties that listens to the evidence and arguments presented by both parties and renders a decision. *see also* ARBITRATION.

COURT OF INTERNATIONAL TRADE (CIT) American court having jurisdiction over any civil action against the United States arising from U.S. federal laws governing import transactions. The court hears antidumping, product classification, and countervailing duty matters as well as appeals of UNFAIR TRADE PRACTICE cases from the INTERNATIONAL TRADE COMMISSION. The court was originally established in 1890, and its principal offices are located in New York City. The court is empowered to hear and determine cases arising at any port or place within the jurisdiction of the United States. The judges are appointed for life by the president, subject to Senate confirmation.

COVERED DIFFERENTIAL the difference between the similar short-term exchange rates of two CONVERTIBLE CURRENCIES after concessions have been made for the FORWARD PREMIUM or DISCOUNT on one of the currencies.

COVERED INTEREST ARBITRAGE

1. ARBITRAGING the difference in value between an international purchase of a short-term investment vehicle covered by a simultaneous purchase of a FUTURES CONTRACT for the same amount in the opposite direction (the net investment position is offset by a reverse transaction eliminating the exchange risk). The investor hopes to make money with the net difference in value of the investment vehicles. For example, an investor purchases a 6-month German government bond while simultaneously purchasing a 6-month put option contract on the bond. This can also be termed an interest and foreign exchange futures combination arbitrage.
2. a method of benefiting from the interest rate difference between various international money markets, by borrowing money in one market and lending it in another at a higher interest rate.
3. interest and amortization payments covered from the operating profits of a concern.

COVERED UNDER CARNET imported goods protected from customs duties by the convention on the ATA CARNET for the Temporary Admission of Goods (ATA Convention). Such items normally include samples of commercial goods not meant for domestic consumption intended primarily to demonstrate a product's advantages and characteristics.

CPCM *see* COMITE PERMANENT CONSULTATIF DU MAGHREB.

CPT *see* CARRIAGE PAID TO.

CRAWLING PEG *see* CRAWLING PEG SYSTEM.

CRAWLING PEG SYSTEM a procedure in which a currency EXCHANGE RATE(S) is altered frequently (multiple times a year), generally to adjust for rapid inflation. Between changes, the EXCHANGE RATE(S) for the currency remains fixed. Instead of the whole amount of a revaluation or devaluation taking place at once, it is spread in small percentages over a number of months. *see also* EXCHANGE RATE(S) CLASSIFICATIONS.

CREDIT HEDGE *see* HEDGING.

CRÉDIT MIXTE *see* MIXED CREDIT.

CREDIT PROTOCOL financial management methods for aid and export credits as detailed in the 1978 EEC/OECD Arrangement. It covers such areas as repayment of credits, syndicated credits, credit terms, and average repayment periods for export credits.

CREDIT RISK INSURANCE insurance designed to cover risks of nonpayment for delivered goods.

CREDIT TRANCHES the INTERNATIONAL MONETARY FUND'S (IMF) basic policy on the use of its general resources. Credit is made available in four tranches, each equivalent to 25% of a member's quota.

A first credit tranche purchase raises the IMF's holdings of the purchasing member's currency to no more than 25% of quota. Generally, a member may request use of the IMF's resources in the first credit tranche if it demonstrates that it is making reasonable efforts to overcome its BALANCE OF PAYMENTS difficulties. Also, a member may request use of the first credit tranche as part of a standby arrangement.

Subsequent purchases are made in the upper credit tranches. These resources are made available if a member adopts policies that provide appropriate grounds for expecting that the member's balance of payments difficulties will be resolved within a reasonable period. Use of these resources is almost always made under a standby or an extended arrangement.

CREDIT TRANSACTIONS
1. commercial credit transactions including credit balances on ARBITRAGE transactions.
2. methods for managing intergovernmental and EXPORT transactions developed by the INTERNATIONAL MONETARY FUND.
3. EXPORT CREDIT transaction as detailed in the 1978 EEC/OECD Arrangement on export credits.
4. national currency balances required involving transactions in time deposits between credit institutions.

CREN *see* CORPORATION FOR RESEARCH AND EDUCATIONAL NETWORKING.

CRISIS IN THE GULF Persian Gulf War fought primarily in Kuwait and Iraq during January and February 1991. The crisis was precipitated in August 1990, when Iraq, led by President Saddam Hussein, invaded and annexed Kuwait. The United Nations Security Council passed several resolutions demanding that Iraq unconditionally withdraw from Kuwait by January 1991. When Iraq refused to withdraw, a military strike by the UN forces occurred. The United Nations was victorious, and Iraq was forced to sign terms of surrender, which included withdrawal and renunciation of its claim to Kuwait as its 19th province.

CRITICAL CIRCUMSTANCES a determination made by the U.S. Assistant Secretary for Import Administration (of the U.S. DEPART-

MENT OF COMMERCE'S INTERNATIONAL TRADE ADMINISTRATION) as to whether there is a reasonable basis to believe or suspect that there is a history of dumping in the United States or elsewhere of the merchandise under consideration, or that the IMPORTER knew or should have known that the exporter was selling this merchandise at less than FAIR VALUE, and there have been massive IMPORTS of this merchandise over a relatively short period. This determination is made if an allegation of critical circumstances is received from the petitioner. *see also* TARIFF ACT OF 1930.

CROSS BORDER LEASING a popular form of financing capital investments in many developing countries. The OVERSEAS PRIVATE INVESTMENT CORPORATION (OPIC) has designed insurance packages to cover both CAPITAL and OPERATING LEASES. The insurance is available to U.S. investors leasing to private-sector entities. Transactions must have an average life of 3 years.

CROSS-BORDER SUPPLY a MODE OF SUPPLY under the GENERAL AGREEMENT ON TRADE-IN SERVICES involving temporary movement across national borders without requiring physical movement of buyer or seller, as when the service can be provided by long-distance communication. *see also* MOVEMENT OF NATURAL PERSONS; CONSUMER MOVEMENT; PRODUCER PRESENCE; TEMPORARY PRODUCER MOVEMENT.

CROSS-CULTURAL TRAINING the process of making employees and their dependents aware of cultural differences between HOME and HOST COUNTRY cultures. *see also* CULTURAL EMPATHY; CULTURAL ASSIMILATION; CULTURAL ASSIMILATOR; CULTURAL ORIENTATION; ENVIRONMENTAL BRIEFING; FIELD EXPERIENCE; LANGUAGE TRAINING; LOCALIZATION; SENSITIVITY TRAINING.

CROSS LICENSING the transfer of technology between different firms. *see also* LICENSING; LICENSING AGREEMENT.

CROSS RATE the EXCHANGE RATE computed for a currency, using the rates from two other currencies. Example: DM (Deutsche Mark) 1.5 per U.S. dollar and the SwF (Swiss franc) 1.3 per U.S. dollar. The cross rate would be SwF 1.3/DM1.5 equals SwF 0.867 per DM.

CROSS SUBSIDIZATION process where the profit from one activity of an enterprise is used to offset the loss on another activity. This is particularly crucial in EXPORT subsidization where a product's price can be lowered less than its cost of manufacture in order to penetrate a foreign market. In U.S. law this could lead to a finding by the INTERNATIONAL TRADE COMMISSION that IMPORTS are causing, or are likely to cause, harm to a U.S. industry. Subsequently, this could result in an injury determination as the basis for a Section 201 AFFIRMATIVE DUMPING DETERMINATION case in conjunction with the U.S. DEPARTMENT OF COMMERCE'S determinations on dumping and subsidization.

CROSS TRADER a shipping company of a third country that operates a service between another third country and a member country.

Example: an American trading company contracts with a shipping company located in Argentina to purchase items from a Chilean company to be exported to Mexico, which is a NAFTA member.

CROWN CORPORATION a government-owned corporation organized for public purposes managed in a businesslike manner having an appointed board of directors enjoying a certain degree of financial and supervisory freedom from the government.

CRUZEIRO former unit of currency, Brazil (100 centavos equal 1 cruzeiro).

CSCE *see* CONFERENCE ON SECURITY AND COOPERATION IN EUROPE.

CSP *see* COMMON STANDARD LEVEL OF EFFECTIVE PROTECTION.

CSS *see* CUSTOMIZED SALES SURVEY.

CTD *see* COMMITTEE ON TRADE AND DEVELOPMENT.

CTIS *see* CENTER FOR TRADE AND INVESTMENT SERVICES.

CTL *see* CONSTRUCTIVE TOTAL LOSS.

CTM the largest labor union in Mexico with over 5 million members. In May 1992 the CTM and other Mexican labor unions joined a TRIPARTITE voluntary NATIONAL ACCORD FOR RAISING PRODUCTIVITY AND QUALITY (ANEPC).

CTP *see* COMPOSITE THEORETICAL PERFORMANCE; EXCHANGE RATE(S) CLASSIFICATIONS.

CUBAN PESO unit of currency, Cuba (100 centavos equal 1 Cuban peso).

CUENTAS DE GRUPO (Spanish) *see* CORPORATION.

CULTURAL ADIAPHORA a policy of religious tolerance first advocated by the German scholar and religious reformer Melanchthon (1497–1560). He advocated harmony between Protestantism and Roman Catholicism as well as brought Protestant factions closer together. Cultural adiaphora advocates bringing different religions and cultures closer together.

CULTURAL ADOPTION
1. a policy of respecting the cultures and rights of other people and nations.
2. the promotion and encouragement of human rights and fundamental freedoms advocated under the Universal Declaration of Human Rights resolution adopted in December 1948 by the United Nations General Assembly. The declaration proclaims the personal, civil, political, economic, social, and cultural rights of humans by recognizing the rights and freedoms of others by achieving morality and public order while protecting the general welfare.
3. a policy sponsored by the COUNCIL OF EUROPE, organization of European states, established in 1949, for accomplishing unity

among the member nations on the basis of political liberty rather than geographic location. The council advocates that the member states achieve the various social and economic rights outlined in the European Convention for the Protection of Human Rights and Fundamental Freedoms (1950). These include the rights to a fair wage, to strike, and to social security, including social and medical assistance if it is needed.

4. necessary conditions for achieving a single currency by the Member States under the MAASTRICHT TREATY.

CULTURAL ASSIMILATION a training program devised to assist employees and their dependents to adjust to the cultural differences in foreign countries. *see also* CROSS-CULTURAL TRAINING; CULTURAL ASSIMILATOR.

CULTURAL ASSIMILATOR a learning method designed to introduce individuals of one CULTURE to some of the basic values, attitudes, beliefs, customs and role perceptions of another culture. *see also* CROSS-CULTURAL TRAINING; CULTURAL ASSIMILATION.

CULTURAL BORROWING the evolution and development of cultures through the process of borrowing various elements from other national cultures. An area where this is particularly true is in the development of writing and language systems. The great number of words in the English vocabulary resulted from extensive, constant borrowing from every major language, especially from Latin, Greek, French, and the Scandinavian languages, and from numerous minor languages. The mass media have become an extremely important influence in cultural borrowing. It is expected that the mass media will produce standardized pronunciation and more uniform phonetic spelling. The English language has been constantly enriched by linguistic borrowing, and it has demonstrated infinite possibilities of communication. Through cultural borrowing and adaptation, the English language has become the chief international language.

CULTURAL CAVEAT caution advised whenever seeking to embrace another culture's behavior patterns or customs.

CULTURAL EMPATHY a comprehension of the cultural differences between countries and how those differences affect society and business.

CULTURAL EXCHANGE programs encouraging people to visit foreign countries to further their study or training, to teach, or to give artistic or athletic performances while allowing foreign nationals to visit the host country for the same purposes. Cultural exchange programs trace their origin to the enactment in 1946 of the Fulbright Act, introduced by the U.S. Senator J. William Fulbright. The Fulbright Act encouraged reciprocal exchange of outstanding scholars between countries. Since 1949 more than 100,000 nationals from countries around the world have visited the United States, and

Americans from every state and territory have participated in these exchange programs.

UNESCO also has an exchange program among member nations, of persons working in the mass communications media including film, press, radio, books, and periodicals.

CULTURAL EXCLUSIVES behavior or practices excluded for those not part of a particular culture. Cultural exclusives may include participating in another religion's practices or marrying into another culture.

CULTURAL IMPERIALISM the rationale whereby powerful nations feel compelled to extend and maintain control or influence over weaker nations or peoples. States acting under cultural imperialism consider it to be a "missionary activity" to exercise control over a less powerful nation. Example: during Britain's colonial period the British felt that it was the "white man's burden" to civilize "backward" peoples. To a great extent Germany's imperialism under Hitler was founded on a belief in the inherent superiority of the German national culture. The desire of the United States to "protect the free world" and of the former Soviet Union to "liberate" the peoples of Eastern Europe and the Third World are also examples of imperialism driven by moral and cultural concerns.

CULTURAL LAG a lapse in time that occurs between a cultural development in one nation before another reacts to it. Example: while early American architecture reflects an English influence, a period of time transpired before it was adopted.

CULTURAL MOSAIC a medley or heterogeneity of cultures living in an area reflecting great complexity and variety. Example: the city of Philadelphia, Pennsylvania is noted for its mosaic of neighborhoods, most of which are regularly referred to by their proper names, such as Germantown, Manayunk, East Falls, and Queen Village. Many of the city's neighborhoods retain the ambiance of the ethnic groups who settled in them. Major districts include South Philadelphia, which is known as an Italian neighborhood, and West and North Philadelphia, which are predominantly African-American neighborhoods.

CULTURAL PROPERTIES PRESERVATION LAW a Korean law that prohibits the exporting or carrying of important cultural properties, such as crafts, paintings, and sculptures, out of Korea.

CULTURAL UNIVERSALS
1. the religion, social organization, structure, economic organization, and cultural materials including architecture, art, clothing, tools, and weapons.
2. Universal Declaration of Human Rights, resolution adopted in December 1948 by the UNITED NATIONS General Assembly. It proclaims the personal, civil, political, economic, social, and cultural rights of human beings.

CULTURE all socially transmitted behavior patterns of a human society including the arts, beliefs, institutions, and all other products of human work and thought. Culture is transferred to subsequent generations experientially and by learning.

CULTURE SHOCK a condition of confusion and discomfort affecting a person suddenly exposed to a foreign culture. Factors contributing to culture shock are the inability to communicate in a foreign country's native language including the inability to understand signs as well as unfamiliarity with a new culture.

CURRENCY BOARD an extreme form of PEGGED EXCHANGE RATE in which management of both the EXCHANGE RATE and the MONEY SUPPLY are taken away from the CENTRAL BANK and given to an agency with instructions to back every unit of circulating domestic currency with a specified amount of foreign currency.

CURRENCY CONTRACT PERIOD the period immediately following the devaluation of a currency, when contracts negotiated before the devaluation become due. The effects of such a contract on the BALANCE OF TRADE depend on the currency in which the contract is written. Example: prior to a devaluation one U.S. dollar is equal to one unit of currency of another country. After devaluation the exchange rate adjusts to US$1.10. If a U.S. EXPORTER has a contract to sell goods for US$10,000, the exporter will still receive US$10,000 even after devaluation. However, if the contract was written in a foreign currency, the exporter would then be able to convert each unit of foreign currency into US$1.10 allowing the exporter to receive a gain on the devaluation. A similar relationship would also exist with a U.S. IMPORTER contracting to purchase goods from a foreign firm.

CURRENCY FORECAST a column published each Monday in the JOURNAL OF COMMERCE that follows the fluctuation in the U.S. dollar and how those fluctuations affect U.S. firms overseas.

CURRENCY GYRATIONS *see* FLOATING EXCHANGE RATES; FLUCTUATING EXCHANGE RATES.

CURRENCY INCONVERTIBILITY a situation when a firm is unable to convert local currency into a CONVERTIBLE CURRENCY and transfer those remittances outside the HOST COUNTRY. The OVERSEAS PRIVATE INVESTMENT CORPORATION (OPIC) provides currency inconvertibility coverage which compensates U.S. investors if they are unable to convert insured remittances outside the host country. OPIC inconvertibility coverage encompasses earnings, returns of capital, principal and interest payments, technical assistance fees and other remittances related to investment projects. The coverage, however, does not protect against the devaluation of a country's currency.

CURRENCY OPTION CONTRACT an agreement that allows the individual purchasing the option the right, but not the obligation, to buy or sell a foreign currency at a set rate of exchange within a specified period of time.

CURRENCY SWAPS *see* SWAP.

CURRENCY UNION a region in which rates of exchange are fixed.

CURRENT ACCOUNT *see* BALANCE OF PAYMENTS.

CURRENT ACCOUNT BALANCE measures the transactions (exports minus imports) of goods, services, income, and UNILATERAL TRANSFERS between residents and nonresidents of a country. *see also* BALANCE OF PAYMENTS.

CURRENT RATE METHOD involves the use of the EXCHANGE RATE in effect on the balance sheet date when translating financial statements of a foreign subsidiary. *see also* FUNCTIONAL CURRENCY; TEMPORAL METHOD; TRANSLATION.

CUSCAR type of UN/EDIFACT message that is used to convey data about a U.S. CUSTOMS goods declaration.

CUSDEC type of UN/EDIFACT message that is used to convey data about a U.S. CUSTOMS goods declaration.

CUSTODY BILL OF LADING BILL OF LADING issued by American warehouses as a receipt for goods stored. *see also* CLAUSED BILL OF LADING; ORDER BILL OF LADING; STRAIGHT BILL OF LADING.

CUSTOMARY LAW in INTERNATIONAL LAW, the establishment and acceptance of practices of nations toward each other. *see also* COMMON LAW SYSTEM.

CUSTOMER SATISFACTION doctrine that implies that the quality of service a firm provides has been acceptable to its customers.

CUSTOMIZED SALES SURVEY (CSS) a fee-based INTERNATIONAL TRADE ADMINISTRATION service that provides firms with key marketing, pricing, and foreign representation information about their specific products. Overseas staff conduct on-site interviews to provide data in nine marketing areas about the product, such as sales potential in the market, comparable products, distribution channels, going price, competitive factors, and qualified purchasers. Additional information may be provided to clients at an additional charge. This product was formerly known as the COMPARISON SHOPPING SERVICE.

CUSTOMS
1. an area designated by a government, where goods being imported into a country or exported out of a country can be inspected by an authorized Customs official. The examination of the goods is necessary to determine the goods' origin and destination, the value of the goods, and their dutiable status. *see also* DUTY; EXPORT LEVY; IMPORT DUTY.
2. the authorities designated to collect duties levied by a country on IMPORTS and EXPORTS. The term also applies to the procedures involved in such collection.

CUSTOMS ACT the Canadian Customs and Excise Offshore Application Act, which authorizes a Canadian Dominion Customs Appraiser to supervise IMPORT procedures.

CUSTOMS AND ECONOMIC UNION OF CENTRAL AFRICA *see* CENTRAL AFRICAN CUSTOMS AND ECONOMIC UNION.

CUSTOMS BOND a guarantee required by a foreign government when it wants assurances that a company will REEXPORT machinery or equipment temporarily shipped into the country, usually for a construction project or a trade show, rather than selling it locally. *see also* BOND SYSTEM.

CUSTOMS BOND COVERAGE insurance provided by the OVERSEAS PRIVATE INVESTMENT CORPORATION (OPIC) for a loss resulting from a wrongful calling by a foreign government of a guaranty for a CUSTOMS BOND.

CUSTOMS BROKER *see* CUSTOMSHOUSE BROKER.

CUSTOMS CLASSIFICATION a business classification developed by the Convention on Nomenclature for the Classification of Goods in Customs TARIFFS. Customs Cooperation Council's Recommendation of January 1, 1975, designed to enable statistical data on international trade collected on the basis of the Brussels Nomenclature to be expressed in terms of the second revision of the STANDARD INTERNATIONAL TRADE CLASSIFICATION.

CUSTOMS CLEARING AGENT an agent of a nation's Customs authority charged with the responsibility of regulating the commerce of IMPORTED and EXPORTED goods including imposing tariffs and duties on goods in order to clear them for import.

CUSTOMS COOPERATION COUNCIL (CCC) (French: Conseil de Coopération Dounaière, CCD) an international organization consisting of representatives of about 150 countries. The council serves as a technical body that studies and seeks to resolve the various countries' customs problems in an attempt to harmonize customs operations and promote TRADE. The council was established in 1950, and its headquarters is in Brussels, Belgium.

CUSTOMS COOPERATION COUNCIL NOMENCLATURE (CCCN) customs TARIFF nomenclature formerly used by many countries, including most European nations but not the United States. It has been superseded by the HARMONIZED SYSTEM nomenclature to which most major trading nations, including the United States, adhere.

CUSTOMS ELECTRONIC BULLETIN BOARD (CEEB) electronic bulletin board accessible with a computer and modem providing information on rulings, quotas, currency conversion rates, Customs valuation provisions, directives, and other Customs news. The service is provided by the U.S. CUSTOMS SERVICE.

CUSTOMS DECLARATION (FORM 2976-A) form included in all mail packages used to describe the contents and value of the package.

CUSTOMS DUTY tax imposed on IMPORTS by the Customs authority of a country. In British usage the distinction between Customs duty and excise duties depends on whether the goods are imported (Customs duties) or British produced (excise duties). *see also* AD VALOREM; ANTIDUMPING/COUNTERVAILING DUTY SYSTEM; ANTIDUMPING DUTY; COUNTERVAILING DUTY; DUTY.

CUSTOMS FREE ZONE *see* FREE-TRADE ZONE.

CUSTOMS HARMONIZATION
1. international Customs standards created by the International Convention on the Simplification and Harmonization of Customs Procedures developed by the CUSTOMS COOPERATION COUNCIL (CCC). Customs harmonization is a method seeking to foster international TRADE and cooperation by simplifying and harmonizing Customs procedures and operations. The convention (also known as the KYOTO CONVENTION) was adopted in May 1973 in Kyoto, Japan, as a core legal instrument with three original annexes on Customs procedures. Nearly 30 additional annexes (each covering a different area of Customs procedures and operations) have since been created. To ensure worldwide harmonization, the convention is also open to nonmembers of the CCC, which are state members of the United Nations or its specialized agencies. A country is required only to accept the convention itself and at least one of the annexes to become a contracting party. (When the United States became party to the convention, effective January 1984, it accepted 20 of the annexes and entered certain reservations with respect to some of their provisions.) The annexes contain definitions, standards, and recommended practices, and countries can reserve against any standard or recommended practice in a particular annex. There is also a provision obligating countries to review their national legislation every 3 years to determine if reservations can be removed.
2. EEC-wide norms and standards designed to remove NONTARIFF MEASURES.

CUSTOMS IMPORT VALUE (CIV) value of merchandise appraisal by the U.S. CUSTOMS SERVICE. Methodologically, the Customs Import Value is similar to the F.A.S. (FREE ALONGSIDE SHIP) value because it is based on the value of the product in the foreign COUNTRY OF ORIGIN and excludes charges incurred in bringing the merchandise to the United States (import duties, ocean freight, insurance, etc.); however, it differs in that the U.S. Customs Service, not the IMPORTER or EXPORTER, has the final authority to determine the value of the good.

CUSTOMS PRIVILEGED FACILITIES an area established by a government to facilitate the exchange, transfer, movement, or use of goods between countries having international trade restrictions. *see also* EXPORT PROCESSING ZONE; FOREIGN TRADE ZONE (FTZ); FREE-TRADE ZONE (FTZ); FREE PERIMETERS; FREE PORT.

CUSTOMS PROCESSING FEE a surcharge of 0.8% of the C.I.F. value on imported goods assessed by Mexican CUSTOMS authorities.

CUSTOMS UNION an agreement between two or more countries to remove TRADE barriers with each other and to establish common TARIFF and nontariff policies with respect to IMPORTS from countries outside of the agreement. The EUROPEAN COMMUNITY is the best-known example. The two primary trade effects of a Customs union are:
- trade creation—the shift from consumption of domestic production toward consumption of member imports and
- trade diversion—the shift from trade with nonmember countries in favor of trade with member countries.

CUSTOMS VALUATION CODE Customs valuation accord developed by the Convention on the Valuation of Goods for Customs Purposes in Brussels, Belgium, on December 15, 1950. It provided for more uniformity in the procedures of arriving at import valuations for imposing duties.

CUSTOMS VALUATION METHOD the determination by CUSTOMS of the dutiable value of the imported goods. Generally, the Customs value of all merchandise exported to the United States will be the TRANSACTION VALUE for the goods. If the transaction value cannot be used, then certain secondary bases are considered. The secondary bases of value, in order of precedence for use are: transaction value of identical merchandise, transaction value for similar merchandise, DEDUCTIVE AND COMPUTED VALUE.

CUSTOMSHOUSE BROKER (CHB or CUSTOMS BROKER) any person who is licensed in accordance with Part III of Title 19 of the U.S. Code of U.S. Federal Regulations (Customs regulations) to transact Customs business on behalf of others. Customs business is limited to those activities involving transactions with Customs concerning the entry and admissibility of merchandise; its classification and valuation; and the payment of duties, taxes, or other charges assessed or collected by Customs upon merchandise by reason of its importation, or the refund, rebate, or drawback thereof.

CV see COMMANDITAIRE VENNOOTSCHAP; CONSTRUCTED VALUE.

CVD see COUNTERVAILING DUTY.

CVM see BRAZILIAN SECURITIES COMMISSION.

CWC see CHEMICAL WEAPONS CONVENTION.

CWO see CASH WITH ORDER.

CXT see COMMON EXTERNAL TARIFF.

CYBERTERRORISM attacks on computer networks or systems, generally by hackers working with or for terrorist groups, which can include denial-of-service attacks, insertion of viruses, or stealing of data.

CYPRUS POUND unit of currency, Cyprus (1000 mils equal 1 Cyprus pound).

D

D/A vessel discharges afloat when D/A is prefixed to the word *clause.*

D/A SIGHT DRAFT (DOCUMENTS (AGAINST) ACCEPTANCE SIGHT DRAFT) a bill of exchange that must be paid when payment is requested. A method of payment for goods in which documents transferring title are delivered to the buyer as soon as he/she signs an acceptance, stamped on a draft, guaranteeing payment of the draft.

DAC *see* DEVELOPMENT ASSISTANCE COMMITTEE.

DACON registrations to select firms to be considered for short lists (that is, a select list of firms to be invited to submit proposals) as well as to review the qualifications of firms proposed by the borrower. Registration eligibility includes minimum size and experience requirements. Consulting firms are not required to register; registration does not constitute the World Bank's endorsement of the company's qualifications or the bank's approval of the company's appointment for any specific project. The use of the acronym DACON is not limited to the World Bank; for example, the INTER-AMERICAN DEVELOPMENT BANK also maintains data on consultants in its separately administered DACON. *see also* DATA ON CONSULTING FIRMS.

DAES *see* DYNAMIC ASIAN ECONOMIES.

DAEMON a program that runs continuously to handle particular kinds of events on a UNIX system. A mailer daemon accepts incoming E-MAIL as well as returning it, if the address is inappropriate, with a terse message to the sender indicating the nature of the failure.

DAF, NAMED PLACE OF DELIVERY *see* DELIVERED AT FRONTIER.

DAIRY EXPORT INCENTIVE PROGRAM (DEIP) one of four EXPORT subsidy programs operated by the U.S. Department of Agriculture (USDA). It helps U.S. EXPORTERS meet prevailing world prices for targeted dairy products and destinations. The USDA pays cash to U.S. exporters as bonuses, allowing them to sell certain U.S. dairy products in targeted countries at prices below the exporter's costs of acquiring them. The DEIP is used to help products produced by U.S. farmers meet competition from subsidizing countries.

DALASI unit of currency, Gambia (100 bututs equal 1 dalasi).

DAMAGES money compensation for loss or damage.

DANGER PAY a bonus given to employees as an incentive to accept extremely dangerous working conditions. Example: during World

War II American merchant seaman were given danger pay to become a part of the crew of the Liberty Ships sent to Europe to provide needed war material. These ship convoys had to pass through a gauntlet of German submarines and sustained an extremely high loss rate due to torpedo attacks.

DANGEROUS GOODS items capable of presenting a risk to the health and safety of individuals or property normally requiring special attention when shipped.

DANIDA *see* DANISH INTERNATIONAL DEVELOPMENT ASSISTANCE.

DANISH INTERNATIONAL DEVELOPMENT ASSISTANCE (DANIDA) Danish development assistance directed toward alleviating poverty by promoting economic growth and social development. Following a May 1991 restructuring of Danish aid administration, DANIDA has ceased to exist as an organization, but is used to denote official Danish cooperation with developing countries. That reorganization established SOUTH GROUP in the Ministry of Foreign Affairs as the locus of development assistance. South Group headquarters are in the Ministry of Foreign Affairs, Copenhagen, Denmark.

DANUBE COMMISSION commission agreed to in Belgrade, Yugoslavia, in 1949. It provides a CUSTOMS TARIFF for river basins entering the Black Sea and the western half of Caspian Sea. It also regulates navigation and shipping on the Danube River. Members included Austria, Belgrade, Czechoslovakia, Hungary, and Romania.

DARPA *see* DEFENSE ADVANCED RESEARCH PROJECTS AGENCY.

DASH
  1. acronym for Dual Access Storage Handling.
  2. West African term indicating a form of bribery.

DATA ACT OF 1973 (SWEDEN) *see* DATA INSPECTION BOARD.

DATA ENCRYPTION STANDARD (DES) a popular, standard ENCRYPTION scheme.

DATA INSPECTION BOARD privacy protection board established in Sweden by the DATA ACT OF 1973, requiring all private and public organizations to register their databases and forbidding them from distributing outside the country certain information regarding individual CITIZENS. The purpose of this legislation was to limit the distribution of data supplied by individuals on various applications (i.e., credit cards) to other firms for other uses without the individuals' consent.

DATA ON CONSULTING FIRMS (DACON) computerized roster of consulting firms interested in doing business on WORLD BANK-financed projects. The bank uses DACON registrations to select consulting companies to be considered for short lists (that is, a select list of firms to be invited to submit proposals) as well as to review the qualifications of firms proposed by the borrower. Registration eligibility includes minimum size and experience requirements. Consulting firms are not required to register; registration does not constitute the bank's endorsement of the firm's qualifications or the bank's approval of the firm's appointment for any specific project. The use of the acronym DACON is not limited to the World Bank; for example, the INTER-AMERICAN DEVELOPMENT BANK also maintains data on consultants in its separately administered DACON.

DATA PRIVACY the requirement that a business must protect the privacy of any personal data collected and processed in the operations of a business. *see also* TRANSBORDER DATA FLOW.

DATA TRANSFER *see* TRANSBORDER DATA FLOW.

DATE DRAFT (D/D) DRAFT that matures a specified number of days after the date it is issued, without regard to the date of acceptance. *see also* BILL OF EXCHANGE; D/A SIGHT DRAFT (DOCUMENTS (AGAINST) ACCEPTANCE SIGHT DRAFT); DOCUMENTS AGAINST PAYMENT; SIGHT DRAFT.

DATE OF ISSUE arbitrary date on a CONTRACT or on a financial instrument fixed as the date from which the term runs. *see also* LETTER OF CREDIT; SIGHT DRAFT.

DBGLS *see* DEVELOPMENT BANK OF THE GREAT LAKES STATES.

DBP *see* DEVELOPMENT BANK OF THE PHILIPPINES.

DCS *see* DEFENSE CONVERSION SUBCOMMITTEE.

DD abbreviation for Double Deck; a demand DRAFT.

D/D *see* DATE DRAFT.

DDN *see* DEFENSE DATA NETWORK.

DDN NIC *see* DEFENSE DATA NETWORK NETWORK INFORMATION CENTER.

DDU *see* DELIVERED DUTY UNPAID.

DEADWEIGHT maximum carrying capacity of a ship.

DEALER foreign-based business agent acting as an intermediary between a foreign-based EXPORTER and a home market IMPORTER.

DEBT BUY-BACKS a financial arrangement whereby a debtor nation repurchases (buys back) its debt from an issuing agent at a discount for cash.

DEBT-EQUITY SWAPS *see* SWAP.

DEBT FORGIVENESS a bank debt write-off of large portions of a nation's international debt because of the lack of payment. Banks can either forgive portions of the capital or interest or some combination. This is often accomplished by selling the debt note at a steep discount to a third party in an attempt to recover at least a portion of the original loan. Debt forgiveness occurred frequently during the 1980s when many banks attempted to recover a portion of their loans to some THIRD-WORLD nations.

DEBT-FOR-NATURE SWAP swap arranged by a private conservation group to use the proceeds of debt conversions to finance conservation projects relating to parkland or tropical forests.

DEBT INSTRUMENT a written promise to repay a debt. *see also* FINANCIAL INSTRUMENTS.

DEBT MANAGEMENT AND FINANCIAL ANALYSIS SYSTEM (DMFAS) a computerized financial management system created by the UNITED NATIONS CONFERENCE ON TRADE AND DEVELOPMENT (UNCTAD) at the solicitation of members of the PARIS CLUB in managing and rescheduling their international debt. DMFAS is provided in three different language versions and is subsidized by the UNITED NATIONS DEVELOPMENT PROGRAM (UNDP) as technical assistance. *see also* EXTERNAL DEBT; DEBT RESCHEDULING; DEBT REDUCTION TECHNIQUES.

DEBT MARKET
1. a financial market where issued debt securities are purchased and sold. One such market is the New York Bonds Exchange. A measure of the debt market is the Dow Jones Bond Averages.
2. the overall market for international primary and secondary debt issues.

DEBT OVERHANG a negotiated repayment method with the creditors of a nation's external debt whereby payments are ordered according to a formula often based on its economic ability to pay rather than the originally agreed to debt schedule. Because of their economic inability to pay during the 1980s, many THIRD-WORLD nations had large debt overhangs with their international creditors. *see also* FOREIGN DEBT OVERHANG.

DEBT REDUCTION TECHNIQUES procedures used by creditors for international debtors experiencing difficulty in complying with the terms of loans. Debt reduction techniques are intended to assist the debtor nation in meeting the terms of the loan. They include DEBT RESCHEDULING, DEBT-EQUITY SWAPS, DEBT BUY-BACKS, and EXCHANGE OF DEBT CLAIMS.

DEBT RESCHEDULING methods used by PARIS CLUB creditors for decreasing the national debt owed by nations to international creditors. Debt rescheduling methods include the TORONTO TERMS for debt reduction, which include partial cancellation of a debt and rescheduling of the remainder, consolidation of all international debts, the development of an extended payment schedules, concessional below-market interest rates, and grace periods where no payments are made while the debtor nation develops an economic infrastructure. *see also* DEBT REDUCTION TECHNIQUES; VENICE TERMS.

DEBT SERVICING the ability to pay the principal and interest of a nation's FOREIGN DEBT also referred to as the EXTERNAL DEBT. Debt servicing requires cash payments to pay the interest and reduce the total principal of the loan.

DEBT SWAPS *see* SWAP.

DEBTOR NATION nation that is owed fewer FOREIGN currency obligations than it owes other nations. *see also* BALANCE OF PAYMENTS; INTERNATIONAL MONETARY FUND.

DECs *see* DISTRICT EXPORT COUNCILS.

DECENTE a term used by Mexicans when referring to something with a concern for it being proper or respectable.

DECENTRALIZED a condition where an organization grants decision-making authority to regional parts of an organization. International organizations often use the decentralized approach to their operations to facilitate their ability to adapt to localized national market states. In these cases decision making is done at the HOST COUNTRY level rather than at the headquarters level.

DECEX an agency of the Ministry of Economy in Brazil responsible for the control of IMPORTS and EXPORTS. All firms engaging in international trade must register with DECEX.

DECK CARGO CARGO that is stored on the deck of a ship as contrasted with BELLY CARGO.

DECLARATION a form completed by the ASSURED and forwarded to the MARINE INSURANCE company when reporting shipments coming within the terms of the policy.

DECLARATION BY FOREIGN SHIPPER a statement by the SHIPPER in the foreign country attesting to certain facts. Example: articles shipped from the United States to an insular possession and then returned must be accompanied by a declaration by the shipper in the insular possession, indicating that, to the best of his/her knowledge, the articles were exported directly from the United States to the insular possession and remained there until the moment of their return to the United States.

DECLARATION OF PARTICULARS RELATING TO CUSTOMS VALUE *see* D.V.1.

DECLARED VALUE FOR CARRIAGE value of goods declared to the CARRIER by the shipper for the purposes of determining charges and establishing the liability of the carrier. *see also* DECLARED VALUE FOR CUSTOMS; DEDUCTIVE VALUE; TRANSACTION VALUE; VALUATION; VALUATION CLAUSE

DECLARED VALUE FOR CUSTOMS value of a shipment according to the CUSTOMS laws of the destination country required to be declared by the shipper on the shipping documents or by the importer when the goods are presented for customs clearance. *see also* DECLARED VALUE FOR CARRIAGE; DEDUCTIVE VALUE; TRANSACTION VALUE; VALUATION; VALUATION CLAUSE.

DECONSOLIDATION *see* BREAK-BULK.

DECOUPLE provision of support to a business, such as a farm, in a manner that does not provide an incentive to increase production. Farm SUBSIDIES that are decoupled are included in the GREEN BOX and are therefore permitted by the WORLD TRADE ORGANIZATION (WTO). *see also* GENERAL AGREEMENT ON TARIFFS AND TRADE (GATT).

DEDUCTIVE VALUE method used to determine the value of imported merchandise if the TRANSACTION VALUE of IDENTICAL MERCHANDISE or of SIMILAR MERCHANDISE cannot be determined. The deductive value method is to be used by CUSTOMS unless the IMPORTER has designated the COMPUTED VALUE as the designated method of appraising the value of the merchandise. Basically, the deductive value is the resale price in the United States after importation of the goods, with deductions for certain items. These items are as follows: commissions or profit and general expenses, transportation/insurance costs, and customs duties/federal taxes.

DEEP INTEGRATION economic INTEGRATION that goes well beyond removal of formal TRADE BARRIERS and includes various ways of reducing the international burden of differing national regulations, such as MUTUAL RECOGNITION and HARMONIZATION. *see also* SHALLOW INTEGRATION.

DEFAULT the inability of a debtor nation to make timely interest and/or principal payments on its INTERNATIONAL DEBT. Nations that are in default on all or a portion of their EXTERNAL DEBT jeopardize their credit rating, making future financing very difficult and expensive.

DEFENSE ADVANCED RESEARCH PROJECTS AGENCY (DARPA) a U.S. Department of Defense agency that manages development of new military technology. DARPA (formerly ARPA) originally helped to fund the creation of today's INTERNET.

DEFENSE COMMUNICATIONS AGENCY (DCA) *see* DEFENSE INFORMATION SYSTEMS AGENCY.

DEFENSE CONVERSION the transfer of defense production capabilities to nondefense production, either nondefense industrial products (e.g., pumps and valves) or consumer goods. The term is applicable to the conversion of U.S. defense activity as well as the retraining of defense personnel to enable them to obtain nondefense employment.

The Russians, according to their Defense Conversion Law, have a broader definition, which includes the possibility of a plant maintaining its defense production while expanding its nondefense production for other purposes, including the generation of hard-currency exports.

DEFENSE CONVERSION SUBCOMMITTEE (DCS) a U.S. federal subcommittee of the Intergovernmental U.S.–Russia Business Development Committee, which promotes trade between U.S. industry and the Russian defense sector. The DCS helps identify investment opportunities by supporting changes in U.S. government EXPORT control and other policies limiting opportunities for U.S. industry to participate in Russian defense conversion activities and identifying prospective business contacts for U.S. industry. Established in June 1992, the subcommittee's membership includes the Departments of Commerce, Defense, Energy, Labor, and State; the AGENCY FOR INTERNATIONAL DEVELOPMENT (AID); the EXPORT–IMPORT BANK OF THE UNITED STATES; and the OVERSEAS PRIVATE INVESTMENT CORPORATION (OPIC).

DEFENSE DATA NETWORK (DDN) a global communications network serving the U.S. Department of Defense composed of MILNET, other portions of the INTERNET, and classified networks that are not part of the Internet. The DDN is used to connect military installations and is managed by the DEFENSE INFORMATION SYSTEMS AGENCY.

DEFENSE DATA NETWORK NETWORK INFORMATION CENTER (DDN NIC) a U.S. Department of Defense agency, often called "The NIC." The DDN NIC's primary responsibility is assigning INTERNET network addresses and Autonomous System numbers, administering the root domain, and providing information and support services to the DDN. It is also a primary repository for REQUEST FOR COMMENTS (RFC). *see also* AUTONOMOUS SYSTEM; INTERNET REGISTRY.

DEFENSE EXPORTS WORKING GROUP *see* DEFENSE TRADE WORKING GROUP.

DEFENSE INFORMATION SYSTEMS AGENCY (DISA) formerly called the Defense Communications Agency (DCA), this is the U.S. government agency responsible for managing the DDN portion of the INTERNET. Currently, DISA administers the DDN and supports the user assistance services of the DDN NIC. *see also* DEFENSE DATA NETWORK.

DEFENSE MEMORANDA OF UNDERSTANDING (MOU) defense cooperation agreements signed by the U.S. Department of Defense (DOD) with allied nations. They are related to research, development, or production of defense equipment or reciprocal procurement of defense items. *see also* COPRODUCTION.

DEFENSE PRIORITIES AND ALLOCATION SYSTEM (DPAS) a program administered by the U.S. DEPARTMENT OF COMMERCE'S BUREAU OF EXPORT ADMINISTRATION (BXA) for the purpose of:
- assuring the timely availability of industrial resources to meet current national defense requirements and
- providing a framework for rapid industrial expansion in case of a national emergency.

The authority for DPAS extends from Title I of the U.S. DEFENSE PRODUCTION ACT (DPA) of 1950, as amended. Although the DPAS is designed to be largely self-executing, Special Priorities Assistance (SPA) may be provided, including

- timely delivery of items needed to fill priority-rated defense contracts,
- granting priority rating authority, and
- resolving production and delivery conflicts between rated defense contracts.

DEFENSE PRODUCTION ACT (DPA) U.S. Statute charging the U.S. DEPARTMENT OF COMMERCE with identifying critical defense-related industries, assessing their capability to meet peacetime and national security needs, identifying current and potential production constraints, and proposing remedial actions as appropriate. Title I of the DPA requires that

- contracts or orders relating to certain approved defense and energy programs be accepted and performed on a preferential basis over all other contracts and orders and
- materials, facilities, and services be allocated in such a manner as to promote approved programs.
  see also DEFENSE PRIORITIES AND ALLOCATION SYSTEM.

DEFENSE TECHNOLOGY SECURITY ADMINISTRATION (DTSA) a U.S. Department of Defense (DOD) organization that reviews applications for the EXPORT of items that are subject to the dual-use license controls of the U.S. DEPARTMENT OF COMMERCE and the munitions controls of the U.S. Department of State. DTSA has about 130 to 140 staff and administers DOD technology security policy so that the United States is not technologically surprised on the battlefield. DTSA reviews applications involving dual-use items for reasons of national security, proliferation cases, and munitions controls. *see also* FOREIGN DISCLOSURE AND TECHNICAL INFORMATION SYSTEM.

DEFENSE TRADE ADVISORY GROUP (DTAG) group established by the U.S. Department of State in March 1992 to provide consultation and coordination with U.S. defense exporters. DTAG members are drawn from the U.S. defense industry, associations, academia, and foundations and include technical and military experts, the Department of State, and observers from other U.S. government agencies. Members of the committee are appointed by the U.S. Assistant Secretary of State for Politico-Military Affairs. DTAG has three main working groups:

- Policy Working Group (PWG), which provides advice on broad issues of defense trade, technology transfer, and commercial arms sales in an effort to aid the fifty states in regulating commercial munitions exports.
- Regulatory Working Group (RWG), which provides advice on possible changes and improvements to regulations and procedures related to defense exports of munitions articles, technical data, and software related to defense articles.

- Technical Working Group (TWG), which provides advice on technical issues related to the U.S. MUNITIONS LIST (USML).

DEFENSE TRADE CONTROLS (DTC) (formerly the U.S. Office of Munitions Control, OMC) agency at the U.S. Department of State that administers licenses for the EXPORT of defense articles and services including arms, ammunition, and implements of war. These items are listed in the DEFENSE TRADE REGULATIONS formerly known as the INTERNATIONAL TRAFFIC IN ARMS REGULATIONS (ITAR) and the U.S. MUNITIONS LIST (USML). DTC is involved in the COMMODITY JURISDICTION (CJ) process.

DEFENSE TRADE REGULATIONS (DTR) (formerly known as the INTERNATIONAL TRAFFIC IN ARMS REGULATIONS (ITAR) regulations administered by the U.S. Department of State to control the EXPORT of weapons and munitions.

DEFENSE TRADE WORKING GROUP (DTWG) officials from the U.S. Departments of Commerce, Defense, and State and the U.S. TRADE REPRESENTATIVE was established in 1990 to coordinate agency policies and resources in areas concerned with defense expenditures. The group works with industry to identify ways to target industry needs and increase the success of industry EXPORT efforts by minimizing government impediments, streamlining procedures, and improving the availability of market information. The DTWG includes three subgroups:

- The Defense Exports Working Group, chaired by the U.S. DEPARTMENT OF COMMERCE, which helps implement administration defense export policy and enhances U.S. government support for U.S. defense exporters.
- The European Defense Cooperation Group, chaired by the U.S. Department of State, which coordinates interagency input to U.S.-NATO International Staff for the NATO Council on National Armaments Directors (CNAD) study on defense trade.
- The Technology Transfer and Third Party Reexport Group, chaired by the U.S. Department of Defense, which works with industry to define a more proactive technology transfer regime than could be implemented within the limits of U.S. national security and industrial competitiveness interests.

DEFERRAL (OF FOREIGN SOURCE INCOME) the delay of the payment of taxes earned in a foreign country until such income is remitted to the parent company. *see also* EX-QUAY.

DEFERRED AIR FREIGHT air freight with less urgency, delivered over a period of days. *see also* PRIORITY AIR FREIGHT.

DEFERRED PAYMENT CREDIT a type of LETTER OF CREDIT providing for payment some time after presentation of shipping documents by the EXPORTER.

DEFICIT (in the BALANCE OF PAYMENTS) a negative balance of international payments to settle debts with another nation. These situations can occur with transactions in goods, services, income, and unilateral transfers, which constitute the CURRENT ACCOUNT, and transactions in financial assets and liabilities, which constitute the CAPITAL ACCOUNT.

DEFINITIONAL MISSIONS (DMS) *see* TRADE AND DEVELOPMENT AGENCY.

DEG *see* DEUTSCHE FINANZIERUNGSGESELLSCHAFT FÜR BETEILIGUNGEN IN ENTWICKLUNGSLÄNDERN GMBH (GERMAN FINANCING COMPANY FOR INVESTMENTS IN DEVELOPING COUNTRIES).

DEINDUSTRIALIZE CAPITAL OUTFLOWS going from one developed nation to another when investment returns are more advantageous. This can occur when a nation is experiencing inflation and its currency undergoes a period of DEVALUATION. It can also occur when one nation's cost of business is not competitive with another. The net effect is to decapitalize a nation's productive capacity.

DEL CREDERE AGENT term used in the United Kingdom when a third party acts as an agent guaranteeing payment from a buyer to a seller in an international trade transaction. In Canada the EXPORT DEVELOPMENT CORPORATION (EDC) performs this function while in the United States it is performed by the OVERSEAS PRIVATE INVESTMENT CORPORATION (OPIC).

DEL CREDERE RISK risk that a counterparty is either unable or unwilling to fulfill his or her payment obligations. *see also* CREDIT RISK INSURANCE; COUNTRY RISK; COUNTRY RISK ANALYSIS; RISK AVERSION; RISK POSITION; WAR RISK INSURANCE.

DELINCUENCIA ORGANIZADA a Spanish idiom referring to the well-established illicit drug trade occurring between Colombia and the United States.

DELIVERED AT FRONTIER the fulfillment of the seller's obligations when the goods have arrived at the frontier—but before "the customs border" of the country named in the sales contract. The term is primarily intended to apply to goods by rail or road but is also used irrespective of the mode of transport.

DELIVERED/DUTY PAID (DDP) term, followed by words naming the buyer's premises, denoting the seller's maximum obligation. If the parties wish the seller to clear the goods for IMPORT but some of the cost payable upon the import of the goods should be excluded—such as a VALUE-ADDED TAX (VAT) and/or other similar taxes—this is made clear by adding words to this effect (e.g., "exclusive of VAT and/or taxes"). "Delivered/Duty Paid" may be used irrespective of the mode of transport.

DELIVERED DUTY UNPAID (DDU) seller is obligated to deliver when the goods that have been made available at the named place in the country of importation. The seller (EXPORTER) has to bear the costs and risks involved in bringing the goods thereto (excluding DUTIES, taxes and other official charges payable upon importation as well as the costs and risks of carrying out CUSTOMS formalities). The buyer (IMPORTER) has to pay any additional costs and bear any risks caused by failure to clear the goods for import in time. *see also* INCOTERMS; TERMS OF SALE.

DELIVERED EX QUAY (DEQ) seller (EXPORTER) fulfills the obligation to deliver when the goods have been made available to the buyer on the QUAY at the named port of destination, cleared for importation. The seller has to bear all risks and costs including DUTIES, taxes, and other charges of delivering the goods. *see also* INCOTERMS; TERMS OF SALE.

DELIVERED EX SHIP (DES) seller (EXPORTER) fulfills the obligation to deliver when the goods made have been available to the buyer on the QUAY (WHARF) at the named port of destination, cleared for importation. The seller has to bear all risks and costs including DUTIES, taxes, and other charges of delivering the goods to the shipping dock. *see also* INCOTERMS; TERMS OF SALE.

DELIVER-TO PARTY person or entity who physically receives the shipped merchandise (also known as the ship-to party).

DELIVERY act of transferring the physical possession of merchandise, or the act of the actual or of constructive placement of goods or property within the possession or control of another.

DELIVERY CARRIER transport CARRIER whose responsibility it is to place a SHIPMENT at the disposal of the buyer.

DELIVERY INSTRUCTIONS specific information provided to the INLAND CARRIER concerning the arrangement made by the FREIGHT FORWARDER to deliver the merchandise to the particular pier or steamship line. Not to be confused with DELIVERY ORDER, which is used for IMPORT CARGO.

DELIVERY ORDER document from the CONSIGNEE, SHIPPER, or owner of FREIGHT ordering the DELIVERY of freight to another party. *see also* SHIPPING ORDER.

DELIVERY VERIFICATION CERTIFICATE (DVC) a form used to track imported merchandise from the custody of the IMPORTER to the custody of a manufacturer and is used to substantiate a manufacturing DRAWBACK claim. The DVC is also known as a CERTIFICATE OF DELIVERY (U.S. CUSTOMS SERVICE form).

An EXPORT license may be issued with a requirement for DELIVERY verification by the U.S. Customs Service in the receiving country. When delivery verification is required by a foreign government for goods imported into the United States, the U.S. Customs Service will certify a delivery verification certificate. A U.S. export license may require submission of a similar form from an importing country.

DEMAND-SIDE ECONOMICS a field of economic thought first developed by the British economist John Maynard Keynes. In his book *The General Theory of Employment, Interest, and Money* (1935), Keynes explained that the economic cycles of prosperity and depression occur when the total or aggregate demand for goods and services by consumers, business investors, and governments rises or falls. In demand-side economics Keynes advocated that business and government take an active role in stimulating demand through increased investment as well as with the government spending more and consequently having larger budget deficits. The opposing point of view is developed in SUPPLY-SIDE ECONOMICS.

DÉMARCHE official discussion with another government carried out under instructions.

DE MINIMIS term used for an amount that is small enough to be ignored or too small to be taken seriously. Used to restrict legal provisions, including laws regarding international trade, to amounts of activity or trade that, are not trivially small.

DEMISE lease of property; a demise charter is a BAREBOAT CHARTER. *see also* CHARTER; CHARTER PARTY; CHARTER VESSEL; CHARTERER.

DEMOGRAPHY science of human population analysis. Through the statistical examination of data, demography determines population trends and predicts future developments and probabilities based on
- age, natality and fatality rates, marital and migration patterns, population density and distribution, parentage, physical condition, race, occupation;
- changes in the population as a result of birth, marriage, migration and immigration;
- impact of economic conditions on population trends;
- statistics of crime, illegitimacy, and suicide by geographic and population sector; and
- levels of education.
  see also CENSUS INTERFACE SYSTEM.

DEMURRAGE financial charges or damages assessed for excess time taken to load or unload a vessel causing delay of a scheduled departure. Demurrage refers only to situations in which the CHARTER or SHIPPER, rather than the vessel's operator, is at fault.

DENATIONALIZATION DEPARTMENT OF EXTERNAL AFFAIRS *see* PRIVATIZATION.

DEP *see* DEPARTMENT OF EXPORT PROMOTION.

DEPARTMENT OF COMMERCIAL REGISTRATION the office within the Ministry of Commerce in Thailand, with which all firms interested in doing business in Thailand must register.

DEPARTMENT OF EXPORT PROMOTION (DEP) the Ministry of Commerce in Thailand established to promote Thai-made products in overseas markets as well as to assist individuals doing business in Thailand.

DEPARTMENT OF REGIONAL ECONOMIC EXPANSION *see* INDUSTRY, SCIENCE AND TECHNOLOGY CANADA.

DEPARTMENT OF REGIONAL INDUSTRIAL EXPANSION *see* INDUSTRY, SCIENCE AND TECHNOLOGY CANADA.

DEPARTMENT OF TRADE AND INDUSTRY (DTI) *see* BRITISH OVERSEAS TRADE BOARD.

DEPENDENCY
1. a term used to describe a country as relying on one principal COMMODITY or product to sell or on one specific country as a customer or supplier;
2. a political subdivision under the control of a nation of which it does not form an integral part. Examples of dependencies include the Loyalty Islands in the southern Pacific Ocean included as a dependency in the French territory of New Caledonia. Self-governing British dependencies are the British Virgin Islands, Anguilla, and Montserrat in the Leeward Islands; the Cayman Islands in the Caribbean Sea; and the Falkland Islands, or Islas Malvinas, in the southern Atlantic Ocean, east of the Strait of Magellan and northeast of the southern tip of South America.

DEPENDENCY THEORY theory that LESSER-DEVELOPED COUNTRIES are poor because they allow themselves to be exploited by DEVELOPED COUNTRIES through international trade and investment.

DEPENDENT DEVELOPMENT an understanding by the LESS-DEVELOPED COUNTRIES (LDCS) that:
• their development is part of a dependent relationship with the developed countries.
• the developed countries purposely seek to dominate the LDCs through global economic control using high interest rates while maintaining low COMMODITY prices by manipulating the markets.
    This has led to charges of American imperialism as well as efforts to affect actions of the world powers through political voting blocks in the United Nations General Assembly.

DEPENDENT VISA a permit that allows a family to accompany an employee at his/her assignment in another country. *see also* EXIT VISA; EXIT/REENTRY VISA; MULTIPLE-ENTRY VISA; RESIDENCY VISA; SINGLE-ENTRY VISA; WORK PERMIT; WORK VISA.

DEPOSIT OF ESTIMATED DUTIES ANTIDUMPING DUTIES that must be deposited upon entry of merchandise, which is the subject of an antidumping duty order for each manufacturer, producer, or EXPORTER equal to the amount by which the foreign market value exceeds the U.S. price of the merchandise. *see also* TARIFF ACT OF 1930.

DEPRECIATION loss of market value of one currency against another. When the foreign exchange needs of a country exceed total receipts from abroad and are unable to receive foreign credits, the exchange value of the currency of the country tends to decline. Under these conditions its currency depreciates.

DEPUTY CHIEF OF MISSION (DCM) individual who assists the CHIEF OF MISSION or the ambassador in a consulate or TRADE MISSION. The DCM is almost always a career U.S. FOREIGN SERVICE OFFICER.

DEQ *see* DELIVERED EX QUAY.

DERIVATIVE MARKET *see* DERIVATIVES.

DERIVATIVES leveraged instruments that are linked to either specific financial instruments or indicators (such as foreign currencies, government bonds, share price indices, or interest rates) or to particular COMMODITIES (such as gold, sugar, or coffee) that may be purchased or sold at a future date. Derivatives may also be linked to a future exchange, according to contractual arrangement, of one asset for another. The instrument, which is a contract, may be tradable and have a market value. Among derivative instruments are options (on currencies, interest rates, COMMODITIES, or indices), traded financial futures, warranties, and arrangements such as currency and interest rate SWAPS.

DERIVATIVES MARKET a market designed to protect or minimize risk against any future occurrences. Example: a FORWARD CONTRACT can protect an investor against FLUCTUATING EXCHANGE RATES. *see also* DERIVATIVES.

DEROGATION a departure from the established rules, as when a country's policies are said to constitute a derogation from the GENERAL AGREMENT ON TARIFFS AND TRADE (GATT).

DES *see* DELIVERED EX SHIP.

DESTABILIZATION SPECULATION two forms of currency speculation:
- selling a falling currency either by selling the currency, short selling the currency future, or purchasing currency put options.
- purchasing a rising currency either by purchasing the currency, purchasing the currency future, or purchasing currency call options.
  The next result of destabilization speculation is to cause extreme currency volatility with wide swings in currency prices during any periods of price fluctuation.

DESTINATION place to which a SHIPMENT is CONSIGNED.

DESTINATION CONTROL STATEMENT statement required to be placed on commercial INVOICES and BILLS OF LADING by EXPORTERS for most EXPORT sales. These statements alert foreign recipients of goods and documents that diversion contrary to U.S. law is prohibited. Destination control statements are discussed in the U.S. Code of Federal Regulations (15 CFR §786.5 and §786.6).

DETENTION international shipping charges and fees levied by transportation companies beyond the time the goods should have been delivered. Essentially the goods have been kept in detention by the transportation company, hence the name. Because detention charges are very similar to DEMURRAGE, additional international shipping charges are often referred to as "demurrage and detention."

DETERMINATION
1. verification and certification for customs purposes of the origin of materials, merchandise, or property.
2. determination of origin decision is pivotal in establishing the required CUSTOMS DUTIES, an order with the full force of law issued by an ADMINISTRATIVE LAW JUDGE (ADJ) concerning matters such as trade and commerce.

DETRACCIONES taxes on agricultural products exported from Uruguay.

DEUTSCHE FINANZIERUNGSGESELLSCHAFT FÜR BETEIL-IGUNGEN IN ENTWICKLUNGSLÄNDERN GmbH (DEG) (English: German Financing Company for Investments in Developing Countries) German finance company that promotes direct private-sector investment in developing countries and provides advisory services in planning and implementing jointly financed and managed companies. DEG operations emphasize matching small and medium-sized German companies with similar third-world counterparts. *see also* DEUTSCHE GESELLSCHAFT FÜR TECHNISCHE ZUSAMMENARBEIT; KREDITANSTALT FÜR WIEDERAUFBAU.

DEUTSCHE GESELLSCHAFT FÜR TECHNISCHE ZUSAM-MENARBEIT (GTZ) (English: German Agency for Technical Cooperation) German agency that provides advisory services to German and other national organizations, selects and trains experts, and releases project funds. GTZ plans, executes, and monitors technical cooperation projects and programs in conjunction with partner organizations in developing countries. *see also* DEUTSCHE FINANZIERUNGSGESELLSCHAFT FÜR BETEILIGUNGEN IN ENTWICKLUNGSLÄNDERN GMBH; KREDITANSTALT FÜR WIEDERAUFBAU.

DEUTSCHE MARK unit of currency, Germany (100 pfennig equal 1 deutsche mark).

DEVALUATION an official act reducing the rate at which one currency is exchanged for another in international currency markets. This normally occurs when a chronic imbalance exists in a nation's BALANCE OF PAYMENTS, which weakens the international acceptance of the currency as legal tender.

An official devaluation happens when a nation has been maintaining a fixed EXCHANGE RATE(S) relative to other major foreign currencies. When a FLOATING EXCHANGE RATE(S) is maintained—that is, currency values are not fixed but are set by market forces—a decline in a currency's value is known as a DEPRECIATION.

A currency devaluation reduces the value of a nation's currency in terms of other currencies. After a devaluation, a nation will have to exchange more of its own currency in order to obtain a given amount of foreign currency. This causes the price of imports to rise, potentially causing inflation, while the price of the nation's exports declines, making them more competitive to foreign consumers.

DEVANNING unloading of CARGO from a CONTAINER. *see also* STRIPPING.

DEVELOPED COUNTRY a nation characterized by a relatively high standard of living as measured by per capita income, life expectancy, infant mortality, high literacy rates and high per capita levels of education. The economy of developed countries is distinguished by a strong industrial base with a large service sector. Generally speaking, the majority of the developed countries of the world are in the Northern Hemisphere.

Example: the United States in 1998 had a per capita GNP of $27,195, while the male life expectancy was 77 and the female was 80. The infant mortality rate was 14.5 per 1,000.

DEVELOPING COUNTRY a nation characterized by low per capita income, life expectancy, literacy rates, and per capita levels of education while having high infant mortality rates. Developing countries normally have an underdeveloped economy that is highly agricultural with a small industrial base.

Example: India in 1998 had a per capita GNP of $350, while the male life expectancy was 62 years and the female was 63.7. The infant mortality rate was 71 per 1,000j.

DEVELOPMENT ASSISTANCE (DA) specific economic assistance provided by the U.S. AGENCY FOR INTERNATIONAL DEVELOPMENT (AID). DA includes "functional" accounts that emphasize long-term development objectives for Agriculture, Rural Development and Nutrition; Population Planning; Health; Child Survival Fund; AIDS Prevention and Control; Education and Human Resources Development; Private Sector; Energy and Environment; and Science and Technology Corporation, as well as the Development Fund for Africa, and other assistance—the Special Assistance Initiatives and Humanitarian and Technical Assistance for the former Soviet republics. *see also* ECONOMIC SUPPORT FUND.

DEVELOPMENT ASSISTANCE COMMITTEE (DAC) committee consisting of most members of the ORGANIZATION OF ECONOMIC COOPERATION AND DEVELOPMENT (OECD). The DAC coordinates member country aid policies and EXPORT credits to LESSER-DEVELOPED COUNTRIES.

DEVELOPMENT BANK OF THE GREAT LAKES STATES (DBGLS) (French: Banque du Développement des États du Grand Lac, BDEGL) bank providing technical and financial assistance to promote socio-economic development among its members: Burundi, Rwanda, and Zaire. The bank was established in 1977, and its headquarters is in Goma, Zaire. *see also* ECONOMIC COMMUNITY OF THE GREAT LAKES COUNTRIES.

DEVELOPMENT BANK OF THE PHILIPPINES the principal source of medium- and long-term credit in the Philippines. These funds are made available from government equity, proceeds from the sale of bonds, loans from the CENTRAL BANK, and other OFFICIAL DEVELOPMENT ASSISTANCE (ODA) funds.

DEVELOPMENT CENTER OF THE ORGANIZATION OF ECONOMIC COOPERATION AND DEVELOPMENT (OECD) a unit established in 1961 within the OECD that makes available pertinent information to any nation, particularly the LESS-DEVELOPED COUNTRIES (LDC), on every major field of economic activity. Its principal focus is
- to foster employment and economic growth among nonmember nations,
- to assist in economic expansion in nonmember nations in the process of development, and
- to expand world trade.

DEVELOPMENT CONTRIBUTION the contribution of a proposed OVERSEAS PRIVATE INVESTMENT CORPORATION (OPIC) project to the economic and social development of the HOST COUNTRY. OPIC will examine each project for the following factors:
- increased availability of goods and services of better quality or at lower cost;
- development of skills through training;
- transfer of technological and managerial skills;
- foreign exchange earnings or savings;
- host country tax revenues; and
- increases in stimulation of other local enterprises.
  see also ECONOMIC CONTRIBUTION.

DEVELOPMENT FUND FOR AFRICA (DFA) fund administered by the U.S. AGENCY FOR INTERNATIONAL DEVELOPMENT (AID). It channels all U.S. development assistance to sub-Saharan Africa. The fund has emphasized certain sectors, including agricultural production in connection with the preservation of natural resources, health, voluntary family planning, education, and income generation. It was enacted by U.S. Congress in 1987. *see also* AFRICAN DEVELOPMENT FOUNDATION.

DEVELOPMENT PHASE the period of time an OVERSEAS PRIVATE INVESTMENT CORPORATION (OPIC) project involving mineral and natural resource development is initiated until its completion. To encourage U.S. investment in this sector, OPIC provides specialized insurance coverage during the EXPLORATION and development phases. *see also* CURRENCY INCONVERTIBILITY; EXPROPRIATION; POLITICAL VIOLENCE.

DEVIATION a change in a vessel's destination or the use of a route other than that described in the BILL OF LADING.

DFA *see* DEVELOPMENT FUND FOR AFRICA.

DFI *see* DIRECT FOREIGN INVESTMENT.

DFP *see* DUTY-FREE PORT.

DFZ *see* DUTY-FREE ZONE.

DHL an international air courier service.

DIALUP a temporary, as opposed to dedicated, connection between machines established over a standard phone line.

DIARIO OFICIAL the official government gazette in Mexico. The gazette is responsible for the publication of all current legislative activities. Example: on June 27, 1991, it published the Law for the Promotion and Protection of Industrial Property.

DIESEL PETROLEUM PRICES a daily listing of various grades and prices available for diesel petroleum appearing in the JOURNAL OF COMMERCE. These prices are used by many government and local municipalities in bid solicitations.

DIFFERENTIAL amount added to or deducted from a base shipping rate between two given locations to determine a new rate for another location.

DIFFERENTIATED PRODUCT applied to products produced by a country, even though there are many firms within the country whose products are the same, if buyers identify products based on COUNTRY OF ORIGIN.

DIGITAL CIRCUIT an electric circuit where the voltages represent a small set of values (e.g., 0 or 1). Digital circuits are the primary circuitry found in computers. *see also* ANALOG CIRCUIT.

DILLON ROUND The fifth ROUND of MULTILATERAL TRADE NEGOTIATIONS that was held under the auspices of the GENERAL AGREEMENT ON TARIFFS AND TRADE (GATT), beginning in 1960 and ending in 1961. It was named after C. Douglas Dillon, U.S. Undersecretary of State under Eisenhower and Treasury Secretary under Kennedy. *see also* WORLD TRADE ORGANIZATION (WTO).

DIPLOMAT official representatives of a government in foreign affairs. Most diplomats are career officers employed in a designated national foreign service. Example: in the United States, diplomats may be recruited as Foreign Service Reserve officers, although their term of service may be limited to 5 or 10 years.

Often times distinguished citizens are appointed by nations to serve as ambassadors. However, in the U.S., career officers predominate in the foreign service. *see also* TITLE AND RANK.

DIPLOMATIC IMMUNITY the exemption of DIPLOMATS from a host country's criminal laws as well as not being liable to any form of arrest or detention including not being in its civil and administrative jurisdiction. Additionally, diplomats are exempt from the host state's direct taxes. Even though diplomatic immunity does protect diplomats from the application of a host country's laws, those who do break the law are normally returned home as PERSONAE NON GRATAE. Diplomats have a duty to honor the laws and regulations of the host country and avoid interposing themselves in its internal affairs.

DIPLOMATIC MISSION an embassy, or foreign mission, located in a foreign country directed by an ambassador with a career DIPLOMAT staff. A mission consists of sections for public, economic and commercial affairs, information and cultural and consular affairs, and management matters. In addition, a mission often includes a number of ATTACHÉS from other government departments. Military attachés normally are assigned to foreign missions, but agricultural, commercial, labor, and cultural attachés are also common.

Foreign service officers usually staff foreign missions except for the attachés who are drawn from their respective agencies back home. Citizens of the host country are often hired as translators and for nonsensitive jobs.

DIPLOMATIC STATUS *see* DIPLOMATIC IMMUNITY.

DIRECCIÓN NACIONAL DE ADUANAS term used when referring to CUSTOMS in Uruguay. Prior to placing an order for goods with a supplier from another country, the IMPORTER in Uruguay is required to obtain an IMPORT LICENSE from the BANCO DE LA REPUBLICA ORIENTAL DE URUGUAY (BROU), pay the surcharges, clear the goods through the Dirección Nacional de Aduanas (customshouse), and pay the remaining taxes.

DIRECCIÓN NACIONAL DE CORREOS the National Post Office in Uruguay. It operates locally and internationally, delivering letters and parcels through its offices throughout Uruguay.

DIRECT EXPORTING commercial activity occurring between an EXPORTER and an IMPORTER without the intervention of a third-party agent of any kind. If the goods are subsequently reexported without any substantive modifications of the trade items, then the original importer is considered an agent for the subsequent international trade. This would then disqualify the original shipment from being classified as a direct EXPORT because of its subsequent TRANSSHIPMENT.

DIRECT FOREIGN INVESTMENT (DFI) *see* DIRECT INVESTMENT.

DIRECT INVESTMENT investment made to acquire a lasting interest in an enterprise operating in an economy other than that of the investor. The investor's purpose is to have an effective voice in the management of the enterprise.

In the United States, direct investment is defined as the ownership or control, directly or indirectly, by one person of 10% of more of the voting securities of an incorporated business enterprise or an equivalent interest in an unincorporated business enterprise. Direct investment transactions are not limited to transactions in voting securities. The percentage ownership of voting securities is used to determine if direct investment exists, but once it is determined that it does, all parent-affiliate transactions, including those not involving voting securities, are recorded under direct investment. *see also* FOREIGN DIRECT INVESTMENT IN THE UNITED STATES; FOREIGN PERSON; U.S. AFFILIATE.

DIRECT LOAN PROGRAM a program of the EXPORT–IMPORT BANK OF THE UNITED STATES (EXIMBANK) providing financing for the sale of U.S. EXPORTS faced by foreign competition backed by subsidized financing. The EXIMBANK provides direct loans to foreign buyers of American products and INTERMEDIARY LOANS to individuals making loans to foreign buyers. The loans can be made up to 85% of the value of the American goods being exported. *see also* COMMERCIAL BANK GUARANTEE PROGRAM; LEASE GUARANTEES; WORKING CAPITAL GUARANTEE PROGRAM.

DIRECT MAIL COLLECTION (DMC) seller (EXPORTER) forwards documents and instructions for collecting payment directly to a collecting BANK in a foreign country, without going through the intermediary of the seller's own domestic bank. *see also* TERMS OF PAYMENT.

DIRECT QUOTE the number of units of the local currency given for one unit of a foreign currency. *see also* EXCHANGE RATE; FOREIGN EXCHANGE; INDIRECT QUOTE.

DIRECT SELLING a situation where the EXPORTER decides to enter the foreign market without the use of an intermediary. The exporter deals directly with the distributors or final customers in the foreign country. This allows the exporter greater control over his/her marketing efforts and should allow him/her to earn higher profits. *see also* DIRECT EXPORT; INDIRECT EXPORT.

DIRECTION DES RELATIONS ECONOMIQUES EXTERIEURES (DREE) the main policy-making agency for EXPORT promotion and credit activities located in the French Ministry of Economic Affairs, Finance and Budget. DREE oversees the activities of other agencies that provide domestic and overseas export assistance, including the French Center for Foreign Commerce (CENTRE FRANÇAIS DU COMMERCE EXTÉRIEUR, CFCE) and the French equivalent of the U.S. AND FOREIGN COMMERCIAL SERVICE (the Poste d'Expansion Economique). DREE also coordinates France's interagency position on trade issues, negotiates bilateral trade agreements, and participates in the multilateral trade talks in the EUROPEAN COMMUNITY and the GENERAL AGREEMENT ON TARIFFS AND TRADE.

Within France, CFCE is the primary point of contact for export promotion services, whereas overseas, the Poste d'Expansion Economique provides promotional services to French firms. Through a network of regional offices in France, CFCE counsels exporters and organizes overseas trade events. CFCE also gathers and distributes trade information.

DIRECTION OF TRADE refers to the countries toward which a country's EXPORTS are sent and from which its IMPORTS are brought, in contrast to the commodity composition of its exports and imports. *see also* BILATERAL TRADE.

DIRECTORY OF U.S. EXPORTERS an annual reference guide published by the JOURNAL OF COMMERCE containing profiles on U.S. firms actively exporting. Information includes location, company executives, type of merchandise exported, annual tonnage, dollar volume, and bank references. *see also* DIRECTORY OF U.S. IMPORTERS.

DIRECTORY OF U.S. IMPORTERS an annual reference guide published by the JOURNAL OF COMMERCE containing profiles on U.S. firms actively importing. Information includes location, company executives, type of merchandise imported, annual tonnage, dollar volume and bank references. *see also* DIRECTORY OF U.S. EXPORTERS.

DIRIGENTE a social security contribution program for managers in Italy. *see also* ANNUITY PLAN; CASORAN (ALGERIA); COMPENSATION; GOSI (SAUDI ARABIA); PROVIDENT FUND; SAVINGS PLANS; SUPERANNUATION; TOTALIZATION AGREEMENT.

DIRIGISME a French term meaning a state planned and controlled economy. A dirigiste economy is one that is heavily controlled by the government such as in a communist nation or socialist economy. Typically this kind of an economy is characterized by many state-owned corporations and industries.

DIRTY BOMB a makeshift nuclear device that is created from radioactive nuclear waste material.

DIRTY CARGO an unclean CARGO transported in bulk on board a ship or in containers having disposable liners. Examples of dirty cargo are animal products including animal waste and used paper. Dirty cargo may present health or fire hazards, which require ships having high-quality ventilation and fire protection systems.

DIRTY FLOAT a system in which the float of exchange rates is partially determined by government intervention or restrictions to limit appreciation or depreciation; sometimes known as managed float. *see also* CLEAN FLOAT.

DIRTY MONEY money earned through criminal, illicit, or unlawful international business activities. Two types of dirty money are BLACK MONEY and GRAY MONEY.

DISA *see* DEFENSE INFORMATION SYSTEMS AGENCY.

DISC *see* DOMESTIC INTERNATIONAL SALES CORPORATION.

DISCHARGE unloading of passengers or CARGO from a vessel, vehicle, or aircraft. *see also* DISCHARGING; VES.

DISCHARGING process of unloading of CARGO from a CARRIER or contents from a container. *see also* DISCHARGE.

DISCLOSURE MEETING an informal meeting at which the INTERNATIONAL TRADE ADMINISTRATION (ITA) discloses to parties to the proceeding the methodology used in determining the results of an antidumping investigation or administrative review. A disclosure meeting is generally held promptly after the preliminary or final determinations of an investigation or promptly after the preliminary or final results of a review. *see also* TARIFF ACT OF 1930.

DISCOUNT decreasing the price of a bill of exchange or some other financial security. Example: an EXPORTER may grant a discount to an IMPORTER for a cash payment. *see also* FACTORING.

DISCOUNTED BILL an accepted DRAFT against which a loan is made and the interest is deducted immediately. *see also* DISCOUNT; DISCOUNTING.

DISCOUNTING
1. the reduction of the value of a negotiable instrument in order to consummate a sale.
2. an institutional loan given to a business after pledging a customer's debt obligation to it as collateral.

DISCOUNTING OF ACCEPTED BILLS OF EXCHANGE *see* PURCHASE OF DRAWINGS UNDER A DOCUMENTARY CREDIT.

DISCOUNTING OF DRAWING UNDER A LETTER OF CREDIT *see* PURCHASE OF DRAWINGS UNDER A DOCUMENTARY CREDIT.

DISCREPANCY a term used when referring to a situation in which the documents presented to the ADVISING BANK by the EXPORTER do not conform to the LETTER OF CREDIT. *see also* BILL OF LADING; CERTIFICATE OF INSPECTION; CERTIFICATE OF INSURANCE; CERTIFICATE OF ORIGIN; COMMERCIAL INVOICE.

DISCRETIONARY LICENSING *see* LICENSING.

DISHONOR a refusal on the part of an individual or firm, on whom a DRAFT is drawn and who owes the indicated amount, to accept or to pay it when due. *see also* BILL OF EXCHANGE; DOCUMENTS AGAINST PAYMENT; SIGHT DRAFT.

DISMISSAL OF PETITION a determination made by the U.S. DEPARTMENT OF COMMERCE'S INTERNATIONAL TRADE ADMINISTRATION (ITA) that the petition does not properly allege the basis on which antidumping duties may be imposed, does not contain information deemed reasonably available to the petitioner supporting the allegations, or is not filed by an appropriate interested party. This dismissal causes termination of the proceeding. *see also* TARIFF ACT OF 1930.

DISPATCH an amount paid by a vessel's operator to a CHARTER if loading or unloading is completed in less time than stipulated in the charter agreement.

DISPUTE COVERAGE insurance coverage provided by the OVER-SEAS PRIVATE INVESTMENT CORPORATION (OPIC), protecting the investor in the event of contractual disputes due to unpaid invoices, contract repudiation, and other disputes that may arise during the performance of a contract. To be eligible for a claim, a U.S. contractor must invoke the disputes resolution mechanism in its contract with the foreign government buyer.

DISPUTE SETTLEMENT PANEL *see* DISPUTE SETTLEMENT SYSTEM.

DISPUTE SETTLEMENT SYSTEM a mechanism developed for the purpose of resolving international trade disputes between two or more parties. There are two types of dispute settlement systems:

- BINATIONAL DISPUTE-SETTLEMENT MECHANISM: a treaty that develops a procedure by two or more parties or nations to an international trade agreement that facilitates the resolution of any subsequent trade disputes.
- WORLD TRADE ORGANIZATION (WTO): an organization established by the GENERAL AGREEMENT ON TARIFFS AND TRADE (GATT) for the purpose of resolving trade disputes between member countries. Under the terms of the treaty, the WTO has the authority to resolve disputes between member states without respect to national sovereignty.

DISTRIBUTION a line at the beginning of a USENET posting that limits it to a particular country, region, or NETWORK. Distribution lines are useful for posting messages intended for a particular audience on the INTERNET.

DISTRIBUTION LICENSE (DL) a special license that allows the holder to make multiple exports of authorized COMMODITIES to foreign consignees who are approved in advance by the BUREAU OF EXPORT ADMINISTRATION (BXA). The procedure also authorizes approved foreign consignees to reexport among themselves and to other approved countries. Applicants and consignees must establish Internal Control Programs to ensure the proper distribution of items under the DL. Each program must include comprehensive procedures for ensuring that the items exported will be used only for legitimate end uses.

DISTRIBUTION SERVICE service that accepts one SHIPMENT from a single SHIPPER and, at a point of destination, separates the shipment and distributes it to many receivers. *see also* CONSOLIDATED CONTAINER; CONSOLIDATED SHIPMENT; CONSOLIDATOR.

DISTRIBUTOR an EXPORTER or foreign agent in a home-based country acting as an IMPORTER for the purpose of marketing and selling the exporter's products and services. In certain situations the distributor may be designated an authorized distributor by the exporter with specific authority to represent its interests. A distributor may sell directly for a supplier and maintain an inventory of the supplier's products.

Domestic distributors market goods and services for domestic companies and may have no relationship with exporters or importers.

DISTRICT EXPORT COUNCILS (DECS) a voluntary auxiliary of U.S. AND FOREIGN COMMERCIAL SERVICE district offices to support EXPORT expansion activities. There are 51 DECs with 1,500 members that help with workshops and also provide counseling to less experienced EXPORTERS.

DIVERSIFICATION STRATEGY a strategy used when a multinational firm develops a program for evaluating and selecting countries to enter and commit resources. A diversification strategy involves producing or selling goods in many countries to avoid an overreliance on one market. *see also* CONCENTRATION STRATEGY.

DIVERSIFIED PORTFOLIO a portfolio that includes a variety of assets whose prices are not likely all to change together. In international economics the term refers to the holding assets denominated in different currencies.

DIVERSION any change in the billing of a SHIPMENT once it has been received by the CARRIER at point of origin and prior to DELIVERY at destination.

DIVERSIONARY DUMPING EXPORT sales by foreign producers to a third-country market at less than FAIR VALUE where the product is then further processed and shipped to another country.

DIX ETHERNET *see* ETHERNET.

DJIBOUTI FRANC unit of currency, Djibouti (100 centimes equal 1 Djibouti franc).

DL *see* DISTRIBUTION LICENSE.

DLO abbreviation for dispatch loading only.

Dm
   1. decimeter (one tenth of a meter long).
   2. dekameter (10 meters long).

DM abbreviation for the DEUTSCHE MARK.

DMC *see* DIRECT MAIL COLLECTION.

DOA *see* DOCUMENTS ON ACCEPTANCE.

DOBRA unit of currency, São Tomé and Principe.

DOCK loading or unloading platform at an industrial location, carrier terminal, a ship's berth, or WHARF.

DOCK EXAMINATION U.S. CUSTOMS examination that requires that FREIGHT be opened for a thorough inspection rather than just a visual one. *see also* CUSTOMS PRIVILEGED FACILITIES; CUSTOMSHOUSE BROKER.

DOCK RECEIPT a receipt used to transfer accountability when the EXPORT item is moved by the domestic CARRIER to the port of embarkation and left with the international carrier for export. After the ground carrier delivers the export item to the international shipper, the dock receipt is used as documentation to prepare a BILL OF LADING (BL).

DOCUMENTARY COLLECTION documents used for financing exports. These documents consist of an IMPORTER'S draft BILL OF EXCHANGE conveyed with certain commercial documents including BILL OF LADING, shipper's INVOICE, IRREVOCABLE LETTER OF CREDIT, and related documents.

The EXPORTER can also be paid with a SIGHT DRAFT without documents, termed a "clean collection," whereupon the exporter receives payment upon delivery whereas the importer receives all the ownership documentation. *see also* BILL OF EXCHANGE; COLLECTIONS; DRAFT; EXPORT FINANCING.

DOCUMENTARY CREDIT bank instrument issued for an IMPORTER to be credited to an EXPORTER. The bank has the responsibility of authorizing payments or drafts to be made to another bank. The two types of documentary credits are SIGHT DOCUMENTARY CREDITS and TERM DOCUMENTARY CREDITS.

DOCUMENTARY DRAFT a type of commercial DRAFT that is payable only upon the presentation of supporting title documentation such as a BILL OF LADING, customs or EXPORT INVOICE, or INSURANCE POLICY. *see also* SIGHT DOCUMENTARY DRAFTS; TERM DOCUMENTARY DRAFTS.

DOCUMENTARY LETTER OF CREDIT a LETTER OF CREDIT where the issuing bank stipulates that certain documents must accompany a DRAFT. The documents assure the applicant (IMPORTER) that the merchandise has been shipped and that title to the goods has been transferred to the importer.

DOCUMENTARY STAMP TAX special stamps that must be affixed to certain documents in business transactions in the Philippines. Documentary stamp taxes are collected on BILLS OF LADING, DRAFTS, BILLS OF EXCHANGE, INSURANCE POLICIES, WAREHOUSE RECEIPTS, etc.

DOCUMENTS AGAINST ACCEPTANCE *see* DOCUMENTS ON ACCEPTANCE (DOA).

DOCUMENTS AGAINST PAYMENT (D/P) a method of payment where the goods are shipped without a LETTER OF CREDIT or another form of guaranteed payment. The IMPORTER must sign the DRAFT and make payment before receiving the necessary documents to pick up the goods. *see also* SIGHT DRAFT.

DOCUMENTS KIT/AID an information packet provided by the AGENCY FOR INTERNATIONAL DEVELOPMENT (AID) with complete information on all AID-sponsored programs and procedures.

DOCUMENTS ON ACCEPTANCE (DOA)
1. an IMPORTER'S agreement to accept a TIME DRAFT for the EXPORTER'S goods and materials in order to receive the ownership documentation.
2. instructions given by a SHIPPER to a BANK indicating that documents transferring TITLE to goods should be delivered to the IMPORTER (or DRAWEE) only upon the IMPORTER'S ACCEPTANCE (signature on) of the attached DRAFT.

DOHA DECLARATION document agreed on by the trade ministers of the member countries of the WORLD TRADE ORGANIZATION (WTO) at the DOHA MINISTERIAL meeting. It initiates negotiations on a wide range of trade issues. A distinctive feature of the declaration is the emphasis placed on the interests of DEVELOPING COUNTRIES. *see also* DOHA ROUND; GENERAL AGREEMENT ON TARIFFS AND TRADE (GATT).

DOHA MINISTERIAL The WORLD TRADE ORGANIZATION (WTO) ministerial meeting held in Doha, Qatar, in November 2001, at which it was agreed to begin a new round of MULTILATERAL TRADE NEGOTIATIONS, the DOHA ROUND.

DOHA ROUND round of MULTILATERAL TRADE NEGOTIATIONS begun January 2002 as a result of agreement at the DOHA MINISTERIAL. Also referred to as the Doha Development Round.

DOLLAR
1. official unit of currency in Australia, Bahamas, Barbados, Bermuda, Canada, Hong Kong, Jamaica, New Zealand, Singapore, Taiwan, Trinidad and Tobago, and the United States. Each nation's CENTRAL BANK issues dollars. The dollar is represented with the $ sign, and each has a different value.
2. The American dollar is often regarded as an international unit of currency and is accepted throughout the world as a form of payment. *see also* DOLLAR STANDARD.

DOLLAR GLUT superabundance of U.S. dollars throughout international financial markets, causing a general decline in the value of the currency.

DOLLAR OVERHANG the impact of having a surplus of U.S. dollars controlled by international monetary centers. This resulted from large U.S. deficits financed by large international purchases of American governmental debt instruments denominated in U.S. dollars. As a result, the dollar is often subject to market volatility.

DOLLAR STANDARD the central importance of the American dollar to the international monetary system because of the size of the American economy and the extent of its international trade. However, on August 15, 1971, U.S. President Richard M. Nixon suspended the convertibility of the dollar into gold because of a loss of confidence in the dollar resulting from the persistent U.S. BALANCE OF PAYMENTS deficits at that time. Subsequently, the SMITHSONIAN AGREEMENT was achieved with representatives of the ten major world currencies who met in Washington, DC, in December 1971 to revise the system agreed on at the BRETTON WOODS CONFERENCE. This created a free-floating value system for the world's currencies.

DOLLARIZATION adoption by a country other than the United States of the U.S. dollar as local currency. *see also* FOREIGN EXCHANGE

DOLLY piece of equipment with wheels, used to move FREIGHT with or without a tractor.

DOMAIN a heavily used term in the INTERNET. It can be used in the ADMINISTRATIVE DOMAIN context or the DOMAIN NAME SYSTEM (DNS) context.

DOMAIN NAME SYSTEM (DNS) a general-purpose distributed, replicated, data query service. The principal use is the lookup of computer host addresses based on host names. The style of host names now used in the INTERNET is called domain name, because they are the style of names used to look up anything in the DNS. Some important domains are .COM (commercial), .EDU (educational), .NET (network operations), .GOV (U.S. government), and .MIL (U.S. military). Most countries also have a domain. Example: .US (United States), .UK (United Kingdom), .AU (Australia).

DOMESTIC AGENT MIDDLEMAN *see* MANUFACTURER'S EXPORT AGENT.

DOMESTIC COMMERCE the commercial market of a particular country. Example: goods being IMPORTED into a country can be sent directly to a FOREIGN TRADE ZONE (FTZ). As long as the goods remain in the zone or are EXPORTED to another country, no DUTIES are collected. However, if the goods are released and are entered into the domestic commerce, they are then subject to the laws and regulations concerning imports, including the payment of applicable duties and taxes.

DOMESTIC CONTENT REQUIREMENT (DCR) a requirement imposed by a nation that imported goods have a certain percentage of components manufactured within the country using domestic materials and labor. DCR is both a nationalistic as well as an economic issue in that nations have domestic political concerns and an intense interest in BALANCE OF PAYMENTS.

DOMESTIC DEBT a long-term national financial liability created by CURRENT ACCOUNT DEFICITS. Nations finance their domestic debt by selling bonds to domestic as well as international investors. A large domestic debt can create international monetary market uncertainties affecting the value of its currency.

DOMESTIC EXPORTS exports of domestic merchandise including COMMODITIES that are grown, produced, or manufactured in the United States and commodities of foreign origin that have been substantially changed in the United States, including U.S. foreign trade zones, from the form in which they were imported, or which have been enhanced in value by further manufacture in the United States.

DOMESTIC INTERNATIONAL SALES CORPORATION (DISC) the predecessor of the FOREIGN SALES CORPORATION, which took on a new definition as a result of the 1984 Tax Reform Act. DISCs can now provide a tax deferral on up to $10 million of EXPORTS so long as the funds remain in export-related investments.

DOMESTIC LAW the laws and legal system of a country, which may be constrained by international obligations, such as membership in organizations like the WORLD TRADE ORGANIZATION (WTO). It is possible that a domestic law might be inconsistent with such obligations and must be changed, because it can be seen as a threat to the country's sovereignty. *see also* SOVEREIGN.

DOMESTIC SUPPORT the policy of a country that assists a domestic industry, including a SUBSIDY to production, payment not to produce, PRICE SUPPORT, and other means of increasing the income of producers. *see also* PROTECTIONISM; PROTECTIONIST TRADING PRACTICES; TRADE BARRIERS.

DOMESTIC VALUE ADDED method of determining the value added to a product by domestic manufacturers. The formula for determining domestic value added is

Domestic Value Added = Market Price – Imported Components

Example: if a product's value is $20 and it consists of $12 in imported components, its domestic value added is $8 ($20 – $12).

DOMESTICATION the incremental transformation of foreign capital assets into domestic capital assets through purchases by the domestic country. Through domestication a home country seeks to purchase those capital assets deemed essential to protecting and preserving the domestic national interest. This could extend from property and technology to the outright purchase of foreign business assets. *see also* CONFISCATION; EXPROPRIATION; NATIONALIZATION.

DOMICILE the place where a DRAFT or ACCEPTANCE is made payable.

DOMINICAN PESO unit of currency, Dominican Republic (100 centavos equal 1 Dominican peso).

DONG unit of currency, Vietnam.

DOOR-TO-DOOR shipping service from shipper's loading dock door to consignee's unloading dock door.

DOUANE French term for CUSTOMS DUTY. Thus, certain items imported into France may be subject to paying a douane.

DOUBLE-COLUMN TARIFF TARIFF schedule with two rates, one for preferred trading partners and one for IMPORTS from nonpreferred trading countries. *see also* GENERALIZED SYSTEM OF PREFERENCES (GSP); MOST-FAVORED-NATION (MFN) TREATMENT.

DOUBLE-STACKED CONTAINER TRAIN (DST) a train having two freight or CARGO CONTAINERS stacked on top of each other. While a disadvantage of such a configuration is a doubling in the weight carried by the container cars, the freight-carrying capacity of the container train is nonetheless doubled.

DOWN
1. computers and other types of equipment that are not available for use.
2. INTERNET site that is not functioning.

DOWNLOAD a file transfer from a HOST system to your computer. Various PROTOCOLS are used for checking the file as it is being copied to ensure that information is not inadvertently destroyed or corrupted during the process. *see also* UPLOAD.

DOWNSTREAM DUMPING the sale by foreign producers at below cost to a producer in its domestic market. The product is then further processed and shipped to another country.

DOWNSTREAM PRICING the ability of a large commercial producer to control a particular COMMODITY's market value through its extensive utilization as a manufacturing component. Example: Hershey Foods Corporation may have more control over the price of cocoa than any other single market factor.

D/P *see* DOCUMENTS AGAINST PAYMENT.

DP abbreviation for direct port.

DPA *see* DEFENSE PRODUCTION ACT.

DPAS *see* DEFENSE PRIORITIES AND ALLOCATION SYSTEM.

DRACHMA unit of currency, Greece (100 lepta equal 1 drachma).

DRAFT a negotiable financial vehicle issued by an IMPORTER's bank for payment to an EXPORTER upon the proper DOCUMENTARY COLLECTION. *see also* DOCUMENTARY DRAFT.

DRAFT BILL OF EXCHANGE written, unconditional order for payment from one person (the DRAWER) to another (the DRAWEE). It directs the drawee to pay a specified sum of money, in a given currency, at a specific date to the drawer. A SIGHT DRAFT calls for immediate payment (on sight), whereas a TIME DRAFT calls for payments at a readily determined future date.

DRAGO DOCTRINE a doctrine named after the Argentine jurist, statesman, and writer Luis María Drago (1859–1921). He was foreign minister of Argentina from 1902 to 1903, and later became a member of the Permanent Court of Arbitration at The Hague, the Netherlands. The Drago Doctrine was articulated in a 1902 note sent to the U.S. Department of State concerning armed naval units sent by Great Britain, Germany, and Italy to blockade several Venezuelan ports because Venezuela had refused to pay claims arising from international loans. The doctrine stated that public indebtedness in the form of bonds, owed by a sovereign American state to citizens of a European state, must not be collected by armed intervention of the European state on American territory. Drago considered the doctrine as a corollary to the Monroe Doctrine and wanted it recognized as such.

The Hague Conference of 1907 adopted the Drago Doctrine in a modified form. It stated the government of one nation shall not use armed force to recover debts due from another nation until after the case has been submitted to international arbitration and the debtor nation refuses to cooperate.

DRAWBACK a rebate by a government, in whole or in part, of CUSTOMS DUTIES assessed on imported merchandise that is subsequently exported. Drawback regulations and procedures vary among countries.

DRAWBACK SYSTEM a part of the U.S. CUSTOMS SERVICE'S AUTOMATED COMMERCIAL SYSTEM, which provides the means for processing and tracking of drawback claims.

DRAWEE the individual or company on whom a DRAFT is drawn and who owes the indicated amount.

DRAWER The individual or company that issues or signs a DRAFT and thus stands to receive payment of the indicated amount from the DRAWEE.

DRAY vehicle used to haul CARGO or goods. *see also* CELL; CONSOLIDATED CONTAINER; CONTAINER; DRAYAGE.

DRAYAGE charge made for hauling FREIGHT or carts, DRAYS, or trucks. *see also* CONTAINER FREIGHT CHARGE; SPECIAL RATES.

DREE *see* DIRECTION DES RELATIONS ECONOMIQUES EXTERIEURES.

DROP-OFF DELIVERY of a SHIPMENT by a SHIPPER to a CARRIER for transportation. *see also* DROP-OFF CHARGE; DROP SHIP.

DROP-OFF CHARGE charge made by a transportation company for DELIVERY of a CONTAINER. *see also* DROP-OFF.

DROP SHIP shipment by an EXPORTER (foreign supplier) directly to an IMPORTER (domestic customer) with all shipping expenses to be included in the price.

DROP SHIPMENT shipment of goods direct from a manufacturer to a dealer or consumer, avoiding delivery to an intermediary.

DRY-BULK CONTAINER CONTAINER designed to carry any of a number of free-flowing dry solids such as grain or sand. *see also* DRY CARGO CONTAINER; GONDOLA CAR.

DRY CARGO CARGO that does not require temperature controls. *see also* HAZARDOUS MATERIAL; PERISHABLE FREIGHT.

DRY-CARGO CONTAINER any shipping CONTAINER designed to transport goods other than liquids. *see also* DRY-BULK CONTAINER; GONDOLA CAR.

D/S marine abbreviation for days after sighting.

DST *see* DOUBLE-STACKED CONTAINER TRAIN.

DTC *see* DEFENSE TRADE CONTROLS.

DTSA *see* DEFENSE TECHNOLOGY SECURITY ADMINISTRATION.

DTWG *see* DEFENSE TRADE WORKING GROUP.

DUAL CURRENCY BOND a bond that is designated in one currency but pays interest in another currency at a fixed rate of exchange. The repayment value is set in a different currency, often dollars, at a rate determined at the time of issue.

DUAL EMPLOYMENT CONTRACT an employment agreement covering an employee residing and working in one country, while traveling and working in another country. *see also* EMPLOYMENT AGREEMENT; EMPLOYMENT CONDITIONS; EMPLOYMENT CONTRACT.

DUAL EXCHANGE RATES existence of two or more exchange rates for a single currency. *see also* EXCHANGE CONTROLS; IMPORT DEPOSIT REQUIREMENTS; LICENSING; MULTIPLE EXCHANGE RATE; MULTIPLE EXCHANGE RATE SYSTEM; TWO-TIER MARKET.

DUAL IMPERATIVE a term referring to the demands placed on a firm to understand the needs of their national market, while still attempting to justify their activities on a global scale.

DUAL PRICING the sale of identical products in different markets for different prices. This often reflects DUMPING practices.

DUAL-USE GOODS materials and equipment that can be used in peaceful nuclear programs but that also have potential military applications, particularly in atomic weapons. Items that are classified as dual-use goods may have international trade restrictions imposed on them by certain governments.

DUALISM a term used when noting that a country shows growth in a certain area of the economy while other areas continue in a less developed condition.

DUMPING the sale of a COMMODITY in a foreign market at less than FAIR VALUE. Dumping is generally recognized as unfair because the practice can disrupt markets and injure producers of competitive products in an importing country. Article VI of the GENERAL AGREEMENT ON TARIFFS AND TRADE (GATT) permits imposition of antidumping duties equal to the difference between the price sought in the importing country and the normal value of the product in the exporting country.

With price-to-price dumping, the foreign producer can use its sales in the high-priced market (usually the home market) to subsidize its sales in the low-priced EXPORT market. The price difference is often due to protection in the high-priced market.

Price-cost dumping indicates that the foreign supplier has a special advantage. Sustained sales below cost are normally possible only if the sales are somehow subsidized.

DUMPING MARGIN the amount by which the imported merchandise is sold in the United States below the home market or third-country price or the CONSTRUCTED VALUE (that is, at less than its FAIR VALUE). For example, if the U.S. "purchase price" is $200 and the fair value is $220, the dumping margin is $20. This margin is expressed as a percentage of the United States price. In this example, the margin is 10%. *see also* TARIFF ACT OF 1930.

DUNNAGE materials placed around cargo to prevent shifting or damage to the goods while in transit.

DURABLE GOODS any product that is not consumed through use.

DUTIABLE items subject to an IMPORT tax. *see also* AD VALOREM DUTY; COMPOUND DUTY; DUTY; SPECIFIC DUTY.

DUTIABLE LIST items listed in a country's TARIFF schedule for which it charges IMPORT DUTY. *see also* CLASSIFICATION; COMMODITY GROUPINGS; CUSTOMS COOPERATION COUNCIL NOMENCLATURE; HARMONIZED TARIFF SCHEDULE; STANDARD INDUSTRIAL CLASSIFICATION; TARIFF SCHEDULE; TARIFF SCHEDULES OF THE UNITED STATES ANNOTATED (TSUSA).

DUTY tax imposed on IMPORTS by the customs authority of a country. Duties are generally based on the value of the goods (AD VALOREM DUTIES), some other factors such as weight or quantity (SPECIFIC DUTIES), or a combination of value and other factors (COMPOUND DUTIES).

DUTY DRAWBACK *see* DRAWBACK.

DUTY FREE a term used when referring to goods entering into a country, and being exempt from customs duties.

DUTY-FREE PORT (DFP) *see* FOREIGN TRADE ZONE.

DUTY-FREE SHOP *see* FOREIGN TRADE ZONE.

DUTY-FREE ZONE (DFZ) *see* FOREIGN TRADE ZONE.

DUTY PAID FOREIGN GOODS imported goods that have cleared CUSTOMS with all applicable DUTIES and taxes having been collected. Domestic goods or duty paid foreign goods taken into a FREE-TRADE ZONE are viewed as EXPORTS by the customs authorities of the HOST COUNTRY. Upon shipment of these goods into the free-trade zone, they become eligible for any export incentive, tax refund, or DUTY DRAWBACK payment.

DUTY REMISSION a program that a nation may have for refunding a DUTY charged to an IMPORTER if the imported item is reexported. Example: if an importer reexports a machinery component that was charged a duty after being assembled into a final product, the importer would qualify for a duty remission assuming the nation had such a program.

D.V.1. (DECLARATION OF PARTICULARS RELATING TO CUSTOMS VALUE) *see* SINGLE ADMINISTRATIVE DOCUMENT.

DVC *see* DELIVERY VERIFICATION CERTIFICATE.

DW abbreviation for deadweight; the capacity of a ship expressed in long tons (2240 pounds).

DYNAMIC ASIAN ECONOMIES (DAES) a collective reference, currently comprising six Asian countries: Hong Kong, Korea, Malaysia, Singapore, Taiwan, and Thailand.

E

E.&.O.E. abbreviation for errors and omissions excepted.

EAA *see* EXPORT ADMINISTRATION ACT.

EAC *see* EXPORT ASSISTANCE CENTER.

EADB *see* EAST AFRICAN DEVELOPMENT BANK.

EAEC *see* EAST AFRICAN ECONOMIC COMMUNITY; EAST ASIAN ECONOMIC CAUCUS.

EAI *see* ENTERPRISE FOR THE AMERICAS INITIATIVE.

EAITC *see* EXTERNAL AFFAIRS AND INTERNATIONAL TRADE CANADA.

E.A.O.N. abbreviation for except as otherwise noted.

EARB *see* EXPORT ADMINISTRATION REVIEW BOARD.

EARLY HARVEST term used in TRADE negotiations, meaning agreement to accept the results of part of the negotiations before negotiations on all issues are completed.

EARN *see* EUROPEAN ACADEMIC AND RESEARCH NETWORK.

EASEMENT right to use another person's property.

EAST AFRICAN DEVELOPMENT BANK (EADB) development bank created in 1967 to promote economic development among Kenya, Tanzania, and Uganda. Bank headquarters are in Kampala, Uganda.

EAST AFRICAN ECONOMIC COMMUNITY (EAEC) an agreement in 1967 between Kenya, Uganda, and Tanzania to remove TRADE BARRIERS with each other and to establish common TARIFF and nontariff policies with respect to IMPORTS from countries party to the agreement. This agreement was terminated in 1978 when political conflict evolved between Tanzania and Uganda. *see also* CUSTOMS UNION.

EAST ASIAN ECONOMIC CAUCUS (EAEC) a regional consultative forum proposed by Malaysia in late 1990 under the name of East Asian Economic Grouping. Participation is limited to Asian nations.

EAST ASIAN ECONOMIC GROUPING *see* EAST ASIAN ECONOMIC CAUCUS (EAEC).

EAST CARIBBEAN DOLLAR unit of currency Leeward and Windward Islands (100 cents equal 1 Caribbean dollar).

EASTERN AND SOUTHERN AFRICAN TRADE AND DEVELOPMENT BANK official bank for the PREFERENTIAL TRADE

AREA of the eastern and southern African states. *see also* REGIONAL DEVELOPMENT BANKS.

EASTERN CARIBBEAN CENTRAL BANK (ECCB) eastern Caribbean development bank established in October 1983. The ECCB promotes economic development, monetary stability and credit, and exchange among eight member nations. Bank headquarters is in Basseterre, Saint Kitts.

EASTERN EUROPE BUSINESS INFORMATION CENTER (EEBIC) a DEPARTMENT OF COMMERCE service initiated in January 1990. The EEBIC provides information on trade and investment opportunities, trade regulations and legislation, sources of financing, and government and industry contacts in the former eastern bloc. The center maintains a 24-hour automated flashfax system.

E.B. abbreviation for eastbound.

EBB *see* ECONOMIC BULLETIN BOARD.

EBOLA a severe, typically fatal disease in nonhuman primates (such as monkeys, chimpanzees, and gorillas) and in humans.

EBOMB (OR E-BOMB) electromagnetic bomb that produces a brief pulse of energy that affects electronic circuitry,. At low levels, the pulse temporarily disables electronics systems, including computers, radios, and transportation systems, and at high levels it completely destroys circuitry, causing mass disruption of infrastructure while sparing life and property.

EBONE a pan-European INTERNET BACKBONE service.

EBRD *see* EUROPEAN BANK FOR RECONSTRUCTION AND DEVELOPMENT.

EC *see* EUROPEAN COMMISSION; EUROPEAN COMMUNITY.

EC92 *see* EUROPE 1992.

ECA *see* UNITED NATIONS ECONOMIC COMMISSION FOR AFRICA.

ECASS *see* EXPORT CONTROL AUTOMATED SUPPORT SYSTEM.

ECB *see* EUROPEAN CENTRAL BANK.

ECCAS *see* ECONOMIC COMMUNITY OF CENTRAL AFRICAN STATES.

ECCB *see* EASTERN CARIBBEAN CENTRAL BANK.

ECCN *see* EXPORT CONTROL CLASSIFICATION NUMBER.

ECD *see* EXPORTER COUNSELING DIVISION.

ECE *see* ECONOMIC COMMISSION FOR EUROPE.

ECGD *see* EXPORT CREDIT GUARANTEE DEPARTMENT.

ECJ *see* EUROPEAN COURT OF JUSTICE.

ECL *see* EXPORT CONTROL LIST.

ECLAC *see* UNITED NATIONS ECONOMIC COMMISSION FOR LATIN AMERICA AND THE CARIBBEAN.

ECLS *see* EXPORT CONTACT LIST SERVICE.

ECO *see* ECONOMIC COOPERATION ORGANIZATION.

ECODUMPING *see* ENVIRONMENTAL DUMPING.

ECO-LABEL a voluntary mark awarded by the EUROPEAN COMMUNITY (EC) to producers who can demonstrate that their product is significantly less harmful to the environment than similar products. The EC environment ministers agreed to the concept of an eco-label in March of 1992. The EC commission and member states are drafting proposals for eco-labeling criteria with the intention of providing a clear commercial benefit for developing less-polluting products and processes.

ECOTERRORISM sabotage intended to hinder activities that are considered damaging to the environment.

ECONOMIC AND MONETARY UNION (EMU) a provision of the MAASTRICHT TREATY. The EMU has three essential elements: the establishment of the single currency called the EURO; the creation of a single monetary policy overseen by the EUROPEAN CENTRAL BANK; and closer coordination of Member States' economic and budgetary policy. *see also* CONVERGENCE CRITERIA.

ECONOMIC AND SOCIAL COMMISSION FOR ASIA AND THE PACIFIC (ESCAP) the successor to the Economic Commission for Asia and the Far East (ECAFE) originally established in 1947. ESCAP was established by the United Nations in 1974 and is composed of three committees on regional economic cooperation, on the environment and sustainable development, and on poverty alleviation through economic growth and social development. In addition, there are two other committees on statistics and on transport and communications. There are also two special bodies on least-developed and landlocked developing countries and on developing Pacific island countries. ESCAP has annual meetings.

ESCAP has 48 members states within the geographical range from the Cook Islands to Iran. However, its membership does include five nonregional members—France, the Netherlands, the Russian Federation, the United Kingdom, and the United States. The Executive Secretary of ESCAP is in Pakistan. *see also* UNITED NATIONS REGIONAL ECONOMIC COMMISSIONS.

ECONOMIC AND SOCIAL COMMISSION FOR WESTERN ASIA (ESCWA) *see* UNITED NATIONS REGIONAL ECONOMIC COMMISSIONS.

ECONOMIC AND SOCIAL COUNCIL (ECOSOC) UNITED NATIONS council created in 1945 to coordinate its economic and social work. The ECOSOC undertakes studies and makes recommendations on development, world trade, industrialization, natural resources, human rights, the status of women, population, narcotics, social welfare, science and technology, crime prevention, and other issues. The council structure includes five regional commissions and six functional commissions. The functional commissions include Commission on Human Rights, Commission on Narcotic Drugs, Commission for Social Development, Commission on the Status of Women, Population Commission, and the Statistical Commission. *see also* UNITED NATIONS REGIONAL ECONOMIC COMMISSIONS.

ECONOMIC BULLETIN BOARD (EBB) a personal computer-based economic bulletin board operated by the U.S. DEPARTMENT OF COMMERCE in Washington, DC. The EBB is an on-line source for trade leads and statistical releases from the U.S. Bureau of Economic Analysis, the U.S. Census Bureau, the INTERNATIONAL TRADE ADMINISTRATION, the U.S. Bureau of Labor Statistics, the U.S. Federal Reserve Board, Department of the Treasury, and other federal agencies.

ECONOMIC COMMISSION FOR AFRICA (ECA) UN commission established in 1958 to establish measures for the economic and social development of Africa in order to increase the living standards of African nations. The commission's work includes the entire African continent, Madagascar, and the other African islands. ECA has 52 African member states. *see also* UNITED NATIONS REGIONAL ECONOMIC COMMISSIONS.

ECONOMIC COMMISSION FOR EUROPE (ECE) *see* UNITED NATIONS REGIONAL ECONOMIC COMMISSIONS.

ECONOMIC COMMISSION FOR EUROPE (UN/ECE) UN commission established in 1947 for the purpose of generating and improving economic relationships among its members and with other countries of the world. It is also interested in strengthening intergovernmental cooperation, particularly in the environment, transport, statistics, trade and economic analysis. The UN/ECE also has programs in agriculture, timber, human settlements, chemicals, and other areas. It emphasizes providing assistance to countries of Central and Eastern Europe changing from centrally planned to market economies. The membership consists of 46 members including the United States, Canada, Switzerland, and Israel. The Executive Secretary is in Austria.

ECONOMIC COMMISSION FOR LATIN AMERICA AND THE CARIBBEAN (ECLAC) UN economic commission created in 1948 for the purpose of increasing economic activity in Latin America and the Caribbean and for building strong economic relations between Latin American, Caribbean, and other countries in the world. Furthermore, ECLAC works closely with many other regional intergovernmental organizations in the economic and social field as well as provides economic and statistical information. The geographical territory of the commission is Latin America and the Caribbean.

ECLAC has 42 members, and its headquarters is in Santiago, Chile.

see also UNITED NATIONS REGIONAL ECONOMIC COMMISSIONS.

ECONOMIC COMMUNITY OF CENTRAL AFRICAN STATES
(ECCAS) (French: Communauté Economique des États de l'Afrique Centrale, CEEAC) Central African economic association created by the CUSTOMS AND ECONOMIC UNION OF CENTRAL AFRICA to promote regional economic cooperation, eliminate trade restrictions, and establish a Central African Common Market. Members include Burundi, the Cameroon, Central African Republic, Chad, Congo, Equatorial Guinea, Gabon, Rwanda, São Tomé and Principe, and Zaire. The community was established in 1983 (became operational in 1985); headquarters is in Libreville, Gabon.

ECONOMIC COMMUNITY OF THE GREAT LAKES COUNTRIES
(French: Communauté Economique des Pays des Grands Lacs, CEPGL) Central African economic community created in September 1976 to promote regional economic cooperation and integration. The community is associated with the DEVELOPMENT BANK OF THE GREAT LAKES STATES (Banque de Développement des États des Grands Lacs). Community members include Burundi, Rwanda, and Zaire. Headquarters is in Gisengi, Rwanda.

ECONOMIC COMMUNITY OF WEST AFRICAN STATES
(ECOWAS) an economic association of 16 West African nations aimed at creating a full customs union (not yet achieved) as well as social and cultural fellowship. ECOWAS was established in May 1975 by the Treaty of Lagos (first operating in November 1976). Its members include Benin, Burkina Faso, Cape Verde, Côte d'Ivoire, Gambia, Ghana, Guinea, Guinea-Bissau, Liberia, Mali, Mauritania, Niger, Nigeria, Senegal, Sierra Leone, and Togo. The community's headquarters is in Abuja, Nigeria.

ECONOMIC CONTRIBUTION
contribution to the BALANCE OF PAYMENTS and employment effects on the U.S. economy for any project being considered by the OVERSEAS PRIVATE INVESTMENT CORPORATION (OPIC). Such factors as the level of U.S. procurement, net financial flows, and net project EXPORTS to the United States are taken into consideration. Projects that can demonstrate a potential for positive effects on the U.S. economy are of special interest to OPIC.

ECONOMIC COOPERATION ORGANIZATION (ECO)
a southern Asian economic association fostering cooperation to improve socio-economic conditions among the populations of its members. The organization was founded in 1964, and its headquarters is in Tehran, Iran. Members include Afghanistan, Azerbaijan, Iran, Kazakhstan, Kyrgyzstan, Pakistan, Tajikistan, Turkmenistan, Turkey, and Uzbekistan.

ECONOMIC DATA ABROAD
daily column appearing in the JOURNAL OF COMMERCE. It provides comments on economic outlooks and performance in foreign countries.

ECONOMIC EXPOSURE a firm's FOREIGN EXCHANGE risk in areas such as product pricing, material costs, and location of investment. *see also* FLOATING EXCHANGE RATES; FLUCTUATING EXCHANGE RATES; TRANSACTION EXPOSURE; TRANSLATION EXPOSURE.

ECONOMIC INTEGRATION the strategy of countries actively working together in establishing regulations and laws that lead to the ultimate elimination of TRADE BARRIERS among countries coming together to form larger trading groups. *see also* COMMON MARKET.

ECONOMIC OFFICERS embassy officials who analyze and report on macroeconomic trends and trade policies and their implications for U.S. policies and programs. Economic officers represent a nation's interests and arrange and participate in economic and commercial negotiations. *see also* COMMERCIAL OFFICERS.

ECONOMIC POLICY COUNCIL (EPC) council established by U.S. Executive Order in 1985 to address major trade policy issues in a single forum as a means of reducing tensions between different groups, such as the Trade Policy Committee and the Senior Interagency Group. The council was modified in the OMNIBUS TRADE AND COMPETITIVENESS ACT OF 1988. Membership includes the U.S. Departments of Treasury (chair pro tem), State, Agriculture, Commerce, Labor, and Transportation; the OMB; the U.S. TRADE REPRESENTATIVE (USTR); the Council of Economic Advisers; and the Assistant to the President for Science and Technology.

ECONOMIC RESEARCH SERVICE (ERS) an economic research arm of the U.S. Department of Agriculture providing expertise, data, models, and research information about the agricultural economies and policies of foreign countries, the agricultural trade and development relationships between foreign countries and the United States, and U.S. agricultural policies.
Topics include:
- agricultural trade and trade policies and their relationship to the economic, technical, and political factors affecting agricultural trade among countries;
- economic and agricultural market structure, efficiency, and performance of foreign countries;
- technical production systems of foreign countries; and
- foreign governments' production, consumption, monetary, and trade policies.

ECONOMIC SANCTIONS economic penalties, such as prohibiting trade, stopping financial transactions, or barring economic and military assistance, used for foreign policy purposes to achieve the goal of influencing a target nation. Sanctions can be imposed selectively including stopping only certain trade and financial transactions or aid programs, or comprehensively for halting all economic relations with the target nation.

Even though sanctions can be imposed to serve multiple goals, the measures are more successful in achieving the less ambitious and often unarticulated goals of
- upholding international norms by punishing the target nation for unacceptable behavior and
- deterring future objectionable actions.

Sanctions are usually less successful in achieving the most prominently stated goal of making the target country comply with the sanctioning nation's stated wishes.

ECONOMIC SOLIDARITY PACT (ESP) program initiated in December 1987 by the Mexican government when its economy was characterized by accelerating inflation, speculation against the PESO, problems in financing public sector expenditures, and collapse of the stock market. The ESP combined tight fiscal and monetary policies with price, wage, and exchange rate controls and rapid trade liberalization. In December 1988 the program was modified and renamed the PACT FOR STABILITY AND ECONOMIC GROWTH (PSEG).

ECONOMIC STABILIZATION FUND (ESF) a fund used to stabilize the U.S. dollar in times of foreign exchange volatility. The fund is administered jointly by the U.S. Treasury Department and the U.S. Federal Reserve Board, through its New York offices. Fund resources, appropriated by Congress, are usually provided 50% by Treasury and the U.S. federal government. Although not a major role, the fund has also been used in SWAP agreements with other countries to support their currencies. The fund was established by the U.S. Gold Reserve Act of 1934.

ECONOMIC SUPPORT FUND (ESF) an AGENCY FOR INTERNATIONAL DEVELOPMENT (AID) appropriation account for funding economic assistance to countries based on considerations of economic and foreign policy interests of the United States, often in conjunction with military base rights or access rights agreements. Country allocations are determined by the U.S. Department of State consistent with congressional earmarks. To the extent possible, the use of ESF conforms to basic policy directions underlying development assistance. Funds can be used for COMMODITY imports, BALANCE OF PAYMENTS support, or cash grants for budget support. *see also* DEVELOPMENT ASSISTANCE.

ECONOMIC UNION an agreement between two or more countries to remove TRADE BARRIERS with each other and to establish common TARIFF and nontariff policies with respect to IMPORTS from countries outside the agreement. The agreement also allows for free movement of labor and capital and unified MONETARY, FISCAL, and tax POLICIES among members. *see also* COMMON MARKET; CUSTOMS UNION; FREE-TRADE AREA; TRADING BLOC.

ECONOMIC ZONES designated regions in a country that operate under rules that provide special investment incentives, including

DUTY-FREE treatment for IMPORTS and for manufacturing plants that reexport their products. The term *economic zone* is currently used in the People's Republic of China and the FORMER SOVIET UNION. *see also* FREE-TRADE ZONE.

ECONOMIE SOUTERRAINE (French) *see* HIDDEN ECONOMY.

ECONOMIES OF SCALE the reduction in the cost per unit of producing goods with increasing output because fixed costs are being allocated over more units produced. *see also* ECONOMIES OF SCOPE.

ECONOMIES OF SCOPE the reduction in the cost per unit of producing goods through the coordination of two or more manufacturing processes or products. Example: when a firm produces different models of a similar product on the same manufacturing line, the firm reduces unit production costs by eliminating the need for additional manufacturing lines. *see also* ECONOMIES OF SCALE.

ECOSOC Economic and Social Council. *see also* UNITED NATIONS REGIONAL ECONOMIC COMMISSIONS.

ECOTOURISM a broad term that encompasses nature tourism, adventure tourism, ethnic tourism, responsible or wilderness-sensitive tourism, soft-path or small-scale tourism, low-impact tourism, and sustainable tourism. Other forms of ecotourism are scientific, educational, or academic tourism (such as biotourism, archetourism, and geotourism). The definition of the term stresses the destinations and objectives of ecotourism from the traveler's point of view.

ECOWAS *see* ECONOMIC COMMUNITY OF WEST AFRICAN STATES.

ECRT *see* EUROPEAN COMMUNITY OF RESEARCH AND TECHNOLOGY.

ECSC *see* EUROPEAN COAL AND STEEL COMMUNITY.

ECU *see* EUROPEAN CURRENCY UNIT.

EDB *see* EXPORTER DATA BASE.

EDC *see* EXPORT DEVELOPMENT CORPORATION.

EDF *see* EUROPEAN DEVELOPMENT FUND.

EDGE ACT CORPORATIONS banks that are subsidiaries either to bank holding companies or other banks established to engage in international banking and foreign investment and business transactions.

EDI *see* ELECTRONIC DATA INTERCHANGE.

EDIFACT *see* ELECTRONIC DATA INTERCHANGE FOR ADMINISTRATION, COMMERCE, AND TRANSPORTATION.

EDO *see* EXPORT DEVELOPMENT OFFICE.

E.E. abbreviation for errors excepted.

EEA *see* EUROPEAN ECONOMIC AREA.

EEBIC *see* EASTERN EUROPE BUSINESS INFORMATION CENTER.

EEC *see* EUROPEAN ECONOMIC COMMUNITY.

EEC-EFTA LINKAGE the agreement in 1972 between the EUROPEAN ECONOMIC COMMUNITY (EEC) and the EUROPEAN FREE TRADE ASSOCIATION (EFTA). The agreement formed a single European FREE-TRADE AREA. *see also* COMMON MARKET; CUSTOMS UNION; ECONOMIC UNION; EUROPEAN ECONOMIC SPACE; RECIPROCITY.

EEF *see* EXTENDED FUND FACILITY.

E. & O.E. *see* ERRORS AND OMISSIONS EXCEPTED.

EEP *see* EXPORT ENHANCEMENT PROGRAM.

EES *see* EUROPEAN ECONOMIC SPACE.

EE.UU an abbreviation used in Mexico for the United States.

EEZ *see* EXCLUSIVE ECONOMIC ZONE.

EFF *see* ELECTRONIC FRONTIER FOUNDATION.

EFFECTIVE ACCESS *see* RECIPROCITY.

EFFECTIVE EXCHANGE RATE a weighted average of the exchange rate of a country's currency and that of its most important trading partners, with each currency weighted by the comparable significance of each country's level of trade.

EFFECTIVE MARKET ACCESS *see* RECIPROCITY.

EFFECTIVE RATE OF PROTECTION the percentage by which the prices of domestically produced goods are protected by TARIFFS. These charges increase the costs of imported goods so as to deter individuals from purchasing them.

EFFECTS DOCTRINE legal principle that guides courts in the United States to uphold the EXTRATERRITORIAL APPLICATION of U.S. antitrust laws.

EFFICIENCY OF FOREIGN EXCHANGE MARKETS situation occurring when the future SPOT RATE for FOREIGN EXCHANGE has been accurately established by the FORWARD RATE.

EFTA *see* EUROPEAN FREE TRADE ASSOCIATION.

EGYPTIAN POUND unit of currency, Egypt (100 piastres equal 1 Egyptian pound).

EIB *see* EUROPEAN INVESTMENT BANK.

EIS *see* EXECUTIVE INFORMATION SYSTEMS; EXPORT INFORMATION SYSTEM.

EL COLOSUS DEL NORTE a Mexican expression referring to the United States.

EL FINANCIERO (INTERNATIONAL EDITION) a weekly Mexican publication printed in English similar in style to the *Wall*

Street Journal or *Barrons*. The publication includes information on new rules and regulations; political, economic, and trade news; and data on the Mexican stock market. A useful publication for firms interested in doing business in Mexico on an ongoing basis.

EL MACHO MAXIMO a term used by Mexicans when referring to their president.

ELAIN *see* ELECTRONIC LICENSE APPLICATION AND INFORMATION NETWORK.

ELAN *see* EXPORT LEGAL ASSISTANCE NETWORK.

ELECTRONIC DATA INTERCHANGE (EDI) the electronic transmission of data from one business to another business via computer. It emphasizes direct electronic communication as a replacement for paper documents.

ELECTRONIC DATA INTERCHANGE FOR ADMINIS-TRATION, COMMERCE, AND TRANSPORTATION (EDI-FACT) an international syntax used in the interchange of electronic data. Customs bureaus use EDIFACT to interchange data with the importing trade community.

ELECTRONIC FRONTIER FOUNDATION (EFF) a foundation established to address social and legal issues arising from the impact on society of the increasingly pervasive use of computers as a means of communication and information distribution.

ELECTRONIC FUNDS TRANSFER system of transferring funds from one account to another using electronic pulses instead of paper. *see also* TELEGRAPHIC TRANSFER CLAUSE.

ELECTRONIC LICENSE APPLICATION AND INFORMATION NETWORK (ELAIN) a U.S. BUREAU OF EXPORT ADMINISTRATION (BXA) 24-hour on-line service that allows exporters to submit license applications electronically through value-added network vendors. ELAIN is reached by calling BXA's EXPORT LICENSING VOICE INFORMATION SYSTEM (ELVIS).

ELECTRONIC LICENSING a term used to describe the process whereby an EXPORTER submits his EXPORT license applications electronically. *see also* ELECTRONIC LICENSE APPLICATION AND INFORMATION NETWORK (ELAIN).

ELECTRONIC MAIL (E-MAIL) a telecommunications system whereby a computer user can exchange messages with other computer users (or groups of users) via a communications NETWORK. Electronic mail is one of the most popular uses of the INTERNET.

ELECTRONIC VISA INFORMATION SYSTEM (ELVIS) electronic data system through which participating foreign governments transmit electronically to the U. S. government details of shipments of QUOTA-controlled textile goods shipped to the United States. *see also* QUOTA STATUS; QUOTA SYSTEM; PROTECTIONIST TRADING PRACTICES; TEXTILE SURVEILLANCE BODY (TSB).

ELIGIBILITY CRITERIA a term used when referring to standards established by the OVERSEAS PRIVATE INVESTMENT CORPORATION (OPIC) in evaluating projects. All projects considered for OPIC financing must be commercially and financially sound. They must be within the demonstrated competence of the proposed management, which must have a proven record of success in the same or closely related business, as well as a significant and continuing financial risk in the enterprise.

ELVIS *see* ELECTRONIC VISA INFORMATION SYSTEM; EXPORT LICENSE VOICE INFORMATION SYSTEM.

E-MAIL *see* ELECTRONIC MAIL.

E-MAIL ADDRESS a NETWORK address that is used to send ELECTRONIC MAIL to a specified destination. For example an author's address is *shartman@nyit.edu*

EMBARGO a form of TRADE BARRIER that prohibits all trade.

EMBASSY the office in the capital city of a country where the AMBASSADOR sits. *see also* TITLE AND RANK.

EMC *see* EXPORT MANAGEMENT COMPANY.

EMCF *see* EUROPEAN MONETARY AND COOPERATION FUND.

EMIGRATION the MIGRATION of people out of a country. *see also* IMMIGRATION.

EMS *see* EXPORT MANAGEMENT SYSTEM; EUROPEAN MONETARY SYSTEM.

EMU *see* ECONOMIC AND MONETARY UNION.

EN *see* EUROPEAN NORM.

ENABLING CLAUSE Part I of the GENERAL AGREEMENT ON TARIFFS AND TRADE (GATT) framework that permits developed country members to give more favorable treatment to developing countries and special treatment to the least-developed countries, notwithstanding the most-favored-nation provisions of the GATT.

ENCAPSULATION a layered protocols method where a layer adds a header to the protocol data unit (pdu) from the layer above. For example, a data packet could contain several headers ranging from the physical layer, and NETWORK layer INTERNET PROTOCOL (IP), to the application protocol data.

ENCRYPTION the manipulation of a data packet in order to prevent any but the intended recipient from reading that data. There are many types of data encryption, and they are the basis of computer network security. *see also* DATA ENCRYPTION STANDARD.

END OF CONTRACT GRATUITY financial incentive provided to encourage employees to accept and complete assignments in other countries. *see also* BENEFIT GRATUITY; FOREIGN SERVICE PREMIUM.

END-USE CERTIFICATE a Canadian government document issued to importers designating the specific use of the goods being imported.

END-USE TARIFF a DUTY RATE that is dependent upon the end use of the product being imported. Example: books being imported into Canada for use in schools will carry a lower rate of DUTY than the same book imported and sold commercially. *see also* AD VALOREM DUTY; COMPOUND DUTY; SPECIFIC DUTY.

ENDORSEMENT a signature on the reverse side of a negotiable instrument for the purpose of transferring TITLE from one person to another.

ENFORCEMENT refers to Part 787 of the EXPORT ADMINISTRATION REGULATIONS. Part 787 explains those actions considered to be violations of the Export Administration Regulations. This part also discusses record keeping requirements for transactions subject to these regulations, and it explains sanctions that may be imposed by the OFFICE OF EXPORT ENFORCEMENT for violations.

ENHANCED PROLIFERATION CONTROL INITIATIVE (EPCI) a series of measures announced in December 1990 by the United States to reduce certain chemical and biological weapons proliferation risks. Under the initiative, the United States requires licenses for exports of
- precursor chemicals that can be used in making chemical weapons and whole chemical plants to make such precursors;
- potential chemical and biological weapon-related industrial facilities, related designs, technologies, and equipment; and
- any items to destinations that raise proliferation concerns when the EXPORTER knows, or is informed by the U.S. DEPARTMENT OF COMMERCE of such concerns.

  The initiative also calls for
- penalties on U.S. firms and individuals that promote the spread of chemical weapons and missile technology;
- control lists of dual-use equipment and technologies related to chemical and biological weapons and missiles, and of countries to which exports of such items should be controlled, and
- multilateral adoption of the initiative's measures.

ENHANCED STRUCTURAL ADJUSTMENT FACILITY (ESAF) a system by which the INTERNATIONAL MONETARY FUND lends concessional resources to assist poor countries. These countries have extended BALANCE OF PAYMENTS deficits and pursue orderly plans for correcting the deficits and promoting medium-term economic structural adjustment and macroeconomic programs. Although similar to the STRUCTURAL ADJUSTMENT FACILITY (SAF), ESAF has triple the resources available for supporting structural adjustment and monitors performance more closely. Both facilities use the POLICY FRAMEWORK PAPER as a means for attracting additional support structural adjustment. ESAF was established in December 1987. Repayments are required to be made in 5.5 to 10 years. More than 60 countries are eligible for assistance under ESAF and SAF.

EN ROUTE refers to goods, passengers, or vessels in transit. *see also* ESTIMATED TIME OF ARRIVAL; ESTIMATED TIME OF DEPARTURE; IN-TRANSIT.

ENROUTE EXPENSES reimbursements to employees for essential expenses connected with traveling between the HOME country and the foreign assignment. These expenses include items such as hotel, taxi, meals, and telephone.

ENTENTE COUNCIL *see* CONSEIL DE L'ENTENTE.

ENTERPRISE FOR THE AMERICAS INITIATIVE (EAI) an initiative, launched in June 1990, supporting the development of a new economic relationship between the United States and Latin America. The EAI has trade investment, debt, and environment aspects. Trade aspects include efforts to advance free-trade agreements with markets in Latin America and the Caribbean, particularly with groups of countries that have associated for purposes of trade liberalization. As part of this process, the United States seeks to enter into framework agreements on trade and investment with interested countries or groups of countries. These agreements set up intergovernmental councils to discuss and, where appropriate, to negotiate the removal of trade and investment barriers. Investment aspects include the establishment of an INVESTMENT SECTOR LOAN PROGRAM and the MULTI-LATERAL INVESTMENT FUND to support investment reforms.

ENTERPRISE UNIPERSONNELLE A RESPONSABILITE LIMITEE (EURL) (French, meaning sole ownership limited liability company) a company form that combines the features of both a corporation and a partnership. This form of organization can be established with only one shareholder.

ENTREPOT an intermediary storage facility where goods are kept temporarily for distribution within a country or for reexport.

ENTREPOT TRADE IMPORT and EXPORT of goods without the further processing of the goods; usually refers to a party who buys and sells as a middleman. *see also* ENTREPOT.

ENTRY (CUSTOMS) a statement of the kinds, quantities, and values of goods imported together with DUTIES, if any, declared before a CUSTOMS official.

ENTRY DOCUMENTS paperwork required by an IMPORTER at the time the GOODS are being cleared through CUSTOMS. These documents must be filed at a location specified by the Customs officials within a specified period of time. For goods being imported into the United States, these documents consist of:
- Entry Manifest, Customs Form 7533; or application and Special Permit for Immediate Delivery, Customs Form 3461, or other form of merchandise release required by Customs;

- evidence of right to make entry (i.e., BILL OF LADING, AIR WAYBILL, or CARRIER'S CERTIFICATE);
- commercial invoice;
- packing list if appropriate; and
- other documents necessary to determine merchandise admissibility.

ENTRY PAPERS those documents that must be filed with the CUSTOMS officials describing goods imported, such as consumption entry, OCEAN BILL OF LADING or Carrier Release, and COMMERCIAL INVOICE.

ENTRY SUMMARY title of Customs Form 7501.

ENTRY SUMMARY DOCUMENTATION documents prepared by CUSTOMS following the presentation of entry and inspection of goods. At this time the entry summary documentation is filed and estimated duties are deposited within ten working days of the release of the merchandise at a designated customs house. Entry summary documents consist of:

- the entry package returned to the IMPORTER, broker, or his/her authorized agent after merchandise is permitted release;
- Entry Summary (Customs Form 7501), and
- other invoices and documents necessary for the assessment of duties, collection of statistics, or the determination that all IMPORT requirements have been satisfied.

ENTRY SUMMARY SELECTIVITY SYSTEM a part of the U.S. CUSTOMS SERVICE'S AUTOMATED COMMERCIAL SYSTEM, provides an automated review of entry data to determine whether team or routine review is required. Selectivity criteria include an assessment of risk by IMPORTER, TARIFF number, COUNTRY OF ORIGIN, manufacturer, and value. Summaries with Census warnings, as well as quota, ANTIDUMPING, and COUNTERVAILING DUTY entry summaries are selected for team review. A random sample of routine review summaries is also automatically selected for team review.

ENTRY SUMMARY SYSTEM the minimum amount of documentation needed to secure the release of imported merchandise. It is a part of the U.S. CUSTOMS SERVICE'S AUTOMATED COMMERCIAL SYSTEM and contains data on release, summary, rejection, collection, liquidation, and extension or suspension.

ENTRY VALUE the U.S. CUSTOMS SERVICE defines entry value (or entered value) as the value reflected on the entry documentation submitted by the IMPORTER.

ENVIRONMENTAL DUMPING the EXPORT of a good from a country with weak or poorly enforced environmental regulations. *see also* DUMPING; ECODUMPING.

ENVIRONMENTAL SCANNING the orderly evaluation of external conditions that may have an impact on the firm's operations.

ENVIRONMENTAL SUBSIDY a SUBSIDY for adapting existing facilities to new environmental laws or regulations that is NONACTIONABLE under the rules of the WTO.

EOMMEX *see* HELLENIC ORGANIZATION FOR SMALL & MEDIUM SIZED ENTERPRISES & HANDICRAFTS.

EOTC *see* EUROPEAN ORGANIZATION FOR TESTING AND CERTIFICATION.

EPC *see* ECONOMIC POLICY COUNCIL; EUROPEAN PATENT CONVENTION.

EPIC *see* EUROPEAN PRIVATIZATION AND INVESTMENT CORPORATION.

EPO *see* EUROPEAN PATENT OFFICE.

EPZs *see* EXPORT PROCESSING ZONES.

EQUALIZATION money allotted to the customer if the goods are picked up at a destination other than the one named on the BILL OF LADING.

EQUATION OF EXCHANGE an equation that states that the price level times the quantity of transactions is equal to money times the velocity of money.

EQUITABLE TREATMENT a type of FRIENDSHIP, COMMERCE, AND NAVIGATION (FCN) treaty whereby laws applicable to the marketing and distribution of goods in a signatory country are applied sensibly in accordance with appropriate laws to all goods denoted as foreign.

EQUIVALENCE OF ADVANTAGES *see* RECIPROCITY.

EQUIVALENT ACCESS *see* RECIPROCITY.

EQUIVALENT TREATMENT *see* RECIPROCITY.

ERLC *see* EXPORT REVOLVING LINE OF CREDIT.

ERM *see* EUROPEAN EXCHANGE RATE MECHANISM; EXCHANGE RATE(S) MECHANISM.

ERRORS AND OMISSION EXCEPTED (E. & O.E.) a phrase appearing together with the shipper's signature on an invoice, whereby the shipper disavows responsibility for any typographical errors or unintentional omissions.

ERS *see* ECONOMIC RESEARCH SERVICE.

ESA *see* EUROPEAN SPACE AGENCY.

ESAF *see* ENHANCED STRUCTURAL ADJUSTMENT FACILITY.

ESCAP *see* UNITED NATIONS ECONOMIC AND SOCIAL COMMISSION FOR ASIA AND THE PACIFIC.

ESCAPE CLAUSE a clause, which can be invoked under GENERAL AGREEMENT ON TARIFFS AND TRADE (GATT) Article XIX, allowing countries to temporarily violate their GATT obligations to the degree and time necessary to protect a domestic industry from serious injury.

Countries taking such actions, however, must consult with affected contracting parties to determine appropriate compensation for the violation of GATT rights or be subject to retaliatory trade actions.

SECTION 201 of the TRADE ACT OF 1974 requires the U.S. INTERNATIONAL TRADE COMMISSION to investigate complaints filed by domestic industries or workers claiming that they are injured or threatened by rapidly rising imports.

Section 203 of the act provides that if the ensuing investigation establishes that the complaint is valid, relief may be granted in the form of adjustment assistance, which may be training, technical, and financial assistance, or temporary IMPORT restrictions in the form of tariffs, quotas, TARIFF rate quotas, and/or orderly marketing agreements. Import restrictions imposed under the escape clause authority are limited in duration. They may last no longer than 5 years but can be extended by the president for a 3-year period.

ESCB *see* EUROPEAN SYSTEM OF CENTRAL BANKS.

ESCROW ACCOUNT a special bank account into which earnings from sales (e.g., CONVERTIBLE CURRENCY proceeds from EXPORTS) are accumulated. These revenues are set aside for subsequent acquisition of goods and services from a foreign supplier. The escrowed money, usually interest bearing, is disbursed by the bank to the foreign supplier under payment terms and against documents specified in the supplier's sale contract.

ESCUDO unit of currency, Portugal (100 centavos equal 1 escudo).

ESCWA *see* ECONOMIC AND SOCIAL COMMISSION FOR WESTERN ASIA.

ESF *see* ECONOMIC STABILIZATION FUND; ECONOMIC SUPPORT FUND.

ESP *see* EXPORTER'S SALES PRICE.

ESPIRITU (Spanish) *see* ALMA.

ESSENTIAL INDUSTRY ARGUMENT a position held by individuals that a specific industry, which is important to the security of the nation, must be protected during peacetime, so that should a country be at war, the country would then not be dependent on a foreign source of supply. This argument is thus used to generate support for the imposition of TRADE BARRIERS. *see also* PROTECTIONISM.

EST. abbreviation for estimated.

EST. WT. abbreviation for estimated weight.

ESTABLISHMENT *see* RIGHT OF ESTABLISHMENT.

ESTADOUNIDENSE a term often used both verbally and in written form in Mexican news stories when referring to a person from the United States. *see also* EE.UU.

ESTIMATED TIME OF ARRIVAL (ETA) the projected date and time a shipment is scheduled to arrive at its destination or the projected date and time an employee can be expected at his/her foreign assignment. *see also* ESTIMATED TIME OF DEPARTURE (ETD).

ESTIMATED TIME OF DEPARTURE (ETD) the projected date and time a shipment is scheduled to depart or the projected date and time an employee is scheduled to depart from home for his/her foreign assignment. *see also* ESTIMATED TIME OF ARRIVAL (ETA).

ET AL. Latin abbreviation for *and others*.

ETA *see* EUROPEAN TECHNICAL APPROVAL.

ETC *see* EXPORT TRADING COMPANY.

ETHERNET a 10-Mb/s standard for LANs. Computer hosts may be connected to a coaxial cable where they contend for network access using a Carrier Sense Multiple Access system with a data Collision Detection paradigm. *see also* LOCAL AREA NETWORK; TOKEN RING.

ETHNOCENTRISM a conviction held by individuals that their own group is superior to others. It can also be used to describe a firm's opinion that the way a firm conducts business at home will also work abroad. *see also* POLYCENTRISM.

ETHNOGRAPHIC term used to describe different groups of people with loyalty to different nations. *see also* ETHNOSTRUCTURE.

ETHNOSTRUCTURE the different characteristics of the population among people living in a country with loyalties to different nations. *see also* MULTICULTURALISM.

ETSI *see* EUROPEAN TELECOMMUNICATIONS STANDARDS INSTITUTE.

ETUC *see* EUROPEAN TRADE UNION CONFEDERATION.

EU *see* EUROPEAN UNION.

EUCLID *see* EUROPEAN COOPERATION FOR THE LONG TERM IN DEFENSE.

EUR 1 FORM a document required by the African, Caribbean, and Pacific (ACP) countries that are members of the Lomé Convention, in order to qualify for preferential duties. *see also* FORM A.

EURATOM *see* EUROPEAN ATOMIC ENERGY COMMUNITY.

EUREKA *see* EUROPEAN RESEARCH COORDINATION AGENCY.

EURIBOR *see* EURO INTERBANK OFFERED RATE.

EURL *see* ENTERPRISE UNIPERSONNELLE À RESPONSABILITÉ LIMITÉE.

EURO a single European currency that will replace the currencies of the eleven nations comprising the EUROPEAN MONETARY UNION in several stages. First, the EXCHANGE RATES between the national currencies and the euro were fixed on January 1, 1999. Second, the participating members of the EMU will introduce euro notes and coins into their economies beginning January 1, 2002. At that time, the members will have six months to remove their national currencies from circulation. The euro notes will be denominated in units from 5 to 500, while coins will range from one cent to 2 euros.

The benefits of the euro are clear. The new European currency will lower the operating costs of all firms, once they have completed the conversion process to the euro. There will be greater price transparency and increased competition across the market as the consumer is better able to price-compare without any concern for exchange rates.

Companies will also benefit from greater transparency in agent/distributor commissions throughout Europe, simplification of compensation plans, and greater transparency in reporting revenues to national tax authorities and to headquarters.

In May 1998, 11 of the 15 EUROPEAN UNION (EU) members achieved the CONVERGENCE CRITERIA established in the MAASTRICHT TREATY, and agreed to participate in the first round of the Monetary Union on January 1, 1999. The European Monetary Union member countries are Austria, Belgium, Finland, France, Germany, Ireland, Italy, Luxembourg, Netherlands, Portugal, and Spain. The United Kingdom and Denmark met the convergence criteria, but decided not to participate in the first round. Greece did not meet the convergence criteria and Sweden did not meet the criterion. Economists believe that the remaining four EU members will join the monetary union by the time that notes and coins enter circulation in 2002.

One euro corresponds to 100 cents or euro-cents. There will be seven or eight euro notes and eight euro coins. The euro coins and notes will be the same size in all EMU member countries. There might be national symbols, but any euro coin or note will be valid throughout the EMU. Its value will be that of the basket ECU, that is, a combination of national currencies at their exchange rate of a given day.

EURO INTERBANK OFFERED RATE a euro-denominated interest rate charged by large banks among themselves on euro-denominated loans. *see also* LONDON INTERBANK OFFERED RATE.

EURO ZONE countries of the EUROPEAN MONETARY UNION, that have adopted the common currency, the EURO. *see also* MAASTRICHT TREATY.

EUROBOND *see* EURODOLLARS.

EUROCOM a trading company subsidiary of BANCO NATIONAL DE MEXICO (BANAMEX). EUROCOM buys and sells Mexican products on commission and provides various services to Mexico's MAQUILADORA industry. EUROCOM, with the support of BANAMEX, focuses on grains and seeds, lamina steel/iron, and powdered milk importation. *see also* BANCOMEXT.

EUROCOMMERCIAL PAPER unsecured debt obligations coming due within 1 year, issued and offered by nonbank corporations in the EUROMARKET.

EUROCURRENCY
1. the deposit of one nation's currency in another country.
2. any currency traded outside the control of the issuing country.
see also EURODOLLARS.

EUROCURRENCY DEPOSIT an account into which TRANSFERABLE and CONVERTIBLE CURRENCY of a Western European country has been deposited by a nonresident individual or company of the country of the currency. Example: an American (individual or subsidiary) residing in Germany makes a deposit of FRENCH FRANCS into a bank in Italy.

EURODOLLAR DEPOSIT a U.S. dollar denominated account of a nonresident of the United States.

EURODOLLARS deposits of U.S. dollars in banks or other financial institutions located outside the borders of the United States. In every other way, Eurodollars are identical to any other U.S. dollars. These same dollars are also called OFFSHORE DOLLARS, or depending where the money is on deposit, ASIAN DOLLARS. The use of Euro in connection with dollars reflects the beginnings of holding deposits offshore. Likewise, a EUROCURRENCY (or external currency) is the deposit of one nation's currency in another country. A Eurobond is a bond denominated in a currency and traded in a market outside of the issuing country.

EUROLIRA *see* EUROCURRENCY.

EUROMARKETS financial centers located anywhere in the world where EUROCURRENCIES are bought and sold.

EUROMARKS *see* EUROCURRENCY.

EUROPE 1992 refers to the idea of the accomplishment by the year 1992 of a single, united ECONOMIC UNION of European states represented by the EUROPEAN ECONOMIC COMMUNITY (EEC). The formal and complete unification has not occurred to date; it remains an ongoing process. *see also* COMMON MARKET; DELORS REPORT.

EUROPE WITHOUT FRONTIERS *see* EUROPE 1992.

EUROPEAN ACADEMIC AND RESEARCH NETWORK (EARN) a computer NETWORK connecting European academic and research institutions with ELECTRONIC MAIL and file transfer services using the BITNET protocol.

EUROPEAN ATOMIC ENERGY COMMUNITY (EURATOM) European organizations established in 1958 for the common development of Europe's nuclear resources. *see also* EUROPEAN COMMUNITY.

EUROPEAN BANK FOR RECONSTRUCTION AND DEVELOPMENT (EBRD) European constituted bank providing assistance to nations through direct loans. The loans are designed to facilitate the development of market-oriented economies and to promote private and entrepreneurial initiatives. The EBRD's charter mandates that at least 60% of EBRD lending contribute to privatization of state-owned enterprises. The remaining 40% may fund public infrastructure or environmental projects that promote private-sector development, as well as state-owned enterprises that operate in a competitive fashion. EBRD was established in May 1990 and began financing operations in June 1991. EBRD headquarters is in London, England.

EUROPEAN CENTER FOR NUCLEAR RESEARCH *see* CENTRE EUROPÉEN DE RECHERCHE NUCLEAIRE.

EUROPEAN CENTRAL BANK (ECB) a European bank envisioned by the MAASTRICHT TREATY, which would be created to oversee performance of economic policy and EXCHANGE RATE(S), policy tasks conferred on the European System of Central Banks. The ECB would have the exclusive right to issue bank notes within the EUROPEAN COMMUNITY. The national central banks would be the sole subscribers to and holders of the capital of the ECB. The funding formula for the ECB would be based both on a member state's population and on its gross domestic product. The ECB will form, together with the national central banks, the European System of Central Banks.

EUROPEAN COAL AND STEEL COMMUNITY (ECSC) (French: Communauté Européen du Charbon et de l'Acier) European coal and steel organization providing activities to operate a common market in coal and steel and to remove barriers to trade in coal, coke, steel, pig-iron, and scrap iron.

EUROPEAN COMMISSION (EC) one of the five major institutions of the EUROPEAN COMMUNITY (EC). The commission is responsible for ensuring the implementation of the TREATY OF ROME and community rules and obligations; submitting proposals to the Council of Ministers; executing the council's decisions; reconciling disagreements among council members; administering EC policies, such as the COMMON AGRICULTURAL POLICY and coal and steel policies; taking necessary legal action against firms or member governments; and representing the community in trade negotiations with non-member countries.

EUROPEAN COMMITTEE FOR ELECTROTECHNICAL STANDARDIZATION (CENELEC) a non-profit-making international organization under Belgian law. CENELEC seeks to harmonize electrotechnical standards published by the national organizations and to remove technical barriers to trade that may be caused by differences in standards. CENELEC members include Austria, Belgium, Denmark, Finland, France, Germany, Greece, Iceland, Ireland, Italy, Luxembourg, the Netherlands, Norway, Portugal, Spain, Sweden, Switzerland, and the United Kingdom.

EUROPEAN COMMITTEE FOR STANDARDIZATION (CEN) (French: Comité Europeen de Normalisation) an association of the national standards organizations of 18 countries of the EUROPEAN ECONOMIC COMMUNITY (EEC) and of the EUROPEAN FREE TRADE ASSOCIATION (EFTA). CEN membership is open to the national standards organization of any European country that is, or is capable of becoming, a member of the EEC or EFTA. CEN develops voluntary standards in building, machine tools, information technology, and all sectors excluding the electrical ones covered by CENELEC. CEN is involved in accreditation of laboratories and certification bodies as well as quality assurance.

EUROPEAN COMMUNITY (EC) the name given to the 1967 merger of three European supranational communities: the EUROPEAN COAL AND STEEL COMMUNITY (ECSC) (or Schuman Plan), created in 1952; the COMMON MARKET, or EUROPEAN ECONOMIC COMMUNITY, which established the EUROPEAN MONETARY SYSTEM; and the EUROPEAN ATOMIC ENERGY COMMUNITY. Austria, Belgium, Britain, Denmark, Finland, France, Germany (originally West Germany), Greece, Ireland, Italy, Luxembourg, the Netherlands, Portugal, Spain, and Sweden are full members. The memberships of Norway and Turkey are still under consideration.

The organization provides for the gradual elimination of intraregional CUSTOMS DUTIES and other TRADE BARRIERS, applying a common external TARIFF against other countries and providing for gradual adoption of other integrating measures, including a COMMON AGRICULTURAL POLICY (CAP) and guarantees of free movement of labor and capital. The original six members were Belgium, France, West Germany, Italy, Luxembourg, and the Netherlands. Denmark, Ireland, and the United Kingdom became members in 1973; Greece acceded in 1981 and Spain and Portugal in 1986.

Since 1967, the European Community has been served by four common institutions:

• the EC Commission,
• the EC Council,
• the European Parliament, and
• the EUROPEAN COURT OF JUSTICE.

The present 15 member states of the EC are also members of the ECSC and Euratom. *see also* EUROPEAN UNION.

EUROPEAN COMMUNITY OF RESEARCH AND TECHNOLOGY (ECRT) a program originating from the SINGLE EUROPEAN ACT of July 1987 whereby members of the EUROPEAN ECONOMIC COMMUNITY would cooperate on research and technology issues enabling them to compete more effectively in those areas with the United States and Japan.

EUROPEAN CONFERENCE OF POSTAL AND TELECOMMUNICATIONS ADMINISTRATIONS *see* CONFERENCE EUROPÉEN DES ADMINISTRATIONS DES POSTES ET DES TÉLÉCOMMUNICATIONS.

EUROPEAN COOPERATION FOR THE LONG TERM IN DEFENSE (EUCLID) a coordinated defense R&D initiative approved in a June 1989 meeting of the INDEPENDENT EUROPEAN PROGRAM GROUP (IEPG). EUCLID was designed to overcome deficiencies in European defense R&D spending, minimize individual nations' duplicative efforts, improve planning, and overcome legal and administrative obstacles. EUCLID is divided into 11 technological categories:

- modern radar technology,
- microelectronics,
- composite structures,
- modular avionics,
- electric gun,
- artificial intelligence,
- signature manipulation,
- opto-electronic devices,
- satellite surveillance technologies including verification,
- underwater acoustics, and
- "human factors," including technology for training and simulation.
  Each of the 11 categories is assigned a lead coordinating nation.

EUROPEAN COURT OF JUSTICE (ECJ) European court located in Luxembourg, Belgium, and established in 1958 to support the interpretation and application of EUROPEAN COMMUNITY law. The court has jurisdiction to settle actions brought by

- the EUROPEAN COMMISSION (EC) against member states for failing to implement EC legislation, and
- the member states against EC institutions, referrals for interpretations from national courts where a question of EC law is at issue, and individuals under a provision of EC law.

EUROPEAN CURRENCY UNIT (ECU) a basket of specified amounts of each EUROPEAN COMMUNITY (EC) CURRENCY. Amounts were determined according to the economic size of EC members, all of whose currencies participate in the ECU basket. In the EUROPEAN MONETARY SYSTEM (EMS) the ECU is used as a basis for setting central rates in the EXCHANGE RATE mechanism, as an accounting unit, and as a reserve instrument and means of settlement among the EMS central banks. The ECU is not used by individuals.

Under provisions of the MAASTRICHT TREATY, on January 1, 1999, the ECU adopted the EURO as the single European currency in Stage III of the European Monetary System. On January 1, 1999, the participating currencies are irrevocably fixed against the euro. The euro will be used as a transaction currency and may be used in pricing, tax accounting, or other commercial applications approved by the respective governments. In addition, the EUROPEAN CENTRAL BANK and its policies come formally into force.

The composition of the basket comprising the ECU was frozen on November 1, 1993, in accordance with a provision of the Maastricht Treaty, which entered into force on November 1.

EUROPEAN DEFENSE COOPERATION GROUP *see* DEFENSE TRADE WORKING GROUP.

EUROPEAN DEVELOPMENT FUND (EDF) the principal means by which the EUROPEAN ECONOMIC COMMUNITY (EEC) provides aid, concessionary finance, and technical assistance to developing countries. The fund was originally established in 1958 to grant financial aid to dependencies of the six nations that founded the EEC.

EUROPEAN ECONOMIC AREA (EEA) a European FREE-TRADE AREA (FTA) that became effective in January 1994. It consists of the fifteen members of the EUROPEAN UNION and three members of the EFTA (Iceland, Norway and Switzerland). The EEA, encompassing an area inhabited by 370 million people, allows for the free movement of goods, persons, services and capital throughout all member countries. It has also opened up cooperation in other areas, including research and development, environment, promotion of tourism, social and consumer policy.

Significant differences exist between the EEA and full membership in the EUROPEAN ECONOMIC COMMUNITY (EEC). The EEA is an FTA, not a CUSTOMS UNION. Border controls between the EEC and EFTA, although relaxed, are expected to continue. EFTA will not adopt the EEC's Common Customs Tariff nor participate in the Common Commercial Policy or Common Agricultural Policy. EFTA nations will continue to set their own TARIFFS for third countries subject to the GENERAL AGREEMENT ON TARIFFS AND TRADE (GATT) and OECD agreements.

EUROPEAN ECONOMIC COMMUNITY (EEC) organization formally merged with the EUROPEAN COMMUNITY (EC) in 1967. Frequent use of the term European Community has become common as a reference to the EUROPEAN ECONOMIC COMMUNITY (EEC). *see also* COMMON MARKET.

EUROPEAN ECONOMIC SPACE (EES) *see* EUROPEAN ECONOMIC AREA.

EUROPEAN EXCHANGE RATE MECHANISM (ERM) *see* EXCHANGE RATE MECHANISM.

EUROPEAN FREE TRADE ASSOCIATION (EFTA) a regional organization established in December 1959 by the Stockholm Convention as an alternative to the COMMON MARKET. EFTA was designed to provide a FREE-TRADE AREA (FTA) for industrial products among member countries. In contrast with the EUROPEAN COMMUNITY (EC), EFTA does not have a common external TARIFF nor a common agricultural trade policy. Original EFTA members included the United Kingdom, Austria, Denmark, Norway, Portugal, Sweden, and Switzerland. The United Kingdom, Denmark, and Portugal left the association when they joined the EC. EFTA currently has seven members: Austria, Finland, Iceland, Liechtenstein, Norway, Sweden, and Switzerland; Austria and Sweden have applied for EC membership. Association headquarters is in Geneva, Switzerland.

EUROPEAN INVESTMENT BANK (EIB) an independent public institution based in Luxembourg set up by the TREATY OF ROME in 1957 to contribute to balanced and steady development in the EUROPEAN COMMUNITY (EC). The EIB provides loans and guarantees to companies and public institutions to finance regional development, structural development, and achieve cross-border objectives. The EIB has emphasized regional development and energy, with Italy, Greece, and Ireland receiving major support.

EUROPEAN MONETARY AND COOPERATION FUND (EMCF) a European fund created in 1973 used to keep account of short-term borrowings and support currencies through intervention in foreign exchange markets at the request of member states. Originally the fund was intended to support the EUROPEAN CURRENCY UNIT and support a reserve system of central banks, but the fund was revised and linked with the EUROPEAN MONETARY SYSTEM (EMS) in 1979. It uses the BANK FOR INTERNATIONAL SETTLEMENTS (BIS) as its agent.

EUROPEAN MONETARY INSTITUTE (EMI) European currency institution created under provisions of the MAASTRICHT TREATY to manage the national currency reserves of EUROPEAN COMMUNITY (EC) central banks and encourage international acceptance of the EUROPEAN CURRENCY UNIT (ECU). The EMI is also intended to strengthen coordination of monetary policies among European Community member states and to study and develop the infrastructure and procedures required for the conduct of a single monetary policy. The EMI was established on January 1, 1994.

EUROPEAN MONETARY SYSTEM (EMS) monetary system in Europe created in 1979 to support monetary stability, move Europe toward closer economic integration, and avoid disruptions in trade resulting from fluctuations in currency exchange rates. EMS members deposit gold and dollar reserves with the EUROPEAN MONETARY COOPERATION FUND (EMCF) in exchange for the issuance of EUROPEAN CURRENCY UNITS (ECU). The EMS has three main features: the ECU, credit mechanisms to support member countries, and the EUROPEAN EXCHANGE RATE(S) MECHANISM. All EC members, except Greece and the United Kingdom, participate in the EXCHANGE RATE(S) MECHANISM of the EMS.

EUROPEAN MONETARY UNION *see* MAASTRICHT TREATY.

EUROPEAN NORM (EN) the EN mark is a designation of a standards directive issued by CEN (Comité Européen de Normalisation) or CENELEC (Comité Européen de Normalisation Electrotechnique). Notations regarding EN generally do not appear on the product. *see also* CONFORMITE EUROPEENE.

EUROPEAN ORGANIZATION FOR TESTING AND CERTIFICATION (EOTC) organization created in April 1990 by the EUROPEAN COMMUNITY (EC) Commission under a memorandum of agreement with CEN/CENELEC and the EUROPEAN FREE TRADE

ASSOCIATION (EFTA) countries. EOTC promotes mutual recognition of tests, test and certification procedures, and quality systems within the European private sector for product areas or characteristics not covered by EC legislative requirements. The EOTC headquarters is in Brussels, Belgium.

EUROPEAN PARLIAMENT (EP) *see* EUROPEAN COMMUNITY.

EUROPEAN PATENT CONVENTION (EPC) an agreement between European nations to centralize and standardize patent law and procedure. The EPC took effect in 1977 and established a single European patent through application to the European Patent Office in Munich. Once granted, the patent matures into a bundle of individual patents—one in each member country designated by the patent applicant. Patent applicants must indicate the countries in which they wish to have patent protection.

EUROPEAN PATENT OFFICE (EPO) (German: Europäisches Patentamt; French: Office Européen de Brevets) European patent office established in October 1973 headquartered in Munich, Germany. The EPO promotes easier, cheaper, and more reliable patent protection by establishing a single procedure for granting patents on the basis of a single European patent law. Standards are available in English from the World Intellectual Property Organization. EPO membership is not open to the United States, but close relations are maintained through the U.S. DEPARTMENT OF COMMERCE's Patent and Trademark Office.

EUROPEAN PRIVATIZATION AND INVESTMENT CORPORATION (EPIC) private consulting firm dedicated to providing advisory services related to the restructuring and PRIVATIZATION of Central and Eastern European companies.

EUROPEAN RESEARCH COORDINATION AGENCY (EUREKA) European research agency that coordinates advanced technology projects being carried out by European industry. The agency was created in 1985 and is headquartered in Brussels, Belgium. Its membership includes the EUROPEAN COMMUNITY (EC) countries plus Norway, Sweden, Finland, Switzerland, Austria, Iceland, and Turkey.

EUROPEAN SNAKE the mechanism by which the European Inner Six (Belgium, Federal Republic of Germany, France, Italy, Luxembourg, and the Netherlands) agreed (in March 1972) to limit the fluctuation in the BILATERAL EXCHANGE RATES against the U.S. dollar to ±2.25%. The system lasted until March 1973. *see also* MANAGED FLOATING EXCHANGE RATE SYSTEM.

EUROPEAN SPACE AGENCY (ESA) European agency that designs and coordinates the construction of satellite and launching systems. Members include Austria, Belgium, Denmark, France, Germany, Ireland, Italy, the Netherlands, Norway, Spain, Sweden, Switzerland, and the United Kingdom.

EUROPEAN SYSTEM OF CENTRAL BANKS (ESCB) European CENTRAL BANK system envisioned by the TREATY OF MAASTRICHT for the primary purpose of maintaining price stability within the EUROPEAN COMMUNITY (EC). The ESCB would be composed of the European Central Bank and the central banks of the member states. It would be independent of national governments and community authorities.

EUROPEAN TECHNICAL APPROVAL (ETA) a favorable technical assessment of the fitness for use of a product for an intended use, based on the fulfillment of the essential requirements for building works for which the product is used, as provided for under the EC Construction Products Directive (89/106/EEC). A European technical approval may be granted to products for which there is neither a harmonized European standard, nor a recognized national standard, nor a mandate for a harmonized standard and to a product that differs significantly from harmonized or recognized national standards. Such approval permits free circulation of the products within the member countries of the EUROPEAN COMMUNITY (EC) and the EUROPEAN FREE TRADE ASSOCIATION (EFTA).

EUROPEAN TELECOMMUNICATIONS STANDARDS INSTITUTE (ETSI) (French: Institut Européen des Normes des Télécommunication; German: Europäisches Institut für Telekommunikationsstandards) European telecommunications standards established in March 1988 in response to the inability of the European Conference of Postal and Telecommunications Administrations (CEPT) to keep up with the schedule of work on common European standards and specifications agreed to in the 1984 Memorandum of Understanding between CEPT and the EC. ETSI has a contractual relationship with the EC to pursue standards development for telecommunications equipment and services, and it cooperates with other European standards bodies such as CEN/CENELEC. ETSI membership includes the telecommunications administrations that constitute the CEPT as well as manufacturers, service providers, and users. *see also* CONFERENCE EUROPEENNE DES ADMINISTRATIONS DES POSTES ET DES TELECOMMUNICATIONS.

EUROPEAN TRADE UNION CONFEDERATION (ETUC) the primary organization that speaks for European trade unions. Founded in 1973, the ETUC consists of more than 30 organizations in 20 Western European countries and has over 40 million members. The confederation's principal goal is to influence European policies affecting workers. It is active with the EUROPEAN COMMUNITY, the COUNCIL OF EUROPE, the EUROPEAN FREE TRADE ASSOCIATION (EFTA), and the OECD Trade Union Advisory Committee. ETUC headquarters is in Brussels, Belgium.

EUROPEAN UNION (EU) an umbrella reference to the EUROPEAN COMMUNITY (EC) and to two European integration efforts introduced by the MAASTRICHT TREATY: Common Foreign and Security Policy (including defense) and Justice and Home Affairs (principally cooperation between police and other authorities on crime, terrorism, and immigration issues). The term *European Union* was introduced in November 1993 (when the Maastricht Treaty on European Union became effective). The term *European Community* continues to exist as a legal entity within the broader framework of the EU.

EUROPOUNDS *see* EUROCURRENCY.

EUROSTAT *see* STATISTICAL OFFICE OF THE EUROPEAN COMMUNITY.

EUROSTERLING *see* EUROCURRENCY.

EUROTERM a phrase originated by European economists and traders when referring to the supporters of the European ECONOMIC MONETARY UNION (EMU).

EUROTERRORISM associated with left-wing terrorism of the 1960s, 1970s, and 1980s involving the Red Brigade, Red Army Faction, and November 17th Group, among other groups that targeted American interests in Europe and NATO. Other groups include Orange Volunteers, Red Hand Defenders, Continuity IRA, Loyalist Volunteer Force, Ulster Defense Association, and First of October Anti-Fascist Resistance Group.

EUROTYPES term used to describe a consumer after the European ECONOMIC MONETARY UNION has been successfully formed. *see also* EUROPE 1992.

EUROYEN *see* EUROCURRENCY.

EUTELSAT a 26-member country STRATEGIC ALLIANCE formed to increase the capacity and improve the capability of the telecommunications infrastructure in Europe.

EVENTS OF COMPENSATION terms under which the OVERSEAS PRIVATE INVESTMENT CORPORATION will compensate for the following losses:
* The FOREIGN BUYER refuses to participate in the DISPUTE SETTLEMENT SYSTEM (procedure) or frustrates its operation with respect to a valid claim.
* The foreign buyer refuses to pay an award in the insured's favor.
* The procedure yields an award in favor of the foreign buyer, and the award can be proven to have been obtained through fraud, corruption or duress, or, if there is a written record of the proceedings, is unsupported by substantial evidence in that record.
* Due to changed conditions in the project country, it is too dangerous or would be futile for the insured to pursue dispute settlement.

EVERGREEN CLAUSE
1. a special clause found in a LETTER OF CREDIT, providing for a regular expiration date with an automatic extension. The clause usually appears in STANDBY or REVOLVING LETTERS OF CREDIT.
2. a clause appearing in agency/distributor contracts allowing the distributor to automatically renew the contract without changes, making termination very difficult.

EVERYTHING BUT ARMS term given by the EUROPEAN UNION to its decision in 2001 to eliminate QUOTAS and TARIFFS on all products except arms from the world's 48 poorest countries.

EVIDENCE ACCOUNT an umbrella agreement contracted between a Western supplier and a government agency in a developing country (e.g., an industrial ministry or a provincial or state authority), which is designed to facilitate reciprocal trade flows. The agreement stipulates trade conditions between the Western company, other independent firms designated by it, and commercial organizations under the jurisdiction of the developing country signatory. It also requires that the cumulative payment turnovers for the trade goods, not payments of individual transactions, be balanced in an agreed-upon proportion within a specified period of time (typically 1 to 3 years). Trade flows are monitored, and financial settlements occur through banks designated by the agreement's signatories.

EVIDENCE OF ORIGIN information presented in the EXPORTER'S CERTIFICATE OF ORIGIN certifies that the goods described are eligible for a preferential rate of duty under a trade program.

EVIDENCE OF RIGHT TO MAKE ENTRY documents required by an IMPORTER to support his/her right to clear a shipment through customs. Goods may be entered only by the owner, purchaser, or a licensed CUSTOMSHOUSE BROKER. When the goods are consigned "to order," the BILL OF LADING properly endorsed by the CONSIGNOR may serve as evidence of the right to make an entry. An AIR WAYBILL may be used for merchandise arriving by air. *see also* ENTRY DOCUMENTS; ENTRY SUMMARY DOCUMENTATION; ORDER BILL OF LADING.

EX DOCK (IMPORT USAGE ONLY) the seller's obligation to place the specified goods at the specified price on the IMPORT dock clear of all customs and duty requirements. The buyer must do nothing further than pick up the goods within a prescribed time limit.

EX FACTORY sale term where the buyer gains ownership of goods when they leave the VENDOR's dock. *see also* EX WORKS; INCOTERMS.

EX-"FROM" a quoted price that applies only at the point of origin when used in pricing terms such as EX FACTORY (at the seller's factory) or EX DOCK (dock at the IMPORT point). In practice, this kind of quotation indicates that the seller agrees to place the goods at the disposal of the buyer at the specified place within a fixed period of time.

EX MILL (EX WAREHOUSE, EX MINE, EX FACTORY) the seller's obligation to place the specified quantity of goods at the specified price at his mill loaded on trucks, railroad cars, or any other specified means of transport. The buyer must accept the goods in this manner and make all arrangements for transportation.

EX QUAY trade term meaning that the seller makes the goods available to the buyer on the quay (wharf) at the destination named in the sales contract. The seller has to bear the full cost and risk involved in bringing the goods there. There are two "Ex Quay" contracts in use:

- Ex Quay "duty paid" and
- Ex Quay "duties on buyer's account," in which the liability to clear goods for import is to be met by the buyer instead of by the seller.

EX SHIP trade term meaning that the seller will make the goods available to the buyer on board the ship at the destination named in the sales contract. The seller bears all costs and risks involved in bringing the goods to the destination.

EX WORKS (EXW) at a named point of origin (examples: ex factory, ex mill, ex warehouse). Under this term, the price quoted applies only at the point of origin and the seller agrees to place the goods at the disposal of the buyer at a specified place on the date or within the period fixed. All other charges are for the account of the buyer.

EXCELSIOR a distinguished Mexican daily newspaper.

EXCEPTION RATES shipping rates set higher because the COMMODITY requires special handling and care, such as live animals.

EXCEPTIONS a unique occurrence in a MULTILATERAL or BILATERAL TRADE AGREEMENT, that when it occurs, the relationship between the parties is altered.

EXCESS CAPACITY state that occurs when a firm has output capabilities for which there is inadequate demand. This can often act as an incentive for a firm to become involved in exporting.

EXCESS-CURRENCY COUNTRY a country where the local currency supply available to the U.S. government for conducting official business exceeds U.S. requirements for the 2 years following the year for which the designation is made.

EXCEL *see* EXPORT CREDIT ENHANCED LEVERAGE.

EXCHANGE CONTROL AUTHORITY *see* CENTRAL BANK.

EXCHANGE CONTROLS an IMPORT restriction applied by a country with an adverse trade balance, reflecting a desire to control the outflow of CONVERTIBLE CURRENCIES from a country. *see also* IMPORT DEPOSIT REQUIREMENTS; IMPORT LICENSE; IMPORT RESTRICTIONS; MULTIPLE EXCHANGE RATES.

EXCHANGE EXPOSURE an inherent valuation risk occurring when assets or liabilities from financial statements are expressed in a foreign currency. When financial statements are valued using foreign currencies, appreciation or depreciation may occur.

EXCHANGE MARKET the market on which national currencies are exchanged for one another.

EXCHANGE PERMIT a government permit required by the IMPORTER'S government to enable the firm to convert its own country's currency into foreign currency with which to pay a seller in another country. *see also* IMPORT LICENSE.

EXCHANGE RATE(S) the price of one currency expressed in terms of another (i.e., the number of units of one currency that may be exchanged for one unit of another currency).

Influences on exchange rates include differences between interest rates and other asset yields between countries; investor expectations about future changes in a currency's value; investors' views on the overall quantity of dollar-denominated assets in circulation; arbitrage; and CENTRAL BANK EXCHANGE RATE(S) support. *see also* EXCHANGE RATE CLASSIFICATIONS.

EXCHANGE RATE CLASSIFICATIONS the following are the different types of possible EXCHANGE RATE(S) regimes and how they work:
- SINGLE-CURRENCY PEG. The country PEGS to a major currency—usually the U.S. dollar or the French franc—with infrequent adjustment of the parity.
- COMPOSITE CURRENCY PEG. The country pegs to a basket of currencies of major trading partners to make the pegged currency more stable than if a single-currency peg were used. The weights assigned to the currencies in the basket may reflect the geographical distribution of trade, services, or capital flows. They may also be standardized, as in SPECIAL DRAWING RIGHTS (SDR) and the EUROPEAN CURRENCY UNIT (ECU).
- Limited flexibility vis-à-vis a single-currency peg. The value of the currency is maintained within certain margins of the peg.
- Limited flexibility through cooperative agreements. This applies to countries in the EXCHANGE RATE(S) MECHANISM of the EUROPEAN MONETARY SYSTEM (EMS) and is a cross between a peg of individual EMS currencies to each other and a float of all these currencies jointly vis-à-vis non-EMS currencies.
- Greater flexibility through adjustment to an indicator. The currency is adjusted more or less automatically to changes in selected indicators. A common indicator is the real EFFECTIVE EXCHANGE RATE(S), which reflects inflation-adjusted changes in the currency vis-à-vis major trading partners.
- Greater flexibility through MANAGED FLOAT. The CENTRAL BANK sets the rate but varies it frequently. Indicators for adjusting the rate include, for example, the BALANCE OF PAYMENTS position, reserves, and PARALLEL MARKET developments. Adjustments are not automatic.
- Full flexibility through an independent float. Rates are determined by market forces. Some industrial countries have floats—except for the EMS countries—but the number of developing countries in this category has been increasing. *see also* CRAWLING PEG SYSTEM.

EXCHANGE RATE MECHANISM (ERM) a program through which member countries of the EUROPEAN ECONOMIC COMMUNITY (EEC) agree to maintain parity in EXCHANGE RATES among their currencies. Limits are set on the amounts by which exchange rates may vary between any two currencies. If an exchange rate reaches the limit, the CENTRAL BANKS of the two countries intervene in the market to ensure that the limit is not exceeded. The ERM was established in 1979 with agreement by Belgium, France, West Germany, Luxembourg, the Netherlands, and Denmark to limit fluctuation in the bilateral exchange rates between their currencies to ±2.25%. Italy, which was also a member, did not limit fluctuation to ±2.25% until 1990. Spain joined in 1989, the United Kingdom in 1990, and Portugal in 1992, each agreeing to a wider band of 6% fluctuation in the bilateral exchange rates in the value of their currencies against other ERM members. Disruptions in September 1992 led to the withdrawal of Italy and the United Kingdom and to some parity realignments. The ERM has since resumed, with provisions allowing currency fluctuations of 15%.

EXCHANGE RATE REGIME rules under which a country's EXCHANGE RATE is determined. *see also* FLOATING EXCHANGE RATES; PEGGED EXCHANGE RATE; MANAGED FLOAT; CURRENCY BOARD; EXCHANGE CONTROLS; EXCHANGE RATE MECHANISM (ERM).

EXCHANGE RATE RISK a risk that losses can arise as a result of a change in the value of a currency. *see also* FLUCTUATING EXCHANGE RATES.

EXCHANGE RATE SPREAD the difference in the price of a currency between what it is bought and sold for.

EXCISE TAX a surcharge assessed on the manufacture of certain categories of products either produced or imported for domestic use.

EXCLUSIVE ECONOMIC ZONE (EEZ) the rights of coastal states to control the living and nonliving resources of the sea for 200 miles off their coasts while allowing freedom of navigation to other states beyond 12 miles, as agreed at the sixth session of the Third UN Conference on the LAW OF THE SEA (UNCLOS). The EEZ also gives the coastal states the responsibility for managing the conservation of all natural resources within the 200-mile limit.

EXCULPATORY CLAUSE contractual clause that releases one party from liability in case of wrongdoing by the other party involved.

EXECUTIVE INFORMATION SYSTEMS a system of collecting decentralized and geographically dispersed data and providing uniform organizational information to management for their immediate attention.

EXERCISE PRICE the price at which a currency can be bought or sold by contract on or before a future date.

EXHIBITION exhibits set up by organizations either in the United States or abroad for the purpose of promoting their goods or services. These exhibits are attended by potential customers and are an excellent opportunity to make new and valuable customers. *see also* CATALOG EXHIBITIONS; CERTIFIED TRADE FAIR PROGRAM; MATCHMAKER TRADE DELEGATIONS; TRADE MISSIONS.

EXIMBANK *see* EXPORT–IMPORT BANK OF THE UNITED STATES.

EXIT/REENTRY VISA permit issued by a government granting permission to a foreign resident to temporarily leave and then reenter the HOST COUNTRY. *see also* EXIT VISA; MULTIPLE-ENTRY VISA; RESIDENCY VISA; SINGLE-ENTRY VISA; WORK VISA.

EXIT VISA permit allowing a foreign resident to leave the HOST COUNTRY. *see also* EXIT/REENTRY VISA.

EXON-FLORIO section 721 of the U.S. Defense Production Act, which provides the president with authority to investigate proposed or pending mergers, acquisitions, and takeovers by or with foreign persons to determine their effects on national security. The provision also grants the president authority to suspend or block those transactions that lead to control of a domestic company by a foreign person if the president determines that the foreign purchaser might take actions that would threaten the national security. *see also* COMMITTEE ON FOREIGN INVESTMENT IN THE UNITED STATES; FOREIGN DIRECT INVESTMENT IN THE UNITED STATES.

EXPANSIONISTIC PRICING a radical form of PENETRATION PRICING. It differs only in that the price will be even lower in an attempt to secure a larger share of the potential buyers at extremely low prices. This strategy is considered suitable for MULTINATIONAL COMPANIES doing business in LESS-DEVELOPED COUNTRIES (LDC).

EXPAT *see* EXPATRIATE.

EXPATRIATE any person working and/or living outside his/her own country. This individual is normally a professional or management employee relocated from one country for employment in another.

EXPATRIATE ALLOWANCE a supplementary payment made to an employee for accepting an international assignment. *see also* COMPLETION ALLOWANCE; DANGER PAY; EXPATRIATE; EXPATRIATE PREMIUM; FOREIGN SERVICE PREMIUM; HARDSHIP ALLOWANCE.

EXPATRIATE FAILURE the early return of an EXPATRIATE to his/her HOME COUNTRY before his/her period of assignment has concluded.

EXPATRIATE PREMIUM *see* EXPATRIATE ALLOWANCE.

EXPIRATION DATE the date by which the complete set of documents required in the LETTER OF CREDIT, without DISCREPANCIES, must be presented to the ADVISING BANK. There is no way of correcting the discrepancy of presenting the documents late. The letter of credit will then be valid only if the buyer accepts the documents with the discrepancy.

EXPIRY DATE *see* EXPIRATION DATE.

EXPLORATION PHASE the phase during which a firm is evaluating an investment involving mineral or natural resource development in a less than developed or developing country. To encourage U.S. investment in this sector, the OVERSEAS PRIVATE INVESTMENT CORPORATION (OPIC) provides insurance covering intangible costs as well as tangible assets. OPIC provides coverage against CURRENCY INCONVERTIBILITY, EXPROPRIATION, and POLITICAL VIOLENCE during the exploration phase. *see also* DEVELOPMENT PHASE.

EXPORT sending or transporting goods out of a country for sale in another country. In international sales, the EXPORTER is usually the seller or the seller's agent. *see also* DIRECT EXPORT; INDIRECT EXPORT; IMPORT.

EXPORT ABC'S a weekly column appearing every Friday on the Export Opportunities page of the JOURNAL OF COMMERCE. It examines important considerations to successful exporting, such as government regulations, labeling rules, and shipping insurance.

EXPORT ADMINISTRATION *see* EXPORT ADMINISTRATION ACT.

EXPORT ADMINISTRATION ACT (EAA) U.S. law passed in 1979, as amended, authorizing the president to control exports of U.S. goods and technology to all foreign destinations, as necessary for the purpose of national security, foreign policy, and short supply.

 As the basic EXPORT administration statute, the EAA is the first big revision of export control law since enactment of the U.S. Export Control Act of 1949. The EAA is not a permanent legislation; it must be reauthorized—usually every 3 years. There have been reauthorizations of the EAA in 1982, 1985 (the EXPORT ADMINISTRATION AMENDMENTS ACT), and 1988 (Omnibus Amendments of 1988) that have changed provisions of the basic act.

EXPORT ADMINISTRATION REGULATIONS (EAR) U.S. EXPORT regulations providing specific instructions on the use and types of licenses required and the types of COMMODITIES and technical data under control.

EXPORT AND IMPORTS PERMITS ACT Canadian legislation establishing the basis of authority for government control of exports out of and imports into Canada. *see also* AREA CONTROL LIST; EXPORT CONTROL LIST (ECL); IMPORT CONTROL LIST.

EXPORT ASSISTANCE CENTER (EAC) system established by the state of Texas to link agencies, associations, and local governments in efforts to increase exports by assisting current and prospective exporters. The U.S. AND FOREIGN COMMERCIAL SERVICE overseas posts has been considering using the Texas model to develop similar EXPORT assistance networks.

EXPORT BROKER an individual or company that brings together buyers and sellers for a fee but does not take part in actual sales transactions.

EXPORT BULLETIN a weekly account of U.S. cargoes departing U.S. ports appearing in the JOURNAL OF COMMERCE. The report provides information on who is shipping what to where from 47 U.S. ports to markets around the world.

EXPORT BUYER a domestic-based marketing intermediary who purchases for goods for sales to customers in other countries. This term is often used when referring to an intermediary who purchases closeout or discontinued items. *see also* INDIRECT EXPORTING.

EXPORT CARRIER the vessel on which a COMMODITY is EXPORTED from the United States to another country. In the event that the shipment is made via rail, truck, or airplane, the export carrier then means the rail car, truck, or airplane.

EXPORT CLEARANCE Part 786 of the U.S. EXPORT ADMINISTRATION REGULATIONS. This section covers procedures that must be followed to clear outgoing shipments through CUSTOMS and to assure that the validated EXPORT LICENSE is properly used. Additional topics included in this section include using the validated license, the SHIPPER'S EXPORT DECLARATION, conformity of shipping documents, DESTINATION CONTROL STATEMENTS, and SHIPPING TOLERANCES.

EXPORT COMMISSION HOUSE an organization that, for a commission, acts as a purchasing agent for a FOREIGN BUYER. *see also* EXPORT BUYER; INDIRECT EXPORTING.

EXPORT CONTACT LIST SERVICE (ECLS) an INTERNATIONAL TRADE ADMINISTRATION (ITA) service that provides mailing lists of prospective overseas customers from ITA's file of foreign firms (the Foreign Traders Index). The ECLS identifies manufacturers, distributors, retailers, service firms, and government agencies. A summary of the information on the company includes contact information, product and service interests, and other data.

EXPORT CONTROL AUTOMATED SUPPORT SYSTEM (ECASS) automated EXPORT control support system implemented by the U.S. DEPARTMENT OF COMMERCE in 1985 to replace a paper-based system. The system currently provides
- electronic submission of application forms directly with the use of value-added network vendors.
- optical character recognition of applications submitted on paper; paperless workstations for all licensing officers to review the application, route it to other officers, branches, or external agencies, and to enter their final action along with most riders and conditions.
- automated audit of all licenses issued.
- real time management reporting on Licensing Officer workloads, average processing times, counts and times by license type, destination country, COMMODITY code, and other data.

EXPORT CONTROL CLASSIFICATION NUMBER (ECCN)
(formerly Export Control Commodity Number) a five-character number for every EXPORT product that identifies the category, product group, type of control, and country group level of control as specified in the U.S. COMMERCE CONTROL LIST.

EXPORT CONTROL COMMODITY NUMBER *see* EXPORT CONTROL CLASSIFICATION NUMBER.

EXPORT CONTROL LIST (ECL) a list of all Canadian goods subject to EXPORT CONTROL by means of an EXPORT PERMIT. *see also* EXPORT AND IMPORT PERMITS ACT.

EXPORT CONTROLS
1. governmental restrictions on goods leaving the country. The reasons given for the imposition of these controls are national security, foreign policy, and short supply.
2. a type of INTERNATIONAL COMMODITY AGREEMENT.

EXPORT COUNSELING term used when referring to assistance given Canadian EXPORTERS through the International Trade Centers of the Department of External Affairs and International Trade Canada.

EXPORT CREDIT
1. special delayed payment terms or financial facilities offered to FOREIGN BUYERS.
2. programs providing financing to help businesses compete more effectively and expand or develop EXPORT markets. *see also* EXPORT–IMPORT BANK OF THE UNITED STATES (EXIMBANK); OVERSEAS PRIVATE INVESTMENT CORPORATION (OPIC).

EXPORT CREDIT ENHANCED LEVERAGE (EXCEL) program developed in 1990 by the WORLD BANK in conjunction with a working group of the International Union of Credit and Investment Insurers (the BERNE UNION). The objective of EXCEL is to provide EXPORT CREDITS at consensus rates for private sector borrowers in highly indebted countries, which would previously have been too great a risk for most agencies to cover.

EXPORT CREDIT GUARANTEE DEPARTMENT (ECGD) a part of the British Department of Industry and Trade, the ECGD is the primary source of official government EXPORT credit. The ECGD helps exporters by providing
- insurance against the risk of not being paid for exports and
- guarantees to banks for exporters of capital goods, under which finance can be obtained for EXPORT business, often at a favorable rate of interest.

Subject to Parliamentary approval, ECGD's short-term underwriting division, the Insurance Service Group, is to be privatized. The medium- and long-term underwriting group is introducing a new system for assessing premiums that will more realistically reflect the risk involved. The department was originally established in 1919, and its headquarters is in London, England.

EXPORT CREDIT GUARANTEE PROGRAMS *see* GENERAL SALES MANAGER.

EXPORT DECLARATION a formal statement made to the Director of CUSTOMS at a port of exit declaring full particulars about goods being exported. *see also* SHIPPER'S EXPORT DECLARATION.

EXPORT DEVELOPMENT CORPORATION (EDC) Canada's official EXPORT credit agency, responsible for providing export credit insurance, loans, guarantees, and other financial services to promote Canadian export trade.

EXPORT DEVELOPMENT OFFICE (EDO) offices staffed by U.S. AND FOREIGN COMMERCIAL SERVICE officers in seven cities (Tokyo, Sydney, Seoul, Milan, London, Mexico City, and Sao Paulo) to provide services to U.S. exporters. EDOs perform market research to identify specific marketing opportunities and products with the greatest sales potential and to organize EXPORT promotion events. When not in use for trade exhibitions, EDOs with exhibit and conference facilities are made available to individual firms or associations.

EXPORT DISINCENTIVES policies that may serve to deter U.S. EXPORTS, such as TRADE SANCTIONS, export controls, and domestic and regulatory policies having a coincidental impact of handicapping U.S. competitiveness.

EXPORT DRAFT an order for the IMPORTING party to pay the seller for the EXPORTED goods. *see also* BILL OF EXCHANGE; DATE DRAFT; D/A SIGHT DRAFT (DOCUMENTS (AGAINST) ACCEPTANCE SIGHT DRAFT) DOCUMENTS AGAINST ACCEPTANCE; DOCUMENTS AGAINST PAYMENT; SIGHT DRAFT.

EXPORT DUTY a tax imposed on exports by the government authorities of a country. *see also* EXPORT LEVY.

EXPORT EDUCATION a term used when referring to training programs coordinated through a Canadian International Trade Center to instruct firms in the development and implementation of basic EXPORT marketing plans, which show where and how to sell goods.

EXPORT ENHANCEMENT ACT OF 1992 a U.S. Statute requiring the TRADE PROMOTION COORDINATING COMMITTEE (TPCC) to issue an annual report containing "a government wide strategic plan for U.S. federal trade promotion efforts" including a description of its implementation. The legislation requires the TPCC to establish in its strategic plan priorities for federal trade promotion and explain the rationale for these priorities. The act also requires the TPCC to include in the plan a strategy for bringing federal trade promotion activities into line with the new priorities and for improving their coordination. The TPCC is further required to propose in the plan a means for eliminating overlap among federal trade promotion activities and increasing cooperation between state and federal trade promotion efforts.

The act requires that the TPCC include in its strategic plan a proposal to the U.S. President for an annual unified budget for federal trade promotion activities. This budget is to

- reflect the new priorities and improved interagency coordination, and
- eliminate funding for areas of overlap and duplication among federal agencies.

EXPORT ENHANCEMENT PROGRAM (EEP) one of four EXPORT subsidy programs operated by the U.S. Department of Agriculture. It is intended to enhance U.S. trade policy strategies and objectives and to expand U.S. agricultural exports. Under the EEP, the Agriculture Department's COMMODITY CREDIT CORPORATION provides bonuses to U.S. exporters to enable them to be price competitive and thereby sell U.S. agricultural products in targeted overseas markets in which competitor countries are making subsidized sales. EEP-eligible COMMODITIES have included wheat, wheat flour, rice, frozen poultry, barley, barley malt, table eggs, feed grains, and vegetable oil.

EXPORT FINANCING *see* EXPORT CREDIT.

EXPORT HOUSE either a buying agent or merchant. An EXPORT merchant purchases goods for his/her own account, takes TITLE, and sells them. As an export agent who retains the role of principal throughout the transaction, the export house promotes the EXPORTER'S products overseas, assumes the credit risk of the FOREIGN BUYER, and coordinates all the physical and clerical responsibilities associated with the shipment. *see also* EXPORT COMMISSION HOUSE.

EXPORT–IMPORT BANK OF JAPAN (JEXIM) Japan's official provider of EXPORT CREDITS. About 10% of JEXIM's business is providing export credits. The bank's main role is to disburse about half the funds available under the trade surplus recycling program (the Nakasone facility). *see also* JAPAN INTERNATIONAL COOPERATION AGENCY; OVERSEAS ECONOMIC COOPERATION FUND.

EXPORT–IMPORT BANK OF THE UNITED STATES (EXIMBANK) an independent U.S. agency chartered in 1934 to finance the EXPORT of U.S. goods and services. EXIMBANK offers four major export finance support programs: loans, guarantees, working capital guarantees, and insurance. EXIMBANK undertakes some of the risk associated with financing the production and sale of American-made goods. It provides financing to overseas customers for American goods when lenders are not prepared to finance the transactions; and enhances a U.S. EXPORTER'S ability to match foreign government subsidies by helping lenders meet lower rates, or by giving financing incentives directly to foreign buyers. *see also* PRIVATE EXPORT FUNDING CORPORATION (PEFCO).

EXPORT INCENTIVE programs and certain tax procedures that open new markets or provide financial benefits to EXPORTERS. *see also* DOMESTIC INTERNATIONAL SALES CORPORATION (DISC); DUTY DRAWBACK; FOREIGN SALES CORPORATIONS (FSC); FOREIGN TRADE ZONES (FTZ).

EXPORT INFORMATION SYSTEM (EIS) a classified automated information system for EXPORT licensing operations maintained by the U.S. Department of Energy. *see also* EXPORT CONTROL AUTOMATED SUPPORT SYSTEM.

EXPORT INSTABILITY fluctuations in EXPORT earnings and prices for goods and services due primarily to changes in the economic and political/legal environment. *see also* FLUCTUATING EXCHANGE RATES.

EXPORT INSURANCE a policy taken out by EXPORTERS enabling them to reduce the COMMERCIAL RISKS (such as buyer insolvency or failure to pay) and POLITICAL RISKS (such as war or CURRENCY INCONVERTIBILITY). *see also* EXPORT DEVELOPMENT CORPORATION; EXPORT–IMPORT BANK OF THE UNITED STATES (EXIMBANK); FOREIGN CREDIT INSURANCE ASSOCIATION (FCIA).

EXPORT JOBBER a domestic-based marketing intermediary who purchases and takes TITLE to goods and resells them to FOREIGN BUYERS without taking possession of the goods. The goods move directly from the supplier to the buyer. *see also* INDIRECT EXPORTING.

EXPORT LEGAL ASSISTANCE NETWORK (ELAN) an American group of attorneys with experience in international trade who provide free initial consultations to small businesses on EXPORT-related matters. It is sponsored by the U.S. Small Business Administration.

EXPORT LEVY *see* EXPORT DUTY.

EXPORT LICENSE
1. a government document (also known as an INDIVIDUALLY VALIDATED LICENSE) authorizing EXPORTS of specific goods in specific quantities to a particular destination. This document may be required in some countries for most or all exports and in other countries only under special circumstances.
2. a permit required to engage in the export of certain commodities and quantities to certain destinations. The list of such goods is found in the comprehensive Export Schedule issued by the U.S. Bureau of Foreign Commerce.

EXPORT LICENSE NUMBER a number assigned to an INDIVIDUALLY VALIDATED LICENSE authorizing EXPORTS of specific goods in specific quantities to a specific destination.

EXPORT LICENSE VOICE INFORMATION SYSTEM (ELVIS) a U.S. BUREAU OF EXPORT ADMINISTRATION (BXA) 24-hour on-line service that allows EXPORTERS to obtain recorded information on such topics as COMMODITY classifications, emergency handling procedures, and seminars as well as to order information.

EXPORT LIMITATION a provision that limits the recipient country's volume of exports of COMMODITIES that are the same as, or like, the commodities being furnished by the United States under P.L. 480 (FOOD FOR PEACE) sales agreement. The EXPORT of the actual commodities is also prohibited, with the latter prohibition being termed an export restriction.

EXPORT LIMITATION PERIOD the period during which the recipient country must restrict exports of COMMODITIES that are considered to be the same as, or like, those supplied under P.L. 480 (FOOD FOR PEACE).

EXPORT MANAGEMENT COMPANY (EMC) a private company that serves as the EXPORT department for several manufacturers, soliciting and transacting export business on behalf of its clients in return for a commission, salary, or retainer plus commission. An EMC maintains close contact with its clients and is supply-driven. An EMC may take title to the goods it sells, making a profit on the markup, or it may charge a commission, depending on the type of products being handled, the overseas market, and the manufacturer-client's needs.

EXPORT MANAGEMENT SYSTEM (EMS) an optional program a company can consider establishing to ensure that their EXPORTS and export decisions are consistent with EXPORT ADMINISTRATION REGULATIONS. It involves the establishment of mechanisms within the company that provide checks and safeguards at key steps in the order-processing system, helping to manage better the overall export process. The objective of the program is to preclude exporters from making shipments that are contrary to U.S. export controls and therefore inconsistent with the company's best interests.

EXPORT MERCHANT
1. a producer or merchant who sells directly to a foreign purchaser without going through an intermediate such as an EXPORT BROKER.
2. a company that buys products directly from manufacturers and then packages and marks the merchandise for resale under its own name.

EXPORT OPPORTUNITIES BULLETIN a column appearing daily in the JOURNAL OF COMMERCE. It consists of EXPORT trade leads taken from U.S. DEPARTMENT OF COMMERCE publications and provides information on the product description, the name and address of the overseas buyer, and the address of the foreign commercial officer at the U.S. Embassy. *see also* TRADE OPPORTUNITIES PROGRAM (TOP).

EXPORT-ORIENTED INDUSTRIALIZATION the policies and practices of developing nations of increasing the EXPORT of primary products (agricultural and raw materials) but aggressively promoting the exporting of manufactured goods, as an important part of their development strategy.

EXPORT PACKERS firms involved in the preparation of goods for EXPORT. *see also* CONTAINERIZATION; PALLETIZATION; SHRINK WRAPPING.

EXPORT PERMIT *see* EXPORT LICENSE.

EXPORT PESSIMISM a term used to describe the expectations of less than developed countries that an EXPORT-ORIENTED INDUSTRIALIZATION program will not be successful in its development strategies because of the increasing protectionist and technological practices of developed countries.

EXPORT PROCESSING ZONE (EPZ) a form of FREE-TRADE ZONE that provides incentives for industrial or commercial EXPORT activity. Export processing zones are located in developing countries and are usually in defined areas, industrial parks, or facilities that provide free-trade zone benefits and usually offer additional incentives, such as exemption from normal tax and business regulations. The zones, which began appearing around 1975, are sometimes referred to as SPECIAL ECONOMIC ZONES or Development Economic Zones. *see also* FOREIGN TRADE ZONE.

EXPORT PROMOTION SERVICES (EPS) the collective programs a nation has to help companies sell products abroad. These programs may include business counseling, training, and representational assistance, as well as market research information, trade fair opportunities, and EXPORT financing assistance.

EXPORT QUOTAS specific restrictions or target objectives on the value or volume of exports of specified goods imposed by the government of the exporting country. These restraints may be intended to protect domestic producers and consumers from temporary shortages of certain materials or as a means to moderate world prices of specified COMMODITIES. Commodity agreements sometimes contain explicit provisions to indicate when EXPORT quotas should go into effect among producers. Export quotas are also used in connection with orderly marketing agreements and voluntary restraint agreements.

EXPORT RATE a freight rate specially established for application on EXPORT traffic and generally lower than the domestic rate.

EXPORT RESTRAINT AGREEMENTS *see* VOLUNTARY RESTRAINT AGREEMENTS.

EXPORT RESTRAINTS restrictions on the number of EXPORTS that are allotted for certain FOREIGN markets. *see also* TRADE BARRIERS; VOLUNTARY EXPORT RESTRICTION (VER); VOLUNTARY RESTRAINT AGREEMENT (VRA).

EXPORT REVOLVING LINE OF CREDIT (ERLC) a form of financial assistance provided by the U.S. *S*mall Business Administration (SBA). The ERLC guarantees loans to U.S. firms to help bridge the working capital gap between the time inventory and production costs are disbursed until payment is received from a foreign buyer. SBA guarantees 85% of the ERLC subject to a $750,000 guarantee limit. The ERLC is granted on the likelihood of a company satisfactorily completing its EXPORT transaction. The guarantee covers default by the EXPORTER but does not cover default by a foreign buyer. Failure on the buyer's side is expected to be covered by LETTERS OF CREDIT or export credit insurance.

EXPORT SALE a transaction entered into between an EXPORTER and a foreign buyer. The transaction must be in written form and include the following:
- the exporter must agree to EXPORT the COMMODITY and specify the quantity;
- the foreign buyer agrees to receive the commodity;
- a fixed price must be established; and
- the method of payment and terms of sale must be stated.

EXPORT STATISTICS a measure of the total physical quantity or value of merchandise (except for shipments to U.S. military forces overseas) moving out of the United States to foreign countries, and whether such merchandise is exported from within the U.S. Customs territory, from a U.S. Customs bonded warehouse, or from a U.S. FOREIGN TRADE ZONE.

EXPORT SUBSIDIES direct government payments or other economic inducements given to domestic producers of goods that are sold in foreign markets. The GENERAL AGREEMENT ON TARIFFS AND TRADE (GATT) recognizes that EXPORT subsidies may distort trade, unduly disturb normal commercial competition, and hinder the achievement of GATT fair trade objectives; however, it does not clearly define what practices constitute an export subsidy. *see also* SUBSIDY.

EXPORT SUPPORT PROGRAMS a variety of federal government agencies, as well as a number of state and local ones, that offer programs to assist exporters with their financing needs. Some are guarantee programs that require the participation of an approved lender; others provide loans or grants to the EXPORTER or a foreign government. The aim of the programs is to improve exporters' access to credit rather than to subsidize the cost at below market levels. *see also* EXPORT–IMPORT BANK OF THE UNITED STATES (EXIMBANK); OVERSEAS PRIVATE INVESTMENT CORPORATION (OPIC).

EXPORT TARGETING any coordinated effort on the part of a government to increase the EXPORT competitiveness of a specific firm or industry.

EXPORT TARIFF *see* EXPORT DUTY.

EXPORT TAX a tax on exports. *see also* EXPORT DUTY; LEVY.

EXPORT TRADE CERTIFICATE OF REVIEW a certification of partial immunity from U.S. antitrust laws that can be granted based on the EXPORT TRADING COMPANY ACT legislation by the U.S. DEPARTMENT

OF COMMERCE with U.S. Department of Justice concurrence. Any prospective or present U.S.-based EXPORTER with antitrust concerns may apply for certification.

EXPORT TRADE INFORMATION term used when referring to programs provided through the Canadian INTERNATIONAL TRADE CENTERS. The programs assist Canadian exporters in identifying and qualifying direct leads of potential buyers, distributors, and licensees from both private and public sources. The U.S. DEPARTMENT OF COMMERCE also offers similar programs to U.S. EXPORTERS. *see also* BUREAU OF SOURCING SUPPLIERS (BOSS); INTERNATIONAL TRADE DATA BANK (ITDB); TRADE PROMOTION EVENTS (TPE).

EXPORT TRADING COMPANY (ETC) a company doing business in the United States principally to EXPORT goods or services produced in the United States or to facilitate such exports by unaffiliated persons. The ETC can be owned by foreigners and can IMPORT, BARTER, and arrange sales between third countries, as well as export. An ETC is demand-driven and transaction-oriented. Generally, an ETC takes title to the products involved, but may work on a commission basis.

EXPORT TRADING COMPANY ACT OF 1982 American statute that initiates the EXPORT TRADE CERTIFICATE OF REVIEW program that provides antitrust preclearance for EXPORT activities; permitting bankers' banks and bank holding companies to invest in ETCs; establishing a Contact Facilitation Service within the U.S. DEPARTMENT OF COMMERCE designed to facilitate contact between firms that produce exportable goods and services and firms that provide export trade services.

EXPORT TRADING COMPANY MATCHMAKING PROJECT a U.S. DEPARTMENT OF COMMERCE program created to assist manufacturers and service companies in selecting the EXPORT assistance firms most appropriate for them. The project has created an extensive computerized data base of EXPORT TRADING, marketing, and consulting firms that can be used by firms to identify the export organization that is best suited to assisting them. *see also* MATCHMAKER EVENTS; MATCHMAKER SERVICES; MATCHMAKER TRADE DELEGATIONS.

EXPORTER an individual, manufacturer, intermediary, or merchant who sells and/or ships goods and services to a foreign IMPORTER.

EXPORTER COUNSELING DIVISION (ECD) a division of the U.S. BUREAU OF EXPORT ADMINISTRATION (BXA) responsible for providing information to U.S. EXPORTERS on rules and regulation pertaining to the shipment of U.S. goods to other countries.

EXPORTER DATA BASE (EDB) a data base, operating on a pilot basis since 1992, developed by the U.S. Commerce Department's INTERNATIONAL TRADE ADMINISTRATION (ITA) and the U.S. CENSUS BUREAU. The EDB links COMMODITY data from millions of U.S. EXPORT declarations to the bureau's various databases on the business characteristics of U.S. firms. It provides data on the number of exporters, their distribution in cities and states, and their economic characteristics.

EXPORTER'S CERTIFICATE OF ORIGIN a document completed by the EXPORTER certifying that the goods described therein are eligible for a preferential rate of DUTY under some trade program such as the NORTH AMERICAN FREE TRADE AGREEMENT (NAFTA).

EXPORTER'S EMPLOYER IDENTIFICATION NUMBER same as the EXPORTER'S U.S. Internal Revenue Service Employer Identification Number. If no such number has been assigned to an individual exporter, that individual's social security number, preceded by the symbol SS, is applicable. *see also* SHIPPER'S EXPORT DECLARATION.

EXPORTER'S SALES PRICE (ESP) a statutory term used to refer to the United States sales prices of merchandise that is sold or is likely to be sold in the United States, before or after the time of importation, by or for the account of the EXPORTER. Certain statutory adjustments are made to permit a meaningful comparison with the foreign market value of such or similar merchandise (e.g., IMPORT DUTIES). U.S. Selling and administrative expenses and freight are deducted from the U.S. price. *see also* TARIFF ACT OF 1930.

EXPORTS FOR EXPORTER'S OWN ACCOUNT a transaction involving a shipment made by an EXPORTER that is unsold at time of shipment. Example: shipments on CONSIGNMENT to a selling agent of the exporter.

EXPOSURE NETTING *see* NETTING.

EXPROPRIATION government seizure of foreign-owned assets. Such seizure is not contrary to international law as long as just and fair compensation is promptly paid. *see also* CONFISCATION; NATIONALIZATION.

EXTENDED FUND FACILITY (EFF) an arrangement by which the INTERNATIONAL MONETARY FUND (IMF) may provide assistance to its members to enable them to meet their BALANCE OF PAYMENTS (BOP) needs for longer periods and in larger amounts than are available under the IMF's CREDIT TRANCHE policies.

EXTERNAL AFFAIRS AND INTERNATIONAL TRADE CANADA (EAITC) new title given to the Canadian DEPARTMENT OF EXTERNAL AFFAIRS. The purpose of the EAITC is to assist in the worldwide development and implementation of international trade policy in Canada.

EXTERNAL DEBT
  1. the international financial obligations of a firm. *see also* FOREIGN DEBT; FOREIGN DEBT LOAD; INTERNATIONAL DEBT; INTERNATIONAL DEBT LOAD.

2. the U.S. dollar financial obligations owed by governments to international financial institutions (i.e., the World Bank), governments, and private banks.

EXTERNAL TRADE ACT OF 1987 legislation enabling the Korean government to deal more effectively with the dynamic trade environment both at home and abroad. The legislation provided for a gradual transition toward a free and open trading system, a reduction of EXPORT and IMPORT restrictions and protection of FAIR TRADE.

EXTERNAL VALUE purchasing power of a currency abroad that is converted using the exchange rate. *see also* CONVERTIBLE CURRENCY; HARD CURRENCY; SOFT CURRENCY.

EXTINCTION PRICING a pricing strategy used by large low-cost producers to deliberately reduce prices so as to eliminate weaker existing competitors from international markets. *see also* EXPANSIONISTIC PRICING; PENETRATION PRICING.

EXTRADITION the mechanism by which individuals either charged or convicted of a crime are returned to the country from which they have fled. *see also* EXTRADITION TREATY.

EXTRADITION TREATY a signed agreement between countries to return to the country from which individuals either charged or convicted of a crime have fled.

EXTRANET secure private network that uses INTERNET protocols and the public telecommunication system to share part of a business's information or operations with suppliers, vendors, partners, customers, or other businesses. An extranet can be viewed as part of a company's INTRANET that is extended to users outside the company. The same benefits that web technologies have brought to corporate intranets are now starting to accelerate business among other businesses.

Extranets can be used to exchange large volumes of data, share product catalogs and news with trading partners, collaborate with other companies on joint development efforts, develop joint training programs with other companies, and provide or access applications among companies.

EXTRATERRITORIAL APPLICATION OF LAWS attempts by a government to extend the application of its laws outside its territorial borders. *see also* EXTRATERRITORIALITY.

EXTRATERRITORIALITY a situation whereby a government extends the application of its laws to the citizens or the foreign operations of a company. *see also* EFFECTS DOCTRINE.

EXW *see* EX WORKS.

F

F-1 VISA a specialized term used to describe a VISA required by a foreign student for entry into the United States.

F2F face to face (E-MAIL abbreviation). An actual meeting between those who have been corresponding on the INTERNET.

F/A abbreviation for free astray.

F.A.A. abbreviation for free of all average.

FAAS *see* FOREIGN AFFAIRS ADMINISTRATIVE SUPPORT.

FACET *see* FUTURE AUTOMATED COMMERCIAL ENVIRONMENT TEAM.

FACILITATING INTERMEDIARY an individual or firm who provides services or makes arrangements for expediting the shipment to its overseas destination. Examples: financial institutions (i.e., banks), CUSTOMS HOUSE BROKERS, FREIGHT FORWARDERS, and insurance companies.

FACILITATION any program designed to expedite the flow of international commerce.

FACILITY LICENSE license permitting firms in the United States or abroad to provide prompt service for equipment exported from the United States; produced abroad by a subsidiary, affiliate, or branch of a U.S. firm; or produced abroad by a manufacturer who uses parts imported from the United States in the manufactured product. For complete information see Section 773.7 of the U.S. Export Administration Regulations. *see also* BUREAU OF EXPORT ADMINISTRATION (BXA); EXPORT LICENSE; INDIVIDUALLY VALIDATED LICENSE; SERVICE SUPPLY LICENSE.

FACTOR a financial institution that specializes in the financing of accounts receivable. *see also* FACTORING; FACTORING HOUSES; FORFAITING.

FACTOR ENDOWMENT a country has or does not have one or more of the factors of production—land, labor, or capital.

FACTOR MOBILITY the free movement across borders of economic resources that go into the production of goods. These factors include
* property resources including land,
* human resources including labor, and
* capital.

FACTORAGE commission or other compensation paid to a FACTOR. *see also* FACTORING; FACTORING HOUSE; FACTOR'S LIEN; FORFAITING.

FACTORING the DISCOUNTING of a foreign account receivable that does not involve a DRAFT. The EXPORTER transfers title to its foreign accounts receivable to a factoring house for cash at a discount from the face value. Factoring is often done without recourse to the exporter. EXPORT factoring allows an exporter to ship on OPEN ACCOUNT, by which goods are shipped without guarantee of payment, that is, a LETTER OF CREDIT. The FACTOR assumes financial ability of the customer to pay and handles collections on the receivables. *see also* FACTORING HOUSES; FORFAITING.

FACTORING HOUSES certain companies that purchase EXPORT receivables (e.g., INVOICES to foreign buyers), at a discounted price, usually about 2% to 4% less than their face value.

FACTOR'S LIEN right of a FACTOR to retain the principal's merchandise until the factor receives full compensation from the principal. *see also* FACTORAGE; FACTORING; FACTORING HOUSE; FORFAITING.

FACTORY DOOR COST the cost to produce a product that does not add any marketing or general administration costs.

FAIR PRICE the price to which the EXPORT price is compared in ANTIDUMPING cases which is either the price charged in the exporter's own domestic market or some measure of their cost, both adjusted to include any transportation cost and tariff needed to enter the importing country's market. *see also* DUMPING; GENERAL AGREEMENT ON TARIFFS AND TRADE (GATT).

FAIR TRADE *see* UNFAIR TRADE.

FAIR TRADING ACT OF 1986 legislation passed in New Zealand that prohibits any person from trading in a manner that is misleading or deceptive or that is likely to mislead or deceive. The Fair Trading Act also deals with product safety standards, consumer information standards, and safety of services in New Zealand.

FAIR VALUE the reference against which U.S. purchase prices of imported merchandise are compared during an ANTIDUMPING INVESTIGATION. Generally expressed as the weighted average of the EXPORTER's domestic market prices, or prices of exports to third countries during the period of investigation.

In some cases fair value is the CONSTRUCTED VALUE. Constructed value is used if there are no, or virtually no, home market or third-country sales or if the number of such sales made at prices below the cost of production is so great that remaining sales above the cost of production provide an inadequate basis for comparison. *see also* TARIFF ACT OF 1930.

FAK *see* FREIGHT ALL KINDS.

FALKLAND ISLAND POUND unit of currency, Falkland Islands (100 pence equal 1 Falkland Island pound)

FALLOUT the descent to the earth's surface of particles contaminated with radioactive material from a radioactive cloud.

FAM TOUR familiarization tour for travel agents or journalists planned and executed by a destination or region, usually in cooperation with an international airline.

FAO *see* FOOD AND AGRICULTURE ORGANIZATION.

FARNET a nonprofit corporation, established in 1987, whose mission is to advance the use of computer NETWORKS to improve research and education.

FAS *see* FOREIGN AGRICULTURAL SERVICE; FREE ALONGSIDE SHIP.

FASB *see* FINANCIAL ACCOUNTING STANDARDS BOARD.

FAST TRACK procedures for approval of trade agreements were included by Congress in trade legislation in 1974, in 1979, and again in the 1988 Trade Act. Fast track provides two guarantees essential to the successful negotiation of trade agreements:
- a vote on implementing legislation within a fixed period of time and
- a vote, up or down, with no amendments to that legislation.

Provisions in the U.S. OMNIBUS TRADE ACT OF 1988 include that the foreign country request negotiation of an FTA and that the president give the Congress a 60-legislative-day notice of intent to negotiate an FTA. During the 60-legislative-day period, a committee can disapprove fast track authority by a majority vote. Disapproval would likely end the possibility of FTA negotiations. The 60 legislative days can translate into 5 to 10 months of calendar time, depending on the congressional schedule. Formal negotiations would begin following this 60-day congressional consideration period.

FATAH political organization created in the 1960s and led by Yasser Arafat.

FATWA a legal ruling regarding Islamic Law.

FAVORABLE CONSIDERATION a COCOM review policy under which an application for the application of EXPORT of eligible items will be subject to a 4-week COCOM review period with a presumption of approval unless specific objections are raised at the proposed transaction.

FAX an electronic device used to transmit printed documents over phone or electronic wire; derived from facsimile transmission. *see also* TELEX.

FAZ *see* FOREIGN ACCESS ZONE.

FBIS *see* FOREIGN BROADCAST INFORMATION SERVICE.

FBP *see* FOREIGN BUYER PROGRAM.

FBSEA *see* FOREIGN BANK SUPERVISION ENHANCEMENT ACT.

FCA *see* FREE CARRIER (FCA) TO A NAMED PLACE.

FC&S *see* FREE OF CAPTURE AND SEIZURE.

FCIA *see* FOREIGN CREDIT INSURANCE ASSOCIATION.

FCIB *see* FOREIGN CREDIT INTERCHANGE BUREAU.

FCIL *see* FOREIGN CAPITAL INDUCEMENT LAW.

FCN *see* FRIENDSHIP, COMMERCE, AND NAVIGATION TREATY.

FCO *see* FOREIGN AND COMMONWEALTH OFFICE.

FCPA *see* FOREIGN CORRUPT PRACTICES ACT.

F.C. & S. *see* FREE OF CAPTURE AND SEIZURE.

FCSC *see* FOREIGN CLAIMS SETTLEMENT COMMISSION.

F.D. abbreviation for free discharge.

FDIUS *see* FOREIGN DIRECT INVESTMENT IN THE UNITED STATES.

FEASIBILITY STUDIES (FSs) *see* TRADE AND DEVELOPMENT AGENCY.

FECA *see* FOREIGN EXCHANGE CONTROL ACT.

FEDERACION MUNDIAL DE INSTITUCIONES FINANCIERAS DE DESAROLLO (FEMIDE) *see* WORLD FEDERATION OF DEVELOPMENT FINANCING INSTITUTIONS.

FEDERAL GRAIN INSPECTION SERVICE (FGIS) U.S. agency responsible for certifying that grain produced in the United States meets the official U.S. standards for grain. As part of its responsibilities, FGIS works with international traders. Before any grain can be exported from the United States, it must first be certified by FGIS as having met a specific standard. FGIS staff explain the national inspection system, U.S. grain standards, and COMMODITY inspection programs; conduct briefings and tours; assess foreign inspection and weighing techniques; and respond to inquiries about quality and quantity of U.S. grain exports. FGIS agencies in eight states are delegated authority to perform official EXPORT services at ports.

FEDERAL INFORMATION EXCHANGE (FIX) one of the junctions between the American governmental internets and the INTERNET.

FEDERAL INSPECTION SITE location at which international merchandise is processed and inspected by one or more federal agencies. *see also* CUSTOMS; U.S. CUSTOMS SERVICE.

FEDERAL MARITIME COMMISSION (FMC) an independent U.S. agency that regulates oceanborne transportation in the foreign commerce and in the domestic offshore trade of the United States.

FEDERAL NETWORKING COUNCIL (FNC) the coordinating group of representatives from those U.S. federal agencies involved in the development and use of federal networking, especially those networks using TCP/IP and the INTERNET. Current members include representatives from U.S. Departments of Defense and Energy, DEFENSE ADVANCED RESEARCH PROJECTS AGENCY, National Science Foundation, NASA, and Health and Human Services.

FEDERAL OPERATIONS TAX (IOF) a federal tax imposed by the government of Brazil on loans, insurance polices, and short-term security and investment fund investments and on the closing of certain exchange contracts for services.

FEDERAL RESERVE SYSTEM the CENTRAL BANK of the United States and the coordinator of MONETARY POLICY. *see also* FISCAL POLICY; MONEY SUPPLY.

FEDERAL TRADE COMMISSION (FTC) independent U.S. regulatory agency established in 1914 as a companion piece of legislation to the CLAYTON ANTITRUST ACT. The FTC has the responsibility of preventing restrictive trade practices by enforcing antitrust laws, preventing false and deceptive advertising, regulating the labeling and packaging of commodities, and collecting data concerning business conditions and making it available to Congress, the president, and the public. The FTC has the authority to request relevant trade information from corporations, to issue cease-and-desist orders, and to prosecute violators.

FEDERATION INTERNATIONALE DES ASSOCIATIONES DE TRANSITAIRES (FIATA) *see* INTERNATIONAL AIR TRANSPORT ASSOCIATION (IATA).

FEEDER VESSEL vessel used to connect to a line vessel that directly services a port. *see also* LINE HAUL; LINE HAUL VESSEL.

FEES payments made to individuals or firms for the performance of certain services abroad.

FEMA *see* FOREIGN EXTRATERRITORIAL MEASURES ACT OF 1984.

FEOID *see* FOREIGN EXCHANGE OPERATIONS AND INVESTMENT DEPARTMENT.

FETs *see* FOREIGN ECONOMIC TRENDS.

FEU forty-foot (12.2 m) equivalent units—two 20-foot (6.1 m) CONTAINERS = 1 FEU.

F.F.A. abbreviation for free from average.

FFP *see* FOOD FOR PROGRESS.

FGIS *see* FEDERAL GRAIN INSPECTION SERVICE.

FI *see* FREE IN.

F.I.A. abbreviation for full interest admitted.

FIAS *see* FOREIGN INVESTMENT ADVISORY SERVICE.

FIBER DISTRIBUTED DATA INTERFACE (FDDI) a high-performance (100Mb/s) LOCAL AREA NETWORK standard. Fiber optics is used with a version of TOKEN RING.

FICTITIOUS VALUE an assumed or imaginary value. A fictitious or arbitrary value cannot be used in determining the value of the goods for customs purposes. *see also* ARBITRARY VALUE; COMPUTED VALUE; DEDUCTIVE VALUE; TRANSACTION VALUE.

FIDEICOMISOS (FEE TRUSTS) the mechanism in laws created by the National Foreign Investment Commission of Mexico allowing increased foreign participation in industry sectors where Mexican laws restrict foreign DIRECT INVESTMENT.

FII *see* FOREIGN INVESTMENT INSURANCE.

FIJI DOLLAR unit of currency, Fiji Islands (100 cents equal 1 Fiji dollar).

FILE SERVER
1. a computer that functions to develop information about international trade and transportation through the compilation and analysis of statistical data.
2. a computer/storage device dedicated to storing files. Any user on the NETWORK can store files on the server.

FILE TRANSFER the copying of a file from one computer to another over a computer network. *see also* FILE TRANSFER PROTOCOL; KERMIT.

FILE TRANSFER PROTOCOL (FTP) a computer PROTOCOL that allows a user on one host to access and transfer files to and from another host over a network. Also, FTP is usually the name of the program the user invokes to execute the protocol on the INTERNET.

FILER
1. the process of issuing a user identification and password along with the other necessary security identifiers; also, unique user identification.
2. the entity responsible for submission of data to the government; names and addresses of parties licensed to act as representatives in the transaction of business (ITDS Standard Data Set).

FILIAL AV UTENLANDSK AKSJESELSKAP a branch of a foreign company or corporation in Norway.

FINAL DETERMINATION decision made by the INTERNATIONAL TRADE ADMINISTRATION after an investigation whether an EXPORTER'S sales are at less than FAIR VALUE. This determination usually is made within 75 days after the date a preliminary determination is made. If the final determination is affirmative and follows a negative preliminary determination, the matter is referred to the INTERNATIONAL TRADE COMMISSION for a determination of the injury caused or threatened by the sales at less than fair value. Where the preliminary determination was negative, the ITC must render a decision not later than 75 days after the affirmative final determination. A negative final determination by the U.S. Assistant Secretary for Import Administration terminates an ANTIDUMPING INVESTIGATION. *see also* TARIFF ACT OF 1930.

FINAL TRADE GOODS term used when referring to the goods that are the result of a processing activity taking place in an EXPORT PROCESSING ZONE.

FINANCED EXPORT OPPORTUNITIES a U.S. AGENCY FOR INTERNATIONAL DEVELOPMENT (AID) publication that provides pertinent details of individual proposed procurements under formal competitive bid procedures, usually required by foreign country public sector agencies.

FINANCIAL ACCOUNTING STANDARDS BOARD the organization responsible for the setting of financial accounting standards in the United States.

FINANCIAL DOCUMENTS refers to BILLS OF EXCHANGE, DRAFTS, promissory notes, checks, or any other instrument used for the obtaining payment of money.

FINANCIAL INSTITUTION *see* BANK.

FINANCIAL INSTITUTION BUYER CREDIT POLICY a program of the EXPORT–IMPORT BANK OF THE UNITED STATES (EXIMBANK). It is a single-buyer policy insuring individual short-term loans by financial institutions to foreign buyers for the importation of U.S. goods and services.

FINANCIAL INSTRUMENT document that is evidence of a monetary transaction, such as a DRAFT, BILL, a check and a promissory note. *see also* DOCUMENTARY DRAFT; LETTER OF ASSIGNMENT; LETTER OF CREDIT (L/C); SIGHT DRAFT.

FINANCIAL RISKS *see* TRANSACTION RISK; TRANSLATION RISK.

FINES, PENALTIES, AND FORFEITURES SYSTEM (FPFS) a part of the CUSTOMS' AUTOMATED COMMERCIAL SYSTEM used to assess, control, and process penalties resulting from violations of law or Customs regulations. FPFS provides retrieval of case information for monitoring case status.

F.I.O. *see* FREE IN AND OUT.

FIRA *see* FOREIGN INVESTMENT REVIEW AGENCY.

FIREWALL protective barrier that is a collection of components configured to enforce a specific access control policy between a trusted NETWORK and an untrusted network.

FIRM SURVEILLANCE the power of the INTERNATIONAL MONETARY FUND (IMF) to oversee the EXCHANGE RATE policies of member nations.

FIRST WORLD COUNTRIES Western, industrialized, non-Communist countries. *see also* DEVELOPED COUNTRY; DEVELOPING COUNTRY; LESS-DEVELOPED COUNTRIES; LESSER-DEVELOPED COUNTRIES.

FISCAL ECONOMICS *see* KEYNESIAN ECONOMICS.

FISCAL POLICY use of government taxation and spending policies to achieve desired economic goals. *see also* MONETARY POLICY.

FISCALISM *see* KEYNESIAN ECONOMICS.

FISHER EFFECT the relationship between interest rates and inflation in two countries. Example: if the interest rates in the HOME COUNTRY were lower than those of another country, the inflation rate in the home country should also be lower, so that the real interest rates would be equal. *see also* INTERNATIONAL FISHER EFFECT (IFE).

FISHYBACK the moving of CARGO in containers via ocean liners. *see also* CONTAINERIZATION.

FIT *see* FOREIGN INDEPENDENT TOUR.

FIVE DRAGONS term used to describe the emerging economies of Hong Kong, Singapore, South Korea, Taiwan, and Thailand. *see also* FIVE TIGERS; NEWLY INDUSTRIALIZED COUNTRY.

FIVE-K COUNTRIES those countries as defined under Section 5k of the EXPORT ADMINISTRATION ACT (EAA). Such countries are eligible for some or all of the same treatment as COCOM countries in relation to EXPORT control requirements if those countries maintain comparable export control programs. *see also* COORDINATING COMMITTEE ON MULTILATERAL EXPORT CONTROLS.

FIVE TIGERS an expression used when referring to Hong Kong, Taiwan, Singapore, South Korea, and Thailand. *see also* NEWLY INDUSTRIALIZED COUNTRY.

FIX *see* FEDERAL INFORMATION EXCHANGE.

FIXED CHARGES charges that do not increase or decrease with a change in volume. *see also* VARIABLE CHARGES.

FIXED EXCHANGE *see* FIXED EXCHANGE RATES.

FIXED EXCHANGE RATES a system under which the price of one currency in relation to another currency is fixed by intergovernmental agreement and government intervention in the world currency exchange markets. *see also* FLOATING EXCHANGE RATES; FLUCTUATING EXCHANGE RATES.

FIXED INTEREST RATE a loan that has an interest rate that remains valid for the life of the loan regardless of whether other rates rise or fall.

FIXED PRICE a selling technique in which no negotiating of the price takes place. *see also* VARIABLE PRICE.

FIXING setting of a price by a known method at regular times. For example, the establishment of an official EXCHANGE RATE, interest rate, or security or COMMODITY price. *see also* COMMODITY RATE; PRICE.

F.I.W. abbreviation for FREE IN WAGON.

FLAG symbol of a country or registry of a vessel. *see also* FLAG OF CONVENIENCE.

FLAG OF CONVENIENCE reference to a ship registered under the flag of a nation that offers conveniences in the areas of taxes, crew, and safety requirements.

FLEXIBLE EXCHANGE RATES *see* FLOATING EXCHANGE RATES.

FLIGHT OF CAPITAL movement of capital to avoid loss or increase gain. *see also* CAPITAL INFLOW; CAPITAL OUTFLOW.

FLOATING *see* FLOATING CURRENCY; FLOATING EXCHANGE RATE.

FLOATING CURRENCY a currency whose value will fluctuate in response to the supply and demand for that currency. *see also* FIXED EXCHANGE RATE; FLEXIBLE EXCHANGE RATE; FLOATING EXCHANGE RATE.

FLOATING EXCHANGE RATE a system under which the price of one currency in relation to another currency is determined by the supply and demand for that currency in the currency market. *see also* CLEAN FLOAT; DIRTY FLOAT.

FLOATING (INSURANCE) CONTRACT an insurance contract that automatically covers all EXPORT shipments. *see also* FLOATING POLICY; MARINE INSURANCE; OPEN INSURANCE POLICY.

FLOATING INTEREST RATE a situation in which the interest rate set for a loan is made to rise or fall in reference to some appropriate index such as LIBOR or the prime rate. *see also* FLOATING-RATE NOTES OR BONDS; VARIABLE INTEREST RATE.

FLOATING POLICY a MARINE INSURANCE policy that applies to all shipments made by an EXPORTER over a period of time rather than one shipment only. Same as OPEN INSURANCE POLICY.

FLOATING-RATE NOTE or **BOND** a DEBT INSTRUMENT that contains a FLOATING or VARIABLE INTEREST RATE pegged to a fluctuating rate such as the 6-month LIBOR rate.

FLORENCE AGREEMENT also called the Agreement of the Importation of Educational, Scientific and Cultural Materials of 1950. The agreement provides for the nonassessment of CUSTOMS DUTIES and other charges on the importation of specified types of books, publications, and documents and educational, scientific, and cultural materials.

FLORIN unit of currency, Netherlands Antilles (100 cents equal 1 N.A. florin) *see also* GUILDER.

FLOTSAM floating debris or wreckage of a ship and its CARGO.

FLUCTUATING EXCHANGE RATE *see* FLOATING EXCHANGE RATE.

FMC *see* FEDERAL MARITIME COMMISSION.

FMD *see* FOREIGN MARKET DEVELOPMENT PROGRAM.

FMS abbreviation for Foreign Military Sales. *see also* CONVENTIONAL ARMS TRANSFER.

FMV *see* FOREIGN MARKET VALUE.

FNC *see* FEDERAL NETWORKING COUNCIL.

FO *see* FREE OUT.

F.O.B. *see* FREE ON BOARD.

F.O.B. AIRPORT the seller's obligation to deliver the goods to the air CARRIER at the airport of departure. The risk of loss of or damage to the goods is transferred from the seller to the buyer when the goods have been so delivered.

F.O.B. FREIGHT ALLOWED the same as F.O.B. NAMED INLAND CARRIER, except the seller pays the freight charges of the inland CARRIER.

F.O.B. FREIGHT PREPAID the same as F.O.B. NAMED INLAND CARRIER, except the seller pays the freight charges of the inland CARRIER.

F.O.B. NAMED INLAND CARRIER a BILL OF LADING (B/L) obtained by the seller placing the goods on the named CARRIER at the specified inland point. The buyer pays for the transportation.

F.O.B. NAMED PORT OF EXPORTATION seller is responsible for placing the goods at a named point of exportation at the seller's expense. Some European buyers use this form when they actually mean F.O.B. VESSEL.

F.O.B. VESSEL seller is responsible for goods and preparation of EXPORT documentation until actually placed aboard the vessel.

FOGS NEGOTIATIONS in the URUGUAY ROUND, this portion of the negotiations dealt with the functioning of the GENERAL AGREEMENT ON TARIFFS AND TRADE (GATT) system and resulted ultimately in the formation of the WORLD TRADE ORGANIZATION (WTO) and its DISPUTE SETTLEMENT SYSTEM.

FOLLOWUP a USENET posting that is a response to an earlier message.

FOMEX *see* FONDO PARA EL FOMENTO DE LAS EXPORTACIONES DE PRODUCTOS MANUFACTURADOS.

FONAPRE *see* FUND FOR PREVENTIVE ASSISTANCE.

FONATUR *see* NATIONAL FOUNDATION FOR TOURISM—MEXICO.

FONDO FINANCIERO PARA EL DESARROLLO DE LA CUENCA DEL PLATA (FONPLATA) (English: Plata Basin Financial Development Fund) fund that finances prefeasibility and feasibility studies, engineering designs, and projects for its member countries, Argentina, Bolivia, Brazil, Paraguay, and Uruguay. The fund encourages cofinancing with international development institutions to increase project impact. Loan financing is available for infrastructure, industrial development, livestock education, and health projects. FONPLATA was established in 1976, and its headquarters is in Sucre, Bolivia. The fund is an outgrowth of the April 1969 Plata Basin Treaty of August 1970, which sought to coordinate development of the region, including navigation, control of aquatic resources, and the use of natural resources.

FONDO PARA EL FOMENTO DE LAS EXPORTACIONES DE PRODUCTOS MANUFACTURADOS (FOMEX) an EXPORT fund, established as a trust by the Mexican government to increase employment and to increase the balance of payments and the international reserve levels. FOMEX uses loans and loan guarantees to help exporters of manufactured goods and services and importers who wish to substitute imports with nationally produced goods.

FONPLATA *see* FONDO FINANCIERO PARA EL DESARROLLO DE LA CUENCA DEL PLATA.

FOOD AND AGRICULTURAL ORGANIZATION (FAO) a specialized agency of the United Nations established in 1945 to combat hunger and malnutrition. The FAO serves as a coordinating body between government representatives, scientific groups, and nongovernmental organizations to carry out development programs relating to food and agriculture. Its headquarters is in Rome, Italy.

FOOD FOR DEVELOPMENT *see* FOOD FOR PEACE.

FOOD FOR PEACE U.S. program also known as P.L. 480, originally established by the 1954 Agricultural Trade and Development Act. It is the primary means by which the United States provides foreign food assistance. The three primary objectives of the program are to:
- expand U.S. agricultural exports,
- provide humanitarian relief, and
- aid the economic development of developing countries.
  see also FOOD FOR PROGRESS.

FOOD FOR PROGRESS (FFP) established by the 1985 U.S. Farm Bill and administered by the U.S. Department of Agriculture. The program donates surplus government-owned agricultural COMMODITIES or Title I of U.S. P.L. 480 funds to needy countries for development and agricultural reform purposes. *see also* FOOD FOR PEACE.

FOR YOUR INFORMATION (FYI) a subseries of requests for comments that are not technical standards or descriptions of protocols. FYIs convey general information about topics related to TCP/IP PROTOCOL SUITE or the INTERNET. *see also* STD.

FORCE MAJEURE   the title of a standard clause in a marine contract exempting the parties for nonfulfillment of their obligations as a result of conditions beyond their control, such as earthquakes, floods, or war.

FORDTIS   *see* FOREIGN DISCLOSURE AND TECHNICAL INFORMATION SYSTEM.

FOREIGN   something unfamiliar or coming from the outside. Located away from an individual's HOME COUNTRY such as several trips to foreign cities.

FOREIGN ACCESS ZONE (FAZ)   a term adopted by Japan for its form of free-trade zone. FAZs are the outgrowth of Japan's effort to improve its trade balance and to stimulate regional economic areas. FAZs are intended to be established around airports and seaports, with facilities warehouses, CARGO sorting, distribution, IMPORT processing, wholesale merchandising, design-in centers, and exhibition halls on an international scale. The FAZ concept emphasizes imports rather than processing and job creation. It extends from the July 1992 Law on Extraordinary Measures for the Promotion of Imports and the Facilitation of Foreign Direct Investment in Japan. Passage of the law is linked to the STRUCTURAL IMPEDIMENTS INITIATIVE. *see* FREE-TRADE ZONE.

FOREIGN ACCOUNTS RECEIVABLE FINANCING   a method of financing EXPORTS whereby
- the EXPORTER uses the line of credit it has with its bank to borrow funds, in turn extending credit to its buyers. The exporter would use a TIME DRAFT to state that the payment is due after the buyer accepts the DRAFT, for example 30 days after acceptance.
- the exporter transfers title of its foreign accounts receivable to a factoring house or an organization that specializes in financing accounts receivable for cash at a discount from the face value. *see also* EXPORT FINANCING.

FOREIGN ACCOUNTS RECEIVABLE PURCHASES   a method of EXPORT FINANCING whereby an EXPORTER sells its ACCEPTED BILLS OF EXCHANGE or TIME DRAFTS that have been accepted by the FOREIGN BUYER. In this case, the bank purchases the time draft that a creditworthy foreign buyer has accepted or agreed to pay at some specified future date. The bank accepts the obligation of paying the draft, usually for a customer, for a fee. *see also* BANKER'S ACCEPTANCE; FACTORING; FORFAITING.

FOREIGN AFFAIRS ADMINISTRATIVE SUPPORT (FAAS)   a program used by the U.S. Department of State (DOS) to define the additional costs it incurs for providing services necessary to support the overseas operations of agencies external to DOS. Under FAAS, DOS funds core costs required for its own programs, whereas the supported agencies fund incremental costs of their service requirements. These latter costs are shared through the application of workload factors that measure agency participation in the services.

FOREIGN AFFILIATE *see* AFFILIATE.

FOREIGN AFFILIATE OF A FOREIGN PARENT an affiliate of a major foreign corporation, which itself has an American affiliate.

FOREIGN AGRICULTURAL SERVICE (FAS) an agency of the U.S. Department of Agriculture that collects foreign market information regarding agricultural production and trade, develops foreign markets for U.S. agricultural products, and represents U.S. agricultural interests overseas multilaterally. FAS maintains over 60 counselor and attaché posts, located in U.S. embassies and consulates, and about 15 Agricultural Trade Offices (ATOs) that provide market development and trade promotion services in overseas locations. FAS also administers USDA's EXPORT credit and concessional sales programs. FAS headquarters is located in Washington, DC.

FOREIGN AND COMMONWEALTH OFFICE (FCO) equivalent to the U.S. *S*tate Department in Britain's Diplomatic Service with posts in about 170 countries. Among its functions, the FCO supports overseas trade and EXPORT promotion services in cooperation with Britain's DEPARTMENT OF TRADE AND INDUSTRY.

FOREIGN ASSETS CONTROL (OFAC) the U.S. Treasury Department's Office of Foreign Assets Control. It administers and sanctions programs involving specific countries and restricts the involvement of U.S. persons in third-country strategic exports.

FOREIGN ASSISTANCE ACT OF 1961 U.S. legislation authorizing the formation and operation of the TRADE AND DEVELOPMENT PROGRAM (TDP) within the framework of the U.S. INTERNATIONAL DEVELOPMENT COOPERATION AGENCY (USIDCA).

FOREIGN ASSISTANCE ACT OF 1991 U.S. act that replaced the Support for East European Democracy (SEED) Act. The Foreign Assistance Act allows support to 26 countries, including all Eastern European nations and most of the former Soviet republics.

FOREIGN AVAILABILITY the existence of selected foreign COMMODITIES or technology subject to EXPORT control as determined by a review of the U.S. BUREAU OF EXPORT ADMINISTRATION (BXA). The reviews use four criteria to determine foreign availability: comparable quality, availability-in-fact, foreign source, and adequacy of available quantities that would render continuation of the U.S. control ineffective in meeting its intended purpose. A positive determination of foreign availability means that a non-U.S. origin item of comparable quality may be obtained by one or more proscribed countries in quantities sufficient to satisfy their needs so that U.S. exports of such an item would not make a significant contribution to the military potential of such countries.

FOREIGN BANK SUPERVISION ENHANCEMENT ACT (FBSEA) an act passed in 1991 that increased the U.S. Federal Reserve's supervisory powers over foreign banks by
- requiring Federal Reserve review before a foreign bank enters or expands in the United States,
- tightening the standards for entry and expansion that must be considered by the Federal Reserve,
- requiring Federal Reserve Board approval of U.S. representative offices of foreign banks, and
- requiring that each U.S. office of a foreign bank be examined at least once a year by the Federal Reserve.

  see also INTERNATIONAL BANKING ACT.

FOREIGN BOND   international bond denominated in the currency of the country where it is issued.

FOREIGN BRANCH OFFICE   a sales or other office maintained in a foreign country and staffed by direct employees of the EXPORTER. *see also* BRANCH OFFICE.

FOREIGN BROADCAST INFORMATION SERVICE (FBIS) a U.S. agency disseminating information obtained from foreign radio and television broadcasts and news and technical data reports together with the U.S. JOINT PUBLICATION RESEARCH SERVICE (JPRS). FBIS publishes political, military, economic, environmental news, commentary, scientific, and other information. The FBIS and JPRS agencies have radio transmissions, newspapers, books, and periodicals.

FOREIGN BUYER/FOREIGN SELLER   a person whose place of doing business with respect to the transaction is outside the United States.

FOREIGN BUYER PROGRAM (FBP)   a joint industry INTERNATIONAL TRADE ADMINISTRATION (ITA) program to assist EXPORTERS in meeting qualified foreign purchasers for their product or service at trade shows held in the United States. ITA selects leading U.S. trade shows in industries with high EXPORT potential. Each show selected for the FBP receives promotion through overseas mailings, U.S. embassy and regional commercial newsletters, and other promotional techniques. ITA trade specialists counsel participating U.S. exhibitors.

FOREIGN CLAIMS SETTLEMENT COMMISSION (FCSC) an independent quasijudicial agency within the U.S. Justice Department authorized to determine claims of U.S. nationals for loss of property in specific foreign countries. These losses have occurred either as a result of nationalization of property by foreign governments or from damage and loss of property as a result of military operations in specific conflicts.

FOREIGN COMMERCE   trade between individuals or legal entities in different countries.

FOREIGN CONCERN any partnership, corporation, company, association, or other entity of, or organized under the laws of, any jurisdiction other than the United States.

FOREIGN CORRUPT PRACTICES ACT (FCPA) U.S. law prohibiting U.S. individuals, companies, and direct foreign subsidiaries of U.S. companies from offering, promising, or paying anything of value to any foreign government official in order to obtain or retain business.

FOREIGN CREDIT INSURANCE ASSOCIATION (FCIA) an affiliate of the EXIMBANK that offers POLITICAL and COMMERCIAL RISK insurance. The insurance protects mostly short-term credit extended for the sale of consumer goods, raw materials, COMMODITIES, spare parts, and other items normally sold on terms of up to 180 days. Coverage is also available for some bulk commodities sold on 360-day terms and capital and quasicapital goods sold on terms up to 5 years.

FOREIGN CREDIT INTERCHANGE BUREAU the international division of the National Association of Credit Managers headquartered in New York.

FOREIGN CURRENCY SWAPS transaction that occurs when the currency of one country is traded for the currency of another country with an understanding that the transaction will be reversed at some later date. *see also* SWAP.

FOREIGN DEBT *see* EXTERNAL DEBT.

FOREIGN DEBT OVERHANG *see* DEBT SERVICING.

FOREIGN DIRECT INVESTMENT IN THE UNITED STATES (FDIUS) the ownership or control, directly or indirectly, by a single foreign person or individual, or related group of individuals, company, or government, of 10% or more of the voting securities of an incorporated U.S. business enterprise or an equivalent interest in an unincorporated U.S. business enterprise, including real property. Such a business is referred to as a U.S. affiliate of a foreign direct investor. *see also* COMMITTEE ON FOREIGN INVESTMENT IN THE UNITED STATES; FOREIGN PERSON PORTFOLIO INVESTMENT.

FOREIGN DISCLOSURE AND TECHNICAL INFORMATION SYSTEM (FORDTIS) a classified information system that contains an automated database of munitions and dual-use EXPORT licenses. The system is maintained by the U.S. Defense Department's DEFENSE TECHNOLOGY SECURITY ADMINISTRATION (DTSA). *see also* EXPORT CONTROL AUTOMATED SUPPORT SYSTEM.

FOREIGN ECONOMIC TRENDS (FETS) reports prepared by U.S. embassies abroad to describe foreign country economic and commercial trends and trade and investment climates. The reports describe current economic conditions; provide updates on the principal factors influencing developments and the possible impacts on American exports; and review newly announced foreign government policies as well as consumption, investment, and foreign debt trends.

FOREIGN EXCHANGE (F/X)
  1. the currency or credit instruments of a foreign country.
  2. transactions involving the purchase or sale of currencies.

FOREIGN EXCHANGE BROKER an individual that specializes in the trade of FOREIGN EXCHANGE by bringing buyers and sellers together.

FOREIGN EXCHANGE CONTRACT CONTRACT for the sale or purchase of FOREIGN EXCHANGE specifying an EXCHANGE RATE and DELIVERY date. *see also* EXCHANGE RATE CLASSIFICATIONS; FORWARD CONTRACT; FORWARD COVER; FORWARD RATE; FUTURES CONTRACT; SPOT RATE.

FOREIGN EXCHANGE CONTROL ACT legislation that regulates FOREIGN EXCHANGE transactions, the EXCHANGE RATE system, and the payment and receipt of foreign exchange in Korea. The act imposes restrictions on such transactions and sets forth the principles by which they are to be regulated.

FOREIGN EXCHANGE CONTROLS *see* EXCHANGE CONTROLS.

FOREIGN EXCHANGE OPERATIONS AND INVESTMENTS DEPARTMENT (FEOID) the department of the CENTRAL BANK OF THE PHILIPPINES responsible for approving the REPATRIATION of profits, capital gains, and dividends accruing to nonresidents of the Philippines.

FOREIGN EXCHANGE OPTION an arrangement in which a purchaser and a seller of foreign currencies agree on a specific rate of exchange at a future date. The purchaser may choose to exercise or pass up the option, thus setting a limit on unfavorable exchange rates. The seller is given a fee for tendering the option. Purchasers may exercise the option at any time. In the European option currency exchange is made on the originally established date, whereas in the American option, exchange is made within a couple of days of the purchaser exercising the option. *see also* FORWARD EXCHANGE RATE.

FOREIGN EXCHANGE RATE *see* EXCHANGE RATE.

FOREIGN EXCHANGE RESERVES all gold, SPECIAL DRAWING RIGHTS (SDR), U.S. dollars, and all other CONVERTIBLE CURRENCIES being held in a country's treasury. *see also* CENTRAL BANK.

FOREIGN EXPATRIATE *see* EXPATRIATE.

FOREIGN EXPORTS EXPORTS of foreign merchandise reexports consisting of commodities of foreign origin that have entered the United States for consumption or into Customs-bonded warehouses or U.S. FOREIGN TRADE ZONES (FTZS), and that, at the time of exportation, are in substantially the same condition as when imported.

FOREIGN EXTERNAL DEBT *see* EXTERNAL DEBT.

FOREIGN EXTRATERRITORIAL MEASURES ACT OF 1984 (FEMA) (Canadian) legislation allowing the Canadian government to prevent any person or company operating in Canada from following any U.S. law that hinders trade between Canada and any other country. *see also* EXTRATERRITORIALITY.

FOREIGN FINANCING type of financing when a company goes into a foreign country's capital market and borrows funds in local currency. Example: an American company borrows LIRA in Italy or YEN in Japan.

FOREIGN FLAG a reference to a CARRIER not registered in the United States that flies the American flag. The term applies to air and sea transportation.

FOREIGN FREIGHT FORWARDER a corporation carrying on the business of forwarding who is not a SHIPPER or CONSIGNEE. The foreign FREIGHT FORWARDER receives compensation from the shipper for preparing documents and arranging various transactions related to the international distribution of goods. Also, a BROKERAGE FEE may be paid to the forwarder from steamship lines if the forwarder performs at least two of the following services:
1. coordinates the movement of the CARGO to shipside,
2. prepares and processes the ocean bill of lading,
3. prepares and processes dock receipts or delivery orders,
4. prepares and processes consular documents or export declarations,
5. pays the ocean freight charges on shipments.

FOREIGN INCOME income earned by Americans from work performed in another country.

FOREIGN INDEPENDENT TOUR (FIT) a foreign itinerary having prepaid travel arrangements tailored to meet a traveler's specific wishes.

FOREIGN INVESTMENT *see* COMMITTEE ON FOREIGN INVESTMENT IN THE UNITED STATES; FOREIGN DIRECT INVESTMENT IN THE UNITED STATES; NET FOREIGN INVESTMENT.

FOREIGN INVESTMENT ADVISORY SERVICE (FIAS) a joint facility established in 1986 of the INTERNATIONAL FINANCE CORPORATION (IFC) and the MULTILATERAL INVESTMENT GUARANTEE AGENCY to help developing countries increase the inflow of foreign investment. The service provides advice at the request of member governments on formulating a general framework of legal, accounting, and regulatory policies and institutions and procedures to attract and assess investment interest.

FOREIGN INVESTMENT INSURANCE (FII) an insurance program of the Canadian EXPORT DEVELOPMENT CORPORATION that protects Canadian investments in foreign countries. The FII provides POLITI-

CAL RISK coverage against losses resulting from INCONVERTIBILITY, EXPROPRIATION, and wars, revolutions, and insurrections. *see also* FOREIGN CREDIT INSURANCE ASSOCIATION (FCIA); OVERSEAS PRIVATE INVESTMENT CORPORATION (OPIC).

FOREIGN INVESTMENT LAW legislation usually found in socialist command economies that outlines restrictions pertaining to the operation of foreign firms doing business in their countries.

FOREIGN INVESTMENT REVIEW AGENCY (FIRA) an agency created in 1974 by the Canadian government with the objective of:
- evaluating DIRECT INVESTMENT in Canada and guaranteeing that any investment had to have a direct benefit to Canada, such as increased employment, and
- regulating the movement of foreign capital in Canada.
  FIRA was modified and replaced by INVESTMENT CANADA.

FOREIGN INVOICE ACCEPTANCE *see* ACCEPTANCE.

FOREIGN MARKET DEVELOPMENT PROGRAM (FMD) also known as the COOPERATOR PROGRAM. It is one of several U.S. Department of Agriculture (USDA) programs designed to encourage the development, maintenance, and expansion of commercial EXPORT markets for U.S. agricultural COMMODITIES and products. Under FMD, USDA considers proposals with preference given to activities promising early results and lasting benefits in commercial export markets. Funds may be used for trade servicing, consumer promotion, and market research and to provide technical assistance to actual or potential foreign purchasers.

FOREIGN MARKET RESEARCH *see* INDUSTRY SUBSECTOR ANALYSIS.

FOREIGN MARKET VALUE (FMV) the price at which merchandise is sold, or offered for sale, in the principal markets of the country from which it is exported. If information on foreign home market sales is not useful, the foreign market value is based on prices of exports to third countries or constructed value. Adjustments for quantities sold, circumstances of sales, and differences in the merchandise can be made to those prices to ensure a proper comparison with the prices of goods exported to the United States. *see also* TARIFF ACT OF 1930.

FOREIGN MILITARY SALES (FMS) *see* CONVENTIONAL ARMS TRANSFER.

FOREIGN-OWNED AFFILIATE IN THE UNITED STATES a business in the United States in which there is sufficient foreign investment to be classified as a direct foreign investment. To determine fully the foreign owners of a U.S. affiliate, three entities must be identified: the FOREIGN PARENT, the ULTIMATE BENEFICIAL OWNER (UBO), and the FOREIGN PARENT GROUP. All these entities are persons in the broad sense: thus they may be individuals; business enterprises; governments; religious, charitable, or other nonprofit organizations; associated groups; estates; and trusts.

A U.S. affiliate may have an ultimate beneficial owner that is not the immediate foreign parent. Moreover, the affiliate may have several ownership chains above it, if it is owned at least 10% by more than one foreign person. In such cases, the affiliate may have more than one foreign parent, UBO, and/or foreign parent group.

FOREIGN PARENT the first foreign person or entity outside the United States in an affiliate's ownership chain that has a direct investment in the affiliate. The foreign parent consists only of the first person or entity outside the United States in the affiliate's ownership chain. All other affiliated foreign persons are excluded.

FOREIGN PARENT GROUP (FPG) a group consisting of:

- the FOREIGN PARENT.
- any foreign person or entity, proceeding up the foreign parent's ownership chain, that owns more than 50% of the party below it, up to and including the ultimate beneficial owner (UBO).
- any foreign person or entity, proceeding down the ownership chains of each of these members, that is owned by more than 50% by the party above it. A particular U.S. affiliate may have several ownership chains above it, if it is owned at least 10% by more than one foreign party. In such cases, the affiliate may have more than one foreign parent, UBO, and/or foreign parent group.

FOREIGN PERSON any person resident outside the United States or subject to the jurisdiction of a country other than the United States. *Person* is any individual, branch, partnership, association, associated group, estate, trust, corporation, or other organization whether or not organized under the laws of any state, and any government including a foreign government, the U.S. government, a state or local government, or any agency, corporation, financial institution, or other entity or instrumentality thereof, including a government-sponsored agency. *see also* FOREIGN PARENT; FOREIGN PARENT GROUP; U.S. AFFILIATE.

FOREIGN POLICY CONTROLS foreign policy regulations distinct from national security controls, COCOM, or other international agreements that are imposed to further U.S. foreign policy. The controls are typically imposed in response to developments in a country or countries—such as considerations regarding terrorism and human rights—or to developments involving a type or types of COMMODITIES and their related technical data. Foreign policy controls expire annually, unless extended.

FOREIGN REMITTANCES transfer of any monetary instrument across national boundaries. *see also* TELEGRAPHIC TRANSFER PAYMENT; TRANSFER PAYMENT.

FOREIGN SALES AGENT an individual or company that serves as the foreign representative of a domestic supplier and seeks sales abroad for the supplier.

FOREIGN SALES CORPORATION (FSC) a corporation created to secure U.S. tax exemption on a portion of earnings derived from the sale of U.S. products in foreign markets. To qualify for special tax treatment, an FSC must be a foreign corporation, maintain an office outside the U.S. territory, maintain a summary of its permanent books of account at the foreign office, and have at least one director resident outside of the United States.

FOREIGN SERVICE part of the U.S. Department of State that aids in maintaining relations between the United States and other nations. The Foreign Service was established by Congress in 1924 and supports the President and the Secretary of State in pursuing America's foreign policy objectives. Foreign Service functions include representing U.S. interests; operating U.S. overseas missions; assisting Americans abroad; public diplomacy and reporting; and communicating and negotiating political, economic, consular, administrative, cultural, and commercial affairs. The Foreign Service comprises officers from the U.S. Departments of State, Commerce, and Agriculture and the United States Information Service. *see also* COMMERCIAL OFFICERS; ECONOMIC OFFICERS.

FOREIGN SERVICE INSTITUTE (FSI) U.S. agency founded in 1946 under the FOREIGN SERVICE to train U.S. foreign and civil service officials. Training courses cover administrative, consular, economic, commercial, political work, foreign languages, and diplomatic life overseas.

FOREIGN SERVICE NATIONAL (FSN) HOST COUNTRY national employed by a U.S. mission overseas.

FOREIGN SERVICE OFFICER (FSO) *see* TITLE AND RANK.

FOREIGN SERVICE PREMIUM *see* EXPATRIATE ALLOWANCE.

FOREIGN SOURCE INCOME income or compensation given to an employee outside the United States (the HOME COUNTRY).

FOREIGN SUBSIDIARY a company that is owned and controlled by another company (the parent company) and is situated in a country other than the HOME COUNTRY of the owner. *see also* BRANCH; BRANCH OFFICE; FOREIGN AFFILIATE.

FOREIGN TAX CREDIT the accounting credit taxpayers are authorized to take against any taxes payable in their HOME COUNTRY for taxes levied on the same income by a foreign government.

FOREIGN TRADE DIVISION (FTD) the division in the U.S. DEPARTMENT OF COMMERCE's Census Bureau that compiles and disseminates official U.S. IMPORT and EXPORT STATISTICS. The division also maintains international COMMODITY classification systems and conducts methods research, including international comparability of trade statistics.

FOREIGN TRADE ORGANIZATION (FTO) a governmentally controlled trading organization that regulates the IMPORT and EXPORT of goods. An FTO is usually found in centrally planned economies.

FOREIGN TRADE REPORTS (FT410) a U.S. DEPARTMENT OF COMMERCE monthly publication that provides a statistical record of the shipments of all merchandise exported from the United States to foreign countries, including both quantity and dollar value of these exports to each country during the month covered by the report.

FOREIGN TRADE STATISTICAL REPORTING (FTSR) *see* SHIPPER'S EXPORT DECLARATION.

FOREIGN TRADE ZONE ENTRY a form declaring goods that are brought duty-free into a FOREIGN TRADE ZONE (FTZ) for further processing or storage and subsequent exportation and/or consumption.

FOREIGN TRADE ZONES-SUBZONES (FTZ-SZ) the U.S. form of FREE-TRADE ZONES. These zones are restricted-access sites in or near ports of entry, that operate under public utility principles to create and maintain employment by encouraging operations in the United States that might otherwise have been carried on abroad. Goods brought into a zone for a bona fide CUSTOMS reason are exempt from state and local ad valorem tax. The zones are licensed by the U.S. DEPARTMENT OF COMMERCE's Foreign Trade Zone Board and operate under the supervision of the U.S. CUSTOMS SERVICE. QUOTA restrictions do not normally apply to foreign goods stored in zones, but the board can limit or deny zone use in specific cases on public interest grounds. Domestic goods moved into a zone for EXPORT may be considered exported upon entering the zone for purposes of excise tax rebates and drawback. A foreign trade subzone is a non-contiguous zone site located at a manufacturing plant.

FOREIGN TRADERS INDEX (FTI) the U.S. AND FOREIGN COMMERCIAL SERVICE headquarters compilation of overseas contact files, intended for use by domestic businesses. This includes background information on foreign companies, address, contact person, sales figures, size of company, and products by SIC code.

FOREIGNER *see* FOREIGN.

FOREX *see* FOREIGN EXCHANGE.

FOREX BROKER *see* FOREIGN EXCHANGE BROKER.

FOREX TRADING acronym for FOREIGN EXCHANGE trading.

FORFAIT GUARANTEE PROGRAM a nonrecourse financing guarantee program of the AGENCY FOR INTERNATIONAL DEVELOPMENT (AID) providing assistance to U.S. firms in securing financing for the EXPORT of durable goods, machinery, spare parts, automotive equipment, and tools to AID-assisted DEVELOPING COUNTRIES. These guarantees are for periods up to 5 years with a maximum value of $1 million. *see also* FORFAITING.

FORFAITING a form of supplier credit in which an EXPORTER surrenders possession of EXPORT receivables, which are usually guaranteed by a bank in the IMPORTER'S country, by selling them at a discount to a forfaiter in exchange for cash. These instruments may also carry the guarantee of the foreign government. In a typical forfaiting transaction, an exporter approaches a forfaiter before completing a transaction's structure. Once the forfaiter commits to the deal and sets the discount rate, the exporter can incorporate the discount into the selling price. Forfaiters usually work with bills of exchange or promissory notes, which are unconditional and easily transferable debt instruments that can be sold on the secondary market. *see also* FACTORING.

FORFEITURE
1. loss of property for failure to comply with the law.
2. a form of debt repayment where a buyer who borrows funds to finance a purchase repays the factor over a period of time in several installments.

FORINT unit of currency, Hungary (100 fillérs equal 1 forint).

FORM A a CERTIFICATE OF ORIGIN that may have to be presented to U.S. CUSTOMS to obtain DUTY-FREE treatment under programs such as the GENERALIZED SYSTEM OF PREFERENCES (GSP) or CARIBBEAN BASIN INITIATIVE (CBI). The requirement for a Form A for merchandise covered by a FORMAL ENTRY may be waived by the District Director of U.S. Customs where he/she determines appropriate, or if the imported articles are for household or personal use and/or not intended for resale or brought in for the account of others. The IMPORTER will, however, be required to produce it for GSP duty-free treatment if requested to do so by U.S. Customs. The EXPORTER in the DEVELOPING COUNTRY must supply this form. Also called UNCTAD Certificate of Origin Form A.

FORMAL RULINGS *see* BINDING TARIFF CLASSIFICATION RULINGS.

FORMER SOVIET UNION (FSU) a collective reference to republics comprising the former Soviet Union. The term has been used both including and excluding the Baltic republics, Estonia, Latvia, and Lithuania. The term includes the other 12 republics of Russia, Ukraine, Belarus, Moldova, Armenia, Azerbaijan, Uzbekistan, Turkmenistan, Tajikistan, Kazakhstan, Kyrgizstan, and Georgia.

FORTY-FOOT EQUIVALENT UNIT *see* TWENTY-FOOT EQUIVALENT UNIT.

FORWARD CONTRACT an agreement, usually between an individual or firm and financial institution, to exchange one currency for the currency of another country, at a specified rate at some set date in the future. *see also* EXCHANGE RATE CLASSIFICATIONS; FORWARD COVER; FORWARD RATE; FUTURES CONTRACT; SPOT RATE.

FORWARD COVER the manner by which a firm is able to protect itself against fluctuations in the exchange rate from the time the contract is accepted and the date when payment is due. *see also* FORWARD CONTRACT; FORWARD RATE; HEDGING.

FORWARD DISCOUNT the percentage difference the FORWARD RATE is below the SPOT RATE. *see also* FORWARD PREMIUM; TRADING AT A DISCOUNT; TRADING AT A PREMIUM.

FORWARD EXCHANGE RATE the price set between two parties for delivery of a foreign currency on an agreed future date. If that date occurs within a week, the agreement is called a spot transaction; if the date is more than a week in the future, the arrangement is called a forward exchange transaction. *see also* FOREIGN EXCHANGE OPTION.

FORWARD FOREIGN EXCHANGE *see* FORWARD EXCHANGE RATE.

FORWARD INTEGRATION occurs when a manufacturer of a product used in the manufacture of another product decides to expand to the next level, by producing the complete product as compared to just the components.

FORWARD POSITION the situation that reflects the difference between outstanding obligations that a FOREIGN EXCHANGE TRADE has for forward purchases and the sale of a foreign currency at a specific time.

FORWARD PREMIUM the percentage difference the FORWARD RATE is above the SPOT RATE. *see also* FORWARD DISCOUNT; TRADING AT A DISCOUNT; TRADING AT A PREMIUM.

FORWARD RATE *see* FORWARD EXCHANGE RATE.

FOUL BILL OF LADING a receipt for goods issued by a CARRIER with an indication that the goods were damaged when received.

FOUR TIGERS an expression used when referring to Hong Kong, Taiwan, Singapore, and South Korea. *see also* FIVE TIGERS; NEWLY INDUSTRIALIZED COUNTRY.

FOURTH WORLD term used when referring to those countries categorized as LEAST DEVELOPED COUNTRY (LDC). *see also* LESS-DEVELOPED COUNTRIES; THIRD WORLD.

F.O.W. abbreviation for first open water.

F.P.A. *see* FREE OF PARTICULAR AVERAGE.

FPAAC *see* FREE OF PARTICULAR AVERAGE AMERICAN CONDITIONS.

FPAEC *see* FREE OF PARTICULAR AVERAGE ENGLISH CONDITIONS.

FPFS *see* FINES, PENALTIES, AND FORFEITURES SYSTEM.

FPG *see* FOREIGN PARENT GROUP.

FPO abbreviation for Fleet Post Office used in addressing mail to a FOREIGN SERVICE POST. *see also* APO.

FRACTIONAL CURRENCY any currency that is smaller than a standard money unit.

FRAMEWORK AGREEMENT agreements reached at the TOKYO ROUND that called for consideration to be given "to improvements in the international framework for the conduct of world trade." Four separate agreements make up what is known as the framework agreement. They concern
- differential and more favorable treatment for, and reciprocity and fuller participation by, developing countries in the international framework for trade;
- trade measures taken for balance of payments purposes;
- safeguard actions for development purposes; and
- an understanding on notification, consultation, dispute settlement, and surveillance in the GENERAL AGREEMENT ON TARIFFS AND TRADE (GATT).

Generally, bilateral framework agreements contain similar objectives. They are based on a statement of agreed principles regarding the benefits of open trade and investment, increased importance of services to economies, the need for adequate intellectual property rights protection, the importance of observing and promoting internationally recognized worker rights, and the desirability of resolving trade and investment problems expeditiously. The parties establish a Council on Trade and Investment to monitor trade and investment relations, hold consultations on specific trade and investment matters of interest to both sides, and work toward removing impediments to trade and investment flows. The framework agreements do not bind signatories to implement specific trade liberalization measures. *see also* ENTERPRISE FOR THE AMERICAS INITIATIVE.

FRANC AREA *see* CURRENCY AREA.

FRANC ZONE (French: Zone Franc, ZF) a MONETARY UNION among countries whose currencies are linked to the FRENCH FRANC at a fixed rate of exchange: Benin, Burkina, the Cameroon, Central African Republic, Chad, Comoros, Congo, Equatorial Guinea, France, Gabon, Côte d'Ivoire, Mali, Niger, Senegal, and Togo. These countries have agreed to hold their reserves primarily in French francs and to transact exchanges on the Paris market. The zone was established in May 1951 under the auspices of a French government agency: Comité Monétaire de ZF.

FRANCHISING the granting of an exclusive license by a company (franchisor) to a domestic or foreign company (franchisee) to sell its products or services for a FEE (ROYALTY). *see also* LICENSING.

FRANCHISING AGREEMENT the contractual agreement between the franchisor and the franchisee. *see also* FRANCHISING.

FRANCO free from DUTIES, transportation charges, and other levies. *see also* DUTY FREE.

FRANCOPHONE a national of a country whose predominant language is French. *see also* ANGLOPHONE.

FR. & C.C. abbreviation for free of riot and civil commotion.

FREDERICKSBURG PLAN formal guidelines developed to address the establishment of uniform international telecommunications standards. The meeting took place at Fredericksburg, Virginia, in 1990, and its participants included the U.S. Committee Tl, the EUROPEAN TELECOMMUNICATIONS STANDARDS INSTITUTE (ETSI), and Japan's Telecommunication and Technology Committee (TTC).

FREE ALONGSIDE SHIP (FAS) a named port of EXPORT. Under FAS, the seller quotes a price for the goods that includes charges for delivery of the goods alongside a vessel at the port of departure. The seller handles the cost of unloading and wharfage; loading, ocean transportation, and insurance are left to the buyer. FAS is also a method of export and IMPORT valuation.

FREE-ASTRAY term that describes a SHIPMENT dropped off at the wrong location and forwarded to the proper location free of charge.

FREE CARRIER (FCA) TO A NAMED PLACE term replacing the former "FOB named inland port" to designate the seller's responsibility for the cost of loading goods at the named shipping point. It may be used for multimodal transport, container stations, and any mode of transport, including air.

FREE DOMICILE term describing a situation in which the SHIPPER pays all the transportation charges and applicable duties. *see also* DELIVERED DUTY PAID.

FREE ECONOMIC ZONE *see* FREE TRADE ZONE.

FREE IN a pricing term indicating that the charterer of a vessel is responsible for the cost of loading goods onto the vessel.

FREE IN AND OUT (F.I.O.) term used to indicate that cost of loading and unloading a vessel is borne by the charterer.

FREE IN WAGON CARGO that is free of all charges. *see also* FREE IN AND OUT; FREE ON BOARD (F.O.B.).

FREE LIST statement of items that do not require the payment of DUTIES.

FREE MARKET market where there is unrestricted trading of GOODS with prices determined by supply and demand. Internationally, a FREE MARKET refers to an unrestricted movement of goods in and out of the country, unhampered by the existence of TARIFFS or other TRADE BARRIERS. *see also* CUSTOMS PRIVILEGED FACILITIES; FREE TRADE; FREE TRADE AGREEMENT; FREE-TRADE AREA; PROTECTIONISM; PROTECTIONIST TRADING PRACTICES.

FREE OF CAPTURE AND SEIZURE (F.C. & S.) an EXPORT insurance clause providing that loss is not insured if due to capture, seizure, confiscation, and like actions, whether legal or not, or from such acts as piracy, civil war, rebellion, and civil strife.

FREE OF DUTY *see* DUTY FREE.

FREE OF PARTICULAR AVERAGE (FPA) an EXPORT MARINE INSURANCE clause providing that partial loss or damage is not insured.
- American condition FPAAC—Partial loss not insured unless caused by the vessel being sunk, stranded, burned, on fire, or in collision.
- English conditions FPAEC—Partial loss not insured unless a result of the vessel being sunk, stranded, burned, on fire, or in collision.

   see also AVERAGE; FREE OF PARTICULAR AVERAGE; FREE OF PARTICULAR AVERAGE ENGLISH CONDITIONS (FPAEC); GENERAL AVERAGE; INCHMAREE CLAUSE; MARINE CARGO INSURANCE.

FREE OF PARTICULAR AVERAGE ENGLISH CONDITIONS (FPAEC) a clause included in EXPORT MARINE INSURANCE policies. It is the same as the FREE OF PARTICULAR AVERAGE AMERICAN CONDITIONS (FPAAC) except that partial losses under the PERILS OF THE SEA clause are fully recoverable if the vessel has been stranded, sunk or burned, been on fire or in a collision, without requiring that the damage actually be caused by one of these perils. *see also* FREE OF PARTICULAR AVERAGE; GENERAL AVERAGE; INCHMAREE CLAUSE.

FREE ON BOARD (F.O.B.) at a named port of EXPORT, the seller quotes the buyer a price that covers all costs up to and including delivery of goods aboard a vessel at a port. FOB is also a method of EXPORT valuation.

FREE ON RAIL/FREE ON TRUCK (FOR/FOT) synonymous terms since the word *truck* relates to the railway wagons. The terms should be used only when the goods are to be carried by rail.

FREE OUT (F.O.) a pricing term indicating that the cost of unloading goods from the vessel is borne by the charterer.

FREE PERIMETERS similar to a FREE PORT; however, they are confined to a remote or underdeveloped region of a country. They are normally established to serve the local consumption requirements of the remote regions that are unable to be serviced through normal domestic distribution channels. Although goods being shipped into these areas are not exempt from TARIFF and IMPORT control mechanisms, they are, however, subject to fewer import controls than would be applied elsewhere. These privileges are normally limited to products such as foodstuffs, medicines, capital goods, and urgently required consumer goods.

FREE PORTS a form of FREE-TRADE ZONE that usually encompasses an entire port area. Examples include Hong Kong and Singapore.

FREE TIME time allowed IMPORTERS-CONSIGNEES to take physical delivery of CARGO before storage or DEMURRAGE is assessed.

FREE TRADE the unimpeded exchange and flow of goods and services between trading partners regardless of national borders.

FREE TRADE AGREEMENT (FTA) an arrangement that establishes unimpeded exchange and flow of goods and services between trading partners regardless of national borders. An FTA does not, as opposed to a common market, address labor mobility across borders, common currencies or uniform standards or other common policies such as taxes. Member countries of a FREE-TRADE AREA apply their individual TARIFF rates to countries outside the free-trade area.

FREE TRADE AGREEMENT OF 1989 *see* CANADA–U.S. FREE TRADE AGREEMENT.

FREE-TRADE AREA (FTA) a cooperative arrangement among two or more nations, pursuant to the GENERAL AGREEMENT ON TARIFFS AND TRADE (GATT), whereby trade barriers are removed among the members. The arrangement generally includes a customs union with a common external TARIFF, although there are exceptions in which members maintain individually separate tariff schedules for external countries.

FREE-TRADE ZONE (FTZ) a generic term referring to special commercial and industrial areas at which special customs procedures allow the importation of foreign merchandise including raw materials, components, and finished goods without the requirement that DUTIES be paid immediately. They are sometimes called customs-free zones or duty-free zones. If the merchandise is later exported, duty-free treatment is given to reexports. The zones are usually located in or near ports of entry. Merchandise brought into these zones may be stored, exhibited, assembled, processed, or used in manufacture prior to reexport or entry into the national customs territory. When manufacturing activity occurs in free-trade zones, it usually involves a combination of foreign and domestic merchandise and usually requires special governmental authority. Types of free trade zones include FREE PORTS, TRANSIT ZONES, FOREIGN TRADE ZONES, and foreign trade subzones. *see also* DRAWBACK; ECONOMIC ZONES; EXPORT PROCESSING ZONES; FOREIGN ACCESS ZONES; FREETRADE AREA; TRANSIT ZONES.

FREE ZONE an area within a country—a seaport, airport, warehouse, or any designated area—regarded as being outside its Customs territory where IMPORTERS may bring goods of FOREIGN origin without paying Customs duties and taxes, pending their eventual processing, transshipment or REEXPORTATION. *see also* DRAWBACK; ECONOMIC ZONES; EXPORT PROCESSING ZONES; FOREIGN ACCESS ZONES; FREE-TRADE AREA; FREE TRADE ZONE; TRANSIT ZONES.

FREEDOM SUPPORT ACT (FSA) U.S. law signed in October 1992, authorizing a range of programs to support free market and democratic reforms in Russia, Ukraine, Armenia, and other states of the former Soviet Union.

FREELY CONVERTIBLE CURRENCY *see* CONVERTIBLE CURRENCY.

FREELY FLOATING EXCHANGE RATE SYSTEM a system in which EXCHANGE RATES are determined by market forces rather than government intervention or restrictions. *see also* CLEAN FLOAT; DIRTY FLOAT; MANAGED FLOATING EXCHANGE RATE SYSTEM.

FREENET a bulletin board system offering E-MAIL, communications, and other information services. Freenets are nonprofit organizations, and they are a member of the National Public Telecomputing Network (NPTN). The mission of freenets is to provide widely available free computer telecommunication services.

FREEWARE software that is distributed free of charge.

FREIGHT goods in the process of being shipped or being designated for shipment from the seller to the buyer by a COMMON CARRIER. *see also* CARGO.

FREIGHT ALL KINDS (FAK) a shipping classification. Goods classified FAK are usually charged higher rates than those marked with a specific classification and are frequently in a container that includes various classes of CARGO.

FREIGHT BROKER (DOMESTIC) *see* FREIGHT FORWARDER (DOMESTIC).

FREIGHT/CARRIAGE PAID TO . . . similar to C & F. The seller pays the freight for the carriage of the goods to the named destination. However, the risk of loss of or damage to the goods, as well as of any cost increases, is transferred from the seller to the buyer when the goods have been delivered into the custody of the first CARRIER and not at the ship's rail. The term can be used for all modes of transport including multimodal operations and container or "roll on–roll off" traffic by trailer and ferries. When the seller has to furnish a BILL OF LADING, waybill, or carrier's receipt, he/she duly fulfills this obligation by presenting such a document issued by the person with whom he/she has contracted for carriage to the named destination.

FREIGHT CARRIAGE . . . AND INSURANCE PAID TO similar to FREIGHT/CARRIAGE PAID TO . . . but with the addition that the seller has to procure transport insurance against the risk of loss of damage to the goods during the carriage. The seller contracts with the insurer and pays the insurance premium.

FREIGHT CHARGE charge assessed for transporting FREIGHT.

FREIGHT CLAIM demand upon a CARRIER for the payment of overcharge or loss or damage sustained by SHIPPER or CONSIGNEE.

FREIGHT FORWARDER an independent business that handles EXPORT shipments for compensation. At the request of the SHIPPER, the forwarder makes the actual arrangements and provides the necessary services for expediting the shipment to its overseas destination. The forwarder takes care of all documentation needed to move the shipment from origin to destination, making up and assembling the necessary documentation for submission to the bank in the EXPORTER'S name. The forwarder arranges for CARGO insurance, makes the necessary overseas communications, and advises the shipper on overseas requirements of marking and labeling. The forwarder operates on a fee basis paid by the exporter and often receives an additional percentage of the freight charge from the common CARRIER. An export freight forwarder must be licensed by the FEDERAL MARITIME COMMISSION (FMC) to handle ocean freight and by the INTERNATIONAL AIR TRANSPORT ASSOCIATION (IATA) to handle air freight. An ocean freight forwarder dispatches shipments from the United States via common carriers, books or arranges space for the shipments, and handles the shipping documentation.

FREIGHT FORWARDER (DOMESTIC) a firm whose business involves contracting with carriers on behalf of EXPORTERS arranging for the shipment of the goods to the CONSIGNEE. *see also* FREIGHT FORWARDER.

FREIGHT VILLA a term used to describe a second house in Japan, which is used solely for the purpose of storing personal household effects.

FREIGHTER ship or airplane used to carry CARGO.

FRENCH COMMUNITY *see* CURRENCY AREA; FRANC ZONE.

FRENCH FRANC unit of currency in France, French Guyana, Guadaloupe, Martinique, Monaco, Reunion, St. Martin, and St. Pierre-Miquelon (100 centimes equal 1 French franc).

FRIENDSHIP, COMMERCE, AND NAVIGATION TREATY international agreement that specifies the rights and responsibilities of a country with regard to other countries and communication and transportation infrastructures.

FRINGE BENEFITS assorted forms of indirect compensation provided an employee upon acceptance of an international ASSIGNMENT.

FRONT END series of initial system events pertaining to data submission; also used to refer to the user interface portion of a system.

FRONTIER TRANSACTIONS *see* BALANCE OF PAYMENTS.

FS abbreviation for a feasibility study. *see also* TRADE AND DEVELOPMENT AGENCY.

FSA *see* FREEDOM SUPPORT ACT.

FSC *see* FOREIGN SALES CORPORATION.

FSI *see* FOREIGN SERVICE INSTITUTE.

FSN *see* FOREIGN SERVICE NATIONAL.

FSU *see* FORMER SOVIET UNION.

FT abbreviation for the measure of foot; also for FOREIGN TRADE.

FTA *see* FREE TRADE AGREEMENT; FREE-TRADE AREA.

FTA COMMISSION commission established under the authority of the CANADA–U.S. FREE TRADE AGREEMENT. The commission is co-chaired by the U.S. TRADE REPRESENTATIVE (USTR) and the Canadian Minister of International Trade. The commission is responsible for supervising the implementation of the agreement and takes part in the BINATIONAL DISPUTE SETTLEMENT MECHANISM.

FTA SELECT (AUTO) PANEL representatives of the U.S. TRADE REPRESENTATIVE (USTR) and the Canadian Minister of International Trade responsible for reporting on the state of the North American automotive industry and to submit recommendations on steps that can be taken to improve the competitiveness in the domestic and international markets.

FTD *see* FOREIGN TRADE DIVISION.

FTI *see* FOREIGN TRADERS INDEX.

FTP *see* FILE TRANSFER PROTOCOL.

FTSR *see* FOREIGN TRADE STATISTICAL REPORTING.

FTZs *see* FOREIGN TRADE ZONES.

FUNCTION major work element that accomplishes the mission or business of an organization, such as accounting, marketing, etc. A subfunction is a component of a function such as accounts receivable, accounts payable, etc. in the accounting function, or in data processing, a process performed by the computer on data.

FUNCTIONAL CURRENCY the currency of the principal economic environment in which the firm is operating. The firm is required to use the functional currency when using the CURRENT RATE METHOD in translating their financial statements. *see also* CONSOLIDATION; REPORTING CURRENCY; TEMPORAL METHOD; TRANSLATION.

FUNCTIONAL DISCOUNTS special allowances provided middlemen during the introductory stages of a marketing program. The objectives of such discounts are to compensate the middlemen for their efforts in selling, stocking, delivery, promotion, etc., and to encourage them to exert an additional effort on behalf of the firm and their marketing program.

FUNCTIONAL INTERMEDIARY an individual or firm, such as EXPORT PACKER or COMMON CARRIER, who provides services that physically alter the product enabling the product to be shipped to the customer. *see also* FACILITATING INTERMEDIARY.

FUNCTIONAL TRADE AGREEMENT a bilateral or multilateral understanding limited in scope used to MANAGE TRADE. *see also* FRAMEWORK AGREEMENT; VOLUNTARY EXPORT RESTRICTIONS; VOLUNTARY RESTRAINT AGREEMENT.

FUND FOR PREVENTIVE ASSISTANCE (FONAPRE) fund created in 1984 that is also called the Banking Fund for Savings Protection in Mexico. FONAPRE is headed by the Finance Secretariat and is similar in some ways to the U.S. Federal Deposit Insurance Corporation (FDIC). Unlike the FDIC, it has the option of selecting which checking accounts, saving accounts, and other conventional deposits it protects.

FUNDAMENTAL DISEQUILIBRIUM a macroeconomic condition characterized by an unusually large and continuous CURRENT ACCOUNT BALANCE, which might lead to an uncontrollable flow of capital into or out of the country. *see also* BALANCE OF PAYMENTS.

FUNDAMENTALISM conservative religious authoritarianism. Fundamentalism is not specific to Islam; it exists in all faiths. Characteristics include literal interpretation of scriptures and a strict adherence to traditional doctrines and practices.

FUNGIBLES goods that are identical to other goods of the same nature. *see also* IDENTICAL GOODS; SIMILAR GOODS; SIMILAR MERCHANDISE.

FURNISHING ALLOWANCE the reimbursement to an employee for the cost of furnishing his/her accommodations at the ASSIGNMENT location.

FUTURE ARRIVALS a column appearing daily in the JOURNAL OF COMMERCE. It lists the due dates for vessels scheduled to arrive at Atlantic ports. Vessels are also listed in alphabetical order with expected arrival dates at other North American ports.

FUTURE AUTOMATED COMMERCIAL ENVIRONMENT TEAM group established by the Deputy Commissioner of Customs in 1993 to develop a concept for redesigning the Customs AUTOMATED COMMERCIAL SYSTEM (ACS).

FUTURES CONTRACT an agreement stipulating an EXCHANGE RATE for exact amounts of currency with definite maturity dates in advance of a future transaction. *see also* FORWARD CONTRACT; FORWARD RATE.

FUTURES MARKET a market for exchange of currencies in the future. Participants contract to exchange currencies, not today, but at a specified calendar date in the future, and at an agreed to EXCHANGE RATE. *see also* FORWARD CONTRACT; FORWARD RATE; FUTURES CONTRACT.

F/X *see* FOREIGN EXCHANGE.

G

GAB *see* GENERAL ARRANGEMENTS TO BORROW.

GAMBIA RIVER BASIN DEVELOPMENT ORGANIZATION (French: Organisation pour la Mise en Valeur du Fleuve Gambie, OMVG) organization that promotes the construction of dams for hydroelectric and irrigation purposes. The organization was established in June 1978, and its headquarters is in Dakar, Senegal. Members include Gambia, Guinea, Guinea-Bissau, and Senegal.

GANG group of STEVEDORES under a supervisor, assigned to load or unload a portion of a vessel.

GANGWAY opening through which a ship is boarded.

GANTRY CRANE specialized machine for the raising or lowering of CARGO mounted on a structure spanning an open space on a ship. *see also* APPURTENANCE; SLING.

GAP ANALYSIS analysis of the difference between projected market potential and actual sales of an international firm. These differences can result from changes in usage patterns, competitive activity, incomplete product lines, or an inadequate distribution network.

GASTARBEITER (German) *see* GUEST WORKERS.

GATEWAY
1. in the context of travel activities, a major airport or seaport.
2. internationally, the port where customs clearance takes place.
3. a communications device/program that passes data between communication NETWORKS having similar functions but dissimilar implementations.

GATS *see* GENERAL LICENSE (AIRCRAFT ON TEMPORARY SOJOURN).

GATS *see* GENERAL AGREEMENT ON TRADE-IN SERVICES.

GATT *see* GENERAL AGREEMENT ON TARIFFS AND TRADE.

GATT AGREEMENTS *see* ROUNDS.

GATT CUSTOMS VALUATION CODE the agreed-upon formula to be used by GATT members in determining the value of goods being imported into their country. The code states that the DUTIABLE value of merchandise is determined by customs, and it is basically the TRANSACTION VALUE, the price the buyer actually pays the seller.

GATT DISPUTE SETTLEMENT SYSTEM *see* DISPUTE SETTLEMENT SYSTEM.

GATT PANEL a panel of neutral representatives that may be established by the GATT Secretariat under the dispute settlement provisions of the GENERAL AGREEMENT ON TARRIFS AND TRADE (GATT) to review the facts of a dispute, render findings of GATT law, and recommend action.

GATT STANDARDS CODE product standards code negotiated and accepted during the Tokyo Round in the 1970s. It is designed to eliminate the use of standards, technical regulations, and conformity assessment (certification) procedures as unnecessary barriers to trade. The standards code is administered by the GATT Secretariat in Geneva, Switzerland. The U.S. DEPARTMENT OF COMMERCE'S National Institute of Standards and Technology is responsible for several provisions of the standards code that relate to the establishment of a U.S. inquiry point, a standards information center, and a technical office for nonagricultural products.

GAUGE FOR INTERNATIONAL MARKET STRATEGIES (GIMS) a model developed by James D. Goodnow used to gauge international market strategies in determining the appropriate method used by a firm in entering a foreign market (i.e., INDIRECT EXPORT, DIRECT EXPORTING, LICENSING, ASSEMBLY, CONTRACT MANUFACTURING, JOINT VENTURE, WHOLLY OWNED SUBSIDIARY).

GCC *see* GULF COOPERATION COUNCIL.

GCCI *see* GLOBAL CONTRACT COMPREHENSIVE INSURANCE.

GCG *see* GENERAL LICENSE (SHIPMENTS TO AGENCIES OF COOPERATING GOVERNMENTS).

GCT *see* GENERAL LICENSE (GCT).

G-DEST *see* GENERAL LICENSE (G-DEST).

GDP *see* GROSS DOMESTIC PRODUCT.

GE *see* GENERAL EXCEPTION.

GEF *see* GLOBAL ENVIRONMENTAL FACILITY.

GEISHA BOND bond issued on the Japanese market in currencies other than the YEN. *see also* SAMURAI BOND; SUSHI BOND.

GEM *see* GLOBAL EXPORT MANAGER.

GEMSU *see* GERMAN ECONOMIC MONETARY AND SOCIAL UNION.

GENERAL AGREEMENT ON TARIFFS AND TRADE (GATT) a binding contract among over 100 governments. GATT was established in 1947 as an interim measure pending the establishment of the International Trade Organization, under the Havana Charter. GATT has provided the legal framework for international trade with its primary mission being the reduction of trade barriers. Its headquarters is in Geneva, Switzerland. *see also* ROUNDS; STANDARDS.

GENERAL AGREEMENT ON TRADE-IN SERVICES (GATS) an agreement, negotiated in the URUGUAY ROUND, that brings international trade-in services into the WTO. It arranges for countries to provide NATIONAL TREATMENT to foreign service providers and for them to select and negotiate the service sectors to be covered under GATS. *see also* MODES OF SUPPLY.

GENERAL ARRANGEMENTS TO BORROW (GAB) an agreement under which the INTERNATIONAL MONETARY FUND (IMF) may borrow monies from major industrial nations (Belgium, Canada, France, Germany, Italy, Japan, the Netherlands, the United Kingdom, the United States, Sweden, and Switzerland). The GAB were established in 1962 and amended several times. They were originally designed to enable the participants to strengthen the IMF by lending to it specified amounts of their currencies. These loans would be made when supplementary resources were needed to help finance purchases by GAB participants in circumstances where such financing would forestall or cope with an impairment of the international monetary system. The GAB were amended to include an associated agreement with Saudi Arabia and to permit the fund to use the arrangements to finance transactions with nonparticipants under certain conditions on purchases involving upper credit tranche conditionality.

GENERAL ASSEMBLY the main deliberative body of the United Nations. The General Assembly may consider any issues within the overall purview of the United Nations Charter and make recommendations to the SECURITY COUNCIL. Concurrence on general issues requires a simple majority of its membership, whereas a two-thirds majority of the members present and voting is necessary on issues deemed to be extremely important. As of November 1999, the membership of the General Assembly consisted of 185 nations. The General Assembly is located in the United Nations headquarters in New York.

GENERAL AVERAGE the loss resulting from a deliberate sacrifice of any part of the vessel or CARGO in an attempt to save the vessel and the remainder of the cargo. The cost of such a loss is shared (or averaged) on a prorated basis by the ship owner and all remaining cargo owners.

GENERAL CARGO RATE rate a CARRIER charges for the shipment of CARGO that does not have a special class rate or COMMODITY rate.

GENERAL CARGO VESSELS vessels designed to handle BREAK BULK CARGO such as bags, cartons, cases, crates, and drums, either individually or in unitized or palletized loads. *see also* CONTAINER SHIP; HATCH.

GENERAL COMMODITY RATE FREIGHT rate applicable to all COMMODITIES except those for which specific rates have been filed. *see also* SPECIFIC COMMODITY RATE.

GENERAL EXCEPTION a COCOM EXPORT licensing policy for items whose technical parameters exceed certain parameters. In the event the items being exported exceed those parameters, the general exception policy includes an 8-week cocom review with no presumption of approval. *see also* ADMINISTRATIVE EXCEPTION NOTE (AEN); FAVORABLE CONSIDERATION (FC).

GENERAL EXPENSES any direct and indirect costs of marketing goods. *see also* CUSTOMS VALUATION METHOD; COMPUTED VALUE METHOD; TRANSACTION VALUE METHOD.

GENERAL EXPORT LICENSE any various EXPORT licenses covering EXPORT COMMODITIES for which Validated Export Licenses are not required. No formal application or written authorization is needed to ship exports under a General Export License. *see also* INDIVIDUAL VALIDATED LICENSE (IVL).

GENERAL IMPORTS a measure of the total physical arrivals of merchandise from foreign countries, whether such merchandise enters consumption channels immediately or is entered into bonded warehouses or FOREIGN TRADE ZONES under CUSTOMS custody.

GENERAL LIABILITY unlimited responsibility for an obligation, such as the payment of debts of a business.

GENERAL LICENSE (GL) licenses, authorized by the U.S. BUREAU OF EXPORT ADMINISTRATION (BXA), that permit the EXPORT of goods and technology to specified countries without the need for a validated license. No prior written authorization is required, and no INDIVIDUAL VALIDATED LICENSE (IVL) is issued.

There are over 20 different types of general licenses, each represented by a symbol. These general licenses exist to accommodate the various exporting situations that the BXA has determined should not require an IVL.

GENERAL LICENSE—BAGGAGE authorization for individuals leaving the United States for any destination to take with them as personal baggage the following items: personal effects, household effects (including personal computers), vehicles, and tools of the trade (including highly technical ones), provided that certain conditions concerning these items are complied with by the EXPORTER.

GENERAL LICENSE—CREW limited authorization for a member of the crew on an exporting CARRIER to EXPORT personal and household items among his/her effects.

GENERAL LICENSE (GATS) (Aircraft on Temporary Sojourn) authorized departure of foreign registry civil aircraft on temporary sojourn in the United States from the United States and of U.S. civil aircraft for temporary sojourn abroad.

GENERAL LICENSE (GCG) (Shipments to Agencies of Cooperating Governments) limited authorization for the EXPORT of COMMODITIES for official use of any agency of a cooperating government within the territory of the cooperating government.

GENERAL LICENSE (GCT) limited authorization of EXPORTS to eligible countries of all "A" level COMMODITIES, except those specifically excluded in certain EXPORT CONTROL COMMODITY NUMBERS (ECCNS) on the COMMODITY CONTROL LIST, to COCOM and CoCom participating countries. Exports may be made under GCT only when intended for use or consumption within the importing country, REEXPORT among and consumption within eligible countries, or reexport in accordance with other provisions of the EXPORT ADMINISTRATION REGULATIONS (EAR).

GENERAL LICENSE (G-DEST) authorization of limited shipments of commodities to destinations not requiring a validated license. The majority of all items exported fall under the provisions of General License G-DEST.

GENERAL LICENSE (GFW) limited authorization of exports to most free-world destinations of certain COMMODITIES subject to national security controls. In most cases, these commodities have performance characteristics that permit the United States to approve EXPORTS to controlled countries with notification only to other COCOM governments.

GENERAL LICENSE (GIFT) authorization, subject to various provisions and limitations, of the EXPORT of gift parcels by an individual in the United States.

GENERAL LICENSE (GIT) limited authorization of the EXPORT from the United States of COMMODITIES that originate in one foreign country and are destined to another foreign country.

GENERAL LICENSE (GLOG) limited authorization of the EXPORT of unprocessed western red cedar timber harvested from federal, state, and other public lands in Alaska, all private lands, and land held in trust for recognized Indian tribes by federal or state agencies.

GENERAL LICENSE (GLR) authorization, subject to various provisions and limitations, for the return or repair of COMMODITIES and the replacement of parts.

GENERAL LICENSE (GLV) authorization, subject to various provisions and limitations, for the single shipment of a COMMODITY when the shipment does not exceed the value limit specified in the GLV paragraph of the EXPORT CONTROL CLASSIFICATION NUMBER (ECCN).

GENERAL LICENSE (G-NGO) authorization, subject to various provisions and limitations, for nongovernmental, nonprofit organizations to EXPORT donated items necessary to carry out small-scale humanitarian projects in Vietnam.

GENERAL LICENSE (GTDA) authorization of EXPORTS to all destinations of technical data that are in the public domain and generally available.

GENERAL LICENSE (GTDR) general license used when exporting technical data to free-world destinations. The information does not qualify under GTDA and an IVL is not required. The EXPORTER may use a GTDR. Certain GTDR shipments must be accompanied by a written assurance from the foreign CONSIGNEE stating that neither the technical data nor the direct product thereof will be shipped to COUNTRY GROUPS Q, S, W, Y, Z, or the People's Republic of China. Lower-level technology may be shipped without written assurance. This is generally referred to as GTDU.

GENERAL LICENSE (G-TEMP) authorization, subject to various provisions and limitations, for the temporary EXPORT of COMMODITIES and software for temporary use abroad for a period generally not to exceed 12 months.

GENERAL LICENSE (GTF-U.S.) authorization, subject to various provisions and limitations, for the EXPORT of COMMODITIES that were
- imported into the United States for display at an exhibition or trade fair and
- either entered under bond or permitted temporary free importation under bond providing for their EXPORT and are being exported in accordance with the terms of such bond.

GENERAL LICENSE (GUS) authorization of the EXPORT to any destination of COMMODITIES and software for personal or official use of personnel and agencies of the U.S. government.

GENERAL LICENSE (GVN) authorization, subject to various provisions and limitations, for EXPORT to Vietnam of low-level items to be used by the EXPORTER to open offices or do feasibility studies in connection with contracts to be executed after lifting of the embargo. The exporter must have obtained a license from the U.S. Treasury Department for the activities.

GENERAL LICENSE—PLANE STORES authorization, subject to various provisions and limitations, for the EXPORT on aircraft of U.S. or foreign registry departing from the United States of usual and reasonable kinds and quantities of COMMODITIES necessary to support the operation of an aircraft, provided the commodities are not intended for unloading in a foreign country and are not exported under a BILL OF LADING as CARGO.

GENERAL LICENSE—SAFEGUARDS authorization, subject to various provisions and limitations, for the EXPORT to the INTERNATIONAL ATOMIC ENERGY AGENCY (IAEA) and the EUROPEAN ATOMIC ENERGY COMMUNITY (EURATOM).

GENERAL LICENSE—SHIP STORES authorization, subject to various provisions and limitations, for the EXPORT of usual and reasonable kinds and quantities of the COMMODITIES to support the operations of a vessel, provided the commodities are not intended for unloading in a foreign country and are not exported under a BILL OF LADING as CARGO.

GENERAL ORDER merchandise not entered within 5 working days after arrival of the CARRIER at CUSTOMS and stored at the expense of the IMPORTER. *see also* DEMURRAGE; GENERAL ORDER WAREHOUSE.

GENERAL ORDER WAREHOUSE warehouse where CUSTOMS sends merchandise that has not been claimed within 5 days of arrival. *see also* DEMURRAGE; GENERAL ORDER.

GENERAL SALES MANAGER (GSM) two programs, GSM-102 and GSM-103, of the U.S. Department of Agriculture's COMMODITY CREDIT CORPORATION that provide guarantees for the repayment of commercial credit extended to finance U.S. agricultural EXPORT sales. The programs differ principally in the length of their terms of coverage. The GSM-102 program (for General Sales Manager) provides coverage for terms extending from 6 months to 3 years. Guarantees are extended to U.S. banks confirming foreign letters of credit issued to assist foreign importers who wish to buy U.S. exports and to help primarily developing countries that may face difficulties in obtaining a loan. The GSM-103 program provides coverage for terms extending from 48 months to 10 years. Guarantees are extended to foreign importers who wish to buy U.S. exports and to help primarily developing countries that may face difficulties in obtaining a loan.

GENERAL TARIFF a TARIFF that applies to countries that do not enjoy either preferential or MOST-FAVORED-NATION TARIFF TREATMENT. Where the general tariff rate differs from the most-favored-nation rate, the general tariff rate is usually the higher rate.

GENERAL TRADING COMPANIES firms that are involved either in importing products for local distribution to consumers or other companies, or in representing firms in identifying customers for their products in other countries. *see also* SOGO SHOSHA.

GENERALIZED SYSTEM OF PREFERENCES (GSP) a framework under which developed countries give preferential TARIFF treatment to manufactured goods imported from certain developing countries. GSP is one element of a coordinated effort by the industrial trading nations to bring developing countries more fully into the international trading system. The U.S. GSP scheme is a system of nonreciprocal tariff preferences for the benefit of these countries. The U.S. conducts annual GSP reviews to consider petitions requesting modification of product coverage and/or country eligibility. U.S. GSP law requires that a beneficiary country's laws and practices relating to market access, intellectual property rights protection, investment, EXPORT practices, and workers' rights be considered in all GSP decisions.

GENERALLY ACCEPTED ACCOUNTING PRINCIPLES the recognized consensus within a country at a particular time as to which economic resources and obligations should be recorded as assets and liabilities and which changes in them should be measured, what information should be disclosed and how it should be disclosed, and which financial statements should be prepared.

GENEVA CONVENTION FOR THE PROTECTION OF PRODUCERS OF PHONOGRAMS AGAINST UNAUTHORIZED DUPLICATION OF THEIR PHONOGRAMS a multilateral treaty providing for the protection of intellectual property around the world through cooperation among states. The agreement is administered by the WORLD INTELLECTUAL PROPERTY ORGANIZATION.

GENEVA PROTOCOL 1925 the first treaty to prohibit the use of biological weapons.

GEOCENTRISM (GEOCENTRIC ORGANIZATION) a characteristic of a firm that does not view any one country as more important than any other for the firm. It refers to the process of the firm taking a worldwide or global orientation toward doing business internationally. Example: the products developed in one country are marketed concurrently to other countries around the world.

GEOGRAPHIC CODES a list of countries meeting the requirements as AGENCY FOR INTERNATIONAL DEVELOPMENT (AID) eligible sources. Many AID agreements require that COMMODITIES be purchased from the United States or from selected free-world countries. To meet these requirements, a COMMODITY must be produced in and shipped from an eligible country.

GEOGRAPHIC HOLE the absence of a multinational firm in a particular market that the firm views as important, but that can be viewed as harmful to the firm's overall international marketing program.

GERMAN REUNIFICATION the unification of the Federal Republic of Germany (West Germany) and the Democratic Republic of Germany (East Germany).

GERM WARFARE the use of biological agents to harm targeted people either directly, by bringing the people into contact with the agents or indirectly, by infecting animals and plants, which would in turn harm the people.

GESELLSCHAFT MIT BESCHRANKTE HAFTUNG (GmbH) (German, meaning limited liability company) a German corporation with separate legal personality. Its shareholders participate in the original share capital with their initial contributions but are not liable to the company's creditors. One person alone can form a limited liability company, but legal entities may also be shareholders. The company name of a limited liability company must either be derived from the purpose of its business or—as in the case of LIMITED PARTNERSHIPS—from the name of the shareholder or a combination of both. It must always state "with limited liability" (mbH).

GFW *see* GENERAL LICENSE (GFW).

GIBRALTAR POUND unit of currency, Gibraltar (100 pennies equal 1 Gibraltar pound).

GIE *see* GROUPEMENT D'INTERET ECONOMIQUE.

GIF acronym for Graphic Interchange Format. A format developed in the mid 1980s by CompuServe, a commercial NETWORK, for use in transmitting photo-quality graphic images. GIFs are widely used on-line.

GIFT *see* GENERAL LICENSE (GIFT).

GILT-EDGED MARKET all marketable securities in the United Kingdom, with the exception of Treasury Bills.

GILTS securities issued by the British and Irish governments, and also those issued by local British authorities.

GIT *see* GENERAL LICENSE.

GLANDERS an infectious bacterial disease known to cause inflammation in horses, donkeys, mules, goats, dogs, and cats.

GLASNOST a Russian word made popular by former Soviet President Gorbachev meaning openness. It referred to an official political policy of the Soviet Union of openness of information between the Soviet Union, its citizens, and the world community.

GLOBAL ALLIANCING an international marketing strategy involving the formation of cooperative relationships between firms so as to reduce overall operating costs through the sharing of common fixed expenses, thereby allowing the cooperating firms to have more profitable comprehensive global marketing operations.

GLOBAL BANKER a column appearing in the JOURNAL OF COMMERCE. It discusses capital flows, financing, and trends in the global marketplace for funds.

GLOBAL BOND bond that can be traded immediately in any United States capital market and in the EUROMARKET.

GLOBAL CASH MANAGEMENT the establishment of a centralized system to control cash flow in a multinational firm. The objective of such a program is to ensure effective acquisition and use of funds so as to maximize the return. Cash management is more complex in multinational firms because of the potential for government control of foreign exchange transactions, fluctuating exchange rates, etc.

GLOBAL CONTRACT COMPREHENSIVE INSURANCE a program of the EXPORT DEVELOPMENT CORPORATION in Canada that provides insurance coverage for Canadian exporters against nonpayment of invoices for either commercial or political reasons. The coverage is initiated at the time the goods are ordered and remains in effect until payment is received. *see also* COMMERCIAL RISKS; POLITICAL RISKS.

GLOBAL CORPORATION *see* MULTINATIONAL CORPORATION.

GLOBAL ENVIRONMENTAL FACILITY (GEF) jointly administered program by the WORLD BANK and the UNITED NATIONS DEVELOP-

MENT PROGRAMS (UNDP) aimed at four global problems: climate change, pollution of international waters, destruction of biodiversity, and depletion of the stratospheric ozone. The facility was started in 1990 as a pilot project to help developing countries protect the environment and to transfer environmentally benign technology to these nations.

GLOBAL EXPORT MANAGER (GEM) an electronic system for collecting and disseminating trade leads and business opportunities. GEM is maintained by the NATIONAL ASSOCIATION OF STATE DEVELOPMENT AGENCIES (NASDA).

GLOBAL MARKETING *see* INTERNATIONAL MARKETING.

GLOBAL MARKET SURVEYS foreign market industry reports prepared and distributed by the U.S. DEPARTMENT OF COMMERCE. These surveys provide comprehensive, in-depth research performed on location in overseas markets. Reports cover market size and outlook, market characteristics, and competitive and end-user analysis for selected industry subsectors in a particular country.

GLOBAL QUOTA a quota on the total imports of a product from all countries.

GLOBAL SCANNING the orderly collection of information regarding a multinational's external environment, analyzing it and forecasting the impact these environmental forces have on the firm. The forces that could have an impact on the firm include political, legal, economic, technological, and cultural.

GLOBAL SERVICES COMPREHENSIVE INSURANCE a program of the EXPORT DEVELOPMENT CORPORATION in Canada that supplies insurance coverage for Canadian exporters that provide services against nonpayment of invoices for either commercial or political reasons. The coverage is in effect while the services are being performed and remains in effect until payment is received. *see also* COMMERCIAL RISKS; POLITICAL RISKS.

GLOBAL SHIPMENTS COMPREHENSIVE INSURANCE a program of the EXPORT DEVELOPMENT CORPORATION in Canada that provides insurance coverage for Canadian exporters against nonpayment of invoices for either commercial or political reasons. The coverage is initiated at the time the goods are shipped and remains in effect until payment is received. *see also* COMMERCIAL RISKS; POLITICAL RISKS.

GLOBAL SOURCING the acquisition by a domestic company of materials and supplies from foreign suppliers for domestic production or distribution.

GLOBAL STRATEGY the program for defining and achieving the organization's global marketing objectives.

GLOBAL SYSTEM OF TRADE PREFERENCES *see* GENERALIZED SYSTEM OF PREFERENCES.

GLOBALIZATION the increasing worldwide integration of markets for goods, SERVICES, and capital that attracted special attention in the late 1990s.

GLOG *see* GENERAL LICENSE.

GmbH *see* GESELLSCHAFT MIT BESCHRANKTE HAFTUNG.

G-NGO *see* GENERAL LICENSE (G-NGO).

GNP *see* GROSS NATIONAL PRODUCT.

GNU abbreviation for GNu's Not UNIX. A free version of the UNIX operating system being developed by the Free Software Foundation. GNU is not finished, but another FREEWARE adaptation of UNIX is in wide use.

GOING GLOBAL refers to the worldwide trade program being undertaken by the Canadian government through the year 2000.

GOLD EXCHANGE STANDARD a system under which currency values are set in terms of gold. *see also* BRETTON WOODS CONFERENCE.

GOLD EXPORT POINT the amount of gold content equal to one unit of a foreign country's currency plus shipping costs between two countries. *see also* MINT PARITY.

GOLD IMPORT POINT the amount of gold content equal to one unit of a foreign country's currency minus shipping costs between two countries. *see also* MINT PARITY.

GOLD KEY SERVICE a U.S. INTERNATIONAL TRADE ADMINISTRATION service that provides customized information for U.S. firms visiting a country—market orientation briefings, market research, introductions to potential business partners, an interpreter for meetings, assistance in developing a market strategy, and help in putting together a follow-up plan. Trade specialists design an agenda of meetings, screen and select the right companies, arrange meetings with key people, and go with U.S. representatives to ensure that no unforeseen difficulties occur.

GOLD POOL an agreement of the GROUP OF TEN to establish a gold reserve to be used by the market in London, England, to maintain and prevent the official price of gold rising above U.S.$35.00 per ounce. The Gold Pool replaced the TWO-TIER GOLD MARKET in 1968.

GOLD RESERVES gold retained by a nation's monetary agency that forms the backing of currency that the nation has issued. *see also* GOLD EXCHANGE STANDARD; GOLD EXPORT POINT; GOLD IMPORT POINT; GOLD POOL; GOLD STANDARD.

GOLD STANDARD refers to the now defunct international monetary system under which each country established the value of its currency in terms of gold. *see also* FLOATING EXCHANGE RATE.

GONDOLA CAR an open railway car with sides and ends, used principally for hauling CARGO such as coal or sand.

GOOD NEIGHBORLY TREATMENT an agreement between nations not to interfere in the internal affairs of each other. *see also* FRIENDSHIP, COMMERCE, AND NAVIGATION TREATY (FCN).

GOODS *see* COMMODITY.

GOODS AND SERVICES TAX the consumption tax in Canada. *see also* VALUE-ADDED TAX (VAT).

GOODS OF THE SAME CLASS OR KIND goods that fall within a group or range of goods produced by a particular industry or industry sector and that include identical or similar goods. *see also* CUSTOMS VALUATION; IDENTICAL GOODS; SIMILAR GOODS.

GOPHER a distributed information service that makes available hierarchical collections of information across the INTERNET. Gopher uses a simple protocol that allows a single Gopher client to access information from any accessible Gopher server, providing the user with a single "Gopher space" of information. Public domain versions of the client and server are available. *see also* ARCHIE; ARCHIVE SITE; PROSPERO.

GOURDE unit of currency, Haiti (100 centimes equal 1 gourde).

GOVERNMENT ACCOUNTS *see* CANADA ACCOUNT.

GOVERNMENT PROCUREMENT CODE *see* AGREEMENT OF GOVERNMENT PROCUREMENT.

GOVERNMENT PROCUREMENT POLICIES AND PRACTICES a nontariff barrier to trade involving the discriminatory purchase by official government agencies of goods and services from domestic suppliers, even in cases where the domestic suppliers' prices are higher or their quality is inferior as compared with competitive goods that could be imported.

GRADUATION a term used when a country is removed from any preferential TARIFF listings for a specific product or taken off the entire list as a result of industrial development. *see also* GENERALIZED SYSTEM OF PREFERENCES.

GRANDFATHER CLAUSE a GENERAL AGREEMENT ON TARIFFS AND TRADE (GATT) provision that allows the original contracting parties to exempt from general GATT obligations mandatory domestic legislation that is inconsistent with GATT provisions but that existed before the GATT was signed. Newer members may also "grandfather" domestic legislation if that is agreed to in negotiating the terms of accession. (U.S. legislation also provides for "grandfather clauses.")

GRANTEE
1. one to whom a grant is made; a grant being the giving or permitting as a right or privilege, an authority, a power, a license, or a property.

  2. a corporation to which the privilege of establishing, operating, and maintaining a FOREIGN TRADE ZONE (FTZ) in the United States has been granted by the Foreign Trade Zone Board. *see also* FREE PORT; FREE ZONE.

GRAY MARKET GOODS
  1. products that are fakes, frauds, copies, or counterfeits of authentic products.
  2. imported goods bearing a genuine trademark but imported by a party other than the trademark holder or authorized IMPORTER.

GRAY MARKETING the process of planning, pricing, promoting, and distributing GRAY MARKET GOODS.

GRAY MONEY *see* DIRTY MONEY.

GREEN BOX a category of SUBSIDIES permitted under the WORLD TRADE ORGANIZATION AGRICULTURE AGREEMENT.

GREEN CARD an identity card (VISA) issued by the U.S. Immigration and Naturalization Service entitling a FOREIGN national to enter and reside in the United States as a permanent resident.

GREEN CLAUSE a special clause found in a LETTER OF CREDIT, providing for a regular expiration date with an automatic extension. The clause usually appears in STANDBY or REVOLVING LETTERS OF CREDIT.

GREEN CONSUMER refers to ever-increasing environmentally conscious buyers and users of products, particularly in DEVELOPED COUNTRIES. This movement means that international marketers will have to review materials being used, pricing programs, product formulations, etc., so as to appeal to this new consumer.

GREEN CUSTOMS LABEL (FORM 2976) a declaration form that must be completed and attached by an individual sending a letter or package containing DUTIABLE items via the postal service.

GREEN FIELD INVESTMENT foreign DIRECT INVESTMENT that involves construction of a new plant, rather then the purchase of an existing plant or firm.

GREY LIST list of disreputable end users in nations of concern for missile proliferation from the U.S. intelligence community.

GRID fixed margin within which exchange rates are allowed to fluctuate. *see also* FLEXIBLE EXCHANGE RATES; FLOATING CURRENCY; FLOATING EXCHANGE RATES; FLUCTUATING EXCHANGE RATE.

GROSS DOMESTIC PRODUCT (GDP) a measure of the market value of all goods and services produced within the boundaries of a nation, regardless of asset ownership. Unlike GROSS NATIONAL PRODUCT (GNP), GDP excludes receipts from that nation's business operations in foreign countries, as well as the share of reinvested earnings in foreign affiliates of domestic corporations.

GROSS NATIONAL PRODUCT (GNP) a measure of the market value of goods and services produced by the labor and property of a nation. Includes receipts from that nation's business operation in foreign countries, as well as the share of reinvested earnings in foreign affiliates of domestic corporations.

GROSS WEIGHT the full weight of a shipment, including goods and packaging. *see also* TARE WEIGHT.

GROUP OF FIVE (G-5) similar to the GROUP OF SEVEN (G-7), except Canada and Italy do not belong.

GROUP OF SEVEN (G-7) group of seven major industrialized countries who have met annually since 1976 in summit meetings to discuss economic and political issues. The seven are the United States, Canada, Japan, Britain, France, Germany, and Italy (plus the EUROPEAN UNION). *see also* G-8.

GROUP OF EIGHT (G-8) the G-7 countries plus Russia, which have met as a full economic and political summit since 1998.

GROUP OF TEN (G-10) established in 1962, 10 of the wealthiest industrial members of the INTERNATIONAL MONETARY FUND (IMF) "stand ready to lend currencies to the IMF up to specified amounts when their resources are needed" under the IMF'S GENERAL AGREEMENTS TO BORROW (GAB). The finance ministers of these countries comprise the Group of 10 (also called the PARIS CLUB). Members include Belgium, Canada, France, Germany, Italy, Japan, the Netherlands, Sweden, Switzerland, the United Kingdom, and the United States. Although they number 11 with the addition of Switzerland in 1984, the numerical name persists.

GROUP OF ELEVEN (G-11) established in 1984, this group includes the largest debtor nations in Latin America (also known as the CARTAGENA GROUP). Members include Argentina, Bolivia, Brazil, Chile, Colombia, Dominican Republic, Ecuador, Mexico, Peru, Uruguay, and Venezuela.

GROUP OF FIFTEEN (G-15) established in 1990, this group consists of relatively prosperous or large developing countries. The G-15 discusses the benefits of mutual cooperation in improving their international economic positions. Members include Algeria, Argentina, Brazil, Egypt, India, Indonesia, Jamaica, Malaysia (a very active member), Mexico, Nigeria, Peru, Senegal, Venezuela, the former Yugoslavia, and Zimbabwe.

GROUP OF TWENTY-FOUR (G-24) a grouping of finance ministers from 24 developing country members of the INTERNATIONAL MONETARY FUND (IMF). The group, representing 8 countries from each of the African, Asian, and Latin American country groupings in the GROUP OF SEVENTY-SEVEN, was formed in January 1972 to counterbalance the influence of the GROUP OF TEN.

GROUP OF SEVENTY-SEVEN (G-77) a grouping of developing countries that received its name in connection with 77 countries issuing a joint statement in Geneva, Switzerland, in 1964. The G-77's primary focus is serving as a caucus for articulating members' collective interests primarily in areas of promoting economic cooperation among developing countries and in negotiations on economic matters with developing countries. G-77 membership has increased since 1964 to over 125 countries.

GROUPEMENT D'INTERET ECONOMIQUE (GIE) (French, meaning economic interest grouping) a joint venture that has features of both a partnership and a corporation. The GIE is used by enterprises that wish to set up a joint activity on a trial basis to cooperate, but not to merge. The GIE must be an extension of some activity of its members, frequently marketing, research, and management. AIRBUS INDUSTRIES GROUP is an example of a GIE.

GROUPISM refers to the individual's role in Japanese organizations. The concept states that individuals must do what is best for the organization as a whole rather than what might be best for the individual. The interests of the group override those of the individuals, and all individuals are required to be subservient to the wishes of the group. *see also* NEMAWASHI; TATEMAE.

GSM *see* GENERAL SALES MANAGER.

GSP *see* GENERALIZED SYSTEM OF PREFERENCES.

GST *see* GOODS AND SERVICES TAX.

GTDA *see* GENERAL LICENSE (GTDA).

GTDR *see* GENERAL LICENSE (GTDR).

G-TEMP *see* GENERAL LICENSE (G-TEMP).

GTF-U.S. *see* GENERAL LICENSE (GTF-U.S.).

GTZ *see* DEUTSCHE GESELLSCHAFT FÜR TECHNISCHE ZUSAMMENARBEIT.

GUARANI unit of currency, Paraguay (100 centimos equal 1 guarani).

GUERNSEY POUND unit of currency, Guernsey (100 pennies equal 1 Guernsey pound).

GUEST WORKERS foreign workers who are legally brought in by a government to perform certain types of jobs over a specified time. These workers normally come from countries that have many refugees or that have high birth rates.

GUINEA-BISSAU PESO unit of currency, Guinea-Bissau (100 centavos equal 1 Guinea-Bissau peso).

GUINEAN FRANC unit of currency, Guinea (Conakry) (100 cauris equal 1 Guinean franc).

GULDEN unit of currency, the Netherlands (100 cents equal 1 gulden).

GULF COOPERATION COUNCIL (GCC) Persian Gulf council established in May 1981, seeking to strengthen cooperation (in areas such as agriculture, industry, investment, security, and trade) among its 6 members: Bahrain, Kuwait, Qatar, Oman, Saudi Arabia, and the United Arab Emirates. The GCC, created in response to the outbreak of the Iran–Iraq war, established the Gulf Standards Organization in November 1982 and the Gulf Investment Corporation in 1984. The presidency of the GCC rotates yearly among members. Council headquarters is in Riyadh, Saudi Arabia.

GUS *see* GENERAL LICENSE (GUS).

GUYANA DOLLAR unit of currency, Guyana (100 cents equal 1 Guyana dollar).

GVN *see* GENERAL LICENSE (GVN).

H

H-1 VISA a specialized term used by U.S. immigration to describe a temporary worker of distinguished merit and ability being allowed to enter into the United States. The VISA is a stamp on the foreign national's passport issued by a U.S. consular officer that allows the individual to enter the United States and conduct business. *see also* B-1 VISA; L-1 VISA; WORK PERMIT; WORK VISA.

HABATSU (Japanese) a term used when making reference to an individual's followers or supporters. These individuals follow their leader on the basis of their own self-interest or personal loyalties. *see also* KANRYOHA; KEIBATSU; NOMENKLATURA.

HABITAT *see* UNITED NATIONS COMMISSION ON HUMAN SETTLEMENTS.

HAGUE AGREEMENT CONCERNING THE INTERNATIONAL DEPOSIT OF INDUSTRIAL DESIGNS a MULTILATERAL TREATY, also known as the Hague Act of 1960, that promotes protection of intellectual property around the world through cooperation among states, and administers various "unions," each founded on a multilateral treaty and dealing with the legal and administrative aspects of intellectual property. The treaty is administered by the WORLD INTELLECTUAL PROPERTY ORGANIZATION, which was established in 1967 (came into force in 1970), and became a specialized agency of the United Nations in December 1974. The headquarters is in Geneva, Switzerland.

HALLMARK impression made on gold and silverware introduced in the beginning of the fourteenth century in England to identify the quality of the metal used.

HAMAS a radical Islamic organization that operates primarily in the West Bank and Gaza Strip whose goal is to establish an Islamic Palestinian state in place of Israel.

HAMBURG RULES an adaptation to the UNITED NATIONS CONVENTION ON THE CARRIAGE OF GOODS BY SEA. It refers to the guidelines provided for by the UNITED NATIONS CONFERENCE ON TRADE AND DEVELOPMENT regarding the level of liability for a sea carrier for loss or damage to goods in transit. The Hamburg Rules allowed for an increase in a carrier's liability with the aim of creating a sense of equity between shippers and ship owners. *see also* CODE OF CONDUCT FOR LINER CONFERENCES; UNITED NATIONS CONFERENCE ON TRADE AND DEVELOPMENT (UNCTAD).

HANDSHAKE electronic connection methodology used by two modems in order to take turns sending and receiving data in an orderly way.

HARBOR FEES charges assessed to harbor users for maintenance purposes.

HARBORMASTER officer who attends to the berthing, etc. of ships in a harbor. *see also* PILOT.

HARD CURRENCY the currency of a nation that may be exchanged for that of another nation without restriction. Sometimes referred to as convertible currency. Hard-currency countries typically have sizable exchange reserves and surpluses in their BALANCE OF PAYMENTS (BOP). *see also* SOFT CURRENCY.

HARD LOAN FOREIGN loan that must be paid in HARD MONEY. *see also* HARD CURRENCY; HARD MONEY; SOFT CURRENCY; WORLD BANK.

HARD MONEY currency of a nation that has stability in the country and abroad. *see also* HARD CURRENCY; SOFT CURRENCY.

HARDSHIP ALLOWANCE an additional form of direct compensation when an individual is placed at a location that is less than desirable. This payment is usually made over and above the EXPATRIATION PREMIUM. *see also* DANGER PAY; EXPATRIATE ALLOWANCE; FOREIGN SERVICE PREMIUM.

HARD SIDE (OF INTERNATIONAL MARKETING) those elements of marketing dealing with areas that can be quantified, such as profits, costs, and logistics strategies. *see also* SOFT SIDE (OF INTERNATIONAL MARKETING).

HARMONIZATION the changing of government regulations and practices, as a result of an INTERNATIONAL AGREEMENT, to make those of different countries the same or more compatible.

HARMONIZE the process of bringing about a state of mutual agreement. *see also* HARMONIZED SYSTEM.

HARMONIZED CODE *see* HARMONIZED SYSTEM.

HARMONIZED SYSTEM (HS) a system for classifying goods in international trade, developed under the auspices of the CUSTOMS COOPERATION COUNCIL. Beginning on January 1, 1989, the new HS numbers replaced previously adhered to schedules in over 50 countries, including the United States.

   For the United States, the HS numbers and four additional digits are the numbers that are entered on the actual EXPORT and IMPORT documents. Any other COMMODITY code classification number (SITC, end-use, etc.) are just rearrangements and transformations of the original HS numbers.

HARMONIZED SYSTEM COMMITTEE a unit of the CUSTOMS COOPERATION COUNCIL that serves to study and make recommendations in resolving the various countries' customs problems in an attempt to harmonize customs operations and promote trade. The council was established in 1950 and is headquartered in Brussels, Belgium. *see also* HARMONIZED SYSTEM; U.S. INTERNATIONAL TRADE COMMISSION (USITC).

HARMONIZED TARIFF SCHEDULE (HTS) *see* HARMONIZED SYSTEM.

HARMONIZED TARIFF SCHEDULE OF THE UNITED STATES (HTSUS) *see* HARMONIZED SYSTEM.

HARTER ACT legislation protecting a ship's owner against claims for damage resulting from the behavior of the vessel's crew, provided the ship left port in proper condition.

HATCH opening in the deck of a vessel that gives access to the CARGO hold. *see also* GENERAL CARGO VESSELS.

HAULAGE local transport of goods; also, the charge(s) made for hauling FREIGHT on carts, DRAYS, or trucks; also called cartage or DRAYAGE.

HAZARDOUS MATERIAL substance or material that has been determined by the U.S. Secretary of Transportation to be capable of posing an unreasonable risk to health, safety, and property when transported in commerce, and that has been so designated. *see also* DRY CARGO; PERISHABLE FREIGHT.

HEADER the element of a data packet that comes before the actual data, and provides source and destination addresses, error checking, and other fields. A header is also that part of an ELECTRONIC MAIL MESSAGE that comes before the body of a message and has, as well as other things, the message originator, date, and time.

HEARING an inquiry that is held at the request of an interested party in ANTIDUMPING PETITION for the purpose of allowing interested persons to express their views orally to officials of the U.S. DEPARTMENT OF COMMERCE. The hearing is held prior to the Commerce Department's (INTERNATIONAL TRADE ADMINISTRATION) final determination or before the final results of an administrative review are published. *see also* TARIFF ACT OF 1930.

HEAVILY INDEBTED POOR COUNTRIES name given to those countries with large debts, which are then the focus of initiatives to forgive that debt as a means of assisting development. *see also* DEVELOPING COUNTRIES; DEVELOPMENT ASSISTANCE; DEVELOPMENT ASSISTANCE COMMITTEE; LESS-DEVELOPED COUNTRIES.

HEAVY LIFT refers to articles too heavy to be lifted by a ship's tackle. *see also* GANTRY CRANE; HEAVY LIFT CHARGE; HEAVY LIFT VESSEL.

HEAVY LIFT CHARGE charge made for lifting articles too heavy to be lifted by a ship's tackle. *see also* HEAVY LIFT.

HEAVY LIFT VESSEL vessel with HEAVY LIFT cranes and other equipment designed to be self-sustaining in the handling of heavy CARGO.

HECKSCHER-OHLIN THEORY trade theory that advances the concept of COMPARATIVE ADVANTAGE requiring the endowment and cost of factors of production. This thory explains why nations with large labor forces focus on producing LABOR INTENSIVE goods, whereas countries with more capital than labor focus on producing CAPITAL INTENSIVE goods. *see also* FACTOR ENDOWMENT; FACTOR MOBILITY.

HEDGE a form of protection used by firms to guard against FLUCTUATING EXCHANGE RATES. For example, a firm could enter into a FORWARD CONTRACT as a way to eliminate the risks associated with an unfavorable change in an EXCHANGE RATE.

HEDGE RATIO amount of future exchange contracts, OPTIONS, or underlying financial instruments, purchased or sold against a position to accomplish a HEDGE of the position.

HELLENIC EXPORT PROMOTION PROGRAM (HEPO) an international trade association formed to promote the interests of Greek manufacturers in foreign markets.

HELLENIC ORGANIZATION FOR SMALL & MEDIUM SIZED ENTERPRISES & HANDICRAFTS an international trade association formed to promote the interests of small to medium-sized Greek handicraft manufacturers.

HELMS-BURTON ACT United States law enacted in 1996 that penalized companies for doing business in Cuba. *see also* EMBARGO; TRADE BARRIER.

HELSINKI ACCORD agreement that deals with the rights of people to migrate freely. The tourism portions of the accord encourage
• tourism and tourism studies;
• preservation of artistic, historic, and cultural heritages of signatories;
• lowering of fees and documentation needed for international travel; and
• other efforts to encourage cooperation on tourism among countries.
   The accord was signed in 1975 and has been subsequently modified, recognizing the end of the division of Europe and of the Cold War. *see also* CONFERENCE ON SECURITY AND COOPERATION IN EUROPE (CSCE).

HEMORRHAGIC FEVERS describes a severe multisystem syndrome wherein the overall vascular system is damaged and the body becomes unable to regulate itself. The symptoms are commonly accompanied by hemorrhage; however, the bleeding itself is not usually life threatening. Some types of hemorrhagic fever viruses cause only relatively mild illnesses.

HETARCHY an organizational structure in management whereby all parties are considered equal, with no subordinate–superior relationship found in the organization. It is often used when referring to the management of affiliated companies where it is not clear that one company is superior to the other. *see also* HIERARCHY; KEIRETSU.

HEZBOLLAH one of many terrorist organizations that seek the destruction of Israel and the United States.

HICKENLOOPER AMENDMENT OF 1961 an amendment to an American law providing for the suspension of all foreign aid to any country that nationalizes American-owned property in that country or that has attempted to abrogate an existing contract without attempting to reach a settlement within a reasonable period of time. *see also* CONFISCATION; EXPROPRIATION; NATIONALIZATION; PRIVATIZATION.

HIDDEN DAMAGE the condition of goods that have been damaged while in transit that is not visible from a simple external examination of the packages. Insurance carriers normally have strict time limitations for the placing of such claims. *see also* OBVIOUS DAMAGE; PILFERAGE.

HIDDEN ECONOMY *see* BLACK MARKET.

HIERARCHY a superior–subordinate relationship between and among companies. *see also* HETARCHY.

HIGH-CONTEXT CULTURE a society where meaning is communicated between and among individuals through the use of extensive nonverbal methods of communication rather than what is explicitly stated. *see also* LOW-CONTEXT CULTURE; SITUATIONAL CONFORMITY.

HIGH DENSITY cargo whose weight is high in relation to its volume. A shipping company charges freight according to weight or volume, whichever yields the highest freight charge, resulting in high-density freight being charged on a weight basis. *see also* HEAVY LIFT CHARGE.

HIGH-PERFORMANCE COMPUTING AND COMMUNICATIONS (HPCC) an advanced computer system having high-speed computing, communications, information technologies, multiple processor, advanced network systems, and other special-purpose and experimental features, including advanced software.

HIJRAH CALENDAR a 12-month lunar calendar used in Middle Eastern Islamic countries.

HIPC *see* HEAVILY INDEBTED POOR COUNTRIES.

HITCHMENT combination of portions of a SHIPMENT with different geographical regions that move under one BILL OF LADING from SHIPPER to CONSIGNEE. *see also* CONSOLIDATED SHIPMENT.

HOFS German-style beer halls found in Korea. The presence of these establishments has increased dramatically over the past several years, and customers are expected to purchase a dish of snacks or food with their beer.

HOLD space below deck in a vessel used to carry CARGO.

HOLD FOR PICKUP FREIGHT to be held at the CARRIER's destination location for pickup by the recipient.

HOLD HARMLESS CONTRACT agreement by which one party accepts responsibility for all damages and other liability that arise from a transaction, relieving the other party of any such liability.

HOLDER *see* QUOTA HOLDER.

HOME BIAS preference, by consumers, for products produced in their country, as opposed to otherwise identical IMPORTS. *see also* HOME COUNTRY; HOST COUNTRY.

HOME COUNTRY the country in which a company engaged in international trade and investment is headquartered. *see also* HOST COUNTRY.

HOME LEAVE a special allowance provided by employers covering the expense of trips back to the HOME COUNTRY. The frequency of such trips is related to the degree of hardship at the overseas assignment. The purpose of such leave is to allow the employee to renew family and business relationships, in an attempt to minimize any potential adjustment problems at time of repatriation.

HOME MARKET PRICE *see* FOREIGN MARKET VALUE.

HOMOCIDE BOMBINGS term to replace the old "suicide bombings."

HOMOLOGATION OF AN AUTOMOBILE the certification by a country that a vehicle conforms to its safety and emission standards—primarily that a vehicle has been manufactured or modified to meet a country's standards.

HONG family-owned business empire in Hong Kong.

HONG KONG DOLLAR unit of currency, Hong Kong (100 cents equal 1 Hong Kong dollar).

HONNE (Japanese) the innermost feelings that Japanese hide from others when involved in groups. *see also* GROUPISM; TATEMAE.

HONOR to pay or to accept a DRAFT complying with the terms of credit.

HORIZONTAL EXPORT TRADING COMPANY an EXPORT TRADING COMPANY that exports a range of similar or identical products supplied by a number of manufacturers or other producers. Example: Webb-Pomerene Organizations, trade-group organized EXPORT trading companies, and an export trading company formed by an association of agricultural cooperatives.

HORN OF AFRICA northeastern area of Africa consisting of Djibouti, Ethiopia, Somalia, and Sudan.

HOST a computer providing a communication vehicle for other computers on a NETWORK. A host supports application programs including electronic mail, Telnet, and FTP.

HOST ADDRESS *see* INTERNET ADDRESS.

HOST COUNTRY the country in which a business is operating outside of its headquarters. *see also* HOME COUNTRY.

HOST GOVERNMENT the government of the country in which a firm is operating outside of its headquarters.

HOST NATIONAL a CITIZEN of the country in which a business is operating outside of its headquarters.

HOUSE AIR WAYBILL BILL OF LADING issued by a FREIGHT FORWARDER for consolidated air freight shipments. *see also* AIR WAYBILL (AWB).

HOUSE-TO-HOUSE term usually used to indicate a CONTAINER yard-to-container yard shipment. *see also* DOOR-TO-DOOR; PIER-TO-PIER; POINT-TO-POINT.

HOUSING ALLOWANCE payments made to employees for reimbursement of accommodation costs at an assignment location. Can also be referred to as foreign housing.

HPCC *see* HIGH-PERFORMANCE COMPUTING AND COMMUNICATIONS.

HS *see* HARMONIZED SYSTEM.

HT abbreviation for height.

HTS *see* HARMONIZED TARIFF SCHEDULE.

HTSUS *see* HARMONIZED TARIFF SCHEDULE OF THE UNITED STATES.

HUB
1. a centralized location to which CARGO is directed and from which it is distributed to other areas.
2. a device used in a network to connect several computers for the purpose of transmitting data and messages.

HUB AND SPOKE ROUTING aircraft routing service pattern that feeds traffic from many cities into a central hub designed to connect with other flights to final destinations. The system maximizes operating flexibility by connecting many markets through a central hub with fewer flights than would be required to connect each pair of cities in an extensive system.

HULL outer shell of a vessel.

HUMAN COWORKING MODEL ORGANIZATION an organizational model found in Japan based on the concept of GROUPISM. The interests of the group supersede those of the individual. *see also* MACHINE MODEL ORGANIZATION.

HUMAN SHIELD volunteers from around the world who traveled to Iraq to stand at strategic sties to try to deter allied bombing.

HUMANITARIAN LICENSE a special license authorized by Section 773.5 of the U.S. EXPORT ADMINISTRATION REGULATIONS (EAR) that allows the shipment of goods donated to meet basic human needs. Supplement 7 to Part 773 lists the kinds of items that meet these basic human needs.

HUMP that part of a rail track that is elevated so that when a car is pushed up "on the hump" and uncoupled, it runs down the other side by gravity.

HUNDREDWEIGHT PRICING special pricing for multiple-piece SHIPMENTS traveling to one destination that is rated on the total weight of the shipment as opposed to being rated on a per-package basis.

HYPOTEK/CREDIT SOCIETY a society of lenders in Norway that provides financing to foreign-owned businesses, subject to the quality of their collateral and the project.

I

IACAC *see* INTER-AMERICAN COMMERCIAL ARBITRATION COMMISSION.

IACC *see* INTERNATIONAL ANTICOUNTERFEITING COALITION.

IACO *see* INTER-AFRICAN COFFEE ORGANIZATION.

IADB *see* INTER-AMERICAN DEVELOPMENT BANK.

IAEA *see* INTERNATIONAL ATOMIC ENERGY AGENCY.

IAEL *see* INTERNATIONAL ATOMIC ENERGY LIST.

IAF *see* INTERNATIONAL ACCREDITATION FORUM.

IAIGC *see* INTER-ARAB INVESTMENT GUARANTEE CORPORATION.

IARCs acronym for international agricultural research centers. *see also* CONSULTATIVE GROUP ON INTERNATIONAL AGRICULTURAL RESEARCH.

IASC *see* INTERNATIONAL ACCOUNTING STANDARDS COMMITTEE.

IATA *see* INTERNATIONAL AIR TRANSPORT ASSOCIATION.

IAU *see* INTERNATIONAL ACCOUNTING UNIT.

IBA *see* INTERNATIONAL BANKING ACT.

IBC *see* INTERNATIONAL BANKING CENTER.

IBEC *see* INTERNATIONAL BANK FOR ECONOMIC COOPERATION.

IBF *see* INTERNATIONAL BANKING FACILITY.

IBOR *see* INTERBANK OFFERED RATE.

IBOS *see* INTERNATIONAL BUSINESS OPPORTUNITIES SERVICE.

IBRACON *see* BRAZILIAN INSTITUTE OF ACCOUNTANTS.

IBRD *see* INTERNATIONAL BANK FOR RECONSTRUCTION AND DEVELOPMENT.

IBRS *see* INTERNATIONAL BUSINESS REPLY SERVICE.

IC *see* IMPORT CERTIFICATE.

ICA *see* INTERNATIONAL COMMODITY AGREEMENT.

ICAC *see* INTERNATIONAL CONFEDERATION OF AGRICULTURAL CREDIT.

ICAO *see* INTERNATIONAL CIVIL AVIATION ORGANIZATION.

ICB *see* INTERNATIONAL COMPETITIVE BIDDING.

ICC *see* INTERNATIONAL CHAMBER OF COMMERCE.

ICCEC *see* INTERGOVERNMENTAL COUNCIL OF COPPER EXPORTING COUNTRIES.

ICE CLAUSE a standard clause in the chartering of ocean vessels. It dictates the course a vessel master may take if the ship is prevented from entering the loading or discharge port because of ice or if the vessel is threatened by ice while in the port. The clause establishes rights and obligations of both vessel owner and charterer if these events occur.

ICELANDIC KRONA unit of currency, Iceland (100 eyrir equal 1 króna).

ICEP *see* INSTITUTO DO COMÉRCIO DE PORTUGAL.

ICFTU *see* INTERNATIONAL CONFEDERATION OF FREE TRADE UNIONS.

ICGEB *see* INTERNATIONAL CENTER FOR GENETIC ENGINEERING AND BIOTECHNOLOGY.

ICHCA *see* INTERNATIONAL CARGO HANDLING COORDINATION ASSOCIATION.

ICJ *see* INTERNATIONAL COURT OF JUSTICE.

ICMS *see* IMPOSTO DOBRE CIRCULACAO DE MERCADORIAS Y SERVICOS.

ICO *see* INTERNATIONAL COCOA ORGANIZATION; INTERNATIONAL CONGRESS OFFICE.

ICON *see* INDEXED CURRENCY OPTION NOTE.

ICPO *see* IRREVOCABLE CORPORATE PURCHASE ORDER.

ICSHT *see* INTERNATIONAL CENTER FOR SCIENCE AND HIGH TECHNOLOGY.

ICSID *see* INTERNATIONAL CENTRE FOR SETTLEMENT OF INVESTMENT DISPUTES.

ICSU *see* INTERNATIONAL COUNCIL OF SCIENTIFIC UNIONS.

ICTF *see* INTERMODAL CONTAINER TRANSFER FACILITY.

ICTP *see* INTERNATIONAL CENTER FOR THEORETICAL PHYSICS.

IDA *see* INTERNATIONAL DEVELOPMENT ASSOCIATION.

IDB *see* INTER-AMERICAN DEVELOPMENT BANK; INTERNATIONAL DATA BASE.

IDENTICAL GOODS *see* SIMILAR GOODS.

IDENTICAL MERCHANDISE *see* SIMILAR GOODS.

IDENTICAL RECIPROCITY *see* RECIPROCITY.

IDENTICAL TREATMENT an example of a FRIENDSHIP, COMMERCE, AND NAVIGATION (FCN) TREATY. Identical treatment specifies the rights and responsibilities of a country in relation to other countries concerning laws and regulations governing the marketing of goods and so ensuring that these regulations apply in exactly the same way whether the goods are produced domestically or imported.

IDIN *see* INTERNATIONAL DEVELOPMENT INFORMATION NETWORK.

IDR *see* INTERNATIONAL DEPOSITORY RECEIPT.

IDRC *see* INTERNATIONAL DEVELOPMENT RESEARCH CENTER.

IE *see* INFREQUENT EXPORTER.

IEA *see* INTERNATIONAL ENERGY AGENCY.

IEB *see* INTERNATIONAL EXHIBITIONS BUREAU.

IEC *see* INTERNATIONAL ELECTROTECHNICAL COMMISSION.

IEEPA *see* INTERNATIONAL EMERGENCY ECONOMIC POWERS ACT.

IEP *see* INTERNATIONAL ECONOMIC POLICY.

IEPG *see* INDEPENDENT EUROPEAN PROGRAM GROUP.

IESC *see* INTERNATIONAL EXECUTIVE SERVICE CORPS.

IFAC acronym for Industry Functional Advisory Committee. *see also* INDUSTRY CONSULTATIONS PROGRAM.

IFAD *see* INTERNATIONAL FUND FOR AGRICULTURAL DEVELOPMENT.

IFC *see* INTERNATIONAL FINANCE CORPORATION.

IFE *see* INTERNATIONAL FISHER EFFECT.

IFRB *see* INTERNATIONAL FREQUENCY REGISTRATION BOARD.

IFS *see* IN-FLIGHT SURVEY.

IFU *see* INDUSTRIALIZATION FUND FOR DEVELOPING COUNTRIES.

IGADD *see* INTERGOVERNMENTAL AUTHORITY ON DROUGHT AND DEVELOPMENT.

IGC *see* INTERAGENCY GROUP ON COUNTERTRADE.

IGP *see* INTERIOR GATEWAY PROTOCOL.

IIB *see* INTERNATIONAL INVESTMENT BANK.

IIC *see* INTER-AMERICAN INVESTMENT CORPORATION.

IINREN *see* INTERAGENCY INTERIM NATIONAL RESEARCH AND EDUCATION NETWORK.

IIPA *see* INTERNATIONAL INTELLECTUAL PROPERTY ALLIANCE.

IIT *see* INSTRUMENTS OF INTERNATIONAL TRAFFIC.

IL industrial list. *see also* INTERNATIONAL INDUSTRIAL LIST.

ILO *see* INTERNATIONAL LABOR ORGANIZATION.

IMMEDIATE DELIVERY a procedure that provides for immediate release of a shipment being imported into the United States. This is accomplished by making application for a Special Permit for Immediate Delivery on U.S. Customs Form 3461 prior to the arrival of merchandise. If the application is approved, the shipment is released expeditiously following arrival.

IMMEDIATE TRANSPORTATION ENTRY a CUSTOMS form declaring goods for transportation by a bonded CARRIER from a port of entry to a bonded warehouse at an inland port, or another port of entry.

IMF *see* INTERNATIONAL MONETARY FUND.

IMF QUOTA amount of money that each member country is required to contribute to the INTERNATIONAL MONETARY FUND, partly in their own currency and partly in U.S. dollars, gold, or other member-country currencies. A country's quota is based on its GROSS DOMESTIC PRODUCT (GDP). Countries having voting power in the IMF in proportion to their IMF quotas.

IMI *see* INTERNATIONAL MARKET INSIGHTS.

IML *see* INTERNATIONAL MUNITIONS LIST.

IMMIGRANT VISA a stamp in a foreign national's passport issued by a U.S. consular officer, which creates a legal presumption that there are no apparent reasons to deny entry for permanent residency in the United States. *see also* NONIMMIGRANT VISA.

IMMIGRATION entry of FOREIGN nationals into a country for the purpose of establishing permanent residence.

IMO *see* INTERNATIONAL MARITIME ORGANIZATION.

IMPAIRMENT an injury or damage. The OVERSEAS PRIVATE INVESTMENT CORPORATION (OPIC) provides EXPROPRIATION insurance coverage, which indemnifies against any ABROGATION, impairment, REPUDIATION, or BREACH OF CONCESSIONAL AGREEMENTS between a U.S. company and a foreign government. *see also* OVERSEAS PRIVATE INVESTMENT CORPORATION; EXPROPRIATION.

IMPLIED CONDITIONS certain implied conditions that are not written into MARINE INSURANCE policies but that are so basic to understanding between the underwriter and the assured that the law gives them much the same effect as if written. In many other types of CONTRACTS, there also may be IMPLIED CONDITIONS, for example, if a seller implies that his or her goods are fit for the purpose they purport to serve. *see also* FREE OF PARTICULAR AVERAGE; GENERAL AVERAGE; MARINE CARGO INSURANCE; PARTICULAR AVERAGE.

IMPORT bringing goods or services into one country from another for trade or sale. *see also* EXPORT.

IMPORT ALLOCATION CERTIFICATE a document that must be completed and submitted to a FOREIGN EXCHANGE bank by an IMPORTER in Japan, as a prerequisite to the securing of an IMPORT permit. The requirement for such a certificate is mandated by Japan's MINISTRY OF INTERNATIONAL TRADE AND INDUSTRY (MITI).

IMPORT AUTHORIZATION requirement that IMPORTS be authorized by a special agency before entering a country; similar to IMPORT LICENSING.

IMPORT BRIEFS a daily column appearing in the JOURNAL OF COMMERCE. The column lists items of interest to importers.

IMPORT BULLETIN a weekly report published by the JOURNAL OF COMMERCE. The report details all foreign cargoes entering ports in the United States. The Import Bulletin lists incoming CARGO by COMMODITY group, describing the cargo in terms of its nature, the quantity, the port of origin, the vessel, and the name of the CONSIGNEE in the United States.

IMPORT CERTIFICATE (IC) a means by which the government of the country of ultimate destination exercises legal control over the internal channeling of the COMMODITIES covered by the IMPORT certificate.

IMPORT COMPETING an industry that competes with imports.

IMPORT CONTROL LIST *see* EXPORT AND IMPORT PERMITS ACT.

IMPORT CONTROLS *see* COMMERCIAL CONTROLS; EXPORT CONTROLS; TRADE BARRIERS.

IMPORT CREDIT commercial LETTER OF CREDIT issued for the purpose of financing the importation of goods. *see also* BACK-TO-BACK BORROWING; BACK-TO-BACK LETTER OF CREDIT.

IMPORT DEPOSIT REQUIREMENTS a government policy by which an IMPORTER must post a deposit prior to the release of FOREIGN EXCHANGE by the government, in order to IMPORT goods into the country. *see also* IMPORT LICENSING.

IMPORT DUTY a tax placed on goods entering into a country. *see also* AD VALOREM DUTY; SPECIFIC DUTY.

IMPORT LEADS a column appearing on Tuesdays and Fridays in the JOURNAL OF COMMERCE. The column lists foreign manufacturers looking for buyers in the United States.

IMPORT LICENSE a document required and issued by some national governments authorizing the importation of goods.

IMPORT MERCHANT a merchant who buys overseas for his/her own account for the purpose of later resale, handling all details of IMPORT documentation and transportation. Usually the merchant specializes in one or two COMMODITIES.

IMPORT QUOTA a means of restricting imports by issuing licenses to IMPORTERS, assigning each a quota, after determining the total amount of any COMMODITY that is to be imported during a period. Import licenses may also specify the country from which the IMPORTER must purchase the goods.

IMPORT QUOTA AUCTIONING the process of auctioning the right to IMPORT specified quantities of QUOTA-restricted goods.

IMPORT RATE a rate established specifically for application on IMPORT traffic; when so published, it is generally less than a domestic rate.

IMPORT RELIEF any of several measures imposed by a government to temporally restrict IMPORTS of a product or COMMODITY to protect domestic producers from competition. *see also* EXPORT SUBSIDIES; IMPORT QUOTAS; IMPORT RESTRICTIONS; SUBISIDIES; TARIFF.

IMPORT RESTRICTIONS controls on the volume of goods coming into a country with an adverse trade balance (or for other reasons) from other countries. Import restrictions include the imposition of TARIFFS or IMPORT QUOTAS, restrictions on the amount of foreign currency available to cover imports, a requirement for IMPORT deposits, the imposition of import surcharges, or the prohibition of various categories of imports.

IMPORT-SENSITIVE PRODUCERS domestic manufacturer whose economic viability is threatened by quality, price, or service competition from imported products. *see also* IMPORT RELIEF; IMPORT SUBSTITUTION.

IMPORT SUBSTITUTION a strategy that emphasizes the replacement of IMPORTS with domestically produced goods, rather than the production of goods for EXPORT, to encourage the development of domestic industry.

IMPORT SURCHARGE a uniformly levied tax on most or all IMPORTS, in addition to existing TARIFFS.

IMPORT TARIFF a tax placed on goods entering into a country. *see also* AD VALOREM DUTY; DUTY; SPECIFIC DUTY.

IMPORTER a person primarily liable for the payment of duties on the merchandise purchased from an EXPORTER, or an authorized agent acting on the IMPORTER's behalf. The importer may be
- a CONSIGNEE,
- the IMPORTER OF RECORD, or
- the actual owner of the merchandise if the actual owner has filed with CUSTOMS a declaration acknowledging ownership along with a superseding bond.

IMPORTER DISTRIBUTOR a merchant who IMPORTS goods, usually on an exclusive territory arrangement, maintains an inventory, and, through a sales staff, sells to retailers.

IMPORTER NUMBER identification number assigned by the U.S. CUSTOMS SERVICE to each IMPORTER to track entries and other transactions.

IMPORTER OF RECORD the owner or purchaser of the goods as defined by the U.S. CUSTOMS SERVICE, or, when designated by the owner, purchaser, or CONSIGNEE, a licensed CUSTOMS BROKER.

IMPORTERS MANUAL USA reference book detailing specific requirements for importing 135 different product groups into the United States and other important information.

IMPORTS COMMODITIES of foreign origin as well as goods of domestic origin returned to a country with no change in condition or after having been processed and/or assembled in other countries. For statistical purposes, imports are classified by type of transaction:
- merchandise entered for immediate consumption (duty-free merchandise and merchandise on which duty is paid on arrival),
- merchandise withdrawn for consumption from CUSTOMS-bonded warehouses and FOREIGN TRADE ZONES, and
- merchandise entered into Customs-bonded warehouses and U.S. foreign trade zones from foreign countries.

IMPORTS FOR CONSUMPTION total of merchandise that has physically cleared through U.S. CUSTOMS either entering domestic consumption channels immediately or entering after withdrawal for consumption from BONDED WAREHOUSES under Customs custody or from U.S. FOREIGN TRADE ZONES. *see also* CONSUMPTION ENTRY.

IMPOST tax, usually an IMPORT DUTY.

IMPOSTO DE IMPORTACAO an IMPORT DUTY levied on goods being imported into Brazil, based on the CIF value of the imported goods.

IMPOSTO SOBRE CIRCULACAO DE MERCADORIAS E SERVICOS (ICMS) a state value-added tax placed on goods imported into Brazil. The tax is based on the sum of the CIF value, the IMPORT DUTY, the IPI tax and any other additional customs charges.

IMPOSTO SOBRE PRODUCTOS INDUSTRIALIZADOS (IPI) the federal value-added tax paid by importers in Brazil. It is based on the CIF value and any IMPORT DUTY that has been paid.

IMPOUND to seize or hold; or to place in protective custody by order of a court.

IN BOND procedure under which goods are transported, stored, or handled, before CLEARANCE and release by CUSTOMS, and the government's interest is secured by indemnity bonds. *see also* IN-BOND SHIPMENT; IN-BOND SYSTEM; SURETY BOND; TARIFF.

IN-BOND INDUSTRY an industry based on the importation of components into a FREE-TRADE ZONE without the payment of DUTIES. The components are processed and reexported.

IN-BOND SHIPMENT IMPORT or EXPORT SHIPMENT that has not been cleared by U.S. CUSTOMS officials. *see also* FREE-TRADE ZONE; IN-BOND INDUSTRY; IN-BOND SYSTEM.

IN-BOND SYSTEM a part of the U.S. CUSTOMS SERVICE AUTOMATED COMMERCIAL SYSTEM (ACS) that controls merchandise from the point of unloading at the port of entry or exportation. The system works with the input of departures (from the port of unloading), arrivals, and closures (accountability of arrivals).

IN CASE OF NEED *see* CASE OF NEED (PRINCIPAL'S REPRESENTATIVE).

INCENTIVE force that motivates people to greater activity or increased efficiency.

INCHMAREE CLAUSE a contractual clause indemnifying losses resulting from a potential defect in the vessel's hull or machinery and losses resulting from errors in navigation of the vessel by the master or crew as long as the damage does not result from want of due diligence by the owner of the vessel.

INCIDENTAL SERVICES the U.S. AGENCY FOR INTERNATIONAL DEVELOPMENT-authorized reimbursement for services such as costs for the installation or erection of equipment or the training of individuals responsible for the operation and maintenance of the equipment.

INCOME money or its equivalent, earned or accrued, arising from the sale of goods or services.

INCOME DISPARITY inequality of income; normally refers to differences in average PER CAPITA INCOME across countries. *see also* INEQUALITY.

INCOMPLETE SPECIALIZATION production of goods that compete with IMPORTS.

INCONVERTIBILITY COVERAGE *see* CURRENCY INCONVERTIBILITY.

INCOTERMS a codification of terms maintained by the INTERNATIONAL CHAMBER OF COMMERCE (ICC). This is used in foreign trade contracts to define which parties incur the costs and at what specific point the costs are incurred.

INDEMNIFY to compensate for actual loss sustained. *see also* INSURED VALUE; INDEMNITY; LANDED VALUE; MARINE CARGO INSURANCE.

INDEMNITY
1. compensation to make a person whole from a loss already sustained.
2. contract or assurance by which one engages to secure another against an anticipated loss.

INDENT a requisition for goods, enumerating conditions of the sale. Acceptance of an indent by a seller constitutes his/her agreement to the conditions of the sale.

INDEPENDENT ACTION the right of a CONFERENCE member to depart from the common FREIGHT rates, terms, or conditions of the conference without the need for prior approval of the conference.

INDEPENDENT EUROPEAN PROGRAM GROUP (IEPG) an intergovernmental organization that is not formally part of the NORTH ATLANTIC TREATY ORGANIZATION (NATO), but whose membership includes all the EUROPEAN COMMUNITY (EC) members of the alliance, plus Norway and Turkey. Established in 1976, IEPG's objectives are to promote European cooperation in research, development, and production of defense equipment; improve transatlantic armaments cooperation; and maintain a healthy European defense industrial base.

INDEPENDENT STATES *see* COMMONWEALTH OF INDEPENDENT STATES.

INDEXED term used in finance that means "measured by" and/or "adjusted according to," thus an interest rate on a note may be, by agreement, "indexed" or adjusted according to the market at the time the interest is due. Or a note denominated in a foreign currency may have its EXCHANGE RATE "indexed" or adjusted according to the market rate in effect at the time of payment. *see also* INDEXED CURRENCY BORROWINGS.

INDEXED CURRENCY BORROWINGS borrowings in a foreign currency where the rate of interest is linked to an agreed scale, and/or the RATE OF EXCHANGE at repayment is linked to an agreed scale. *see also* INDEXED.

INDEXED CURRENCY OPTION NOTE (ICON) a debt repayment instrument whose value is partially determined by the EFFECTIVE EXCHANGE RATE between two currencies. Interest payments, made in one currency, are lowered if the rate of exchange exceeds a prearranged rate.

INDIGENOUS EMPLOYEE an alternative term used when referring to a local/national employed by the firm. The term is seldom used because of concerns of prejudice.

INDIRECT EXPORTING sale by the EXPORTER to the buyer through a domestically located intermediary. *see also* EXPORT BROKER; EXPORT COMMISSION HOUSE; EXPORT JOBBER; EXPORT MANAGEMENT COMPANY (EMC); PIGGYBACK EXPORTING; TRADING HOUSE.

INDIRECT QUOTE a quote for FOREIGN EXCHANGE that is given in terms of the number of units of the foreign currency for one unit of the domestic currency.

INDIVIDUALLY VALIDATED LICENSE (IVL) written approval by which the U.S. DEPARTMENT OF COMMERCE grants permission, which is valid for 2 years, for the EXPORT of a specified quantity of products or technical data to a single recipient. IVLs also are required, under certain circumstances, as authorization for the reexport of U.S.-origin COMMODITIES to new destinations abroad.

INDUSTRIAL DEVELOPMENT PROGRAMS (PDTI) a series of limited benefits provided by the Brazilian government to promote investment in Brazil. Companies seeking these benefits must obtain approval from the appropriate government agencies.

INDUSTRIAL ESPIONAGE the act or practice of spying by using operatives to obtain secret information about a business competitor. This may or may not be followed by the unauthorized use of proprietary information.

INDUSTRIAL LIST (IL) *see* INTERNATIONAL INDUSTRIAL LIST.

INDUSTRIAL POLICY a plan or course of action, by a government, intended to influence and determine decisions influencing the development of a country's industrial sectors and the direction of its industrial growth.

INDUSTRIAL PRICE INDEX a leading indicator of inflation developed by the Center for International Business Cycle Research at Columbia University. The index appears daily in the JOURNAL OF COMMERCE.

INDUSTRIAL RELATIONS the relations between the management of a firm and its employees.

INDUSTRIAL SABOTAGE the intentional act of property destruction or obstruction of the normal operations of a firm.

INDUSTRIAL TARGETING a government policy of providing assistance to specific industries. Example: it can be used to describe the process by which a country selects a particular industry for special attention in areas such as EXPORT promotion.

INDUSTRIAL TRAINING PROGRAM (SENAI) a program operated by the Brazilian government to improve the quality of the unskilled labor force coming from regions other than the principal metropolitan areas. *see also* COMMERCIAL TRADE SCHOOL PROGRAM (SENAC).

INDUSTRIALIZATION FUND FOR DEVELOPING COUNTRIES (IFU) a revolving fund sponsored by Danish companies that invests in joint venture companies in the developing countries. Its resources were made available by the Danish government. IFU takes part in joint ventures as a shareholder and can provide loans or guarantees for loans. The fund was established by Denmark in 1967, and its headquarters is in Copenhagen. Since 1978, fund operations have been financed solely from the return on investments in developing countries and from other financial assets, with no public financial subsidy.

INDUSTRIALIZATION THROUGH IMPORT SUBSTITUTION *see* IMPORT SUBSTITUTION.

INDUSTRY CONSULTATIONS PROGRAM an advisory committee structure created by the TRADE ACT OF 1974, and expanded by the TRADE AGREEMENTS ACT OF 1979. The program is operated jointly by the U.S. DEPARTMENT OF COMMERCE and the U.S. TRADE REPRESENTATIVE (USTR). Members of the committees are appointed by the U.S. Secretary of Commerce and the USTR. *see also* ADVISORY COMMITTEE ON TRADE POLICY AND NEGOTIATIONS.

INDUSTRY FUNCTIONAL ADVISORY COMMITTEE (IFAC) *see* INDUSTRY CONSULTATIONS PROGRAM.

INDUSTRY POLICY ADVISORY COMMITTEE (IPAC) *see* INDUSTRY CONSULTATIONS PROGRAM.

INDUSTRY SECTOR ADVISORY COMMITTEE (ISAC) *see* INDUSTRY CONSULTATIONS PROGRAM.

INDUSTRY, SCIENCE, TECHNOLOGY CANADA (IST) the department of the Canadian government responsible for the development and implementation of trade and regional expansion programs. *see also* DEPARTMENT OF EXTERNAL AFFAIRS; INTERNATIONAL TRADE CENTERS.

INDUSTRY SUBSECTOR ANALYSIS (ISA) overseas market research for a given industry subsector (such as cardiological equipment for the medical equipment industry) that presents basic information about a foreign market such as market size, competitive environment, primary end users, best prospects products, and market access information.

INEQUALITY differences in PER CAPITA INCOME or household income across populations within a country or across countries. *see also* INCOME DISPARITY.

INFANT INDUSTRY a newly established industry in a country as compared to one well established in that country. *see also* INFANT INDUSTRY ARGUMENT.

INFANT INDUSTRY ARGUMENT the argument that a newly established industry in a DEVELOPING COUNTRY needs protection from foreign IMPORTS until such time as its labor force is trained and production techniques have been mastered. The argument is based on the theory that the new firm will not survive due to low-cost IMPORTS from experienced foreign competitors.

IN-FLIGHT SURVEY (IFS) a means of providing data on visitor characteristics, travel patterns, and spending habits and for supplying data on the U.S. international travel dollar accounts as well as estimating BALANCE OF PAYMENTS needs. It is administered by the U.S. Immigration and Naturalization Service to U.S. and foreign travelers departing the United States. The IFS covers about 70% of U.S. carriers and 35% of foreign carriers who voluntarily choose to participate. Sample results are expanded to universe estimates to account for nonresponse of passengers on each sampled flight, for coverage of all flights on each major airline route, and for all international routes. The basis for the expansion is the number of passengers departing the United States.

INFONAVIT (NATIONAL HOUSING FUND) a Mexican government program that provides economic assistance to employees and is financed by an assessment on employers. In Mexico, employers are required to establish a bank account for each employee, which includes two subaccounts: one for deposits to the employee's pension fund and one for deposits into the employee's National Housing Fund (INFONAVIT) account. Employers must contribute 2% of each worker's salary to the pension account and 5% to the INFONAVIT account.

INFORMAL ENTRY simplified IMPORT ENTRY procedure accepted at the option of CUSTOMS for any baggage or commercial SHIPMENT that does not exceed $2000. *see also* ENTRY (CUSTOMS); ENTRY DOCUMENTS; ENTRY PAPERS.

INFORMATION TECHNOLOGY INITIATIVE 6 (IT06) sixth initiative of the National Performance Review calling for the development of an international trade data system sponsored by the U.S. government that will meet the needs of U.S. federal agencies involved in international trade as well as the trade information needs of businesses and the general public.

INFORMED COMPLIANCE term for the improved ability of an entity (such as a company) to comply with federal rules and regulations through easy access to up-to-date information.

INFRASTRUCTURE the underlying base or foundation of an economy, including the basic facilities, services, and installations needed for functioning, such as transportation and communications systems, water and energy supplies, and public institutions including schools, that will allow it to function more effectively.

INFREQUENT EXPORTER (IE) as defined by the U.S. DEPARTMENT OF COMMERCE'S INTERNATIONAL TRADE ADMINISTRATION (ITA), a company that has some EXPORT experience—usually averaging between 1 and 50 export shipments per year—but that still needs assistance to increase the size of its export market or to expand into new ones.

INHALATION ANTHRAX contracted by inhaling anthrax spores. The disease results in pneumonia, sometimes meningitis, and finally death.

INHERENT VICE an insurance term referring to any defect or other characteristics of a product that could result in damage to the product without external cause. Insurance policies may specifically exclude losses caused by inherent vice.

INITIAL NEGOTIATING RIGHT (INR) a right held by one GATT country to seek compensation for an impairment of a given bound

TARIFF rate by another GATT country. INRs stem from past negotiating concessions and allow the INR holder to seek compensation for an impairment of TARIFF concessions regardless of its status as a supplier of the product in question.

INJURY a finding by the U.S. INTERNATIONAL TRADE COMMISSION (ITC) that IMPORTS are causing, or are likely to cause, harm to a U.S. industry. An injury determination is the basis for a SECTION 201 case. It is also a requirement in all antidumping and most countervailing duty cases (ANTIDUMPING/COUNTERVAILING DUTY SYSTEM), in conjunction with U.S. DEPARTMENT OF COMMERCE determinations on DUMPING AND SUBSIDIZATION.

INLAND BILL OF LADING a BILL OF LADING (B/L) (a waybill on rail or the pro forma bill of lading in trucking) used in transporting goods overland to the EXPORTER's international CARRIER. It is used to document the transportation of the goods between the port and the point of origin or destination. Although a through bill of lading can sometimes be used, it is usually necessary to prepare both an inland bill of lading and an ocean bill of lading for EXPORT shipments. It should contain information such as marks, numbers, steamship line, and similar information to match with a dock receipt.

INLAND CARRIER a transportation line that hauls EXPORT or IMPORT CARGO traffic between ports and inland points.

INLAND WATERWAY a navigable body of water, such as a river, channel, or canal, within the boundaries of a country intended for use in the carriage of goods.

INMARSAT *see* INTERNATIONAL MARITIME SATELLITE ORGANIZATION.

INNER SIX the 6 members of the EUROPEAN ECONOMIC COMMUNITY (EEC) from 1958 to 1973. *see also* EUROPEAN FREE TRADE ASSOCIATION; OUTER SEVEN.

INOCULATION REQUIREMENTS the requirement initiated by a country that all visitors be inoculated with a vaccine in order to protect them against a particular disease.

INPI *see* INSTITUTO NACIONAL DE PROPRIEDADE INDUSTRIAL.

INR *see* INITIAL NEGOTIATING RIGHT.

INSA-DONG the main antique district in Korea. This area contains many old book stores and galleries with an emphasis on old and modern furniture. The area is very popular with business visitors.

INSPECTION CERTIFICATE *see* CERTIFICATE OF INSPECTION; INSPECTION CERTIFICATION.

INSPECTION CERTIFICATION a certificate attesting to the specifications of goods shipped required by some purchasers and countries. Inspection certificates are usually obtained from independent testing organizations.

INSPECTION SERVICES a service performed by an independent testing organization attesting to the specifications of the goods being shipped. The inspection company will issue documents certifying that the merchandise was in good condition immediately prior to shipment. *see also* CERTIFICATE OF INSPECTION; INSPECTION CERTIFICATE.

INSTITUTE OF ELECTRICAL AND ELECTRONICS ENGINEERS (IEEE) a professional association, founded in 1963, for scientists and engineers in electrical engineering. It has 274,000 members and 70 local groups with a staff of 500. It publishes an annual membership directory, the monthly *Spectrum*, and the periodical *Standards*. It is located in New York City.

INSTITUTO DO COMERCIO EXTERNO DE PORTUGAL (ICEP) Portuguese Foreign Trade Institute, whose activities are under the authority of the Ministry of Commerce and Tourism and include the promotion of Portuguese EXPORTS and direct foreign investment.

INSTITUTO NACIONAL DE PROPRIEDADE INDUSTRIAL (INPI) the government bureau in Brazil that studies grants and maintains records of patents. The patent issued by the government confers upon the inventor the sole right to make, use, and sell that invention for a predetermined period of time. To be eligible for patent protection in Brazil, the invention must be novel and not previously patented or used in Brazil. The invention must be capable of being produced or applied to an industrial process and not be obvious from a developmental viewpoint. Under current law, pharmaceutical, medical, and food products and their processes cannot be patented.

INSTRUMENT any written document that gives formal expression to a legal agreement or act.

INSTRUMENT PAYABLE TO THE BEARER a check or other redeemable note payable to the holder. *see also* LETTER OF CREDIT.

INSTRUMENTS OF INTERNATIONAL TRAFFIC (IIT) equipment used in the shipment of merchandise in international traffic including lift vans, CARGO vans, shipping tanks, skids, pallets, caul boards, and cores for textile fabrics. These are designated as instruments of international traffic within the meaning of section 3221, TARIFF ACT OF 1930, as amended.

INSURANCE CERTIFICATE a certificate used to assure the CONSIGNEE that insurance is provided to cover loss of or damage to the CARGO while in transit.

INSURANCE CERTIFICATION a document used when the EXPORTER provides the insurance; it specifies the amount and type of coverage and is a negotiable instrument.

INSURED VALUE the value of the goods being covered for loss or damage while in transit. The insurance typically compensates the owner of merchandise for losses in excess of those that can be legally recovered from the carrier that are sustained from fire, shipwreck, piracy, and various other causes. The insured value is normally computed by adding the invoice cost, freight expenses, miscellaneous costs, and insurance premium plus a percentage, usually 10%. This would normally represent the LANDED VALUE. *see also* MARINE CARGO INSURANCE.

INTANGIBLE PROPERTY *see* INTELLECTUAL PROPERTY RIGHTS.

INTEGRATED CARGO SERVICE blend of all segments of the CARGO system providing the combined services of CARRIER, FREIGHT FORWARDER, handler, and agent.

INTEGRATED CARRIERS CARRIERS that have both air and ground fleets, or other combinations, such as sea, rail, and truck. Because they usually handle thousands of small parcels an hour, they are less expensive and offer more diverse services than regular carriers.

INTEGRATED SERVICES DIGITAL NETWORK (ISDN) an emerging digital telecommunications technology that is beginning to be offered by the major world telephone carriers. ISDN is capable of carrying voice and digital network services in a single medium, making it possible to provide data and voice services through a single "wire." ISDN standards are specified through the CONSULTATIVE COMMITTEE ON INTERNATIONAL TELEPHONE & TELEGRAPH (CCITT).

INTEGRATED TARIFF OF THE EUROPEAN COMMUNITY (TARIC) a publication that presents the regulations pertaining to import of products into the EC as well as for some exports. TARIC adopts the provisions of community legislation, the HARMONIZED SYSTEM, and the combined nomenclature (CN).

INTEGRATION (ECONOMIC) refers to reducing TRADE BARRIERS among countries to transactions and to movements of goods, capital, and labor, including HARMONIZATION of laws, regulations, and STANDARDS. *see also* COMMON MARKET; CUSTOMS UNION; DEEP INTEGRATION; FREE-TRADE AREA; SHALLOW INTEGRATION.

INTELLECTUAL PROPERTY original piece of work that can be copyrighted or trademarked to confirm ownership.

INTELLECTUAL PROPERTY RIGHTS (IPR) a generic phrase encompassing intangible property rights, including, among others, patents, trade and service marks, copyrights, industrial designs, rights in semiconductor chip layout designs, rights in trade secrets, and software. *see also* BERNE CONVENTION; CAPRI PROJECT; PARIS CONVENTION; PATENT COOPERATION TREATY; TREATY ON INTERNATIONAL REGISTRATION OF AUDIOVISUAL WORKS; WORLD INTELLECTUAL PROPERTY ORGANIZATION (WIPO).

INTELPOST a high-speed international electronic mail service that operated between the postal system of the United States and other countries. The service has been discontinued.

INTELSAT *see* INTERNATIONAL TELECOMMUNICATIONS SATELLITE ORGANIZATION.

INTER-AFRICAN COFFEE ORGANIZATION (French: Organisation Inter-Africaine de Café) an INTERNATIONAL COMMODITY GROUP with headquarters in Abdijan, Côte d'Ivoire, that consists of 22 African countries involved in the production of coffee. The purpose of the group is to exchange information on achieving optimal production and prices for the COMMODITY.

INTERAGENCY GROUP ON COUNTERTRADE (IGC) executive group established in December 1988 under an Executive Order of the president of the United States. The IGC reviews policy and negotiates agreements with other countries on COUNTERTRADE and offsets. It operates at the Assistant Secretary level with the U.S. DEPARTMENT OF COMMERCE as chair. Its membership includes 11 other U.S. agencies: the Departments of Agriculture, Defense, Energy, Justice, Labor, State, and Treasury; the AGENCY FOR INTERNATIONAL DEVELOPMENT; the Federal Emergency Management Agency; the U.S. TRADE REPRESENTATIVE (USTR); and the Office of Management and Budget.

INTERAGENCY INTERIM NATIONAL RESEARCH AND EDUCATION NETWORK (IINREN) an emerging INTERNET NETWORK system. It is planned that this networking infrastructure will manage the gigabit NATIONAL RESEARCH AND EDUCATION NETWORK (NREN) database.

INTER-AMERICAN COMMERCIAL ARBITRATION COMMISSION (IACAC) the commission, associated with the ORGANIZATION OF AMERICAN STATES, follows provisions of the UNITED NATIONS Commission on International Trade Law. The IACAC administers a system for arbitrating and conciliating international commercial disputes throughout the Western Hemisphere. IACAC was originally established in 1934, and its headquarters is in Washington, DC.

INTER-AMERICAN DEVELOPMENT BANK (IADB or IDB) (Spanish: Banco Interamericano de Desarrollo, BID) a regional financial institution that helps accelerate economic and social development in Latin America and the Caribbean. The bank was established in 1959 and began operations in October 1960. IADB's headquarters is in Washington, DC. The 28 regional members include Argentina, Bahamas, Barbados, Belize, Bolivia, Brazil, Canada, Chile, Colombia, Costa Rica, Dominican Republic, Ecuador, El Salvador, Guatemala, Guyana, Haiti, Honduras, Jamaica, Mexico, Nicaragua, Panama, Paraguay, Peru, Suriname, Trinidad and Tobago, the United States, Uruguay, and Venezuela. The IDB also includes 16 nonregional members: Austria, Belgium,

Denmark, Finland, France, Germany, Israel, Italy, Japan, the Netherlands, Norway, Portugal, Spain, Sweden, Switzerland, and the United Kingdom. *see also* CARIBBEAN DEVELOPMENT BANK; INTER-AMERICAN INVESTMENT CORPORATION.

INTER-AMERICAN INVESTMENT CORPORATION (IIC) a multilateral investment corporation that promotes the economic development of Latin American and Caribbean regional member countries by stimulating the establishment, expansion, and modernization of medium- and small-scale private enterprises. The IIC works directly with private enterprises in these countries and neither seeks nor requires government guarantees. The corporation makes direct investments such as equity participation, loans, and purchases of debt instruments, as well as direct investment through other financial institutions. The corporation also finances feasibility studies, underwrites securities, provides technical and managerial assistance, and helps entrepreneurs in mobilizing additional capital. The IIC is affiliated with the INTER-AMERICAN DEVELOPMENT BANK. It was established in 1986, and its headquarters is in Washington, DC.

INTER-AMERICAN TREATY OF RECIPROCAL ASSISTANCE *see* RIO TREATY.

INTER-ARAB INVESTMENT GUARANTEE CORPORATION (IAIGC) Arab development corporation established in 1965. It stimulates capital transfers among members by providing investment risk coverage and by supporting development studies. Its headquarters is in Kuwait, and nearly all Arab countries are members.

INTERBANK DEALINGS interbank business relationships. *see also* INTERBANK MARKET; INTERBANK TRANSACTIONS.

INTERBANK MARKET the FOREIGN EXCHANGE market between and among BANKS. *see also* DIRECT QUOTE; EXCHANGE RATE; FORWARD RATE; INDIRECT QUOTE; SPOT RATE.

INTERBANK OFFERED RATE (IBOR) the rate of interest at which banks lend to other prime banks. Terms are established for the length of loan and individual foreign currencies. A number of financial centers offer an IBOR including Abu Dhabi (ADIBOR), Bahrain (BIBOR), Brussels (BRIBOR), Hong Kong (HKIBOR), London (LIBOR), Luxembourg (LUXIBOR), Madrid (MIBOR), Paris (PIBOR), Saudi Arabia (SAIBOR), Singapore (SIBOR), and Zurich (ZIBOR). *see also* LONDON INTERBANK OFFERED RATE.

INTERBANK RATE rate of interest charged by a bank on a loan to another bank. *see also* INTERBANK OFFERED RATE (IBOR); LONDON INTERBANK OFFERED RATE (LIBOR).

INTERBANK TRANSACTIONS any transactions between BANKS involving FOREIGN EXCHANGE as compared to those taking place between banks and nonbank customers.

INTERCHANGE AGREEMENT agreement that specifically lays out the terms of leasing equipment from a CARRIER.

INTERCHANGE POINT point where one CARRIER delivers FREIGHT to another carrier.

INTEREST ARBITRAGE the transfer of short-term funds from one market to a market in another country in order to profit from a higher interest rate.

INTEREST RATE the rate of return on bonds, loans, or deposits.

INTEREST RATE DIFFERENTIAL the difference in interest rates between one country and another. The INTERNATIONAL FISHER EFFECT (IFE) suggests that interest differentials between countries are a predictor of future changes in the SPOT RATE in the FOREIGN EXCHANGE market. According to the IFE, the currency of the country with the lower rates will strengthen in the future.

INTEREST RATE SWAPS *see* SWAPS.

INTER ALIA an allowable adjustment when computing the value for goods being IMPORTED. The primary basis for CUSTOMS value is normally the TRANSACTION VALUE. Regulations provide for adjustments to the price actually paid or payable in cases where certain specific elements, which are considered to form a part of the value for customs purposes, are incurred by the buyer but are not included in the price actually paid or payable for the imported goods.

INTERFERENCE WITH OPERATIONS (IWO) a special program of the OVERSEAS PRIVATE INVESTMENT CORPORATION (OPIC). This insurance coverage provides the insured coverage against cessation of operations for 6 months or more caused by political violence. Compensation for such cessation is based on the amount of the investment, less returns of capital. Compensation must be repaid to OPIC, without interest, if within 5 years the political violence has abated and the insured can resume operations.

INTERGOVERNMENTAL AUTHORITY ON DROUGHT AND DEVELOPMENT (IGADD) African authority formed in 1986 that coordinates efforts in its members' region to build food security, stop desertification, and reclaim arid zones for food production. IGADD's headquarters is based in Djibouti and its members include Djibouti, Ethiopia, Kenya, Somalia, the Sudan, and Uganda. Financing stems primarily from Djibouti and Ethiopia.

INTERGOVERNMENTAL COUNCIL OF COPPER EXPORTING COUNTRIES (French: Conseil Inter-Gouvernemental des Pays Exportateurs de Cuivre) an INTERNATIONAL COMMODITY GROUP that is headquartered in Neuilly-sur-Seine, France, and includes the following copper-producing countries as members: Chile, Indonesia, Peru, Zaire, and Zambia, with Australia, Mauritania, and Papua New Guinea as associate members. The purpose of the group is to promote higher copper prices in the marketplace, which should provide member countries with higher earnings.

INTERIM COMMITTEE a group of people temporarily delegated to perform a function, such as investigating, considering, reporting, or acting on matters pertaining to international trade.

INTERINDUSTRY TRADE trade in which a country's EXPORTS and IMPORTS are in different industries. *see also* COMPARATIVE ADVANTAGE; HECKSCHER-OHLIN THEORY.

INTERLINE SHIPPING movement of a single SHIPMENT in two or more CARRIERS.

INTERMEDIARY LOAN PROGRAM—EXIMBANK a program that provides fixed interest rate loans to a responsible party that extends a loan to a buyer of U.S. EXPORTS. The purpose of the loan is to provide assistance to U.S. firms facing competition from other countries that are backed by subsidized financing. *see also* COMMERCIAL BANK GUARANTEE PROGRAM; DIRECT LOAN PROGRAM; LEASE GUARANTEES; WORKING CAPITAL GUARANTEE PROGRAM.

INTERMEDIATE CONSIGNEE the bank, forwarding agent, or other intermediary (if any) that acts in a foreign country as an agent for the EXPORTER, the purchaser, or the ultimate CONSIGNEE, for the purpose of effecting delivery of the EXPORT to the ultimate consignee.

INTERMEDIATE CREDIT GUARANTEE PROGRAM *see* EXPORT CREDIT GUARANTEE PROGRAMS.

INTERMEDIATE GOODS goods sent into an EXPORT PROCESSING or FREE-TRADE ZONE that have received some processing and will undergo further processing as they become part of another product.

INTERMEDIATION COSTS a term used when referring to the business costs for the development, maintenance, and use of foreign markets. They refer to those expenditures such as time and labor for a multinational firm necessary for the attainment of a goal.

INTERMITTANT DUMPING dumping that occurs for short periods of time, presumably to dispose of temporary surpluses of goods and not intended to eliminate competition. *see also* GENERAL AGREEMENT ON TARIFFS AND TRADE (GATT); SPORADIC DUMPING.

INTERMODAL the transportation of goods using a variety of modes, either ocean, air, or truck.

INTERMODAL COMPATIBILITY ability of a SHIPMENT of goods to be transported from one form of transportation to another. *see also* INTERMODAL; INTERMODAL CONTAINER TRANSFER FACILITY (ICTF); INTERMODAL TRANSPORT.

INTERMODAL CONTAINER TRANSFER FACILITY (ICTF) a location where CARGO is transferred from one mode of transportation to another. Example: transferring cargo from a ship to a truck or from a truck to a rail car.

INTERMODAL MOVEMENT *see* INTERMODAL.

INTERMODAL TRANSPORT coordinated transport of FREIGHT using multiple methods of transportation. *see also* INTERMODAL; INTERMODAL COMPATABILITY; INTERMODAL CONTAINER TRANSFER FACILITY (ICTF).

INTERMODAL TRANSPORTATION *see* INTERMODAL.

INTERNAL DEBT an obligation relating to the domestic affairs of a nation or a business to pay something to someone else.

INTERNALIZATION the desire of the parent company to retain control over its foreign operations, principally because it is less costly when dealing within the same corporate family as opposed to contracts with other companies. These costs will be lower due to the use of experienced managers, a common corporate culture, and the elimination of lengthy negotiations with the other company, and potential problems involving the enforcement of the agreement can be eliminated.

INTERNATIONAL
1. relating to or involving dealings outside one's own country that are between one country and other countries, or with a country other than its own.
2. extending across or surpassing the national boundaries of a country.

INTERNATIONAL ACCOUNTING STANDARDS COMMITTEE a multinational private-sector organization formed in 1973 by an agreement of the professional accounting organizations of Australia, Canada, France, Germany, Ireland, Japan, Mexico, the Netherlands, the United Kingdom, and the United States to develop worldwide accounting standards. It now consists of individuals from over 49 countries including employees, investors, creditors, suppliers, customers, and regulatory and taxing authorities.

INTERNATIONAL ACCOUNTING UNIT (IAU) a unit of measure that is based on the exchange rates of the 16 NATO member countries and that is reevaluated every 6 months. NATO infrastructure projects are usually denominated in International Accounting Units.

INTERNATIONAL ACCREDITATION FORUM (IAF) a group of international accreditation bodies created in January 1993 that joined together to promote international recognition of accreditation for quality systems (ISO 9000) registrars. Signatories include representatives of accrediting bodies in Australia, Canada, Japan, Mexico, the Netherlands, New Zealand, and the United States.

INTERNATIONAL AGREEMENTS a broad classification of legally binding arrangements between nations. The arrangements include TREATIES, CONVENTIONS, PROTOCOLS, ANNEXES, ACCORDS, and MEMORANDA OF UNDERSTANDING. Other common titles include note, pact, declaration, statute, constitution, and process-verbal. The title is not a controlling factor in making distinctions among arrangements. Some titles are not used consistently, and titles are often used as synonyms, with subtlety in differentiation resulting in an inability to apply certitude in definition. When a treaty or an executive agreement is first published by the United States, it is assigned a TIAS number and published in slip form in the treaties and other International Acts Series. TIAS, published by the U.S. Department of State, is a series of individual pamphlets.

INTERNATIONAL AGRICULTURAL RESEARCH CENTERS (IARCs) *see* CONSULTATIVE GROUP ON INTERNATIONAL AGRICULTURAL RESEARCH.

INTERNATIONAL AIR TRANSPORT ASSOCIATION (IATA) an international trade association serving airlines, passengers, shippers, travel agents, and governments. Established in 1945, the association promotes safety, standardization in forms (baggage checks, tickets, weigh bills), and aids in establishing international airfares. IATA headquarters is in Geneva, Switzerland.

INTERNATIONAL AND TERRITORIAL OPERATIONS general commercial activities outside the territory of the United States, including operations between U.S. points separated by foreign territory or major expanses of international waters.

INTERNATIONAL ANTICOUNTERFEITING COALITION (IACC) a nonprofit organization seeking to advance INTELLECTUAL PROPERTY RIGHTS (IPR) protection on a worldwide basis by promoting laws, regulations, and directives designed to render theft of IPR unattractive and unprofitable. Founded in 1978, the IACC is located in Washington, DC.

INTERNATIONAL ATOMIC ENERGY AGENCY (IAEA) a specialized agency of the United Nations acting as the primary international enforcement organization for a system of safeguards ensuring that nonnuclear weapons states do not divert shipments of sensitive nuclear-related equipment from peaceful applications to the production of nuclear weapons. Before a supplier state of nuclear materials or equipment may approve an EXPORT to a nonnuclear weapons NPT (NUCLEAR NONPROLIFERATION TREATY) signatory state, it must receive assurances that the recipient will place the material under IAEA safeguards. Subsequent to shipment, the recipient state must allow IAEA officials to verify the legitimate end use of the exported materials or equipment. Established in July 1957, the IAEA gives advice and technical assistance to developing countries on nuclear power development, nuclear safety, radioactive waste management, and related efforts. Safeguards are the technical means applied by the IAEA to verify that nuclear equipment or materials are used exclusively for peaceful purposes. The IAEA's headquarters is in Vienna, Austria.

INTERNATIONAL ATOMIC ENERGY LIST (IAEL) one of three lists maintained by COCOM. The IAEL comprises strictly nuclear-related items that are also of commercial value. It consists of materials, facilities, nuclear-related equipment, and software. The U.S. Department of State, which has the lead in U.S. negotiations concerning the IAEL, relies on U.S. Department of Energy experts.

INTERNATIONAL BANK FOR ECONOMIC COOPERATION (IBEX) an international financial institution serving as the CENTRAL BANK OF THE COUNCIL OF MUTUAL ECONOMIC ASSISTANCE (CMEA). The CMEA was established in 1949 ostensibly to create a common market. The CMEA was a Soviet initiative with Bulgaria, Czechoslovakia, Hungary, Poland, and Romania as founder members. The council was later joined by the German Democratic Republic, Mongolia, Cuba, and Vietnam; Yugoslavia held associate status. Members normally received some products, particularly oil and gas from the former Soviet Union, at below-market prices. The CMEA was succeeded in 1991 by the ORGANIZATION FOR ECONOMIC COOPERATION (OIEC). The IBEX functioned in two major ways:

1. it acted as the central bank for MULTILATERAL settlement of trade balances among CMEA members; and
2. it provided credit to members, enabling expanded trade among member countries.

INTERNATIONAL BANK FOR RECONSTRUCTION AND DEVELOPMENT (IBRD) a bank established in December 1945 as part of the WORLD BANK to help countries reconstruct their economies after World War II. IBRD assists developing member countries by lending to government agencies and by guaranteeing private loans for such projects as agricultural modernization or infrastructure development. The bank's headquarters is in Washington, DC.

INTERNATIONAL BANKING the process of either borrowing and lending funds to domestic firms for the purpose of financing EXPORT sales or providing credit to foreign buyers to finance purchases.

INTERNATIONAL BANKING ACT (IBA) a U.S. legislative framework for governing the activities of foreign banks, which previously had been governed only by state laws. Established in 1978, the IBA developed a policy of national treatment for U.S. offices of foreign banks by
- limiting any new multistate branching activities to activities more comparable to those of U.S. banks,
- placing the foreign bank offices under the same reserve requirements that apply to U.S. banks,
- limiting foreign bank involvement in U.S. securities, and
- making federal deposit insurance available to U.S. offices of foreign banks if they choose to engage in retail banking.
  see also FOREIGN BANK SUPERVISION ENHANCEMENT ACT.

INTERNATIONAL BANKING CENTERS areas where financial institutions are located to conduct international trade-related business, including the buying and selling of foreign currencies, arranging for international collections, and financing for foreign trade. *see also* INTERNATIONAL FINANCIAL CENTERS; OFFSHORE BANKING UNIT.

INTERNATIONAL BANKING FACILITY (IBF) one of four categories of foreign banking in the United States. An IBF may be a domestic bank or an office of a foreign bank. In either circumstance, the IBF maintains asset and liability accounts that are segregated from domestic activity and limited to financing international trade. IBFs are exempted from such requirements as reserve levels and obligations to make some insurance premiums. In the United States, eligibility requirements limit IBFs to business with other IBFs and with non-U.S. residents. U.S. banks may structure operations to draw foreign customer deposits and loans to their domestic offices. *see also* OFFSHORE BANKING UNIT.

INTERNATIONAL BUNKER PRICES a weekly listing appearing on Tuesdays in the JOURNAL OF COMMERCE. It provides quotations for ships' bunker fuel obtained during the course of the week.

INTERNATIONAL BUSINESS OPPORTUNITIES SERVICE (IBOS) a WORLD BANK subscription package that includes information on upcoming projects and business opportunities. The Service includes

- the Monthly Operational Summary (MOS) listing all projects in the pipeline;
- Technical Data Sheets (TDSs), published for each approved loan, listing identifying information, procurement methods, cofinancing, and similar data;
- general procurement notices, issued for projects involving international competitive bidding;
- specific procurement notices describing specific items to be procured and bidding requirements; and
- major contract award notices identifying successful bidders for contracts that were recently awarded.

    see also INTERNATIONAL COMPETITIVE BIDDING; LIMITED INTERNATIONAL BIDDING; LOCAL COMPETITIVE BIDDING.

INTERNATIONAL BUSINESS REPLY SERVICE (IBIS) a service of the U.S. Postal Service similar to the Domestic Business Reply Service. It allows mail to be distributed to and deposited in certain foreign countries for return to the addressee in the United States without charge, with the postage being collected from the U.S. recipient at time of delivery.

INTERNATIONAL CALENDAR a listing of forthcoming conferences, seminars, meetings, courses, and workshops concerned with international trade, appearing each Monday in the JOURNAL OF COMMERCE.

INTERNATIONAL CARGO HANDLING COORDINATION ASSOCIATION (ICHCA) an international CARGO association that
- collects, edits, and disseminates technical information relating to cargo handling by all modes of transport;
- maintains consultative status with the International Standards Organization for the development of standards relating to cargo-handling equipment (such as hooks, containers, wire slings, spreaders, and pallets);
- maintains a library for members' use; and
- represents members' interests on an international basis.

There is an ICHCA U.S. National Section. The ICHCA Secretariat General is in London, England.

INTERNATIONAL CENTER FOR GENETIC ENGINEERING AND BIOTECHNOLOGY (ICGEB) *see* UNITED NATIONS INDUSTRIAL DEVELOPMENT ORGANIZATION (UNIDO).

INTERNATIONAL CENTER FOR SCIENCE AND HIGH TECHNOLOGY (ICHST) *see* UNITED NATIONS INDUSTRIAL DEVELOPMENT ORGANIZATION (UNIDO).

INTERNATIONAL CENTER FOR THEORETICAL PHYSICS (ICTP) *see* INTERNATIONAL ATOMIC ENERGY AGENCY.

INTERNATIONAL CENTRE FOR SETTLEMENT OF INVESTMENT DISPUTES (ICSID) an affiliate of the WORLD BANK, ICSID is a public international organization that provides facilities for the conciliation and arbitration of investment disputes between contracting states and nationals of other contracting states. The centre's objective is to promote an atmosphere of mutual confidence between states and foreign investors conducive to increasing the flow of private international investment. The centre does not itself engage in conciliation or arbitration but assists in the initiation and conduct of conciliation and arbitration proceedings. Recourse to conciliation and arbitration under the ICSID convention is entirely voluntary. However, once the parties have consented, they are bound to carry out their undertakings and, in the case of arbitration, to abide by the award. All contracting states, whether or not they are parties to the dispute, are required to recognize awards rendered pursuant to the convention as binding and to enforce the pecuniary obligations imposed thereby. The centre also conducts and publishes research in foreign investment law. ICSID was created under a treaty, the United Nations Convention on the Settlement of Investment Disputes Between States and Nationals of Other States (the ICSID Convention), in October 1966. The centre's headquarters is in Washington, DC.

INTERNATIONAL CHAMBER OF COMMERCE (ICC) private body created in 1919 to promote free trade and private enterprise and to represent business interests at national and international levels. Members include national councils from 60 countries. The ICC's headquarters is in Paris, France. *see also* INCOTERMS.

INTERNATIONAL CHANNEL EFFICIENCY a ratio based on the degree to which the effective output in achieving the desired distribution objectives in the marketing and supplying of goods to intermediaries is compared to the total input investments (transportation, warehousing, etc.).

INTERNATIONAL CHANNEL LAG COEFFICIENT a gauge of the skill with which a channel of distribution is functioning. The international channel lag coefficient is a ratio of controllable to uncontrollable marketing costs. The higher the coefficient, the more costly it is for the firm to distribute its products internationally.

INTERNATIONAL CIVIL AVIATION ORGANIZATION (ICAO) a UNITED NATIONS specialized agency that promotes international cooperation in civil aviation. The ICAO council adopts standards and recommended practices concerning air navigation, prevention of unlawful interference, and facilitation of border-crossing procedures for international civil aviation. Operating since 1947, ICAO includes almost all United Nations members. Its headquarters is in Montreal, Canada.

INTERNATIONAL COCOA ORGANIZATION (ICO) an INTERNATIONAL COMMODITY GROUP established in 1973 and with headquarters in London. Its membership consists of 18 EXPORT-producing countries and 22 importing countries. The purpose of the ICO is to make sure that the producing countries make available the product to the market on a regular basis, maintain buffer stocks in the event demand exceeds supply and the world price exceeds the agreed-to price level, and coordinate the purchase of the commodity by producing countries in the event supply exceeds demand and the price drops below the agreed-to price level.

INTERNATIONAL COFFEE AGREEMENT an agreement signed by 67 countries, representing all the world's major exporters and importers of coffee. The INTERNATIONAL COFFEE ORGANIZATION (ICO) acted as a forum for market participants since the early 1960s but has not regulated markets since July 1989, when consuming and exporting country members were unable to agree on EXPORT quotas. Since suspending export quotas, the ICO has been acting mainly as a center for meetings and as a collector of statistics on the coffee market. The ASSOCIATION OF COFFEE PRODUCING COUNTRIES, a new pact comprising 28 members that account for 85% of world coffee exports, has been seeking to strengthen world coffee prices through an export-retention plan.

INTERNATIONAL COFFEE ORGANIZATION (ICO) *see* INTERNATIONAL COFFEE AGREEMENT.

INTERNATIONAL COMMODITY AGREEMENT (ICA) an international understanding, usually reflected in a legal instrument, that relates to trade in a particular basic COMMODITY and is based on terms negotiated and accepted by most of the countries that export and IMPORT commercially significant quantities of the commodity. Some commodity agreements (such as exist for coffee, cocoa, natural rubber, sugar, and tin) center on economic provisions intended to defend a price range for the commodity through the use of buffer stocks or export quotas or both. Other commodity agreements (such as existing agreements for jute and jute products, olive oil, and wheat) promote cooperation among producers and consumers through improved consultation, exchange of information, research and development, and export promotion.

INTERNATIONAL COMMODITY GROUP an organization of producer countries trading in a particular basic COMMODITY, combined to establish an INTERNATIONAL CARTEL.

They combine resources in an attempt to secure competitive prices from suppliers and supply producers with reliable data on production levels, consumption, production, and transportation costs. *see also* COMMON FUND FOR COMMODITIES; INTERNATIONAL COMMODITY AGREEMENT; UNITED NATIONS CONFERENCE ON TRADE AND DEVELOPMENT.

INTERNATIONAL COMMODITY ORGANIZATION *see* INTERNATIONAL COMMODITY GROUP.

INTERNATIONAL COMPETITIVE BIDDING (ICB) one of several forms of procurement made with WORLD BANK financing. Even though the World Bank provides financing from its loans for the contracts and ensures that agreed procurement procedures are observed, the borrower, not the World Bank, is always responsible for procurement. ICB requires that

- all goods or works to be procured through ICB be internationally advertised through the United Nations (in the publication *Development Business*) and at least one major local newspaper;
- bids be entertained in the bidder's or other currencies in which expenses would normally be incurred or in an international currency specified by the borrower;
- payments be made in the currencies in the bids, without requirement to accept any portion of payment in countertrade;
- documents be in an international language (English, French, or Spanish);
- bids be openly reviewed; and
- contracts be awarded to the lowest evaluated responsive bid.

ICB permits a margin of preference to be given to domestic goods and, under certain conditions, to domestic contracting services in developing countries. *see also* INTERNATIONAL BUSINESS OPPORTUNITIES SERVICE; LIMITED INTERNATIONAL BIDDING; LOCAL COMPETITIVE BIDDING.

INTERNATIONAL CONFEDERATION OF AGRICULTURAL CREDIT (ICAC) *see* CONFEDERATION INTERNATIONALE DU CREDIT AGRICOLE (COCA).

INTERNATIONAL CONFEDERATION OF FREE TRADE UNIONS (ICFTU) a confederation of more than 140 national organizations from nearly 100 countries to promote the trade union movement by recognizing workers' organizations and the rights of workers to bargain collectively. ICFTU organizes and educates free-trade unions in the developing world primarily through its three regional organizations: APRO for Asia and the Pacific located in New Delhi, India; AFRO in Africa; and ORIT in Latin America (Mexico City). Established in 1949, ICFTU headquarters is in Brussels, Belgium.

INTERNATIONAL CONGRESS OFFICE (ICO) a U.S. TRAVEL AND TOURISM ADMINISTRATION office that persuades international associations to select the United States as venues for their meetings. The ICO operates out of the American Embassy in Paris.

INTERNATIONAL CONVENTION ON THE SIMPLIFICATION AND HARMONIZATION OF CUSTOMS PROCEDURES a convention, developed by the CUSTOMS COOPERATION COUNCIL (CCC), that seeks to foster international trade and cooperation by simplifying and harmonizing CUSTOMS procedures and operations. (The term *customs procedure* is not used in the narrow sense of the treatment assigned to imported goods; it covers all provisions relating to a particular sphere of customs activity.) The convention (also known as the KYOTO CONVENTION) was adopted in May 1973 in Kyoto, Japan, as a core legal instrument with three original ANNEXES on customs procedures. Nearly 30 additional annexes (each covering a different area of customs procedures and operations) have since been created. To ensure worldwide harmonization, the convention is also open to nonmembers of the CCC that are state members of the UNITED NATIONS or its specialized agencies. A country is required to accept only the convention itself and at least one of the annexes to become a contracting party. (When the United States became party to the convention, effective January 1984, it accepted 20 of the annexes and entered certain reservations with respect to some of their provisions.) The annexes contain definitions, standards, and recommended practices. Countries can reserve against any standard or recommended practice in a particular annex. There is also a provision obligating countries to review their national legislation every 3 years to determine if reservations can be removed.

INTERNATIONAL COUNCIL OF SCIENTIFIC UNIONS (ICSU) a nongovernmental organization that coordinates international activity in the different branches of science and their applications. Founded in 1931, the ICSU is the successor to the International Research Council, which was created in 1919. The council seeks to break the barriers of specialization through international interdisciplinary programs and research bodies.

There are two categories of ICSU members:
- national, multidisciplinary scientific academies or research councils that promote cooperation and research and
- international organizations that promote cooperation in a single field of science (scientific unions).

The council has a small headquarters office in Paris, France.

INTERNATIONAL COURT OF JUSTICE (ICJ) the principal judicial organ of the UNITED NATIONS. Established in 1945, the ICJ decides cases submitted to it by states and gives advisory opinions on legal questions submitted to it by the GENERAL ASSEMBLY or SECURITY COUNCIL or by UN specialized agencies. The court is composed of 15 judges elected by the General Assembly and the Security Council from a list of persons nominated by the national groups in the Permanent Court of Arbitration. The seat of the court is in The Hague, the Netherlands.

INTERNATIONAL CRIMINAL POLICE ORGANIZATION (INTERPOL) the coordinating organization for the worldwide criminal police. It was established in Vienna in 1923, reorganized in Paris in 1946, and serves more than 125 member nations. The goal of INTERPOL is to provide assistance among authorities globally, focusing on counterfeiting, forgery, smuggling, and the narcotics trade.

INTERNATIONAL DAIRY ARRANGEMENT an international agreement resulting from the TOKYO ROUND of MULTILATERAL TRADE NEGOTIATIONS. The agreement was signed by 16 members of the GENERAL AGREEMENT ON TARIFFS AND TRADE (GATT) including Argentina, Australia, Bulgaria, Egypt, the EUROPEAN ECONOMIC COMMUNITY (EEC), Finland, Hungary, Japan, New Zealand, Norway, Poland, Romania, South Africa, Sweden, Switzerland, and Uruguay. The principal aim of the agreement was to promote the growth of dairy products worldwide through the reduction of TRADE BARRIERS.

INTERNATIONAL DATA BASE (IDB) an automated data bank containing statistical tables of demographic, economic, and social data for all countries of the world maintained by the CENTER FOR INTERNATIONAL RESEARCH. Data categories include population; vital statistics; health and nutrition; fertility, migration; foreign-born and refugee statistics; provinces and cities; marital status; family planning; ethnic, religious, and language groups; literacy and education; labor force, employment, income, and gross national product; and household size and housing indicators. IDB data users include governments, private firms, research institutions, and international organizations.

INTERNATIONAL DEBT *see* EXTERNAL DEBT.

INTERNATIONAL DEBT RATING the classification given to banks, municipalities, and other major borrowers of capital according to their ability to pay their obligations as they come due. An organization will be charged a higher rate of interest from a financial institution as its rating is lowered. Debt ratings can be affected by the number of loans in LESS-DEVELOPED COUNTRIES (LDC), the repayment record of these LDCs, and the percentage of high-risk loans found in their portfolio.

INTERNATIONAL DEBT RATING SERVICES independent firms that provide the classifications given to financial institutions and major corporate borrowers with regard to their creditworthiness. Examples: Dun & Bradstreet and Moody's Investment Service.

INTERNATIONAL DEPOSITORY RECEIPT (IDR) a negotiable bank-issued certificate representing ownership of stock securities by an investor outside the country of origin. The securities backing the receipt remain in the custody of the issuing bank or a correspondent.

INTERNATIONAL DEVELOPMENT ASSOCIATION (IDA) a part of the WORLD BANK GROUP, the IDA is an association created to lend money to developing countries at no interest and for a long repayment period. It was created in 1959 and began operations in November 1960. The IDA provides development assistance through SOFT LOANS to meet the needs of many developing countries that cannot afford development loans at ordinary rates of interest and in the time span of conventional loans. The Association's headquarters is in Washington, DC. *see also* WORLD BANK.

INTERNATIONAL DEVELOPMENT INFORMATION NETWORK (IDIN) a collaboration among 5 regional associations and the ORGANIZATION OF ECONOMIC COOPERATION AND DEVELOPMENT (OECD) involved in the collection, review, and distribution of information concerning research on common economic and social issues affecting members. The 5 regional associations include EADI (Europe), CODESRIA (Africa), ADIPA (Asia), CLACSO (Latin America), and AICARDES (Middle East/Arab). *see also* DEVELOPMENT CENTER OF THE ORGANIZATION OF ECONOMIC COOPERATION AND DEVELOPMENT; EUROPEAN COMMUNITY OF RESEARCH AND TECHNOLOGY.

INTERNATIONAL DEVELOPMENT RESEARCH CENTER (IDRC) a private organization created by Canadian federal legislation to provide support for the development and promotion of scientific and technical programs benefiting developing countries. The Canadian government supports the program to generate additional orders for Canadian goods and services.

INTERNATIONAL ECONOMIC POLICY (IEP) former department of the INTERNATIONAL TRADE ADMINISTRATION (ITA) of the U.S. DEPARTMENT OF COMMERCE responsible for providing commercial and economic information on specific countries for interested companies. The IEP staff provides briefings for firms on how to do business in specific markets and assistance on any problems a firm may be encountering in another country. Currently these services are concentrated in the ITA subdivision called the U.S. AND FOREIGN COMMERCIAL SERVICE (US&FCS), which maintains a network of international trade specialists in the United States and commercial officers in foreign cities to help American companies do business abroad. *see also* ECONOMIC POLICY COUNCIL.

INTERNATIONAL ELECTROTECHNICAL COMMISSION (IEC) commission that was established in 1906 to deal with questions related to international standardization in the electrical and electronic engineering fields. The members of the IEC are the national committees, one for each country, that are required to be as representative as possible of all electrical interests in the country concerned: manufacturers, users, governmental authorities, and teaching and professional bodies. They are composed of representatives of the various organizations that deal with questions of electrical standardization at the national level. Most of them are recognized and supported by their governments.

INTERNATIONAL EMERGENCY ECONOMIC POWERS ACT (IEEPA) U.S. act passed in 1977 to extend emergency powers previously granted to the President by the Trading with the Enemy Act of 1917 (which authorized the President to exercise extraordinary powers when the United States is at war). IEEPA enables the President, after declaring that a national emergency exists because of a threat from a source outside the United States, to investigate, regulate, compel, or prohibit virtually any economic transaction involving property in which a foreign country or national has an interest.

INTERNATIONAL ENERGY AGENCY (IEA) agency founded in 1974 as a forum for energy cooperation among 21 member nations. The IEA helped participating countries prepare to reduce the economic risks of oil supply disruptions and to reduce dependence on oil through coordinated and cooperative research efforts.

INTERNATIONAL EXECUTIVE SERVICE CORPS (IESC) a nonprofit organization funded by the AGENCY FOR INTERNATIONAL DEVELOPMENT that recruits retired U.S. executives and technical advisers to counsel businesses in developing nations on a volunteer basis. IESC's program includes short-term technical and managerial assistance and long-range trade and investment services. IESC was founded in 1964, and its headquarters is in Stamford, Connecticut.

INTERNATIONAL EXHIBITIONS BUREAU (IEB) international agency that governs the frequency of international exhibitions and oversees the guarantees and facilities that the host nation is required to offer. By agreement, member states may mount international exhibitions only after the events have been registered with IEB. Member states are also precluded from participating in exhibitions in nonmember states in the absence of agreement by the bureau. The IEB was originally created in 1928 and was revised in 1972. Its headquarters is in Paris, France.

INTERNATIONAL FINANCE CENTERS major cities in which financial institutions, such as commercial banks, are located and are conducting business resulting from international trade, according to internationally accepted principles and practices.

INTERNATIONAL FINANCE CORPORATION (IFC) a financial arm of the WORLD BANK, the IFC promotes private-sector investment in developing countries. Established in 1956, the IFC charges market rates and seeks profitable returns. *see also* AFRICA ENTERPRISE

FUND; AFRICA PROJECT DEVELOPMENT FACILITY; AFRICAN MANAGEMENT SERVICES COMPANY; CARIBBEAN/CENTRAL AMERICA BUSINESS ADVISORY SERVICE.

INTERNATIONAL FINANCING the strategies and motivations of firms for direct foreign investment, international banking operations, lending, and investment criteria.

INTERNATIONAL FISHER EFFECT (IFE) a theory that implies that the level of interest rates in a country is a predictor of changes in the spot exchange rate. The theory is based on the works of Irving Fisher, an American economist and professor at Yale University, known for his work in monetary economic theory. According to the IFS, the currency of the country with the lower inflation rate will strengthen, whereas the currency of the country with the higher inflation rate will weaken. *see also* INTEREST RATE DIFFERENTIAL.

INTERNATIONAL FREIGHT BROKER *see* FREIGHT FORWARDER.

INTERNATIONAL FREIGHT FORWARDER *see* FREIGHT FORWARDER.

INTERNATIONAL FREQUENCY REGISTRATION BOARD (IFRB) (French: Comité International d'Enregistrement des Fréquences) an organizational entity under the INTERNATIONAL TELECOMMUNICATIONS UNION (ITU). Located in Geneva, IFRB is composed of 5 full-time elected officials with a rotating chairmanship. IFRB maintains the International Frequency Register, monitors and analyzes all ITU records of frequency use around the world, and makes determinations as to whether or not certain systems are in compliance with the Radio Regulations.

INTERNATIONAL FUND FOR AGRICULTURAL DEVELOPMENT (IFAD) an international agricultural fund created in 1976 (began operations in December 1977) that provides financial support for programs that improve agricultural policies and increase food production among its 140 member nations. The fund also seeks to improve nutrition in developing countries. IFAD's headquarters is in Rome, Italy.

INTERNATIONAL IMPORT CERTIFICATE a statement issued by the government of the country of destination of U.S. goods certifying that the imported products will be disposed of responsibly in the designated country. It is the responsibility of the U.S. EXPORTER to notify the CONSIGNEE to obtain the certificate. The IMPORTER certificate should be retained in the U.S. exporter's files, and a copy should be submitted with the application for an INDIVIDUALLY VALIDATED LICENSE (IVL). *see also* STATEMENT OF ULTIMATE CONSIGNEE AND PURCHASER.

INTERNATIONAL INDUSTRIAL LIST the COCOM industrial list that contains dual-use items whose export is controlled for strategic reasons.

INTERNATIONAL INSTITUTE FOR THE UNIFICATION OF PRIVATE LAW (UNIDROIT) originally established in 1926 at the initiative of Italy and associated with the League of Nations, the institute studies methods for coordinating and unifying the private and trade laws of member countries. The institute's headquarters is in Rome, Italy.

INTERNATIONAL INTELLECTUAL PROPERTY ALLIANCE (IIPA) bilateral and multilateral efforts by U.S. copyright-based industries to improve the international protection of copyrighted works. IIPA is composed of trade associations, each representing a significant segment of the U.S. copyright community. IIPA was formed in 1984, and its headquarters is in Washington, DC.

INTERNATIONAL INVESTMENT *see* FOREIGN DIRECT INVESTMENT IN THE UNITED STATES; PORTFOLIO INVESTMENT.

INTERNATIONAL INVESTMENT BANK (IIB) an international financial institution formed by members of the COUNCIL FOR MUTUAL ECONOMIC ASSISTANCE (CMEA). The IIB was a result of the Agreement on Multilateral Payment in Transferable Rubles, which created the INTERNATIONAL BANK FOR ECONOMIC COOPERATION (IBEC). The function of the IBEC involved the settlement of CMEA member trade balances and the extension of short-term credit to members. It was the role of the IIB to extend medium- to long-term credit for the development of projects in areas such as energy, health, education, agriculture, industry, and transportation infrastructure development. *see also* ORGANIZATION FOR ECONOMIC COOPERATION (OIEC); COUNCIL FOR MUTUAL ECONOMIC ASSISTANCE.

The fall of the communist governments of most of the European members in 1989 and 1990 and the end of the use of the RUBLE as a basis for trade between members in 1991 brought about the dissolution of the council in 1991.

INTERNATIONAL INVESTMENT POSITION the balance of the amount and distribution of a country's assets in a foreign country relative to the foreign country's investment in the home country.

INTERNATIONAL JOINT COMMISSION a joint U.S-Canadian commission established by the Boundary Waters Treaty of 1909. It is responsible for the investigation of pollution complaints in the Great Lakes, and arbitrates disputes pertaining to United States-Canadian use of boundary waters relating to fishing, navigation, sanitation, energy use, and irrigation in the Great Lakes, and the Atlantic, Pacific, and Arctic Oceans.

INTERNATIONAL JUTE COMMISSION (IJC) an INTERNATIONAL COMMODITY AGREEMENT that was initiated in January 1991 under the authorization of the UNITED NATIONS CONFERENCE ON TRADE AND DEVELOPMENT (UNCTAD). The IJC represents the producer and consumer countries of jute production. The main purpose of the association is to promote cooperation among producers and consumers through improved consultation, exchange of information, research and development, and EXPORT promotion.

INTERNATIONAL LABOR ORGANIZATION (ILO) originally established in 1919 by the League of Nations, the ILO became a specialized agency of the United Nations in 1946. It seeks to promote improved working and living conditions by establishing standards that reduce social injustice in areas such as employment, pay, health, working conditions, and freedom of association among workers. Its headquarters is in Geneva, Switzerland.

INTERNATIONAL LEAD AND ZINC STUDY GROUP an INTERNATIONAL COMMODITY GROUP established in London in 1959 and consisting of 31 member countries from Western and Eastern Europe. The organization was established with the primary purpose of ensuring the supply of the commodity in desired quantities at reasonable prices. *see also* COUNCIL FOR MUTUAL ECONOMIC ASSISTANCE; INTERNATIONAL CARTEL.

INTERNATIONAL LOANS a column that appears periodically in the JOURNAL OF COMMERCE. It lists loans being made by the WORLD BANK and other financial institutions. The information furnished in the column provides leads for companies supplying the goods and services financed by these loans.

INTERNATIONAL MARITIME BUREAU (IMB) the division of the INTERNATIONAL CHAMBER OF COMMERCE responsible for policing acts of fraud, piracy, and other forms of criminal activity during the transportation of goods internationally. Agents for the International Maritime Bureau search for stolen or diverted CARGO and ships and false or stolen documents and passports. Agents for the IMB travel around the world under the authority of the IMB MULTILATERAL TREATY to which all members of the ORGANIZATION OF ECONOMIC COOPERATION AND DEVELOPMENT (OECD) have consented. *see also* INTERNATIONAL CHAMBER OF COMMERCE; INTERNATIONAL CRIMINAL POLICE ORGANIZATION (INTERPOL).

INTERNATIONAL MARITIME ORGANIZATION (IMO) a specialized agency of the United Nations established in 1948. The IMO facilitates cooperation on technical matters affecting merchant shipping and traffic, including improved maritime safety and prevention of marine pollution. Its headquarters is in London, England.

INTERNATIONAL MARITIME SATELLITE ORGANIZATION (INMARSAT) an international partnership of signatories from 67 nations. The partnership provides mobile satellite capacity to its signatories, who, in turn, use the capacity to provide worldwide mobile satellite services to their maritime, aeronautical, and land-mobile customers—including shipping, cruise, fishing, research and offshore exploration industries, and airlines. INMARSAT began service in 1976. COMSAT is the U.S. signatory to INMARSAT.

INTERNATIONAL MARKET INSIGHTS (IMI) staff reports prepared by American embassies and consulates. An IMI covers developments in a single country that are of interest to traders and investors. Topics may include new laws, policies and procedures, new trade regulations, and marketplace changes.

INTERNATIONAL MARKET RESEARCH SURVEYS *see* INDUSTRY SUBSECTOR ANALYSIS.

INTERNATIONAL MARKETING CHANNEL the path used by a firm through which the firm's products reach the final consumer or user in the EXPORT process. This includes any individual or firm who provides services or makes arrangements for expediting the shipment to its overseas destination or provides services that physically alter the product, enabling the product to be shipped to the customer. *see also* FACILITATING INTERMEDIARY; FUNCTIONAL INTERMEDIARY.

INTERNATIONAL MONETARY FUND (IMF) fund established in December 1945 to promote international monetary harmony. It monitors the exchange rate and monetary policies of member nations and provides credit for member countries that experience temporary balance of payments deficits. Each member has a quota, expressed in SPECIAL DRAWING RIGHTS (SDRS), which reflects both the relative size of the member's economy and that member's voting power in the fund. Quotas also determine the members' access to the financial resources of, and their shares in, the allocation of special drawing rights by the fund. The IMF, funded through members' quotas, may supplement resources through borrowing. The IMF has a membership of approximately 175 countries. *see also* COMPENSATORY AND CONTINGENCY FINANCING FACILITY; CREDIT TRANCHE; ENHANCED STRUCTURAL ADJUSTMENT FACILITY; EXTENDED FUND FACILITY; GENERAL ARRANGEMENTS TO BORROW; RESERVE TRANCHE; STAND-BY ARRANGEMENTS.

INTERNATIONAL MONETARY SYSTEM a financial system, including the institutions, rules, and procedures of different countries, that enables international trade to function effectively. These systems are used for effecting international payments between countries and the settling of international BALANCE OF PAYMENT obligations. The initial international monetary system, in effect from the late 19th to early 20th century was the GOLD STANDARD. It was replaced by the gold bullion standard, which was discontinued in the 1930s. Prior to the end of World War II, the allied powers met at the Bretton Woods resort in New Hampshire and established EXCHANGE RATES for most currencies, linking the U.S. dollar to gold. By 1973, the system was not functioning as well, and it was discontinued and replaced by the current system of FLOATING EXCHANGE RATES.

INTERNATIONAL MUNITIONS LIST (IML) one of three lists controlled by the 17-member COORDINATING COMMITTEE FOR MULTILATERAL EXPORT CONTROLS (COCOM). The IML contains 23 categories and is similar in coverage to, but less restrictive than, the U.S. MUNITIONS LIST (USML).

INTERNATIONAL ORGANIZATION FOR MIGRATION (IOM) assists countries in meeting individual needs arising from immigration and emigration. The organization was established in 1951, and its headquarters is in Geneva, Switzerland.

INTERNATIONAL POSTAL MONEY ORDERS a service available to individuals in the United States interested in transferring funds to individuals or firms in countries who have agreements with the U.S. Postal Service for the exchange of postal money orders.

INTERNATIONAL POW WOW an annual trade fair, sponsored by the Travel Industry Association of America, that brings together over 1,200 international buyers (tour operators and wholesalers) from 55 countries. The buyers are chosen through international selection criteria and purchase packages that they sell to their respective travel retailers. The International POW WOW promotes foreign tourism to the United States.

INTERNATIONAL PRODUCT LIFE CYCLE *see* PRODUCT LIFE CYCLE.

INTERNATIONAL RADIO CONSULTATIVE COMMITTEE (CCIR) (French: Comité International des Radiocommunications) a subsidiary organization of the INTERNATIONAL TELECOMMUNICATIONS UNION, the CCIR studies and issues recommendations on technical and operating questions connected with radiocommunications. The CCIR is located in Geneva, Switzerland, and the U.S. Department of State is the U.S. member.

INTERNATIONAL RESERVES the total of the currency on hand plus the commercial bank reserves held against deposits, as required by law. International reserves are the means of settling international debts. *see also* FOREIGN EXCHANGE.

INTERNATIONAL RUBBER AGREEMENT (IRA) an INTERNATIONAL COMMODITY AGREEMENT signed in 1987 under the authorization of the UNITED NATIONS CONFERENCE ON TRADE AND DEVELOPMENT (UNCTAD) as the replacement to the former agreement from 1979. The agreement centers on economic provisions intended to defend a price range for the commodity through the use of buffer stocks or EXPORT quotas or both.

INTERNATIONAL RUBBER ORGANIZATION the INTERNATIONAL COMMODITY ORGANIZATION responsible for the administration of the INTERNATIONAL RUBBER AGREEMENT.

INTERNATIONAL RUBBER STUDY GROUP (IRSG) an INTERNATIONAL COMMODITY GROUP, established in 1944 and headquartered in London, to provide a forum for the examination of problems influencing synthetic and natural rubber. The IRSG includes members from 30 countries who are either natural rubber consumer or synthetic rubber producer countries. *see also* INTERNATIONAL CARTEL; INTERNATIONAL COMMODITY AGREEMENT.

INTERNATIONAL SERVICE FOR NATIONAL AGRICUL-TURAL RESEARCH (SNAR) *see* CONSULTATIVE GROUP ON INTERNATIONAL AGRICULTURAL RESEARCH.

INTERNATIONAL SOCIAL SECURITY ASSOCIATION (ISSA) group of organizations responsible for the administration of social security. Established in 1927, ISSA aims to protect and develop social security throughout the world. The association works closely with the INTERNATIONAL LABOR ORGANIZATION (ILO). The ISSA secretariat is located in the ILO building in Geneva, Switzerland.

INTERNATIONAL STANDARDS ORGANIZATION (ISO) a worldwide federation of national bodies, established in 1947, representing approximately 90 member countries. The scope of the International Standards Organization covers standardization in all fields except electrical and electronic engineering standards, which are the responsibility of the INTERNATIONAL ELECTROTECHNICAL COMMISSION (IEC). However, the ISO does develop standards for computers and communications. Together, the ISO and IEC form the specialized system for worldwide standardization—the world's largest nongovernmental system for voluntary industrial and technical collaboration at the international level.

The result of ISO technical work is published in the form of International Standards. There are, for example, ISO standards for the quality grading of steel; for testing the strength of woven textiles; for storage of citrus fruits; for magnetic codes on credit cards; for automobile safety belts; and for ensuring the quality and performance of such diverse products as surgical implants, ski bindings, wire ropes, and photographic lenses. *see also* INTERNATIONAL ACCREDITATION FORUM.

INTERNATIONAL STANDARDS ORGANIZATION 9000–9004 (ISO 9000) the general name for the quality standard accepted throughout the EUROPEAN ECONOMIC COMMUNITY. It was initially adopted in 1987. ISO is a series of documents on quality assurance published by the Geneva-based International Standards Organization. The five documents outline standards for developing Total Quality Management and a Quality Improvement Process. 9000 consists of guidelines for the selection and use of the quality systems contained in 9001–9003. 9001 outlines a model for quality assurance in design, development, production, installation, and servicing. 9002 outlines a model for quality assurance in production and installation. 9003 outlines a model for quality assurance for final inspection and testing. 9004 is not a standard but contains guidelines for quality management and quality system elements.

INTERNATIONAL STANDARDS ORGANIZATION INFORMATION NETWORK (ISONET) an agreement between standardizing bodies to make information on standards, technical regulations, and related matters readily available. ISONET links the information centers of national standards bodies with each other and with the ISO Information Centre in Geneva, Switzerland. National members of ISONET are responsible for serving as the international reference point for information about the standards, technical regulations, and certification systems that operate in the individual member's country and for providing their own nationals with information on national, foreign, regional, and international technical rules.

INTERNATIONAL SUGAR AGREEMENT (ISA) an INTERNATIONAL COMMODITY AGREEMENT signed in 1987 by 43 exporting and 11 importing members. It differs from many of the other COMMODITY agreements in that the ISA does not exclusively represent the interests of the producer relative to the consumer countries. It is, however, a collaborative agreement whereby members agree to collaborate in the collection and distribution of production and consumption statistics, information on taxation programs affecting sugar consumption, information on the development of artificial sugar substitutes, and any other condition that can either promote or retard the production and distribution of sugar. *see also* INTERNATIONAL SUGAR ORGANIZATION.

INTERNATIONAL SUGAR ORGANIZATION the INTERNATIONAL COMMODITY ORGANIZATION responsible for the administration of the INTERNATIONAL SUGAR AGREEMENT (ISA).

INTERNATIONAL SWAPS AND DERIVATIVES ASSOCIATION (ISDA) an association, established in 1985, as a not-for-profit corporation, with headquarters in New York City. The ISDA promotes orderly practices in the swap market, conducts research on the volume and quality of transactions, and promotes public understanding. Its members include over 140 institutions worldwide representing dealers in swaps, corporations, software firms, and law firms. The ISDA, formerly known as the International Swap Dealers Association, changed its name in August 1993. *see also* DERIVATIVES.

INTERNATIONAL TAKEOVER the bid by a foreign company to seize control in the open market of a domestic company.

INTERNATIONAL TELECOMMUNICATIONS CONVENTION OF 1973 convention that granted to a country the right to intercept and withhold any communication affecting that country's national security.

INTERNATIONAL TELECOMMUNICATIONS SATELLITE ORGANIZATION (INTELSAT) a nonprofit cooperative of about 120 countries that jointly own and operate a global communications satellite system serving the world. Created in 1964 under a multilateral agreement, the system is used primarily for international communications and by many countries for domestic communications. In 1991 the INTELSAT system comprised a network of 16 satellites in geosynchronous orbit over the Atlantic, Indian, and Pacific Ocean regions, with service to about 1,500 international and domestic earth station antennas. COMSAT is the U.S. representative to and participant in INTELSAT.

INTERNATIONAL TELECOMMUNICATIONS SERVICES transborder services provided via cable, radio, or satellite. These service offerings have traditionally been international message telephone service (IMTS), telex, and telegraph, but during the 1980s they grew to include privately leased lines, overseas value-added services, and international 800 services.

INTERNATIONAL TELECOMMUNICATION UNION (ITU) (French: Union Internationale des Télécommunications, UIT) a specialized agency of the UNITED NATIONS with responsibilities for developing operational procedures and technical standards for the use of the radio frequency spectrum, the satellite orbit, and the international public telephone and telegraph network. ITU develops telecommunications standards in the form of recommendations covering all technical aspects of systems and equipment including interfaces, methods of operation, and principles governing the fixing of tariffs and rates to be charged. There are over 160 member nations of the ITU. The Radio Regulations that result from ITU conferences have treaty status and provide the principal guidelines for world telecommunications. In the case of the United States, they are the framework for development of the U.S. national frequency allocations and regulations. The ITU has four permanent organs: the General Secretariat, the INTERNATIONAL FREQUENCY REGISTRATION BOARD (IFRB), THE INTERNATIONAL RADIO CONSULTATIVE COMMITTEE (CCIR), and the INTERNATIONAL TELEGRAPHY AND TELEPHONE CONSULTATIVE COMMITTEE (CCITT). The union is located in Geneva, Switzerland. The Department of State is the U.S. member. *see also* INTERNATIONAL FREQUENCY REGISTRATION BOARD; INTERNATIONAL RADIO CONSULTATIVE COMMITTEE; INTERNATIONAL TELEGRAPHY AND TELEPHONE CONSULTATIVE COMMITTEE.

INTERNATIONAL TELECOMMUNICATIONS USER GROUP a professional association that provides telecommunications management with information on the impact of transborder data flow regulations in each country where the firm is conducting business.

INTERNATIONAL TELEGRAPHY AND TELEPHONE CONSULTATIVE COMMITTEE (CCITT) (French: Comité Consultatif International Télégraphique et Téléphonique) a subsidiary organization of the INTERNATIONAL TELECOMMUNICATION UNION located in Geneva, Switzerland. The CCITT studies and issues recommendations on standards and specifications on technical, operating, and TARIFF questions connected with telephony, data transmission, and telegraphy. The U.S. Department of State is the U.S. member. *see also* INTERNATIONAL TELECOMMUNICATION UNION.

INTERNATIONAL TIN AGREEMENT *see* INTERNATIONAL TIN COUNCIL.

INTERNATIONAL TIN COUNCIL (ITC) an INTERNATIONAL COM-MODITY GROUP responsible for the administration of the International Tin Agreement. The ITC centered on economic provisions intended to defend a price range for tin through the use of buffer stocks or EXPORT QUOTAS. Under the auspices of the UNITED NATIONS CONFERENCE ON TRADE AND DEVELOPMENT, the agreement was signed in 1966, renewed in 1971, renegotiated and resigned in 1976, extended for 1 year in 1981, and ceased active operation in 1983 due to the collapse in the world tin market. Although the ITA is presently inactive, it remains in existence. Its membership includes 20 producing and consuming countries, plus the EUROPEAN ECONOMIC COMMUNITY (EEC), which is treated as a single trading entity.

INTERNATIONAL TRADE business of buying and selling goods beyond national borders.

INTERNATIONAL TRADE ADMINISTRATION *see* U.S. INTERNATIONAL TRADE ADMINISTRATION.

INTERNATIONAL TRADE ADVISORY COMMITTEE a trade advisory group initiated by the Canadian government in 1989 to support private-sector input concerning the implementation of the U.S.-Canada FREE TRADE AGREEMENT of 1989. The committee consists of 45 people from a variety of areas, including labor, consumer groups, industry, agriculture, and academia. *see also* SECTORAL ADVISORY GROUPS ON INTERNATIONAL TRADE (SAGIT).

INTERNATIONAL TRADE CENTER (ITC) units found within the regional office of INDUSTRY, SCIENCE AND TECHNOLOGY CANADA (ISTC), the purpose of which is to coordinate on behalf of the department of EXTERNAL AFFAIRS AND INTERNATIONAL TRADE in Canada. These centers have been set up to assist Canadian firms in increasing the EXPORT of their products. The ITC provides a wide variety of services including EXPORT COUNSELING, education, trade information, financing, and insurance. *see also* DEPARTMENT OF EXTERNAL AFFAIRS; EXPORT DEVELOPMENT CORPORATION (EDC); CANADIAN INTERNATIONAL DEVELOPMENT AGENCY (CIDA).

INTERNATIONAL TRADE CENTRE UNCTAD/GATT an organization established in 1964 under the authorization of the GENERAL AGREEMENT ON TARIFFS AND TRADE (GATT) to provide assistance to DEVELOPING COUNTRIES in the promotion of EXPORTS. The International Trade Centre assists in the development and implementation of export promotion programs and provides information, guidance, and training to exporters relative to financing, logistics, and marketing in these developing countries. *see also* UNITED NATIONS CONFERENCE ON TRADE AND DEVELOPMENT (UNCTAD).

INTERNATIONAL TRADE COMMISSION (ITC) an independent U.S. government agency concerned with IMPORTS, import duties, and the effect of imports on U.S. industry. The commission has 6 commissioners who review and make recommendations concerning countervailing duty and antidumping petitions submitted by U.S. industries seeking relief from imports that benefit unfair trade practices. Known as the U.S. Tariff Commission before its mandate was broadened by the TRADE ACT OF 1974.

INTERNATIONAL TRADE COMMISSION CALENDAR a listing of hearings, briefings, and reports due the following month from the U.S. INTERNATIONAL TRADE COMMISSION. The column appears the third Monday of every month in the JOURNAL OF COMMERCE.

INTERNATIONAL TRADE DATA BANK (ITDB) a Canadian-generated computerized database providing data on the movement of COMMODITIES by country and product classification for the ORGANIZATION FOR ECONOMIC COOPERATION AND DEVELOPMENT (OECD), ORGANIZATION OF PETROLEUM EXPORTING COUNTRIES (OPEC), TRADING BLOCKS such as the EUROPEAN ECONOMIC COMMUNITY, and LESS-DEVELOPED COUNTRIES (LDCS). The ITDB is available to Canadian exporters through the network of INTERNATIONAL TRADE CENTER OFFICES. *see also* BUREAU OF SOURCING SUPPLIERS (BOSS); NATIONAL TRADE DATA BANK; TRADE OPPORTUNITIES PROGRAM; TRADE PROMOTION EVENTS; WORLD INFORMATION NETWORK.

INTERNATIONAL TRADE DATA SYSTEM an electronic system that integrates the different U.S. government trade and transportation data processes into a system that provides a standard means of gathering, processing, storing and disseminating IMPORT and EXPORT trade data.

INTERNATIONAL TRADE DEVELOPMENT CENTERS (ITDCs) U.S. programs and services provided to U.S. farmers and agribusinesses to enhance exports of agricultural and forestry COMMODITIES and related products. Activities include developing and promoting programs unique to a region's products, conducting research, providing market information, and offering conferences and seminars for exports. Grants for the ITDCs are administered by the U.S. Agriculture Department's Cooperative State Research Service.

INTERNATIONAL TRADE LOAN PROGRAM a program of the U.S. Small Business Administration that makes available long-term loans to small businesses for the development and expansion of export markets. The program enables them to compete more effectively against foreign competition by providing funds for the purchase or upgrade of facilities and equipment or any other improvement that will be used in the production of goods and services in the United States. *see also* EXPORT REVOLVING LINE OF CREDIT (ERLC); SMALL BUSINESS INVESTMENT COMPANY (SBIC).

INTERNATIONAL TRAFFIC IN ARMS REGULATIONS (ITAR) international agreements administered by the U.S. State Department to control the EXPORT of U.S. defense articles and services. The provisions implemented in the ITAR are governed by the ARMS EXPORT CONTROL ACT. Direct commercial sales of U.S.-origin defense products, components, technologies, and services are controlled under the ITAR by the State's Office of Defense Trade Controls. *see also* DEFENSE TRADE REGULATIONS.

INTERNATIONAL TRANSACTION NUMBER (ITC) unique identifier that ITDS DATA ELEMENTS will associate with an international trade transaction, or a unique number assigned by the initiating party that identifies an international trade transaction.

INTERNATIONAL TRANSFER OF TECHNOLOGY *see* TECHNOLOGY TRANSFER.

INTERNATIONAL VINE AND WINE STUDY GROUP an INTERNATIONAL COMMODITY GROUP established in 1924 and headquartered in Paris, France. The group provides information on the technical, scientific, and economic problems of growing, harvesting, and processing wine.

INTERNATIONAL VALUE-ADDED NETWORK SERVICES (IVANS) advanced telecommunications services, such as voice mail and electronic banking. IVANS agreements play a growing role in maintaining the competitiveness of American firms and provide benefits for consumers worldwide.

INTERNATIONAL WHEAT COUNCIL (IWC) an INTERNATIONAL COMMODITY GROUP founded in 1949 with its headquarters located in London, England, initially responsible for the execution of a series of International Wheat Agreements, referred to as Wheat Trade Conventions (WTC). The initial WTC signed in 1949 included 5 exporting and 40 importing countries, accounting for 50% of the global wheat trade. The WTC was established to defend a price range for the COMMODITY through the use of buffer stocks or EXPORT quotas or both and to promote cooperation among producers and consumers through improved consultation, exchange of information, research and development, and export promotion. The agreement was extended through 1983, at which time it collapsed because the IWC was not able to generate any consensus on pricing levels; however, it was subsequently renegotiated in 1986. *see also* ROUND OF TRADE NEGOTIATIONS.

INTERNATIONAL WOOL STUDY GROUP an INTERNATIONAL COMMODITY GROUP consisting of 42 producer-consumer members, established in 1949 and headquartered in London, England. The organization was established with the primary purpose of assuring the supply of the COMMODITY in desired quantities at reasonable prices and providing members with a forum for the examination of problems influencing wool production and marketing.

INTERNET the term Internet usually refers to a collection of NETWORKS interconnected with ROUTERS. The Internet is the largest network in the world. It is a three level hierarchy composed of BACKBONE networks (e.g., NSFNET, MILNET), midlevel networks, and stub networks. The Internet is a multiprotocol network.

INTERNET ADDRESS (IP) address that uniquely identifies a node on the INTERNET. *see also* IP ADDRESS.

INTERNET CONTROL MESSAGE PROTOCOL (ICMP) an addition to the INTERNET PROTOCOL (IP). It provides error messages, test packets, and informational messages related to IP.

INTERNET PROTOCOL (IP) the NETWORK layer for the TCP/IP INTERNET PROTOCOL SUITE. It is a connectionless, best-effort packet switching protocol. *see also* PACKET SWITCHING; REQUEST FOR COMMENTS; TCP/IP PROTOCOL SUITE.

INTERNET RELAY CHAT (IRC) an international protocol that provides synchronous conferencing. IRC is a NETWORK of servers that manage connections with individual CLIENT programs.

INTERNET SOCIETY (ISOC) a nonprofit, professional membership organization that facilitates and supports the technical evolution of the INTERNET; stimulates interest in and educates the scientific and academic communities, industry, and the public about the technology, uses, and applications of the Internet; and promotes the development of new applications for the system. The society provides a forum for discussion and collaboration in the operation and use of the global Internet infrastructure. The Internet Society publishes a quarterly newsletter, the *Internet Society News*, and holds an annual conference. The development of Internet technical standards takes place under the auspices of the Internet Society with substantial support from the Corporation for National Research Initiatives under a cooperative agreement with the U.S. federal government.

INTERPOL *see* INTERNATIONAL CRIMINAL POLICE ORGANIZATION.

INTERSTATE CARRIER a U.S. transportation company whose business extends beyond the boundaries of one state.

INTERSTATE COMMERCE trade, transport, and communication between or among the several states of the United States.

INTERTEMPORAL TRADE a country IMPORTS in one time period paying for the imports with EXPORTS in a different time period, earlier or later.

INTERVENTION CURRENCY a CONVERTIBLE CURRENCY used by a government's monetary authority (i.e., CENTRAL BANK) when acting in a FOREIGN EXCHANGE market to limit the amount by which an EXCHANGE RATE may fluctuate. If an exchange rate reaches the limit, the monetary authorities will usually intervene in the market to ensure that the limit is not exceeded. *see also* CLEAN FLOAT; DIRTY FLOAT; MANAGED FLOATING EXCHANGE RATE SYSTEM.

INTI unit of currency, Peru (OBSOLETE). *see also* NUEVOS SOLES.

INTIFADA (INTIFADAH) actions originally characterized by civil disobedience by the Palestinians that escalated into the use of terror.

INTRANET closed internal computer network.

IN-TRANSIT description of an international shipment that passes through the territory of a particular country without entering the commerce of that country.

INV abbreviation for INVOICE.

INVESTMENT CLIMATE conditions found in HOST COUNTRIES that could affect the success or failure of a DIRECT INVESTMENT in a foreign country. *see also* INVESTMENT CLIMATE STATEMENTS (ICSS).

INVESTMENT CLIMATE STATEMENTS (ICSs) statements prepared occasionally by the commercial sections of the U.S. embassies for the U.S. and Foreign Commercial Service, covering 67 individual countries. The ICSs provide statistics and analyses of policies and issues affecting the climate for direct investment in the individual country.

INVESTMENT FINANCE PROGRAMS investment programs offered by the OVERSEAS PRIVATE INVESTMENT CORPORATION (OPIC) through the use of direct loans, loan guarantees, and equity techniques that provide medium- to long-term funding and permanent capital to ventures involving significant equity and management participation by U.S. businesses.

INVESTMENT MISSION a program of the OVERSEAS PRIVATE INVESTMENT CORPORATION that brings business groups of U.S. executives to selected countries to meet HOST COUNTRY government officials, local business leaders, and potential JOINT VENTURE partners who play key roles in bringing proposed ventures to fruition.

INVESTMENT ONE-STOP ACTION CENTER a government department within the Philippine Council for Investments, Trade, Tourism, Agriculture, Natural Resources, Transportation, Communication, and Services. The purpose of the council is to coordinate the investment development efforts of the government. The One-Stop Action Center enables the government to attend to the investor's needs or problems immediately when establishing a business or investing in the Philippines.

INVESTMENT PROMOTION SERVICES *see* UNITED NATIONS INDUSTRIAL DEVELOPMENT ORGANIZATION.

INVESTMENT SECTOR LOAN PROGRAM (ISLP) administered by the INTER-AMERICAN DEVELOPMENT BANK (IDB) as part of the ENTERPRISE FOR THE AMERICAS INITIATIVE, ISLP supports investment sector reforms in Latin America and the Caribbean. The IDB evaluates the need for reform in individual countries and, with input from several U.S. government agencies, negotiates the terms for investment sector loans. *see also* ENTERPRISE FOR THE AMERICAS INITIATIVE.

INVISIBLE BARRIERS TO TRADE government regulations and cultural conditions that do not directly restrict TRADE but hinder it with excessive and obscure requirements. *see also* NONTARIFF BARRIERS (NTB); TARIFF BARRIER.

INVISIBLE TRADE *see* INVISIBLES.

INVISIBLE TRADE BALANCE BALANCE OF TRADE created by the IMPORT and EXPORT of services. *see also* INVISIBLES.

INVISIBLES areas of nonmerchandise INVISIBLE TRADE that include expenses such as freight and insurance and most types of services and investment.

INVOICE a statement of charges prepared by a seller and submitted to the purchaser of goods or services.

INVOICE ACCEPTANCE *see* FOREIGN INVOICE ACCEPTANCE.

INWARD FOREIGN MANIFEST a U.S. CUSTOMS SERVICE–mandated document requiring the complete listing by BILL OF LADING (BIL) number or AIR WAYBILL (AWB) number of an arriving carrier's CARGO. It lists the commercial particulars of the goods, including: CONSIGNORS, CONSIGNEES, marks and numbers, number and kind of packages, their weights or measures, descriptions and quantities of the goods, their port of loading, and intended PORT OF DISCHARGE.

IOM *see* INTERNATIONAL ORGANIZATION FOR MIGRATION.

IPAC acronym for Industry Policy Advisory Committee. *see also* INDUSTRY CONSULTATIONS PROGRAM.

IPR *see* INTELLECTUAL PROPERTY RIGHTS.

IR *see* INTERNET REGISTRY.

IRISH POUND unit of currency, Republic of Ireland (100 pence equal 1 Irish pound).

IRREVOCABLE CORPORATE PURCHASE ORDER a purchase order completed by a buyer on corporate letterhead that indicates the type and quantity of products being ordered from a supplier. *see also* SALES AGREEMENT.

IRREVOCABLE LETTER OF CREDIT a LETTER OF CREDIT that obligates the issuing bank to pay the EXPORTER when all terms and conditions have been met. None of the terms and conditions may be changed without the consent of all parties to the letter of credit.

IRREVOCABLE TRANSFERABLE LETTER OF CREDIT *see* IRREVOCABLE LETTER OF CREDIT; LETTER OF CREDIT.

ISA *see* INDUSTRY SUBSECTOR ANALYSIS.

ISAC acronym for Industry Sector Advisory Committee. *see also* INDUSTRY CONSULTATIONS PROGRAM.

ISDA *see* INTERNATIONAL SWAPS AND DERIVATIVES ASSOCIATION.

IsDB *see* ISLAMIC DEVELOPMENT BANK.

ISLAMIC CONFERENCE ORGANIZATION *see* ORGANIZATION OF THE ISLAMIC CONFERENCE.

ISLAMIC DEVELOPMENT BANK (IsDB) (sometimes IDB) Islamic bank that finances economic aid and social development in member countries. The bank also supports Muslim communities in nonmember countries. Membership is open to all countries that are members of the Islamic Conference. Members include Afghanistan, Algeria, Bahrain, Bangladesh, Benin, Brunei, Burkina, the Cameroon, Chad, Comoros, Djibouti, Egypt, Gabon, the Gambia, Guinea, Guinea-Bissau, Indonesia, Iran, Iraq, Jordan, Kuwait, Lebanon, Libya, Malaysia, Maldives, Mali, Mauritania, Morocco, Niger, Oman, Pakistan, the Palestine Liberation Organization, Qatar, Saudi Arabia, Senegal, Sierra Leone, Somalia, Sudan, Syria, Tunisia, Turkey, Uganda, the United Arab Emirates, and Yemen. The bank was created in 1973. Its headquarters is in Jeddah, Saudi Arabia.

ISLAMIC LAW law of Islam termed the Shari'ah. In Islamic law, any distinction between civil law and religious law is very difficult to make. Islamic law specifies the moral goals of the community. In Islamic society, therefore, the word *law* has broader significance than it does in the Western world since Islamic law contains both legal and moral mandates. Thus not all Islamic law can be stated as formal legal rules or enforced by the courts. A great deal depends on individual conscience.

From a business standpoint, the Law of Transactions Code is perhaps the most relevant part of Islamic law. In addition to specifying the legal and illegal capacity to transact based primarily upon being at least 15 years of age as well as having the ability to make rational judgments (*rashid*), it specifies four basic types of transactions and has the Doctrine of Riba. The four basic types of transactions include Bay, Ijarah, Hibah, and Ariyah, which relate primarily to real estate transactions. The Doctrine of Riba prohibits usurious transactions defined as charging any form of interest on loans or investments. However, it is possible to receive "considerations," which include management fees as well as having the right to an equity capital position.

ISLP *see* INVESTMENT SECTOR LOAN PROGRAM.

ISNAR acronym for International Service for National Agricultural Research. *see also* CONSULTATIVE GROUP ON INTERNATIONAL AGRICULTURAL RESEARCH.

ISO *see* INTERNATIONAL STANDARDS ORGANIZATION.

ISO DEVELOPMENT ENVIRONMENT (ISODE) software that allows OPEN SYSTEMS INTERCONNECTION services to use a TCP/IP PROTOCOL SUITE network. Pronounced *eye-so-dee-eee.*

ISONET *see* INTERNATIONAL STANDARDS ORGANIZATION INFORMATION NETWORK.

ISAA *see* INTERNATIONAL SOCIAL SECURITY ASSOCIATION.

ISSUANCE the execution, validation, and tender of delivery of a CON-TRACT or FINANCIAL INSTRUMENT to the appropriate party. *see also* ISSU-ING BANK; LETTER OF CREDIT (L/C).

ISSUANCE DATE OF THE DOCUMENTS date indicated on documents as their date of preparation.

ISSUING BANK the bank that opens the LETTER OF CREDIT on the advice of the IMPORTER in favor of the EXPORTER and agrees to pay all DRAFTS drawn against it by the BENEFICIARY, who is normally the EXPORTER. *see also* ADVISING BANK; DOCUMENTARY CREDIT.

ISTITUTO NAZIONALE PER IL COMMERCIO ESTERO (ICE) (English: Institute of Foreign Trade) an Italian agency that promotes EXPORTS through a network of domestic and foreign offices. Although ICE obtains overall policy direction and funding from the Ministry of Foreign Trade (Ministero del Commercio con l'Estero), it functions as an autonomous public corporation. The Ministry of Foreign Affairs (Ministero degli Affari Esteri) provides additional support through its overseas embassies and consulates; however, ICE's overseas officers are independent of these organizations.

ITA *see* INTERNATIONAL TIN AGREEMENT.

ITAEWON DISTRICT the principal shopping district in Korea catering to foreign clientele.

ITAR *see* INTERNATIONAL TRAFFIC IN ARMS REGULATIONS.

ITC *see* INTERNATIONAL TRADE CENTER; INTERNATIONAL TRADE COMMISSION; INTERNATIONAL TRANSACTION NUMBER.

ITDCs *see* INTERNATIONAL TRADE DEVELOPMENT CENTERS.

ITDS DATA ELEMENTS specific data list used by the International Trade Data System to facilitate the entry, exit, and IN-TRANSIT movement of goods between the United States and FOREIGN countries.

ITEM-BY-ITEM TARIFF REDUCTION a negotiating strategy used by parties to the GENERAL AGREEMENTS ON TARIFFS AND TRADE (GATT) during MULTILATERAL TRADE NEGOTIATIONS. Rather than negotiating on a general across-the-board TARIFF reduction, the parties choose to limit negotiations to specific product classes, followed by a discussion of specific products within the product class. This technique is especially successful when discussing tariff reductions on products that are so important to the country's economy that any changes can cause serious economic problems.

IT06 *see* INFORMATION TECHNOLOGY INITIATIVE 6.

ITU *see* INTERNATIONAL TELECOMMUNICATION UNION.

IVL *see* INDIVIDUALLY VALIDATED LICENSE.

J

J CURVE AND REAL EXCHANGE RATES the CURRENT ACCOUNT may initially worsen before improving in response to real depreciation in EXCHANGE RATES, because it takes time for the growth of IMPORT volumes to decline in response to higher import prices. This phenomenon is known as the J-curve effect because the downward movement followed by an upward movement in the current account resembles the letter *J*.

J-1 VISA a specialized term used by U.S. immigration to describe an exchange visitor to the United States. The visa is a stamp on the foreign national's passport issued by a U.S. consular officer that allows the individual to enter the United States and conduct business.

JAMAICA ACCORDS (JAMAICA AGREEMENT) an agreement in January 1976 by the members of the INTERNATIONAL MONETARY FUND (IMF) to accept a system of controlled FLOATING EXCHANGE RATES and to diminish the importance of gold in international transactions by abolishing the official price and allowing it to fluctuate in the world market. The agreement was formally ratified by the U.S. Congress and the president of the United States in April 1978. *see also* GOLD STANDARD; MANAGED FLOAT.

JAMAICA DOLLAR unit of currency, Jamaica (100 cents equal 1 Jamaica dollar).

JAPAN CORPORATE PROGRAM program initiated by the U.S. DEPARTMENT OF COMMERCE to help increase U.S. EXPORTS to Japan. The program was initiated in January 1991, following selection of 20 companies to participate in a 5-year pilot project to improve U.S. knowledge of, and access to, the Japanese market. As part of the 5-year commitment to the program, the companies arrange four visits a year to Japan, including two by their chief executives; publish their product literature in Japanese; participate in at least one trade promotion event in Japan each year; and modify products to enhance consumer acceptance and promote sales in Japan. The Department of Commerce supports the 20 firms with market data, arranges introductory meetings with prospective Japanese buyers, and recommends market development strategies.

JAPAN DEVELOPMENT BANK (JDB) founded in 1951 to aid in developing and diversifying the Japanese economy, the JDB is a nonprofit organization owned entirely by the Japanese government. U.S. companies may participate in JDB funding activity under the bank's Loan Division in the International Department. The International Department disburses loans to foreign companies under two primary loan programs: Promotion of Foreign Direct Investment in Japan and

Facilities for Import Products. The other loan programs of JDB are also available to foreign-owned companies under the principle of equal treatment of clients regardless of nationality.

JAPAN EXPORT INFORMATION CENTER (JEIC) center that provides information on doing business in Japan, market entry alternatives, market information and research, product standards and testing requirements, TARIFFS, and NONTARIFF barriers. The center maintains a commercial library and participates in private- and government-sponsored seminars on doing business in Japan. JEIC is operated by the INTERNATIONAL TRADE ADMINISTRATION of the U.S. DEPARTMENT OF COMMERCE.

JAPAN EXTERNAL TRADE ORGANIZATION (JETRO) Japanese organization legally operating under the aegis of the MINISTRY OF INTERNATIONAL TRADE AND INDUSTRY (MITI), which administers the EXPORT programs of the Japanese government independently. MITI subsidizes about 60% of JETRO's total annual expenditures and, technically, has final decision-making authority over JETRO management and programs. Originally established to help Japanese firms export, JETRO also assists American companies seeking to export to Japan and promotes Japanese direct investment in the United States and U.S. direct investment in Japan.

JAPAN, INC. an American expression used when referring to the impression of the close relationship among the private sector, the MINISTRY OF INTERNATIONAL TRADE AND INDUSTRY (MITI), and the Ministry of Finance in Japan enabling them to dominate the world marketplace. MITI occupies a central position in Japan's economic bureaucracy and is regarded as one of the three most powerful and prestigious ministries of the central government (along with the Ministry of Finance and the Ministry of Foreign Affairs). In formulating and implementing Japan's trade and industrial policies, MITI is responsible for funding most of Japan's EXPORT promotion programs. The ministry also supervises the export financing programs of the EXPORT–IMPORT BANK OF JAPAN (JEXIM), operates several types of export insurance programs, supports research organizations, and facilitates various types of overseas technical and cooperation training programs.

JAPAN INTERNATIONAL COOPERATION AGENCY (JICA) Japanese agency that administers the bilateral grant portion of Japan's OFFICIAL DEVELOPMENT ASSISTANCE (ODA). JICA covers both
- grant aid cooperation (offered without the obligation of repayment) and
- technical cooperation (offering trainees, experts, equipment, project-type technical cooperation, and development studies).

The agency was established in August 1974, and its headquarters is in Tokyo, Japan. *see also* EXPORT–IMPORT BANK OF JAPAN (JEXIM); OVERSEAS ECONOMIC COOPERATION FUND.

JAPAN SEA BASIN a proposal initiated by the Japanese MINISTRY OF INTERNATIONAL TRADE AND INDUSTRY (MITI) and Japanese educators, that Japan, the former Union of Soviet Socialist Republics (USSR), South Korea, North Korea, and China should form a regional economic cooperation zone to promote economic cooperation among members. The purpose of the proposed zone would be to provide Japan with an abundant supply of inexpensive labor and raw materials, promote economic reforms among the nonmarket economies in the region, and create a dependence on Japan by the other members for its ability to provide technology and investment capital. *see also* ASSOCIATION OF SOUTHEAST ASIAN NATIONS; DEPENDENT DEVELOPMENT; YEN DIPLOMACY.

JAPAN SPECIAL FUND (JSF) a fund created by the Japanese government that provides grants of financial aid to MULTILATERAL DEVELOPMENT BANKS for project feasibility studies and disaster assistance. *see also* AFRICAN DEVELOPMENT BANK; ASIAN DEVELOPMENT BANK; EUROPEAN BANK FOR RECONSTRUCTION AND DEVELOPMENT; INTER-AMERICAN DEVELOPMENT BANK; WORLD BANK.

JCIT *see* JOINT COMMITTEE FOR INVESTMENT AND TRADE.

JDB *see* JAPAN DEVELOPMENT BANK.

JEIC *see* JAPAN EXPORT INFORMATION CENTER.

JEMAAH ISLAMIAH (JI) a terrorist organization that has as its principal goal the creation of a unified Southeast Asian Islamic state, stretching from southern Thailand, through the Malay Peninsula, encompassing Singapore and continuing across the Indonesian archipelago into the southern Philippines.

JET LAG a temporary disruption of an individual's body clock resulting from travel across several time zones, typically in high-speed aircraft.

JETRO *see* JAPAN EXTERNAL TRADE ORGANIZATION.

JETSAM articles from a ship or ship's CARGO that are thrown overboard, usually to lighten the load in times of emergency or distress, and that sink or are washed ashore.

JETTISON the voluntary throwing overboard of either CARGO or the ship's material, including equipment, to protect other property from a common danger.

JEXIM *see* EXPORT–IMPORT BANK OF JAPAN.

JICA *see* JAPAN INTERNATIONAL COOPERATION AGENCY.

JIHAD a struggle against oppression, whether political, religious, personal, or spiritual.

JINMYAKU (Japanese) an individual's personal network of friends and associates. This network is not a result of family ties but rather one based on an individual's personal and company loyalties. *see also* HABATSU; KEIBATSU; KONE; NOMENKLATURA; PAIPU.

JIT *see* JUST IN TIME.

JOINT AGENT a person having authority to transact business for two or more transportation lines.

JOINT AND SEVERAL LIABILITY liability for damages imposed on two or more individuals or legal entities that are responsible together and individually, allowing the party harmed to seek full remedy against any number of the wrongdoers.

JOINT COMMITTEE FOR INVESTMENT AND TRADE (JCIT) U.S. and Mexican joint committee established in October 1990 to demonstrate a commitment to greater economic cooperation. The committee identifies trade and investment opportunities and coordinates trade promotion events.

JOINT PUBLICATION RESEARCH SERVICE (JPRS) *see* FOREIGN BROADCAST INFORMATION SERVICE.

JOINT RATE single through rate on CARGO moving via two or more CARRIERS. *see also* GENERAL CARGO RATE; GENERAL COMMODITY RATE.

JOINT STOCK ASSOCIATION *see* JOINT STOCK COMPANY.

JOINT STOCK COMPANY an unincorporated business enterprise with ownership interests represented by shares of stock. *see also* CORPORATION; JOINT VENTURE; LIMITED (LIABILITY); LIMITED LIABILITY COMPANY; LIMITED PARTNERSHIP.

JOINT VENTURE a business undertaking in which more than one company shares ownership, control of production, and/or marketing, profits, and losses.

JONES ACT U.S. law that prohibits FOREIGN ships from transporting goods or people between one U.S. location and another. *see also* CABOTAGE; TRADE BARRIERS.

JORDANIAN DINAR unit of currency, Jordan (1000 fils equal 1 Jordanian dinar).

JOURNAL OF COMMERCE a daily newspaper providing coverage on developments in international trade, commerce, and transportation. It has a daily SHIPCARD section that contains a daily guide on ocean liner services and a comprehensive listing of ship arrivals for major North American ports. The *Journal of Commerce* is owned and published by The Economist Group of London.

JPRS Joint Publication Research Service. *see also* FOREIGN BROADCAST INFORMATION SERVICE.

JSF *see* JAPAN SPECIAL FUND.

JUDICIAL REVIEW the process whereby a higher court reexamines an action or a judicial determination of a lower court in order to correct possible errors. In matters involving disputes in international trade, the U.S. COURT OF INTERNATIONAL TRADE has jurisdiction over any civil action against the United States arising from federal laws governing IMPORT transactions. The court hears antidumping, product classification, and countervailing duty matters, as well as appeals of unfair trade practice cases from the U.S. INTERNATIONAL TRADE COMMISSION. *see also* BINATIONAL DISPUTE SETTLEMENT MECHANISM.

JURAT statement signed by a person authorized to take an oath certifying to the authenticity of a document or affidavit.

JURISDICTION the areas over which an authority has the right and power to interpret and apply the law. In international law, jurisdiction is based on provisions of MULTILATERAL or BILATERAL AGREEMENTS. *see also* DOMESTIC JURISDICTION.

JURISDICTIONAL CLAUSE a provision included in a contract between an IMPORTER and an EXPORTER providing a mechanism by which disputes can be settled. The clause will stipulate the laws under which the contract will be governed. *see also* ARBITRATION CLAUSE.

JURISDICTIONAL RULE OF REASON the principle of law that balances the interests of one country against those of another country. *see also* ACTS OF STATE DOCTRINE; COMITY; CONFLICT OF LAWS.

JURISTIC ACT action intended to have, and capable of having, a legal effect, such as the creation, termination, or modification of a legal right. *see also* JURISDICTION; JURISDICTIONAL CLAUSE.

JUST IN TIME (JIT) an inventory management system. JIT requires that materials and components used in the production process be delivered as they are needed in the production process. The concept attempts to reduce carrying costs by minimizing inventory requirements. JIT was introduced to Japan by Dr. Edward Deming, an American statistician and manufacturing efficiency expert. It is used extensively in Japan as well as throughout the world.

K

KANGERA BASIN ORGANIZATION (KBO) (French: Organisation pour la Management et le Développement du Bassin de la Riviere Kangera) organization established in 1978 and headquartered in Kigali, Rwanda. Officially known as the Organization for the Management and Development of the Kangera Basin, the KBO promotes integrated exploitation and management of water and land resources in the Kangera Basin. KBO members includes Burundi, Rwanda, Tanzania, and Uganda.

KAPEIK unit of currency, Republic of Belarus.

KAPITAALVENNOOTSCHAP (Dutch) *see* CORPORATION.

KARBOVANETZ unit of currency, Ukraine (1 karbovanetz equals 1 Russian ruble).

KBO *see* KANGERA BASIN ORGANIZATION.

KCAB *see* KOREAN COMMERCIAL ARBITRATION BOARD.

KDD *see* KOKUSAI DENSHIN DENWA.

KEELAGE charges paid by a ship entering or remaining in certain PORTS. *see also* PORT CHARGE.

KEIBATSU (Japanese) familial relationships resulting from marriage among the elite in Japan to simplify the buildup of contacts. *see also* HABATSU; JINMYAKU.

KEIDANREN (English: Japanese Federation of Economic Organizations) organization established in 1946 as a private, nonprofit economic organization representing virtually all branches of economic activity in Japan.

KEIRETSU the horizontally and vertically linked industrial structure of post-war Japan. The horizontally linked groups include a broad range of industries linked via banks and general trading firms. There are 8 major industrial groups, sometimes referred to as Kigyo Shudan: Mitsubishi, Mitsui, Sumitomo, Fuyo, DKB, Sanwa, Tokai, and IBJ. The vertically linked groups (such as Toyota, Matsushita, and Sony) are centered around parent companies, with subsidiaries frequently serving as suppliers, distributors, and retail outlets. Common characteristics among the groups include crossholding of company shares, intragroup financing, joint investment, mutual appointment of officers, and other joint business activities. The keiretsu system emphasizes mutual cooperation and protects affiliates from mergers and acquisitions. Ties within groups became looser after the oil shocks of the 1970s as a result of decreasing dependence on banks for capital.

KEIZAI DOYUKAI (Japanese) a group of powerful business leaders responsible for the development of strategic international business policy in Japan. The group is referred to as the Committee for Economic Development, and its members come from the top ZAKAI members. *see also* KEIDANREN; KEIRETSU; NIKKEIREN.

KENGEN (Japanese) the legitimate use of power by a Japanese manager resulting from the position he/she is in. *see also* HIGH-CONTEXT CULTURE; KEN'I; NEMAWASHI; SITUATIONAL CONFORMITY; YOROSHIKU TANOMU.

KEN'I (Japanese) the ability of a Japanese manager to control employees on the basis of one's personal power derived from the manager's character rather than his/her position. *see also* KENGEN.

KENNEDY ROUND the sixth set in a series of MULTILATERAL TRADE NEGOTIATIONS held under the authority of the GENERAL AGREEMENT ON TARIFFS AND TRADE (GATT). The negotiations were initiated in 1963, and the U.S. government was given the authorization to participate under the TRADE EXPANSION ACT OF 1962. The legislation granted the President general authority to negotiate, on a reciprocal basis, reductions of up to 50% in U.S. TARIFFS. The act explicitly eliminated the PERIL POINT PROVISIONS that had limited U.S. negotiating positions in earlier GATT rounds, and instead called on the Tariff Commission, the U.S. INTERNATIONAL TRADE COMMISSION, and other federal agencies to provide information regarding the probable economic effects of specific tariff concessions. *see also* ANTIDUMPING CODE; LIBERALIZATION; ROUND OF TRADE NEGOTIATIONS.

KENYA SHILLING unit of currency, Kenya (100 cents equal 1 Kenya shilling).

KERBEROS the security system of the Massachusetts Institute of Technology Project Athena. It is based on symmetric key cryptography. *see also* ENCRYPTION.

KERMIT a widely used file transfer PROTOCOL developed by Columbia University. Because Kermit runs in most operating environments, it is a very useful method for transferring computer files. *see also* FILE TRANSFER PROTOCOL (FTP).

KEY CURRENCY major currency in the global economy. Key currencies include the U.S. DOLLAR, the BRITISH POUND, the German MARK, the SWISS FRANC, the FRENCH FRANC, the Dutch GUILDER, the Japanese YEN, and the CANADIAN DOLLAR.

KEY INDUSTRY an industry that, on the basis of its size or influence exerted over other industry sectors, may affect a significant portion of a country's economy. In establishing policies relating to foreign investment, countries have been careful to prevent foreign control over certain key industries.

KEYNESIAN ECONOMICS economic theory named after English economist and monetary expert John Maynard Keynes. He advocated active government involvement in the economy as the most reliable way to control the effects of fluctuations in the business cycle. During recessionary times, deficit spending and easier monetary policies stimulate business activity. *see also* MONETARISM.

KEYNESIANISM *see* KEYNESIAN ECONOMICS.

KFAED *see* KUWAIT FUND FOR ARAB ECONOMIC DEVELOPMENT.

KFTA *see* KOREA FOREIGN TRADE ASSOCIATION.

KfW *see* KREDITANSTALT FÜR WIEDERAUFBAU.

KG
   1. abbreviation for kilogram.
   2. *see* KOMMANDITGESELLSCHAFT.

KGAA *see* KOMMANDITGESELLSCHAFT AUF AKTIEN.

KHUN the word used in Thailand for Mr., Mrs., Ms, or Miss. When addressing a Thai, the person should use the Thai's first name when referring to them, placing *Khun* ahead of it.

KICKBACKS illegal commissions paid in a business transaction. In the United States kickbacks are prohibited by the Robinson Patman Act. *see also* BRIBERY.

KILLFILE a file used by an individual to filter USENET postings by excluding messages on certain topics or from certain people, which a user does not want seen or read.

KINA unit of currency, Papua New Guinea (100 toea equal 1 kina).

KINSHIP relationships between people by blood, marriage, adoption, or common ancestor. Kinship is the basis upon which people relate to other people. In INTERNATIONAL MARKETING, kinship or relationships between people will enable the marketer to better determine the consuming unit for some goods, whether it be a household or family, and whether the decision-making process takes place in a larger unit and in different ways.

KIOSK small structure suitable for use as a newsstand, display stand, bandstand, study, or stand.

KIP unit of currency, Laos.

KIPO *see* KOREAN INDUSTRIAL PROPERTY OFFICE.

KNEECAPPING a common punishment used by Northern Ireland's Irish Republican Army that involves breaking or shooting the kneecaps of those accused of collaborating with the British.

KNOCKED DOWN describing an article that is taken apart and folded or telescoped in such a way as to reduce its bulk at least 66²/₃% from its normal shipping cubage when set up or assembled. *see also* FREIGHT ALL KINDS (FAK).

KNOWN LOSS evident loss, as opposed to a concealed loss or damage to contents within a package; a loss that the insured and/or the insurer is aware of at the time the insurance is effected. *see also* HIDDEN DAMAGE; OBVIOUS DAMAGE; PILFERAGE.

KOBACO *see* KOREA BROADCASTING ADVERTISING CORPORATION.

KOBO unit of currency, Nigeria (100 kobos equal 1 naira).

KOKUSAI DENSHIN DENWA (KDD) company that was, for more than a century, Japan's sole supplier of international telecommunications services and today remains Japan's leading international CARRIER. Even though its history can be traced back to 1871 to its predecessor organizations, KDD was established in 1953. KDD is Japan's signatory to INTELSAT and INMARSAT.

KOMMANDITGESELLSCHAFT (KG) (German, meaning LIMITED PARTNERSHIP). It differs from a GENERAL PARTNERSHIP in that only the general partner (Komplementaer) has full personal liability for the liabilities of the partnership, whereas the remaining (limited) partners' (Kommanditist) liability is limited to the specific amount of their contribution. The company must carry the name of one personally liable partner with reference to the existence of a company. The name of the general partner with unlimited liability may not be left out.

KOMMANDITGESELLSCHAFT AUF AKTIEN (KGAA) (German, meaning LIMITED PARTNERSHIP by shares) a combination of the elements of a stock company and a limited partnership. At least one general partner has unlimited liability, whereas limited shareholders have an interest in the stated capital divided into shares without being personally liable for the debts of the company.

KONCERNREGNSKABER (Danish) *see* CORPORATION.

KONE (Japanese) an individual's contacts with key people. *see also* JINMYAKU; PAIPU.

KONKURS (German) an application for bankruptcy.

KONTRAKT (Danish) *see* CONTRACT.

KONZERNRECHNUNGSLEGUNG (German) *see* CORPORATION.

KORAN the sacred book of the Islamic religion. It is the direct word of God revealed to the Prophet Mohammed. It is the foundation upon which all followers base their beliefs. If an item does not appear in the Koran, it will be rejected by the faithful. A firm working in such an environment—introducing new products, methods, procedures, or routines—may encounter many difficulties. *see also* ISLAMIC LAW.

KOREA BROADCASTING ADVERTISING CORPORATION (KOBACO) an organization that acts as the sales agent for the television and radio stations in Korea. Advertisers can purchase broadcasting time either from KOBACO or through advertising agencies. When advertisers or agencies submit a request to purchase media time, the commercials must first be submitted to KOBACO for preview. After the review, the advertiser will be offered a specific time slot and duration over which the advertisements can appear and begin negotiations for a contract with KOBACO.

KOREA COMMERCIAL ARBITRATION BOARD an organization responsible for the settlement of commercial disputes in Korea. The basic framework for arbitration was codified into law by the Arbitration Act of 1966. In cases where a party requests assistance from the board to settle a claim, the board acts as an intermediary for an exchange of opinions and position. If appropriate, the board will offer recommendations to the parties as to how the dispute may be resolved.

KOREA CUSTOMS TARIFF SCHEDULE a comprehensive list of the goods that may be imported into Korea and the IMPORT duties applicable to each product. Since 1968 the Korea Customs Tariff Schedule has been based on the HARMONIZED COMMODITY DESCRIPTION AND CODING SYSTEM.

KOREA FOREIGN TRADE ASSOCIATION (KFTA) a nonprofit, private business organization of Korean companies that provides information and services concerning trade both for members and for foreign businesses. KFTA, with its headquarters in Seoul, maintains some U.S. offices.

KOREA TRADE PROMOTION CORPORATION (KOTRA) a nonprofit organization established by the Korean government in 1962 to promote foreign trade. The corporation now also serves as an IMPORT promotion center offering a variety of free services in trade, investment, and international economic cooperation. KOTRA, with headquarters in Seoul, has a network of domestic and overseas offices, including several U.S. sites.

KOREAN INDUSTRIAL PROPERTY OFFICE (KIPO) the office responsible for the processing of applications for the registration of patents, copyrights, and trademarks in Korea.

KOREAN TRADEMARK LAW law that provides the owner with protection from unauthorized use for a period of 10 years from the date of registration, which can be renewed every 10 years upon application for renewal.

KORUNA unit of currency, Czech Republic (100 haler equal 1 koruna).

KOTRA *see* KOREA TRADE PROMOTION CORPORATION.

KRAGOWA IZBA GOSPODARCZA the Polish CHAMBER OF COMMERCE.

KREDITANSTALT FÜR WIEDERAUFBAU (KFW) (English: Reconstruction Loan Corporation) German loan corporation that promotes the establishment of German companies in developing countries and promotes new technologies by German companies in developing countries. KFW provides assistance to developing countries in the form of loans, grants, materials, or services. KFW mines volume and use of funds, repayment conditions, interest rates, fund-release procedures, and monitoring requirements. *see also* DEUTSCHE FINANZIERUNGSGESELLSCHAFT FÜR BETEILGUNGEN IN ENTWICKLUNGSLÄNDERN GmbH; DEUTSCHE GESELLSCHAFT FÜR TECHNISCHE ZUSAMMENARBEIT.

KRONA unit of currency, Sweden (100 øre equal 1 Swedish krone).

KRONA unit of currency, Faroe Islands, Iceland (100 øre equal 1 króna).

KRONE
1. unit of currency, Denmark (100 øre equal 1 Danish krone).
2. unit of currency, Norway (100 øre equal 1 Norwegian krone).

KROON unit of currency, Estonia (100 senti equal 1 kroon).

KTNET TRADE AUTOMATION SYSTEM an on-line electronic computer network that links over 18,000 licensed traders and 2,000 transportation companies, customs officers, and banks in Korea.

KUROI KIRI (Japanese) *see* BRIBERY.

KUWAIT DINAR unit of currency, Kuwait (1000 fils equal 1 Kuwaiti dinar).

KUWAIT FUND FOR ARAB ECONOMIC DEVELOPMENT (KFAED) a Kuwaiti independent public institution that assists Arab and other developing countries in developing their economies by granting them concessional loans for development programs and by financing preinvestment studies of ways to expand production capacities. Fund operations, originally restricted to Arab countries, were extended to cover other developing countries in July 1974. In March 1981 the objectives of the fund were extended to include participation in the capital and resources of development institutions and other types of establishments. These recipients have included the ARAB FUND FOR ECONOMIC AND SOCIAL DEVELOPMENT (ESD), the AFRICAN DEVELOPMENT BANK, the AFRICAN DEVELOPMENT FUND, the ARAB BANK FOR ECONOMIC DEVELOPMENT IN AFRICA, the INTER-ARAB INVESTMENT GUARANTEE CORPORATION, the INTERNATIONAL DEVELOPMENT ASSOCIATION (IDA), the INTERNATIONAL FUND FOR AGRICULTURAL DEVELOPMENT, and the Special Program of Assistance for African Countries. The KFAED was established in December 1961 and its headquarters is in Safat, Kuwait.

KWACHA
  1. unit of currency, Malawi (100 tambala equal 1 kwacha).
  2. unit of currency, Zambia (100 ngwee equal 1 kwacha).

KWANZA unit of currency, Angola.

KYAT unit of currency, Myanmar (100 pyas equal 1 kyat).

KYOTO CONVENTION *see* INTERNATIONAL CONVENTION ON THE SIM-
PLIFICATION AND HARMONIZATION OF CUSTOMS PROCEDURES.

L

L. abbreviation for BRITISH POUND. Symbol is £.

L-1 VISA a specialized term used by U.S. immigration to describe a visitor entering the United States as an intracompany transfer. The visa is a stamp on the foreign national's passport issued by a U.S. consular officer, which allows the individual to enter the United States and conduct business.

L.&R. abbreviation for lake and rail transport.

L.A. abbreviation for letter of authority.

LA ZONE FRANC *see* FRANC ZONE.

LAARI unit of currency, Republic of Maldives (100 laari equal 1 rufiyaa).

LABELING requirement to label imported goods with information about how and where they were produced. *see also* COUNTRY OF DEPARTURE; COUNTRY OF ORIGIN; MARKING (MARKS).

LABOR ABUNDANT country where its endowment of labor is large compared to other countries. *see also* FACTOR ENDOWMENT; HECKSCHER-OHLIN THEORY.

LABOR INTENSIVE an activity where labor costs are a larger portion of total cost than material or capital. *see also* CAPITAL INTENSIVE.

LABOR MARKET the mix of workers available for hire by a firm and the mix of different labor costs associated with these workers. Each country has a different blend of these workers and their costs, and international companies can gain advantages by selecting states, countries, or areas of countries that provide a labor market with a suitable mix of workers at a suitable cost that satisfies the company's staffing requirements.

LAES *see* LATIN AMERICAN ECONOMIC SYSTEM.

LAFTA acronym for Latin America Free Trade Association. *see also* LATIN AMERICAN INTEGRATION ASSOCIATION (LAIA).

LAG STRATEGY a strategy used by a firm to delay the payment of payables due in a foreign currency with the anticipation that it will strengthen or delay the receipt of foreign currency receivables because the currency is expected to weaken. It is the opposite of a LEAD STRATEGY.

LAGTING one of the two parliamentary bodies in Norway. Legislation is vested in the Parliament, called STORTINGET. Lagting consists of 157 members elected through a general election based on proportional representation. Of the 157 members, 39 of them form the Lagting, whereas the balance form the ODELSTING. All legislation is initially reviewed by the Odelsting followed by the Lagting. Subsequently, the legislation is forwarded to the King for assent by the Council.

LAIA *see* LATIN AMERICAN INTEGRATION ASSOCIATION.

LAISSER PASSER a document, accorded by a host government to foreign diplomatic personnel, that permits them to pass freely across the border of that country.

LAISSEZ-FAIRE a concept referring to minimal government interference in the economic activity of a society. The doctrine of laissez-faire economics was described in Adam Smith's treatise *Wealth of Nations* in 1776. It held that businesses' pursuit of self-interest would provide the maximum good for all. *see also* MERCANTILISM; SOCIALISM.

LAKE CHAD BASIN COMMISSION (LCBC) commission that recommends plans for developing the Chad Basin in northeastern Africa and coordinates research programs. The commission was established in 1964 and its headquarters is in N'Djamena, Chad. LCBC members include the Cameroon, Chad, Niger, and Nigeria.

LAN *see* LOCAL AREA NETWORK.

LANDBRIDGE movement of CONTAINERS from a FOREIGN country by vessel, transiting a country by rail or truck, then being loaded aboard another vessel for DELIVERY to a second foreign country. *see also* MICROBRIDGE; MINIBRIDGE.

LANDED VALUE a term used in MARINE CARGO INSURANCE to refer to the wholesale market value of the goods, at the destination on the final day of discharge.

LANHAM ACT OF 1947 federal legislation governing trademarks and other symbols for identifying goods sold in interstate commerce.

LARGE-SCALE INDUSTRIAL TRANSFER the transfer of technology when a manufacturing facility is transferred from its center of operations to another location, so that the firm can take advantage of available lower operating costs, such as a favorable LABOR MARKET. *see also* TECHNOLOGY TRANSFER.

LASH (LIGHTER ABOARD SHIP) an open or covered vessel that transfers CARGO between ship and shore, used mainly in harbors and inland waterways. Lighters are generally used for shorter hauls, barges for longer ones. These vessel are particularly beneficial in shallow ports where deep water vessels do not have sufficient space for maneuvering or an adequate amount of space to dock or anchor. A LASH must measure at least 820 feet long with a deck crane, which would allow it to load and unload barges through a stern section that projects over the water.

LASSA FEVER an acute, commonly fatal, viral disease characterized by high fever, ulcers of the mucous membranes, headaches, and disturbances of the gastrointestinal system.

LAT. abbreviation for latitude.

LATIN AMERICAN ASSOCIATION OF DEVELOPMENT FINANCING INSTITUTIONS Latin American association that promotes cooperation among members in ways that support the integration of Latin American economies, including efforts to improve the flow of information among members and to encourage the study of problems of common interest. Members include 24 Latin American countries and several countries in Europe and North America. The association was established in January 1968, and its headquarters is in Lima, Peru.

LATIN AMERICAN ASSOCIATION OF INTERNATIONAL TRADING COMPANIES a regional industry association initially proposed in Caracas, Venezuela, in October 1987 and formally established in coordination with the INTER-AMERICAN DEVELOPMENT BANK (IDB), the UNITED NATIONS CONFERENCE ON TRADE AND DEVELOPMENT (UNCTAD), and the LATIN AMERICAN ECONOMIC SYSTEM (LAES) in Rio de Janeiro, Brazil, in September 1988. Its members included representatives from Argentina, Brazil, Colombia, Cuba, Ecuador, El Salvador, Panama, Peru, Uruguay, and Brazil. The purpose of the association to was promote EXPORTS from the region. *see also* LATIN AMERICAN INTEGRATION ASSOCIATION (LAIA).

LATIN AMERICAN ECONOMIC SYSTEM (LAES) (Spanish: Sistema Económico Latinoamericano, SELA) organization established in October 1975 that promotes economic and social integration among approximately 26 Latin American and Caribbean member states. LAES seeks to present a united view for Latin America before agencies of the EUROPEAN ECONOMIC COMMUNITY (EEC) and the UNITED NATIONS. The LAES headquarters are in Caracas, Venezuela.

LATIN AMERICAN EXPORT BANK *see* BANCO LATINOAMERICANO DE EXPORTACIONES.

LATIN AMERICAN FREE TRADE ASSOCIATION (LAFTA) *see* LATIN AMERICAN INTEGRATION ASSOCIATION.

LATIN AMERICAN INTEGRATION ASSOCIATION (LAIA) (Spanish: Asociación Latinoamericana de Integración, ALADI) successor to the LATIN AMERICAN FREE TRADE ASSOCIATION (LAFTA) created in 1960. LAIA is the successor to LAFTA, but LAFTA remains and is more flexible than LAIA. LAIA, whose membership includes Argentina, Bolivia, Brazil, Chile, Colombia, Ecuador, Mexico, Paraguay, Peru, Uruguay, and Venezuela, has been declining as a major Latin American integration effort in favor of regional efforts, such as MERCOSUR. Association headquarters are in Montevideo, Uruguay.

LATINO an Hispanic person of Latin American descent.

LAUNDERING the process of disguising the source or nature of illegal or doubtful funds in international business transactions by placing them into legitimate deals through an intermediary by means of investments, transfer, or deposits. *see also* DIRTY MONEY; OFFSHORE BANKING.

LAW OF BLOOD a country's nationality ruling stating that infants acquire the citizenship of their parents at birth.

LAW OF COMPARATIVE ADVANTAGE *see* COMPARATIVE ADVANTAGE.

LAW OF ONE PRICE principle that identical goods should sell for the same price throughout the world in an environment of FREE TRADE.

LAW OF THE SEA the rights of coastal states to control the living and nonliving resources of the sea for 200 miles off their coasts while allowing freedom of navigation to other states beyond 12 miles, as agreed at the sixth session of the Third United Nations Conference on the Law of the Sea (UNCLOS) in 1982.

LAW OF THE SOIL a country's nationality ruling stating that an individual acquires the citizenship of the country where the person is born.

LAY DAYS the dates between which a chartered vessel is to be available in port for loading of CARGO.

LAY ORDER the document that indicates the period during which IMPORTED merchandise may remain at the place of unloading without some action being taken for its disposition.

LAYER levels of more or less independent computer communication network protocols. The lowest layer governs direct host-to-host communication between the hardware at different HOSTS; the highest layer consists of user applications. Each layer builds on the layer beneath it. For each layer, programs at different hosts use protocols appropriate to the layer to communicate with each other. TCP/IP PROTOCOL SUITE has 5 layers of protocols; OPEN SYSTEMS INTERCONNECTION has 7. The advantages of different layers of protocols is that the methods of passing information from one layer to another are specified clearly as part of the protocols, and changes within a protocol layer are prevented from affecting the other layers. This greatly simplifies the task of designing and maintaining communication programs.

L/C abbreviation for LETTER OF CREDIT.

LC MAIL mail that includes letters and packages paid at the letter rate of postage. *see also* AO MAIL.

LCB *see* LOCAL COMPETITIVE BIDDING.

LCBC *see* LAKE CHAD BASIN COMMISSION.

LCL *see* LESS THAN CARLOAD; LESS THAN CONTAINER LOAD.

L.&D. abbreviation for loss and damage.

LD50 a dose of a substance that kills 50% of those infected.

LDC *see* LESS-DEVELOPED COUNTRY.

LDG abbreviation for loading.

LEAD TIME period of time needed to prepare for an action. *see also* ESTIMATED TIME OF ARRIVAL (ETA); ESTIMATED TIME OF DEPARTURE (ETD).

LEAGUE OF ARAB STATES (or ARAB LEAGUE) a North African and Middle Eastern regional grouping of countries aimed at improving relations among Arab nations. Members include Algeria, Bahrain, Djibouti, Egypt, Iraq, Jordan, Kuwait, Lebanon, Libya, Mauritania, Morocco, Oman, Palestine, Qatar, Saudi Arabia, Somalia, Sudan, Syria, Tunisia, United Arab Emirates, Yemen Arab Republic, and Yemen People's Democratic Republic. The league was established in March 1945, and its headquarters is in Cairo, Egypt. *see also* ARAB BANK FOR ECONOMIC DEVELOPMENT IN AFRICA; ARAB FUND FOR ECONOMIC AND SOCIAL DEVELOPMENT.

LEASE GUARANTEE PROGRAM a program where the EXPORT–IMPORT BANK OF THE UNITED STATES (EXIMBANK) provides guarantees of commercial loans to foreign buyers of U.S.-manufactured goods or services. These guarantees cover 100% of principal and interest against both political and commercial risks of nonpayment. Long-term guarantees are available only for major projects, large capital goods, and/or project-related services.

LEAST-DEVELOPED COUNTRIES *see* LESSER-DEVELOPED COUNTRIES.

LEBANESE POUND unit of currency, Lebanon. *see also* LIVRE.

LEGACY SYSTEM existing automated system that continues to function within an agency at the time of transition to a different system.

LEGAL ENTITY any individual, proprietorship, partnership, CORPORATION, association, or other organization that has, in the eyes of the law, the capacity to make a CONTRACT or an agreement, and the ability to assume an obligation and to discharge an indebtedness.

LEGAL TENDER any money that is recognized as being lawful for use by a debtor to pay a creditor, who must accept same in the discharge of a debt unless the contract between the parties specifically states that another type of money is to be used. *see also* CONVERTIBLE CURRENCY; CURRENCY INCONVERTIBILITY; HARD CURRENCY; SOFT CURRENCY.

LEGAL WEIGHT the weight of the goods plus any immediate wrappings that are sold along with the goods. Example: the weight of a tin can as well as its contents. *see also* NET WEIGHT.

LEI unit of currency, Moldava.

LEMPIRA unit of currency, Honduras (100 centavos equal 1 lempira).

LENDER OF LAST RESORT an institution that has the capacity and willingness to make loans when no one else can. Within a country, the CENTRAL BANK may play that role, because it can create money.

LEONE unit of currency, Sierra Leone.

LEONTIEF PARADOX the results of a study undertaken by Wassily Leontief, which showed that U.S. producers of LABOR-INTENSIVE products were more successful in exporting their products than producers of CAPITAL-INTENSIVE products.

LESS-DEVELOPED COUNTRY (LDC) a country with low per capita GROSS NATIONAL PRODUCT (GNP). Terms such as THIRD WORLD, poor, DEVELOPING COUNTRY, and underdeveloped have also been used to describe less-developed countries.

LESS THAN CARLOAD (LC) an amount of CARGO that is too small to fill a single rail car.

LESS THAN CONTAINER LOAD (LCL) an amount of CARGO too small to fill a single shipping container.

LESS THAN FAIR VALUE (LTFV) a determination made by the Assistant Secretary for Import Administration of the U.S. DEPARTMENT OF COMMERCE'S INTERNATIONAL TRADE ADMINISTRATION (ITA) as to whether there is a reasonable basis to believe or suspect that there is a history of DUMPING in the United States or elsewhere of the merchandise under consideration or that the IMPORTER knew or should have known that the EXPORTER was selling this merchandise at less than fair value and there have been massive imports of this merchandise over a relatively short period. *see also* ANTIDUMPING DUTY; TARIFF ACT OF 1938; OMNIBUS TRADE ACT OF 1988.

LESS THAN TRUCKLOAD shipment that does not completely fill a truck or that weighs less than the weight required for the application of the truckload freight rate, which is usually a lower freight rate than that applied to less-than-truckload cargo. *see also* LESS THAN CARLOAD (LC); LESS THAN CONTAINER LOAD (LCL).

LESSER-DEVELOPED COUNTRIES (LLDCs) (sometimes also known as Least-Developed Countries) classification developed by the UNITED NATIONS to give some guidance to donor agencies and countries about an equitable allocation of foreign assistance. The criteria for designating a country an LLDC, originally adopted by the UN Committee for Development Planning in 1971, have been modified several times. Criteria have included low per-capita income, literacy, and manufacturing share of the country's total GROSS DOMESTIC PRODUCT. There is continuing concern that the criteria should be more robust and less subject to the possibility of easy fluctuation of a country between LESS-DEVELOPED COUNTRY and Lesser-Developed Country status.

LETTER OF ASSIGNMENT document with which the assignor assigns rights to a third party. *see also* ASSIGNMENT OF LETTER OF CREDIT; BACK-TO-BACK LETTER OF CREDIT; BACK-TO-BACK LOAN; BACK-TO-BACK BORROWING.

LETTERA DI ACCREDITAMENTO (Italian) *see* LETTER OF CREDIT.

LETTER OF CREDENCE an official document carried by a representative who is sent by a country to represent it in country-to-country relations that conveys the individual's credentials as a diplomatic envoy to a foreign government. *see also* DIPLOMAT; TITLE AND RANK.

LETTER OF CREDIT (L/C) a financial document issued by a bank at the request of the CONSIGNEE guaranteeing payment to the shipper for CARGO if certain terms and conditions are fulfilled. Normally it contains a brief description of the goods, documents required, shipping date, and expiration date after which payment will no longer be made. Upon receipt of the documentation, the bank is either paid by the buyer or takes title to the goods themselves and proceeds to transfer funds to the seller. The banks insist upon exact compliance with the terms of the sale and will not pay if there are discrepancies. *see also* IRREVOCABLE LETTER OF CREDIT; REVOCABLE LETTER OF CREDIT; CONFIRMED LETTER OF CREDIT; DOCUMENTARY LETTER OF CREDIT.

LETTER OF INDEMNITY document that serves to protect the CARRIER/owner financially against possible repercussions in connection with the release of goods without presentation of an original BILL OF LADING. *see also* INDEMNIFY; INDEMNITY.

LETTER OF INTENT a document that describes the preliminary understanding between parties who intend to make a CONTRACT or join together in another action.

LEU unit of currency, Romania (100 ban equal 1 leu).

LEV unit of currency, Bulgaria (100 stotinka equal 1 lev).

LEVEL PLAYING FIELD a situation where all parties in a negotiation are of equal strength and are negotiating under similar conditions. The term can be used in conjunction with some international negotiations, such as the MULTILATERAL TRADE NEGOTIATIONS of the GENERAL AGREEMENT ON TARIFFS AND TRADE (GATT).

LEVY
1. to impose and collect a tax or TARIFF.
2. a tax or tariff. *see also* DUTY.

LIAISON OFFICE an office established in another country to provide a means of communication between HOME COUNTRY organization groups and units and organization groups or units located in a foreign country.

LIB *see* LIMITED INTERNATIONAL BIDDING.

LIBERALIZATION to relax or decontrol. Liberalization is used in international business when referring to trade liberalization, agreements by or among countries to reduce TARIFF and NONTARIFF TRADE BARRIERS. These impediments can include
- IMPORT policies (tariffs and other import charges, quantitative restrictions, import licensing, and customs barriers);
- standards, testing, labeling, and certification;
- government procurement;
- EXPORT subsidies;
- lack of intellectual property protection;
- service barriers;
- investment barriers; and
- other barriers (e.g., barriers encompassing more than one category or barriers affecting a single sector).
  see also GENERAL AGREEMENT ON TARIFFS AND TRADE (GATT); ROUNDS.

LIBERATION KIP unit of currency, Laos (former) (100 ats equal 1 Liberation kip). *see also* KIP.

LIBERIAN DOLLAR unit of currency, Liberia (100 cents equal 1 Liberian dollar).

LIBID *see* LONDON INTERBANK BID RATE.

LIBOR *see* LONDON INTERBANK OFFERED RATE.

LIBYAN DINAR unit of currency, Libya (1000 dirhams equal 1 Libyan dinar).

LICENSED PRODUCTION
1. a compensatory form of COUNTERTRADE transaction called OFFSETS, which involves transfer of technical information under direct commercial arrangements between an EXPORTER/manufacturer and a foreign government or producer, in which the exporter provides permission for all or part of the EXPORT contract to be produced OFFSHORE. *see also* OFFSET DEALS.
2. a transfer of technical information under direct commercial arrangements between a U.S. manufacturer and a foreign government or producer.

LICENSING a contractual arrangement in which the licensor's patents, trademarks, service marks, copyrights, or know-how may be sold or otherwise made available to a licensee for compensation negotiated in advance between the parties. Such compensation, known as royalties, may consist of a lump sum royalty, a running royalty (royalty based on volume of production), or a combination of both. Companies frequently license their patents, trademarks, copyrights, and know-how to a foreign company that then manufactures and sells products based on the technology in a country or group of countries authorized by the LICENSING AGREEMENT. *see also* FRANCHISING; LICENSED PRODUCTION.

LICENSING AGREEMENT a formal agreement between a company (licensor), and another company in the domestic or a foreign country (licensee)that makes available the licensor's patents, trademarks, copyrights, and know-how to the licensee for manufacturing and selling products in a country or group of countries. *see also* LICENSED PRODUCTION; LICENSING.

LICENSING CODE *see* AGREEMENT ON IMPORT LICENSING.

LIFE-CYCLE PROCESSING an accounting approach in which a company sets product prices based on recovering costs over the life cycle of the product. U.S. authorities dispute the validity of this approach because projections of future yield improvements cannot be verified at the time of DUMPING calculations.

LIFETIME EMPLOYMENT the practice of firms in Japan and certain other countries in which workers are practically guaranteed employment with the firm for the balance of their lives, seldom leaving for employment opportunities with other firms.

LIFFE *see* LONDON INTERNATIONAL FINANCIAL FUTURES AND OPTIONS EXCHANGE.

LIFT ON/LIFT OFF (LO/LO) the method by which CARGO is loaded onto and removed from a vessel, such as by the use of a crane.

LIFT VAN wooden or metal CONTAINER used for packing household goods and personal effects.

LIGHTER an open or covered vessel that transfers CARGO between ship and shore, used mainly in harbors and inland waterways. Lighters are generally used for shorter hauls, barges for longer ones.

LIGHTER ABOARD SHIP (LASH) floatable large CONTAINER (LIGHTER) used in the combined ocean and inland waterway transport of goods. *see also* LASH (LIGHTER ABOARD SHIP).

LIGHTERAGE (LTGE) the use of a small vessel to transfer CARGO from shallow water to a deep-water vessel anchored offshore or to transfer cargo between vessels themselves. *see also* LASH; LIGHTER.

LIKE PRODUCT any product with similar characteristics that can be substituted for any other product with similar characteristics. *see also* DETERMINATION; FINAL DETERMINATION.

LILANGENI unit of currency, Swaziland (100 cents equal 1 lilangeni). *see also* EMALANGENI.

LIMEAN *see* LONDON INTERBANK MEAN RATE.

LIMITATION PERIOD maximum period set by statute within which a legal action can be brought or a right enforced. A statute may prohibit, for example, any individual or legal entity from bringing an action for breach of CONTRACT more than one year after the breach occurred.

LIMITED APPOINTMENT appointees restricted to the U.S. AND FOREIGN COMMERCIAL SERVICE (US&FSC) (or to other foreign services) from the private sector or from the U.S. federal government who are noncareer officers assigned overseas for a limited time.

LIMITED INTERNATIONAL BIDDING (LIB) one of several forms of procurement made with WORLD BANK financing. In some circumstances (such as small purchases, urgent need, or few suppliers), suppliers or contractors of specialized goods and services participate by invitation rather than in response to an advertisement. *see also* INTERNATIONAL BUSINESS OPPORTUNITIES SERVICE; INTERNATIONAL COMPETITIVE BIDDING; LOCAL COMPETITIVE BIDDING.

LIMITED (LIABILITY) two types of limited companies in the United Kingdom:
- a private limited company to which the public cannot be invited to subscribe for shares issued.
- a PUBLIC LIMITED COMPANY (PLC) that can raise funds through share issues. Before a limited company can "go public," it must have a minimum share capital. A private limited company requires no minimum share capital. The investor's liability is limited to the amount of the investment.

LIMITED LIABILITY COMPANY a company that has selected a form of business ownership that allows the owners of the business to limit their liability to the amount of their investment.

LIMITED PARTNERSHIP a type of partnership agreement where the limited partner is treated as an investor only, and his/her liability is limited to the amount he/she has invested into the business.

LINE HAUL direct movement of FREIGHT between two major ports by a single ship. *see also* FEEDER VESSEL; LINE HAUL VESSEL.

LINE HAUL VESSEL vessel on a regularly defined schedule. *see also* LINE HAUL; FEEDER VESSEL.

LINE RELEASE SYSTEM a part of U.S. Department of Customs' AUTOMATED COMMERCIAL SYSTEM (ACS) designed for the release and tracking of shipments through the use of personal computers and bar code technology. To qualify for line release, a COMMODITY must have a history of invoice accuracy and be selected by local CUSTOMS districts on the basis of high volume. To release the merchandise, Customs reads the bar code into a personal computer, verifies that the bar code matches the invoice data, and enters the quantity. The CARGO release is transmitted to the Automated Commercial System, which establishes an entry and the requirement for an entry summary and provides the AUTOMATED BROKER INTERFACE (ABI) system participants with release information.

LINEAR REDUCTION OF TARIFFS *see* ACROSS THE BOARD TARIFF REDUCTIONS.

LINER vessel carrying passengers and CARGO that operates on a route with a fixed schedule.

LINER SHIPPING shipping services transporting CARGO on a regular basis between ports in different countries. *see also* CONFERENCE.

LINER TERMS conditions under which a shipping company will transport goods, including the amount payable for FREIGHT and the cost both for loading and discharge of the vessel.

LINGUA FRANCA (Italian: *lingua* meaning language and *franca* meaning Frankish, European, or the language of commerce) the medium of communication used most commonly in an area or region. Every major trading area of the world has a lingua franca. Example: Latin Americans have Spanish; Europeans have English and French among the EUROPEAN ECONOMIC COMMUNITY (EEC), Russian or German in Eastern Europe; Asians have Chinese in Asia and Southeast Asia, English with the rest of the world.

LINKAGE (LINKING) the generation of demand in a second or third international market based upon the entrance into that market of the product from the initial market. Example: the Japanese initially exported their cars to Canada, and as demand increased they were persuaded to manufacture cars in Canada. Once the manufacturing operations were established in Canada, the Japanese car manufacturers used them as a spring board to REEXPORT vehicles to the United States. Now that they have established operations in the United States, the network is complete. The initial linkage between the Japanese car manufacturers in Canada and the United States was to take advantage of the CANADIA–U.S. FREE TRADE AGREEMENT OF 1989.

LINKING SCHEME requirement that, the IMPORTER must buy a certain amount of the same product from local producers in order to get an IMPORT LICENSE.

LIQUID ASSETS anything owned by a company that can be quickly converted to cash. Example: U.S. Treasury bills, common stocks, CONVERTIBLE CURRENCIES, and TRANSFERABLE CURRENCY.

LIQUIDATED DAMAGES sum of money that a contracting party agrees to pay to the other party for breaching an agreement.

LIQUIDATION the point at which a country's CUSTOMS service determines the rate of DUTY and its final amount. Liquidation is accomplished by posting a notice on a public bulletin board at the customshouse. *see also* LIQUIDATION SYSTEM.

LIQUIDATION SYSTEM the part of the U.S. Department of Customs' AUTOMATED COMMERCIAL SYSTEM that closes the file on each entry and establishes a batch filing number essential for recovering an entry for review or enforcement purposes. An entry liquidation is a final review of the entry. U.S. P.L. 95-410 (Customs Procedural Reform and Simplification Act of 1978) requires that all liquidations be performed within 1 year from the date of consumption entry or final withdrawal on a warehouse entry. Three 1-year extensions are permitted.

LIQUIDITY a country's international reserves held in TRANSFERABLE CURRENCIES, which are available to settle a temporary BALANCE OF PAYMENT disequilibrium.

LIQUIDITY CRISIS A financial crisis that occurs because of lack of LIQUIDITY. Usually means that a CENTRAL BANK runs short of the INTERNATIONAL RESERVES needed to PEG its EXCHANGE RATES and/or to service its foreign loans. *see also* EXCHANGE RATE MECHANISM (ERM).

LIRA unit of currency, Cyprus, Italy, Malta, Turkey, San Marino, and Vatican City.

LIVING ALLOWANCE *see* COST DIFFERENTIAL.

LIVRE unit of currency, Lebanon (*see also* LEBANESE POUND).

LLOYDS OF LONDON English association of insurance underwriters, the oldest of its kind in the world; not in itself an insurance company.

LLOYDS REGISTRY English society, independent of LLOYDS OF LONDON, which surveys and classifies the ships of the world according to their description, condition, seaworthiness, and compliance with codes and protocols; also establishes standards for maintenance and construction. (Correct name: Lloyds Register of Shipping.)

LO/LO *see* LIFT ON/LIFT OFF.

LOADING physical placing of CARGO into a truck or a shipping CONTAINER, or onto a vessel.

LOADING BERTH a space at a pier for a vessel to dock or anchor in preparation for loading.

LOAN GUARANTEES a program of the Canadian EXPORT DEVELOPMENT CORPORATION (EDC) whereby it provides repayment guarantees to banks and financial institutions for private-sector loans to creditworthy foreign buyers of Canadian goods and services. *see also* EXPORT FINANCING; EXPORT–IMPORT BANK OF THE UNITED STATES (EXIMBANK).

LOAN PREDISBURSEMENT INSURANCE a Canadian EXPORT DEVELOPMENT CORPORATION (EDC) program providing production risk coverage to Canadian EXPORTERS from the date the EXPORT FINANCING is approved until disbursement is made to the exporter under the terms of the loan.

LOAN SUPPORT FOR SERVICES a Canadian EXPORT DEVELOPMENT CORPORATION (EDC) program that makes available its financing abilities supporting EXPORT transactions involving services provided by Canadian firms that should ultimately lead to contracts for Canadian goods (i.e., consulting and feasibility studies).

LOAN (TO FOREIGN IMPORTERS) a medium- and long-term financing program of the Canadian EXPORT DEVELOPMENT CORPORATION (EDC) providing assistance to foreign buyers of Canadian capital goods and services.

LOCAL AREA NETWORK (LAN) a localized computer data NETWORK linking several computers together. Because of their small size, LANs can be optimized to transfer data at high speed. *see also* ETHERNET; FIBER DISTRIBUTED DATA INTERFACE; TOKEN RING.

LOCAL COMPETITIVE BIDDING (LCB) one of several forms of procurement made with WORLD BANK financing. The LCB method is generally used for contracts involving
- labor-intensive activities,
- small value,
- locally procurable services or goods priced below the world market,
- intermittent work, and
- activities to be performed at numerous sites.
    see also INTERNATIONAL BUSINESS OPPORTUNITIES SERVICE; INTERNATIONAL COMPETITIVE BIDDING; LIMITED INTERNATIONAL BIDDING.

LOCAL CONTENT REQUIREMENT *see* DOMESTIC CONTENT REQUIREMENT (DCR).

LOCAL HIRE a person hired in a particular country for work in that country. It also has a special meaning in that the employee is not a citizen of the country. Example: an American residing in England is hired to work for a British firm in England. *see also* LOCAL NATIONAL.

LOCAL NATIONAL a person hired by a company for employment in a country of which he/she is a citizen.

LOCALS *see* LOCAL NATIONAL.

LOG OFF the disconnect procedure from a HOST system.

LOG ON/LOG IN identification procedure used when connecting to a HOST computer or public-access site. *see also* LOG OFF.

LOI ROYER legislation that regulates the establishment and expansion of retail stores in France. It took effect in 1973 and provides existing retailers with veto power over the establishment of any large-scale retailers attempting to enter the market. There are similar laws in Belgium, Italy, and Japan. *see also* DAITEN HO.

LOMBARD RATE one of the official interest rates in Germany used to regulate the money market. Other countries use the term Lombard to describe rates that function somewhat like the Lombard rate. Example: the Swiss have their own Lombard rate. In France, it's called the Central Bank Intervention rate, but it performs the same function.

LOME CONVENTION an agreement concluded at Lomé, Togo in February 1975 that entered into force in April 1976. The original convention was followed by several additional Lomé Conventions, which expanded the scope of the original agreement. The convention is between the EUROPEAN COMMUNITY (EC) and 62 African, Caribbean, and Pacific states (ACP) (mostly former colonies of the EC members). The agreement covers some aid provisions as well as trade and TARIFF preferences for the ACP countries when shipping to the EC. Lomé grew out of the 1958 TREATY OF ROME's "association" with the 18 African colonies/countries that had ties with Belgium and France. The ACP members are Angola, Bahamas, Barbados, Benin, Botswana, Burkina Faso, Burundi, Cameroon, Cape Verde, Central African Republic, Chad, Comoros, Congo, Côte d'Ivoire, Djibouti, Dominica, Equatorial Guinea, Ethiopia, Fiji, Gabon, Gambia, Ghana, Grenada, Guinea, Guinea-Bissau, Guyana, Jamaica, Kenya, Lesotho, Liberia, Madagascar, Malawi, Mali, Mauritius, Mauritania, Mozambique, Namibia, Niger, Nigeria, Papua New Guinea, Rwanda, Saint Lucia, Saint Vincent, Samoa, São Tomé and Principe, Senegal, Seychelles, Sierra Leone, Solomon Islands, Somalia, Sudan, Suriname, Swaziland, Tanzania, Togo, Trinidad and Tobago, Uganda, Zaire, Zambia, and Zimbabwe.

LONDON CLUB a creditor cartel of commercial banks that evolved in the early 1980s. Debt rescheduling (constructing new repayment profiles over a specific period of time) was a primary function of the club. The Brady deals on debt restructuring (renegotiating the entire stock of outstanding debt at a discount) obviated the need to reschedule repayments every couple of years. In some respects, the BANK ADVISORY COMMITTEE has replaced the London Club. The PARIS CLUB, also concerned with debt repayment, is an association of official creditors.

LONDON INTERBANK BID RATE (LIBID) the rate of interest paid for funds in the London interbank market. The bid to LIBOR's offer has been used as a reference for floating rate payments for especially strong borrowers.

LONDON INTERBANK MEAN RATE (LIMEAN) the midpoint of the LIBOR (LONDON INTERBANK OFFERED RATE) spread. LIMEAN has been used as a reference for floating rate payments.

LONDON INTERBANK OFFERED RATE (LIBOR) the most prominent of the interbank offered rates. LIBOR is the rate of interest at which banks in London lend funds to other prime banks in London. LIBOR is frequently used as a basis for determining the rate of interest payable on Eurodollars and other Eurocurrency loans. The effective rate of interest on these Eurocredits is LIBOR plus a markup negotiated between lender and borrower. *see also* INTERBANK OFFERED RATE.

LONDON INTERNATIONAL FINANCIAL FUTURES AND OPTIONS EXCHANGE (LIFFE) Europe's leading futures exchange, LIFFE trades in futures contracts including short-term interest rates, government bonds, stock indices, and traded options on these instruments. The exchange was established in 1982 to provide a means for hedging interest rates and currency exposures against volatility. Originally called the London International Financial Futures Exchange, LIFFE merged in March 1992 with the London Traded Options Market (LTOM) and retained the original acronym.

LONDON METALS a daily column in the JOURNAL OF COMMERCE that lists the spot and future prices in POUNDS per metric ton for those metals trading most actively in London. *see also* COMEX METAL WAREHOUSE; SPOT METALS.

LONDON OIL FUTURES a daily column in the JOURNAL OF COMMERCE that provides a list of quotations on futures trading of crude and home heating oil from the International Petroleum Exchange in London. *see also* OIL FUTURES TRADING; OIL OPTIONS; PETROLEUM PRICES; SPOT PRODUCT PRICES.

LONG-DATED FORWARD a foreign exchange contract whose maturity exceeds 1 year; a few have extended over 10 years.

LONG POSITION the purchase of foreign currency for delivery in the future. Example: if an individual predicts that the future SPOT RATE of a foreign currency will be higher than the current FORWARD RATE, the individual will recommend taking a long position in that currency. *see also* FLUCTUATING EXCHANGE RATES; SHORT POSITION.

LONGSHOREMAN laborer who loads and unloads ships at a seaport.

LONG-TERM AGREEMENT ON INTERNATIONAL TRADE IN COTTON AND TEXTILES the INTERNATIONAL COMMODITY AGREEMENT that was replaced by the MULTIFIBER ARRANGEMENT (MFA).

LOON (LOONIE) a term used to refer to the CANADIAN DOLLAR coin minted by the Bank of Canada in 1989 to replace all paper notes in circulation.

LOSS OF INTENT document, such as a written memorandum, that describes the preliminary understanding between parties who intend to make a contract or join together in another action, such as a JOINT VENTURE or a corporate merger.

LOTI *see* MALOTI.

LOT LABELS labels attached to each piece of a multiple-lot SHIPMENT for identification purposes.

LOUVRE ACCORD accord developed in February 1987 that attempted to stop the U.S. dollar's fall and to stabilize currency relationships by introducing reference ranges among the G-7 currencies. *see also* PLAZA ACCORD.

LOW-CONTEXT CULTURE a society where meaning is communicated between and among individuals more through the use of language and less through the use of nonverbal methods of communication. *see also* HIGH-CONTEXT CULTURE; SITUATIONAL CONFORMITY.

LOWER DECK CONTAINERS CARRIER-owned CONTAINERS specially designed as an integral part of the aircraft to fit in the CARGO compartments of a wide-body aircraft. *see also* BELLY PITS OR HOLDS.

LTD an abbreviation for Limited. *see also* LIMITED LIABILITY COMPANY.

LTFV *see* LESS THAN FAIR VALUE.

LTGE abbreviation for lighterage. *see also* LIGHTER.

LTL *see* LESS THAN TRUCKLOAD.

LUCRO DA EXPLORACAO a special 10-year income tax exemption on operating profits offered by the Brazilian government for new agricultural and industrial investment in the SUDENE region. A similar exemption is also offered for investment in the SUDAM area (Amazon Basin States).

LUSOPHONE COUNTRIES those countries in which the official language is Portuguese. These countries are Angola, Brazil, Cape Verde, Guinea-Bissau, Mozambique, Portugal, and São Tomé and Principe.

LUXEMBOURG FRANC unit of currency, Luxembourg (100 centimes equal 1 Luxembourg franc).

LVs an abbreviation for luncheon vouchers issued in the United Kingdom. LVs are similar to food stamps issued by the U.S. government.

M

MAASTRICHT TREATY the TREATY OF EUROPEAN UNION (named for the Dutch town in which the treaty was signed). The treaty creates a European Union by
- committing the 12 member states of the EUROPEAN ECONOMIC COMMUNITY (EEC) to both EUROPEAN MONETARY UNION (EMU) and political union,
- introducing a single currency (EUROPEAN CURRENCY UNIT, ECU),
- establishing a EUROPEAN SYSTEM OF CENTRAL BANKS (ESCB),
- creating a EUROPEAN CENTRAL BANK (ECB), and
- broadening EEC integration by including both a common foreign and security policy (CFSP) and cooperation in justice and home affairs (CJHA).

The treaty, negotiated in 1991 and signed in February 1992, entered into force on November 1, 1993. It envisioned EMU being achieved in three stages. A first stage (encompassing treaty negotiations and lasting through January 1, 1994) concluded with ratification of treaty amendments needed to establish EMU, including participation by all 12 EEC member states in the EUROPEAN EXCHANGE RATE MECHANISM.

The second stage involved using the EUROPEAN MONETARY INSTITUTE (EMI) to support development of a single currency (the ECU) and development of the ECB.

The Madrid Summit of Heads of State and Government decided on the details of entry into stage three. In December 1995, the Council of Ministers adopted a detailed changeover scenario in order to clarify the process of introducing the single currency for all economic agents and European citizens. This involves irrevocable fixing of exchange rates and the debut of the ECB with transfer of powers necessary for administering economic and monetary union. Since January 1999, the EURO has been the single currency for all member states of the EMU.

MAC ADDRESS the computer firmware address of a device connected to a NETWORK. *see also* ETHERNET; TOKEN RING.

MACHINE MODEL ORGANIZATION the Japanese view of the European and North American business organization; that is, one based on the importance of profits, so that nothing stands in the way of the firm's pursuit of profits. *see also* HUMAN COWORKING MODEL ORGANIZATION.

MACROECONOMICS study of statistics of the economy as a whole rather than as single economic units.

MADE-TO-MEASURE TARIFF TARIFF set to raise the price of an imported good as compared to the domestic price, so as to leave domestic producers unaffected. *see also* DUTY; SCIENTIFIC TARIFF; TARIFF ANOMALY; TARIFF BARRIER; TARIFF ESCALATION.

MADRID AGREEMENT CONCERNING THE INTERNATIONAL REGISTRATION OF MARKS a MULTILATERAL TREATY signed by 22 nations (the Madrid Union) in 1891 to promote the protection of intellectual property around the world through cooperation among states. The treaty provided for the creation of a central registration organization for patents and trademarks. Since the late 1970s, the treaty has been administered by the WORLD INTELLECTUAL PROPERTY ORGANIZATION (WIPO), which is responsible for coordinating the legal and administrative aspects of the treaty.

MAGHREB COMMON MARKET a MULTILATERAL AGREEMENT signed by Algeria, Libya, Mauritania, Morocco, and Tunisia. The union was established in February 1989 to foster integration of the Maghreb economy. The union also seeks to join the ARAB MAGHREB UNION (AMU) and the GULF COOPERATION COUNCIL states in a COMMON MARKET. It was the successor to the MAHGREB PERMANENT CONSULTATIVE COMMITTEE. *see also* MAGHREB STATES.

MAGHREB PERMANENT CONSULTATIVE COMMITTEE a regional organization founded in Tunis in 1964 to promote economic cooperation among member countries. Its members included Algeria, Mauritania, Morocco, Libya, and Tunisia. In response to political differences with other members, Libya withdrew from the organization in 1970. The long-range goal of this initial committee was ultimately to form a COMMON MARKET among its members. *see also* ARAB MAGHREB UNION (AMU); MAGHREB COMMON MARKET; MAGHREB STATES.

MAGHREB STATES the three North African nations of Algeria, Morocco, and Tunisia. The EUROPEAN COMMUNITY (EC) concluded a trade and aid agreement in 1976 with these states. The term *Maghreb states* sometimes also includes Libya and Mauritania. The five Maghreb states created the ARAB MAGHREB UNION (AMU). *see also* MAGHREB COMMON MARKET; MAGHREB PERMANENT CONSULTATIVE COMMITTEE.

MAGNA CARTA FOR COUNTRYSIDE AND BARANGAY BUSINESS ENTERPRISES a program of the Philippine government to encourage the development of small-scale business enterprises outside of Metro Manila and other highly urbanized areas. It exempts small businesses from all taxes, including income tax, VALUE-ADDED TAX, license and building permit fees, and other business taxes, except real property and capital gains tax, IMPORT DUTIES, and other miscellaneous taxes on imported goods.

MAI *see* MULTILATERAL AGREEMENT ON INVESTMENT.

MAIL BRIDGE a method of forwarding electronic mail messages conforming to predetermined administrative criteria between two or more computer NETWORKS. *see also* ELECTRONIC MAIL; MAIL GATEWAY.

MAIL ENTRIES a type of ENTRY that allows an IMPORTER to use the mails to IMPORT merchandise into the United States. This type of entry offers the following benefits to the importer:
- ease in clearing shipments through CUSTOMS,
- savings on shipping charges,
- no entry required on DUTY-FREE merchandise not exceeding US$1250 in value, and
- no need to clear shipments personally if under US$1250 in value.

MAIL SERVER a software program that responds to ELECTRONIC MAIL requests for information by distributing the appropriate data or files.

MAILING LIST
1. a list of ELECTRONIC MAIL addresses, used by a MAIL EXPLODER, to forward messages to groups of people. Generally, a mailing list is used to discuss a certain set of topics, and different mailing lists discuss different topics. A mailing list may be moderated. This means that messages sent to the list are actually sent to an individual who determines whether or not to send the messages on to everyone else.
2. a conference where messages are delivered as E-MAIL to participants instead of to a USENET NEWSGROUP. To join a mailing list, a message is sent to a specific E-MAIL address, which is often a computer that automates the process.

MAKE BULK *see* CONSOLIDATED SHIPMENT.

MALA FIDE in bad faith; a seller's representation that goods are usable for a particular purpose when in fact the seller knows that the goods are not. *see also* BONA FIDE.

MALAGASY FRANC unit of currency, Madagascar (1 ariary equals 5 Malagasy francs).

MALDIVIAN RUPEE *see* RUFIYAA.

MALOTI (LOTI) unit of currency, Lesotho (100 sente equal 1 maloti).

MALTESE LIRA unit of currency, Malta (100 cents equal 1 Maltese lira).

MANAGED FLOAT *see* DIRTY FLOAT.

MANAGED FLOATING EXCHANGE RATE SYSTEM the policy of government intervention in managing short-term fluctuations in EXCHANGE RATES. It is a system wherein a CENTRAL BANK might intercede at times to secure a politically agreeable exchange rate different from the one resulting from free-market supply and demand. *see also* DIRTY FLOAT; MONETARISM.

MANAGED TRADE any international transaction affected by non-market factors such as NONTARIFF (trade) BARRIERS and quantitative limitations.

MANAGEMENT CONTRACT
1. an agreement wherein a firm provides another firm with management personnel to perform management functions for it.
2. a situation where a former owner of a foreign investment that has been expropriated by a foreign government has been requested to continue supervising the operations until such time as the local management has been trained.

MANAGEMENT INFORMATION BASE (MIB) the range of information a simple network management protocol (SNMP) management station can retrieve from a NETWORK device (e.g., ROUTER). There are minimal MIB standards. As a minimum, any SNMP manager should interface to any SNMP agent with a properly defined MIB. *see also* CLIENT–SERVER MODEL; DISTRIBUTED DATABASE.

MANAGING AGENTS foreign-based intermediaries hired by firms to exclusively represent the firms in business dealings with foreign governments. These representatives normally have the authority, perhaps even power of attorney, to make commitments on behalf of the firms they represent.

MANAUS FREE ZONE a FREE-TRADE ZONE in Brazil that offers special tax incentives to firms investing in the underdeveloped Amazon region. Foreign goods processed in the free-trade zone and reexported are exempt from IMPORT DUTIES and the federal VALUE-ADDED TAX.

MANIFEST a document that summarizes all CARGO aboard the vessel by port of loading and discharge. When the steamship line has processed all the BILLS OF LADING, the ship's manifest is then prepared.

MANO RIVER UNION (MRU) a northwestern African union that advances common policies and cooperation on TARIFFS and CUSTOMS regulations, on development projects, and in other economic areas. The union instituted a common external tariff in 1977. The MRU was established in 1973; headquarters is in Freetown, Sierra Leone.

MANUFACTURE IDENTIFICATION NUMBER (MID) a data element used by CUSTOMS.

MANUFACTURED IMPORTS PROMOTION ORGANIZATION (MIPRO) a nonprofit organization established in 1978 by the joint efforts of the Japanese government and the private sector to promote IMPORTS of foreign-manufactured products by hosting exhibitions and providing a wide range of market information. MIPRO's activities are broadly classified into three categories:
• holding imported product trade exhibitions for buyers and the general public;

- disseminating information regarding imported products and the Japanese market; and
- promoting sales of foreign products to Japanese consumers to promote recognition of the quality of imported goods.

MANUFACTURER'S EXPORT AGENT

1. an individual or firm that purchases products directly from the manufacturer, packing and marking the products according to its own specifications. The individual or firm then sells overseas through its contacts in its own name and assumes all risks for accounts. see also EXPORT MANAGEMENT COMPANY (EMC).
2. An individual or firm that serves as the foreign representative of a number of noncompeting firms and seeks sales abroad. The individual or firm receives a commission on all sales. see also INDIRECT EXPORT.

MANUFACTURER'S REPRESENTATIVE
a foreign-based individual that serves as the foreign representative of an EXPORTING manufacturer who seeks sales abroad for the EXPORTER.

MAQUILADORA
Mexico's "in-bond" industry program that allows foreign manufacturers to ship components into Mexico duty-free for assembly and subsequent reexport. Industry established under the maquiladora program is Mexico's second largest source of foreign revenue (following oil exports).

The maquiladora program was established in 1965. In December 1989, the Mexican government liberalized the maquiladora program to make this a more attractive and dynamic sector of the economy. As a result, maquiladora operations may IMPORT (DUTY- and import license-free) products not directly involved in production, but that support production, including computers and other administrative materials and transportation equipment.

MAQUILADORA INDUSTRY see MAQUILADORA.

MAQUILADORA SYSTEM see MAQUILADORA.

MARCHE DU TRAVAIL (French) see LABOR MARKET.

MARGIN

1. the difference between the SPOT and FORWARD price quoted for a foreign currency. see also DISCOUNT; LONG POSITION; PREMIUM; SHORT POSITION.
2. money placed on deposit with a broker, to finance futures trading.

MARGIN CALL
telephone call by a futures or an options exchange or by a broker to clients for additional collateral to that previously posted when the futures, options, or securities were purchased without posting their full value.

MARGINAL COST
increase in the total cost of production that results from manufacturing one more unit of output.

MARGINAL PROPENSITY TO IMPORT economic theory that discusses the relationship between adjustments in expenditures, savings, and IMPORTS, with changes in national income. The marginal propensity to import refers to the change in the level of imports by a country given a change in the level of national income.

MARINE BILL OF LADING a receipt for the CARGO and a contract for transportation between a shipper and the ocean carrier. It may also be used as an instrument of ownership that can be bought, sold, or traded while the goods are in transit. To be used in this manner, it must be a negotiable "Order" Bill-of-Lading. *see also* CLEAN BILL OF LADING; ON-BOARD BILL OF LADING; INLAND BILL OF LADING.

MARINE CARGO INSURANCE insurance indemnifying loss of, or damage to, goods at sea. *see also* MARINE INSURANCE.

MARINE EXTENSION CLAUSE a clause appearing in MARINE CARGO INSURANCE POLICIES providing continued coverage on GOODS during deviation, delay, reshipment, and transshipment, or any other modification in the normal shipment of the goods beyond the control of the ASSURED.

MARINE INSURANCE indemnification for the owner of merchandise for losses in excess of those that can be legally recovered from the CARRIER and that are sustained from fire, shipwreck, piracy, and various other causes. Three of the most common types of marine insurance coverage are FREE OF PARTICULAR AVERAGE (FPA), WITH PARTICULAR AVERAGE (WPA), and ALL RISK COVERAGE. *see also* MARINE CARGO INSURANCE.

MARINE INSURANCE CERTIFICATE a certificate used to assure the CONSIGNEE that insurance is provided to cover loss of or damage to the CARGO while in transit via ocean vessel.

MARINE MAMMAL PROTECTION ACT U.S. law adopted in 1972 prohibiting the taking (harassing, hunting, capturing, or killing) of marine mammals, and also prohibiting the import of any marine mammal product or any fish that has been associated with the taking of marine mammals. *see also* TUNA-DOLPHINE CASE.

MARINE SURVEYOR an individual who is a specialist responsible for determining the nature, extent, and cause of loss and/or damage of the goods while in transit via oceangoing vessel. *see also* INSURANCE CERTIFICATION; MARINE CARGO INSURANCE; MARINE EXTENSION CLAUSE; MARINE INSPECTION CERTIFICATE.

MARITIME relating to commerce or navigation by sea. *see also* MARITIME ADMINISTRATION.

MARITIME ADMINISTRATION a division of the U.S. DEPARTMENT OF COMMERCE responsible for the administration of laws for the maintenance of a merchant marine for the purpose of national defense and commerce.

MARITIME CALENDAR a column appearing each Friday in the JOURNAL OF COMMERCE. The column lists all seminars, workshops, courses, and meetings involving maritime issues.

MARK unit of currency, Germany (100 pfennig equal 1 mark). *see also* DEUTSCHE MARK.

MARK SHEET an IMPORT declaration that must be submitted to the FOREIGN EXCHANGE bank in Japan by the Japanese IMPORTER to secure foreign exchange to IMPORT goods in excess of ¥1 million. *see also* IMPORT ALLOCATION CERTIFICATE; QUANTITY RESTRICTIONS.

MARKET ACCESS the openness of a national market to foreign products. Market access reflects a government's willingness to permit IMPORTS to compete relatively unimpeded with similar domestically produced goods.

MARKET DISRUPTION the situation created when a surge of IMPORTS in a given product line causes sales of domestically produced goods in a particular country to decline to an extent that the domestic producers and their employees suffer major economic hardship.

MARKET ECONOMY economic system where resources are allocated and production is determined by market forces rather than by government decree. *see also* COMMAND ECONOMY.

MARKET-ORIENTED COOPERATION PLAN (MOCP) plan established in 1990 aimed at improving long-term business relations between Japan's automotive manufacturers and U.S. auto parts suppliers.

MARKET-ORIENTED SECTOR-SELECTIVE (MOSS) talks begun in January 1985 as bilateral trade discussions between the United States and Japan in an effort to remove many trade barriers at once in a given sector. MOSS talks have focused on six sectors:
- telecommunications,
- medical equipment and pharmaceuticals,
- electronics,
- forest products,
- auto parts, and
- air CARGO.

Overall, the talks focus high-level attention on reducing certain market obstacles and opening communication channels to resolve follow-up disputes.

MARKET PRICE price established in the market where buyers and sellers meet to buy and sell similar products. *see also* MARKET ACCESS; MARKET DISRUPTION; PRICE ESCALATION; PRICE SUPPRESSION.

MARKET PROMOTION PROGRAM (MPP) program authorized by the U.S. Food, Agriculture, Conservation, and Trade Act of 1990 administered by the U.S. Department of Agriculture's Foreign Agricultural Service. Under the MPP, surplus stocks or funds from the COMMODITY CREDIT CORPORATION are used to partially reimburse agricultural organizations conducting specific foreign market development projects for eligible products in specified countries. Proposals for MPP programs are developed by trade organizations and private firms. Activities financed by the programs vary from COMMODITY to commodity and include activities such as market research, construction of a three-story wood demonstration building, construction of a model feed mill, and consumer promotion activities. MPP is broader in scope than the U.S. TARGETED EXPORT ASSISTANCE (TEA) PROGRAM, repealed by the 1990 U.S. Farm Bill, whose purpose was to assist exports of commodities hurt by unfair foreign trade practices.

MARKETING BOARDS agencies established in different countries responsible for managing the supply of agricultural products, in an attempt to stabilize prices and farm incomes. Example: the DAIRY EXPORT INCENTIVE PROGRAM (DEIP) is one of four EXPORT SUBSIDY programs operated by the U.S. Department of Agriculture (USDA), that help U.S. EXPORTERS meet prevailing world prices for targeted dairy products and destinations. The USDA pays cash to U.S. exporters as bonuses, allowing them to sell certain U.S. dairy products in targeted countries at prices below the exporter's costs of acquiring them. DEIP is used to help products produced by U.S. farmers meet competition from subsidizing countries. *see also* COMMON AGRICULTURAL POLICY.

MARKETING YEAR an alternative term used when referring to the reporting period for a COMMODITY in various governmental reports.

MARKING (MARKS) letters, numbers, and other symbols placed on CARGO packages to facilitate identification.

MARKKA unit of currency, Finland (100 penni equal 1 markka).

MARKS *see* MARKING.

MARKS OF ORIGIN the physical markings on a product that indicate the country of origin where the article was produced. CUSTOMS rules require marks of origin of most countries.

MARKUP terminology used by the WORLD TRADE ORGANIZATION (WTO), to refer to the extent to which an APPLIED TARIFF exceeds the BOUND RATE.

MARSHALL LERNER CONDITION economic theory that provides the conditions under which a DEVALUATION of a currency will help reduce a deficit in a country's BALANCE OF PAYMENTS. The theory assumes perfect elasticities in IMPORT and EXPORT supply. That is, the quantity supplied is affected by a change in the price. Example: a 10% devaluation will lead to a greater than 10% increase in exports, thus increasing foreign exchange receipts, which improves the country's balance of payments.

MARSHALL PLAN a plan implemented by the United States and many nations of Europe to promote economic recovery after World

War II. The plan was initially proposed in 1947 by Secretary of State George Marshall. The program distributed more than US$12 billion in aid from 1948 to 1951 and was administered by the Economic Cooperation Administration (ECA). It has also been referred to as the European Recovery Program.

MASTER'S PROTEST a sworn statement given by the captain of an oceangoing vessel describing any unusual happening that may have occurred during the voyage.

MATADOR BOND bond issued on the Spanish market, denominated in currencies other than the PESETA.

MATCHED SALES TECHNIQUE a technique used by firms to circumvent foreign government-imposed price controls. This approach couples the purchase of the price-controlled item with another item not subject to price controls.

MATCHMAKER EVENTS U.S. trade delegations organized and led by the U.S. International Trade Administration to help new-to-EXPORT and new-to-market firms meet prescreened prospects who are interested in their products or services in overseas markets. Matchmaker delegations usually target two major country markets and limit trips to a week or less. This approach is designed to permit U.S. firms to interview a maximum number of prospective overseas business partners with a minimum of time away from their home office. The program includes U.S. embassy support, briefings on market requirements and business practices, and interpreter services. Matchmaker events, based on specific product themes and end users, are scheduled for a limited number of countries each year.

MATCHMAKER PROGRAM (MKR) *see* MATCHMAKER EVENTS.

MATCHMAKER SERVICES *see* MATCHMAKER EVENTS.

MATCHMAKER TRADE DELEGATIONS *see* MATCHMAKER EVENTS.

MATERIAL CONTRACT TERMS terms in a CONTRACT that describe the goods, fix price, and set the delivery date.

MATE'S RECEIPT a receipt issued by a deck officer on a merchant ship acknowledging receipt of CARGO. This form of receipt is normally seen in instances where cargo is being shipped via CHARTERED vessel. *see also* BILL OF LADING; DOCK RECEIPT.

MATURITY DATE the date that the buyer is formally obligated to pay a note, DRAFT, or ACCEPTANCE to the seller or his/her representative.

MAURITIUS RUPEE unit of currency, Mauritius (100 cents equal 1 Mauritius rupee).

MAXI-DEVALUATION a major DEVALUATION of the currency of a country. This is usually required in a country with significant inflation problems and where existing devaluations have not been large enough to compensate for inflation. This has occurred in markets such as Brazil with the devaluation of the CRUZEIRO.

MAXIMUM INSURED AMOUNT (MIA) represents the contractually stipulated maximum allowable amount of actual insurance provided by the OVERSEAS PRIVATE INVESTMENT CORPORATION (OPIC). The difference between the CURRENT INSURED AMOUNT (CIA) and the MIA is called the STANDBY AMOUNT.

MAXIMUM PRICE SYSTEM specification of the highest price permitted for an import. *see also* MINIMUM PRICE SYSTEM.

MCCA abbreviation for Mercado Común Centroamericano. *see also* CENTRAL AMERICAN COMMON MARKET.

MDBs *see* MULTILATERAL DEVELOPMENT BANKS.

MDSE abbreviation for merchandise.

MEASUREMENT CARGO CARGO on which the transportation charge is assessed on the basis of measurement.

MEDIUM OF EXCHANGE any COMMODITY that is widely accepted in payment for goods and services and in settlement of debts. *see also* BARTER; COUNTERPURCHASE; COUNTERTRADE.

MEDIUM-TERM BULK AGRICULTURE CREDITS INSURANCE AND GUARANTEE PROGRAM a program of the Canadian EXPORT DEVELOPMENT CORPORATION (EDC), which provides insurance to Canadian EXPORTERS of bulk COMMODITIES on credit terms. *see also* COMMERCIAL RISKS; EXPORT FINANCING; POLITICAL RISKS; SHORT-TERM BULK AGRICULTURAL CREDITS INSURANCE.

MELTING POT a place where immigrants of different cultures or races abandon their distinctiveness, adopt new cultural values, and form an integrated society. It is a term often used when referring to the demographic structure of the United States. *see also* MULTICULTURALISM.

MEMORANDA OF UNDERSTANDING *see* INTERNATIONAL AGREEMENTS.

MEMORANDUM BILL OF LADING duplicate copy of the BILL OF LADING.

MEMORANDUM TARIFFS publications containing rule and rate information extracted from official TARIFFS.

MERCADO COMUN CENTROAMERICANO (MCC) *see* CENTRAL AMERICAN COMMON MARKET.

MERCANTILISM one of the first economic doctrines (1550–1800). The core of the theory holds that a nation's wealth is based on the amount of gold it has in its reserves. Nations with little or no gold reserves could increase their wealth by EXPORTING more than they IMPORT, and governments would control trade because individuals would trade gold for imports. *see also* ABSOLUTE ADVANTAGE; COMPARATIVE ADVANTAGE; TRADE BARRIERS.

MERCHANDISE EXPORTS goods sent or transported abroad or to another country. *see also* BALANCE OF PAYMENTS.

MERCHANDISE IMPORTS goods brought or transported into a country. *see also* BALANCE OF PAYMENTS.

MERCHANDISE TRADE EXPORTS and IMPORTS of goods. *see also* SERVICES.

MERCHANDISE TRADE BALANCE *see* BALANCE OF PAYMENTS.

MERCHANT BANKS *see* BANK.

MERCHANT'S CREDIT LETTER OF CREDIT issued by the buyer with no commitment on the part of a BANK. *see also* REVOCABLE LETTER OF CREDIT.

MERCHANT'S HAULAGE inland move from or to a port that has all arrangements made by the EXPORTER. *see also* LINE HAUL.

MERCOSUR (Spanish; Mercosul in Portuguese; English: Southern Common Market) a common external TARIFF, similar to the European Community's TREATY OF ROME, that establishes and eliminates barriers to trade in services. Mercosur is composed of Argentina, Brazil, Paraguay, and Uruguay. Mercosur entered into force in December 1994 for Argentina and Brazil and December 1995 for Paraguay and Uruguay. While in the SOUTHERN CONE, Chile has not sought entry to Mercosur, but Chile does have an agreement with Argentina that will provide for some similar benefits.

MERGER the combination of the operations of two or more commercial interests or corporations to form a new company. In a merger, the original companies cease to exist and are replaced by a new company.

MERRY-GO-ROUND circulation of money through various sources, completing where it started.

METHOD OF ADVICE means by which a COLLECTING BANK must send all advices to the bank from which the COLLECTION ORDER was received. This method is normally mail; however, if the collecting bank feels the situation is urgent, alternative methods such as TELEX and cable transfers, etc. may be used at the expense of the principal.

METHOD OF ENTRY the method by which a firm enters into a foreign country with its products, technology, human skills, management, or other resources. *see also* ASSEMBLY; CONTRACT MANUFACTURING; DIRECT EXPORT; DIRECT INVESTMENT; EXPORT; INDIRECT EXPORT; JOINT VENTURE; LICENSING; WHOLLY OWNED SUBSIDIARY.

METHOD OF TRANSPORTATION the mode of transport by which the merchandise is shipped (vessel, air, rail, truck, etc.).

METICAL (METICAIS) unit of currency, Mozambique.

MEXICAN NATIONAL FOREIGN TRADE BANK (BAN-COMEXT) *see* BANCONACIONAL DE COMERCIO EXTERIOR (BANCOMEXT).

MEXICAN PESO unit of currency, Mexico (100 centavos equal 1 Mexican peso). *see also* NUEVOS PESO.

MFA *see* MULTIFIBER ARRANGEMENT.

MFN *see* MOST-FAVORED-NATION TREATMENT.

MFN TARIFF tariff level that a member of the GENERAL AGREEMENT ON TARIFFS AND TRADE (GAAT) or WORLD TRADE ORGANIZATION (WTO) charges on a good to other members. *see also* AD VALOREM; GENERALIZED SYSTEM OF PREFERENCES; PERMANENT NORMAL TRADING RELATIONS; SPECIFIC TARIFF.

MFN STATUS status given by the U.S. to some non-members of the WORLD TRADE ORGANIZATION (WTO) where they are charged an MFN TARIFF even though they are eligible for higher tariffs. *see also* PERMANENT NORMAL TRADING RELATIONS.

MHW *see* MINISTRY OF HEALTH AND WELFARE.

MIB *see* MANAGEMENT INFORMATION BASE.

MICROBRIDGE LANDBRIDGE movement in which CARGO originating in or destined to an inland point is railed or trucked to or from the water port for a shipment to or from a FOREIGN country. *see also* MINIBRIDGE.

MID see MANUFACTURE IDENTIFICATION NUMBER.

MIDDLE EAST DEVELOPMENT BANK a proposal for a MULTILATERAL DEVELOPMENT BANK that would be headquartered either in Qatar, the United Arab Emirates, or Kuwait. It would focus on economic growth in the region, with emphasis on the areas of agriculture, transportation, energy, water supply, sanitation, education, and industrial development. *see also* ARAB FUND FOR ECONOMIC AND SOCIAL DEVELOPMENT; ARAB MONETARY FUND; ISLAMIC DEVELOPMENT BANK; OPEC FUND FOR INTERNATIONAL DEVELOPMENT.

MIDDLE PRODUCT a GOOD that has undergone some processing and requires further processing before going to consumers. *see also* CUSTOMS DUTY; CUSTOMS IMPORT VALUE (CIV); CUSTOMS VALUATION METHOD; VALUATION.

MIF *see* MULTILATERAL INVESTMENT FUND.

MIGA *see* MULTILATERAL INVESTMENT GUARANTEE AGENCY.

MIGRATION permanent relocation of people from one country to another. *see also* EMIGRATION; IMMIGRATION; NATION.

MILITARY ASSISTANCE PROGRAM *see* CONVENTIONAL ARMS TRANSFER.

MILITARY CRITICAL TECHNOLOGIES LIST (MTCL) a document listing technologies that the U.S. Defense Department considers to have current or future utility in military systems. The MCTL describes arrays of design and manufacturing know-how; keystone manufacturing, inspection, and test equipment; and goods accompanied by sophisticated operation, application, and maintenance know-how. Military justification for each entry is included in a classified version of the list.

MIME *see* MULTIPURPOSE INTERNET MAIL EXTENSIONS.

MINIBRIDGE movement of CARGO from a port over water, then over land to a port on an opposite coast. *see also* LANDBRIDGE; MICROBRIDGE.

MINIMUM CHARGE lowest rate applicable on each type of CARGO service, no matter how small the shipment.

MINIMUM IMPORT PRICE see MINIMUM PRICE SYSTEM.

MINIMUM PRICE SYSTEM specification of the lowest price permitted for an import. Prices below the minimum may trigger a TARIFF, hence a variable LEVY, or QUOTA. Also referred to as: basic import price, MINIMUM IMPORT PRICE, reference price, and TRIGGER PRICE.

MINISTER COUNSELOR (MC) *see* SENIOR COMMERCIAL OFFICER.

MINISTER OF INTERNATIONAL TRADE *see* TRADE MINISTER.

MINISTERIAL a meeting of ministers. In the circumstance that surround the GENERAL AGREEMENT ON TARIFFS AND TRADE (GATT) and the WORLD TRADE ORGANIZATION (WTO), it is a meeting of the TRADE MINISTERS from the member countries (including the United States and the U.S. TRADE REPRESENTATIVE [USTR]).

MINISTRY OF FOREIGN ECONOMIC RELATIONS AND TRADE (MOFERT) the People's Republic of China (PRC) Ministry of Foreign Economic Relations and Trade was established in March 1982 by combining former separate ministries. MOFERT implements national trade policies through administrative actions, drafts laws, and issues foreign trade regulations. MOFERT does not engage in foreign trade transactions, but facilitates the foreign trading corporations (FTCs) that do.

MINISTRY OF HEALTH AND WELFARE (MHW) Japan's agency responsible for regulating medical products under its Pharmaceutical Affairs Law. The ministry also is charged with determining Japanese health care expenditures.

MINISTRY OF INTERNATIONAL TRADE AND INDUSTRY (MITI) one of the three most powerful and prestigious ministries of the central government (along with the Ministry of Finance and the Ministry of Foreign Affairs) occupying a central position in Japan's economic bureaucracy. In formulating and implementing Japan's trade and industrial policies, MITI is responsible for funding most of

Japan's EXPORT PROMOTION programs (although operation of these programs is left to the JAPAN EXTERNAL TRADE ORGANIZATION, JETRO). The ministry also supervises the export financing programs of Japan's Export–Import Bank, operates several types of export insurance programs, supports research organizations, and facilitates various types of overseas technical and cooperation training programs. Lately, MITI has assumed a role in encouraging imports of foreign products into Japan.

MINISTRY OF POSTS AND TELECOMMUNICATIONS (MPT) Japan's telecommunications regulatory agency. The Ministry is authorized to adjust supply and demand among service providers to ensure that there is not excessive competition in a given market. To do so, MPT issues "administrative guidance" to the industry and recommends "unification" when there appears to be excessive competition in a given market.

MINT PARITY the requirement under the gold standard that each country define the gold content of its currency and that they be prepared to buy or sell gold at the price stated.

MIPRO *see* MANUFACTURED IMPORTS PROMOTION ORGANIZATION.

MISSILE TECHNOLOGY CONTROL REGIME (MTCR) organization established in April 1987 by Canada, France, Germany, Japan, the United Kingdom, and the United States. The purpose of the MTCR is to limit the proliferation of missiles "capable of delivering nuclear weapons," to increase regional stability, and to convey publicly the combined resolve of the partners to address this issue.

The regime expanded to include 23 countries, with the addition of Australia, Austria, Belgium, Denmark, Finland, Greece, Iceland, Ireland, Italy, Luxembourg, the Netherlands, New Zealand, Norway, Portugal, Spain, Sweden, and Switzerland. The MTCR does not have permanent organizations but convenes regular meetings to exchange information and coordinate member country stands. Under the MTCR, each member administers missile-related EXPORT controls independently. After the MTCR agrees that certain goods and technologies should be controlled for missile proliferation reasons, each member must implement the controls in its own domestic legislation. There is no international entity that oversees the implementation and enforcement of MTCR controls.

Items and technology agreed to be controlled by the MTCR partners are listed in the MTCR Annex. The annex is divided into two groups: Category I (consisting of complete rocket and unmanned air vehicle systems and subsystems) and Category II (encompassing components, equipment, technology, materials used in missile design, development, production or use).

MISSILE TECHNOLOGY EXPORT CONTROL GROUP (MTEC) a U.S. Department of State group that reviews trade applications involving missile technology concerns. *see also* OPERATING COMMITTEE.

MITBESTIMMUNG (German) the practice of having representatives of labor unions participate in the management of the firm by becoming members of the board of directors.

MITI *see* MINISTRY OF INTERNATIONAL TRADE AND INDUSTRY.

MIXED CREDIT the practice of combining concessional and market-rate EXPORT credit as an export promotion mechanism.

MIXED ECONOMY an economic system having a blending of private and government ownership. It is a system where the government allows private ownership, but retains control over those enterprises in key sectors.

MIXED TARIFF *see* COMPOUND DUTY.

MIXED VENTURE a form of JOINT VENTURE or partnership where the government establishes a relationship with a private firm.

MIXING REGULATION
1. specification of the proportion of domestically produced content in products sold on the domestic market. *see also* DOMESTIC CONTENT REQUIREMENTS (DCR); TRADE BARRIERS.
2. specification of an amount of domestically produced product that must be purchased by an IMPORTER for given quantities of IMPORTS. *see also* LINKING SCHEME.

MOCP *see* MARKET-ORIENTED COOPERATION PLAN.

MOD ACT refers to the U.S. CUSTOMS Modernization and Informed Compliance Act of 1992.

MODALITY method or procedure as to how negotiations are to be conducted. For example, WORLD TRADE ORGANIZATION (WTO) documents speak of modalities of negotiations.

MODE OF SUPPLY method by which suppliers of internationally traded SERVICES deliver their service to buyers. The four modes are CROSS-BORDER SUPPLY, CONSUMER MOVEMENT, PRODUCER PRESENCE, and MOVEMENT OF NATURAL PERSONS.

MOFERT *see* MINISTRY OF FOREIGN ECONOMIC RELATIONS AND TRADE.

MOL an acronym for the Ministry of Labor.

MOLOTOV COCKTAIL a crude incendiary bomb made of a bottle filled with flammable liquid and fitted with a rag wick.

MONETARISM theory stating that MONEY SUPPLY is the key determinant of economic activity of a country, being far more important than a government's FISCAL POLICY (taxes and expenditures). It is also referred to as the school of supply-side economics. *see also* KEYNESIAN ECONOMICS.

MONETARY POLICY government policy controlled by the CENTRAL BANK aimed at controlling the economy (inflation rates, interest rates, and economic growth) by controlling the MONEY SUPPLY. *see also* FISCAL POLICY.

MONETARY UNION a MULTILATERAL AGREEMENT between countries that have already united in an ECONOMIC UNION including a common currency, complete convertibility of the members' currencies, free movement of capital, and fixed and irrevocable EXCHANGE RATES between the currencies of the members. *see also* COMMON MARKET; DELORS REPORT; ECONOMIC MONETARY UNION.

MONEY any denomination of coin or paper currency of legal tender that passes freely as a MEDIUM OF EXCHANGE.

MONEY CREATION the increase in money supply by the commercial or CENTRAL BANK. *see also* FEDERAL RESERVE SYSTEM; FISCAL POLICY; MONETARY POLICY; MONEY SUPPLY.

MONEY LAUNDERING *see* LAUNDERING (OF MONEY).

MONEY MARKET the market for short-term financial instruments (i.e., commercial paper, treasury bills, discount notes). *see also* MONEY MARKET OPERATIONS.

MONEY MARKET OPERATIONS creating, investing in, buying, and selling short-term obligations in the market for short-term DEBT INSTRUMENTS. *see also* DEBT MARKET.

MONEY SUPPLY the total of coins, paper money, traveler's checks, demand deposits, time accounts, and credit union share drafts held by individuals, banks, and financial institutions in a country.

MONKEYPOX a Russian bioweapons program, which is in the same family as smallpox.

MONOPOLY an organization that controls production and distribution of a product or service for which there are no alternatives. It is characterized by high prices, the absence of competition, and nonresponsiveness to the needs of the consumers. *see also* INTERNATIONAL CARTEL; EXTRATERRITORIALITY; OLIGOPOLY.

MOOR to secure a vessel to an anchor, buoy, or pier. *see also* DISCHARGE; DOCK; MOORAGE.

MOORAGE describing charges assessed for mooring a vessel to a pier or wharf.

MORATORIUM a period of delay during which a nation suspends payments of EXTERNAL DEBTS, both interest and its principal. *see also* DEFAULT; NONPERFORMING ASSETS.

MORDIDA (Spanish) *see* BRIBERY.

MOROCCAN DIRHAM unit of currency, Morocco (100 centimes equal 1 Moroccan dirham).

MOSS *see* MARKET-ORIENTED, SECTOR-SELECTIVE.

MOST-FAVORED-NATION (MFN) TREATMENT commitment that a country will extend to another country the lowest TARIFF rates it applies to any other country. All contracting parties undertake to apply such treatment to one another under Article I of the GENERAL AGREEMENT ON TARIFFS AND TRADE (GATT). When a country agrees to cut tariffs on a particular product imported from one country, the tariff reduction automatically applies to IMPORTS of this product from any other country eligible for most-favored-nation treatment. This principle of nondiscriminatory treatment of imports appeared in numerous bilateral trade agreements prior to establishment of GATT. A country is under no obligation to extend MFN treatment to another country unless both are bilateral contracting parties of GATT or MFN treatment is specified in a bilateral agreement.

MOTHBALLING preservation of a production facility without using it to produce, but keeping the machinery in working order and the supplies available. This may be advantageous should the facility's operating costs be unusually high and the purpose is to have the facility available in time of war, as compared with having it produce in time of peace under a SUBSIDY. *see also* NATIONAL DEFENSE ARGUMENT.

MOTOR CARRIER'S TERMINAL location where loaded or empty shipping CONTAINERS are received or delivered by a motor CARRIER.

MOU *see* RECIPROCAL DEFENSE PROCUREMENT MEMORANDUM OF UNDERSTANDING.

MOVEMENT OF NATURAL PERSONS One of the four MODES OF SUPPLY under the GENERAL AGREEMENT ON TRADE-IN SERVICES, involving temporary movement across national borders by persons employed by or associated with a firm, in order to participate in the firm's business. *see also* CROSS-BORDER SUPPLY; CONSUMER MOVEMENT; PRODUCER PRESENCE; TEMPORARY PRODUCER MOVEMENT.

MPP *see* MARKET PROMOTION PROGRAM.

MPT *see* MINISTRY OF POSTS AND TELECOMMUNICATIONS.

MRAs *see* MUTUAL RECOGNITION AGREEMENTS.

MRU *see* MANO RIVER UNION.

MSA *see* MULTILATERAL STEEL AGREEMENT.

MTCL *see* MILITARY CRITICAL TECHNOLOGIES LIST.

MTCR *see* MISSILE TECHNOLOGY CONTROL REGIME.

MTN *see* MULTILATERAL TRADE NEGOTIATIONS.

MULLAH a Muslim, usually holding an official post, who is trained in traditional religious doctrine and law and doctrine.

MULTIBUYER POLICY a program of the EXPORT–IMPORT BANK OF THE UNITED STATES (EXIMBANK) that provides insurance coverage over all or a reasonable portion of an EXPORTER's short- and medium-term EXPORT credit sales. *see also* NEW-TO-EXPORT POLICY; SINGLE-BUYER POLICY; UMBRELLA POLICY.

MULTICULTURAL (MULTICULTURALISM) the demographic structure of a nation in which several differing cultures are included. Each group retains its own identity and cultural values, while still maintaining allegiance to the resident nation. *see also* MELTING POT.

MULTIDOMESTIC COMPANIES a method whereby a firm manages its international operations, in which the operations in one country are independent from those in other countries.

MULTIFIBER ARRANGEMENT (MFA) an international umbrella compact, authorized by the GENERAL AGREEMENT ON TARIFFS AND TRADE (GATT), that allows contracting parties to negotiate bilaterally quantitative restrictions on textile IMPORTS (which normally would be considered contrary to GATT provisions) to the extent the importing country considers them necessary to prevent market disruption.

The URUGUAY ROUND Agreement on Textiles and Clothing contains an agreed schedule for the gradual phase-out of quotas established pursuant to the MFA over a 10-year transition period, after which textile and clothing trade will be fully integrated into the GATT and subject to the same disciplines as other sectors. *see also* COMMITTEE FOR THE IMPLEMENTATION OF TEXTILE AGREEMENTS.

MULTILATERAL AGREEMENT an international compact in which three or more parties participate. *see also* BILATERAL AGREEMENT.

MULTILATERAL AGREEMENT ON INVESTMENT an agreement to liberalize rules on international DIRECT INVESTMENT that were negotiated in the ORGANIZATION FOR ECONOMIC COOPERATION AND DEVELOPMENT (OECD) but were never completed or adopted because of adverse public reaction.

MULTILATERAL DEVELOPMENT BANKS (MDBs) *see* AFRICAN DEVELOPMENT BANK; ASIAN DEVELOPMENT BANK; EUROPEAN BANK FOR RECONSTRUCTION AND DEVELOPMENT; INTER-AMERICAN DEVELOPMENT BANK; WORLD BANK.

MULTILATERAL INVESTMENT FUND (MIF) an outgrowth of the ENTERPRISE FOR THE AMERICAS INITIATIVE, the fund is administered by the Inter-American Development Bank. It provides program and project grants to advance investment reform and technical assistance for privatization movements in Latin America and the Caribbean and to encourage domestic and foreign investment in the area. The MIF was established in January 1993.

MULTILATERAL INVESTMENT GUARANTEE AGENCY (MIGA) a part of the WORLD BANK Group, MIGA encourages equity investment and other direct investment flows to developing countries through the mitigation of noncommercial investment barriers. Established in April 1988, the agency offers investors guarantees against noncommercial risks. It advises developing member governments on the design and implementation of policies, programs, and procedures related to foreign investments. It also sponsors a dialogue between the international business community and host governments on investment issues. MIGA provides coverage for equity interests, other forms of direct investment, industrial cooperation such as management and service contracts, licensing and franchising agreements, turnkey contracts, and arrangements concerning transfer of technology and know-how in which the investor assumes a stake in the performance of the venture.

MULTILATERAL STEEL AGREEMENT (MSA) the MSA would have addressed the underlying causes of unfair trade in steel by eliminating tariffs, nontariff measures such as quotas, and most subsidies in the steel sector and establishing a dispute-settlement mechanism. The United States and 34 other countries participated in negotiations for an MSA under the general auspices of the GENERAL AGREEMENT ON TARIFFS AND TRADE (GATT). MSA negotiations were suspended in March 1992, coincident with the expiration of the steel voluntary restraint agreements.

MULTILATERAL TRADE any transactions involving the movement of goods and services between four or more countries. *see also* BILATERAL TRADE; MULTILATERAL AGREEMENT; TRILATERAL TRADE.

MULTILATERAL TRADE NEGOTIATIONS (MTN) the eight multilateral ROUNDS of negotiations held under the auspices of the GENERAL AGREEMENT ON TARIFFS AND TRADE (GATT) since 1947.

MULTILATERAL TRADE ORGANIZATION (MTO) *see* GATT; NAFTA.

MULTILATERAL TREATY a legally binding agreement between several countries in written form and governed by international law. *see also* CONVENTION; INTERNATIONAL AGREEMENTS.

MULTIMODAL TRANSPORT transportation that includes at least two methods of transport, such as shipping by rail and by sea.

MULTINATIONAL CORPORATION a business that owns or controls product or service facilities outside the country in which it is based.

MULTINATIONAL ENTERPRISE *see* MULTINATIONAL CORPORATION.

MULTINATIONAL MARKETING *see* INTERNATIONAL MARKETING.

MULTIPLE DECLARATION FORM a form on which an IMPORTER will report IMPORT shipments scheduled to arrive, in order to request insurance coverage. The multiple declaration form allows the importer to report a grouping of shipments, as compared to a SINGLE-DECLARATION FORM. *see also* MARINE CARGO INSURANCE.

MULTIPLE-ENTRY VISA a specialized term used by immigration authorities to describe a visitor who is permitted multiple entries, without the need to reapply for each visit. The visa is a stamp on the foreign national's passport issued by a consular officer that allows the individual to enter the country. *see also* SINGLE-ENTRY VISA.

MULTIPLE EXCHANGE RATE *see* EXCHANGE CONTROLS.

MULTIPLE EXCHANGE RATE SYSTEM a system where a country's CENTRAL BANK will establish different EXCHANGE RATES for different types of transactions. *see also* DUAL EXCHANGE RATES; EXCHANGE CONTROLS; IMPORT DEPOSIT REQUIREMENTS; LICENSING.

MUNDELL–FLEMING MODEL an economic model of an economy with FLUCTUATING EXCHANGE RATES and perfect capital mobility.

MUNICIPAL JURISDICTION *see* DOMESTIC JURISDICTION.

MUNICIPAL PROPERTY TAX (IPTU) an annual tax levied by the Brazilian government on real estate in urban areas. The tax rates are computed on the fair market value of the real estate.

MUNICIPAL SERVICE TAX (ISS) a tax levied by the Brazilian government on most services, with rates ranging from 2% to 5%.

MUSLIM LAW *see* ISLAMIC LAW.

MUSTARD GAS blistering agents that cause severe damage to the eyes, internal organs, and respiratory system.

MUTUAL RECOGNITION acceptance by one country of another country's certification that a satisfactory STANDARD has been met for ability, performance, safety, etc. *see also* GATT STANDARDS CODE; MUTUAL RECOGNITION AGREEMENTS (MRAS).

MUTUAL RECOGNITION AGREEMENTS (MRAs) international agreements negotiated on a sectoral basis (such as telecommunications, medical devices, pharmaceuticals, chemicals, and processed foods) allowing countries to accept each other's final test results, although quality assurances may be required. Under MRAs, the entire testing and certification process may occur outside the importing country. Under MRAs within the EUROPEAN COMMUNITY (EC), a U.S. company would obtain product certification on an EC-wide basis, enabling the firm to market its products throughout the community. Based on private-law contractual negotiations, subcontracting permits a notified body of the EC to delegate some of its testing responsibilities to a third-country testing lab or quality assessment body. However, the notified body retains ultimate responsibility for final decisions relating to EC certification. Formal discussions between representatives of the U.S. government and the EUROPEAN ECONOMIC COMMUNITY (EEC) on entering MRAs began in October 1992.

MUTUALITY OF BENEFITS *see* RECIPROCITY.

MYONG-DONG one of the principal shopping areas in Seoul, Korea. Myong-Dong is the fashion center of Korea, consisting of numerous fashion salons and boutiques that offer styles and creations comparable to Paris and Rome.

N

N.A. GULDEN unit of currency, Netherlands Antilles (100 cents equal 1 GULDEN).

NAC *see* NATIONAL ADVISORY COUNCIL ON INTERNATIONAL MONETARY AND FINANCIAL POLICIES.

NACE *see* NORTH AMERICAN COMMISSION ON THE ENVIRONMENT.

NACIONAL FINANCIERA (NAFIN) Mexican financial agency that promotes growth in priority development areas. NAFIN provides financial assistance to small and medium-sized Mexican businesses, encourages foreign investment in Mexico, and supports technological development in Mexico. NAFIN headquarters is in Mexico City, Mexico.

NADBank *see* NORTH AMERICAN DEVELOPMENT BANK.

NAFIN *see* NACIONAL FINANCIERA.

NAFINSA an acronym used when referring to the Government Development Bank of Mexico. NAFINSA provides loans to foreign firms for direct investment in Mexico and provides facilities for IMPORT products. The purpose of NAFINSA is to provide aid in the development and diversification of the Mexican economy.

NAFO *see* NORTH ATLANTIC FISHERIES ORGANIZATION.

NAFTA *see* NORTH AMERICAN FREE TRADE AGREEMENT.

NAIRA unit of currency, Nigeria (100 kobos equal 1 naira).

NAK *see* NEGATIVE ACKNOWLEDGMENT.

NAL *see* NATIONAL AGRICULTURAL LIBRARY.

NAM *see* NONALIGNED MOVEMENT.

NAMESPACE widely used and distributed set of unique names on the INTERNET.

NARCOTERRORISM the view of many counterterrorist experts that an alliance exists between drug traffickers and political terrorists.

NASDA *see* NATIONAL ASSOCIATION OF STATE DEPARTMENTS OF AGRICULTURE; NATIONAL ASSOCIATION OF STATE DEVELOPMENT AGENCIES.

NATAP *see* NORTH AMERICAN TRADE AUTOMATION PROTOTYPE.

NATION a country with a single, usually independent government.

NATIONAL
1. of, relating to, or belonging to a NATION.
2. a person who is a CITIZEN or a long-term resident of a nation. *see also* NATURALIZATION.

NATIONAL ACCORD FOR RAISING PRODUCTIVITY AND QUALITY (ANEPC) a voluntary agreement among the CTM (Mexico's largest labor union), Mexican labor unions, and the Mexican government. The agreement called for the government and employers to pledge to invest more in upgrading worker skills, whereas organized labor agreed to negotiate workplace understandings with management on improving quality. Employers also pledged to reward workers for productivity increases.

NATIONAL ADVISORY COUNCIL ON INTERNATIONAL MONETARY AND FINANCIAL POLICIES (NAC) U.S. governmental advisory council responsible for coordinating U.S. participation in international financial institutions and the policies and practices of agencies of the U.S. government that make, or participate in making, foreign loans or that engage in foreign financial, exchange, or monetary transactions. With regard to international financial institutions, the council seeks to ensure that their operations are conducted in a manner consistent with U.S. policies and objectives and with lending and other foreign financial activities of U.S. government agencies. The council formulates and reviews policies and programs for use by the U.S. representatives to these institutions and advises the Secretary of the Treasury on
• policies and selected proposed transactions of the institutions;
• proposed actions by these institutions requiring U.S. approval on such subjects as the flotation of securities, increases in quotas and subscriptions, and changes in their articles of agreement; and
• problems relating to the administration and management of the international financial institutions.
  NAC membership includes the Departments of the Treasury (as chair), State, and Commerce; the U.S. TRADE REPRESENTATIVE (USTR), the Federal Reserve System, the U.S. Export–Import Bank, and the International Development Cooperation Agency.

NATIONAL AGENCY FOR ECONOMIC RIGHTS (SNDE) an agency of the Brazilian government responsible for exercising control over the prices of IMPORTS and EXPORTS and investigating cases in which it suspects that DUMPING may have occurred.

NATIONAL AGRICULTURAL LIBRARY (NAL) the NAL serves as the U.S. center for the international agricultural information system. In its international role, the NAL cooperates in database production, compilation of world lists of journals, publication exchange, cooperative indexing, and intern training. The NAL's AGRICOLA database covers all aspects of agriculture via bibliographic records to documents, including international agricultural trade topics such as policy, research, flows of COMMODITIES, and environmental, taxation, and sociological impacts. AGRICOLA is produced solely by the NAL. The NAL's Agricultural Trade and Marketing Information Center (ATMIC) disseminates information on agribusiness, COUNTERTRADE (BARTER), EXPORTS, and trade development. The NAL is located in Beltsville, Maryland. *see also* AGRICULTURAL MARKETING SERVICE (AMS).

NATIONAL ASSOCIATION OF EXPORT COMPANIES a nonprofit organization in the United States that acts as the information provider, support clearinghouse forum, and advocate for those involved in exporting and servicing EXPORTERS.

NATIONAL ASSOCIATION OF STATE DEPARTMENTS OF AGRICULTURE (NASDA) a nonprofit, nonpartisan organization of the 50 U.S. state departments of agriculture and those from the U.S. trust territories of Puerto Rico, Guam, American Samoa, and the Virgin Islands. NASDA's headquarters is in Washington, DC.

NATIONAL ASSOCIATION OF STATE DEVELOPMENT AGENCIES (NASDA) forum formed in 1946 for directors of U.S. state economic development agencies to exchange information, compare programs, and deal with issues of mutual interest. NASDA's organization includes International Trade and Foreign Investment components. Trade activities include maintenance of a State Export Program Database.

NATIONAL BANK OF POLAND (NBP) the CENTRAL BANK of Poland. It is responsible for issuing currency, holding FOREIGN EXCHANGE reserves, administering exchange regulations, and acting as the government's bank. It also functions as the central clearing house for all banks and is responsible for the supervision of all private banks in Poland.

NATIONAL BANK OF ROMANIA the CENTRAL BANK of Romania. It is responsible for the regulation of credit and currency in the economy, establishment of a FOREIGN EXCHANGE policy through the setting of EXCHANGE RATES, and supervision of those entities authorized to conduct foreign exchange transactions. Additionally, it is responsible for maintaining Romania's international foreign reserves and monitoring and controlling the activities of the commercial banks.

NATIONAL COUNCIL ON INTERNATIONAL TRADE DOCUMENTATION (NCITD) a private organization that provides several low-cost publications that contain information on specific documentation commonly used in international trade. NCITD provides a free listing of its publications. NCITD's address is National Council on International Trade Documentation, 350 Broadway, Suite 1200, New York, NY 10013.

NATIONAL CUSTOMS BROKERS & FORWARDERS ASSOCIATION OF AMERICA, INC. (NCBFAA) represents more than 700 member companies including major American FREIGHT FORWARDERS,

CUSTOMS BROKERS, and air cargo agents. The organization facilitates international trade through its expertise in logistics management and IMPORT/EXPORT procedures and regulations. It also expedites the movement of goods across borders. NCBFAA has been in existence for more than 100 years.

NATIONAL DEFENSE ARGUMENT FOR PROTECTION argument that IMPORTS should be restricted to sustain a domestic industry so that it will be available in case of trade disruption due to war. *see also* SUBSIDY; MOTHBALLING; STOCKPILING.

NATIONAL DEFENSE EXECUTIVE RESERVE (NDER) program, operated by the U.S. DEPARTMENT OF COMMERCE BUREAU OF EXPORT ADMINISTRATION (BXA), that recruits and trains experienced business executives and other qualified civilians to serve in key government positions during periods of emergency. These reservists would augment Department of Commerce staff as required to respond to national security emergencies.

NATIONAL ECONOMIC DEVELOPMENT AUTHORITY (NEDA) an independent agency of the government of the Philippines responsible for the development and coordination of programs that bring about optimal use of limited resources for the development of the country.

NATIONAL EXPATRIATE *see* EXPATRIATE.

NATIONAL FOUNDATION OF TOURISM (FONATUR) a private Mexican organization that supports the government's policy of tourism investment. It works with the Secretary of Tourism to identify private investors for designated projects and provides incentives for firms investing in these projects. These incentives can be very complex and differ from project to project. The incentives offered include low-interest loans, tax reductions, labor exemptions, and debt for equity swaps.

NATIONAL INCOME AND PRODUCT ACCOUNTS (NIPA) *see* BALANCE OF PAYMENTS (BOP).

NATIONAL INSTITUTE OF STANDARDS AND TECHNOLOGY (NIST) U.S. governmental body that provides assistance in developing standards. Formerly the National Bureau of Standards.

NATIONAL INTELLIGENCE COUNCIL (NIC) organization made up of the U.S. National Intelligence Officers. It concentrates on problems of particular geographic regions and functional areas such as economics and chemical/biological warfare.

NATIONAL MONETARY COUNCIL (CMN) (Conselho Monetario Nacional) the National Monetary Council in Brazil. The President of the CMN is the Minister of Finance, and the council consists of representatives from both government and the private sector. The CMN is responsible for the formulation of monetary and credit policy. *see also* CENTRAL BANK OF BRAZIL (BACEN).

NATIONAL PHARMACEUTICAL STOCKPILE a stock of vaccines and antidotes stored at Centers for Disease Control and Prevention in Atlanta, to be used against biological warfare.

NATIONAL RESEARCH AND EDUCATION NETWORK (NREN) the realization of an interconnected gigabit computer NETWORK devoted to high-performance computing and communications. *see also* IINREN.

NATIONAL SALARY a form of HOST COUNTRY compensation given to EXPATRIATES. It is often necessary to provide or develop a theoretical HOME COUNTRY base for the purpose of certain benefit plans. *see also* BASE SALARY; U.S. SOURCE INCOME.

NATIONAL SCIENCE FOUNDATION (NSF) a U.S. government agency whose purpose is to promote the advancement of science. NSF funds science researchers, scientific projects, and infrastructure to improve the quality of scientific research. *see also* NSFNET.

NATIONAL SECURITY CONTROLS U.S. national security controls restricting EXPORTS of U.S. goods and technology that would make a significant contribution to the military potential of another country and thus be detrimental to Western countries' national security.

NATIONAL SECURITY COUNCIL (NSC) U.S. security council established by the National Security Act of 1947 to advise the President with respect to the integration of domestic, foreign, and military policies relating to national security.

NATIONAL SECURITY DIRECTIVES (NSDs) policy or procedural guidance signed by the president of the United States. In 1989, the president reorganized the NATIONAL SECURITY COUNCIL (NSC) committee process. As reorganized, under the NSC, there are committees for COCOM, terrorism, nonproliferation, etc. NSDs were known as National Security Decision Directives (NSDDs) before President Bush's reorganization. NSD-1 reorganized the process, and NSD-10 established the committees. The scope of coverage and the players are about the same under the NSD and NSDD processes.

NATIONAL SECURITY DIRECTIVE #53 (NSD #53) specific U.S. National Security time guidelines for outside agency review of EXPORT license applications. This directive also established a series of escalation levels to ensure that disagreements among U.S. agencies are resolved within the time requirements of the EXPORT ADMINISTRATION ACT (EAA). The EAA requires that all DUAL-USE EXPORT license applications referred by the U.S. DEPARTMENT OF COMMERCE to outside agencies for review be completed within 60 days after receipt. The EAA directs that an export license application should be completed within 120 days maximum. In order to clarify those time guidelines, the NATIONAL SECURITY COUNCIL and the president of the United States issued NSD #53 in December 1990.

NATIONAL SECURITY OVERRIDE (NSO) circumstance where U.S. government control is maintained over exports of a COMMODITY because it is deemed a national security-sensitive item, despite a finding of its foreign availability.

The term has also been used in other contexts. For example, under a November 16, 1990 directive, the president of the United States asked interagency control groups to move as many dual-use items as possible from the U.S. Department of State's INTERNATIONAL MUNITIONS LIST to the U.S. DEPARTMENT OF COMMERCE'S COMMERCE CONTROL LIST. In some circumstances, a national security override is applied to prevent transfer of a particular item.

NATIONAL SOVEREIGNTY *see* SOVEREIGN (SOVEREIGNTY).

NATIONAL TOURISM POLICY ACT U.S. legislation, passed in 1981, that created the U.S. TRAVEL AND TOURISM ADMINISTRATION, requiring the establishment of the Tourism Policy Council and the Travel and Tourism Advisory Board.

NATIONAL TRADE DATA BANK (NTDB) international economic and EXPORT promotion information supplied by 19 U.S. agencies. Data are updated monthly and are presented in one of three standard formats: text, time series, or matrix. The NTDB contains data from the U.S. Departments of Agriculture (Foreign Agricultural Service), COMMERCE (Bureau of the Census, Bureau of Economic Analysis, U.S. INTERNATIONAL TRADE ADMINISTRATION (ITA), and National Institute for Standards and Technology), Energy, and Labor (Bureau of Labor Statistics); the Central Intelligence Agency, EXIMBANK, the Federal Reserve System; U.S. INTERNATIONAL TRADE COMMISSION (ITC); OVERSEAS PRIVATE INVESTMENT CORPORATION (OPIC); Small Business Administration; the U.S. TRADE REPRESENTATIVE (USTR); and the University of Massachusetts (MISER data on state origins of exports).

NATIONAL TRADE ESTIMATES REPORT (NTE) an annual report prepared by the U.S. TRADE REPRESENTATIVE (USTR) that identifies significant foreign barriers to and distortions of trade.

NATIONAL TREATMENT process of giving individuals and firms of foreign countries the same competitive opportunities, including market access, as are available to domestic parties.

NATIONALIZATION the process of transferring ownership of foreign-owned private property from a private company to the foreign government with compensation being provided by the government to the company's foreign owners. *see also* CONFISCATION; EXPROPRIATION.

NATO *see* NORTH ATLANTIC TREATY ORGANIZATION.

NATURAL ADVANTAGE an international trade theory referring to an advantage a country has in the production of a particular product due to conditions such as climate or access to certain natural resources. *see also* ABSOLUTE ADVANTAGE; ACQUIRED ADVANTAGE; COMPARATIVE ADVANTAGE.

NATURAL LAW a law or body of laws derived from nature that is binding upon human actions apart from or in conjunction with established laws. It is derived from the Latin *jus naturale* and it is based on reason, fairness, and equity.

NATURAL RESOURCE anything that is provided by nature, such as deposits of minerals, quality of land, old-growth forests, and fish populations. The availability of particular natural resources is an important determinant of COMPARATIVE ADVANTAGE and trade-in products that depend on them. Natural resources constitute primary factor of production, which include land, labor, and capital. *see also* FACTOR ENDOWMENT, HECKSCHER-OHLIN THEORY.

NATURAL RESOURCE-BASED PRODUCTS (NRBPs) a GATT Negotiating Group formed as a direct result of pressure from resource-rich LESS-DEVELOPED COUNTRIES to have an additional forum to deal with their special concerns, including the removal of barriers to trade in natural resource-based products. There are different interpretations among participants as to whether this group includes only three traditional product areas examined during the early 1980s GATT Work Program on NRBPs (nonferrous metals and minerals; fish and fish products; and wood and wood products) or whether the group may also discuss barriers in nontraditional product areas such as energy-based products.

NATURAL TRADE trade that is either free or restricted, but not artificially encouraged by SUBSIDIES.

NATURALIZATION the process of granting full citizenship to a person of foreign birth. In turn, this person pledges to obey and uphold the laws of the state.

NBA *see* NIGER BASIN AUTHORITY.

NBP *see* NATIONAL BANK OF POLAND.

NCBFAA *see* NATIONAL CUSTOMS BROKERS & FORWARDERS ASSOCIATION OF AMERICA, INC.

NCTA *see* NORTHWEST CORRIDOR TRANSIT AGREEMENT.

NDER *see* NATIONAL DEFENSE EXECUTIVE RESERVE.

NEA *see* NUCLEAR ENERGY AGENCY.

NEBS *see* NEW EXPORTERS TO BORDER STATES.

NECESSITY TEST a procedure to determine whether a TRADE BARRIER intended to serve some purpose is necessary for that purpose. *see also* CONSUMPTION EFFECT OF A TARIFF; PRODUCTION EFFECT OF A TARIFF; TRADE DISPUTE ASSISTANCE.

NEGATIVE ACKNOWLEDGMENT (NAK) computer response to receipt of a corrupted packet of information. *see also* ACKNOWLEDGMENT.

NEGATIVE DIFFERENTIAL a circumstance when a calculation for an allowance provided to an employee, such as a COST DIFFERENTIAL, is negative. Example: a negative differential occurs when foreign assignment costs are lower than HOME COUNTRY COSTS.

NEGATIVE LIST a list in an international agreement of those items, entities, or products to which agreement will *not* apply, the commitment being to apply the agreement to everything else. *see also* POSITIVE LIST.

NEGOTIABLE legally capable of being transferred by endorsement or delivery. *see also* LETTER OF CREDIT (L/C); NEGOTIABLE BILL OF LADING; ORDER BILL OF LADING.

NEGOTIABLE BILL OF LADING BILL OF LADING transferred by ENDORSEMENT. *see also* ORDER BILL OF LADING.

NEMAWASHI the Japanese method of arriving at a decision through consensus. The process enables all individuals to participate in the process by allowing them to state their opinions before acceptance of the decision by all members.

NEOMERCANTALISM *see* MERCANTILISM.

NEPALESE RUPEE unit of currency, Nepal (100 piasa equal 1 Nepalese rupee).

NERVE AGENT insecticides developed into chemical weapons. Some of the better known nerve agents include VX, sarin, soman, and tabun. Nerve agents can be inhaled or absorbed through intact skin.

NESTED describing an item that is packed within another.

NET
1. computer NETWORK.
2. abbreviation for INTERNET.

NET CASH payment for goods sold without any deduction allowed from the price.

NET EXPORTS see BALANCE OF TRADE (BOT).

NET FOREIGN ASSET POSITION value of the assets that a country owns abroad minus the value of the domestic assets owned by foreigners. *see also* BALANCE OF INDEBTEDNESS.

NET FOREIGN INVESTMENT the sum of U.S. EXPORTS of goods and services, receipts of factor income, and capital grants received by the United States (net), less the sum of IMPORTS of goods and services by the United States, payments of factor income, and transfer payments to foreigners (net). It may also be viewed as the acquisition of foreign assets by U.S. residents, less the acquisition of U.S. assets by foreign residents.

NET LIQUIDITY BALANCE a statement of a country's accounting position described as the balance of all transactions including all

CURRENT ACCOUNT, long-term capital, and short-term nonliquid asset transactions. *see also* BALANCE OF PAYMENTS.

NET NATIONAL PRODUCT market value of the net output of goods and services produced by the nation's economy. *see also* GROSS DOMESTIC PRODUCT (GDP); GROSS NATIONAL PRODUCT (GNP).

NET PRICE price after all deductions, discounts, and rebates have been taken.

NET WEIGHT (ACTUAL NET WEIGHT) weight of the goods alone without any immediate wrappings. Example: the weight of the contents of a tin can without the weight of the can. *see also* GROSS WEIGHT; LEGAL WEIGHT.

NETTING an important cash management strategy used by multinational firms enabling them to lower the amount of cash flow by moving cash between subsidiaries more quickly and efficiently. The netting process refers to foreign subsidiaries in a net payable position, forwarding funds to a central clearing account and then having the clearing account manager forward these accounts to the net receiver subsidiaries. The advantages of such a process are savings of FOREIGN EXCHANGE conversion costs, savings on transfer charges and commissions, and faster access to funds.

NETIQUETTE a pun on "etiquette" referring to proper behavior on a computer NETWORK.

NETWORK
1. a computer data communications system that interconnects computer systems at various sites. A network may be composed of any combination of individual work stations or LANS. *see also* INTERNET.
2. an electronic trading and communications service developed by the World Trade Centers Association in cooperation with G.E. Information Services that enables a subscriber to place any offers and inquiries on an electronic bulletin board.

NETWORK FILE SYSTEM (NFS) a de facto INTERNET standard NETWORK protocol created by Sun Microsystems Corporation. It enables networked computer systems to easily share files. The protocol has been widely adopted by other companies.

NEUTRAL AIR WAYBILL standard AIR WAYBILL without identification of issuing CARRIER.

NEW CEDI unit of currency, Ghana.

NEW ECONOMY term was used in the late 1990s to suggest that GLOBALIZATION and innovations in information technology had changed the way that the world economy works.

NEW EXPORTERS OVERSEAS (NEXOS) *see* EXPORT SUPPORT PROGRAMS.

NEW EXPORTERS TO BORDER STATES (NEBS) *see* EXPORT SUPPORT PROGRAMS.

NEW EXPORTS TO U.S. SOUTH (NEXUS) *see* EXPORT SUPPORT PROGRAMS.

NEW HAVEN RESIDUAL FUEL a daily column appearing in the JOURNAL OF COMMERCE that lists the prices of heavy fuels from four companies (Buckley, Coastal, Hess, and Wyatt).

NEW INTERNATIONAL ECONOMIC ORDER (NEIO) initiated during the Sixth Special Session of the United National General Assembly in 1974 when it adopted the Charter of Economic Rights and Duties of States. The NEIO is an informal political organization, symbolizing a consensus among the world's developing countries that DEPENDENT DEVELOPMENT is not desirable.

NEW MONEY
1. financing made available to the IMPORTER or EXPORTER in a private commercial venture from private sources on the basis of meeting certain specific conditions.
2. international debt financing funds made available to countries with critical BALANCE OF PAYMENT problems by members of the PARIS CLUB. *see also* GROUP OF TEN.

NEW PRODUCT INFORMATION SERVICE (NPIS) program providing worldwide publicity for new U.S. products available for immediate EXPORT. This information is disseminated through the U.S. DEPARTMENT OF COMMERCE publication COMMERCIAL NEWS USA (CNUSA).

NEW TAIWAN DOLLAR unit of currency, Taiwan. *see also* YUAN.

NEW TECH a regular column appearing in the Transportation and Trade Technology section of the JOURNAL OF COMMERCE. It profiles new products.

NEW-TO-EXPORT an action that results from documented assistance to a company that accommodates a client's first verifiable EXPORT sale. Either the company has not exported to any destination during the past 24 months or prior exports either have resulted from unsolicited orders or were received through a U.S.-based intermediary.

NEW-TO-EXPORT POLICY an EXIMBANK program available to firms beginning to EXPORT or small businesses with an average annual export credit sales volume in the prior 2 years of less than $2 million. The policy provides enhanced coverage at premiums lower than those usually found in regular policies. The coverage covers either political or commercial risks.

NEW-TO-MARKET (NTM) a reportable new-to-market EXPORT action that results from documented assistance to an EXPORTER, which facilitates a verifiable sale in a new foreign market. Either the company has not exported to that market during the past 24 months or previous exports to that market either have resulted from unsolicited orders or were received through a U.S.-based intermediary.

NEW ZEALAND DOLLAR unit of currency, New Zealand (100 cents equal 1 New Zealand dollar).

NEWLY INDEPENDENT STATES (NIS) a collective reference to 12 republics of the former Soviet Union: Russia, Ukraine, Belarus (formerly Byelorussia), Moldova (formerly Moldavia), Armenia, Azerbaijan, Uzbekistan, Turkmenistan, Tajikistan, Kazakhstan, Kirgizstan (formerly Kirghiziya), and Georgia. Following dissolution of the Soviet Union, the distinction between the NIS and the COMMONWEALTH OF INDEPENDENT STATES (CIS) was that Georgia was not a member of the CIS. That distinction dissolved when Georgia joined the CIS in November 1993.

NEWLY INDUSTRIALIZING COUNTRIES (NICs) nations of the THIRD WORLD that have enjoyed rapid economic growth and can be described as middle-income countries (such as Singapore and the Republic of Korea). The term was originated by the ORGANIZATION FOR ECONOMIC COOPERATION AND DEVELOPMENT (OECD).

NEWLY INDUSTRIALIZING ECONOMIES (NIEs) the more advanced developing countries in East Asia. The reference includes Hong Kong, Korea, Singapore, and Taiwan; occasionally its use encompasses other countries such as Indonesia and Thailand.

NEWSGROUP a USENET conference.

NEXOS *see* NEW EXPORTERS OVERSEAS.

NEXUS *see* NEW EXPORTS TO U.S. SOUTH.

NGO *see* NONGOVERNMENTAL ORGANIZATION.

NGULTRUM unit of currency, Bhutan (100 chetrum equal 1 ngultrum).

NIB *see* NORDIC INVESTMENT BANK.

NICs *see* NEWLY INDUSTRIALIZING COUNTRIES.

NICE AGREEMENT CONCERNING THE INTERNATIONAL CLASSIFICATION OF GOODS AND SERVICES FOR THE PURPOSES OF THE REGISTRATION OF MARKS a MULTILATERAL TREATY that promotes the protection of intellectual property around the world through cooperation among states. The treaty is administered by the WORLD INTELLECTUAL PROPERTY ORGANIZATION (WIPO). Also known as the Nice Agreement or the Geneva Act of the Nice Agreement.

NICHE
1. the process of a firm identifying a specific position in the marketplace not usually serviced by a competitor.
2. a strategy employed by international firms to specialize in a particular segment of an already well-developed market.

NICHE MARKETING *see* NICHE.

NICHE STRATEGY *see* NICHE.

NICHERS *see* NICHE.

NIEs *see* NEWLY INDUSTRIALIZING ECONOMIES.

NIGER BASIN AUTHORITY (NBA) (French: Autorité du Bassin du Neiger) the authority regulates navigation, publishes statistics and hydrological forecasts, and promotes environmental control and agricultural and infrastructure development. The NBA fosters coordinated development of the Niger Basin area. The NBA's predecessor organization was established in 1964, and its headquarters is in Niamey, Niger. NBA members include Benin, Burkina Faso, the Cameroon, Chad, Côte d'Ivoire, Guinea, Mali, Niger, and Nigeria.

NIGERIA TRUST FUND (NTF) a Nigerian fund administered by the African Development Bank and established in February 1976. The NTF grants loans on preferential terms to finance projects in Nigeria in cooperation with other lending institutions.

NIHON KEIZAI SHIMBUN the financial daily newspaper in Japan reporting on the activities of the NIKKEI. It is a publication comparable to the *Wall Street Journal* in the United States, *The Financial Times* of London, and the *Globe* and the *Mail* in Toronto, Canada.

NIKKEI the Tokyo Stock Exchange. The Nikkei index is a measure of performance of 225 important stocks listed on the exchange. This index is comparable to the Dow Jones Industrial Average on the New York Stock Exchange or the TSE 300 Composite Index, which measures performance on the Toronto Stock Exchange.

NIKKEIREN the Japanese Federation of Employer's Associations. *see also* ZAIKAI.

NIPPON TELEGRAPH AND TELEPHONE CORPORATION (NTT) Japan's largest telecommunications enterprise, converted from a public corporation to a private enterprise in April 1985. Although competition has been allowed, the Japanese government still owns the majority of NTT stock, and postponement of a decision on NTT divestiture is an issue of considerable importance to market access by foreign companies. NTT was established in 1952.

NIS *see* NEWLY INDEPENDENT STATES.

NIST *see* NATIONAL INSTITUTE OF STANDARDS AND TECHNOLOGY.

NME nonmarket economy. *see also* COMMUNISM.

NNPA *see* NUCLEAR NONPROLIFERATION ACT.

NNPT *see* NUCLEAR NONPROLIFERATION TREATY.

N.O.E. abbreviation for not otherwise enumerated.

N.O.H.P. abbreviation for not otherwise herein provided.

N.O.I.B.N. abbreviation for not otherwise indicated by number or not otherwise indexed by name.

NOMENKLATURA a patronage system common in the former Soviet Union and some other communist states that controlled important committees at various levels of the Communist Party. *see also* HABATSU.

NOMINAL EXCHANGE RATE actual EXCHANGE RATE at which currencies are exchanged on an EXCHANGE MARKET. *see also* REAL EXCHANGE RATE.

NOMINAL INTEREST RATE interest rate actually observed in the market. *see also* REAL INTEREST RATE.

NOMINAL RATE OF PROTECTION a TARIFF rate applied to lower-priced foreign GOODS to protect domestic producers, enabling them to be competitive with the foreign producer. Example: goods valued at US$100 that are imported into the United States and subject to a nominal tariff rate of 10% would generate an additional cost of US$10 for the IMPORTER (domestic buyer). *see also* EFFECTIVE RATE OF PROTECTION.

NOMINAL TARIFF the taxes or DUTIES charged on merchandise being imported into a country. *see also* AD VALOREM DUTY.

NONACTIONABLE SUBSIDY a SUBSIDY that is permitted by the rules of the WORLD TRADE ORGANIZATION (WTO) and is not subject to COUNTERVAILING DUTY (CVD). These include NONSPECIFIC SUBSIDIES, subsidies for industrial research, REGIONAL AIDS, and some ENVIRONMENTAL SUBSIDIES.

NONALIGNED MOVEMENT (NAM) an alliance of THIRD-WORLD states that aims to promote the political and economic interests of DEVELOPING COUNTRIES. The name originated in a declaration of neutrality issued at the Conference of Non-Aligned Countries in Belgrade, Yugoslavia, in September 1961. NAM interests have included ending colonialism/neocolonialism, supporting the integrity of independent countries, and seeking a new international economic order.

NONAUTOMATIC LICENSING import licensing that is discretionary, based on an IMPORT QUOTA, or performance related.

NONCONFERENCE LINE a shipping line that transports ocean CARGO but is not a member of a CONFERENCE. *see also* CONFERENCE LINE.

NONCONVERTIBLE CURRENCY *see* SOFT CURRENCY.

NONGOVERNMENTAL ORGANIZATIONS (NGOs) private-sector nonprofit organizations that contribute to development in developing countries through such activities as development cooperation projects, financial aid, material aid, the dispatch of personnel, the acceptance of trainees, and development education. In this context,

NGOs are accredited by the UNITED NATIONS or its specialized agencies and can lobby and do business with them.

NONIMMIGRANT VISA a term used when allowing a foreigner entrance and permission to establish a temporary residence in the United States.

NONINCOTERMS terms of sales used in international transactions that are common and acceptable between and among those who use them. However, because the use of these terms is limited, they are not legitimized by the INTERNATIONAL CHAMBER OF COMMERCE. *see also* INCOTERMS.

NONMARKET ECONOMY (NME) *see* COMMUNISM.

NONPERFORMING ASSETS loans provided to THIRD-WORLD countries by financial institutions where payment of the principal or interest on the debt has been suspended or canceled. *see also* DEFAULT; EXTERNAL DEBT.

NONPUBLIC RECORD an account of information or facts, recorded in writing as a means of preserving knowledge not available to the general public.

NONRECOURSE FINANCING the process of making funds available to capitalize a TRADE transaction in which the individual providing the capital can receive payment from no one except the issuer who tendered the instrument. *see also* FORFAITING.

NONRESIDENT CONVERTIBILITY the ability of a nonresident of a country to convert currency in a bank to the currency of another country. *see also* CONVERTIBLE CURRENCY.

NONSPECIFIC SUBSIDY a SUBSIDY that is available to more than a single industry and is therefore a NONACTIONABLE SUBSIDY under the rules of the WORLD TRADE ORGANIZATION (WTO).

NONTARIFF BARRIERS (NTBs) barriers or restrictions to trade that are NONTARIFF in nature. The classes of nontariff barriers are
   1. quantitative restrictions such as quotas, "Buy Local Legislation," VOLUNTARY EXPORT RESTRAINTS, and ORDERLY MARKETING ARRANGEMENTS;
   2. administrative regulations such as specific permission requirements, IMPORT/EXPORT LICENSES, FOREIGN EXCHANGE CONTROLS, performance and SURETY bonds;
   3. technical regulations such as packing, labeling, and marking requirements; and
   4. direct price influences such as EXPORT SUBSIDIES and CUSTOMS VALUATION.

NONTARIFF MEASURES (NTMs) an imprecise barrier to IMPORTS. Some of the most commonly used NTMs include IMPORT quotas or other quantitative restrictions; nonautomatic IMPORT licensing,

CUSTOMS surcharges, or other fees and charges; customs procedures; EXPORT subsidies; unreasonable standards or standards-setting procedures; government procurement restrictions, inadequate intellectual property protection, and investment restrictions.

Participants in the TOKYO ROUND attempted to address these barriers through the negotiations of a number of GATT codes, open for signature to all GATT members. Seven codes were negotiated during the Tokyo Round, covering customs valuations, import licensing, subsidies and COUNTERVAILING DUTIES, ANTIDUMPING DUTIES, standards, government procurement, and trade in civil aircraft.

Although the Tokyo Round codes had alleviated some of the problems caused by nontariff measures, overall use of NTMs has increased since conclusion of the Tokyo Round.

NONTRADABLE GOOD a COMMODITY that, by its nature, cannot be traded internationally. *see also* NONTRADED GOODS AND SERVICES.

NONTRADED GOODS AND SERVICES GOODS for which supply and demand exists; however, they are not traded for certain reasons, such as the cost of transportation. *see also* INVISIBLE TRADE.

NONVESSEL OPERATING COMMON CARRIER (NVOCC) a small ocean CARGO shipment consolidator that functions as a carrier; however, it does not own any vessels. The NVOCC consolidates these small shipments and then in turn offers the container loads to ocean carriers. These firms transport cargo for clients, issue BILLS OF LADING, and assume responsibilities for shipments. *see also* FOREIGN FREIGHT FORWARDER.

NONVESSEL OWNING CARRIER (NVOC) a company that consolidates and disperses international containers that originate at, or are bound for, inland ports.

NON-VIOLATION a complaint that a country's action, though not a violation of WORLD TRADE ORGANIZATION (WTO) rules, has nullified or impaired a member's expected benefits from the agreement. *see also* NULLIFICATION.

NORAD *see* NORWEGIAN AGENCY FOR DEVELOPMENT COOPERATION.

NORDIC COUNCIL an all-Nordic-countries group, established in 1952, directed toward supporting cooperation in communications, cultural, economics, environmental, fiscal, legal, and social areas. Members include Denmark, Finland, Iceland, Norway, and Sweden. Council headquarters is in Stockholm, Sweden.

NORDIC INVESTMENT BANK (NIB) a Nordic bank that began operating in December 1975. It promotes economic cooperation and development by providing resources and guarantees for EXPORTS and for capital investment projects. Bank members include Denmark, Finland, Iceland, Norway, and Sweden. Bank headquarters is in Helsinki, Finland.

NORGES BANK the CENTRAL BANK of Norway. It is responsible for administering the exchange control regulations and issuing applicable licenses under existing regulations.

NORGES STATSAUTORISERTE REVISORERS FORENING (NSRF) one of two professional agencies accrediting auditors in Norway. The other is the REGISTRERTE REVISORERS FORENING (RRF). The NSRF is a member of the INTERNATIONAL ACCOUNTING STANDARDS COMMITTEE (IASC), the International Federation of Accountants (IFA), and the Fédération Européene des Experts-Compatables de la CEE (FEE).

NORMAL PRICE the price of the imported goods used for the purposes of levying AD VALOREM DUTIES of CUSTOMS or the value of any goods IMPORTED for home use. *see also* COMPUTED VALUE; TRANSACTION VALUE.

NORMAL QUOTE *see* DIRECT QUOTE.

NORMAL TRADING RELATIONS *see* MOST-FAVORED-NATION (MFN) TREATMENT; PERMANENT NORMAL TRADING RELATIONS.

NORMAL VALUE price charged for a product on the domestic market of the producer and compared with the export price in determining DUMPING has taken place.

NORTH AMERICAN COMMISSION ON THE ENVIRONMENT (NACE) a commission created by the members of the NORTH AMERICAN FREE TRADE AGREEMENT (NAFTA) to enforce their commitment to the environment. The commission's primary goal is to broaden cooperative activities among the principal environmental officials of the three members. It will consider environmental implications of trade-related economic activity, particularly in the area of production, and also promote the assessment and resolution of environmental problems.

NORTH AMERICAN DEVELOPMENT BANK (NADBank) a bank capitalized and governed by the United States and Mexico intended to provide financing related to the NORTH AMERICAN FREE TRADE AGREEMENT (NAFTA). The NADBank will finance projects certified by the BORDER ENVIRONMENT COOPERATION COMMISSION and provide support for community adjustment and investment. Up to 10% of NADBank resources may be made available for community adjustment and investment, which need not be in the border region.

NORTH AMERICAN FREE TRADE AGREEMENT (NAFTA) a free-trade agreement comprising Canada, the United States, and Mexico effective January 1994. NAFTA exceeds 360 million consumers and a combined output of $6 trillion—approximately 20% larger than the EUROPEAN COMMUNITY (EC). NAFTA's consumer population is slightly smaller than the EUROPEAN ECONOMIC AREA (EEA), which has over 380 million consumers. The agreement progressively eliminates almost all United States–Mexico TARIFFS over a 10-year period, with a small number of tariffs for trade-sensitive industries phased out over a 15-year period. Mexico–Canada tariffs are also phased out over a 10-year period. Tariff reduction schedules between the United States and Canada negotiated in the Canadian Free Trade Agreement are retained.

NAFTA eliminates other barriers to trade such as IMPORT licensing requirements and CUSTOMS user fees. It establishes the principle of national treatment, for ensuring that NAFTA-origin products traded between NAFTA countries will receive treatment equal to similar domestic products. It also guarantees service providers of the three countries equal treatment in the NAFTA area, including the right to invest and the right to sell services across borders.

NAFTA establishes five basic principles to protect foreign investors and their investment in the free-trade area:

- nondiscriminatory treatment,
- freedom from performance requirements,
- free transference of funds related to an investment,
- expropriation only in conformity with international law, and
- the right to seek international arbitration for a violation of the agreement's protections.

The agreement contains special provisions for sensitive economic sectors, including agriculture, automotive products, energy, and textiles and apparel. The agreement also created a BORDER ENVIRONMENT COOPERATION COMMISSION and a NORTH AMERICAN DEVELOPMENT BANK (NADBank).

NORTH AMERICAN TRADE AUTOMATION PROTOTYPE trinational initiative to HARMONIZE government processes and standardize data elements across the NORTH AMERICAN FREE TRADE AGREEMENT (NAFTA) countries (United States, Mexico, and Canada), and proof of concept for the International Trade Data System. *see also* TRILATERAL TRADE; TRILATERAL TRADE AGREEMENT.

NORTH ATLANTIC TREATY ORGANIZATION (NATO) military alliance established in 1949 by Belgium, Canada, Denmark, France (which has only partial membership), Great Britain, Iceland, Italy, Luxembourg, the Netherlands, Norway, Portugal, and the United States. It was later joined by Greece and Turkey (1952), West Germany (1955; now Germany), and Spain (1982). With the end of the cold war, NATO's role, originally defense-oriented, is being redefined.

NORTHERN ALLIANCE this was the Taliban's major opposition, before the U.S.-led war in Afghanistan.

NORTHERN CORRIDOR a transportation infrastructure founded in East Africa and served by the port of Mombassa in Kenya. It consists of

- the railway system from Mombassa to Nairobi and continuing to Kampala, Uganda, and beyond that to the border of Uganda and Zaire;

- the highway system that runs from Mombassa to Nairobi, Kenya, proceeding to Kampala, Uganda, and then to Kigali, Rwanda, and finally to Bujumbura, the capital of Burundi; and
- the oil pipeline running from the port of Mombassa to Nairobi, Kenya.

NORTHERN CORRIDOR TRANSIT AGREEMENT (NCTA) a MULTILATERAL TREATY between Burundi, Kenya, Uganda, Tanzania, Rwanda, and Zaire signed on February 19, 1985, concerning the transportation infrastructure known as the NORTHERN CORRIDOR. The purpose of the agreement is to facilitate the movement of goods through the region, to remove or reduce administrative procedures, and to provide the region's land-locked countries with an outlet to the Indian Ocean via the Port of Mombassa.

NORTHWEST ATLANTIC FISHERIES ORGANIZATION (NAFO) an international organization created to manage and protect fishery resources in the northwest Atlantic Ocean. It was established in 1979, and its membership consists of the EUROPEAN ECONOMIC COMMUNITY (EEC), Canada, the United States, Japan, Iceland, Norway, and the former USSR (COMMONWEALTH OF INDEPENDENT STATES, CIS).

NORWEGIAN AGENCY FOR DEVELOPMENT COOPERATION (NORAD) Norwegian agency that provides financing of project EXPORTS from Norway to developing countries for undertakings that contribute to development and can be sustained without future external assistance. About 50% of Norwegian assistance is bilateral aid; the balance is channeled as multilateral aid through United Nations specialized agencies and financial institutions, including regional development banks. NORAD bilateral aid includes provisions for Norwegian private industrial sector participation as suppliers of capital equipment and services and technology. A portion of assistance may involve concessional financing for Norwegian project exports, including mixed credits, export credit guarantees, support for training in connection with project exports, and tied cofinancing on grant basis with the WORLD BANK, the AFRICAN DEVELOPMENT BANK, and the ASIAN DEVELOPMENT BANK. NORAD assistance is subject to the ORGANIZATION FOR ECONOMIC COOPERATION AND DEVELOPMENT'S (OECD) DEVELOPMENT ASSISTANCE COMMITTEE guidelines for development assistance and associated financing. NORAD was established in 1968, and its headquarters is in Oslo, Norway.

NORWEGIAN KRONE unit of currency, Norway (100 øre equal 1 Norwegian krone).

N.O.S. abbreviation for not otherwise specified.

NO SHOW FREIGHT that has been booked on a ship, but has not physically arrived in time to be loaded onto that ship.

NOTARY PUBLIC person commissioned by a state (in the United States) for a stipulated period to administer certain oaths and to attest and certify documents. In some countries, the authority of a notary public is much more extensive.

NOTIFY ADDRESS address mentioned in the transport document to which the CARRIER is to give notice when goods are due to arrive. *see also* CONSIGNEE; NOTIFY PARTY.

NOTIFY PARTY name and address of a party in the transport document to be notified by the shipping company of the arrival of a shipment. *see also* CONSIGNEE; NOTIFY ADDRESS.

NRBP *see* NATURAL RESOURCE-BASED PRODUCTS.

NRC *see* NUCLEAR REGULATORY COMMISSION.

NREN *see* NATIONAL RESEARCH AND EDUCATION NETWORK.

NSC *see* NATIONAL SECURITY COUNCIL.

NSD #53 *see* NATIONAL SECURITY DIRECTIVE #53.

NSDs *see* NATIONAL SECURITY DIRECTIVES.

NSF *see* NATIONAL SCIENCE FOUNDATION.

NSFNET an essential part of academic and research communications funded by the NATIONAL SCIENCE FOUNDATION (NSF). It is a high-speed "NETWORK of networks" that is hierarchical in nature. At the highest level, it is a BACKBONE network currently comprising 16 NODES connected to a facility that spans the continental United States. Attached to that are midlevel networks and attached to the midlevels are campus and local networks. NSFNET also has connections out of the United States to Canada, Mexico, Europe, and the Pacific Rim. NSFNET is part of the INTERNET.

NSG *see* NUCLEAR SUPPLIERS GROUP.

NSO *see* NATIONAL SECURITY OVERRIDE.

N.S.P.F. abbreviation for not specifically provided for.

NTBs *see* NONTARIFF BARRIERS.

NTDB *see* NATIONAL TRADE DATA BANK.

NTE *see* NATIONAL TRADE ESTIMATES REPORT.

NTF *see* NIGERIA TRUST FUND.

NTM *see* NEW-TO-MARKET.

NTMs *see* NONTARIFF MEASURES.

NTSC television transmission and reception format used in the United States. *see also* PAL, SECAM.

NTT *see* NIPPON TELEGRAPH AND TELEPHONE CORPORATION.

NUCLEAR ENERGY AGENCY (NEA) a companion organization to the INTERNATIONAL ENERGY AGENCY, with headquarters in Paris, and an element of the ORGANIZATION FOR ECONOMIC COOPERATION AND DEVELOPMENT (OECD). NEA promotes the safe and effective use of nuclear energy by exchanging information among technical experts, sharing analytical studies, and undertaking joint research and development projects by member countries.

NUCLEAR NONPROLIFERATION ACT (NNPA) U.S. act passed in 1974 that made the U.S. Energy Department responsible for approving arrangements for nuclear exports and transfers. Each arrangement requires U.S. State Department concurrence, as well as consultations with the U.S. ARMS CONTROL AND DISARMAMENT AGENCY (ACDA), the U.S. Nuclear Regulatory Commission, and the U.S. Departments of Defense and Commerce.

NUCLEAR NONPROLIFERATION TREATY (NPT) treaty that became effective in 1970 and was intended to limit the number of states with nuclear weapons to five: the United States, the former Soviet Union, Britain, France, and China. In doing so, the NPT attempts to

- prevent nuclear weapons sales by not assisting other nations with nuclear weapons development,
- halt the nuclear weapons development programs of nonnuclear weapons states, and
- promote nuclear disarmament and the peaceful use of nuclear technologies and materials.

Over 140 states have pledged not to acquire nuclear weapons and to accept the safeguards of the International Atomic Energy Agency over all their nuclear materials.

In May 1995, the treaty was extended indefinitely.

NUCLEAR REGULATORY COMMISSION (NRC) U.S. commission that regulates the transfer of nuclear facilities, materials, and parts with uniquely nuclear applications (such as items associated with nuclear reactors). The U.S. Department of Energy regulates the transfer of information relating to nuclear technology; the U.S. State Department controls defense articles and services, such as nuclear weapons design and test equipment; and the U.S. DEPARTMENT OF COMMERCE controls a range of dual-use items with potential nuclear application.

License applications for the EXPORT of nuclear items are reviewed by the U.S. Department of Energy and may be referred to an interagency working group known as the SUBGROUP ON NUCLEAR EXPORT COORDINATION (SNEC). The SNEC is composed of representatives from the U.S. Departments of State, Defense, and Commerce; the ARMS CONTROL AND DISARMAMENT AGENCY (ACDA); and the NRC. see also INTERNATIONAL ATOMIC ENERGY AGENCY; NUCLEAR SUPPLIERS GROUP; ZANGGER COMMITTEE.

NUCLEAR SUPPLIERS GROUP (NSG) an organization of nuclear supplier nations that coordinates exports of nuclear materials and equipment with the INTERNATIONAL ATOMIC ENERGY AGENCY (IAEA) inspectorate regime. The reason for creating the NSG was to allow member nations some flexibility (which they do not enjoy in the ZANGGER COMMITTEE) in controlling items to nonnuclear weapons states.

The NSG's independence from the NUCLEAR NONPROLIFERATION TREATY (NPT) enables NSG to enlist the cooperation of supplier states that are not signatories to the NPT and thus not involved in the nuclear export control activities of the Zangger Committee. The NSG's control list is more comprehensive than the Zangger Committee's "trigger list"; it requires the imposition of safeguards on exports of nuclear technology in addition to nuclear materials and equipment. The NSG developed a multilateral list for national adoption of export controls on DUAL-USE COMMODITIES with a nuclear application.

NUEVA PALMERA the FREE ZONE in Uruguay.

NUEVOS PESO unit of currency, Mexico (100 centavos equal 1 nuevos peso).

NUEVOS SOL unit of currency, Peru (100 centavos equal 1 nuevos sol).

NULLIFICATION *see* NONVIOLATION.

NVOC *see* NONVESSEL OWNING CARRIER.

NVOCC *see* NONVESSEL OPERATING COMMON CARRIER.

O

O.&R. abbreviation for ocean and rail.

OAPEC *see* ORGANIZATION OF ARAB PETROLEUM EXPORTING COUNTRIES.

OAS *see* ORGANIZATION OF AMERICAN STATES.

OATUU *see* ORGANIZATION OF AFRICAN TRADE UNION UNITY.

OAU *see* ORGANIZATION OF AFRICAN UNITY.

OBL *see* OCEAN BILL OF LADING.

OBRs *see* OVERSEAS BUSINESS REPORTS.

OBU *see* OFFSHORE BANKING UNIT.

OBVIOUS DAMAGE goods that have been damaged while in transit, which damage can be noted by an external examination of the packages. Insurance carriers normally have strict time limitations for the placing of such claims. *see also* HIDDEN DAMAGE; PILFERAGE.

OC *see* OPERATING COMMITTEE.

OCEAN BILL OF LADING (OBL) a receipt for the CARGO and a contract for transportation between a SHIPPER and the ocean CARRIER. It may also be used as an instrument of ownership that can be bought, sold, or traded while the goods are in transit. To be used in this manner, it must be a negotiable ORDER BILL OF LADING. *see also* CLEAN BILL OF LADING; ON-BOARD BILL OF LADING.

OCEAN FREIGHT DIFFERENTIAL (OFD) the amount by which the cost of the ocean freight bill for the portion of COMMODITIES required to be carried on U.S. flag vessels exceeds the cost of carrying the same amount on foreign flag vessels. When applied to agricultural commodities shipped under Food for Peace, OFD is the amount paid by the COMMODITY CREDIT CORPORATION. *see also* OPERATING DIFFERENTIAL SUBSIDY (ODS).

OCEAN FREIGHT FORWARDER *see* FREIGHT FORWARDER.

OCTET a series of 8 consecutive binary digits, or BITS, also called a BYTE, which allows 256 "on–off" combinations. This term is used in NETWORKING, rather than *byte*, because some systems have bytes that are not 8 bits long.

ODA *see* OFFICIAL DEVELOPMENT ASSISTANCE.

ODS *see* OPERATING DIFFERENTIAL SUBSIDY.

OECD *see* ORGANIZATION FOR ECONOMIC COOPERATION AND DEVELOPMENT.

OECD CONSENSUS an international agreement under Organization for Economic Cooperation and Development auspices governing the conditions—such as interest rate, repayment term, and cash down payment—of medium- and long-term official EXPORT credit. It does not apply to strictly private credit. Example: the agreement specifies how governments relate the interest rate on their export credits to market levels. Although informal and nonenforceable, agreement guidelines are regularly observed by the 22 OECD member governments that are "participants" to the agreement.

OECD CONSENSUS GUIDELINES *see* OECD CONSENSUS.

OECF *see* OVERSEAS ECONOMIC COOPERATION FUND.

OECS *see* ORGANIZATION OF EASTERN CARIBBEAN STATES.

OETCA *see* OFFICE OF EXPORT TRADING COMPANY AFFAIRS.

OFAC *see* OFFICE OF FOREIGN ASSETS CONTROL.

OFD *see* OCEAN FREIGHT DIFFERENTIAL.

OFF-LINE describing the state in which a computer is not connected to a HOST system or the NET. *see also* ON-LINE.

OFFENE HANDELSGESELLSCHAFT (OHG) (German, meaning general partnership) characterized by the unlimited and direct liability of all partners who are jointly and severally liable. Their liability cannot be restricted. The partnership must carry the family name of at least one partner with reference to the kind of partnership (such as "& Co.").

OFFER
1. a proposal that is made to a certain individual or legal entity to enter into a CONTRACT, that is definite in its terms, and that indicates the offerer's intent to be bound by an acceptance. *see also* PURCHASE FROM FOREIGN SELLER; PURCHASING AGENT.
2. with respect to securities, the price at which one is ready to sell. *see also* BID (BUY).

OFFER (SELL) *see* BID (BUY).

OFFICE OF DEFENSE TRADE CONTROLS (DTC) the office at the U.S. Department of State that administers the EXPORT control of items on the U.S. MUNITIONS LIST (USML).

OFFICE OF EXPORT LICENSING (OEL) *see* CENTER FOR DEFENSE TRADE.

OFFICE OF EXPORT TRADING COMPANY AFFAIRS (OETCA) an office within the INTERNATIONAL TRADE ADMINISTRATION (ITA) of the U.S. DEPARTMENT OF COMMERCE responsible for promoting the formation and use of U.S. EXPORT intermediaries. It issues EXPORT TRADE CERTIFICATES OF REVIEW providing limited immunity from U.S. antitrust laws. The OETCA informs the business community of the benefits of export intermediaries through conferences, presentations before trade associations and civic organizations, and publications. The major publication on this subject is the Export Trading Company Guidebook, available for purchase through the U.S. Government Printing Office. OETCA provides counseling to businesses seeking to take advantage of the EXPORT TRADING COMPANY ACT OF 1982.

OFFICE OF FOREIGN ASSETS CONTROL (OFAC) an agency within the U.S. Department of the Treasury that maintains controls over transactions (including financial transactions) with EMBARGOED countries.

OFFICE OF INTERNATIONAL COOPERATION AND DEVELOPMENT (OICD) office in the U.S. Department of Agriculture responsible for cooperative international research, scientific and technical exchanges, and liaison with international agricultural organizations. OICD also directs training and technical assistance in efforts in approximately 80 developing countries.

OFFICE OF MANAGEMENT AND BUDGET executive office of the President of the United States that evaluates, formulates, and coordinates management procedures and program objectives within and among federal departments and agencies. It also controls the administration of the federal budget.

OFFICE OF MUNITIONS CONTROL (OMC) *see* DEFENSE TRADE CONTROLS.

OFFICE OF SUPPLY, REPUBLIC OF KOREA (OSROK) a Korean agency responsible for supervising procurement of supplies by Korean government agencies and government-owned enterprises in Korea. All Korean government procurements require a formal public invitation to bid.

OFFICIAL COMMERCIAL CONTROLS *see* COMMERCIAL CONTROLS.

OFFICIAL DEVELOPMENT ASSISTANCE (ODA) U.S. funds provided to developing countries and multilateral institutions provided by official agencies of national, state, or local governments. Each transaction must be
- administered with the promotion of the economic development and welfare of developing countries as its main objective and
- concessional in character and contain a grant element of at least 25% of the total amount.

OFFICIAL RATE the PAR VALUE of a pegged exchange rate. *see also* EXCHANGE RATE MECHANISM (ERM).

OFFICIAL RESERVE ACCOUNT *see* ACCOMMODATING TRANSACTIONS.

OFFICIAL RESERVE TRANSACTIONS transactions by a CENTRAL BANK that cause changes in its OFFICIAL RESERVES. The transactions are usually purchases or sales of its own currency in the EXCHANGE MARKET in exchange for foreign currencies or other foreign-currency-denominated assets. *see also* SPECIAL DRAWING RIGHTS (SDRS); MONETARY POLICY.

OFFICIAL RESERVES the total of a country's holdings of gold, SPECIAL DRAWING RIGHTS, and internationally acceptable currencies.

OFFICIAL SETTLEMENT BALANCE a statement summarizing the net debit or credit position in the OFFICIAL RESERVE ACCOUNT for a country. *see also* ACCOMMODATING TRANSACTIONS.

OFFSET REQUIREMENT a requirement that foreign EXPORTERS purchase domestic products, invest in the importing country, or both, as a condition for importing into a country. *see also* COPRODUCTION; COUNTERTRADE; LICENSED PRODUCTION; OFFSETS; OVERSEAS INVESTMENT; SUBCONTRACTOR PRODUCTION; TECHNOLOGY TRANSFER.

OFFSETS an umbrella label for a broad range of industrial and commercial compensation practices required as a condition of purchase in commercial or government-to-government sales of either military or high-cost civilian hardware. Whether commercial or military, offsets involve overseas production that results in the creation or expansion of industrial capacity in the IMPORTER's country. The compensatory forms of offset include coproduction, licensed production, subcontractor production, overseas investment, and technology transfer.

Countries require offsets for a variety of reasons: to ease (or offset) the burden of large defense purchases on their economies, to increase domestic employment, to obtain desired technology, or to promote targeted industrial sectors. Governments sometimes impose offset requirements on foreign exporters as a condition for approval of major sales agreements in an effort to either reduce the adverse trade impact of a major sale or gain specified industrial benefits for the importing country. In these circumstances, offset requirements may be direct or indirect, depending on whether the goods and services are integral parts of the product. In a direct offset, a U.S. manufacturer selling a product uses a component that is made in the purchasing country. In an indirect offset, the EXPORTER would buy products that are peripheral to the manufacture of its product. *see also* COPRODUCTION; COUNTERTRADE; LICENSED PRODUCTION; OVERSEAS INVESTMENT; SUBCONTRACTOR PRODUCTION; TECHNOLOGY TRANSFER.

OFFSHORE BANKING specific categories of financial transactions taking place outside the domestic jurisdiction of a country. *see also* OFFSHORE BANKING CENTERS; OFFSHORE BANKING UNIT; EURODOLLARS; OFFSHORE FUNDS.

OFFSHORE BANKING CENTER *see* OFFSHORE BANKING UNIT; EUROBANKING.

OFFSHORE BANKING UNIT (OBU) normally a foreign bank that conducts domestic money market, EUROCURRENCY, and foreign exchange settlements. OBUs cannot accept domestic deposits, but their activities are unrestricted by domestic authorities. OBUs are located in major financial centers (known as offshore banking centers) with liberal reserve, tax, and capital market requirements.

OFFSHORE DOLLARS *see* EURODOLLARS.

OFFSHORE FUNDS cash or other negotiable instruments deposited in accounts at financial institutions situated outside the domestic jurisdiction of a country. *see also* OFFSHORE BANKING UNIT (OBU).

OFFSHORE MANUFACTURING the foreign manufacture of goods by a domestic company primarily for IMPORT into its home country.

OHG *see* OFFENE HANDELSGESELLSCHAFT.

OIC *see* ORGANIZATION OF THE ISLAMIC CONFERENCE.

OICD *see* OFFICE OF INTERNATIONAL COOPERATION AND DEVELOPMENT.

OIL FUTURES TRADING a daily column appearing in the JOURNAL OF COMMERCE that provides daily price quotations on futures contracts for home heating oil, unleaded gasoline, crude oil, and propane gas from the New York Mercantile Exchange.

OIL OPTIONS a daily column appearing in the JOURNAL OF COMMERCE that provides quotations on options to buy or sell thousand-barrel lots of crude and heating oil from the New York Mercantile Exchange.

OLD-TO-MARKET (OTM) committed and experienced larger-scale firms, where a significant portion of their manufacturing capability is foreign-sourced. EXPORT sales volume is often in excess of 15% of total sales.

OLIGOPOLY a condition where there are so few market participants that they are capable of significantly affecting supply and prices by individual or collusive actions. *see also* MONOPOLY.

OMA *see* ORDERLY MARKETING AGREEMENT.

OMC Office of Munitions Control. *see also* DEFENSE TRADE CONTROLS.

OMNIBUS INVESTMENTS CODE OF 1987 a compilation of the foreign investment laws administered by the Department of Trade and Industry in the Philippines. It provides foreign and local investors with all the necessary information concerning available government incentive programs promoting investment in the Philippines.

OMNIBUS TRADE AND COMPETITIVENESS ACT OF 1988 a U.S. federal law designed to improve the competitiveness of American industry in international trade. It empowered the U.S. TRADE REPRESENTATIVE (USTR) to enforce U.S. laws in several areas:
- it gave power to protect U.S. rights in trade agreements.

- it enforced antidumping laws.
- it protected U.S. intellectual property.

Additionally, the act provided for fast-track consideration of trade agreements resulting from the Uruguay Round of the GATT talks. It also banned U.S. government purchases from companies that made sales to Communist countries.

OMPI Organisation Mondiale de la Propriété Intellectuelle. *see also* WORLD INTELLECTUAL PROPERTY ORGANIZATION (WIPO).

OMVG Organisation pour la Mise en Valear du Fleuve Gambie. *see also* GAMBIA RIVER BASIN DEVELOPMENT ORGANIZATION.

OMVS Organisation pour la Mise en Valeur de Fleuve Sénégal. *see also* ORGANIZATION FOR THE DEVELOPMENT OF THE SENEGAL RIVER.

O/N abbreviation for order notify.

ON BOARD notation on a BILL OF LADING indicating that goods have been loaded on board or shipped on a named ship. In the case of received-for-shipment bills of lading, the following four parties are authorized to add this "on board" notation:
1. the CARRIER
2. the carrier's agent
3. the master of the ship
4. the master's agent.

see also MARINE BILL OF LADING; ON-DECK BILL OF LADING; ORDER BILL OF LADING; SHORT-FORM BILL OF LADING, STRAIGHT BILL OF LADING.

ON-BOARD BILL OF LADING CARGO certification that has been placed aboard the named vessel and is signed by the master of the vessel or his representative. On LETTER OF CREDIT transactions, an on-board bill of lading is usually necessary for the shipper to obtain payment from the bank. When all BILLS OF LADING (B/L) are processed, a SHIP'S MANIFEST is prepared by the steamship line. This summarizes all CARGO aboard the vessel by port of loading and discharge.

ON-DECK BILL OF LADING BILL OF LADING containing the notation that goods have been placed on deck. *see also* MARINE BILL OF LADING; ON BOARD; ON-BOARD BILL OF LADING; ORDER BILL OF LADING; SHORT-FORM BILL OF LADING; STRAIGHT BILL OF LADING.

ON-LINE describing the state in which a computer is connected to an on-line service, bulletin board system, or INTERNET site. *see also* OFF-LINE.

ONUS OF GOOD FAITH the basis on which all CARGO insurance is governed. Individuals who have their cargo insured do not have a right to abandon cargo or fail to take any action that could result in averting or minimizing a loss or damage. In other words, these individuals must at all times act in the same manner as they would in the event that they were not insured. *see also* MARINE INSURANCE.

OPEC *see* ORGANIZATION OF PETROLEUM EXPORTING COUNTRIES.

OPEC FUND FOR INTERNATIONAL DEVELOPMENT an independent development agency established by the ORGANIZATION OF PETROLEUM EXPORTING COUNTRIES (OPEC) in 1976 with headquarters in Vienna, Austria. The purpose of the agency is to provide assistance to non-oil-producing developing nations with critical BALANCE OF PAYMENT deficits.

OPEN ACCOUNT a trade arrangement in which goods are shipped to a foreign buyer before, and without written guarantee of, payment. Because this method poses an obvious risk to the supplier, it is essential that the buyer's integrity be unquestionable.

OPEN CONFERENCE shipping CONFERENCE in which there are no restrictions on membership other than ability and willingness to serve the trade. *see also* CONFERENCE LINE; FOREIGN FREIGHT FORWARDER; NONCONFERENCE LINE; NONVESSEL OPERATING COMMON CARRIER (NVOCC).

OPEN DOOR TREATMENT an agreement between countries whereby the parties agree to treat nationals of each other's country in an equal and impartial way with regard to trading within the specified territories. *see also* FRIENDSHIP, COMMERCE, AND NAVIGATION TREATY.

OPEN ECONOMY *see* MARKET ECONOMY.

OPEN-END CONTRACT agreement by which the buyer may purchase goods from a seller for a certain time without changes in the price or the CONTRACT terms. *see also* CLOSED-END TRANSACTION.

OPEN INSURANCE POLICY a MARINE INSURANCE policy that applies to all shipments made by an EXPORTER over a period of time rather than to a single shipment.

OPEN MEETING a U.S. legal requirement (Sunshine Act of 1976) that required governmental agencies, as a matter of general policy, to have their hearings and meetings announced in advance and open to the public.

OPEN POSITION a condition existing when you either have more assets than you have liabilities, or more liabilities than you have assets in one currency. A CLOSED or COVERED POSITION exists when your assets and liabilities in a particular currency are equal. *see also* EXPOSURE NETTING.

OPENING BANK the bank that opens the LETTER OF CREDIT on the advice of the IMPORTER in favor of the EXPORTER and agrees to pay all DRAFTS drawn against it by the BENEFICIARY, who is normally the exporter. *see also* ADVISING BANK; DOCUMENTARY CREDIT.

OPERATING COMMITTEE (OC) a committee chaired by the U.S. DEPARTMENT OF COMMERCE acting as the first step in resolving interagency disputes over the disposition of license applications for dualuse items not reviewed by one of the other interagency working groups. The other working groups include:

- the SUBGROUP ON NUCLEAR EXPORT COORDINATION (SNEC), chaired by the U.S. Department of State for applications involving nuclear concerns;
- the Missile Technology Export Control Group (MTEC), chaired by the U.S. Department of State for applications involving missile technology concerns;
- the "Shield," chaired by the U.S. Department of State for applications involving chemical or biological warfare concerns.

These committees review applications and participate in the dispute resolution. Prior to any escalation to the ADVISORY COMMITTEE ON EXPORT POLICY (ACEP), all applications must be reviewed by one of these working groups.

OPERATING DIFFERENTIAL SUBSIDY (ODS) a payment that the U.S. government makes to vessels carrying the American flag to offset the difference in operating costs between U.S. and foreign carriers. *see also* OCEAN FREIGHT DIFFERENTIAL (OFD).

OPERATING LEASES a term used when the lessor maintains ownership of the asset. Whenever coverage is provided to an investor by the OVERSEAS PRIVATE INVESTMENT CORPORATION (OPIC), the U.S. lessor maintains ownership of the assets. EXPROPRIATION and political violence compensation is based on the value of leased assets. Inconvertibility coverage compensates for lease payments that cannot be coverted from local currency to dollars or cannot be transferred outside the HOST COUNTRY.

OPERATION EXODUS a U.S. CUSTOMS SERVICE export enforcement program that was developed in 1981 to help stem the flow of the illegal EXPORT of U.S.-sourced arms and technology to the former Soviet bloc and other prohibited foreign destinations.

OPERATION IRAQI FREEDOM United States-led coalition war aimed at effecting a regime change and freeing the Iraqi people. Operation lasted from March 19 to May 1, 2003.

OPERATOR OF FOREIGN TRADE ZONE a U.S. corporation that operates a FOREIGN TRADE ZONE under the terms of an agreement with a foreign trade zone GRANTEE. *see also* FREE PORTS; FREE ZONE.

OPIC *see* OVERSEAS PRIVATE INVESTMENT CORPORATION.

OPIC FACTSLINE an automated facsimile service, sponsored by the OVERSEAS PRIVATE INVESTMENT CORPORATION (OPIC). This service allows you to request documents for transmission to your facsimile machine on various OPIC programs. To receive a document on your facsimile machine, call (202) 336-8700 from any touch tone phone.

OPTIMAL TARIFF level of a TARIFF that maximizes a country's welfare.

OPTIMUM CURRENCY AREA the ideal area between fixed and flexible EXCHANGE RATES. Example: consider the geographical closeness between the United States and Canada. The rates of the U.S. dollar and the Canadian dollar are closely linked and have a history of being somewhat fixed, yet they float with the rest of the world. Also, the exchange rates of the European Monetary System are fixed within the system; however, they fluctuate with the rest of the world.

OPTIMUM TARIFF the "best" DUTY RATE for goods being IMPORTED into a country. It is the rate that maximizes the net national economic gain that accrues from improvement in the terms of trade of a country. *see also* PROHIBITIVE DUTY.

OPTIMUM TARIFF THEORY a TARIFF theory that states that an EXPORTER will lower the price for its goods when an IMPORT tax is placed on them.

OPTION the privilege to buy or sell FOREIGN EXCHANGE either on a specific date or within a specified period.

OPTIONAL ORIGIN CONTRACTS a transaction involving an EXPORT sales contract between an EXPORTER and a foreign buyer under which the exporter has the option of exporting the COMMODITY from the United States or one or more other exporting countries. The exporter can also choose an export sales contract under which no origin is specified.

ORDER
1. a request to deliver, sell, receive, or purchase goods or SERVICES.
2. an instruction, command, or direction authoritatively given.
3. a designation of the person to whom a BILL OF EXCHANGE is to be paid, or delivery of goods made, a BILL OF LADING (B/L) consigned, or a key word which makes a document negotiable.

ORDER BILL *see* ORDER BILL OF LADING.

ORDER BILL OF LADING a negotiable BILL OF LADING made out to the order of the shipper.

ORDER NOTIFY BILL OF LADING term to provide for surrender of the ORIGINAL BILL OF LADING before FREIGHT is surrendered. *see also* TO ORDER.

ORDERLY MARKETING AGREEMENT (OMA)
1. a BILATERAL agreement between governments by which one government limits EXPORTS to the other. Similar to a voluntary export restriction agreement or a voluntary restraint agreement, it is used to address injury to a domestic industry.
2. The exporting nation undertakes to ensure that international trade in specified sensitive products will not disrupt, threaten, or impair competitive industries or workers in importing countries.

ORGANISATION MONDIALE DE LA PROPRIETE INTELLECTUELLE (OMPI) *see* WORLD INTELLECTUAL PROPERTY ORGANIZATION.

ORGANISATION POUR LA MISE EN VALEUR DU FLEUVE GAMBIE (OMVG) *see* GAMBIA RIVER BASIN DEVELOPMENT ORGANIZATION.

ORGANISATION POUR LA MISE EN VALEUR DU FLEUVE SENEGAL (OMVS) *see* ORGANIZATION FOR THE DEVELOPMENT OF THE SENEGAL RIVER.

ORGANIZACION DE LOS ESTADOS AMERICANOS (OEA) *see* ORGANIZATION OF AMERICAN STATES.

ORGANIZATION FOR ECONOMIC COOPERATION AND DEVELOPMENT (OECD) organization that provides a forum for discussion of common economic and social issues facing the United States, Canada, Western Europe, Japan, Australia, and New Zealand. OECD was founded in September 1960 as successor to the Organization for European Economic Cooperation (OEEC), which had administered European participation in the MARSHALL PLAN. OECD seeks "to achieve the highest sustainable economic growth and employment and a rising standard of living in member countries while maintaining financial stability and thus contribute to the world economy." Members include Australia, Austria, Belgium, Canada, Denmark, Finland, France, Germany, Greece, Iceland, Ireland, Italy, Luxembourg, Japan, the Netherlands, New Zealand, Norway, Portugal, Spain, Sweden, Switzerland, Turkey, the United Kingdom, and the United States. OECD headquarters is in Paris, France. *see also* ARRANGEMENT ON GUIDELINES FOR OFFICIALLY SUPPORTED EXPORT CREDITS.

ORGANIZATION FOR THE DEVELOPMENT OF THE SENEGAL RIVER (French: Organisation pour la Mise en Valeur du Fleuve Sénégal, OMVS) organization that promotes hydroelectric, irrigation, and navigation use of the Senegal river. The organization was established in March 1972, and its headquarters is in Dakar, Senegal. Members include Guinea-Bissau, Mali, Mauritania, and Senegal.

ORGANIZATION OF AFRICAN TRADE UNION UNITY (OATUU) the sole representative of African organized labor as recognized by the ORGANIZATION OF AFRICAN UNITY (OAU) and the INTERNATIONAL LABOR ORGANIZATION (ILO). OATUU is formally nonaligned and independent of all international trade union organizations but maintains relations with trade unions worldwide. OATUU headquarters is in Accra, Ghana.

ORGANIZATION OF AFRICAN UNITY (OAU) founded in May 1963 with 32 African countries, this organization has since grown beyond 50 members. It aims to further African unity and solidarity; to coordinate political, economic, cultural, scientific, and defense policies; and to eliminate colonialism in Africa. Members include Algeria, Angola, Benin, Botswana, Burkina Faso, Burundi, Cameroon, Cape Verde, Central African Republic, Chad, Comoros, Congo, Côte d'Ivoire, Egypt, Equatorial Guinea, Ethiopia, Gabon, the Gambia, Ghana, Guinea, Guinea-Bissau, Kenya, Lesotho, Liberia, Libya, Madagascar, Malawi, Mali, Mauritania, Mauritius, Morocco, Mozambique, Namibia, Niger, Nigeria, Rwanda, São Tomé and Principe, Senegal, Seychelles, Sierra Leone, Somalia, Sudan, Swaziland, Tanzania, Togo, Tunisia, Uganda, Zaire, Zambia, and Zimbabwe. OAU headquarters is in Addis Ababa, Ethiopia.

ORGANIZATION OF AMERICAN STATES (OAS) (Spanish: Organización de los Estados Americanos, OEA) known as the PAN AMERICAN UNION, the OAS is a regional organization created in Bogota, Colombia, in April 1948 (entered into force in December 1951), which promotes Latin American economic and social development. Members include the United States, Mexico, and most Central American, South American, and Caribbean nations. Other members include Antigua and Barbuda, Argentina, the Bahamas, Barbados, Belize, Bolivia, Brazil, Canada, Chile, Colombia, Costa Rica, Cuba (participation suspended), Dominica, Dominican Republic, Ecuador, El Salvador, Grenada, Guatemala, Guyana, Haiti, Honduras, Jamaica, Nicaragua, Panama, Paraguay, Peru, Saint Kitts-Nevis, Saint Lucia, Saint Vincent and the Grenadines, Suriname, Trinidad and Tobago, Uruguay, and Venezuela. The U.S. accredits an Ambassador to the OAS. The OAS secretariat is located in Washington, DC. *see also* SISTEMA DE INFORMACION AL COMERCIO EXTERIOR.

ORGANIZATION OF ARAB PETROLEUM EXPORTING COUNTRIES (OAPEC) Arab petroleum exporting organization created in 1968. Its members include Algeria, Bahrain, Egypt, Iraq, Kuwait, Libya, Qatar, Saudi Arabia, Syria, and the United Arab Emirates. Headquarters is in Cairo, Egypt. *see also* ORGANIZATION OF PETROLEUM EXPORTING COUNTRIES (OPEC).

ORGANIZATION OF EASTERN CARIBBEAN STATES (OECS) Eastern Caribbean organization established in 1981 and intended to promote territorial integrity. Recently the focus includes the founding of an export development agency. Its headquarters is in Saint Lucia. Members include Antigua and Barbuda, Dominica, Grenada, Montserrat, Saint Kitts-Nevis, Saint Lucia, and Saint Vincent and the Grenadines.

ORGANIZATION OF PETROLEUM EXPORTING COUNTRIES (OPEC) an association of the world's oil-producing countries, formed in 1960, with headquarters in Vienna, Austria. The chief purpose of OPEC is to coordinate the petroleum policies of its members: Algeria, Ecuador, Gabon, Indonesia, Iran, Iraq, Kuwait, Libya, Nigeria, Qatar, Saudi Arabia, the United Arab Emirates, and Venezuela. *see also* ORGANIZATION OF ARAB PETROLEUM EXPORTING COUNTRIES.

ORGANIZATION OF THE ISLAMIC CONFERENCE (OIC) Islamic conference established in May 1971 to promote cooperation in cultural, economic, scientific, and social areas among Islamic nations. OIC's headquarters is located in Jeddah, Saudi Arabia. About half the OIC members are also members of the ORGANIZATION OF AFRICAN UNITY (OAU). OIC members include Afghanistan, Algeria, Bahrain, Bangladesh, Benin, Brunei, Burkina Faso, Cameroon, Chad, Comoros, Cyprus, Djibouti, Egypt, Gabon, the Gambia, Guinea, Guinea-Bissau, Indonesia, Iran, Iraq, Jordan, Kuwait, Lebanon, Libya, Malaysia, Maldives, Mali, Mauritania, Morocco, Niger, Nigeria, Oman, Pakistan, Qatar, Saudi Arabia, Senegal, Sierra Leone, Somalia, Sudan, Syria, Tunisia, Turkey, Uganda, the United Arab Emirates, and Yemen.

ORIENTATION VISITS (OVs) *see* TRADE AND DEVELOPMENT AGENCY.

ORIGIN RULE *see* RULES OF ORIGIN.

O.S.&D. abbreviation for over, short and damage.

O.T. abbreviation for on truck or railway.

OTM *see* OLD-TO-MARKET.

OUGUIYA unit of currency, Mauritania.

OUTER SEVEN the members of the EUROPEAN FREE TRADE ASSOCIATION (EFTA), a regional organization established in December 1959 by the Stockholm Convention as an alternative to the Common Market. Original EFTA members included the United Kingdom, Austria, Denmark, Norway, Portugal, Sweden, and Switzerland. *see also* EUROPEAN ECONOMIC COMMUNITY (EEC); INNER SIX.

OUTRIGHT free from reserve or restraint; direct; positive; downright; altogether; complete; and open.

OUTRIGHT FORWARD a FORWARD CONTRACT that is not related to a SPOT MARKET transaction. Example: a firm might be receiving DEUTSCHE MARKS in 60 days and thus enter into a 60-day forward contract to trade Deutsche marks for dollars. *see also* OPTION.

OUTSIDER *see* NONCONFERENCE LINE.

OUTSOURCING a situation where a company will use a foreign supplier to purchase supplies or components to achieve lower costs and improved quality. Risks of outsourcing include currency fluctuations and long lead times.

OUTWARD-ORIENTED STRATEGY *see* EXPORT PROMOTION SERVICES (EPS).

OUTWARD PROCESSING ARRANGEMENTS a term used in the EUROPEAN ECONOMIC COMMUNITY (EEC) when referring to the international marketing concept of independent firms based in different countries agreeing to cooperate in the manufacture, assembly, and distribution of goods. *see also* JOINT VENTURES; LICENSING.

OUTWARD SWAP spot purchase of FOREIGN EXCHANGE and forward resale of the same currency against domestic currency. *see also* BANK

FOR INTERNATIONAL SETTLEMENTS; CENTRAL BANK SWAPS; SWAP ARRANGE-MENTS; SWAP NETWORK.

OVs orientation visits. *see also* TRADE AND DEVELOPMENT AGENCY.

OVER-THE-COUNTER securities trading that takes place outside the normal security exchanges.

OVERALL RECIPROCITY *see* RECIPROCITY.

OVERBASE COMPENSATION additional payments given to an employee on an international assignment over and above the base salary. This additional compensation is usually given to compensate for hardship, danger, etc.

OVERINVOICING provision of an invoice that reports the price as higher than is actually being paid.

OVERNIGHT period in which settlement is required on a transaction, such as a currency trade or a SWAP, on the next business day after the transaction.

OVERSEAS BUSINESS REPORTS (OBRs) marketing studies of America's major trading partners that provide updated EXPORT and economic outlooks, industrial trends, trade regulations, distribution and sales channels, transportation, and the credit situation in individual countries.

OVERSEAS COMMUNICATION TAX a 10% tax imposed by the Philippine government on the amount paid for communications transmitted. The tax is payable by the person paying for the services rendered.

OVERSEAS ECONOMIC COOPERATION FUND (OECF) a Japanese government development financial institution that provides developing countries and areas with grants and long-term, low-interest loans. As a result of difficulty in distinguishing between the fund and the EXPORT–IMPORT BANK OF JAPAN (JEXIM), a 1975 reorganization put OECF in charge of all direct loans to be made as OFFICIAL DEVELOPMENT ASSISTANCE (ODA) with the grant element of 25% or more. The fund was created in 1961, and its headquarters is in Tokyo, Japan. *see also* JAPAN INTERNATIONAL COOPERATION AGENCY.

OVERSEAS INVESTMENT
1. *see* DIRECT INVESTMENT.
2. a component of a type of COUNTERTRADE transactions called direct offsets. That is, the offset agreement involves capital contribution toward the establishment or expansion of a subsidiary or joint venture in a foreign country.
3. an offset agreement involving capital contributed toward the establishment or expansion of a SUBSIDIARY or JOINT VENTURE in a foreign country. *see also* OFFSETS.

OVERSEAS PRIVATE INVESTMENT CORPORATION (OPIC) a government corporation that assists U.S. private investments in

LESS-DEVELOPED COUNTRIES by providing direct loans and loan guarantees, insuring against a broad range of political risks, and providing a variety of investor services. The overseas investments may include distributorships owned by U.S. manufacturers that are consistent with the economic interests of both the United States and the developing country involved. OPIC was formed as a part of the AGENCY FOR INTERNATIONAL DEVELOPMENT in 1961 and became an independent agency 10 years later.

OVERVALUED CURRENCY a currency whose value is supported at a higher level than its market value through government actions.

P

P.A. abbreviation for particular average.

PA'ANGA unit of currency, Tonga (100 seniti equal 1 pa'anga).

PACIFIC BASIN ECONOMIC COUNCIL (PBEC) a private-sector group organized in 1967 to promote regional trade and investment. PBEC currently includes about 1,000 corporations and 14 national membership committees.

PACIFIC ECONOMIC COOPERATION CONFERENCE *see* PACIFIC ECONOMIC COOPERATION COUNCIL.

PACIFIC ECONOMIC COOPERATION COUNCIL (PECC) a nongovernmental organization founded in 1980 and aimed at promoting cooperation in the Asia-Pacific region. Members are drawn from 20 countries and territories: Australia, Brunei, Canada, Chile, China, Hong Kong, Indonesia, Japan, Korea, Malaysia, Mexico, New Zealand, the Pacific Islands, Peru, the Philippines, Russia, Singapore, Taiwan, Thailand, and the United States.

PACIFIC RIM countries and economies bordering the Pacific Ocean. Generally the term *Pacific Rim* has been regarded as a reference to East Asia, Canada, and the United States. At a minimum, the Pacific Rim includes Canada, Japan, the People's Republic of China, Taiwan, and the United States. It may also include Australia, Brunei, Cambodia, Hong Kong/Macau, Indonesia, Laos, North Korea, South Korea, Malaysia, New Zealand, the Pacific Islands, the Philippines, Russia (or the Commonwealth of Independent States), Singapore, Thailand, and Vietnam. As an evolutionary term, usage sometimes includes Mexico, the countries of Central America, and the Pacific coast countries of South America.

PACKING LIST a list showing the number and kinds of items being shipped, as well as other information needed for transportation purposes.

PACT FOR STABILITY AND ECONOMIC GROWTH (PSEG) Mexican legislation that replaced the ECONOMIC SOLIDARITY PACT (ESP). The PSEG was similar to the ESP with the most important modification being a relaxation of the EXCHANGE RATE policy, replacing the exchange rate freeze with a controlled exchange rate policy.

PAGAFES dollar-denominated Mexican treasury bills payable in PESOS (at maturity) using the controlled exchange rate. Because the controlled exchange rate has been eliminated in Mexico, all pagafes have been retired. *see also* AJUSTABONOS; BONDES; CETES; TESOBONOS.

PAIPU (Japanese) the access an individual has to someone who is important or has power. *see also* JINMYAKU; KONE.

PAKISTAN RUPEE unit of currency, Pakistan (100 paisa equal 1 Pakistan rupee).

PAL a transmission and reception format for television used in many European countries. *see also* NTSC; SECAM.

PALLET a platform upon which a shipment rests or on which goods are assembled and secured before being shipped. The use of pallets in shipping goods ensures greater ease in handling and reduces the chance of damage.

PALLET LOADER device employing one or more vertical lift platforms for the mechanical loading or unloading of palletized freight at planeside. *see also* PALLET; PALLETIZATION; PALLET TRANSPORTER; UNITIZATION; UNIT LOAD DEVICE.

PALLET TRANSPORTER vehicle for the movement of loaded PALLETS between the aircraft and the freight terminal. *see also* PALLET; PALLETIZATION; PALLET LOADER; UNIT LOAD DEVICE.

PALLETIZATION the process of using a PALLET on which a large number of individual packages are placed, which consolidates shipments, facilitates handling, and reduces the possibility of any damage occurring during shipment.

PALLETIZING loading and securing of a number of sacks, bags, boxes, or drums on a PALLET base. *see also* PALLET; PALLETIZATION; UNITIZATION; UNIT LOAD DEVICE.

PAN AMERICAN STANDARDS COMMISSION *see* COMISION PANAMERICANA DE NORMAS TECNICAS (COPANT).

PAN AMERICAN UNION *see* ORGANIZATION OF AMERICAN STATES.

PANEL a three-person committee assembled by the WORLD TRADE ORGANIZATION (WTO) to hear evidence in disputes between members. *see also* DISPUTE SETTLEMENT SYSTEM.

PAPER FISH the reduction in the QUOTA of fish not being caught as allowed under the NORTHWEST ATLANTIC FISHERIES ORGANIZATION.

PAPER GOLD *see* SPECIAL DRAWING RIGHTS (SDR).

PAR an equality between the face value of a share of stock or bond for example, and its actual market value. If it can be sold for more, it is "above par"; if it can be sold for less, "below par."

PAR EXCHANGE RATE free market price of one country's money in terms of the currency of another. *see also* FIXED EXCHANGE RATES; FLOATING EXCHANGE RATE; FLUCTUTATING EXCHANGE RATE.

PAR OF EXCHANGE market price of money in one national currency that is exchanged at the official rate for a specific amount in another national currency, or another commodity of value (gold, silver, etc.). *see also* EXCHANGE RATES; FIXED EXCHANGE RATES; FLOATING EXCHANGE RATE; FLUCTUTATING EXCHANGE RATE; MEDIUM OF EXCHANGE.

PAR VALUE
1. the value that a government sets, either by agreement or regulation, on its currency in terms of other currencies. This value of a currency was originally stated in terms of gold or the U.S. dollar; however, now it is being quoted in terms of SPECIAL DRAWING RIGHTS.
2. the face value of a share of stock in a company or the value of a bond trading at 100 cents to the dollar.

PARA TARIFF charge on imports that is not included in a country's TARIFF SCHEDULE.

PARALLEL EXPORTING (PARALLEL IMPORTING, PARALLEL TRADING) the trading of a product by independent operators who are outside the manufacturer's official channel of distribution. The parallel IMPORTER, EXPORTER, or trader may compete with the manufacturer's authorized distributors or subsidiaries, yet the operations are still legal.

PARALLEL MARKET (FOREIGN EXCHANGE) *see* BLACK MARKET.

PARASTATAL ENTERPRISE any company wholly or partly owned or controlled by a government.

PARCEL POST a postal service handling and delivering packages. *see also* PARCEL POST RECEIPT.

PARCEL POST AIR FREIGHT airline service through which a SHIPPER can consolidate a number of parcel post packages, with destination postage affixed by the shipper, for shipment as air freight to the postmaster at another city; meant for subsequent DELIVERY within local postal zones or beyond. *see also* PARCEL POST; PARCEL POST RECEIPT.

PARCEL POST RECEIPT the postal authorities' signed acknowledgment of delivery to them of a shipment made by PARCEL POST.

PARCEL RECEIPT receipt given by a steamship company for a parcel shipment.

PARENT BANK BANK in a major industrial country that sets up a subsidiary in a developing country. *see also* BANK AFFILIATE ETC; BANK HOLDING COMPANY; PARENT COMPANY.

PARENT COMPANY a company engaging in international trade or investing in a foreign country that owns a subsidiary company located there.

PARIS CHARTER FOR A NEW EUROPE a MULTILATERAL AGREEMENT signed by members of the CONFERENCE OF SECURITY AND COOP-

ERATION IN EUROPE (CSCE) in Paris, France, on November 22, 1990. The members committed themselves to a new declaration on human rights and an end to solving problems via military means. *see also* NORTH ATLANTIC TREATY ORGANIZATION (NATO); WARSAW PACT.

PARIS CLUB a popular designation for meetings among representatives of a developing country that wishes to renegotiate its "official" debt (normally excluding debts owed by and to the private sector without official guarantees) and representatives of the relevant creditor governments and international institutions. These meetings usually occur at the request of a debtor country that wishes to consolidate all or part of its debt service payments falling due over a specified period. Meetings are traditionally chaired by a senior official of the French Treasury Department. Comparable meetings occasionally take place in London and in New York for countries that wish to renegotiate repayment terms for their debts to private banks. These meetings are sometimes called creditor clubs. *see also* LONDON CLUB.

PARIS CONVENTION abridgment for The Paris Convention for the Protection of Industrial Property first adopted in 1883. The Paris Convention is the major international agreement providing basic rights for protecting industrial property. It covers patents, industrial designs, service marks, trade names, indications of source, and unfair competition. The United States ratified this treaty in May of 1887. The treaty provides two fundamental rights:
- the principle of national treatment provides that nationals of any signatory nation shall enjoy in all other countries of the union the advantages that each nation's laws grant to its own nationals.
- the right of priority enables any resident or national of a member country to, first, file a patent application in any member country and, thereafter, file a patent application for the same invention in any of the other member countries within 12 months of the original filing and receive benefit of the original filing date.

The resident or national of a member country also can claim the filing date of a trademark application or industrial design filed in another member country within six months of the filing date in his/her own country or country of residence.

PARIS PACT *see* LOUVRE ACCORD.

PARITY
1. equality in amount or value.
2. equivalence of prices of GOODS or SERVICES in different markets. *see also* MARKET PRICE; PRICE ESCALATION; PRICE SUPPRESSION.
3. the relationship between two currencies such that they are exchangeable for each other at PAR or at the official rate of exchange. *see also* EXCHANGE RATE(S); EXCHANGE RATE CLASSIFICATIONS; EXCHANGE RATE SPREAD; SPOT RATE
4. equivalence of prices of farm products (or farm income) to those existing at a former time or to the general cost of living.

PAROL an oral expression.

PAROL CONTRACT one that is verbal only and that has not been put into writing by the parties.

PARTIAL SHIPMENTS when the goods being transported do not represent the whole order as requested by the buyer. Example: EXPORTERS should always request that the LETTER OF CREDIT specify that partial shipments be allowed.

PARTICULAR AVERAGE in MARINE INSURANCE, a partial loss sustained on damage to goods that have been insured. *see also* AVERAGE; GENERAL AVERAGE; FREE OF PARTICULAR AVERAGE; WITH AVERAGE.

PARTNERSHIP an unincorporated business owned and operated by two or more persons, who, according to the agreement of the partnership, share profits, losses, and responsibilities and have general or limited liability. At least one partner must have unlimited liability. *see also* JOINT VENTURE.

PASSIVE INCOME income generated from a firm's operation in a TAX HAVEN country, which is the result of investments in other countries including income from sales and services involving buyers and sellers located elsewhere. Either the buyer or the seller needs to be part of the same organizational structure as the corporation earning the passive income. *see also* ACTIVE INCOME.

PASSPORT
1. an official document issued by a government certifying a person's identity and citizenship and authorizing the person to travel abroad.
2. a permit issued by a foreign country authorizing a person to transport goods or to travel through that country.

PASS-THROUGH (also called TRANSSHIPMENT) a foreign country's use of one country in a trade bloc as a means of gaining preferential treatment from other countries in the bloc.

PATACA unit of currency, Macao (100 avos equal 1 pataca).

PATENT a grant by law of privilege, property, or authority to one or more individuals, including the grant to an inventor of the right to exclude others from making, using, or selling the invention for a term of years.

PATENT COOPERATION TREATY (PCT) a worldwide convention, open to any PARIS CONVENTION country. The PCT entered into force in 1978. Unlike the Paris Convention, which addresses substantive intellectual property rights, the PCT addresses procedural requirements, aiming to simplify the filing, searching, and publication of international patent applications.

PATERNALISM a system in which a leader or an authority figure cares for all people as their father.

PATHOGEN any agent that can cause disease.

PAYABLE IN EXCHANGE requirement that a negotiable instrument be paid in the currency of the place from which it was originally issued.

PAYEE the individual or firm in whose favor a LETTER OF CREDIT is issued or a DRAFT is drawn. The payee can be the EXPORTER or the DRAWER of the draft. It can also be the exporter's BANK or other bearer of the draft upon its maturity. *see also* DRAWEE; PAYER.

PAYER the individual or firm responsible for honoring a DRAFT on its MATURITY DATE. This is normally the IMPORTER, the individual or firm against whom the draft was drawn; however, it can also be the importer's BANK, in the event the IMPORTER defaults and the bank issues an IRREVOCABLE LETTER OF CREDIT. *see also* DRAWEE; DRAWER; PAYEE.

PAYMENT DOCUMENTS a variety of documentation forms that must be completed by the exporting firm to ensure that the EXPORTER receives payment for the goods. Example: one of the most common forms of payment is a LETTER OF CREDIT. An EXPORT letter of credit is issued by the IMPORTER's bank, with a promise to pay the exporter a specified amount upon receipt of certain payment documents specified in the letter of credit within a specified time period. *see also* BILL OF LADING; COMMERCIAL INVOICE; CERTIFICATE OF INSPECTION; CERTIFICATE OF ORIGIN; INSURANCE CERTIFICATE.

PAYMENT IN ADVANCE the IMPORTER remits payment in full to the EXPORTER prior to the receipt of the goods. With this method of payment, the exporter/seller is relieved of any collection problems and has immediate use of the funds. On the other hand, payment in advance may create cash flow problems and increases risks for the importer/buyer.

PAYMENTS SURPLUS excess of the value of a nation's EXPORTS over its IMPORTS. *see also* BALANCE OF PAYMENTS.

PAYOFF *see* MORDIDA.

PBAS *see* POLISH BUSINESS ADVISORY SERVICE.

PBEC *see* PACIFIC BASIN ECONOMIC COUNCIL.

PCT *see* PATENT COOPERATION TREATY.

P.D. abbreviation for per diem; public domain.

PEC *see* PRESIDENT'S EXPORT COUNCIL.

PECC *see* PACIFIC ECONOMIC COOPERATION COUNCIL.

PEFCO *see* PRIVATE EXPORT FUNDING CORPORATION.

PEG to fix an EXCHANGE RATE against some standard, such as another currency. *see also* EXCHANGE RATE MECHANISM.

PEGGED EXCHANGE RATE *see* EXCHANGE RATE MECHANISM.

PEMEX *see* PETROLEOS MEXICANOS.

PENALTY sum of money that the obligor of a debt security undertakes to pay in the event of his failure to perform his obligations under the conditions of the debt security. *see also* SURETY.

PENETRATION PRICING strategy of setting a price sufficiently low as to rapidly reach a mass market. Penetration pricing places a greater emphasis on value to the buyer than on costs in establishing price. *see also* EXPANSIONISTIC PRICING.

PER CAPITA by or for each individual; calculated by taking the number of individuals involved; is divided equally among all. *see also* PER CAPITA INCOME.

PER CAPITA INCOME income per person, usually measured as gross domestic product divided by population.

PERESTROIKA (Russian) a word made popular by the former Soviet Union's President Gorbachev referring to the modernization of its economy. It emphasized replacing the COMMAND ECONOMY with more market-driven initiatives and decentralizing the decision-making power from the central government.

PERFORMANCE proper fulfillment of a contract or obligation according to its terms. *see also* BOND SYSTEM.

PERFORMANCE REQUIREMENTS government-mandated or government-approved activities that investors must undertake, usually as a condition of establishment or operation in a particular country.

PERFORMANCE SECURITY GUARANTEE a program of the Canadian EXPORT DEVELOPMENT CORPORATION that protects financial institutions against any wrongful calling of a performance bond, which is normally issued in the form of a documentary credit, and on behalf of the Canadian EXPORTER in favor of the foreign buyer. *see also* EXPORT FINANCING.

PERFORMANCE SECURITY INSURANCE a program of the Canadian EXPORT DEVELOPMENT CORPORATION providing EXPORTERS with coverage against a wrongful call by a foreign buyer against a DOCUMENTARY CREDIT provided by the buyer's bank to the benefit of the exporter.

PERIL POINT estimated limit beyond which a reduction in TARIFF protection would cause material injury to a domestic industry. *see also* PERIL POINT PROVISION.

PERIL POINT PROVISION a provision in U.S. legislation forbidding the President from negotiating any reduction in U.S. TARIFFS that might result in any INJURY to any U.S. domestic industry. The TRADE EXPANSION ACT OF 1962 explicitly eliminated the Peril Point provision that had limited U.S. negotiating positions in earlier GATT ROUNDS, and instead called on the Tariff Commission, the U.S. INTERNATIONAL TRADE COMMISSION (ITC), and other federal agencies to provide information regarding the probable economic effects of specific tariff concessions.

PERILS OF THE SEA a MARINE INSURANCE term that designates heavy weather, stranding, sinking, collision, and sea water damage as perils of the sea. They are elemental risks of ocean transport. It does not refer to damage resulting from fire, explosion, etc.

PERIOD OF INVESTIGATION the period, usually 6 months, beginning at least 150 days before and continuing 30 days after the first day of the month when an ANTIDUMPING PETITION is filed, during which an EXPORTER's home market (or third country) and U.S. prices and other appropriate facts are investigated to determine whether sales to the United States have been at less than FAIR VALUE. *see also* TARIFF ACT OF 1930.

PERISHABLE FREIGHT FREIGHT subject to decay or deterioration. *see also* DRY CARGO; HAZARDOUS MATERIAL.

PERMANENT INTERSTATE COMMITTEE FOR DROUGHT CONTROL IN THE SAHEL (French: Comité Permanente Interétats de Lutte contre la Sécheresse dans le Sahel, CILSS) committee that provides drought protection assistance to the 9 countries of the Sahel region (Burkina Faso, Cape Verde, Chad, the Gambia, Guinea-Bissau, Mali, Mauritania, Niger, and Senegal) through such forms as food silo construction, agricultural development, road improvement, and desertification prevention. The committee, founded in 1976, works in cooperation with the UNITED NATIONS, the WORLD BANK, the EUROPEAN ECONOMIC COMMUNITY (EEC), and the ORGANIZATION FOR ECONOMIC COOPERATION AND DEVELOPMENT (OECD).

PERMANENT NORMAL TRADING RELATIONS (PNTR) granting of permanent MOST-FAVORED-NATION (MFN) TREATMENT status to a country that is not a member of the WORLD TRADE ORGANIZATION (WTO).

PERSISTENT DUMPING the ongoing tendency of a firm in one country to sell a COMMODITY in a foreign market at less than the fair value price of the goods in the EXPORTER's domestic market.

PERSON *see* FOREIGN PERSON.

PERSONA GRATA a diplomatic representative who is acceptable to the government of the country where he/she is assigned.

PERSONA NON GRATA a diplomatic representative who is no longer acceptable to the government of the country where he/she is assigned.

PESETA unit of currency, Spain.

PETRODOLLARS oil earnings of petroleum-exporting countries in excess of their domestic needs and deposited in dollars in Western banks. However, a large part of the revenues that OPEC countries were unable to spend has been recycled to oil-importing countries in an attempt to balance international accounts.

PETROLEOS MEXICANOS (PEMEX) the state-owned oil monopoly in Mexico.

PHARE PROGRAMME funds provided by the WORLD BANK and EUROPEAN COMMUNITY (EC) for the preparation and implementation of restructuring programs aimed at privatizing the economies of Poland and other former eastern bloc countries.

PHASING *see* TRANSITIONAL MEASURES.

PHILIPPINE INSTITUTE OF CERTIFIED PUBLIC ACCOUNTANTS (PICPA) the accrediting agency for all certified public accountants in the Philippines. The PICPA is a member of the INTERNATIONAL ACCOUNTING STANDARDS COMMITTEE (IASC), the International Federation of Accountants (IFA), the Confederation of ASEAN and Pacific Accountants (PACA), and the ASEAN Federation of Accountants (AFA).

PHILIPPINE PISO unit of currency, Philippines (100 sentimos equal 1 Philippine piso).

PHYSICAL DISTRIBUTION all activities (exclusive of production) involved in moving goods from point of origin to point of destination.

PHYSICAL PRESENCE associated with SECTION 911 of the U.S. Internal Revenue Service Code and qualification for the exclusion of foreign earned income.

PHYTOSANITARY INSPECTION CERTIFICATE a certificate, issued by the U.S. Department of Agriculture, to satisfy IMPORT regulations of foreign countries, indicating that a U.S. shipment has been inspected and is free from harmful pests and plant diseases.

PICKUP AND DELIVERY SERVICE optional additional service for the transport of shipments from SHIPPER'S door to originating carrier's terminal and from terminal of destination to receiver's door, offered by some airlines and railroads and sometimes by other shipping modes. With some transportation services, such as the postal and small-package express services, it is a standard service rather than an option. *see also* DOOR-TO-DOOR; HOUSE-TO-HOUSE; POINT-TO-POINT.

PICKUP ORDER order from a BROKER to a CARRIER to pick up FREIGHT at a location. *see also* DELIVERY INSTRUCTIONS; SERVICE COMMITMENTS.

PIECEMEAL TARIFF REFORM reduction of only one TARIFF by a country that has additional tariffs on other products.

PIERS *see* PORT IMPORT/EXPORT REPORTING SERVICE.

PIER-TO-PIER shipment of CARGO by CARRIER from origin pier to discharge pier. *see also* DOOR-TO-DOOR; HOUSE-TO-HOUSE; POINT-TO-POINT.

PIGGYBACK transportation of truck trailers and containers on specially equipped railroad flatcars. *see also* LANDBRIDGE; MICROBRIDGE; MINIBRIDGE.

PIGGYBACK EXPORTING a foreign distribution operation where another firm's products are sold along with those of another manufacturer. This form of exporting is used by companies that have related or complementary but noncompetitive products. *see also* CARRIER; INDIRECT EXPORTING; RIDER.

PIGGYBACK MARKETING *see* PIGGYBACK EXPORTING.

PIGGYBACKING the assigning by one manufacturer of the EXPORT marketing of its products and distribution to another company. *see also* INDIRECT; EXPORTING; PIGGYBACK EXPORTING.

PILFERAGE any CARGO transit loss or damage. To avoid pilferage, a shipper should avoid mentioning contents or brand names on packages. In addition, strapping, seals, and shrink wrapping are effective means of deterring theft.

PILOT
1. person who flies an airplane.
2. a person whose occupation is to guide ships, particularly along a coast, or into and out of a harbor.

PIPELINE PROTECTION the protection accorded by a country for inventions, usually for pharmaceutical and agrichemical products, that already exist prior to that country's making patent protection available for such inventions.

PIRACY the illegal use of property rights protected by patents, copyrights, and trademarks. Protection for brand names varies from one country to another. In some developing countries barriers to the use of foreign brands or trademarks may exist. In other countries piracy of a company's brand names and counterfeiting of its products are widespread. To protect its products and brand names, a company must comply with local laws on patents, copyrights, and trademarks.

PLAN FILE a computer file that lists anything a UNIX user wants others on the NET to know about them. A plan file is placed in a home directory on a public-access site. Then, anybody who fingers you will get to see this file.

PLATA BASIN FINANCIAL DEVELOPMENT FUND *see* FONDO FINANCIERO PARA EL DESARROLLO DE LA CUENCA DEL PLATA.

PLAZA ACCORD an initiative ratified in a September 1985 meeting in New York by GROUP OF FIVE (G-5) officials to use exchange rates and other macropolicy adjustments as the preferred and necessary means to bring about an orderly decline in the value of the dollar. The agreement, intended to curb increasing U.S. trade imbalances and protectionist action, supported orderly appreciation of the main nondollar currencies against the dollar. *see also* LOUVRE ACCORD.

PLC an abbreviation used in the United Kingdom for a Private Limited Company. It is similar to the use of Inc. for incorporation or Ltd. for a limited liability company.

PLC *see* PRE-LICENSE CHECKS.

PLIMSOLL MARK horizontal line on the outside of a ship that represents the depth to which a vessel may be safely loaded; this mark must stay above the water surface.

PLUNA the state-controlled national airline of Uruguay.

PLURILATERAL among several countries, more than two, which would be bilateral, but not a great many, which would be multilateral.

PLURILATERAL AGREEMENT agreement made in the WORLD TRADE ORGANIZATION (WTO) in which only those member countries that choose to sign on to do so, as opposed to MULTILATERAL AGREEMENTS, in which all members sign on.

PNR abbreviation for the National Revolutionary Party in Mexico.

PNTR *see* PERMANENT NORMAL TRADING RELATIONS.

PO *see* PRINCIPAL OFFICER.

POINT OF ORIGIN location at which a shipment is received by a transportation line from the SHIPPER. *see also* PORT OF DISCHARGE; PORT OF ENTRY; PORT OF EXPORT.

POINT-TO-POINT describing service and rates for shipments in door-to-door service. *see also* DOOR-TO-DOOR; HOUSE-TO-HOUSE; PIER-TO-PIER.

POINT-TO-POINT PROTOCOL (PPP) a telecommunications method for transmitting data packets over serial point-to-point links.

POLICY COORDINATION also called the Economic Policy Coordination or G-7 Process. It refers to the coordination of the seven major economic powers (Canada, France, Germany, Great Britain, Italy, Japan, and the United States), whose finance ministers seek to promote balanced economic growth and stability among exchange rates.

POLICY FRAMEWORK PAPER (PFP) paper that lays out the steps a country will take while receiving structural adjustment assistance from the INTERNATIONAL MONETARY FUND (IMF). It describes the origins of the country's difficulties, corresponding improvement efforts, and requisite financing, as well as probable impacts on environment and society. The paper, updated annually, is developed by the recipient government in collaboration with IMF and the WORLD BANK. By design, it also serves as a vehicle for attracting orderly assistance from other donors. *see also* ENHANCED STRUCTURAL ADJUSTMENT FACILITY.

POLISH BUSINESS ADVISORY SERVICE (PBAS) a project development program that assists small- and medium-sized entrepreneurs with accessing bank financing and developing their businesses. The PBAS provides consulting and technical services to firms and was set up and partially financed by the International Finance Corporation of the WORLD BANK.

POLITICAL RISK normally includes defaults or losses due to action or inaction by governments, including war and civil unrest, expropriations, and inconvertibility of local currency to dollars. Losses due to currency devaluation are not considered a political risk. *see also* COMMERCIAL RISK.

POLITICAL TERRORISM terrorist acts directed at governments and their agents and motivated by political goals (i.e., national liberation).

POLITICAL UNION an agreement among sovereign countries to unite and form a TRADING BLOC that removes barriers to trade, free movement of labor and capital, and harmonizes trade, monetary, fiscal and tax policies among members. *see also* COMMON MARKET; ECONOMIC UNION.

POLITICAL VIOLENCE violence undertaken in a foreign country for political purposes. Examples: declared or undeclared war, hostile action by national or international forces, civil war, revolution, insurrection, and civil strife (including politically motivated terrorism and sabotage).

POLLUTION HAVEN country that, because of its weak or poorly enforced environmental regulations, attracts industries that pollute the environment.

POLYCENTRIC ORGANIZATION a stage in the development of a firm's overseas production capability, where management thinks of its business in terms of multiple countries or regions, each being an integral part of the firm, although the domestic market is still considered the most important.

POLYCENTRISM characteristic of an individual or an organization that feels that any differences must be accounted for in management decisions. In organizations characterized by polycentrism, control is decentralized and organizations are so overwhelmed by differences that they will risk not introducing any productive changes. *see also* ETHNOCENTRISM.

PORT
1. a harbor serving as a PORT OF ENTRY for international shipping.
2. a telecommunications TRANSPORT LAYER value. Each software application has a unique port number associated with it. *see also* TRANSMISSION CONTROL PROTOCOL; USER DATAGRAM PROTOCOL.

PORT CHARGE charge for services performed at ports. *see also* KEELAGE.

PORT MARKS identifying sets of letters, numbers, and/or geometric symbols followed by the name of the PORT of destination, which are placed on EXPORT shipments. Foreign government requirements may be exceedingly strict in the matter of port marks.

PORT OF DISCHARGE port at which a shipment is off-loaded by a transportation line. *see also* POINT OF ORIGIN; PORT OF ENTRY; PORT OF EXPORT.

PORT OF ENTRY PORT at which foreign goods are admitted into a receiving country.

PORT OF EXPORT port, airport, or CUSTOMS point from which an EXPORT shipment leaves a country for a voyage to a FOREIGN country. *see also* POINT OF ORIGIN; PORT OF DISCHARGE; PORT OF ENTRY.

PORT-OF-ORIGIN AIR CARGO CLEARANCE U.S. CUSTOMS SERVICE at foreign airports to facilitate the procedures before arrival in the United States. *see also* CLEAR CUSTOMS.

PORT SHOPPING the practice of EXPORTERS and IMPORTERS choosing a particular port on the basis of their assessment of customs' treatment, rather than on the quality of physical facilities and efficiency.

PORTFOLIO INVESTMENT
1. any foreign investment that is not a direct investment. Foreign portfolio investment includes the purchase of voting securities (stocks) at less than a 10% level, bonds, trade finance, and government lending or borrowing, excluding transactions in official reserves.
2. any managed group of investments including stocks, bonds, or trusts.

PORTS OF THE WORLD a column appearing daily in the JOURNAL OF COMMERCE that alphabetically lists the ports of call serviced by SHIPCARD advertisers and the shipcard numbers for the steamship lines servicing that port.

PORTUGUESE ESCUDO unit of currency, Portugal.

POSITION the total amount of FOREIGN EXCHANGE held by a person, firm, or institution on hand at any given time. *see also* CASH POSITION; LONG POSITION; OPEN POSITION; RISK POSITION; SHORT POSITION.

POSITIVE LIST a list of those items, entities, and products, to which an agreement applies, with no commitment to apply the agreement to anything else. *see also* NEGATIVE LIST.

POST a message placed on a USENET NEWSGROUP for others to see.

POSTDATED CHECK check delivered before its date, generally payable on or after the day its dated.

POSTINDUSTRIAL SOCIETY a society whose political and economic environment has moved away from manufacturing toward a service economy. It is a society whose GROSS DOMESTIC PRODUCT (GDP) comes from predominantly service-oriented industries. *see also* DEVELOPED COUNTRIES; DEVELOPING COUNTRIES.

POST-INITIATED PROMOTION (PIP) a scheduled low-budget trade promotion totally within the budgetary resources at a trade post (TRADE MISSION).

POSTAL TELEGRAPH AND TELEPHONE (PTT) a telephone service provider outside the United States, usually a monopoly, in a particular country.

POSTMASTER the person responsible for taking care of electronic mail problems, answering user queries, and carrying out related responsibilities.

POSTSHIPMENT VERIFICATIONS (PSVs) verifications conducted to determine that a COMMODITY is being used for the purposes for which its EXPORT was licensed. Firms or individuals representing the end user, intermediate consignees, or the purchaser may be subject to inquiries pertaining to the PSV. As part of the PSV process, the U.S. BUREAU OF EXPORT ADMINISTRATION (BXA) forwards a cable to the U.S. EMBASSY or CONSULATE in the respective geographical location to conduct an on-site inspection to ensure that the commodity is physically present and used as stated in the application. PSVs are usually conducted 6 to 8 months subsequent to export of the commodity. PSVs are also conducted by BXA agents.

POTASSIUM IODIDE Federal Drug Administration-approved non-prescription drug for use as a blocking agent to prevent the thyroid gland from absorbing radioactive iodine.

POUND unit of currency of Cyprus, Egypt, England, Falkland/Malvinas Islands, Gibraltar, Guernsey, Ireland, Isle of Man, Jersey, Northern Ireland, Scotland, Saint Helena, Sudan, and Syria.

POURBOIRE *see* BRIBERY.

POW WOW an annual trade show (held in the United States and in Europe) that brings together U.S. sellers and foreign buyers of travel-related services pertaining to travel to the United States.

POW WOW SELECTION COMMITTEE a committee of private-industry representatives in foreign countries who are responsible for selecting invitees to the INTERNATIONAL POW WOW.

POWER OF ATTORNEY—DESIGNATION OF FORWARDING AGENT form that must be completed by the EXPORTER, providing the FREIGHT FORWARDER with the authorization to execute a U.S. SHIPPER'S EXPORT DECLARATION on behalf of the exporter.

PRE-ARRIVAL DATA data transmitted, processed, and resident on a government computer before the shipment arrives at the PORT OF ENTRY.

PRECAUTIONARY PRINCIPLE view that when science has not yet determined whether a new product or process is safe or unsafe, policy should prohibit or restrict its use until it is known to be safe. When applied to TRADE (INTERNATIONAL), this principle has been used as the basis for prohibiting IMPORTS.

PREDATORY DUMPING the sale of a product or COMMODITY by an EXPORTER in a foreign market at less than fair market value, with the aim of eliminating the local producer as a competitor. Once this has been achieved, prices on the goods will then be raised by the exporter-predator. *see also* DUMPING; PERSISTENT DUMPING; SPORADIC DUMPING; ANTIDUMPING DUTY.

PREDATORY PRICING strategy where a producer sets the price for his/her product low enough to drive out competition and deter new firms from entering the market. *see also* EXTINCTION PRICING; PENETRATION PRICING; PREEMPTIVE PRICING.

PREEMPTIVE PRICING a situation where a firm will set the price for its product so low as to discourage competition. The strategy will be to set the price as close as possible to the total cost, and as volume increases, even lower costs will be quoted. The strategy assumes that profits will be made in the long run through market dominance. *see also* EXTINCTION PRICING; PENETRATION PRICING; PREDATORY PRICING.

PREFERENCES bilateral or multilateral trade concessions, normally granted to DEVELOPING COUNTRIES by DEVELOPED COUNTRIES. *see also* GENERALIZED SYSTEM OF PREFERENCES; REVERSE PREFERENCES.

PREFERENTIAL TARIFF tariff that imposes lower rates of DUTY on GOODS imported from some countries. *see also* CARIBBEAN BASIN INITIATIVE (CBI); GENERALIZED SYSTEM OF PREFERENCES (GSP); MOST-FAVORED-NATION (MFN) TREATMENT; NORTHERN AMERICAN FREE TRADE AGREEMENT (NAFTA); PERMANENT NORMAL TRADING RELATIONS (PNTR); PREFERENCES; PREFERENTIAL TRADE AREA (PTA).

PREFERENTIAL TRADE AREA (PTA) a framework under which member countries are given preferential TARIFF treatment for manufactured goods imported from certain countries, either members or nonmembers. *see also* CARIBBEAN BASIN INITIATIVE; GENERALIZED SYSTEM OF PREFERENCES.

PREFERENTIAL TRADE AREA FOR EASTERN AND SOUTHERN AFRICAN STATES southern African trade area established in 1981 that supports economic development and cooperation (agriculture, communications, customs, industry, monetary affairs, natural resources, and trade). Membership includes Burundi, Comoros, Djibouti, Ethiopia, Kenya, Lesotho, Malawi, Mauritius, Rwanda, Somalia, Swaziland, Tanzania, Uganda, Zambia, and Zimbabwe. The PTA's headquarters is in Lusaka, Zambia.

PREFERENTIAL TRADE ARRANGEMENT *see* PREFERENTIAL TRADE AREA (PTA).

PREFERENTIAL TRADE SCHEME *see* PREFERENTIAL TRADE AREA (PTA).

PREFERENTIAL TRADE SYSTEM *see* PREFERENTIAL TRADE AREA (PTA).

PREFERENTIAL TREATMENT reductions in TARIFFS provided by treaty members of a PREFERENTIAL TRADE AREA.

PREFERRED COUNTRY country that has lower rates of DUTY imposed on its GOODS or is given other preferential trade treatment by another country. *see also* PREFERENTIAL TARIFF; PREFERENTIAL TRADE AREA (PTA); PREFERENTIAL TREATMENT.

PREINDUSTRIAL SOCIETY *see* GEMEINSCHAFT.

PRELICENSE CHECKS (PLCs) investigations conducted to determine that dual-use items on an EXPORT license application are destined for a legitimate end use by a reliable end user. Firms or individuals representing the licensee (the applicant), the CONSIGNEE, the purchaser, the intermediate CONSIGNEE, or the end user may be subject to inquiries pertaining to the prelicense check. As part of the process, the BUREAU OF EXPORT ADMINISTRATION (BXA) forwards a cable to the U.S. EMBASSY or CONSULATE in the respective geographical location to conduct an inspection or meet with company representatives to conduct inquiries on BXA's behalf.

PRELIMINARY DETERMINATION the DUMPING determination by the U.S. INTERNATIONAL TRADE ADMINISTRATION (ITA) announcing the results of the investigation conducted within 160 days (or, in extraordinarily complicated cases, 210 days) after a petition is filed or an investigation is self-initiated by the International Trade Administration. If the ITA determines that there is a reasonable basis to believe or suspect that the merchandise under consideration is being sold or is likely to be sold at less than FAIR VALUE, liquidation of all affected entries is suspended, and the matter is referred to the INTERNATIONAL TRADE COMMISSION (ITC). *Preliminary determination* also refers to the decision by the ITC where there is a reasonable indication that an industry in the United States is materially injured, or threatened with material injury, or the establishment of an industry in the United States is materially retarded by reason of the IMPORTS of the merchandise that is the subject of the petition. The ITC must make its decision within 45 days after the date on which the petition is filed or an investigation is self-initiated by the ITA. If this determination is negative, the investigation is terminated. *see also* TARIFF ACT OF 1930.

PREMIUM (IN FOREIGN EXCHANGE) the difference between the SPOT and FORWARD RATES on the FORWARD MARKET. A foreign currency is selling at a premium when the forward rate is higher than the spot rate.

PREMIUM (IN INSURANCE) the amount that the insurance company charges the insured for coverage in the event of loss or damage while the goods are in transit. The amount of the premium is a reflection of the expectation of loss. Premiums quoted for MARINE INSURANCE are normally quoted "per $100 of insured value."

PREPAID notation on a shipping document indicating that the SHIPPER has already paid shipping charges to the CARRIER. *See also* COLLECT CHARGES.

PREPAID CHARGES transportation trade practice under which the SHIPPER pays transportation charges. *see also* COLLECT CHARGES.

PRESENTATION the process of the EXPORTER providing documentation to the bank showing that the goods were shipped by the date specified in the LETTER OF CREDIT.

PRESENTING BANK the collecting bank making presentation of the documents to the DRAWEE, the individual or firm on whom a DRAFT is drawn and who owes the stated amount.

PRESHIPMENT INSPECTION certification of the value, quality, or identity of traded goods done in the exporting country by specialized agencies or firms on behalf of the importing country. *see also* CERTIFICATE OF INSPECTION (OR SPECIAL POLICY); INSPECTION CERTIFICATION.

PRESIDENT'S EXPORT COUNCIL (PEC) council that advises the president of the United States on government policies and programs that affect U.S. trade performance; promote EXPORT expansion; and provide a forum for discussing and resolving trade-related problems among the business, industrial, agricultural, labor, and government sectors.

The council was established by executive order of the president in 1973 and was originally composed only of business executives. The council was reconstituted in 1979 to include leaders of the labor and agricultural communities, Congress, and the Executive Branch.

Twenty-eight private sector members serve "at the pleasure of the President" with no set term of office. Other members include five U.S. Senators and five members of the House; the Secretaries of Agriculture, Commerce, Labor, State, and Treasury; the Chairman of the Export-Import Bank; and the U.S. Trade Representative. The council reports to the president through the U.S. Secretary of Commerce.

PRESIDENT'S EXPORT COUNCIL, SUBCOMMITTEE ON EXPORT ADMINISTRATION (PECSEA) council composed of 25 industry representatives, selected by the U.S. Secretary of Commerce, which advises the PEC, the White House, and Commerce on all EXPORT control matters, including those that affect Commerce, State, Defense, and Energy. It was formed in June 1976.

PREVENTION OF UNFAIR COMPETITION ACT legislation in Korea that protects the foreign investor against unfair competition. A foreign national that is domiciled in or has a business in one of the countries signing the PARIS CONVENTION may make a request for an injunction to halt acts of unfair competition, such as trademark infringement.

PRICE ACTUALLY PAID OR PAYABLE the total payment made or to be made by the buyer to or for the benefit of the seller for the imported goods.

PRICE CONTROL ACT OF 1953 (Norway) legislation authorizing the government to supervise restrictive business practices and dominant enterprises and to issue regulations on prices, profits, production, and distribution.

PRICE DISCRIMINATION sale by a firm to buyers at two different prices. *see also* DUMPING.

PRICE ESCALATION the process by which a price increases as the channel of distribution lengthens, and the increase in the product's price is greater than the added direct cost, such as transportation, insurance, and TARIFFS.

PRICE FLOOR a government-imposed lower limit on the price that may be charged for a product.

PRICE-SPECIE *see* GOLD STANDARD.

PRICE-SPECIE FLOW MECHANISM a process used under the GOLD STANDARD, by which, when a country's BALANCE OF PAYMENTS was in deficit or surplus, there would be an automatic adjustment. When the balance of payments was in a deficit position, the automatic mechanism worked in the following way: a country in a deficit position lost gold and experienced a reduction in the money supply, which in turn caused domestic businesses to reduce prices, which in turn stimulated the exporters and provided little incentive to IMPORT more expensive goods. The process continued until the deficit was eliminated. When the balance of payments was in a surplus position, the automatic mechanism worked in reverse. The surplus caused an increase in the money supply, causing the producers to increase prices, curbing the demand for exports while providing an incentive to import cheap goods.

PRICE SUPPORT SUBSIDY or financial aid offered to specific growers, producers, or distributors, in accordance with governmental regulations, to keep market prices from dropping below a certain minimum level. *see also* EXPORT SUBSIDIES; IMPORT RESTRICTIONS; PROTECTIONISM; PROTECTIONIST TRADING PRACTICES; TRADE BARRIERS.

PRICE SUPPRESSION the process by which the prices on domestically produced goods are forced down as the foreign produced goods competing with them are sold at comparatively lower prices. *see also* UNDERSELLING.

PRICE UNDERTAKING a commitment by an exporting firm to raise its price in an importing-country market, as a means of settling an ANTIDUMPING SUIT and preventing an ANTIDUMPING DUTY.

PRINCIPAL the individual or firm that issues or signs a DRAFT and thus stands to receive payment of the stated amount from the DRAWEE.

PRINCIPAL OFFICER (PO) *see* TITLE AND RANK.

PRINCIPLES OF INTERNATIONAL TRADE *see* GENERAL AGREEMENT ON TARIFFS AND TRADE (GATT).

PRIORITY AIR FREIGHT reserved air freight or air express service in which shipments have a priority after mail and the small package services. *see also* DEFERRED AIR FREIGHT.

PRIORITY FOREIGN COUNTRY a country designated by the U.S. TRADE REPRESENTATIVE (USTR) as engaging in unfair trading acts, policies, and practices. *see also* PRIORITY PRACTICES; SUPER 301.

PRIORITY PRACTICES a country's policies, which present excessive barriers to trade with the United States. The elimination of priority practices would significantly increase the potential for U.S. EXPORTS. If the U.S. TRADE REPRESENTATIVE (USTR) makes a positive determination after weighing all relevant information, a country may be named to the list of
- PRIORITY FOREIGN COUNTRIES,
- the priority watch list, or
- the watch list.

This designation is made by the U.S. government under the authority of the OMNIBUS TRADE AND COMPETITIVENESS ACT OF 1988. *see also* SUPER 301.

PRIVATE CODE secret code system devised to conceal the contents of a message and to reduce the number of words required in a cablegram.

PRIVATE CORPORATION a business corporation with shares that are not traded among the general public. *see also* PUBLIC CORPORATION.

PRIVATE EXPORT FUNDING CORPORATION (PEFCO) a private company, accessed through its member banks and a few EXPORTERS, that works with EXIMBANK in using private capital to finance U.S. EXPORTS. The corporation acts as a supplemental lender to traditional commercial banking sources by making loans to public and private borrowers located outside of the United States who require medium and/or longer-term financing of their purchases of U.S. goods and services.

PRIVATE-SECTOR DEVELOPMENT PROGRAMS a program of the INTER-AMERICAN DEVELOPMENT BANK that promotes the economic development of the regional member countries by stimulating the establishment, expansion, and modernization of private enterprises, especially those of medium and small scale, in Latin America and the Caribbean. The program works directly with private enterprises in these countries and neither seeks nor requires government guarantees. The corporation makes direct investments such as equity participation, loans, and purchases of debt instruments, as well as direct investment through other financial institutions. The corporation also finances feasibility studies, underwrites securities, provides technical and managerial assistance, and helps entrepreneurs in mobilizing additional capital. *see also* INTER-AMERICAN INVESTMENT CORPORATION; ENTERPRISE FOR THE AMERICAS INITIATIVE.

PRIVATE VOLUNTARY ORGANIZATIONS (PVOs) nonprofit, tax-exempt, and nongovernmental organizations governed by a group of private citizens whose purpose is to engage in voluntary, charitable, and development operations overseas. The U.S. AGENCY FOR INTERNATIONAL DEVELOPMENT (AID) has registered over 150 PVOs, which are eligible to receive AID funding.

PRIVATIZATION the transfer of ownership or operation of a government-owned business to private owners or operators. *see also* NATIONALIZATION.

PRIVATIZATION LAW OF 1990 a Polish law, formally known as the State Enterprise Privatization Act of July 1990, enacted as the initial step in the privatization of Polish state-owned enterprises. Privatization may be achieved through transformation or liquidation.

PROCESSED GOOD a good that has been transformed in some way by a production activity. *see also* RAW MATERIAL.

PROCUREMENT the act of obtaining; attainment; acquisition; purchasing; buying.

PROCUREMENT AND LEAD TIME time required by the buyer to select a supplier and to place and obtain a commitment for specific quantities of materials at specified times.

PROCUREMENT INFORMATION BULLETIN—AGENCY FOR INTERNATIONAL DEVELOPMENT (AID) U.S. government publication that announces negotiated procurements by the public sector. Information on individual proposed procurements under formal competitive bid procedures is announced in the AID-financed EXPORT OPPORTUNITIES BULLETIN.

PROCURING AGENT *see* PURCHASING AGENT.

PRODUCER PRESENCE a mode of supply of a traded service in which the producer establishes a presence in the buyer's country by permanent relocation of workers, foreign direct investment, or both. *see also* CONSUMER MOVEMENT; CROSS-BORDER SUPPLY; MOVEMENT OF NATURAL PERSONS.

PRODUCT a GOOD or SERVICE that is produced.

PRODUCT AND SERVICE SECTOR COUNSELING services provided by the industry desk officers of the U.S. INTERNATIONAL TRADE ADMINISTRATION (ITA). The industry desk officers prepare reports on the competitive strength of selected U.S. industries in domestic and international markets for the publication U.S. *Industrial Outlook* (available from the U.S. Government Printing Office). They also promote exports for their industry sectors through marketing seminars, trade missions and trade fairs, foreign buyer groups, business counseling, and information on market opportunities.

PRODUCT GROUPS COMMODITY GROUPINGS used for EXPORT control purposes. *see also* EXPORT CONTROL CLASSIFICATION NUMBER.

PRODUCT LIFE CYCLE the course of the sales and profits of a product over its life. It involves four stages: introduction, growth, maturity, and decline. The INTERNATIONAL PRODUCT LIFE CYCLE holds that as a product moves through its various stages, the location of production will shift internationally.

PRODUCT SHIFTING the change in the production of one product to the production of another, which does not require costly production modification. *see also* PRODUCTION SWITCHING.

PRODUCTION AGREEMENT an agreement where one firm agrees to produce a product for another firm without having any equity ownership in that firm. *see also* ASSEMBLY; CONTRACT MANUFACTURING; LICENSING; PRODUCTION SHARING; PRODUCTION SWITCHING.

PRODUCTION EFFECT OF A TARIFF the increase in domestic production of a product, resulting from an increase in prices on IMPORTED products due to high TARIFFS. *see also* CONSUMPTION EFFECT OF A TARIFF; TRADE EFFECT OF A TARIFF.

PRODUCTION SHARING international production cooperation between independent firms including assembly and distribution of their products. *see also* JOINT VENTURE; LICENSING; MIXED VENTURE.

PRODUCTION SWITCHING the movement of production from one country to another as a result of changing costs. *see also* PRODUCTION AGREEMENTS; PRODUCTION SHARING.

PRODUCTIVITY a measurement of the efficiency of production.

PROFIT
1. value used for the purposes of a constructed value in an ANTIDUMPING DUTY investigation or review. The profit used is the profit normally earned by a producer, from the country of EXPORT, of the same or similar product as that under investigation.
2. the amount remaining after all expenses have been deducted from revenues.

PROFIT SHARING
1. an incentive system where a private enterprise gives a percentage of its profits to its employees.
2. a governmentally owned or subsidized industry having private management, which is compensated wholly or in part through a profit-pooling or sharing arrangement. Private management has

limited investment risk while enjoying the benefits of a profit incentive.

PROFORMA an informal document presented in advance of the arrival of goods or in preparation of the required documents (i.e., LETTER OF CREDIT or IMPORT LICENSE). *see also* PROFORMA INVOICE.

PROFORMA INVOICE an INVOICE provided by a supplier prior to the shipment of merchandise, informing the buyer of the kinds and quantities of goods to be sent, their value, and important specifications (weight, size, and similar characteristics).

PROHIBITED SUBSIDY a SUBSIDY that is prohibited under the rules of the WORLD TRADE ORGANIZATION (WTO), and is specifically designed to distort international trade. *see also* EXPORT SUBSIDIES.

PROHIBITION denial of the right to IMPORT or EXPORT a particular product and, perhaps, to particular countries. *see also* EMBARGO; TRADE BARRIER.

PROHIBITIVE TARIFF a TARIFF that is set at a high enough level that it reduces or eliminates trade in the product subject to the duty. *see also* DUTY; OPTIMUM TARIFF.

PROJECT LICENSE license used by the U.S. BUREAU OF EXPORT ADMINISTRATION (BXA) to authorize large-scale EXPORTS of a wide variety of COMMODITIES and technical data for specified activities. Those activities are restricted to capital expansion, maintenance, repair or operating supplies, or the supply of materials to be used in the production of other commodities for sale. Items intended for resale in the form received are not permitted and must be effected under a DISTRIBUTION LICENSE.

PRONASOL a Mexican government program that targets the estimated 24 million Mexicans who live in extreme poverty and relies heavily on each community's involvement in designing and executing programs. Projects supported by PRONASOL funds usually address some immediate need of a community, such as potable water, sewage, and electrification. Funds are also used for worker training and primary school teaching materials.

PROOF OF DELIVERY evidence that one party has turned over something (CARGO) to another. Commonly, in transportation, a signed, dated acknowledgment of receipt.

PROOF OF INSURANCE *see* CERTIFICATE OF INSURANCE.

PROPRIETOR person who has an exclusive right or interest in property or in a business.

PROPRIETORSHIP a business, usually unincorporated, that is owned and controlled by one person.

PRO RATA BASIS the procedure by which IMPORTED items under ABSOLUTE QUOTA are released when the total quantity of entries filed at the opening of the quota period exceeds the quota. The pro rata basis is the ratio between the quota quantity and the total quantity being offered for ENTRY. This procedure assures an equitable distribution of the quota.

PROSPERO a distributed data file system that provides the user with the ability to create multiple views of a single collection of data files distributed across the INTERNET. Prospero provides a file naming system, and file access is provided by existing access methods (e.g., anonymous FTP and NFS). The Prospero PROTOCOL is also used for communication between clients and servers in the ARCHIE system. *see also* ANONYMOUS FTP; ARCHIVE SITE; GOPHER; NETWORK FILE SYSTEM.

PROTECTED MARKETS buyers and sellers whose markets are protected from disruption by the use of VOLUNTARY EXPORT RESTRAINTS (VERS) of exporters' products to these markets. *see also* MARKET DISRUPTION; RESTRAINED EXPORTERS.

PROTECTION COST OF A TARIFF the effect that TARIFF protection has on industries due to a loss of productive efficiency and changes in consumption. *see also* INFANT INDUSTRY ARGUMENT; TRADE BARRIER.

PROTECTIONISM a government policy to protect inefficient domestic producers through the use of barriers to trade to reduce imports of goods into the country. *see also* GENERAL AGREEMENT ON TARIFFS AND TRADE (GATT); TARIFF; TRADE BARRIERS; QUOTA; RESTRICTIVE STANDARDS.

PROTECTIONIST BUSINESS PRACTICES *see* PROTECTIONIST TRADING PRACTICES.

PROTECTIONIST TRADING PRACTICES any effort on the part of a country to limit or restrict international trade. *see also* PROTECTIONISM; TARIFF ACT OF 1930.

PROTECTIVE ORDER a term for the order in ANTIDUMPING cases under which most business proprietary information is made available to an attorney or other representative of a party to the proceeding. *see also* TARIFF ACT OF 1930.

PROTECTIVE SERVICE service offered by many airlines in which SHIPPERS can arrange to have their shipments under CARRIER surveillance at each stage of transit.

PROTECTIVE TARIFF DUTY or tax on imported products to make them more expensive in comparison to domestic products. *see also* IMPORT QUOTA; IMPORT RESTRICTIONS; PROTECTIONISM; PROTECTIONIST TRADING PRACTICES; TRADE BARRIERS.

PROTEST
1. procedural means by which an IMPORTER, CONSIGNEE, or other designated party may challenge a CUSTOMS decision. *see also* PROTEST SYSTEM.

2. an action required to be taken in some countries to protect one's rights to seek legal remedies when a collection is dishonored. *see also* DOCUMENTS ON ACCEPTANCE; TIME DRAFT.

PROTEST SYSTEM a part of the U.S. CUSTOMS SERVICE AUTOMATED COMMERCIAL SYSTEM that tracks protests from the date they are received through final action. A protest is the legal means by which an IMPORTER, CONSIGNEE, or other designated party may challenge decisions made by a District Director of Customs.

PROTOCOL diplomatic procedures followed between two or more countries. *see also* INTERNATIONAL AGREEMENTS; TITLE AND RANK.

PROTOCOL OF ACCESSION legal document specifying the procedures for a country to join an international agreement or organization. *see also* ACCESSION.

PROTOCOL OF PROVISIONAL APPLICATION (PPA) a legal device that enabled the original contracting parties to accept general GATT obligations and benefits, despite the fact that some of their existing domestic legislation at that time discriminated against IMPORTS in a manner that was inconsistent with certain GATT provisions. Although meant to be "temporary," the protocol has remained in effect, and countries that signed the PPA in 1947 continue to invoke it to defend certain practices that are otherwise inconsistent with their GATT obligations. Countries that acceded to the GATT after 1947 have also done so under the terms of the protocol.

PSVs *see* POSTSHIPMENT VERIFICATIONS.

PTA *see* PREFERENTIAL TRADE AREA; PREFERENTIAL TRADE AREA FOR EASTERN AND SOUTHERN AFRICAN STATES.

PTA BANK *see* EASTERN AND SOUTHERN AFRICAN TRADE AND DEVELOPMENT BANK.

PTT *see* POSTAL TELEGRAPH AND TELEPHONE.

PUBLIC CORPORATION a business corporation with shares traded among the general public, such as through a stock exchange. *see also* PRIVATE CORPORATION.

PUBLIC LIMITED COMPANY *see* LIMITED (LIABILITY).

PUBLISHED RATE
   1. the freight charges for a particular class and quantity of CARGO as published in a carrier's rate schedule.
   2. the service charges of many kinds of public utilities (usually government-regulated enterprises), which are published in rate schedules for public information.

PUERTO RICAN MODEL a U.S. strategy of providing assistance to small Latin American and Caribbean countries whose economy primarily relies on one crop. The model consists of DUTY-FREE access to the United States and tax incentives for U.S. companies relocating to the country. The CARIBBEAN BASIN INITIATIVE program is the basis for this strategy.

PULA unit of currency, Botswana (100 thebe equal 1 pula).

PULL a promotional strategy where the producer directs the effort to inform, persuade, and influence the consumers before they reach the point of purchase. This is usually accomplished through the use of mass media advertising. *see also* PUSH.

PUNITIVE DUTY *see* COUNTERVAILING DUTY.

PUNITIVE TARIFF *see* ANTIDUMPING DUTY; DUTY.

PURCHASE OF DRAWINGS UNDER A DOCUMENTARY CREDIT a means of EXPORT financing whereby the EXPORTER sells TIME DRAFTS to a bank or another lender that a creditworthy foreign buyer has accepted or agreed to pay at a specified future date.

In some cases, banks agree to accept the obligations of paying a draft, usually of a customer, for a fee; this is called a BANKER'S ACCEPTANCE. However, to convert these instruments to cash immediately, an EXPORTER must obtain a loan using the draft as collateral or sell the draft to an investor or a bank for a fee. When the draft is sold to an investor or bank, it is sold at a DISCOUNT.

The exporter receives an amount less than the face value of the draft so that when the draft is paid at its face value at the specified future date, the investor or bank receives more than it paid to the exporter. The difference between the amount paid to the exporter and the face amount paid at maturity is called a discount and represents the fees or interest (or both) the investor or bank receives for holding the draft until maturity.

Some drafts are discounted by the investor or bank without recourse to the exporter in case the party that is obligated to pay the draft defaults. Others may be discounted with recourse to the exporter. In this case the exporter must reimburse the investor or bank if the party obligated to pay the draft defaults. The exporter should be certain of the terms and conditions of any financing arrangement of this nature.

PURCHASE ORDER a purchaser's written OFFER to a supplier formally stating all terms and conditions of a proposed transaction.

PURCHASE PRICE a statutory term used in DUMPING investigations to refer to the U.S. sales price of merchandise that is sold or likely to be sold prior to the date of importation, by the producer or reseller of the merchandise for exportation to the United States. Certain statutory adjustments (e.g., IMPORT DUTIES, commissions, freight) are made, if appropriate, to permit a meaningful comparison with the foreign market value of such or similar merchandise. *see also* TARIFF ACT OF 1930.

PURCHASER within the context of EXPORT controls, the purchaser is that person abroad who has entered into the export transaction with the applicant to purchase the COMMODITIES or technical data for delivery to the ultimate CONSIGNEE.

PURCHASE FROM FOREIGN SELLER a transaction involving the purchase of a COMMODITY from a seller whose place of business is outside the United States.

PURCHASING AGENT an agent who purchases goods in his/her own country on behalf of large foreign buyers such as government agencies and large private corporations.

PURCHASING POWER PARITY a theory that states that exchange rates between currencies are in equilibrium when their purchasing power is the same in each of the two countries.

PUSH a promotional strategy where the producer directs the effort to inform, persuade, and influence the consumers by providing incentives to the marketing intermediaries. This strategy involves direct selling techniques. *see also* PULL.

PVOs *see* PRIVATE VOLUNTARY ORGANIZATIONS.

P.W. abbreviation for packed weight.

Q

QATAR RIYAL unit of currency, Qatar (100 dirhems equal 1 Qatar riyal).

QR *see* QUANTITY RESTRICTION.

QUAD an abbreviation used when referring to the group of four politicians, each of whom hold a cabinet-level position for international trade in their own countries. The members of the group are the Canadian Ministry of International Trade, U.S. TRADE REPRESENTATIVE (USTR), Japan's MINISTER OF INTERNATIONAL TRADE AND INDUSTRY (MITI), and the EUROPEAN ECONOMIC COMMUNITY (EEC) Commissioner for External Relations. *see also* QUADRILATERAL MEETINGS.

QUADRILATERAL MEETINGS meetings involving trade ministers from the United States, the EUROPEAN COMMUNITY (EC), Canada, and Japan to discuss trade policy matters.

QUADRILATERAL TRADE transactions among four countries. *see also* BILATERAL TRADE; MULTILATERAL TRADE; TRILATERAL TRADE.

QUADRILATERAL TRADE AGREEMENT a formal trade agreement among four nations.

QUALITY CONTROL CIRCLES a production system designed to identify and provide solutions for production problems through regular meetings held by small groups of workers.

QUANTITATIVE EXPORT RESTRAINTS *see* VOLUNTARY RESTRAINT AGREEMENT (VRA).

QUANTITATIVE RESTRICTIONS (QRs) explicit limits, usually by volume, on the amount of a specified COMMODITY that may be imported into a country, sometimes also indicating the amounts that may be imported from each supplying country. Compared to TARIFFS, the protection afforded by QRs tends to be more predictable, being less affected by changes in competitive factors. Quotas have been used at times to favor preferred sources of supply. The GENERAL AGREEMENT ON TARRIFS AND TRADE (GATT) generally prohibits the use of quantitative restrictions, except in special cases, such as those cited in Article XX (which permits exceptions to protect public health, national gold stocks, goods of archeological or historic interest, and a few other special categories of goods) or Article XXI (which permits exceptions in the interest of "national security") or for safeguard purposes.

QUANTITY the actual contract quantity specified in the agreement between the EXPORTER and foreign buyer or seller.

QUANTITY CONTROLS limits imposed by a government on the amounts of foreign currency that can be used in a specific transaction.

QUANTITY QUOTA a QUOTA specifying quantity of a GOOD, in units, weight, or volume. *see also* TARIFF QUOTA; TARIFF RATE QUOTAS.

QUANTITY RESTRICTIONS (QR) limits on the amounts of goods that may be EXPORTED or IMPORTED. Also referred to as QUOTAS. *see also* ABSOLUTE QUOTAS; EXPORT QUOTAS; GENERAL AGREEMENT ON TARIFFS AND TRADE (GATT); IMPORT QUOTAS; TARIFF RATE QUOTAS.

QUARANTINE period during which an arriving ship or airplane, including its passengers, crew, and CARGO, suspected of carrying a contagious disease, is held in isolation to prevent the possible spread of the disease.

QUASI INTERNATIONAL LAW rules that refer to the relationships among nations and private legal entities, such as corporations.

QUASI JUDICIAL PROCEDURES means by which governmental agencies or departments responsible for regulating trade make law. *see also* U.S. INTERNATIONAL TRADE COMMISSION (ITC).

QUAY a structure built for the purpose of mooring a vessel; also called a pier. *see also* WHARF.

QUESTIONABLE PAYMENTS *see* BRIBES.

QUETZAL unit of currency, Guatemala (100 centavos equal 1 quetzal).

QUEUE a backup of packets awaiting processing.

QUID PRO QUO mutual consideration; securing an advantage or receiving a concession in return for a similar favor.

QUITAS FISCAL a document required by a foreign resident prior to departing Algeria. The document is issued by the local tax officials for the purpose of verifying that all HOST COUNTRY income taxes have been paid. *see also* FISCAL CLEARANCE.

QUOTA the quantity of goods that may be imported without restriction or additional duties or taxes.

QUOTA STATUS the circumstance existing when a COMMODITY subject to a TARIFF RATE QUOTA cannot be determined in advance of its ENTRY. The QUOTA rates of DUTY are ordinarily assessed on such commodities entered from the beginning of the quota period until such time in the period as it is determined that IMPORTS are nearing the quota level. U.S. District Directors of Customs are then instructed to require the deposit of estimated duties at the over-quota duty rate and to report the time of official presentation of each entry. A final determination of the date and time when a quota is filled is made, and all district directors are advised accordingly.

QUOTA SYSTEM part of the U.S. CUSTOMS SERVICE AUTOMATED COMMERCIAL SYSTEM, controls QUOTA levels (quantities authorized) and quantities entered against those levels. *see also* ABSOLUTE QUOTA; IMPORT RESTRICTIONS; PROTECTIONIST TRADING PRACTICES; TARIFF QUOTA; TRADE BARRIERS.

QUOTA WATCH a column appearing each Tuesday in the JOURNAL OF COMMERCE that provides a listing of textile QUOTA categories that are filled or about to be filled.

QUOTAS AND QUOTA SYSTEM several different types of IMPORT QUOTAS established by U.S. Presidential Proclamations, Executive Orders, or other legislation. Absolute quotas permit a limited number of units of specified merchandise to be entered or withdrawn for consumption during specified periods. Tariff-rate quotas permit a specified quantity of merchandise to be entered or withdrawn at a reduced rate during a specified period. The quota system, a part of the U.S. CUSTOMS SERVICE AUTOMATED COMMERCIAL SYSTEM, controls import quota levels (quantities authorized) and quantities entered against those levels. VISAS control EXPORTS from the country of origin. Visa authorizations are received from other countries and quantities entered against those visas are transmitted back to them. Control of visas and quotas simplifies reconciliation of other countries' exports and U.S. imports. *see also* INTERNATIONAL MONETARY FUND (IMF).

QUOTATION an offer to sell goods at a stated price and under specified conditions.

QUOTED CURRENCY a rate of exchange quoted by relating one currency to another. The currency for which the numerical value is one is called the BASE CURRENCY; the other currency is the quoted currency. Example: if the EXCHANGE RATE between the U.S. dollar and Japanese YEN were quoted at 95 yen, the U.S. dollar would be the base currency, and the yen would be the quoted currency.

QUR'AN the holy book of Islam, considered by Muslims to contain the revelations of God to Mohammed. *see also* KORAN.

R

R.&O. abbreviation for rail and ocean.

R&R *see* REST AND RECREATION LEAVE.

RAIL WAYBILL FREIGHT document that indicates goods have been received for shipment by rail. *see also* AIR WAYBILL; BILL OF LADING.

RAMADAN the ninth month of the Muslim year. During this month Muslims must abstain from eating or drinking from sunrise to sunset. Any consumption of food or drink, or any sexual activity is strictly prohibited during the period of the fast. Soldiers and those individuals who are sick are excused. The Ramadan fast is one of the five "pillars," or basic duties of Islam. It commemorates the first revelation of the KORAN to Muhammad.

RAND unit of currency, South Africa (100 cents equal 1 rand).

RANK IN PERSON the personal rank that a Foreign Service officer maintains even when occupying a job of higher or lower rank.

RARE *see* RESEAUX ASSOCIES POUR LA RECHERCHE EUROPEENNE.

RATE OF EFFECTIVE PROTECTION *see* EFFECTIVE RATE OF PROTECTION.

RATE OF EXCHANGE *see* EXCHANGE RATE.

RATING all MARINE INSURANCE RATES are "per $100.00 of insured value." The rates are included in the policy. Insured value and PREMIUM are usually determined as follows:
- Imports: (Declared Value + Freight + 10%) × Rate = Premium
- Exports: (Invoice Value + Freight + 10%) × Rate = Premium

RATIONALIZATION *see* RATIONALIZED PRODUCTION.

RATIONALIZED PRODUCTION firms producing different components or parts of their product lines in different locations around the world, enabling them to take advantage of lower costs of labor, capital and raw materials. *see also* OUTSOURCING.

RAW MATERIAL a GOOD that has not been transformed by production. *see also* PROCESSED GOOD.

RBP *see* RESTRICTIVE BUSINESS PRACTICE.

R.C.&L. abbreviation for rail, canal, and lake.

RDA *see* AGENTIA ROMANA DE DEZVOLTARE (Romanian Development Agency).

REAL unit of currency of Brazil (100 centavos equal 1 real).

REAL EXCHANGE RATE the NOMINAL EXCHANGE RATE adjusted for inflation.

REAL INTEREST RATE the NOMINAL INTEREST RATE adjusted for inflation.

REAL RIGHTS rights in real estate or in items attached to real estate.

REALIGNMENT simultaneous and mutually coordinated REVALUATION and DEVALUATION of the currencies of several countries. *see also* REVALUATION OF A CURRENCY.

REALIGNMENT OF CURRENCIES simultaneous and mutually coordinated REVALUATION and DEVALUATION of the currencies of several countries. *see also* REVALUATION OF A CURRENCY.

REASONABLE CARE the responsibilities a BANK has in the COLLECTIONS process. All banks will act in good faith and exercise reasonable care. Banks must verify that the documents received appear to be as listed in the collection order and must immediately advise the party for whom the collection order was received of any missing document. *see also* BILL OF EXCHANGE; DRAFT; LETTER OF CREDIT.

REASSEMBLY the INTERNET PROTOCOL process in which a previously fragmented packet is reassembled before being passed to the transport LAYER. *see also* FRAGMENTATION.

REBATE OF DUTIES a rebate by a government, in whole or in part, of customs duties assessed on imported merchandise that is subsequently exported. These regulations and procedures vary among countries. Also called DRAWBACK.

REBATE RATE the rate of interest deductible when a BILL OF EXCHANGE or DRAFT is paid to the beneficiary prior to its MATURITY DATE. *see also* DISCOUNTING; DISCOUNTING OF ACCEPTED BILLS OF EXCHANGE; DISCOUNTING OF DRAWING UNDER A LETTER OF CREDIT.

RECEIPT any written acknowledgment of value received.

RECEIVED FOR SHIPMENT BILL OF LADING a BILL OF LADING (B/L) that confirms the receipt of GOODS by the carrier for transportation on a particular vessel, but not their actual loading on board the vessel nor their actual shipment. *see also* CLEAN BILL OF LADING; ON-BOARD BILL OF LADING; ORDER BILL OF LADING; STRAIGHT BILL OF LADING.

RECEIVING PAPERS paperwork that accompanies a shipment when it is brought to a carrier. *see also* DOCK RECEIPT.

RECIPROCAL DEFENSE PROCUREMENT MEMORANDA OF UNDERSTANDING (MOU) broad bilateral umbrella that seeks to reduce trade barriers on defense procurement. They usually call for the waiver of "buy national" restrictions, customs, and duties to allow the contractors of the signatories to participate, on a competitive basis, in the defense procurement of the other country. These agreements were designed in the late 1970s to promote rationalization, standardization, and interoperability of defense equipment within the NORTH ATLANTIC TREATY ORGANIZATION (NATO). At that time, the MOUs were also intended to reduce the large defense trade advantage the United States possessed over the European allies. The first agreements were signed in 1978.

RECIPROCAL DUMPING the sale by firms from two countries into each others' markets for prices below what each charges at home. *see also* DUMPING.

RECIPROCAL QUOTE the reciprocal of the DIRECT QUOTE (the number of units of the local currency given for one unit of a foreign currency). *see also* INDIRECT QUOTE.

RECIPROCAL TRADE AGREEMENT an international agreement between two or more countries to establish mutual trade concessions that are expected to be of equal value. *see also* RECIPROCITY.

RECIPROCITY the reduction of a country's IMPORT duties or other trade restraints in return for comparable trade concessions from another country.

Reciprocity includes the lowering of CUSTOMS DUTIES on imports in return for TARIFF concessions from other countries, and the negotiated reduction of a country's import duties or other trade restraints in return for similar concessions from another country. Reciprocity is a traditional principle of the GENERAL AGREEMENT ON TARIFFS AND TRADE (GATT) negotiations that implies an approximate equality of concessions accorded and benefits received among or between participants in a negotiation. In practice this principle applies only in negotiations between developed countries. Because of the frequently wide disparity in their economic capacities and potential, the relationship between developed and developing countries is generally not one of equivalence. The concept of relative reciprocity has emerged to characterize the practice by developed countries to seek less than full reciprocity from developing countries in trade negotiations.

RECOMMENDED DETERMINATION RECORD an order issued by an ADMINISTRATIVE LAW JUDGE (ADJ) concerning action to be taken relative to a violation of an order issued by a civil tribunal, such as the U.S. INTERNATIONAL TRADE COMMISSION (ITC). *see also* DETERMINATION; INJURY; PRELIMINARY DETERMINATION; SCOPE DETERMINATION; SPECIAL 301; UNFAIR TRADE PRACTICE.

RECONSIGNMENT
1. change in the name of the CONSIGNOR.
2. change in the place of DELIVERY.
3. relinquishment of shipment at POINT OF ORIGIN.

RED BOX a category of SUBSIDIES that is forbidden under the rules of the WORLD TRADE ORGANIZATION (WTO).

RED CLAUSE a clause appearing in a LETTER OF CREDIT that authorizes the presentation of the CLEAN DRAFT, without documents, accompanied by a statement by the SHIPPER that the proper shipping documents will be submitted at a later date. *see also* TELEGRAPHIC TRANSFER CLAUSE.

REDELIVER
  1. to yield and deliver back a thing.
  2. a demand by CUSTOMS to return to Customs' custody goods for reexamination, detention, REEXPORT, or destruction. *see also* CLEAR CUSTOMS; PROTEST SYSTEM.

REDUCED DEBT SERVICING a technique used by BANKS unwilling to provide additional funds to indebted creditor countries. These banks are given the offer to convert current claims to a repayment of financial obligations by issuing new bonds exempt from future debt reduction measures. *see also* DEBT REDUCTION TECHNIQUES; DEBT SERVICING; PARIS CLUB.

REDUNDANT TARIFF a tariff that, if changed, will not alter the quantity of IMPORTS, either because the TARIFF is prohibitive or because some other policy such as a QUOTA or an EMBARGO, is limiting quantity. *see also* TRADE BARRIERS.

REEFER CONTAINER controlled temperature shipping container (usually refrigerated). *see also* DRY CARGO CONTAINER, GENERAL CARGO VESSELS.

REENTRY SHOCK the normal cultural readjustment that occurs when an individual returns to his/her own HOME COUNTRY. *see also* CULTURE SHOCK; REPATRIATION; REVERSE CULTURE SHOCK.

REENTRY VISA permit issued by a government granting permission to a foreign resident to temporarily leave and then reenter the HOST COUNTRY. *see also* EXIT VISA; MULTIPLE-ENTRY VISA; RESIDENCY VISA; SINGLE-ENTRY VISA; WORK VISA.

REEXPORTS
  1. for EXPORT control purposes, the shipment of U.S.-origin products from one foreign destination to another.
  2. for statistical reporting purposes, exports of foreign-origin merchandise that has previously entered the United States for consumption or into customs-bonded warehouses for U.S. FOREIGN TRADE ZONES.
  Generally, the reshipment of national products from one foreign destination to another.

REFERENCE PRICE *see* MINIMUM PRICE SYSTEM.

REFERENCE ZONE *see* MANAGED FLOAT.

REFG abbreviation for refrigerating; refrigeration.

REFORMA a multilane avenue that runs through the heart of Mexico City. It was designed as an exact duplicate of the Champs Élysées in Paris, France, and is formally known as Paseo de la Reforma.

REFUND amount returned to the CONSIGNOR as a result of the CARRIER having collected charges in excess of the originally agreed-upon charges.

REGIOCENTRISM a business alignment directed toward the needs of regional markets, acknowledging and accepting similarities between regions. Regiocentrism is the third stage through which a firm passes from doing business in its own country to trading with the world. *see also* EPRG (FRAMEWORK); ETHNOCENTRISM; POLYCENTRISM; GLOBALISM.

REGIONAL *see* MIDLEVEL NETWORK.

REGIONAL AID a SUBSIDY directed at a geographic region of a country to assist its development; considered NONACTIONABLE SUBSIDIES under the rules of the WORLD TRADE ORGANIZATION (WTO). *see also* NONSPECIFIC SUBSIDIY; ENVIRONMENTAL SUBSIDY.

REGIONAL COOPERATION FOR DEVELOPMENT an international organization founded in 1964 with headquarters in Tehran, Iran. Its members consist of Iran, Pakistan, and Turkey. The purpose of the group is the economic development of its members. *see also* ORGANIZATION OF THE ISLAMIC CONFERENCE.

REGIONAL DEVELOPMENT BANKS *see* MULTILATERAL DEVELOPMENT BANKS.

REGIONAL DEVELOPMENT PROGRAMS arrangements between the Canadian federal and provincial governments. These arrangements include the distribution of transfer payments from the federal government to the poorer provinces in an attempt to raise the standard of living in these regions and to establish a network of regional development agencies around the country to promote economic growth.

REGIONAL ECONOMIC COMMISSIONS *see* UNITED NATIONS REGIONAL ECONOMIC COMMISSIONS.

REGIONAL ECONOMIC DEVELOPMENT PROGRAMS *see* REGIONAL DEVELOPMENT PROGRAMS.

REGIONAL POLICY *see* REGIONAL AID.

REGIONAL TRADING ARRANGEMENTS business conducted between nations within a formal geographic network. These arrangements can include a common external TARIFF, free labor mobility, and common economic policies, or they could establish an unimpeded exchange and flow of goods and services between trading partners regardless of national borders. Examples: ANDEAN GROUP, ARAB MAHGREB UNION, CARIBBEAN COMMON MARKET, EUROPEAN ECONOMIC COMMUNITY, and NORTH AMERICAN FREE TRADE AGREEMENT.

REGIONALISM the formation or proliferation of PREFERENTIAL TRADE ARRANGEMENTS. *see also* PREFERENCES; PREFERENTIAL TRADE AREA (PTA).

REGIONALIZATION OF TRADE process whereby countries within a region attempt to focus on the importance of trade between members of the region and to move from a customs and economic integration to monetary integration and achieve political integration. It seeks a movement away from regionalism toward trade on much more open, global, and multilateral bases. *see also* CANADA–U.S. FREE TRADE AGREEMENT OF 1989; EUROPE 1992; NORTH AMERICAN FREE TRADE AGREEMENT (NAFTA); PACIFIC ECONOMIC COOPERATION GROUP.

REGISTRERT REVISOR *see* REGISTRERTE REVISORERS FORENING (RRF).

REGISTRERTE REVISORERS FORENING (RRF) one of two professional bodies that qualifies auditors in Norway. The other is NORGES STATSAUTORISERTE REVISORERS FORENING (NSRF). In Norway only state-authorized auditors may audit companies that employ more than 200 people or are publicly owned. All other companies may appoint either a state-authorized auditor or an auditor registered by the RRF.

REGULAR CATALOG SHOW (RCS) *see* CATALOG EXHIBITIONS; TRADE EVENT.

REINVOICING a mechanism used by a domestic unit of an international corporation whereby they would IMPORT merchandise through an offshore company. The offshore company would then reinvoice the merchandise at a higher price, increasing the profits made by the offshore company, while reducing the profits and ultimately the taxes due for the domestic company. These profits are often then returned back to the domestic company in the form of tax-free loans from the offshore affiliates. *see also* TRANSFER PRICING.

REJECTED MERCHANDISE goods that a buyer will either refuse to accept or discard as defective or useless.

RELATIVE PRICE the price of one product as it relates to the price of another product.

RELATIVE PURCHASING POWER PARITY THEORY changes in the EXCHANGE RATES between countries should be proportional to the comparable change in price levels between those countries. *see also* MONETARISM; PURCHASING POWER PARITY THEORY.

RELAY a procedure in which a shipment is shipped to an intermediate port and transferred to another vessel for delivery to the ultimate destination port.

RELOCATION ALLOWANCE direct payments made to an employee relocating from a HOME COUNTRY to a HOST COUNTRY. This allowance is to reimburse the employee's cost of moving personal and household goods and related travel costs. These allowances are also applicable when returning to the home country. *see also* BENEFIT

ALLOWANCE; COST DIFFERENTIAL; COST OF LIVING ALLOWANCE; EDUCATIONAL ALLOWANCE; FURNISHING ALLOWANCE; HOUSING ALLOWANCE; SETTLING-IN ALLOWANCE; UTILITIES ALLOWANCE.

REMEDY the measure recommended by the DISPUTE SETTLEMENT PANEL to resolve the dispute in the WORLD TRADE ORGANIZATION (WTO). The measure will usually bring the offending country into compliance with WTO rules. *see also* BINATIONAL DISPUTE-SETTLEMENT MECHANISM; DISPUTE SETTLEMENT SYSTEM.

REMITTANCE funds forwarded from one person to another as payment for bought items or services.

REMITTING BANK the bank that sends the DRAFT to the overseas bank for collection.

REMOTE LOG-IN an INTERNET PROTOCOL used over a computer NETWORK on a remote computer operating as though it were locally attached. *see also* TELNET.

REMOTE PROCEDURE CALL (RPC) a widely adopted, user-friendly methodology, with many RPC protocols, implementing the client–server network model. It works by having a CLIENT request sent to a remote computer system, whereupon the client is notified of the result.

REPATRIATION
1. the return of assets held in a foreign country.
2. the return of nationals held in foreign countries to their country of birth or citizenship.

REPLEVIN legal action for recovering property brought by the owner or party entitled to repossess the property against a party who has wrongfully kept it.

REPRESENTATIVE *see* FOREIGN SALES AGENT.

REPRESENTATIVE OFFICE an out-of-state office or foreign BANK not authorized to conduct business in that country. The sole purpose of the representative office is to solicit business for its parent bank in those areas where it is authorized to conduct business.

REPRISALS *see* RETALIATION.

REPUBLICAN GUARD the divisions of Saddam Hussein's army that were closest to him.

REPUDIATION the refusal of a foreign government to acknowledge a contract. The OVERSEAS PRIVATE INVESTMENT CORPORATION (OPIC) provides U.S. investors with insurance covering losses due to material changes unilaterally imposed by a host government on project agreements. This is referred to as EXPROPRIATION coverage and includes ABROGATION, IMPAIRMENT, repudiation or BREACH OF CONCESSIONAL AGREEMENTS, production sharing agreements, service contract, risk contract, and other agreements between the U.S. company and the foreign government.

REQUEST FOR QUOTATION negotiating approach whereby the buyer asks for a price QUOTATION from a potential seller for specific quantities of goods. *see also* PROFORMA; PROFORMA INVOICE.

REQUEST/OFFER a negotiating approach whereby requests are submitted by a country to a trading partner identifying the concessions another seeks through negotiations. Compensating offers are similarly tabled and negotiated by delegates of the countries involved.

RESALE PRICE METHODS one of three methods authorized by the U.S. Internal Revenue Code and related regulations allowed in determining an ARM'S LENGTH TRANSACTION. The resale price method uses the sales price received for the goods by the reseller less an appropriate mark up. The other authorized methods are the COMPARABLE UNCONTROLLED PRICE METHOD (market price) and the COST PLUS METHOD. *see also* TRANSFER COST; TRANSFER PAYMENTS; TRANSFER PRICE.

RESCIND to abrogate, annul, avoid, or cancel a CONTRACT; to declare it void in its inception and put an end to it as though it never were.

RESEAUX ASSOCIES POUR LA RECHERCHE EUROPE-ENNE (RARE) European association of research networks.

RESEAUX IP EUROPEEN (RIPE) a collaboration between European NETWORKS that use the TCP/IP PROTOCOL SUITE.

RESERVE CURRENCY *see* FOREIGN EXCHANGE RESERVES.

RESERVE CURRENCY COUNTRY the currencies of the seven major economic powers—Canada, France, Germany, Great Britain, Italy, Japan, and the United States. These countries as a group are referred to as the GROUP OF SEVEN (G-7). The currencies of these countries are referred to as FOREIGN EXCHANGE RESERVES, because they are highly convertible in the world market. *see also* CONVERTIBLE CURRENCY; ORGANIZATION FOR ECONOMIC COOPERATION AND DEVELOPMENT.

RESERVE TRANCHE a position where a member country of the INTERNATIONAL MONETARY FUND (IMF) exceeds its quotas of the IMF's holdings of its currency in the General Resources Account, excluding holdings arising out of purchases made by the member under all policies on the use of the IMF's general resources. A member may purchase up to the full amount of its reserve tranche at any time, subject only to the requirement of BALANCE OF PAYMENTS need. A reserve tranche position does not constitute a use of IMF credit and is not subject to charges or to an expectation or obligation to repurchase.

RESERVED FREIGHT SPACE service by some airlines that enables SHIPPERS to reserve FREIGHT space on designated flights.

RESIDENCY VISA a stamp in a foreign national's passport issued by a consular officer that permits and authorizes the person to establish permanent residency in the country. *see also* DEPENDENT VISA; EXIT/REENTRY VISA; MULTIPLE-ENTRY VISA; WORK PERMIT; WORK VISA.

RESIDENT ALIEN an individual previously admitted into a country on an IMMIGRANT VISA now residing permanently or for an extended period in the country. *see also* NONIMMIGRANT VISA; RESIDENCY VISA; WORK VISA.

RESIDUAL RESTRICTIONS quantitative restrictions that have been maintained by governments before they became contracting parties to the GENERAL AGREEMENT ON TARIFFS AND TRADE (GATT) and, hence, permissible under the GATT grandfather clause. Most of the residual restrictions still in effect are maintained by DEVELOPED COUNTRIES against the IMPORTS of agricultural products.

REST AND RECREATION LEAVE (R&R) a provision authorizing an employee based at a remote or hardship location to leave an assignment location for a short break. These leaves are also provided to employees placed in these locations on an unaccompanied basis.

REST DAY a method of compensation found in some countries, where the employee is compensated for a 7-day period, of which 1 or 2 days are considered paid rest days. Compensation in other countries is based on an hours-worked approach.

RESTRAINED EXPORTERS countries using VOLUNTARY EXPORT RESTRICTIONS (VER) to limit the EXPORT of certain products to certain markets. *see also* PROTECTED MARKETS.

RESTRICTED LETTER OF CREDIT a LETTER OF CREDIT (L/C) that restricts negotiation to the BANK the ISSUING BANK has nominated in the credit. *see also* CONFIRMED LETTER OF CREDIT.

RESTRICTED TRADE trade that is restrained by TARIFFS, transportation costs, or NONTARIFF BARRIERS (NTBS).

RESTRICTIVE BUSINESS PRACTICES (RBPs) actions in the private sector, such as collusion among the largest international suppliers, designed to restrict competition so as to keep prices relatively high. A number of these practices are illegal in the United States and certain other developed countries. *see also* CLAYTON ACT.

RESTRICTIVE TRADE PRACTICES LEGISLATION the European version of the antitrust laws of the United States.

RESTRICTIVE TRADING PRACTICES *see* RESTRICTIVE BUSINESS PRACTICES.

RETAIL TRADE NATIONALIZATION ACT act that prohibits companies not wholly owned by Philippine citizens from engaging directly or indirectly in retail trade. The act does, however, exempt from this prohibition manufacturers and processors that produce goods for sale by commercial and industrial consumers or that sell goods to these consumers, who will use these goods to render services to the general public.

RETALIATION action taken by a country whose EXPORTS are adversely affected by the raising of TARIFFS or other trade-restricting measures by another country. The GATT permits an adversely affected contracting party (CP) to impose limited restraints on IMPORTS from another CP that has raised its trade barriers (after consultations with countries whose trade might be affected). In theory, the volume of trade affected by such retaliatory measures should approximate the value of trade affected by the precipitating change in import protection.

RETORTION a lawful but unfriendly act exercised by one nation upon another in RETALIATION for a similar act perpetrated by the other nation. *see also* GENERAL AGREEMENT ON TARIFFS AND TRADE (GATT).

RETURNED WITHOUT ACTION (RWA) for EXPORT control purposes, the return of a license application without action is used when the application is incomplete, additional information is required, or the product is eligible for a GENERAL LICENSE.

REVALUATION a formal change in the EXCHANGE RATE when the value of a currency rises. A REVALUATION OF A CURRENCY results in a strengthening of the currency. *see also* DEVALUATION.

REVALUATION OF A CURRENCY a strengthening of the value of a county's currency in relation to the currency of other countries. *see also* DEVALUATION; REVALUATION.

REVENUE ARGUMENT FOR A TARIFF the use of a TARIFF to raise revenue for the government. *see also* NATIONAL DEFENSE ARGUMENT; REVENUE EFFECT OF A TARIFF.

REVENUE EFFECT OF A TARIFF funds collected by a government that has assessed DUTIES on IMPORTED goods. *see also* TARIFF.

REVERSE CULTURE SHOCK *see* REENTRY SHOCK.

REVERSE IMPORTS products that are produced overseas by the subsidiaries of multinationals, and are then EXPORTED to the HOME COUNTRY.

REVERSE MISSION an OVERSEAS PRIVATE INVESTOR CORPORATION (OPIC) program that brings groups of foreign government officials and local business leaders to the United States to meet with their American counterparts.

REVERSE PREFERENCES TARIFF advantages once offered by developing countries to IMPORTERS from certain developed countries that granted them preferences. Reverse preferences characterized trading arrangements between the EUROPEAN COMMUNITY (EC) and some developing countries prior to the advent of the GENERALIZED SYSTEM OF PREFERENCES (GSP) and the signing of the LOME CONVENTION.

REVOCABLE LETTER OF CREDIT a LETTER OF CREDIT that can be canceled or altered by the DRAWEE (buyer) after it has been issued by the drawee's bank.

REVOCATION OF ANTIDUMPING DUTY ORDER the revocation of an ANTIDUMPING DUTY ORDER or the suspension of an ANTIDUMP-

ING INVESTIGATION upon application from a party to the proceeding. Ordinarily the application is considered only if there have been no sales at less than FAIR VALUE for at least the 2 most recent years. However, the U.S. INTERNATIONAL TRADE ADMINISTRATION (ITA) may on its own initiative revoke an antidumping duty order or terminate a suspended investigation if there have not been sales at less than fair value for a period of 3 years. *see also* TARIFF ACT OF 1930.

REVOLVING LETTER OF CREDIT a documentary credit issued by a financial institution authorizing continuous drawings to be made over a specified period of time. The LETTER OF CREDIT will automatically be renewed, under similar conditions, each time a drawing is made. The revolving letter of credit can be either confirmed or unconfirmed. *see also* ADVISING BANK; CONFIRMING BANK; ISSUING BANK; DOCUMENTARY DRAFT; EXPORT FINANCING.

RIAL
1. unit of currency, Yemen (North) (100 fils equal 1 rial).
2. unit of currency, Oman (1000 baisa equal 1 rial).

RICARDIAN MODEL the international trade theory introduced by David Ricardo to explain the pattern and the gains from trade in terms of COMPARATIVE ADVANTAGE. *see also* ABSOLUTE ADVANTAGE.

RICIN a stable toxin easily made from the mash that remains after processing castor beans. It can be used as an oral laxative in the form of castor oil, causing diarrhea, nausea, vomiting, abdominal cramps, internal bleeding, liver and kidney failure, and circulatory failure.

RIDER a manufacturer using PIGGYBACK EXPORTING with the foreign distribution operations of another firm's products to sell its own products. A rider is principally used by a smaller firm with no established EXPORT organization or network of international distributors. *see also* CARRIER; INDIRECT EXPORTING.

RIEL unit of currency, Cambodia.

RIGHT OF ESTABLISHMENT the rights of foreign direct investors to establish and operate a business in a foreign country under the same rights granted to businesses operated by citizens of the foreign country. *see also* NATIONAL TREATMENT.

RINGGIT unit of currency, Malaysia (100 sen equal 1 ringgit).

RINGI SYSTEM a decision-making system common in Japanese companies. This system provides the appearance of a form of democratic participative management, whereby decisions are made by low-level managers and circulated to upper levels of management by memorandum. The senior managers then assert their authority either by retarding or blocking approval or by ignoring memoranda that have been circulating. Success in the ringi system is dependent on the ability of the subordinates to satisfy their superiors by anticipating their needs. *see also* NEMAWASHI.

RIO GROUP a political forum of Latin American and Caribbean countries that promotes regional political, economic, and social cooperation. The group comprises 13 countries, including 11 permanent members: Argentina, Bolivia, Brazil, Colombia, Chile, Ecuador, Mexico, Paraguay, Peru, Uruguay, and Venezuela and two rotating members that represent the Central American countries and the Caribbean nations. *see also* RIO TREATY.

RIO TREATY officially called the Inter-American Treaty of Reciprocal Assistance. It is also referred to as the Rio Pact. *see also* ORGANIZATION OF AMERICAN STATES (OAS); RIO GROUP.

RIPE *see* RESEAUX IP EUROPEEN.

RISK AVERSION the extent to which an individual or firm wishes to avoid risk.

RISK POSITION a situation reflecting the net amounts of FORWARD and SPOT locations of a foreign currency being traded by a FOREIGN EXCHANGE BROKER. *see also* FORWARD POSITION; LONG POSITION; OPEN POSITION; POSITION; SHORT POSITION; SQUARE POSITION.

RISK PREMIUM the difference between the FORWARD EXCHANGE RATE and the anticipated future SPOT RATE.

RIVER PLATA BASIN SYSTEM a regional international organization formally referred to as El Sistema de la Cuenca del Plata. The system was established in 1969 under the Treaty of the River Plata Basin. The members include Argentina, Bolivia, Brazil, Paraguay, and Uruguay; it is headquartered in Buenos Aires, Argentina. The purpose of the organization is to promote regional economic integration among the members by the development of commercial policies, projects, and programs using the natural resources of the River Plata Basin.

ROAD WAYBILL transport document that indicates that the road HAULAGE CARRIER has received goods for shipment. *see also* AIR WAYBILL; BILL OF LADING; RAIL WAYBILL.

ROLLBACK an agreement among Uruguay ROUND participants to dismantle all trade-restrictive or distorting measures that are inconsistent with the provisions of the GENERAL AGREEMENT ON TARIFFS AND TRADE (GATT). Measures subject to rollback would be phased out or brought into conformity within an agreed time frame, no later than by the formal completion of the negotiations. The rollback agreement is accompanied by a STANDSTILL commitment on existing trade-restrictive measures. Rollback is also used as a reference to the imposition of quantitative restrictions at levels less than those occurring in the present.

ROLL ON, ROLL OFF a category of ships designed to load and discharge CARGO that rolls on wheels. As the name says, the ships are driven onto the decks of the vessel and driven off. *see also* RO-RO SHIP.

ROLLOVER CREDIT any line of credit that can be borrowed against up to a stated credit limit and into which repayment goes for crediting.

ROMANIAN DEVELOPMENT AGENCY (RDA) *see* AGENTIA ROMANA DE DEZVOLTARE.

ROME CONVENTION a MULTILATERAL TREATY administered by the WORLD INTELLECTUAL PROPERTY ORGANIZATION (WIPO) and responsible for dealing with the legal and administrative aspects of the protection of intellectual property rights.

ROO *see* RULES OF ORIGIN.

RO-RO SHIP acronym for roll on/roll off. A ro-ro vessel is one with ramps that allow CARGO to be driven on or off, which provides it with the capability of transporting different types of vehicles.

ROTFL acronym for rolling on the floor laughing; used by INTERNET users to respond to an amusing NET comment.

ROUND OF TRADE NEGOTIATIONS *see* ROUNDS.

ROUND-TRIP TIME (RTT) a measure of a NETWORK'S message response time.

ROUNDS cycles of multilateral trade negotiations under the GENERAL AGREEMENT ON TARIFFS AND TRADE (GATT), culminating in simultaneous agreements among participating countries to reduce TARIFF and non-tariff trade barriers: 1st Round: 1947, Geneva (creation of the GATT); 2nd Round: 1949, Annecy, France (tariff reduction); 3rd Round: 1951, Torquay, England (accession and tariff reduction); 4th Round: 1956, Geneva (accession and tariff reduction); 5th Round: 1960–1962, Geneva (Dillon Round; revision of GATT, addition of more countries); 6th Round: 1964–1967, Geneva (Kennedy Round); 7th Round: 1973–1979, Geneva (Tokyo Round); 8th Round: 1986–1993, Geneva (Uruguay Round).

ROUTE
1. the itinerary that data traffic follows over a NETWORK to its destination.
2. the route that data and messages follow getting from one computer to another.
3. the course or direction that a shipment moves.

ROYALTY compensation paid under a LICENSING AGREEMENT to a licensor by the licensee.

RPC *see* REMOTE PROCEDURE CALL.

RPFB *see* RUSSIAN PROJECT FINANCE BANK.

RTT *see* ROUND-TRIP TIME.

RUBEL unit of currency, Republic of Belarus.

RUBLE unit of currency, Georgia, Kazakhstan, Republic of Kyrgyz, Russia, Tajikstan, Turkmenistan, and Uzbekistan.

RUBLIS/RUBLI/RUBLU unit of currency, Latvia.

RUFIYAA unit of currency, Republic of Maldives (100 laari equal 1 rufiyaa).

RUIE *see* RUSSIAN UNION OF INDUSTRIALISTS AND ENTREPRENEURS.

RULE-BASED SELECTIVITY risk assessment process based upon user-defined criteria and weights assigned according to established regulations or processes as selection factors. *see also* SELECTIVITY.

RULE-BASED TRADE POLICY institutional arrangements in which national trade policies are governed by internationally agreed-upon rules, as in the GENERAL AGREEMENT ON TARIFFS AND TRADE (GATT) and the WORLD TRADE ORGANIZATION (WTO).

RULES OF NAVIGATION a set of rules based on the 19th-century regulations formally referred to as the International Regulations for Preventing Collisions at Sea. These laws are administered by the INTERNATIONAL MARITIME ASSOCIATION, a specialized agency of the UNITED NATIONS. These rules govern matters affecting merchant shipping, traffic, and maritime safety.

RULES OF ORIGIN regulations used to ascertain where goods being IMPORTED into a country have been produced, for the purpose of determining what DUTIES (if any) are applicable. These regulations are implemented unilaterally, bilaterally, or multilaterally through negotiation. Example: merchandise will be eligible for CARIBBEAN BASIN INITIATIVE (CBI) DUTY-FREE treatment only if the following conditions are met.
- The merchandise must be imported directly from any BENEFICIARY COUNTRY into the CUSTOMS territory of the United States.
- The merchandise must have been produced in a beneficiary country. This requirement is satisfied when
    - the goods are wholly the growth, product, or manufacture of a beneficiary country, or
    - the goods have been substantially transformed into a new and different article of commerce in a beneficiary country, and
    - at least 35% of the appraised value of the article imported into the United States must consist of the cost or value of materials produced in one or more beneficiary countries and/or the direct costs of processing operations performed in one or more beneficiary countries.

see also CERTIFICATE OF ORIGIN.

RUPEE unit of currency, India, Mauritius, Nepal, Pakistan, Seychelles, Sri Lanka.

RUPIAH unit of currency, Indonesia (100 sen equal 1 rupiah).

RUSSIAN COUNTRY FUND a government program of the U.S. OVERSEAS PRIVATE INVESTMENT CORPORATION (OPIC) designed to generate U.S. private-sector investment in the Russian economy. OPIC accomplishes this task by assisting U.S. private investments in Russia through direct loans and LOAN GUARANTEES, insuring against a broad range of political risks, and providing a variety of investor services.

RUSSIAN PROJECT FINANCE BANK (RPFB) a financial institution set up with the assistance of the EUROPEAN COMMUNITY (EC). The bank is intended to develop efficient financial systems in Russia capable of channeling foreign and domestic investment into priority areas by providing medium- and long-term financial and high-quality investment banking advisory services to businesses.

RUSSIAN UNION OF INDUSTRIALISTS AND ENTREPRE-NEURS (RUIE) union that promotes commercial links between Western firms and Russian defense firms. The union, an independent agency created by the Russian central government, consists of hundreds of major enterprises and associations.

RWA *see* RETURNED WITHOUT ACTION.

RWANDA FRANC unit of currency, Rwanda.

S

S&D *see* SPECIAL AND DIFFERENTIAL TREATMENT.

S.A. (SA) *see* SOCIEDAD ANONIMA (Spanish); SOCIETE ANONYME (French).

S.A. DE CV *see* SOCIEDAD ANONIMA DE CAPITAL VARIABLE.

SAARC *see* SOUTH ASIAN ASSOCIATION FOR REGIONAL COOPERATION.

SABIT *see* SPECIAL AMERICAN BUSINESS INTERNSHIP TRAINING PROGRAM.

SACU *see* SOUTHERN AFRICAN CUSTOMS UNION.

SADC *see* SOUTHERN AFRICA DEVELOPMENT COMMUNITY.

SAF *see* STRUCTURAL ADJUSTMENT FACILITY.

SAFE ARRIVAL NOTIFICATION the practice of advising friend and family in the HOME COUNTRY of the safe arrival of employees/ dependents at a remote assignment location.

SAFE HAVEN CURRENCY a politically secure national currency.

SAFE HOUSE building not under surveillance by intelligence or counterintelligence organizations where terrorists can be safe while they plan attacks or rest.

SAFEGUARDS two forms of multilateral safeguards permitted by the GENERAL AGREEMENT ON TARIFFS AND TRADE (GATT):
• a country's right to impose temporary IMPORT controls or other trade restrictions to prevent commercial injury to domestic industry. Article XIX of the GATT permits a country whose domestic industries or workers are adversely affected by increased imports to withdraw or modify concessions the country had earlier granted, to impose, for a limited period, new import restrictions if the country can establish that a product is "being imported in such increased quantities as to cause or threaten serious injury to domestic producers," and to keep such restrictions in effect for such time as may be necessary to prevent or remedy such injury.
• the corresponding right of domestic EXPORTERS not to be deprived arbitrarily of access to markets.

SALES AGREEMENT written document by which a seller agrees to convey property to a buyer for a stipulated price under specified conditions. *see also* IRREVOCABLE CORPORATE PURCHASE ORDER.

SALES COMMISSIONS method of compensating sales personnel, usually based on a percentage of sales.

SALES COMPANY a business established by a company in a foreign country for the purpose of IMPORTING goods or services from the company for sale by the foreign affiliate. *see also* DIRECT EXPORTING.

SALES PROMOTIONS anything used by the marketer to inform, persuade, or influence the end user of the marketer's product that does not include advertising, personal selling, or publicity. Sales promotion items are those that aid in selling and can include displays, premiums, contests, coupons, and gifts. It should be noted that when marketers are considering transferring sales promotion techniques to other markets, they must consider some cultural and legal constraints. Example: laws concerning sales promotions in many countries tend to be more restrictive than those found in the United States or Great Britain.

SALES REPRESENTATIVE an agent who distributes, represents, services, or sells goods on behalf of foreign sellers.

SALES TAX a tax placed by a state or municipality on items at the time of their sale, usually a percentage of the purchase price. *see also* VALUE-ADDED TAX (VAT).

SALMONELLA an infection caused by a gram-negative bacillus, a germ of the *Salmonella* genus. Infection with this bacteria may involve only the intestinal tract, or it may be spread from the intestines to the bloodstream and then to other sites in the body. Signs and symptoms of salmonella enteritis include diarrhea, nausea, abdominal pain, and fever. Dehydration resulting from the diarrhea can cause death, and the disease could cause meningitis or septicemia.

SALVAGE compensation paid for the rescue of a ship, its CARGO, or passengers from a loss at sea; the act of saving a ship or its cargo from possible loss; property saved from a wreck or fire.

SALVENCIA a 20% tax levied on employees on temporary assignment in Venezuela.

SAMARBEIDSAVTALE a JOINT VENTURE in Norway. It may not have a name of its own and its existence cannot be used as a defense against claims made by third parties. A joint venture cannot be registered and has no independent legal identity. There are no bookkeeping or auditing requirements, unless specified in the joint venture agreement.

SAMURAI BOND bond issued on the Japanese market in YEN outside Japan. *see also* GEISHA BOND; SUSHI BOND.

SANCTION a coercive measure adopted usually by a nation, or several nations, against a nation endangering peace and security or violating international law. These actions can be taken either by a collective security system such as the UNITED NATIONS Security Council or General Assembly, or by nation or a group of nations apart from the United Nations system. The term *sanction* is a variation of EMBARGO.

SARIN colorless, odorless gas. Because the vapor is heavier than air, it hovers close to the ground. Although sarin degrades quickly in humid weather, its life expectancy increases as temperature gets higher.

SARL *see* SOCIETE A RESPONSABILITE LIMITEE.

SAS *see* SOCIETE PAR ACTIONS SIMPLIFIEE.

SASO *see* SAUDI ARABIAN STANDARDS ORGANIZATION.

SAUDI ARABIAN RIYAL unit of currency, Saudi Arabia (100 halalas equal 1 Saudi Arabian riyal).

SAUDI ARABIAN STANDARDS ORGANIZATION (SASO) the sole Saudi Arabian government organization to promulgate standards and measurements in the Saudi kingdom. Primarily, SASO promulgates standards for electrical equipment and some food products. Some of these standards have been adopted by the GULF COOPERATION COUNCIL. SASO was established in April 1972.

SBIC *see* SMALL BUSINESS INVESTMENT COMPANY FINANCING.

S.C.&S. abbreviation for strapped, corded, and sealed.

SCHEDULE *see* TARIFF SCHEDULE.

SCHEDULE B a U.S. Bureau of the Census publication based on the HARMONIZED SYSTEM. EXPORT statistics are initially collected and compiled in terms of approximately 8,000 COMMODITY classifications in Schedule B, "Statistical Classification of Domestic and Foreign Commodities Exported from the United States." *see also* TARIFF SCHEDULES OF THE UNITED STATES ANNOTATED.

SCHENGEN AGREEMENT an international agreement ratified on June 19, 1990, by Belgium, Germany, France, Luxembourg, and the Netherlands. They agreed that nationals of the countries signing the agreement will not be subject to customs inspection when entering or leaving any of the Schengen countries. *see also* EUROPE 1992; SINGLE EUROPEAN ACT.

SCHMIR *see* BRIBERY.

SCIENTIFIC TARIFF phrase used when assuming that a TARIFF has been placed on an IMPORTED product as a form of protection providing the domestic producers with the necessary relief to meet the competition. It then would naturally follow that, given this temporary protection, the firms will operate more competitively on the day the tariff is removed. *see also* CONSUMPTION EFFECT OF A TARIFF.

SCO *see* SENIOR COMMERCIAL OFFICER.

SCOPE DETERMINATIONS the product coverage of the ANTIDUMPING/COUNTERVAILING DUTY SYSTEM. The U.S. DEPARTMENT OF COMMERCE will determine—in response to an application from an interested party or on its own initiative—whether a certain product is included within the scope of the antidumping/countervailing duty system.

SCREEN CAPTURE a part of COMMUNICATIONS SOFTWARE that creates a computer file to save whatever information scrolls past on the screen while on-line with a HOST system.

S/D abbreviation for sight draft.

S.D.D. abbreviation for store door delivery.

SDNs *see* SPECIALLY DESIGNATED NATIONALS.

SDRs *see* SPECIAL DRAWING RIGHTS.

SEA *see* SINGLE EUROPEAN ACT.

SEAL a mark or sign that is used to attest the execution of an instrument, contract, or other document.

SEASONAL QUOTA a restriction on the quantity of IMPORTS of a GOOD for a specified period of the year. *see also* ABSOLUTE QUOTAS; IMPORT RESTRICTIONS; PROTECTIONIST TRADING PRACTICES; TARIFF QUOTA; TRADE BARRIERS.

SEASONAL TARIFF a tariff that is levied at different rates at different times of the year, usually on agricultural products. *see also* SPECIFIC TARIFF; VARIABLE LEVY (VL).

SEATO *see* SOUTHEAST ASIA TREATY ORGANIZATION.

SEATTLE MINISTERIAL the MINISTERIAL meeting of the WORLD TRADE ORGANIZATION (WTO) that was held in Seattle in November 1999.

SEAWORTHINESS fitness or safety of a vessel for its intended use.

SECAM format used for television transmission and reception in some European countries. PAL is the format used in other European countries. *see also* NTSC.

SECOFI (SECRETARIA DE COMERCIO Y FOMENTO INDUSTRIAL) the Department of Commerce and Industrial Development and Promotion in Mexico. *see also* SECRETARÍA DE COMERCIO Y FOMENTO INDUSTRIAL.

SECOND OF EXCHANGE duplicate copy of a DRAFT.

SECONDARY BOYCOTT the boycotting of a firm because of its business dealings with a firm that has been boycotted. Example: Ford Motor Company had been on the Arab Boycott BLACKLIST because of their business dealings with Israel. At one time, Toyota had been negotiating a JOINT VENTURE agreement with Ford Motor. However, because of the negotiations, they were threatened with retaliation by the Arab League. Toyota consequently discontinued negotiations with Ford, but they did not indicate that the threatened boycott influenced their decision. *see also* ARAB BOYCOTT OF ISRAEL.

SECONDARY DEVICE an explosive that is detonated after a smaller diversionary device.

SECONDARY TARIFFS charges imposed on IMPORTS in addition to the statutory TARIFF. *see also* IMPORT SURCHARGE.

SECRETARIA DE COMERCIO Y FOMENTO INDUSTRIAL (SECOFI) Mexico's Ministry of Commerce and Industrial Promotion.

SECRETARIAT main administrative office of the UNITED NATIONS containing the Secretary General and staff. Offices of the Secretariat include the Departments of Administration and Management, Peacekeeping Operations, Development Support and Management Services, Economic and Social Information and Policy Analysis, Policy Coordination and Sustainable Development, Legal Affairs, Political Affairs, Public Information, and Humanitarian Affairs. Other United Nations organs associated with the Secretariat include the Development Programme, Children's Fund, Population Fund, Joint Staff Pension Board, International Civil Service Commission, and the Advisory Committee on Administrative and Budgetary Questions. The Secretariat also has numerous special missions. Established in 1946, the headquarters for the Secretariat is in New York.

SECTION 201 the ESCAPE CLAUSE provision of the U.S. TRADE ACT OF 1974, which permits temporary IMPORT relief, not to exceed a maximum of 8 years, to a domestic industry that is seriously injured or threatened with serious injury, due to increased imports. Import relief, granted at the U.S. president's discretion, generally takes the form of increased TARIFFS or quantitative restrictions. To be eligible for section 201 relief, the INTERNATIONAL TRADE COMMISSION (ITC) must determine that
- the industry has been seriously injured or threatened to be injured.
- imports have been a substantial cause (not less than any other cause) of that injury.

Industries need not prove that an unfair trade practice exists, as is necessary under the ANTIDUMPING/COUNTERVAILING DUTY SYSTEM. However, under Section 201, a greater degree of injury—serious injury—must be found to exist, and imports must be a substantial cause (defined as not less than any other cause) of that injury.

If the ITC finding is affirmative, the U.S. president's remedy may be a tariff increase, quantitative restrictions, or orderly marketing agreements. At the conclusion of any relief action, the commission must report on the effectiveness of the relief action in facilitating the positive adjustment of the domestic industry to import competition. If the decision is made not to grant relief, the President must provide an explanation to the Congress.

SECTION 203 of the U.S. TRADE ACT OF 1974 provides that if the ensuing investigation establishes that an import complaint is valid, relief may be granted in the form of adjustment assistance, which may be training and technical and financial assistance, or temporary import restrictions in the form of tariffs, quotas, tariff rate quotas, and/or orderly marketing agreements. Import restrictions imposed under the escape clause authority are limited in duration. They may last no longer than 5 years but can be extended by the president for a 3-year period.

SECTION 232 section of the TRADE EXPANSION ACT OF 1962, as amended, authorizing the U.S. DEPARTMENT OF COMMERCE to determine whether articles are being imported into the United States in quantities or circumstances that threaten national security. Based on the investigation report, the U.S. president can adjust IMPORTS of the article(s) in question.

The U.S. Department of Commerce must report on the effects these imports have on national security and make recommendations for action or inaction within 270 days after starting an investigation. Within 90 days of the report, the president decides whether to take action to adjust imports on the basis of national security. The president must notify Congress of his decision within 30 days.

SECTION 301 section of the GENERAL AGREEMENT ON TARIFFS AND TRADE (GATT) empowering the U.S. TRADE REPRESENTATIVE (USTR) to investigate foreign country trade policy or practice allegations and negotiate the removal of any trade barriers. The USTR may also self-initiate investigations. Specific time frames for conducting the investigations are specified by law. Section 301 requires that GATT's dispute resolution process be invoked where applicable and, if negotiations fail, to retaliate within 180 days from the date that discovery of a trade agreement violation took place. *see also* SPECIAL 301; SUPER 301.

SECTION 337 section of the U.S. TARIFF ACT OF 1930 requiring investigations of unfair practices in IMPORT trade. Under this authority, the INTERNATIONAL TRADE COMMISSION (ITC) applies U.S. statutory and common law of unfair competition to the importation of products into the United States and their sale. Section 337 prohibits unfair competition and unfair importing practices and sales of products in the United States, when these threaten to
- destroy or substantially injure a domestic industry,
- prevent the establishment of such an industry, or
- restrain or monopolize U.S. trade and commerce.

Section 337 also prohibits infringement of U.S. patents, copyrights, registered trademarks, or mask works.

SECTION 416 section of the U.S. Agricultural Act of 1949 that provides for the donation of food and feed COMMODITIES owned by the U.S. Department of Agriculture's COMMODITY CREDIT CORPORATION (CCO) and is focused on people in DEVELOPING COUNTRIES. *see also* FOOD FOR PEACE; FOOD FOR PROGRESS.

SECTORAL ADVISORY GROUP(S) ON INTERNATIONAL TRADE an advisory group established under the auspices of the Canadian government in 1989. It consists of 15 specific industry groups advising the government on matters of international and transborder trade relevant to the CANADA–U.S. FREE TRADE AGREEMENT OF 1989. *see also* INTERNATIONAL TRADE ADVISORY COMMITTEE.

SECTORAL APPROACH TO DATA PRIVACY the approach governments take concerning legislation relative to the issue of privacy with regard to data collection and transmission. Some nations, like the United States, take a sectoral approach, focusing legislation on specific industry sectors such as banking or insurance, whereas others, such as European governments, enact legislation that applies to public and private organizations in all industry sectors.

SECTORAL PRIVATIZATION the process of transferring government ownership of a business in a particular industry to private ownership.

SECTORAL RECIPROCITY the reduction of a country's IMPORT DUTIES or other TRADE restraints in return for comparable trade concessions from another country in specific industrial areas such as the automotive sector or agricultural sector. RECIPROCITY includes the lowering of customs duties on imports in return for TARIFF concessions from other countries; the negotiated reduction of a country's import duties or other trade restraints in return for similar concessions from another country.

SECTORAL TRADE AGREEMENT a bilateral or multilateral agreement focusing on trading relationships for a particular industry segment within the countries. *see also* AUTOMOTIVE PRODUCTS TRADE AGREEMENT; MARKET-ORIENTED COOPERATION PLAN.

SECURED guaranteed payment by the pledge of something valuable. *see also* SECURITY.

SECURITY property pledged as collateral. *see also* SECURED.

SECURITY COUNCIL a primary governing body of the United Nations as defined in its Charter. The Security Council has 5 permanent members and 10 nonpermanent members, 5 of which are elected annually by the GENERAL ASSEMBLY for a term of 2 years. The 5 permanent members of the Security Council are China, France, the Russian Federation, the United Kingdom, and the United States. The council is charged with the responsibility of settling peace disputes and actions that directly threaten peace including breaches of the peace and acts of aggression. Concurrence on all matters requires the affirmative vote of 9 members, including the concurring votes of the 5 permanent members of the council. Procedural matters require an affirmative vote of any 9 members.

A "gentlemen's agreement" reached in 1946 stated that the members of the Security Council, in addition to the 5 permanent members, should be 2 Latin American, 1 Western European, 1 Commonwealth, 1 Eastern European, and 1 Middle Eastern state.

The Security Council is located in the United Nations' main headquarters in New York.

SED *see* SHIPPER'S EXPORT DECLARATION.

SEED *see* SUPPORT FOR EAST EUROPEAN DEMOCRACY.

SEIGNIORAGE benefits under the BRETTON WOODS system that theo-
retically accrue to the United States as issuer of the U.S. dollar, causing the U.S. dollar to be an international RESERVE CURRENCY.

SEIZURE act of taking possession of property.

SELA Sistema Económico Latinoamericano. *see also* LATIN AMERICAN
ECONOMIC SYSTEM.

SELECTIVE when applied to a trade policy, this means one that
affects only some countries, not all. *see also* SAFEGUARDS.

SELECTIVITY process to identify a COMMODITY, CONVEYANCE, or persons associated with the conveyance for further inspection based on
a set of criteria.

SELF-REFERENCE CRITERION an unintentional reference to
one's own cultural values when assessing the behavioral actions of
others coming from a different environment.

SELF-SUFFICIENCY means either not trading at all or IMPORTING
only nonnecessities. *see also* AUTARKY.

SELF-SUFFICIENCY ARGUMENT FOR PROTECTION view
that a country is better off providing for its own needs than depending on IMPORTS. *see also* SELF-SUFFICIENCY; AUTARKY.

SELLER'S MARKET situation that exists when goods cannot easily be SECURED and when the economic forces of business tend to
cause goods to be priced at the vendor's estimate of value. *see also*
BUYER'S MARKET.

**SELLING, GENERAL, AND ADMINISTRATIVE (EXPENSES)
(SGA)** the sum of
- general and administrative expenses (salaries of nonsales personnel, rent, heat, and light),
- direct selling expenses (expenses that are directly tied to the sale of
a specific unit—credit, warranty, and advertising expenses), and
- indirect selling expenses (expenses that are not directly tied to the sale
of a specific unit but are proportionally allocated to all units sold during a certain period—telephone, interest, and postal charges).

SELLING RATE rate at which a BANK is willing to sell FOREIGN
EXCHANGE or to lend money. *see also* BID (BUY); CURRENCY OPTION CON-
TRACT; SPOT QUOTATION; SPOT RATE; SPOT TRANSACTION; SPREAD.

SELVSTENDIG NÆRINGSDRIVENDE FIRMA a sole proprietorship in Norway. In Norway the sole proprietor is responsible for
all his/her debts with all personal as well as business assets. The
name of the enterprise must contain at least the family name of the
owner and must not include anything that might indicate that it is a

partnership or a corporation. Certain activities of a sole proprietorship need to be registered in the commercial register.

SEMICONDUCTOR TRADE ARRANGEMENT a bilateral U.S.–Japan agreement that came into effect on August 1, 1991, replacing the prior 1986 Semiconductor Trade Arrangement. The new arrangement contains provisions to
- increase foreign access to the Japanese semiconductor market and
- deter DUMPING of semiconductors by Japanese suppliers into the U.S. market, as well as in third-country markets.

In evaluating market access improvement, both governments agreed to pay particular attention to market share. The expectation of a 20% foreign market share by the end of 1992 was included in the arrangement. The arrangement explicitly states, however, that the 20% is not a guarantee, a ceiling, or a floor on the foreign market share.

SEMINAR MISSION (SEM) *see* CERTIFIED TRADE MISSIONS.

SEMIPRIVATIZATION those portions of a particular industry owned and operated as government-owned business transferred to private ownership. This normally occurs when there is fear that a country's most valuable resource might be controlled by foreigners and lead to separate control of the country's citizens. Normally, governments deem semiprivatization as necessary to provide required infrastructure improvement resources.

SENAC a Brazilian training program to improve the quality of the unskilled work force from regions other than the principal metropolitan areas. Brazil also operates an industrial training school program (SENAI).

SENAI an industrial training school program operated by the Brazilian government to improve the quality of the unskilled labor force from regions other than the principal metropolitan areas. *see also* SENAC.

S. EN C. *see* SOCIEDAD EN COMANDITA SIMPLE.

SENIOR COMMERCIAL OFFICER (SCO) the senior U.S. and Foreign Commercial Officer at an EMBASSY, who reports in-country to the AMBASSADOR. At major posts, this position carries the title of Commercial Counselor; in key posts, Minister Counselor. Usually reporting to the SCO are a COMMERCIAL ATTACHE and commercial officers. The latter are sometimes assigned to subordinate posts throughout the country.

SENMOSHA a specialized trading company. The senmosha, smaller than a SOGO SOSHA, is an independent company specializing in the trading of high-technology industrial products, such as medical equipment or electronic components, and brand-name items.

SENSITIVITY TRAINING a program in which people learn how to interact with each other by developing a sensitive awareness and understanding of cultural issues.

SEPD *see* STATE EXPORT PROGRAM DATABASE.

SERVER a provider of resources (file servers and name servers). *see also* CLIENT; DOMAIN NAME SYSTEM; NETWORK FILE SYSTEM.

SERVICE scheduled pattern of calls made by a carrier to pick up or discharge CARGO at various locations.

SERVICE A LOAN to pay interest due on a loan.

SERVICE SUPPLY LICENSE authorization for firms in the United States or abroad to provide prompt service for equipment EXPORTED from the United States; produced abroad by a subsidiary, affiliate, or branch of a U.S. firm; or produced abroad by a manufacturer who uses parts imported from the United States in the manufactured product. Part 773.7 of the U.S. EXPORT ADMINISTRATION REGULATIONS provides detailed information regarding SPECIAL LICENSES. *see also* DISTRIBUTION LICENSE; FACILITY LICENSE; HUMANITARIAN LICENSE; PROJECT LICENSE; SPECIAL CHEMICAL LICENSE.

SERVICES that which is intended for use in supplying or serving, offering for repairs or maintenance, or services to the public in response to a need or demand. Services can be categorized into the following areas: construction, trade, transportation, communication, financial, insurance, business and professional, educational, health and recreation, and cultural services.

SETTLEMENT DATE date on which payment for a transaction must be made. *see also* DATE DRAFT (D/D); DOCUMENTS ON ACCEPTANCE (DOA); LETTER OF CREDIT (L/C); SIGHT DRAFT.

SETTLING-IN ALLOWANCE the reimbursement to an employee at an assignment location covering living costs prior to the arrival of his/her household and PERSONAL EFFECTS and movement into permanent accommodations. *see also* RELOCATION ALLOWANCE.

SEVERANCE PAY INDEMNITY FUND (FGTS) contributions made by employers in Brazil. The company deposits 8% of the employee's monthly compensation into a limited-access bank account. In the event an employee is terminated without just cause, the employer is responsible for an additional amount equal to 40% of the company's deposit into the employee's FGTS account accumulated during the time of employment.

SEYCHELLE RUPEE unit of currency, Seychelles (100 cents equal 1 Seychelle rupee).

SEZ *see* SPECIAL ECONOMIC ZONE.

SFSC *see* SHARED FOREIGN SALES CORPORATION.

SGA *see* SELLING, GENERAL, AND ADMINISTRATIVE (EXPENSES).

SHADOW ECONOMY the underground economy. The underground economy is composed of those individuals who provide goods and services to the underground market of industrial users or consumers in a country. The shadow market is also known internationally as the BLACK or PARALLEL MARKET.

SHADOW GOVERNMENT President Bush dispatched about 100 senior civilian managers to live and work secretly outside Washington, activating for the first time a long-standing plan called "Continuity of Operations Plan," to ensure survival of federal rule after catastrophic attack on the nation's capital. Under the plan, high-ranking officials representing their departments rotate in and out of the assignment at one of two fortified locations along the East Coast.

SHALLOW INTEGRATION reduction or elimination of TARIFFS, QUOTAS, and other TRADE BARRIERS in GOODS at the BORDER such as trade-limiting CUSTOMS prcedures. *see also* DEEP INTEGRATION.

SHARED FOREIGN SALES CORPORATION (SFSC) a foreign sales corporation consisting of more than 1 and fewer than 25 unrelated EXPORTERS. *see also* FOREIGN SALES CORPORATION.

SHAREWARE software that is distributed free of charge. However, if the user finds the software to be useful, it should be purchased from the author, whose name and address will be found in a file distributed with the software. *see also* FREEWARE.

SHEKEL *see* SHEQEL.

SHEQEL (SHEQALIM) unit of currency, Israel (100 agora equal 1 sheqel).

SHERMAN ACT legislation of 1890 that bars contracts, combinations, or conspiracies in restraint of trade and makes it a violation of law to monopolize or to attempt to or to conspire to monopolize any trade in interstate or foreign commerce. Jurisdiction requires a direct, substantial, and reasonably foreseeable effect on domestic trade or commerce or on the EXPORT commerce of a person engaged in such commerce in the United States. *see also* CLAYTON ACT.

SHIELD a U.S. interagency EXPORT control committee that reviews licenses involving chemical or biological weapons.

SHIP ARRIVALS a daily schedule of vessel arrivals at all major U.S. ports. It is found daily in the shipcard section of the JOURNAL OF COMMERCE. *see also* SHIP DEPARTURES.

SHIP DEPARTURES a daily schedule of ship departures from all major North American ports. It is found daily in the SHIPCARD section of the JOURNAL OF COMMERCE. *see also* SHIP ARRIVALS.

SHIP FIXTURE BREAKDOWN column appearing daily in the second section of the JOURNAL OF COMMERCE. It is a summary of ship CHARTER agreements provided by the Knight-Ridder Transportation News Ticker.

SHIP SALE REPORT a biweekly report appearing in the JOURNAL OF COMMERCE that tracks sales prices of second-hand bulk carriers and tankers during a 2-week period. This information is compiled by Shipping Intelligence, Inc.

SHIPCARD a daily insert found in the JOURNAL OF COMMERCE that provides a daily guide to ocean shipping liner services. Shipcards are listings of inbound and outbound vessels grouped by general geographic areas from the Atlantic, Gulf, and Pacific Coasts and from the Great Lakes, St. Lawrence Seaway, and Canadian East Coast. *see also* SHIPCARD DIRECTORY.

SHIPCARD DIRECTORY Listings of the outbound and inbound SHIPCARD grouped by general geographic areas from the Atlantic, Gulf, and Pacific Coasts and from the Great Lakes, St. Lawrence Seaway, and Canadian East Coast appearing daily on the back page of the shipcard insert of the JOURNAL OF COMMERCE. The steamship lines, along with their card numbers, are listed alphabetically under each geographic heading.

SHIPMENT all the CARGO carried under the terms of a single BILL OF LADING (B/L).

SHIPMENT CONSOLIDATION *see* CONSOLIDATION.

SHIPMENT RECORD repository of information for each shipment that reflects all activity throughout each step of the shipment life cycle. *see also* MANIFEST; SHIP'S MANIFEST.

SHIPPED ON DECK annotation in a BILL OF LADING that the goods have been shipped on the deck of a vessel. *see also* ON-DECK BILL OF LADING.

SHIPPER the party named on a shipping document responsible for shipping merchandise. The shipper is the party that consigns or receives goods for transportation.

SHIPPER'S AGENT an individual or firm, working as in intermediary, who purchases CARGO capacity from transportation companies (i.e., steamship companies, airlines) and then sells this space to SHIPPERS.

SHIPPER'S ASSOCIATION companies engaged in international trade joining together for the purpose of negotiating freight rates with the shipping companies as a group in an attempt to negotiate more favorable rates.

SHIPPER'S COOPERATIVE a separate company owned by SHIPPERS of goods, who group together to perform the functions of a FOREIGN FREIGHT FORWARDER, on a not-for-profit basis. The services of such a cooperative are available to members and nonmembers in accordance with all regulatory requirements, and profits are distributed only to owner members as patronage dividends.

SHIPPER'S DECLARATION OF CANADIAN ORIGIN document required by U.S. Customs Regulation verifying that goods originating in Canada and being EXPORTED to the United States are in fact Canadian-manufactured goods in accordance with the RULES OF ORIGIN required for the U.S.–CANADA FREE TRADE AGREEMENT.

SHIPPER'S EXPORT DECLARATION (SED) U.S. Treasury Department form containing the complete particulars on individual shipments used to control EXPORTS and act as a source document for official U.S. export statistics. SEDs must be prepared for shipments through the U.S. Postal Service when the shipment is valued over $500. SEDs are required for shipments, other than by the U.S. Postal Service, where the value of COMMODITIES classified under each individual Schedule B number is over $2,500. SEDs must be prepared, regardless of value, for all shipments that require a validated export license or are destined for countries prohibited by the Export Administration Regulations. SEDs are prepared by the EXPORTER and the exporter's agent and delivered to the exporting CARRIER (post office, airline, or vessel line). The exporting carrier presents the required number of copies to the U.S. CUSTOMS SERVICE at the PORT of export.

The U.S. Foreign Trade Statistical Regulations (15 CFR, Part 30) provide the statistical requirements for use by exporters, FREIGHT FORWARDERS, and ocean carriers concerning preparation and filing of SEDs.

SHIPPING CONFERENCE *see* CONFERENCE.

SHIPPING ORDER instructions of SHIPPER to CARRIER for forwarding of goods. *see also* DELIVERY ORDER.

SHIPPING TOLERANCES a means of EXPORTING additional quantities or dollar values that are listed on the INDIVIDUALLY VALIDATED EXPORT LICENSE, without amending the license or applying for a new one. There are several rules for determining the shipping tolerance for a shipment, depending whether the COMMODITY is licensed by number, weight or measure, or dollar value. The Requirements section of the EXPORT CONTROL CLASSIFICATION NUMBER (ECCN) lists the type of unit used in reporting the commodity. If the commodity is reported in dollar value, there is no tolerance. If the commodity is reported as a number of units, there is no tolerance on the number of units; however, there is a 25% tolerance on the total dollar value shown on the license if the commodity is reported in weight or measure. There is a 10% tolerance on the unshipped balance of the weight or measure, and there is a 25% tolerance on the total dollar value shown on the license.

SHIPPING WEIGHT the gross weight in kilograms of shipments, including the weight of moisture content, wrappings, crates, boxes, and containers (other than CARGO vans and similar substantial outer containers).

SHIP'S MANIFEST a list, signed by the captain of a ship, of the individual shipments constituting the ship's CARGO. *see also* MANIFEST; SHIPMENT RECORD.

SHIP'S PAPERS documents a ship must carry to meet the safety, health, immigration, commercial, and CUSTOMS requirements of a PORT of call or of international law.

SHIP'S STORES food, medical supplies, spare parts, and other provisions carried for the day-to-day running of a vessel.

SHORT-FORM BILL OF LADING BILL OF LADING on which the detailed conditions of transportation are not listed in full. *see also* MARINE BILL OF LADING; ON-BOARD; ON BOARD BILL OF LADING; ON-DECK BILL OF LADING; ORDER BILL OF LADING; STRAIGHT BILL OF LADING.

SHORT OF EXCHANGE position of a FOREIGN EXCHANGE trader who has sold more foreign bills than the quantity of bills he or she has in possession to cover sales.

SHORT LIFE CYCLE GOOD any product that becomes obsolete within four years after it has been commercially introduced. *see also* PRODUCT LIFE CYCLE.

SHORT SUPPLY COMMODITIES that may be subject to EXPORT controls to protect the domestic economy from the excessive drain of scarce materials and to reduce the serious inflationary impact of satisfying foreign demand. Items that the U.S. controls for short-supply purposes include petroleum and petroleum products, unprocessed western red cedar, and shipment of horses by sea. The controls are included in the Export Administration Regulations.

SHORT-TERM BULK AGRICULTURAL CREDIT INSURANCE a program of the Canadian EXPORT DEVELOPMENT CORPORATION (EDC) that provides insurance coverage to Canadian EXPORTERS of bulk COMMODITIES on credit terms of up to 365 days. *see also* COMMERCIAL RISKS; POLITICAL RISKS; EXPORT FINANCING.

SHORT WEIGHT notation of a shipment's weight as less than noted on the original BILL OF LADING, indicating loss during shipment. *see also* MARINE CARGO INSURANCE; SHORTAGE; WITH PARTICULAR AVERAGE.

SHORTAGE deficiency in quantity shipped. *see also* SHORT WEIGHT.

SHOT BOOK *see* HEALTH CERTIFICATE.

SHRINK WRAPPING a method of using a strong and flexible plastic film to enclose a load of cartons placed on a PALLET. This technique is used by packers of EXPORT CARGO so that the cargo will be immobilized. It will facilitate handling and reduce the risk of damage.

SHUNTO a spring wage offensive in Japan.

SHUTTLE TRADE trade accomplished by individuals and groups traveling to other countries, buying GOODS, and bringing them home, typically in their luggage, to resell.

SIC *see* STANDARD INDUSTRIAL CLASSIFICATION CODE.

SICE *see* SISTEMA DE INFORMACION AL COMERCIO EXTERIOR.

SICHTPAPIER (German) *see* SIGHT DRAFT.

SIDA *see* SWEDISH INTERNATIONAL DEVELOPMENT AUTHORITY.

SIDE AGREEMENTS an international agreement negotiated specifically for accompanying and building on a trade agreement. The first international agreements of this type were part of the NORTH AMERICAN FREE TRADE ACT (NAFTA). Two side agreements in the areas of labor and the environment were negotiated for the NAFTA agreement. The objective of these two agreements was to promote international cooperation in improving and enforcing labor and environmental standards and conditions.

SIFIDA *see* SOCIETE INTERNATIONALE FINANCIERE POUR LES INVESTISSEMENTS ET LE DEVELOPPEMENT EN AFRIQUE.

.SIG FILE a file named ".sig" or ".signature". that is appended automatically to all the user's outgoing ELECTRONIC MAIL and USENET POSTINGS.

SIGHT DOCUMENTARY CREDIT *see* DOCUMENTARY CREDIT.

SIGHT DRAFT a DRAFT that is to be paid when presented for payment to the DRAWEE. Drafts that are to be paid at a later date, which is often after the buyer receives the goods, are called time drafts or date drafts. A sight draft is used when the seller wishes to retain title to the shipment until it reaches its destination and is paid for. Before the CARGO can be released, the original ocean bill of lading must be properly endorsed by the buyer and surrendered to the carrier, because it is a document that evidences title. *see also* D/A SIGHT DRAFT (DOCUMENTS (AGAINST) ACCEPTANCE SIGHT DRAFT); DOCUMENTS AGAINST PAYMENT (D/P); DOCUMENTARY DRAFT.

SIGNAL-TO-NOISE RATIO
  1. electronic ratio of desired signal-to-noise levels.
  2. (slang) ratio of useful to useless material in a NEWSGROUP.

SIGNATURE SERVICE service designed to provide continuous responsibility for the custody of shipments in transit, so named because a signature is required from each person handling the shipment.

SIGTDOKUMENT (Danish) *see* SIGHT DRAFT.

SII *see* STRUCTURAL IMPEDIMENTS INITIATIVE.

SIJORI *see* SINGAPORE–JAHOR–RIAU GROWTH TRIANGLE.

SILENT LANGUAGE nonverbal forms of communication, such as color, distance, and time. Example: the color black is associated in most Western countries with death, yet white in part of the Far East carries the same connotation. To be successful, an international marketer must match the color of products and advertisements with the consumers' cultural frame of reference.

SILENT PARTNER an individual making a financial investment in a business enterprise who does not participate or play an active role in its management.

SILLE SELSKAP a sleeping partnership in Norway. This is an unlimited partnership in which one or more persons contribute capital and are authorized to share in the organization's profits or losses. In Norway there is no requirement to make public the participation of the sleeping partners, and they have no direct liability for the debts of the partnership.

SIMILAR GOODS goods that, although not comparable in all respects, have equivalent characteristics and component materials enabling them to perform the same functions. *see also* IDENTICAL GOODS.

SIMILAR MERCHANDISE *see* SIMILAR GOODS.

SIMIS *see* SINGLE INTERNAL MARKET INFORMATION SERVICE.

SINGAPORE DOLLAR unit of currency, Singapore (100 cents equal 1 Singapore dollar).

SINGAPORE–JAHOR–RIAU GROWTH TRIANGLE (SIJORI) a subregional economic grouping composed of the nation of Singapore, the Malaysian State of Johor, and Indonesia's Riau Province.

SINGAPORE MINISTERIAL the first ministerial meeting of the WORLD TRADE ORGANIZATION (WTO), held in Singapore in 1996.

SINGAPORE OIL FUTURES a column appearing daily in the JOURNAL OF COMMERCE that lists the prices from the Singapore International Monetary Exchange for crude and fuel oils.

SINGLE ADMINISTRATIVE DOCUMENT (SAD) a CUSTOMS document used within the EUROPEAN ECONOMIC COMMUNITY (EEC) officially referred to as the DECLARATION OF PARTICULARS RELATING TO CUSTOMS VALUE (D.V.1). It was adopted on January 1, 1989, for the purpose of eliminating the many different forms in several languages previously used by the 12 EEC member governments at their borders before authorizing goods to be imported into the country. The SAD functions as an EXPORT declaration, transit document, and IMPORT declaration. The form is used not only within the EEC but also when there is trade between the EEC and the EUROPEAN FREE TRADE ASSOCIATION (EFTA).

SINGLE-BUYER POLICY a program of the EXPORT–IMPORT BANK OF THE UNITED STATES that provides insurance coverage to the U.S. EXPORTER for short- and medium-term credit sales to a single buyer. The policy may be issued for a one-time sale or for a series of shipments to the same buyer. *see also* MULTIBUYER POLICY; NEW-TO-EXPORT POLICY; UMBRELLA POLICY.

SINGLE CURRENCY PEG *see* EXCHANGE RATE CLASSIFICATIONS.

SINGLE DECLARATION FORM a form on which an IMPORTER will report IMPORT shipments scheduled to arrive in order to request insurance coverage. The form is used by the importer to report and request insurance coverage for a single import shipment. The MULTIPLE DECLARATION FORM allows the importer to report a grouping of shipments. *see also* MARINE CARGO INSURANCE.

SINGLE-ENTRY VISA a specialized term used by immigration authorities to describe a visitor who is permitted a one-time entry into a country. Another VISA is required for any future visits. The visa is a stamp on the foreign national's passport issued by a consular officer, which allows the individual to enter the country. *see also* MULTIPLE-ENTRY VISA.

SINGLE EUROPEAN ACT (SEA) the legal and procedural support designed to achieve the single European market in 1992. The SEA revised the EUROPEAN ECONOMIC COMMUNITY (EEC) Treaty and, where not already provided for in the treaty, majority decisions were introduced for numerous votes facing its Council of Ministers, particularly those affecting establishment of the single European Market and the European financial common market. The role of the European Parliament was strengthened; decisions on fiscal matters remained subject to unanimity. SEA entered into force in July 1987 and was the first significant revision of the TREATY OF ROME.

SINGLE INTERNAL MARKET INFORMATION SERVICE (SIMIS) service operated by the U.S. DEPARTMENT OF COMMERCE'S INTERNATIONAL TRADE ADMINISTRATION (ITA) that provides information, assistance, and advice on how to do business in the European Community's internal market.

SINGLE UNDERTAKING a term, in trade negotiations, for requiring participants to accept or reject the outcome of multiple negotiations in a single package, rather than selecting among them.

SI/OGA state/industry-organized, government-approved. *see also* CERTIFIED TRADE MISSIONS.

SISTEMA DE INFORMACION AL COMERCIO EXTERIOR (SICE) (English: Foreign Trade Information System) a data bank that provides foreign trade information to the public and private sectors of member countries of the ORGANIZATION OF AMERICAN STATES (OAS). The system includes information on the U.S. IMPORT and EXPORT markets, markets of other OAS member countries, and trade information on the EUROPEAN COMMUNITY and Japan.

SISTEMA ECONOMICO LATINOAMERICANO (SELA) *see* LATIN AMERICAN ECONOMIC SYSTEM.

SITC *see* STANDARD INTERNATIONAL TRADE CLASSIFICATION.

SKILL INTENSIVE an activity that relies heavily on inputs of skilled labor, usually relative to unskilled labor. *see also* CAPITAL INTENSIVE; LABOR INTENSIVE.

SKILLED LABOR employees who have been trained with the skills required to perform a particular function.

SKY MARSHALS *see* AIR MARSHALS.

SKYJACKING the hijacking of an airliner by terrorists, which was common practice in the 1960s.

SLD abbreviation referring to a ship that has sailed.

S.L.&C. abbreviation for shipper's load and count.

S.L.&T. abbreviation for shipper's load and tally.

SLEEPER CELL a small CELL that keeps itself undetected until such time as they can "awaken" and cause havoc.

SLING a contrivance into which freight is placed to be hoisted into or out of a ship. *see also* GENERAL CARGO VESSELS; HATCH.

SLIP a vessel's BERTH between two piers.

SMALL BUSINESS INVESTMENT COMPANY (SBIC) FINANCING a cooperative agreement between the U.S. SMALL BUSINESS ADMINISTRATION (SBA) and the EXIMBANK to provide equity capital or working capital financing to small businesses above the statutory limit of the SBA. Unlike the SBA, the SBIC is permitted to invest in EXPORT TRADING COMPANIES (ETCS) where banks have an equity participation as long as all other SBIC requirements have been met. *see also* EXPORT REVOLVING LINE OF CREDIT (ERLC); INTERNATIONAL TRADE LOAN PROGRAM.

SMALL AND MEDIUM INDUSTRY PROMOTION CORPORATION (SMIPC) a nonprofit organization that has been promoting the growth and development of small business since 1979. The program was modified in June 1986 to include assistance to overseas investors who wish to establish JOINT VENTURES or enter into LICENSING arrangements with Korean firms.

SMALL PACKAGE SERVICE specialized service to guarantee the DELIVERY of small parcels within specified express time limits.

SMALLPOX the first biological weapon, used during the eighteenth century. There is no specific treatment for smallpox disease, and the only prevention is vaccination.

SMART *see* SOFTWARE FOR MARKET ANALYSIS AND RESTRICTIONS ON TRADE.

SMDS *see* SWITCHED MULTIMEGABIT DATA SERVICE.

SMI *see* STRUCTURE OF MANAGEMENT INFORMATION.

SMIPC *see* SMALL AND MEDIUM INDUSTRY PROMOTION CORPORATION.

SMITHSONIAN AGREEMENT an agreement among the GROUP OF TEN nations, which brought about the end of the WOODS MONETARY SYSTEM. It included new agreements on currency par values, the value of gold, and tariffs. The agreement was achieved in December 1971 at the Smithsonian Institution in Washington, DC. The agreement became necessary when the world currency markets were thrown into disarray when the United States went on the FLOATING EXCHANGE RATE monetary system in August 1971.

SMOOT–HAWLEY TARIFF ACT OF 1930 *see* TARIFF ACT OF 1930.

SMUGGLING moving GOODS across a CUSTOMS frontier in a clandestine manner, evading customs control. It may be goods on which DUTY and taxes have been avoided, or it may be goods that are not permitted to be IMPORTED or EXPORTED.

SNAKE *see* EUROPEAN SNAKE.

SNC *see* SOCIETA IN NOME COLLETTIVO.

SNEC *see* SUBGROUP ON NUCLEAR EXPORT COORDINATION.

S.O. abbreviation for ship's option; shipping order; sellers option.

SOAP *see* SUNFLOWER SEED OIL ASSISTANCE PROGRAM.

SOCIAL DEMOCRACY *see* MIXED ECONOMY.

SOCIAL DUMPING the EXPORT of a GOOD from a country with weak or poorly enforced labor standards, because the exporter has costs that are artificially lower than its competitors in higher-standards countries, constituting an unfair advantage in international trade. *see also* DUMPING, ECODUMPING; ENVIRONMENTAL DUMPING.

SOCIALISM a political/economic system in which government owns or controls the means of producing and distributing goods in critical industries, but allows private or collective ownership in certain noncritical industries. *see also* CAPITALISM; COMMAND ECONOMY; MARKET ECONOMY; NONMARKET ECONOMY.

SOCIEDAD ANONIMA (S.A.) (English: incorporated company) a form of Mexican corporation that must have at least 5 shareholders who may be either Mexican or foreign. Shareholders are liable only up to the amount of their contribution. No shares may be held in the company name. *S.A.* must follow the company name, indicating that it is a corporation.

SOCIEDAD ANONIMA DE CAPITAL VARIABLE (S.A. DE CV) (Spanish: variable capital company) a Mexican corporation similar to S.A., must have at least 5 shareholders, who may be either Mexican or foreign. Each shareholder is liable only up to the amount of his/her contribution. S.A. de CV differs from S.A. in that an S.A.

de CV may own its shares. *S.A. de C.V.* must follow the company name indicating that it is a corporation with variable capital.

SOCIEDAD DE CAPITALES (Spanish) *see* CORPORATION.

SOCIEDAD EN COMANDITA SIMPLE (S. EN C.) (Spanish) *see* LIMITED PARTNERSHIP.

SOCIEDADE DE CAPITAIS (Portuguese) *see* CORPORATION.

SOCIETA A RESPONSABILITA LIMITATA (SRL) a private Italian company.

SOCIETA IN NOME COLLETTIVO (SNC) (Italian) GENERAL PARTNERSHIP in which there is no limit on the liability of the partners.

SOCIETA PER AZIONI (SPA) Italian public corporation that must have at least two shareholders at formation. After formation, the requirement is reduced to one shareholder.

SOCIETE A RESPONSABILITE LIMITEE (SARL) French limited liability company having features of both a CORPORATION and a partnership. The number of partners cannot exceed 50. Partners may be either French or foreign. Partner liabilities are limited to the amount of their contribution, which may be in cash or in kind but not in skills. Even though shares may be freely traded among partners, they may not be transferred to third parties without majority agreement of partners representing at least 75% of the capital.

SOCIETE ANONYME (S.A.) a French form of corporation that must have at least seven shareholders, who may be either French or foreign. Each member is liable only up to the amount of stock owned.

SOCIETE EN COMMANDITE SIMPLE (French) LIMITED PARTNERSHIP composed of general partners, with the managing partner at least having unlimited liability, and silent partners whose liability is limited to the amount of their capital contributions. Silent partners are not permitted to perform any management functions vis-a-vis other partners. In a limited partnership without shares, transfer of shares of the limited partners is allowable only with the consent of all the partners. In a limited partnership with shares (Société en commandité paractions), these are transferred in a manner similar to CORPORATIONS.

SOCIETE EN NOM COLLECTIF (SNC) (French) GENERAL PARTNERSHIP organized with all partners being allocated shares for their contributions, which may be cash, in-kind, or services. There is no required minimum or maximum capital, nor any share par value. Shares in the company are not negotiable and cannot be transferred without agreement of all the partners. Each partner is liable for the totality of the company's debts and obligations.

SOCIETE INTERNATIONALE FINANCIERE POUR LES INVESTISSEMENTS ET LE DEVELOPPEMENT EN AFRIQUE (SIFIDA) a holding company affiliated with the AFRICAN DEVELOP-

MENT BANK (AFDB). The society fosters the formation of profitable business in Africa by identifying and nurturing productive projects, arranging for syndicated loans, and providing EXPORT finance. Major shareholders include the AFDB, the INTERNATIONAL FINANCE CORPORATION (IFC) and more than 100 financial, industrial, and commercial institutions around the world. Its headquarters are in Chène-Bourg, Switzerland.

SOCIETE PAR ACTIONS SIMPLIFIEE (SAS) French private limited company designed for joint ventures. It permits the rights and liability of each shareholder to be defined by mutual agreement between the parties. Only two shareholders are required.

SOCIETY a grouping of people distinguished from other groups by mutual interests, common traditions, collective activities and interests, shared institutions, and a common culture. The *nation-state* is an often-used term denoting society in international business.

SOCIETY FOR WORLDWIDE INTERBANK FINANCIAL TELECOMMUNICATIONS (SWIFT) a cooperative organized under Belgian law, with headquarters in La Hulpe, near Brussels. SWIFT provides communications services to the international banking industry, including payments and administrative messages and, more recently, securities settlements. Traffic in 1991 was about 362 million messages. SWIFT is owned by the member banks—approximately 1,600—including the central banks of most countries. The U.S. Federal Reserve is not a member, but participates in certain types of payments. Securities brokers and dealers, clearing and depository institutions, exchanges for securities, and traveler's checks issuers also participate in SWIFT. SWIFT was organized in 1973 and started operations in 1977.

SODE-NO-SHITA (Japanese) an under-the-table payment. *see also* BRIBE.

SOFT CURRENCY national currencies in which exchange may be made only with difficulty. Soft currency countries typically have minimal exchange reserves and deficits in their balance of payments. *see also* HARD CURRENCY.

SOFT GOODS merchandise manufactured from textiles or the textiles themselves. *see also* COMMODITY.

SOFT LOAN commonly, a loan from a government or multilateral development bank with a long repayment period and below-market interest.

SOFT SIDE (OF INTERNATIONAL MARKETING) those elements of marketing dealing with areas that cannot be quantified, such as culture, business customs, and language differences. *see also* CULTURE; HARD SIDE (OF INTERNATIONAL MARKETING); HIGH-CONTEXT CULTURE; LOW-CONTEXT CULTURE.

SOFTWARE FOR MARKET ANALYSIS AND RESTRICTIONS ON TRADE (SMART) computer programs developed by the UNITED NATIONS CONFERENCE ON TRADE AND DEVELOPMENT (UNCTAD) and the WORLD BANK to provide DEVELOPING COUNTRIES with the information on trade statistics and market information necessary to allow for effective participation in ROUNDS of MULTILATERAL TRADE NEGOTIATIONS. The system is set up and operated out of Geneva, Switzerland, and is funded by the UNITED NATIONS DEVELOPMENT PROGRAM (UNDP).

SOGO/IOGA state/industry-organized, government-supported TRADE MISSIONS to potential buyers or clients overseas. Missions can be undertaken by firms individually or in organized groups. The U.S. DEPARTMENT OF COMMERCE directly sponsors many trade missions and provides support to selected missions organized by state and local governments, Chambers of Commerce, trade associations, and other EXPORT-oriented groups.

SOGO SOSHA a trading company headquartered in Japan engaged in DIRECT EXPORTING. The nearest equivalent in the United States would be a company exporting its own goods or exporting on behalf of other noncompeting companies.

SOLE IMPORTING AGENCY a private or government entity, that has been granted by the government the exclusive right to IMPORT certain GOODS.

SOLOMON ISLAND DOLLAR unit of currency, Solomon Islands (100 cents equal 1 Solomon Island dollar).

SOMALI SHILLING (SHILIN) unit of currency, Somalia.

SOURCE COUNTRY *see* FOREIGN DIRECT INVESTMENT.

SOURCE OF COMMODITIES—AGENCY FOR INTERNATIONAL DEVELOPMENT (AID) policy that limits countries to where COMMODITIES can be purchased. Many AID agreements require that commodities be purchased from the United States. Some agreements do allow purchases from the United States and from selected free-world countries (excluding DEVELOPED COUNTRIES).

SOURCING STRATEGY a plan of action used by a firm as it is related to the purchase of supplies, components, and final products. A firm can decide to source products from both domestic and international locations. *see also* OUTSOURCING.

SOUTH ASIA PREFERENTIAL TRADING ARRANGEMENT *see* SOUTH ASIAN ASSOCIATION FOR REGIONAL COOPERATION.

SOUTH ASIAN ASSOCIATION FOR REGIONAL COOPERATION (SAARC) cooperative association founded in 1985 by seven countries: Bangladesh, Bhutan, India, Maldives, Nepal, Pakistan, and Sri Lanka. It promotes economic, technical, scientific, and social cooperation among members. The South Asian Preferential Trading Arrangement (SAPTA) was established in 1997 as a step toward creating an economic community in south Asia. Members are the original 7 countries.

SOUTH GROUP *see* DANISH INTERNATIONAL DEVELOPMENT ASSISTANCE.

SOUTH PACIFIC BUREAU FOR ECONOMIC COOPERATION (SPEC) a subsidiary organization of the SOUTH PACIFIC FORUM (SPF), which promotes regional cooperation in the development of the island members in partnership with the more industrially developed countries of the region: Australia and New Zealand.

SOUTH PACIFIC COMMISSION regional international organization founded in 1947 and headquartered in Nouméa, Caledonia (an overseas territory of France). Its membership consists of Australia, France, the Netherlands, New Zealand, the United Kingdom, and the United States, and the purpose of the organization is to act as a forum to allow members of the region to cooperate on matters of mutual economic concern. *see also* SOUTHEAST ASIA TREATY ORGANIZATION; UNITED NATIONS ECONOMIC AND SOCIAL COMMISSION FOR ASIA AND THE PACIFIC.

SOUTH PACIFIC FORUM (SPF) a South Pacific regional arrangement for convening 15 governments and territories for deliberations on issues of mutual interest. The forum was established in 1971, and its headquarters is in Suva, Fiji. SPF members include Australia, the Cook Islands, Fiji, Kirbati, Marshall Islands, Micronesia, Nauru, New Zealand, Niue, Papua New Guinea, Samoa, Solomon Islands, Tonga, Tuvalu, and Vanatu.

SOUTHEAST ASIA TREATY ORGANIZATION (SEATO) a mutual defense pact signed in 1955. It was formed under the authority of the Southeast Asia Collective Defense Treaty of 1954, and its signatories included Australia, France, Great Britain, New Zealand, Pakistan, the Philippines, Thailand, and the United States. It was formed in response to the French defeat in Indochina and was designed to oppose communist advances in the region and military threats from the Soviet Union and the People's Republic of China. Lacking support, SEATO was dissolved in 1977. *see also* NORTH ATLANTIC TREATY ORGANIZATION (NATO); WARSAW PACT.

SOUTHERN AFRICA DEVELOPMENT COMMUNITY (SADC) a regional economic pact composed of Angola, Botswana, Lesotho, Malawi, Mozambique, Namibia, Swaziland, Tanzania, Zambia, and Zimbabwe. Since a change in name and focus in mid-1992, the community focuses solely on development, leaving trade matters to the PREFERENTIAL TRADE AREA FOR EASTERN AND SOUTHERN AFRICAN STATES (PTA). Community headquarters are in Gaborone, Botswana. SADC was established in April 1980 as the Southern Africa Development Coordination Conference.

SOUTHERN AFRICAN CUSTOMS UNION (SACU) customs union established in 1910 that includes Botswana, Lesotho, Namibia, South Africa, and Swaziland. SACU provides for the free exchange of goods within the area, a common external TARIFF, and a sharing of custom revenues. External tariffs, excise duties, and several rebate and refund provisions are the same for all SACU members. SACU's revenues are apportioned among its members according to a set formula. These funds constitute a significant contribution to each member's government revenues.

SOUTHERN AFRICAN DEVELOPMENT COORDINATION CONFERENCE *see* SOUTHERN AFRICA DEVELOPMENT COMMUNITY.

SOUTHERN COMMON MARKET *see* MERCOSUR.

SOUTHERN CONE a group of Latin American nations consisting of Argentina, Brazil, Chile, Paraguay, and Uruguay. With the exception of Chile, these countries also comprise the Southern Common Market, or MERCOSUR.

SOUTHERN CONE AXIAL WAY *see* SOUTHERN CONE.

SOVEREIGN (SOVEREIGNTY)
1. an individual who exercises supreme, permanent authority in a nation, such as a king, queen, ruler, monarch, or chief of state.
2. the independence and self-rule power that an independent nation has.
3. the right of a nation to deal with individuals within its own jurisdiction.
4. a British gold coin formerly used in Great Britain and originally worth £1. However, with the abolition of the gold standard the coin is worth significantly more.

SOVEREIGN CREDIT borrowing guaranteed by the government of a SOVEREIGN state. *see also* SOVEREIGN ENTITY.

SOVEREIGN ENTITY a country granted recognition by the UNITED NATIONS, or recognized by custom. *see also* INTERNATIONAL LAW.

SOVEREIGN IMMUNITY practice that grants nations release from litigation in their own courts or in the courts of other countries unless they freely submit. *see also* ACTS OF STATE DOCTRINE; SOVEREIGN (SOVEREIGNTY).

SOVEREIGN RISK risk to a lender that the government of a SOVEREIGN state may DEFAULT on its financial obligations. *see also* POLITICAL RISK.

SPA *see* SOCIETÀ PER AZIONI.

S.P.D. abbreviation for shipped.

SPEC *see* SOUTH PACIFIC BUREAU FOR ECONOMIC COOPERATION.

SPECIAL AMERICAN BUSINESS INTERNSHIP TRAINING (SABIT) PROGRAM originally the Soviet–American Business Internship Training Program, SABIT is a cooperative program that brings business executives and scientists from the former Soviet Union for 3- to 6-month internships to American companies. The program teaches these managers and scientists how to operate in a market economy at the same time that American businesses develop market contacts once their interns return home. Soviet business managers are referred by the U.S. DEPARTMENT OF COMMERCE INTERNATIONAL TRADE ADMINISTRATION to sponsoring U.S. companies, which make the final selection of their interns. The program matches U.S. corporate sponsors with Russian Federation business executives from the same industries. The Independent States provide transportation; the companies provide living expenses and training in management techniques (production, distribution, marketing, accounting, wholesaling, and publishing).

SPECIAL AND DIFFERENTIAL TREATMENT (S&D) the principle that the TOKYO ROUND negotiations should seek to accord particular benefits to the EXPORTS of developing countries, consistent with their trade, financial, and development needs. Among proposals for special or differential treatment are reduction or elimination of tariffs applied to exports of developing countries under the GENERALIZED SYSTEM OF PREFERENCES (GSP), expansion of product and country coverage of the GSP, accelerated implementation of TARIFF cuts agreed to in the Tokyo Round for developing country exports, substantial reduction or elimination of tariff escalation, special provisions for developing country exports in any new codes of conduct covering nontariff measures, assurance that any new multilateral safeguard system will contain special provisions for developing country exports, and the principle that developed countries will expect less than full reciprocity for trade concessions they grant developing countries.

SPECIAL CHEMICAL LICENSE authorization to EXPORT certain chemical and biological equipment described in Section 778.8 of the U.S. EXPORT ADMINISTRATION REGULATIONS (EAR) to preapproved consignees. Section 778.8 prohibits the export of chemical weapons precursors, certain viruses, bacteria, and equipment for their manufacture, from the United States to countries likely to use them in the manufacture of chemical weapons. *see also* SPECIAL LICENSES.

SPECIAL CUSTOMS INVOICE a document, required by some foreign countries, describing a shipment of goods and showing information such as the CONSIGNOR, CONSIGNEE, and value of the shipment. This invoice is certified by a CONSULAR OFFICIAL of the foreign country. It is used by the country's CUSTOMS officials to verify the value, quantity, and nature of the shipment.

SPECIAL DRAWING RIGHTS (SDRs) international reserve assets, created by the INTERNATIONAL MONETARY FUND (IMF) in 1970 and allocated to individual member nations. Within conditions set by the IMF, SDRs can be used by a nation with a deficit in its balance of international payments to settle debts with another nation or with the IMF. The value of SDRs is computed as a weighted average of five currencies: DEUTSCHE MARK, FRENCH FRANC, Japanese YEN, POUND sterling, and U.S. DOLLAR.

SPECIALIZED CREDIT

SPECIAL ECONOMIC ZONE the equivalent of a FOREIGN TRADE ZONE in the former Soviet Union.

SPECIAL IMPORT MEASURES TAX legislation by the Canadian federal government, passed by the federal parliament, giving the CANADIAN IMPORT TRIBUNAL powers similar to the U.S. INTERNATIONAL TRADE COMMISSION (ITC). It was given authority to review, report findings, and make recommendations on appropriate actions concerning COUNTERVAILING DUTIES, DUMPING, ANTIDUMPING PETITIONS, and EXPORT SUBSIDIZATION.

SPECIAL LICENSES procedures established that may be used, when appropriate, in lieu of the INDIVIDUAL VALIDATED LICENSE, in order to facilitate the EXPORT of COMMODITIES requiring a VALIDATED LICENSE. The special licenses generally allow for the export of preapproved commodities, software, and/or technical data to preapproved consignees or destinations. *see also* DISTRIBUTION LICENSE; HUMANITARIAN LICENSE; PROJECT LICENSE; SERVICE SUPPLY/FACILITY LICENSE; SPECIAL CHEMICAL LICENSE.

SPECIAL MARKING REQUIREMENTS any special marking or labeling required on specific products being IMPORTED into the United States by specific agencies (i.e., Food and Drug Administration and Department of Agriculture). These marking requirements are separate and apart from the standard country of origin marking requirements.

SPECIAL RATES rates that apply to CARGO traffic under special conditions and usually to and from a limited number of points.

SPECIAL 301 a U.S. statute created by the OMNIBUS TRADE AND COMPETITIVENESS ACT OF 1988 requiring the U.S. TRADE REPRESENTATIVE (USTR) to review annually the condition of intellectual property protection among U.S. trading partners. Submissions are accepted from industry, after which the USTR, weighing all relevant information, makes a determination as to whether a country presents excessive barriers to trade with the United States by virtue of its inadequate protection of intellectual property. If the USTR makes a positive determination, a country may be named to
- the priority foreign countries list (the most egregious),
- the priority watch list, or
- the watch list.
  see also SECTION 301; SUPER 301.

SPECIAL TRANSACTION GUARANTEES program of the Canadian EXPORT DEVELOPMENT CORPORATION (EDC) that provides BANK and other organization-extending EXPORT FINANCING to foreign buyers of Canadian goods and services, with insurance coverage on nonrecourse supplier financing. The products EXPORTED must be insured with the EDC by the EXPORTER, in order to qualify for the guarantees.

SPECIALIZED CREDIT a special lending program of the Canadian EXPORT DEVELOPMENT CORPORATION (EDC) providing financing to

Canadian EXPORTERS who require funds to purchase Canadian goods for permanent lease to a firm outside Canada, or for use by the Canadian firm outside Canada.

SPECIALLY DESIGNATED NATIONAL (SDN) a U.S. designation of a target government body, representative, intermediary, or front (whether overt or covert) that usually is located in another country and functions as an extension of the sanctioned government. An SDN may also be a third-party company that otherwise becomes owned or controlled by the target government or that operates on its behalf. No criminal linkage is necessary. Ownership by, control by, acting on behalf of, or profiting from trade with the target government or country would suffice to qualify a person for designation as an SDN. The OFFICE OF FOREIGN ASSETS CONTROL (OFAC) of the U.S. Department of the Treasury implements and enforces financial and trade sanctions. OFAC has the authority to include within the definition of sanctioned government those individuals and entities that OFAC has determined are owned by, controlled by, or acting directly or indirectly on behalf of the target government.

SPECIFIC COMMODITY RATE rate applicable to certain classes of COMMODITIES, usually commodities moving in volume shipments. *see also* GENERAL COMMODITY RATE.

SPECIFIC DUTY *see* SPECIFIC TARIFF.

SPECIFIC RATE OF DUTY *see* SPECIFIC TARIFF.

SPECIFIC TARIFF a tax assessed by a government in accordance with its TARIFF schedule on goods as they enter (or leave) a country, dutiable at a specific rate of duty (so much per pound, gallon, etc.) *see also* AD VALOREM TARIFF; DUTY.

SPECIFIC TRANSACTION INSURANCE a program of the Canadian EXPORT DEVELOPMENT CORPORATION (EDC) providing insurance coverage on individual EXPORT shipments of Canadian goods against losses due to COMMERCIAL and POLITICAL RISKS.

SPECULATOR an individual foreign exchange trader who takes positions in different currencies with the objective of gaining a profit.

SPF *see* SOUTH PACIFIC FORUM.

SPILLOVER EFFECTS a situation where a firm would have a marketing program in one country yet create an awareness of the product in another country. This occurs when the medium selected for use in the program is viewed on a cross-national basis.

SPLIT PAY compensation given to the employee on a foreign assignment in a combination of HOME and HOST COUNTRY currencies. Example: a U.S. employee based in Italy could be given a portion of his salary in LIRA and the balance in U.S. dollars. *see also* SPLIT PAYMENTS; SPLIT PAYROLL.

SPLIT PAYMENTS compensation given to an employee on a foreign assignment using a combination of delivery methods and/or currencies. *see also* SPLIT PAY; SPLIT PAYROLL.

SPLIT PAYROLL a situation where an employee is listed on two different payrolls, with each paying a part of the salary. The purpose of using a split payroll is to reduce the income tax level in the HOST COUNTRY.

SPLIT SHIPMENTS shipments that are divided by the exporting transportation company from the ports where the goods are shipped.

SPO KA Z ORGANICZONA ODPOWIEDZIALNO CIA (SP.Z O.O) a limited liability company in Poland.

SPORADIC DUMPING the occasional sale of a COMMODITY in a foreign market at less than FAIR VALUE or at a lower price than domestically. *see also* ANTIDUMPING DUTY; DUMPING; PERSISTENT DUMPING; PREDATORY DUMPING.

SPORE an asexual, usually single-celled reproductive body of plants, such as fungi, mosses, or ferns; a microorganism, as a bacterium, in a resting or dormant state.

SPOT AGAINST FORWARD the extent to which an individual or firm's spot holding of foreign currencies corresponds to FORWARD currency sales. The spot against forward position is calculated by subtracting forward purchases from forward sales. *see also* LONG POSITION; SHORT POSITION.

SPOT CASH immediate cash payment in a transaction. *see also* FORWARD RATE; SPOT DEAL; SPOT RATE.

SPOT CHEMICALS daily listing in the JOURNAL OF COMMERCE of SPOT PRICE quotations or list prices of suppliers on a New York or producing shipping point basis. The quotations posted are based on prices reported in the market or obtained from suppliers and other sources. Prices of various chemicals and products appear in the JOURNAL OF COMMERCE as follows:
    Monday: crude drugs and naval stores
    Tuesday: aromatic chemicals, essential oils, plastic materials, and synthetic textiles
    Wednesday: aromatic solvents, coating resins, coal tar crudes, dry colors, intermediates, paint materials, and pigments
    Thursday: heavy chemicals, including fertilizers and insecticides
    Friday: fine chemicals and paraffin wax

SPOT COMMODITIES daily listing in the JOURNAL OF COMMERCE of SPOT PRICE information for 41 food, grain, textile, metal, and industrial materials.

SPOT DEAL contract for the sale or purchase of a foreign currency, whereby delivery of the currency must be made within 2 business days from the signing of the contract, at the rate in effect on that date. *see also* SPOT RATE.

SPOT EXCHANGE *see* SPOT RATE.

SPOT EXCHANGE RATE *see* SPOT RATE.

SPOT MARKET market for a COMMODITY or FOREIGN EXCHANGE available for immediate delivery. *see also* SPOT AGAINST FORWARD; SPREAD (IN THE FORWARD MARKET); SPREAD (IN THE SPOT MARKET).

SPOT METALS listing appearing daily in the JOURNAL OF COMMERCE of metal prices from aluminum ingots to titanium sponge in commercial quantity and U.S. dollars. It is quoted on the European free market.

SPOT NATURAL GAS a listing appearing each Wednesday in the JOURNAL OF COMMERCE that provides spot natural gas prices as determined by various marketing and trading organizations.

SPOT OPERATIONS FOREIGN EXCHANGE dealing in which settlement of the mutual DELIVERY commitments is made at the latest 2 days after the transaction was carried out. *see also* FORWARD RATE; SPOT RATE; SPOT TRANSACTIONS.

SPOT PRICE price QUOTATION for immediate sale and DELIVERY of a commodity or currency. *see also* FORWARD RATE; SPOT COMMODITIES; SPOT METALS; SPOT PRODUCT PRICES; SPOT RATE.

SPOT PRODUCT PRICES a daily listing in the JOURNAL OF COMMERCE of the spot prices for home heating oil and unleaded gasoline in New York Harbor and on the Gulf Coast.

SPOT QUOTATION *see* SPOT RATE.

SPOT RATE exchange rate quoted for immediate delivery, normally within 2 business days. *see also* FORWARD RATE.

SPOT TRANSACTION *see* FORWARD EXCHANGE RATE.

SPOTTING placing of a container in order for it to be loaded or unloaded.

SPREAD (IN THE FORWARD MARKET) the difference between the SPOT and FORWARD EXCHANGE RATES.

SPREAD (IN THE SPOT MARKET) the difference between the buy (bid) and sell (offer) rates quoted by a FOREIGN EXCHANGE TRADER.

SP.Z O.O an abbreviation for a limited liability company in Poland. *see also* SPO KA Z ORGANICZONA ODPOWIEDZIALNO CIA.

SQUARE POSITION a situation for the FOREIGN EXCHANGE BROKER where the sales and purchases of the same currency are in balance during any normal accounting period. *see also* EXPOSURE NETTING.

S.R.&C.C. *see* STRIKES, RIOTS, AND CIVIL COMMOTIONS.

SRI LANKA RUPEE unit of currency, Sri Lanka (100 cents equal 1 Sri Lanka rupee).

SRL *see* SOCIETÀ A RESPONSABILITÀ LIMITATA.

S.S. abbreviation for shipside.

S/S abbreviation for STEAMSHIP.

SSA abbreviation for sub-Saharan Africa.

S.T. abbreviation for short ton: 2,000 lb.

STABEX an abbreviation for *stabilisation des exports* (French). The program was initiated after the Second LOME CONVENTION between the EUROPEAN COMMUNITY (EC) and 62 AFRICAN, CARIBBEAN, AND PACIFIC (ACP) COUNTRIES (mostly former colonies of the EC members). The arrangement involved making funds available from the EUROPEAN DEVELOPMENT FUND (EDF), the principal means by which the EUROPEAN ECONOMIC COMMUNITY (EEC) provides aid, concessionary finance, and technical assistance to DEVELOPING COUNTRIES. The STABEX arrangements involved making funds available from the EDF in order to stabilize the EXPORT earning of the ACPs when there is a significant change in the world price of nonmineral exports, thus preventing them from obtaining anticipated HARD currency. *see also* SYSMIN.

STABILIZING SPECULATION the means by which a profit can be made on the FOREIGN EXCHANGE market are
- buying a foreign currency when the domestic EXCHANGE RATE is low or dropping in anticipation that the exchange rate will rise and
- selling a foreign currency when the domestic exchange rate is high or increasing on the anticipation that there will be a fall in the rate.

STABLE-VALUED MONEY a currency that is stable and comes from a country with a low inflation rate.

STANDARD INDUSTRIAL CLASSIFICATION (SIC) the classification standard underlying all establishment-based U.S. economic statistics classified by industry.

STANDARD INTERNATIONAL TRADE CLASSIFICATION (SITC) international trade classification system used solely by international organizations for reporting international trade. The SITC has been revised several times. The current version is Revision 3. It was developed by the UNITED NATIONS in 1950.

STANDARD OF LIVING level of material affluence of a nation as measured by per capita output.

STANDARDIZE (STANDARDIZING) a global marketing strategy where the producer standardizes products or services to simplify the procurement and production processes so as to achieve economies of scale in production, marketing, and research and development. *see also* ADAPTATION.

STANDARDS as defined by the Multilateral Trade Negotiations "Agreement on Technical Barriers to Trade" (Standards Code), a technical specification contained in a document that lays down characteristics of a product such as levels of quality, performance, safety, or dimensions. Standards may include, or deal exclusively with, terminology, symbols, testing and test methods, packaging, marking, or labeling requirements as they apply to a product. *see also* GATT STANDARDS CODE.

STANDARDS CODE *see* STANDARDS.

STANDBY AMOUNT the difference between the CURRENT INSURED AMOUNT (CIA) and the MAXIMUM INSURED AMOUNT (MIA). Premiums for most equity investments under the U.S. OVERSEAS PRIVATE INVESTMENT CORPORATION (OPIC) program are calculated for each type of coverage based on the amount of investment at risk during a given year. For other types of investments, premiums are computed on the basis of a contractually stipulated MIA and a CIA that may, within the limits of the contract, be elected by the investor, normally on a yearly basis. The CIA represents the insurance actually in force during any contract year. For EXPROPRIATION and POLITICAL VIOLENCE coverage, the insured must maintain current coverage (CIA) at a level equal to the amount of the investment at risk.

STANDBY ARRANGEMENTS an assurance that a member country of the INTERNATIONAL MONETARY FUND (IMF) will be able to make purchases up to a specified amount from the IMF during a given period, as long as the member has observed the performance criteria and other terms specified in the arrangement. Standby arrangements extend up to 3 years. *see also* INTERNATIONAL MONETARY FUND.

STANDBY COMMITMENT a BANK's commitment to lend money up to a specified amount for a specific period, to be used only in a certain contingency.

STANDBY LETTER OF CREDIT a LETTER OF CREDIT (L/C) that a BANK issues on behalf of its customer to serve as a guarantee to the BENEFICIARY of the L/C that the bank's customer will perform a specified CONTRACT with the beneficiary. If the customer defaults, the beneficiary may draw funds against the L/C as penalties or as payments, whichever the terms of the credit provide. *see also* BOND SYSTEM; PERFORMANCE.

STANDSTILL a commitment of GATT contracting parties not to impose new trade-restrictive measures during the URUGUAY ROUND negotiations. *see also* ROLLBACK.

STATE-CONTROLLED TRADING COMPANY *see* STATE TRADING ENTERPRISES.

STATE EXPORT PROGRAM DATABASE (SEPD) a trade lead system maintained by the NATIONAL ASSOCIATION OF STATE DEVELOPMENT AGENCIES (NASDA). The SEPD includes information on state-operated trade lead systems.

STATE/INDUSTRY-ORGANIZED, GOVERNMENT-APPROVED (S/IOGA) MISSION *see* CERTIFIED TRADE MISSIONS.

STATE-SPONSORED TERRORISM
1. acts of terror initiated by the organization to promote its own interests, with operational assistance from the state.
2. acts of terror initiated by the state to promote the interests of the state or a shared interest (at times with operational assistance from the state).
3. acts of terror executed by the state or its agents in order to achieve its own interests.

The United States State Department lists seven nations as sponsors of terrorism: Cuba, Iran, Iraq, Libya, North Korea, Sudan, and Syria.

STATE TERRORISM acts of terrorism by a government against its own people, such as the acts practiced in Nazi Germany against the Jews or in Iraq practiced against the Kurds.

STATE TRADE MISSION *see* TRADE MISSION.

STATE TRADING ENTERPRISES (STEs) entities established by governments to IMPORT, EXPORT, and/or produce certain products. Examples: government-operated import/export monopolies and marketing boards or private companies that receive special or exclusive privileges from their governments to engage in trading activities.

STATE TRADING NATION *see* STATE TRADING ENTERPRISES.

STATEMENT OF ULTIMATE CONSIGNEE AND PURCHASER (BXA FORM 629P) written assurance that the foreign purchaser of goods will not resell or dispose of them in a manner contrary to the EXPORT LICENSE under which the goods were originally EXPORTED. The EXPORTER must send the statement to the foreign CONSIGNEE and purchaser for completion. The exporter then submits this form along with the export license application.

STATISM political strategy whereby the government plays an active role in running and regulating the economy of the country, with the complete acceptance of it by the population.

STATISTICAL OFFICE OF THE EUROPEAN COMMUNITY (EUROSTAT) statistical office of the EUROPEAN ECONOMIC COMMUNITY (EEC). It provides EEC statistics on economics, finance, foreign trade, services, transportation, industry, population, social conditions, energy, agricultural, forestry, and other topics within the EEC. Eurostat offices are located in Luxembourg.

STATSAUTORISERT REVISOR a state-authorized auditor in Norway. Any firm that employs more than 200 employees or is publicly owned may be audited only by a state authorized auditor. *see also* REGISTRERT REVISOR.

STD a subseries of request for comments that specify INTERNET standards. The official list of Internet standards is in STD 1.

STDS abbreviation for Standards.

STEs *see* STATE TRADING ENTERPRISES.

STEAMSHIP (STEAMER) vessels powered by steam engines. The term is often used to describe powered vessels in general, and companies that operate ocean-going CARGO vessels are often called "steamship companies," despite the fact that the use of steam power for ocean-going vessels is obsolete, the modern standard being diesel engines fueled by oil.

STEAMSHIP CONFERENCE a group of vessel operators joined together for the purpose of establishing freight rates. A shipper may receive reduced rates if the shipper enters into a contract to ship on vessels of conference members only.

STEAMSHIP INDEMNITY indemnity received by an ocean CARRIER and issued by a BANK indemnifying the carrier for any loss incurred for release of goods to the original BILL OF LADING.

STELA *see* SYSTEM FOR TRACKING EXPORT LICENSE APPLICATIONS.

STEREOTYPE a standardized and oversimplified conception, opinion, or image of a group. Example: people from a certain nation or having a particular religion act only in a certain way.

STERLING AREA *see* CURRENCY AREA.

STERLING BLOC the British Commonwealth countries that fixed the price of sterling used in foreign exchange. With a fixed price, sterling was not readily convertible to other currencies. This resulted in trade within the bloc being favored.

STEVEDORE person in charge of the loading and unloading of ships in port.

STOCKPILING the storage of something in order to have it available in the future if the need for it increases. Stockpiling occurs for speculative purposes, by governments to provide for national security and by CENTRAL BANKS managing INTERNATIONAL RESERVES. *see also* MOTHBALLING; NATIONAL DEFENSE ARGUMENT FOR PROTECTION.

STORAGE the keeping of goods in a warehouse or other repository. *see also* BONDED TERINAL; BONDED WAREHOUSES.

STORAGE DEMURRAGE charges made on property remaining on the DOCK past the prescribed "free-time period."

STORAGE IN TRANSIT stopping of FREIGHT traffic at a point between the POINT OF ORIGIN and destination to be stored and reforwarded at a later date.

STORE-DOOR DELIVERY movement of goods to the CONSIGNEE'S place of business, customarily applied to movement by truck.

STORTINGET the house of Parliament in Norway.

STOWAGE the arranging and packing of CARGO in a vessel for shipment. *see also* LOADING; STOWAGE INSTRUCTIONS; SHIP'S MANIFEST; STOWPLAN.

STOWAGE INSTRUCTIONS specific instructions given by the SHIPPER or the shipper's agent concerning the way in which CARGO is to be stowed.

STOWPLAN diagram showing how CARGO containers have been placed on a vessel; also known as stowage plan.

STR abbreviation for steamer.

STRAIGHT BILL OF LADING a nonnegotiable BILL OF LADING in which the goods are consigned directly to a named CONSIGNEE.

STRAIGHT BONDS OR NOTES securities with a fixed interest rate.

STRATEGIC CLUSTERS the grouping of internationally competitive firms near their principal customers and suppliers. *see also* GLOBALIZATION.

STRATEGIC COMMODITY COMMODITY that is capable of contributing significantly to the development, production, or use of military hardware. The fact that the commodity might also have commercial uses does not remove the *strategic* label.

STRATEGIC LEVEL OF CONTROLS COMMODITY groupings used for export control purposes. *see also* EXPORT CONTROL CLASSIFICATION NUMBER.

STREAM-ORIENTED a TRANSMISSION CONTROL PROTOCOL that allows its CLIENT to send data in a continuous stream. The Transmission Control Protocol ensures that all data will be sent to the other end of the NETWORK in the same order without duplicates.

STRIKE CLAUSE insurance clause that may be included in policies to cover against losses as a result of strikes, riots, and civil commotion. *see also* ALL RISK COVERAGE; WAR RISK INSURANCE.

STRIKES, RIOTS, AND CIVIL COMMOTIONS (S.R.&C.C.) an insurance clause excluding insurance of loss caused by labor disturbances, riots, and civil commotions or any person engaged in such actions.

STRIPPING unloading of CARGO from a container; also called DEVANNING.

STRUCTURAL ADJUSTMENT FACILITY (SAF) *see* ENHANCED STRUCTURAL ADJUSTMENT FACILITY.

STRUCTURAL CHANGE condition occurring whenever there are major changes in ownership and/or use of the economic factors of a country. *see also* NEW INTERNATIONAL ECONOMIC ORDER.

STRUCTURAL IMPEDIMENTS INITIATIVE (SII) trade initiative started in July 1989 to identify and solve structural problems that restrict bringing two-way trade between the United States and Japan into better balance. Both the U.S. and Japanese governments chose issues of concern in the other's economy as impediments to trade and current account imbalances. The areas that the U.S. government chose as focus included
- Japanese savings and investment patterns,
- land use,
- distribution,
- KEIRETSU,
- exclusionary business practices, and
- pricing.
  Areas that the Japanese government chose as focus included
- U.S. savings and investment patterns,
- corporate investment patterns and supply capacity,
- corporate behavior,
- government regulation,
- research and development,
- EXPORT promotion, and
- workforce education and training.
  In a June 1990 report, the United States and Japan agreed to schedule future meetings to review progress, discuss problems, and produce annual joint reports.

STRUCTURE OF MANAGEMENT INFORMATION (SMI) the method used to delineate the objects that can be administered with a particular NETWORK management protocol. *see also* MANAGEMENT INFORMATION BASE.

STUFFING loading of CARGO into a container.

SUBCONTRACT PRODUCTION a component of a type of COUNTERTRADE TRANSACTION whereby a U.S.-origin article usually involves a direct commercial arrangement between the U.S. manufacturer and a foreign producer but does not necessarily involve a license of technical information. *see also* COPRODUCTION; DIRECT OFFSETS; INDIRECT OFFSETS; LICENSED PRODUCTION; OFFSETS; OVERSEAS INVESTMENT; TECHNOLOGY TRANSFER.

SUBCONTRACTING the process of manufacturers purchasing components and supplies from other manufacturers.

SUBCONTRACTOR PRODUCTION a direct commercial arrangement between a U.S. manufacturer and a foreign producer. The arrangement does not necessarily involve license of technical information.

SUBGROUP ON NUCLEAR EXPORT COORDINATION (SNEC) an American interagency review panel that monitors and facilitates the interagency processing of specific matters related to activities that, in the determination of any of the members, pose potential policy concerns. The SNEC is composed of the U.S. Departments of State (as chair), Energy (as secretariat), COMMERCE, and Defense; the Arms Control and Disarmament Agency; and the Nuclear Regulatory Commission. The SNEC also includes the Central Intelligence Agency as an observer. Representatives from other agencies may be invited as participants or observers.

SUBNET a region of a NETWORK that may operate independently from the main network. A subnet does share a NETWORK ADDRESS with the main network, but it has a separate subnet number. A subnet is a lower layer of a network.

SUBSIDIARY *see* FOREIGN SUBSIDIARY.

SUBSIDIES any form of direct or indirect financial assistance to a manufacturer of production goods. However, there are various interpretations of the term:
- the GENERAL AGREEMENT ON TARIFFS AND TRADE (GATT) does not directly define subsidies.
- the United States regards a subsidy as a bounty or grant paid for the manufacture, production, or EXPORT of an article. Export subsidies are contingent on exports; domestic subsidies are conferred on production without reference to exports.
   While governments sometimes make outright payments to firms, subsidies usually take a less direct form, including R&D support, tax breaks, loans on preferential terms, and provision of raw materials at below-market prices. *see also* EXPORT SUBSIDIES.

SUBSIDIZED EXPORTS *see* EXPORT SUBSIDIES.

SUBSTANTIATE THE CLAIM a component of the MARINE INSURANCE claim process. The CONSIGNEE must prove that the claim was caused as a result of transit and during the period of insurance coverage. The following steps must be followed to substantiate a claim:
- examine external condition of packages,
- note exceptions on the delivery receipt, and
- record the numbers of packages that appear damaged.

S.U.C.L. abbreviation for set up carload.

SUCRE unit of currency, Ecuador.

SUDAM AREA the Amazon Basin States area of Brazil. It is an area in which the government provides a 10-year tax exemption on operating profit, LUCRO DA EXPLORACAO, for new industrial and agricultural investment. *see also* SUDENE REGION.

SUDANESE POUND unit of currency, Sudan (100 girsh equal 1 Sudanese pound).

SUDENE REGION region comprising the northeast states of Brazil. It is an area in which the government provides a 10-year tax exemption on special operating profit, LUCRO DA EXPLORACAO, for new industrial and agricultural investment. *see also* SUDAM AREA.

SUE AND LABOR CLAUSE common clause found in most MARINE INSURANCE policies that covers the right of an assured to incur an expense in order to minimize a loss before receiving the insurance company's authority to cover that expense. The insurance company will pay these expenses, provided the expenses incurred are reasonable relative to the amount of loss the assured is trying to avoid.

S.U.L.C.L. abbreviation for set up in less than a carload.

SUMMARY INVESTIGATION a 20-day investigation conducted by the U.S. INTERNATIONAL TRADE ADMINISTRATION (ITA) immediately following filing of an ANTIDUMPING PETITION to ascertain if the petition contains sufficient information with respect to sales at "less than FAIR VALUE" and the injury or threat of material injury to a domestic industry caused by the alleged sales at "less than fair value" to warrant the initiation of an antidumping investigation. *see also* TARIFF ACT OF 1930.

SUMMIT CONFERENCE a summit conference is an international meeting at which heads of government are the chief negotiators, major world powers are represented, and the meeting serves substantive rather than ceremonial purposes. The term first came into use in reference to the Geneva Big Four Conference of 1955.

SUNFLOWER SEED OIL ASSISTANCE PROGRAM (SOAP) one of four EXPORT subsidy programs operated by the U.S. Department of Agriculture (USDA) that helps U.S. EXPORTERS meet prevailing world prices for sunflower seed oil in targeted markets. The USDA pays cash to U.S. exporters as bonuses, making up the difference between the higher U.S. cost of acquiring sunflower seed oil and the lower world price at which it is sold.

SUNSET INDUSTRY ARGUMENT the argument that a mature industry should be provided protection, either to help it restore its competitiveness or to cushion its exit from the economy. *see also* INFANT INDUSTRY ARGUMENT.

SUPERFUND *see* U.S. SUPERFUND.

SUPPLIER CREDIT PROTOCOL an agreement between the Canadian EXPORT DEVELOPMENT CORPORATION (EDC) and a foreign BANK that guarantees notes issued by an overseas buyer to a Canadian EXPORTER. *see also* BUYER CREDIT PROTOCOL; FORFAITING.

SUPPLIER CREDITS financing available to an EXPORTER through a process involving the purchase by a BANK of promissory notes issued by a foreign buyer to an exporter. The notes are usually purchased by the bank at a discount prior to the maturity date.

SUPPLY ACCESS assurances that importing countries will, in the future, have fair and equitable access at reasonable prices to supplies of raw materials and other essential imports. Such assurances should include explicit constraints against the use of the EXPORT embargo as an instrument of foreign policy.

SUPPLY-SIDE ECONOMICS *see* MONETARISM.

SUPPORT FOR EAST EUROPEAN DEMOCRACY (SEED) U.S. act, signed into law in November 1989, containing 25 distinct actions to support structural adjustment, private-sector development, trade and investment, and educational, cultural, and scientific activities in Poland and Hungary. Funding for most of the actions was provided by the U.S. AGENCY FOR INTERNATIONAL DEVELOPMENT (AID). The SEED Act expired at the end of fiscal year 1990. Since then support has been provided under the U.S. FOREIGN ASSISTANCE ACT OF 1991.

SUPRANATIONAL INSTITUTIONS organizations or agencies that plan and implement programs that extend beyond or transcend established borders or spheres of influence held by separate nations. *see also* SUPRANATIONAL OBJECTIVES.

SUPRANATIONAL OBJECTIVES directives of international organizations or associations that extend beyond or transcend established borders or spheres of influence held by separate nations. *see also* SUPRANATIONAL INSTITUTIONS.

SURCHARGE an added tax placed on goods being IMPORTED. It can also be referred to as a surtax. *see also* DUTY.

SURETY a guarantee that includes a provision for payment of any increased DUTY that may be found after the goods have cleared CUSTOMS. *see also* SURETY BOND.

SURETY BOND a guarantee included with each ENTRY posted with CUSTOMS to cover any potential DUTIES, taxes, and penalties that may accrue. Bonds may be secured through a resident U.S. surety company but may be posted in the form of U.S. money or certain U.S. government obligations. In the event that a CUSTOMHOUSE BROKER is employed for the purpose of making the entry, the broker may permit the use of his bond to provide the required coverage.

SURETY BOND INSURANCE a program of the Canadian EXPORT DEVELOPMENT CORPORATION (EDC) that provides insurance coverage to the Canadian surety company protecting them against losses associated with failure of a Canadian EXPORTER to comply with a provision of a PERFORMANCE BOND.

SURINAME GULDEN (guilder) unit of currency, Suriname (100 cents equal 1 Suriname gulden).

SURPLUS *see* BALANCE OF PAYMENTS.

SURVEY report by an independent third party, generally a surveyor, who determines the condition of vessels, CARGO, or property (often to support an insurance claim). *see also* MARINE CARGO INSURANCE; MARINE INSURANCE; MARINE SURVEYOR.

SUSHI BOND EURODOLLAR bonds issued by Japanese corporations on the Japanese market for Japanese investors. *see also* GEISHA BOND; SAMURAI BOND.

SUSPENSION OF INVESTIGATION a decision to suspend an ANTIDUMPING INVESTIGATION by the United States if the EXPORTERS who account for substantially all the imported merchandise agree to stop EXPORTS to the United States or agree to revise their prices promptly to eliminate any DUMPING margin. An investigation may be suspended at any time before a final determination is made. No agreement to suspend an investigation may be made unless effective monitoring of the agreement is practicable and is determined to be in the public interest. *see also* TARIFF ACT OF 1930.

SUSPENSION OF LIQUIDATION U.S. action resulting from a preliminary or final affirmative ANTIDUMPING determination, whereby all entries of merchandise subject to the determination are entered or withdrawn for consumption from the warehouse, on or after the date of the publication of the notice in the U.S. FEDERAL REGISTER. U.S. Customs is directed to require a cash deposit or the posting of a bond or other security for each entry affected, which is equal to the estimated amount of the subsidy or the amount by which the FAIR VALUE exceeds the U.S. price. When an administrative review is completed, Customs is directed to collect the final subsidy rate or amount by which the foreign market value exceeds the U.S. price, and to require for each entry thereafter a cash deposit equal to the newly determined subsidy rate or margin of dumping. *see also* TARIFF ACT OF 1930.

SUSTAINABLE DEVELOPMENT environmental principle of providing for the need of the current generation without jeopardizing the environment's ability to provide for future generations.

S.V. abbreviation for sailing vessel.

SWAP ARRANGEMENTS *see* CENTRAL BANK SWAPS; SWAP NETWORK.

SWAP NETWORK a series of bilateral arrangements between the U.S. Federal Reserve and 14 foreign central banks and the BANK FOR INTERNATIONAL SETTLEMENTS (BIS) providing standby reciprocal facilities for obtaining foreign currencies. The facilities provide for the SWAP (simultaneous spot purchase and forward sale) of each other's currency by the Federal Reserve and the respective foreign central bank. Swap drawings typically have a 3-month maturity, with an understanding that they may be more or less automatically rolled over for another 3 months.

SWAPs the exchange of one type of asset or payment for another. Some of the more common forms are cross-border, currency, debt-for-charity, debt-for-COMMODITY, debt-for-debt, debt-for-development, debt-for-equity, debt-for-EXPORT, debt-for-local currency, debt-for-nature, discount, dual currency, interest rate, inward, premium, reverse, and vanilla. Minor variation in names is common.

Currency swaps convert principal from the lender's currency into the debtor's currency and receive interest payments in the debtor's currency. The swap, made to protect the principal from future changes in foreign exchange rates, involves a forward exchange contract to recover the currency involved.

Debt swaps entail replacing the foreign liabilities of a debtor country with ownership or rights of value. A debt-for-equity swap replaces foreign liabilities with a stake in the debtor country's national enterprises; a debt-for-export swap replaces foreign liabilities with an arrangement to receive proceeds from the overseas sale of the debtor country's products or commodities; a debt-for-debt swap replaces an existing foreign liability with a new commitment from the debtor country.

Interest rate swaps involve agreements on the means for exchanging future cash flows. Single-currency interest rate swaps concern exchanging future cash flow in the same currency and offer a means for modifying the impact of future changes in interest rates on a company's profitability. Cross-currency interest rate swaps concern exchanging future cash flows between one currency and another, traded either on a fixed or floating rate, and offer a means for limiting the risk of converting financial interests between currencies.

Swaps also involve arrangements whereby different sellers of similar commodities swap and deliver them to each other's customer if such action saves transportation costs. *see also* DERIVATIVES.

SWEDECORP *see* SWEDISH INTERNATIONAL ENTERPRISE DEVELOPMENT CORPORATION.

SWEDISH INTERNATIONAL DEVELOPMENT AUTHORITY

(SIDA) a Swedish agency responsible to the Ministry for Foreign Affairs that administers the greater portion of Swedish development cooperation. Swedish development assistance is directed toward five goals: economic growth, economic and social equality, economic and political independence, democratic development, and environmental quality. About 50% of Sweden's development assistance is directed toward a limited number of designated "program countries" in Africa, Asia, and Latin America and involves negotiated efforts to integrate external assistance and long-term development strategies. The remaining assistance is allocated to United Nations agencies, international development banks, and about 90 countries. The authority was established in 1965; its headquarters is in Stockholm, Sweden. *see also* SWEDISH INTERNATIONAL ENTERPRISE DEVELOPMENT CORPORATION (SWEDECORP).

SWEDISH INTERNATIONAL ENTERPRISE DEVELOPMENT CORPORATION (SWEDECORP) a Swedish government-funded corporation under Sweden's aid program. Swedecorp supports enterprise development through joint venture investments in developing countries and in Central and Eastern Europe. The corporation also encourages the transfer of industrial and commercial knowledge from Sweden to THIRD-WORLD countries and promotes exports from developing countries to Sweden. The corporation was formed in July 1991 based on a reorganization of international industry assistance programs; its headquarters is in Stockholm, Sweden. *see* SWEDISH INTERNATIONAL DEVELOPMENT AUTHORITY (SIDA).

SWEDISH KRONA (KRONOR) unit of currency, Sweden (100 öre equal 1 Swedish krona).

SWIFT *see* SOCIETY FOR WORLDWIDE INTERBANK FINANCIAL TELECOMMUNICATIONS.

SWING the leeway provided for mutual extension of credit in a BILATERAL TRADE AGREEMENT.

SWISS FRANC unit of currency, Switzerland (100 centimes equal 1 Swiss franc).

SWITCH ARRANGEMENTS a form of COUNTERTRADE in which unused purchase rights under government-to-government trade (clearing agreements) on unwanted goods received by a company in a countertrade transaction are sold at a discount to buyers for cash.

SWITCH DEALS *see* SWITCH ARRANGEMENTS.

SWITCH TRADE *see* SWITCH ARRANGEMENTS.

SWITCH TRANSACTIONS the practice of EXPORTING (or IMPORTING) goods through an intermediary country to final destinations. This is done when the destination country is short of U.S. dollars and the intermediary country has available U.S. dollars and is willing to exchange them for the destination country's currency on goods. Switch transactions must be performed within the various laws concerning EXPORT licenses.

SWITCHED MULTIMEGABIT DATA SERVICE (SMDS) an advanced high-speed public data NETWORK service anticipated to be widely implemented by the major telephone carriers for their data processing networks. *see also* METROPOLITAN AREA NETWORK (MAN).

SYRIAN POUND unit of currency, Syria (100 piastres equal 1 Syrian pound).

SYSMIN acronym for *système mineraux des supports* (French); a program initiated after the second LOME CONVENTION between the EUROPEAN COMMUNITY (EC) and 62 AFRICAN, CARIBBEAN, AND PACIFIC (ACP) COUNTRIES (mostly former colonies of the EC members). The program is similar to STABEX; however, it is designed specifically to protect the mineral producers of the ACP states. The STABEX arrangement involved making funds available from the EUROPEAN DEVELOPMENT FUND (EDF), the principal means by which the EUROPEAN ECONOMIC COMMUNITY (EEC) provides aid, concessionary finance, and technical assistance to DEVELOPING COUNTRIES. SYSMIN, unlike STABEX, does not involve making funds available from the EDF. The purpose of SYSMIN is to provide assistance to ACP states heavily dependent on mining by enabling them to overcome any unforeseen or temporary situations that would affect their EXPORT earning power.

SYSTEM FOR TRACKING EXPORT LICENSE APPLICATIONS (STELA) a U.S. BUREAU OF EXPORT ADMINISTRATION (BXA) computer-generated voice unit that interfaces with the BXA database: ECASS (Export Control Automated Support System). STELA enables a caller to check on an EXPORT license by making a telephone call.

SYSTEMS NETWORK ARCHITECTURE (SNA) a private ownership NETWORKING system implemented by IBM and IBM-compatible mainframe computers.

T

TAA *see* TRADE ADJUSTMENT ASSISTANCE.

TAACs *see* TRADE ADJUSTMENT ASSISTANCE CENTERS.

TA-BAHNG coffee shops in Korea. These coffee shops play a very important role in Korean culture and social life. Prices for a cup of coffee run about 1000 won, and seem very expensive, but customers are allowed sit and talk over their drink for as long as they wish. Koreans tend to meet friends at these shops rather than to invite them into their home.

TABLE OF DENIAL ORDERS (TDO) an alphabetical listing of all U.S. firms and individuals who may be disbarred with respect to either controlled COMMODITIES or general destination (across-the-board) EXPORTS. The TDO appears in Supplements 1 and 2 to U.S. EXPORT ADMINISTRATION REGULATION (EAR) Section 788. Supplement No. 2 includes the geographical version of the list. *see also* TEMPORARY DENIAL ORDER.

TACs *see* TECHNICAL ADVISORY COMMITTEES.

TAISO the daily physical exercise routine practice by Japanese employees at the start of the work day.

TAKA unit of currency, Bangladesh (100 poisha equal 1 taka).

TAKEOFF a point in the development of a LESS-DEVELOPED COUNTRY (LDC) where its infrastructure has adequately matured, an adequate number of associated industries have been established, and domestic capital formation exceeds consumption so that the country's own energy carries the development process forward into the future.

TALIBAN Islamic sect and government that once ruled Afghanistan. Known for savage treatment of women and destruction of ancient artifacts, they believe in Islamic purity and have zero tolerance for other religions.

TAMSA the largest manufacturer of tubing used by the petroleum industry in Mexico. Prior to the crash of the Mexican oil market in 1980, TAMSA was one of the leading EXPORTERS in Mexico. After the crash and the split-up of the former Soviet Union, the EXPORT market dried up and the profitability of TAMSA was significantly affected. Currently TAMSA is devoting a significant portion of its energies to serving the market in Mexico.

TANZANIAN SHILLING (SHILINGI) unit of currency, Tanzania (100 senti equal 1 shilingi).

TARE *see* TARE WEIGHT.

TARE WEIGHT the weight of a container and/or packing materials without the weight of the goods it contains.

TARGETED EXPORT ASSISTANCE PROGRAM (TEA) *see* MARKET PROMOTION PROGRAM.

TARIEF (Dutch) *see* TARIFF.

TARIF (Dutch/French) *see* TARIFF.

TARIFA (Spanish/Portuguese) *see* TARIFF.

TARIFF
1. a tax assessed by a government in accordance with its TARIFF SCHEDULE on goods as they enter (or leave) a country. May be imposed to protect domestic industries from imported goods and/or to generate revenue. Types include AD VALOREM, specific, variable, or some combination.
2. a document defining the applicable rules, rates, and charges for the shipment of goods forming the basis for a contract of CARGO carriage among the SHIPPER, CONSIGNEE, and CARRIER.

TARIFF ACT OF 1930 U.S. act, as amended, that provides for the imposition of ANTIDUMPING DUTIES on IMPORTED merchandise found to have been sold in the United States at "less than FAIR VALUE," if these sales have caused or are likely to cause material injury to, or materially retard the establishment of, an industry in the United States.

The following terms and phrases are commonly used in connection with proceedings under The Tariff Act of 1930, as amended: ADMINISTRATIVE REVIEW, ANTIDUMPING DUTY, ANTIDUMPING DUTY ORDER, ANTIDUMPING INVESTIGATION NOTICE, ANTIDUMPING PETITION, ASSESSMENT, "CLASS OR KIND" OF MERCHANDISE, CONSTRUCTED VALUE, COST OF PRODUCTION, CRITICAL CIRCUMSTANCES, DEPOSIT OF ESTIMATED DUTIES, DISCLOSURE MEETING, DISMISSAL OF PETITION, DUMPING MARGIN, EXPORTER'S SALES PRICE, FAIR VALUE, FINAL DETERMINATION, FOREIGN MARKET VALUE, HEARING, PERIOD OF INVESTIGATION, PRELIMINARY DETERMINATION, PROTECTIVE ORDER, PURCHASE PRICE, REVOCATION OF ANTIDUMPING DUTY ORDER, SECTION 337, SUMMARY INVESTIGATION, SUSPENSION OF INVESTIGATION, and SUSPENSION OF LIQUIDATION.

TARIFF ANOMALY the circumstance where the TARIFF on raw materials or semi-manufactured goods is higher than the tariff on the finished product.

TARIFF BARRIER any TARIFF imposed by a country on goods being imported into the country, regardless of its legitimacy, that prohibits, restricts, or impedes the free flow of goods and services. *see also* NONTARIFF BARRIERS (NTB).

TARIFF BINDING a commitment, under the GENERAL AGREEMENT ON TARIFFS AND TRADE (GATT), by a country not to raise the TARIFF on an item above a specified level. *see also* BOUND RATE.

TARIFF CLASSIFICATION *see* TARIFF HEADING.

TARIFF EQUIVALENT the level of TARIFF that would be the same, in terms of its effect, usually on the quantity of imports, as a given NON-TARIFF BARRIER (NTB). *see also* EXCHANGE CONTROLS; IMPORT LICENSE; ORDERLY MARKETING ARRANGEMENT (OMA); SURETY BONDS; VOLUNTARY EXPORT RESTRICTION (VER).

TARIFF ESCALATION a situation in which TARIFFS on manufactured goods are relatively high, tariffs on semiprocessed goods are moderate, and tariffs on raw materials are nonexistent or very low. The intention of tariff escalation is to reduce competition from exporters' manufactured goods while encouraging the importation of raw materials not otherwise available in the native country.

TARIFF FACTORIES factories established in other countries by multinationals as DIRECT INVESTMENTS, to manufacture, process, or assemble goods in other countries for the purpose of avoiding IMPORT TARIFFS.

TARIFF HEADING the descriptive name attached to a single item in a country's TARIFF SCHEDULE, indicating the product to which it applies. *see also* TARIFF CLASSIFICATION.

TARIFF ITEMS 806 AND 807 section of the TARIFF SCHEDULES OF THE UNITED STATES ANNOTATED (TSUSA), which permit GOODS that have been sent abroad for processing or assembly to be admitted subject to duty only on the VALUE ADDED abroad.

TARIFF JUMPING the establishment of a production facility within a foreign country, through FOREIGN DIRECT INVESTMENT or LICENSING, in order to avoid a TARIFF. *see also* TARIFF FACTORIES.

TARIFF QUOTA application of a higher TARIFF rate to IMPORTED goods after a specified quantity of the item has entered the country at a lower prevailing rate. *see also* TARIFF RATE QUOTAS.

TARIFF RATE QUOTAS QUOTAS that provide for the ENTRY of a specified quantity of the quota product at a reduced rate of duty during a given period. There is no limitation on the amount of the product that may be entered during the quota period, but quantities entered in excess of the quota for the period are subject to higher DUTY RATES.

TARIFF REDUNDANCY *see* REDUNDANT TARIFF.

TARIFF SCHEDULE a comprehensive list of the goods that a country may IMPORT and the IMPORT DUTIES applicable to each product.

TARIFF SCHEDULES OF THE UNITED STATES (TSUS) *see* TARIFF SCHEDULES OF THE UNITED STATES ANNOTATED.

TARIFF SCHEDULES OF THE UNITED STATES ANNOTATED (TSUSA) an official publication of the U.S. INTERNATIONAL TRADE COMMISSION (ITC) embracing the legal text of the Tariff Schedules of the United States together with statistical annotations. This publication was superseded by the HARMONIZED TARIFF SCHEDULE OF THE UNITED STATES ANNOTATED (HTSUSA) for Statistical Reporting Purposes in January 1989.

Effective 1979 to January 1989, the U.S. EXPORT statistics were initially collected and compiled in terms of the COMMODITY classifications in SCHEDULE B, Statistical Classification of Domestic and Foreign Commodities Exported from the United States. Schedule B is a U.S. Bureau of the Census publication and, during this period, was based on the framework of the TSUS. In January 1989, this publication was replaced by Schedule B based on the Harmonized System.

TARIFF SUSPENSION the revocation of a TARIFF, or other trade concession, by a country that has a basis for asserting injuries by a foreign EXPORTER and that time is necessary to protect a domestic industry from further serious injury. *see also* ESCAPE CLAUSE.

TARIFF WALL a trade barrier based on the taxation of IMPORTED goods, erected by a protectionist country to protect its industries from global competition, to generate revenues, and to create a motivation for DIRECT INVESTMENT by the foreign EXPORTER. *see also* ECONOMIC NATIONALISM; INFANT INDUSTRY ARGUMENT; PROTECTIONISM.

TARIFF WAR situation that exists when one nation increases the TARIFF on goods IMPORTED from or EXPORTED to another country, and that country then follows by raising tariffs itself in a retaliatory manner. *see also* IMPORT RESTRICTION; PROTECTIONISM; PROTECTIONIST TRADING TECHNIQUES.

TARIFFA (Italian) *see* TARIFF.

TARIFFY (TARIFFICATION) process of converting NONTARIFF BARRIERS (such as any restriction or QUOTA, charge, or policy, other than traditional CUSTOMS DUTIES, domestic support programs, discriminatory labeling and health standards, and exclusive business practices limiting the access of imported goods) to quantifiable TARIFFS. The purpose of this conversion is to reveal hidden protection being given to the domestic producers, determine the exact cost to all parties affected by the protection, and possibly reduce or eliminate some of these barriers on a multilateral basis. *see also* SUBSIDY; ACROSS THE BOARD TARIFF REDUCTIONS; ITEM-BY-ITEM TARIFF REDUCTIONS.

TATEMAE only form of individual behavior acceptable within a group according to Japanese culture. Tatemae also refers to an individual's "official" behavior when participating in group decision making. *see also* GROUPISM; HONNE; NEMAWASHI.

TAX ABATEMENT/EXEMPTION REGULATING ACT authorized exemption or abatement of CUSTOMS DUTIES for special purposes on goods being IMPORTED into Korea.

TAX CREDIT authorization for a domestic company to reduce taxes payable by the amount of taxes paid to the government in another country.

TAX EQUALIZATION situation where companies withhold an amount equal to the HOME COUNTRY tax obligation of the expatriate employee or PARENT COMPANY national, and the employer pays all HOST COUNTRY taxes. This is necessary because an expatriate can be double taxed: first in the country of assignment and second in the home country.

TAX HAVEN a country that has either no or very little taxation of FOREIGN SOURCE INCOME, making it an ideal place to shelter funds. *see also* OFFSHORE FUNDS.

TAX HAVEN COUNTRIES *see* TAX HAVEN.

TAX HAVEN SUBSIDIARY a division of a multinational company based in a TAX HAVEN COUNTRY in order to minimize the company's income tax obligations.

TAX HOLIDAY period of time during which a government does not charge an enterprise any taxes.

TAX INFORMATION EXCHANGE AGREEMENT (TIEA) a mutual and reciprocal obligation among agreeing countries to exchange information relating to the enforcement of their respective tax laws. A TIEA provides a means by which a signatory government can pursue certain tax evaders, particularly in cases involving large tax claims or drug enforcement. Countries that sign a TIEA agree to
- exchange tax information at the government level in a form admissible to U.S. or host country courts,
- collect information without regard to the taxpayer's nationality,
- establish a means for compelling the production of tax information, and
- ensure that local laws do not prohibit the sharing of tax information.

    A TIEA can support tourism in a signatory country because the agreement facilitates U.S. Internal Revenue Service approval of the destination as a necessary business expense (deductible for U.S. federal income tax purposes) for U.S. citizens and companies that seek to justify attendance at business conventions and seminars in a signatory country.

TAX ON LIQUID FUELS (IVV) a tax levied on the consumer by most municipalities in Brazil on all liquid fuel oil other than diesel. Depending on the municipality, rates vary up to a maximum of 3%.

TAX PROTECTION situation where an employee at an assignment location abroad pays all HOST and HOME COUNTRY taxes, while receiving a reimbursement from the employer for any excess taxes above an agreed figure.

TAX TREATY an agreement between nations as to what income will or will not be taxed by the country where the income is earned.

TBT *see* TECHNICAL BARRIER TO TRADE.

TCI *see* THIRD-COUNTRY INITIATIVE.

TCMD *see* THIRD-COUNTRY MEAT DIRECTIVE.

TCN *see* THIRD-COUNTRY NATIONAL.

TCP/IP PROTOCOL SUITE transmission control protocol over INTERNET PROTOCOL (IP). This is a common shorthand referring to the suite of transport and application protocols that runs over IP. *see also* FTP; ICMP; TELNET.

TDA *see* TRADE AND DEVELOPMENT AGENCY.

TDF *see* TRANSBORDER DATA FLOW.

TDO *see* TABLE OF DENIAL ORDERS.

TEA Targeted Export Assistance Program. *see also* MARKET PROMOTION PROGRAM.

TEA MONEY an allowance negotiated, under a union agreement in Australia, requiring the employer to provide the worker money to purchase refreshments for an approved rest break.

TECH STATS various charts, graphs, tables, and other graphic illustrations of trade-oriented statistics that appear daily in the JOURNAL OF COMMERCE.

TECHNICAL ADVISORY COMMITTEES (TACs) voluntary groups of industry and government representatives who provide guidance and expertise to the U.S. DEPARTMENT OF COMMERCE on EXPORT control matters, including evaluation of technical issues; worldwide availability, use, and production of technology; and licensing procedures related to specific industries. TACs have been set up for
- materials (Materials Technical Advisory Committee, MATAC),
- biotechnology (Biotechnology Technical Advisory Committee, BIOTAC),
- computer systems (CSTAC),
- electronics (ETAC) (formerly semiconductors),
- sensors (STAC) (formerly electronic instrumentation),
- materials processing equipment (MPETAC) (formerly automated manufacturing equipment),
- regulations and procedures (RPTAC),
- telecommunications equipment (TETAC), and
- transportation and related equipment (TRANSTAC).

TECHNICAL ASSISTANCE assistance provided to developing countries, including expert advice and assistance through organizations like the UNITED NATIONS INDUSTRIAL DEVELOPMENT ORGANIZATION (UNIDO) or on the basis of OFFICIAL DEVELOPMENT ASSISTANCE. *see also* TECHNOLOGY TRANSFER; UNITED NATIONS DEVELOPMENT PROGRAM (UNDP).

TECHNICAL BARRIER TO TRADE (TBT) a specification set forth by the GATT STANDARDS CODE specifying characteristics or standards a product must meet (such as levels of quality, performance, safety, or dimensions) in order to be IMPORTED.

TECHNICAL COOPERATION *see* TECHNICAL ASSISTANCE.

TECHNICAL REGULATIONS *see* STANDARDS.

TECHNOLOGY as defined by the U.S. BUREAU OF EXPORT ADMINISTRATION (BXA) regulations, technology and technical data are "information of any kind that can be used, or adapted for use, in the design, production, manufacture, utilization, or reconstruction of articles or materials." Technology can be either tangible or intangible. Models, prototypes, blueprints, or operating manuals (even if stored on recording media) are examples of tangible technology. Intangible technology consists of technical services, such as training, oral advice, information guidance, and consulting.

TECHNOLOGY TRANSFER
1. the transfer of knowledge generated and developed in one place to another, where is it is used to achieve some practical end. Technology may be transferred in many ways: by giving it away (technical journals, conferences, emigration of technical experts, technical assistance programs); by industrial espionage; or by sale (patents, blueprints, industrial processes, and the activities of multinational corporations).
2. an agreement to conduct research and development abroad, to provide technical assistance to a SUBSIDIARY or JOINT VENTURE of OVERSEAS INVESTMENT, or to perform other activities under direct commercial arrangement between a U.S. manufacturer and a foreign entity.

TELEFONOS DE MEXICO (TELMEX) the telephone company in Mexico.

TELEGRAPHIC TRANSFER CLAUSE a clause that can appear in a LETTER OF CREDIT authorizing the ISSUING BANK to release payment to the negotiating bank upon receipt of an authenticated CABLEGRAM (also known as a tested TELEX) from the latter confirming receipt of the necessary documents. *see also* RED CLAUSE.

TELENET a public packet switched NETWORK using the CCITT X.25 protocols. It should not be confused with TELNET.

TELEVISA major television company in Mexico. Televisa has a subsidiary called Video Visa that controls a significant part of the videocassette production, rental, and distribution markets in Mexico.

TELEX an international communications system that uses undersea cables and satellite channels to transmit information in written form between teleprinter terminals in two separate locations. Not used much anymore because information is now transmitted via satellite and phone lines as faxes, ELECTRONIC MAIL (E-MAIL), etc.

TELMEX *see* TELÉFONOS DE MEXICO.

TELNET the INTERNET standard protocol for remote terminal connection service.

TEMPORAL METHOD one of two methods authorized by the FINANCIAL ACCOUNTING STANDARDS BOARD (FASB) Statement No. 52 to be used in translating financial statements. The other method authorized is the CURRENT RATE METHOD. The method to be used is dependent on the FUNCTIONAL CURRENCY, that is the currency of the primary economic environment in which the company is operating. The current rate method is applicable when the functional currency is that of the local currency. The temporal method is applicable when the functional currency is the same as the parent company's reporting currency. *see also* CONSOLIDATION; TRANSLATION.

TEMPORARY ADMISSION permission to IMPORT a good DUTY FREE for use and input in producing for EXPORT. *see also* DRAWBACK; EXPORT PROCESSING ZONE (EPZ); FOREIGN TRADE ZONE; FREE-TRADE ZONE (FTZ).

TEMPORARY DENIAL ORDER an order issued by the U.S. Assistant Secretary of Commerce for EXPORT enforcement for up to 180 days to prevent imminent violation of the export regulations. Denial orders issued after administrative proceedings, which are not temporary, also appear on the TABLE OF DENIAL ORDERS.

TEMPORARY IMPORTATION UNDER BOND (TIB) a bond posted with the U.S. CUSTOMS SERVICE guaranteeing articles brought into the United States by an IMPORTER temporarily and claimed to be exempt from DUTY under Chapter 98, Subchapter XIII, Harmonized Tariff Schedule of the United States (HTS). Items will be EXPORTED within a specified time frame (usually within 1 year from the date of importation). Failure to export these items makes the importer liable for the payment of liquidated damages for breach of the bond conditions. TIB is usually twice the amount of duties and other payments the importer would otherwise be required to pay. Merchandise imported under TIB is usually for sales demonstration, testing, or repair.

TEMPORARY PRODUCER MOVEMENT a method by which suppliers of internationally traded SERVICES deliver their service to buyers through the temporary movement of persons employed by the supplier into the buyer's country. *see also* CROSS-BORDER SUPPLY; CONSUMER MOVEMENT; PRODUCER PRESENCE; and MOVEMENT OF NATURAL PERSONS.

TENDER
1. a small vessel that serves a larger vessel in a port for the purpose of supplying provisions and carrying passengers to and from ship to shore. *see also* LIGHTER; LIGHTER ABOARD SHIP (LASH).
2. an OFFER of MONEY, to supply something or to present something.
3. to satisfy a claim; an unconditional offer to perform coupled with an obvious ability to carry out the offer.
4. A car connected behind a steam railroad locomotive to carry coal and water.

TENOR (OF A DRAFT) designation of DRAFT payment terms as being due at sight, a given number of days after sight, or a given number of days after date.

TERM DOCUMENTARY CREDIT *see* DOCUMENTARY CREDIT.

TERM DOCUMENTARY DRAFT instrument used for EXPORT payment. *see also* ACCEPTANCE FINANCING; BANKER'S ACCEPTANCE; DOCUMENTARY DRAFT; D/A SIGHT DRAFT (DOCUMENTS (AGAINST) ACCEPTANCE SIGHT DRAFT); DOCUMENTS AGAINST PAYMENT (DP); TIME DRAFT.

TERM DRAFT a DRAFT that matures either a certain number of days after acceptance or a certain number of days after the date of the draft. Also referred to as a TIME DRAFT. *see also* DATE DRAFT; SIGHT DRAFT; DOCUMENTARY CREDIT; DOCUMENTARY DRAFT.

TERMINAL a facility that is used by a rail, ship, air, or truck line as a place for receiving and delivering CARGO; loading; unloading; transferring; temporarily storing; recoopering; and similarly handling freight; as well as repairing and servicing equipment. *see also* BONDED WAREHOUSE; WHARF; QUAY.

TERMINAL CHARGE a charge made for services performed at transportation terminals.

TERMINAL EMULATOR a computer program that allows a computer to emulate a terminal. The workstation thus appears as a terminal to the remote HOST.

TERMINATION OF SUSPENDED INVESTIGATION *see* REVOCATION OF ANTIDUMPING DUTY ORDER.

TERMS OF PAYMENT methods by which a firm can receive payment for products sold abroad. *see also* BILL OF EXCHANGE; CONSIGNMENT; DOCUMENTARY DRAFT; LETTER OF CREDIT; OPEN ACCOUNT.

TERMS OF PURCHASE same as TERMS OF SALE. In MARINE INSURANCE the terms of purchase or sale determine when the insurance is in effect.

TERMS OF REFERENCE (TOR) the preparation of a description of the assignment for consultants to be selected by borrowers following WORLD BANK procedures.

TERMS OF SALE delivery and payment terms in a sales agreement. The terms in international business transactions often sound similar to those used in domestic business, but they frequently have very different meanings. Confusion over terms of sale can result in a lost sale or a loss on a sale. For this reason, the EXPORTER must know the terms before preparing a quotation or a PROFORMA invoice. A complete list of important terms and their definitions is contained in *Incoterms 1990*, a booklet issued by ICC Publishing Corporation, Inc., 156 Fifth Avenue, Suite 308, New York, NY 10010. *see also* COST AND FREIGHT (C&F); COST, INSURANCE, AND FREIGHT (CIF); DELIVERED/DUTY PAID (DDP); EX-FACTORY; EX-QUAY; FREE ALONGSIDE SHIP (FAS); FREE ON BOARD (F.O.B.).

TERMS OF TRADE often used incorrectly as the same as TERMS OF SALE. Terms of trade are the values gained from a transaction pertaining to a quantity of EXPORT goods from one country, which can be exchanged for a comparable quantity of IMPORT goods from another country.

TERRORISM defined by the U.S. State Department as "premeditated, politically motivated violence perpetrated against noncombatant targets by subnational groups or clandestine agents, usually intended to influence an audience."

TERRORIST GROUP a group that practices or has significant elements which are involved in TERRORISM.

TESOBONOS U.S. dollar-denominated treasury bills issued by the Mexican government with a 28- or 182-day maturity payable in PESOS at maturity using the FLOATING EXCHANGE RATE. *see also* AJUSTABONOS; BONDES; CETES; PAGAFES.

TEU abbreviation for TWENTY-FOOT EQUIVALENT UNIT. *see also* CONTAINER.

TEXTILE SURVEILLANCE BODY (TSB) an international body that meets in Geneva at the GATT to monitor the MULTIFIBER AGREEMENT (MFA). The TSB receives reports of all textile restrictions and can make recommendations to participants. It can mediate disputes between parties to the MFA but has no binding powers. Membership is balanced between IMPORTING and EXPORTING members.

THEORY OF COUNTRY SIZE theory stating that larger countries are generally more self-sufficient than smaller countries. This is due to the fact that larger countries have more land. Hence, they have a more varied climate and greater amounts of natural resources, plus they IMPORT less of their consumption and EXPORT more of their production.

THIRD-COUNTRY DUMPING perception that the United States is threatened when it is denied FAIR MARKET access to a country when another country dumps goods in that country. Example, the Japanese are selling products in Canada at a price that the U.S. TRADE REPRESENTATIVE (USTR) and the U.S. INTERNATIONAL TRADE COMMISSION (ITC) have calculated to be unfair to comparable products being manufactured in the United States and marketed in Canada. It is then viewed by the United States that the Japanese are guilty of third-country dumping. *see also* DIVERSIONARY DUMPING; DUMPING.

THIRD-COUNTRY INITIATIVE (TCI) initiative created to help countries establish an EXPORT control system on strategic COMMODITIES. Such countries, while not members of COCOM, would establish export control systems that provide levels of protection as close as possible to those provided by COCOM. Such systems include
- IMPORT certifications and delivery verifications,
- controls over reexports of COCOM-origin, controlled goods and indigenous EXPORTS of COCOM-controlled goods,
- cooperation in prelicensing and postshipment checks,
- cooperation on enforcement matters.

The United States supports the third-country initiative through section 5(k) of the EXPORT ADMINISTRATION ACT (EAA), which allows it to provide selected non-COCOM countries with the same licensing benefits provided to COCOM members.

THIRD-COUNTRY MEAT DIRECTIVE (TCMD) a EUROPEAN COMMUNITY (EC) regulation that controls meat IMPORTS based on sanitary requirements. The TCMD requires individual inspection and certification by EC veterinarians of U.S. meat plants wishing to EXPORT to the EC.

THIRD-COUNTRY NATIONALS people working and/or living outside their own country who are not U.S. citizens, but citizens of a third country. *see also* EXPATRIATE.

THIRD OPTION a Canadian political-economic policy in 1973 that attempted to neutralize the perception that the Canadian economy is dependent on the United States by pursuing affiliate membership in the EUROPEAN ECONOMIC COMMUNITY (EEC).

THIRD WORLD a reference to LESS-DEVELOPED COUNTRIES (LDC) located in areas of Asia, Africa, and Latin America. Originally the term was used to differentiate these countries from the Western nations and those that formed the Eastern bloc.

THIRTEENTH MONTH a bonus-type compensation arrangement, common in some foreign countries, where the employee is paid one month's extra salary once a year.

301 SANCTIONS *see* SECTION 301.

THROUGH BILL OF LADING a single BILL OF LADING covering receipt of the CARGO at the point of origin for delivery to the ultimate CONSIGNEE, using two or more modes of transportation.

THROUGH RATE a shipping rate applicable to transportation from point of origin to destination where multiple CARRIERS and multiple modes of transport may be involved. *see also* PUBLISHED RATE.

TIAS *see* TREATIES AND OTHER INTERNATIONAL ACTS SERIES.

TIB *see* TEMPORARY IMPORTATION UNDER BOND.

TIC *see* TRADE INFORMATION CENTER.

TIEA *see* TAX INFORMATION EXCHANGE AGREEMENT.

TIED AID form of an OFFICIAL DEVELOPMENT ASSISTANCE loan made by a government agency of a DEVELOPED COUNTRY that requires a foreign borrower from a DEVELOPING COUNTRY to spend the proceeds in the lender's country. *see also* TIED AID CREDIT; TIED LOAN.

TIED AID CREDIT the practice of providing grants and/or concessional loans, either alone or combined with EXPORT CREDITS, linked to procurement from the donor country.

TIED LOAN a loan made by a government agency that requires a foreign borrower to spend the proceeds in the lender's country.

TIME DRAFT DRAFT that matures either a certain number of days after acceptance or a certain number of days after the date of the draft. *see also* DATE DRAFT; DOCUMENTARY DRAFT; SIGHT DRAFT.

TITLE AND RANK ranking given to various ambassadorial levels. Ambassadors-at-large have a higher rank than a regular AMBASSADOR, depending on circumstances. If at post, the regular ambassador has the higher rank; in other locations, an ambassador-at-large has the higher rank; Heads of Mission are in three classes
- Ambassadors or Nuncios (the papal state equivalent of an Ambassador) accredited to Heads of State.
- Envoys, Ministers, and Internuncios—also accredited to Heads of State. Envoys (or Special Envoys) represent a special interest (such as for Inter-American Affairs); often the special interest is of limited duration (such as Mideast peace talks).
- Chargé d'Affaires—usually accredited to the Minister of Foreign Affairs. The Chargé d'Affaires is the Chief of Mission (COM) at posts to which an Ambassador is not appointed. The Chargé d'Affaires ad Interim is the acting Ambassador (or COM) when the Ambassador (or COM) is out of the country.
    The Deputy Chief of Mission (DCM) is almost always a career officer. Principal officers are the senior officers at constituent posts (that is, at consular establishments). The Deputy Principal Officer is a position at large consulates. An attaché may be either fairly high or fairly low, in terms of rank. An attaché can be anything. A military attaché is of at least medium rank. Functional designations of civilian attachés (such as customs, legal, or science) and foreign service attachés (such as agricultural, commercial, cultural, or science) are not part of the diplomatic title. A diplomatic agent is anybody that has accredited diplomatic status. PERSONA NON GRATA is an official term, used to designate the need for recalling a diplomatic agent. An EMBASSY is the office in the capital city of a country, where the Ambassador sits. A CONSULATE is a diplomatic mission that serves as a constituent post of the embassy.

T.L.O. abbreviation for total loss only.

TM *see* TRADE MISSION.

TNC *see* TRADE NEGOTIATIONS COMMITTEE; TRANSNATIONAL CORPORATION.

TO ORDER term on a financial instrument or title document indicating that it is negotiable and transferable. *see also* ORDER; ORDER BILL OF LADING; ORDER NOTIFY.

TOFC *see* TRAILER ON FLAT CAR.

TOKEN RING a type of LOCAL AREA NETWORK with nodes wired into a ring. Each node constantly passes a control message (token) on to the next; whichever node has the token can send a message. Often, *Token Ring* is used to refer to the IEEE 802.5 token ring standard, which is the most common type of token ring.

TOKYO ROUND the seventh ROUND of MULTILATERAL TRADE NEGOTIATIONS under the GENERAL AGREEMENT ON TARIFFS AND TRADE (GATT) from 1973 to 1979 that culminated in simultaneous agreements among participating countries to reduce TARIFF and NONTARIFF TRADE BARRIERS. The Tokyo Round of negotiations sought to accord particular benefits to the EXPORTS of DEVELOPING COUNTRIES consistent with their trade, financial, and development needs. Among proposals for special or differential treatment were reduction or elimination of tariffs applied to exports of developing countries under the GENERALIZED SYSTEM OF PREFERENCES (GSP), expansion of product and country coverage of the GSP, accelerated implementation of tariff cuts for developing country exports, substantial reduction or elimination of TARIFF ESCALATION, special provisions for developing country exports in any new codes of conduct covering nontariff measures, assurance that any new multilateral safeguard system will contain special provisions for developing country exports, and the principle that developed countries will expect less than full RECIPROCITY for trade concessions they grant developing countries. *see also* AGREEMENT ON ANTIDUMPING PRACTICES; AGREEMENT ON CUSTOMS VALUATION; AGREEMENT ON GOVERNMENT PROCUREMENT; AGREEMENT ON IMPORT LICENSING; AGREEMENT OF THE INTERPRETATION AND APPLICATION OF ARTICLES VI, XVI, AND XXIII OF THE GATT; AGREEMENT ON TRADE IN CIVIL AIRCRAFT; STANDARDS CODE.

TONNE (METRIC TON) 1000 kilograms (2204 lb).

TOP *see* TRADE OPPORTUNITIES PROGRAM.

TOPOLOGY a structure that shows the computers and the NETWORK links between them. It is necessary for a network LAYER to be aware of the current network topology for the packets to reach their final destination.

TOR *see* TERMS OF REFERENCE.

TORONTO TERMS a number of DEBT RESCHEDULING alternatives resulting from the TORONTO SUMMIT in June 1988. *see also* PARIS CLUB.

TOTAL IMPORTS *see* BALANCE OF PAYMENTS.

TOXIN poisonous substance produced by living organisms capable of causing disease when introduced into the tissues of the body.

TPC *see* TRADE POLICY COMMITTEE.

TPCC *see* TRADE PROMOTION COORDINATING COMMITTEE.

TPIS *see* TRADE POLICY INFORMATION SYSTEM.

TPM *see* TRIGGER PRICE MECHANISM.

TPRG *see* TRADE POLICY REVIEW GROUP.

TPRM *see* TRADE POLICY REVIEW MECHANISM.

TPSC Trade Policy Staff Committee. *see also* TRADE POLICY COMMITTEE.

TRACER request to a transportation line to trace a SHIPMENT for the purpose of expediting its movement or establishing DELIVERY.

TRACKING a carrier's system of recording the movement intervals of shipments from origin to destination.

TRADE (INTERNATIONAL) international transactions involving the buying and selling of goods and services between individuals, businesses, and nations for a profit.

TRADE ACCEPTANCE a DRAFT similar to a BANKER'S ACCEPTANCE, with the exception that no bank is involved, and it is sometimes referred to as an accepted bill of exchange. With a trade acceptance, the draft is presented to the IMPORTER by the EXPORTER for acceptance by the importer to pay the amount stated at some fixed future date. *see also* DOCUMENTARY DRAFT.

TRADE ACT OF 1974 U.S. legislation enacted late in 1974 and signed into law in January 1975, granting the president broad authority to enter into international agreements to reduce IMPORT barriers. Major purposes were to
- stimulate U.S. economic growth and maintain and enlarge foreign markets for the products of U.S. agriculture, industry, mining, and commerce;
- strengthen economic relations with other countries through open and nondiscriminatory trading practices;
- protect American industry and workers against unfair or injurious import competition; and
- provide adjustment assistance to industries, workers, and communities injured or threatened by increased imports.

The act allowed the president to extend TARIFF preferences to certain imports from developing countries and set conditions under which MOST-FAVORED-NATION (MFN) treatment could be extended to nonmarket economy countries and provided negotiating authority for the TOKYO ROUND of MULTILATERAL TRADE negotiations.

TRADE ADJUSTMENT ASSISTANCE (TAA) U.S. act eligible for firms and workers that demonstrate that increased IMPORTS of articles similar to or directly competitive with those produced by the company contributed importantly to declines in its sales and/or production and to the separation or threat of separation of a significant portion of the company's workers. These firms receive help through TRADE ADJUSTMENT ASSISTANCE CENTERS (TAAC), primarily in implementing adjustment strategies in production, marketing, and management. TAA for firms is administered by the U.S. DEPARTMENT OF COMMERCE, whereas TAA for workers is administered by the U.S. Department of Labor. Assistance for eligible workers includes training, job search, and relocation allowances, plus reemployment services for workers adversely affected by the increased imports.

TAA was authorized by the TRADE ACT OF 1974.

TRADE ADJUSTMENT ASSISTANCE CENTERS (TAACs) nonprofit, nongovernmental organizations in the United States established to help firms qualify for and receive assistance in adjusting to IMPORT competition. TAACs are funded by the U.S. DEPARTMENT OF COMMERCE as a primary source of technical assistance to certified firms.

TRADE AGREEMENTS ACT OF 1934 legislation authorizing the United States to negotiate mutual reductions of TARIFFS with its trading partners, under the principle of MOST-FAVORED-NATION (MFN).

TRADE AGREEMENTS ACT OF 1979 U.S. legislation authorizing the implementation of trade agreements dealing with nontariff barriers negotiated during the TOKYO ROUND, including agreements that required changes in existing U.S. laws and certain concessions that had not been explicitly authorized by the TRADE ACT OF 1974. The act incorporated into U.S. law the Tokyo Round agreements on dumping, customs valuation, IMPORT licensing procedures, government procurement practices, product standards, civil aircraft, meat and dairy products, and liquor duties. The act also extended the President's authority to negotiate trade agreements with foreign countries to reduce or eliminate nontariff barriers to trade.

TRADE AND DEVELOPMENT AGENCY (TDA) U.S. agency that grants funds for feasibility studies for large projects on the condition that U.S. firms are used to do the study. Should the project sponsor (usually a foreign government) agree to this condition, all interested U.S. companies generally compete for the opportunity to do the feasibility study. The project sponsor chooses the company it wants to do the study and enters into a contractual relationship with that company, with TDA underwriting the expenses. Activities of the TDA include

- Orientation Visits (OVs). TDA occasionally sponsors visits by foreign officials interested in procuring U.S. goods and services for specific projects. Sometimes called "reverse trade missions," OVs provide an opportunity to resolve issues concerning purchases.
- Definitional Missions (DMs). DMs appraise and clarify proposed projects submitted to the TDA. After receiving a request to fund a major study for a new project, TDA usually hires a technically qualified consultant to visit the country and discuss the plan with the project sponsors. The DM is a preliminary report of the feasibility of the project, its potential financing source, possible foreign competition, and the size and scope of the feasibility study that TDA might fund. The information developed by the DM assists TDA in determining whether to provide feasibility-study funding to a project. In addition to making recommendations as to whether the project should be funded, the DM consultant works with the project sponsor to define the work program for the proposed feasibility study.

- Feasibility Studies (FSs). FSs assess the economic, financial, and technical viability of potential projects submitted to the Trade and Development Agency. The host countries must hire U.S. firms to undertake the detailed studies of the technical and economic feasibility of the proposed projects. After a foreign grantee has chosen the U.S. company that will conduct the feasibility study, the GRANTEE and the U.S. company enter into a contract for the feasibility study. The U.S. firms must prepare final reports for TDA.

Formerly known as the Trade and Development Program, TDA was renamed in October 1992 under legislation that expanded the agency's authority by authorizing it to fund architectural and engineering design, to support conceptual and detail design studies, and to provide more resources to support procurement opportunities for U.S. companies at the WORLD BANK and other multilateral lending institutions.

TRADE AND TARIFF ACT OF 1984 legislation authorizing the United States to negotiate with other countries with the aim of establishing FREE-TRADE AREAS (FTA). The act also provided the president with the authority to grant trade preferences, require quantitative limits on the importation of steel, and negotiate FREE TRADE AGREEMENTS. *see also* PREFERENCES; QUANTITATIVE RESTRICTIONS; U.S.–CANADA FREE TRADE AGREEMENT; U.S.–ISRAEL FREE TRADE AGREEMENT.

TRADE BALANCE *see* BALANCE OF PAYMENTS.

TRADE BARRIERS various methods used by governments to prevent the importation of specified trade goods. The U.S. TRADE REPRESENTATIVE (USTR) classifies trade barriers into eight general categories:

- IMPORT policies (tariffs and other import charges, quantitative restrictions, import licensing, and customs barriers);
- standards, testing, labeling, and certification;
- government procurement;
- EXPORT subsidies;
- lack of intellectual property protection;
- service barriers;
- investment barriers; and
- other barriers (e.g., barriers encompassing more than one category or barriers affecting a single sector).

TRADE BLOC (TRADING BLOC) a group of countries banding together for the purpose of increasing trade and investment within the group. These trading blocs establish special trading rules among themselves, such as the EUROPEAN COMMUNITY (EC); ASSOCIATION OF SOUTHEAST ASIAN NATIONS (ASEAN); FREE TRADE AGREEMENTS.

TRADE COMMUNITY IMPORTERS, EXPORTERS, manufacturers, brokers, FREIGHT FORWARDERS, freight CONSOLIDATORS, and CARRIERS directly involved in the sale and transport of INTERNATIONAL TRADE.

TRADE CONCORDANCE the matching of the U.S. HARMONIZED SYSTEM (HS) codes to larger statistical definitions, such as the STANDARD INDUSTRIAL CLASSIFICATION (SIC) code and the STANDARD INTERNATIONAL TRADE CLASSIFICATION (SITC) system. The U.S. Bureau of the Census, the UNITED NATIONS, as well as individual federal and private organizations, maintain trade concordances for the purpose of relating trade and production data.

TRADE CREATION the concept that TRADE generates jobs and benefits the economy of a country. Trade creation is the process that happens when domestic production is affected by the presence of low-cost IMPORTS while business transactions are generated in other areas. *see also* TRADE DEFLECTION; TRADE DIVERSION.

TRADE DEFICIT national TRADE imbalance that occurs when merchandise IMPORTS exceed EXPORTS. *see also* BALANCE OF PAYMENTS; BALANCE OF TRADE; TRADE SURPLUS.

TRADE DEFLECTION process that occurs in a COMMON MARKET having a common external TARIFF among the participating nations or a FREE-TRADE AREA where TRADE BARRIERS are removed among the members. Attempts are made to elude the higher tariffs of other member countries when IMPORTS are shipped into the countries that apply the lowest tariffs. *see also* TRADE CREATION; TRADE DIVERSION.

TRADE DISPUTE any disagreement between nations involving their international trade or TRADE POLICIES. *see also* DISPUTE SETTLEMENT SYSTEM; TRADE WAR.

TRADE DISPUTE ASSISTANCE a U.S. government program to assist in adjusting trade disputes arising between American and foreign traders at the request of either party. Such assistance is limited to informal, conciliatory efforts directed toward removing misunderstandings between the traders, enabling them to settle their differences through friendly negotiations. U.S. firms should submit trade complaints to the District Office of the U.S. DEPARTMENT OF COMMERCE nearest to their place of business. Foreign firms with trade complaints should forward them to the nearest U.S. post abroad.

TRADE DIVERSION the situation in which IMPORTS from FREE-TRADE-AGREEMENT member countries increase, displacing (or substituting) imports from nonmember countries.

TRADE EFFECT OF A TARIFF the reduction in the volume of trade in goods is affected as an outcome of a TARIFF on the goods imposed by the IMPORTING country. *see also* CONSUMPTION EFFECT OF A TARIFF; DUTY; PRODUCTION EFFECT OF A TARIFF.

TRADE EVENT a promotional activity that may include a demonstration of products or services and that brings together in one viewing area the principals in the purchase and sale of the products or services. As a generic term, trade events may include trade fairs, TRADE MISSIONS, TRADE SHOWS, catalog shows, MATCHMAKER EVENTS, and foreign buyer missions.

TRADE EXPANSION ACT OF 1962 U.S. legislation providing authority for U.S. participation in the Kennedy Round of the GATT. The legislation granted the U.S. President general authority to negotiate, on a reciprocal basis, reductions of up to 50% in U.S. TARIFFS.

    The act explicitly eliminated the PERIL POINT PROVISION that had limited U.S. negotiating positions in earlier GATT rounds, and instead called on the Tariff Commission, the U.S. INTERNATIONAL TRADE COMMISSION (ITC), and other federal agencies to provide information regarding the probable economic effects of specific tariff concessions.

TRADE FAIR a stage-setting event in which firms of several nationalities present their products or services to prospective customers in a preformatted setting (usually a booth of a certain size that is located adjacent to other potential suppliers). A distinguishing factor between trade fairs and TRADE SHOWS is size. A trade fair is generally viewed as having a larger number of participants than other trade events, or as an event bringing together related industries.

TRADE FAIR CERTIFICATION PROGRAM (TFC) a program started by the U.S. DEPARTMENT OF COMMERCE in 1983 to promote selected privately organized trade shows. The program helps private-sector organizations in promoting certified international fairs. Commerce assistance includes advertising the fair among foreign customers and helping exhibitors to make commercial contacts.

TRADE FLOW the quantity or value of a country's BILATERAL TRADE with another country.

TRADE IMBALANCE a TRADE SURPLUS or TRADE DEFICIT. *see also* BALANCE OF TRADE (BOT).

TRADE INFORMATION CENTER (TIC) a one-stop source for information on federal programs to assist U.S. exporters.

TRADE LEADS lists developed by various organizations to assist firms in identifying potential EXPORT markets to make contacts leading to representation, distributorships, joint ventures, licensing agreements, or direct sales. *see also* AGRICULTURAL TRADE LEADS; COMMERCIAL NEWS USA (CNUSA); ECONOMIC BULLETIN BOARD (EBB); NATIONAL TRADE DATA BANK (NTDB); TRADE OPPORTUNITIES PROGRAM.

TRADE LIBERALIZATION the process of eliminating TARIFF and NONTARIFF BARRIERS to trade through multilateral negotiations between trading partners and countries that are party to the GENERAL AGREEMENT ON TARIFFS AND TRADE (GATT). *see also* LIBERALIZATION; MULTILATERAL TRADE NEGOTIATIONS; PROTECTIONISM.

TRADE MEASURES *see* NONTARIFF BARRIERS.

TRADE MINISTER the government official primarily responsible for issues of international trade policy. *see also* U.S. TRADE REPRESENTATIVE (USTR).

TRADE MISSION (TM) a group of individuals who meet with prospective customers overseas. Missions visit specific individuals or places with no specific stage setting other than appointments. Appointments are made with government and/or commercial customers, or with individuals who may be a stepping stone to customers.

Trade missions are scheduled in selected countries to help participants find local agents, representatives, and distributors; to make direct sales; or to conduct market assessments. Some missions include technical seminars to support sales of sophisticated products and technology in specific markets. Missions include planning and publicity, appointments with qualified contacts and with government officials, market briefings and background information on contacts, as well as logistical support and interpreter service.

TRADE NAME name under which an organization conducts business, or by which the business or its goods and services are identified.

TRADE NEGOTIATION a negotiation between pairs of governments, or among groups of governments, exchanging commitments to alter their trade policies.

TRADE NEGOTIATIONS COMMITTEE (TNC) the steering group that manages the Uruguay ROUND negotiations. The TNC is composed of all countries participating in the negotiations (that is, it is not limited simply to members of the GATT). The TNC functions at the nonministerial level.

TRADE OPPORTUNITIES PROGRAM (TOP) a U.S. INTERNATIONAL TRADE ADMINISTRATION service that provides sales leads from overseas firms seeking to buy or represent U.S. products and services. Through overseas channels, U.S. foreign commercial officers gather leads and details, including specifications, quantities, end use, and delivery deadlines. TOPs are cabled to Washington and listed on the U.S. DEPARTMENT OF COMMERCE'S ECONOMIC BULLETIN BOARD and redistributed by the private sector.

TRADE POLICY a government plan or course of action intended to influence and determine decisions as they relate to transactions involving two or more nations.

TRADE POLICY COMMITTEE (TPC) a U.S. cabinet-level, interagency trade committee established by the U.S. TRADE EXPANSION ACT OF 1962 chaired by the U.S. TRADE REPRESENTATIVE to provide broad guidance on trade issues.

TRADE POLICY INFORMATION SYSTEM (TPIS) a primary electronic repository of detailed current and historical trade data, including
- U.S. foreign trade data—the detailed U.S. merchandise trade statistics compiled by the Bureau of the Census;
- UNITED NATIONS trade data—trade statistics of over 170 reporting countries on a comparable basis; and

- INTERNATIONAL MONETARY FUND (IMF) and WORLD BANK databases—multicountry statistics on international finance, direction of trade, and developing country debt.

  TPIS provides processing capabilities to

- obtain and disseminate trade data required for formulating and implementing U.S. trade policy and for EXPORT development,
- provide analytical support to the TRADE PROMOTION COORDINATING COMMITTEE, and
- meet the information needs of the U.S. government trade community and the private sector.

TRADE POLICY REVIEW GROUP (TPRG) a U.S. subcabinet group that meets about once a week and reviews American trade policy. The TPRG is an ad hoc creation that was not established by law. TPRG membership is fairly fluid so that agencies that want to participate in a particular discussion can sit at the table. *see also* TRADE POLICY COMMITTEE.

TRADE POLICY REVIEW MECHANISM (TPRM) a GENERAL AGREEMENT ON TARIFFS AND TRADE (GATT) mechanism to review the trade policies of any contracting party to a regularly scheduled review by the GATT Council. The policy of reviews (leading to recommendations on ways to improve a contracting party's trade policies) was created at the Uruguay ROUND midterm ministerial meeting in Montreal.

TRADE POLICY STAFF COMMITTEE (TPSC) *see* TRADE POLICY COMMITTEE.

TRADE PROMOTION encouragement of the progress, growth, or acceptance of trade. *see also* TRADE EVENT; TRADE FAIR; TRADE FAIR CERTIFICATION PROGRAM (TFC); TRADE INFORMATION CENTER (TIC); TRADE MISSION; TRADE OPPORTUNITIES PROGRAM (TOP).

TRADE PROMOTION COORDINATING COMMITTEE (TPCC) mechanism for all U.S. federal agencies to coordinate their trade promotion activities, eliminate duplication, and provide a more focused U.S. government approach to trade promotion. Committee members include 19 U.S. federal agencies. The TPCC formed working groups to aid in coordinating trade promotion programs. Thirteen working groups were operating at the end of 1992:

- Trade Finance;
- Food Production, Machinery, and Processing;
- Energy, Environment, and Infrastructure;
- Technology and Aerospace;
- Services;
- Enterprise for the Americas;
- Eastern Europe;
- Asia and Pacific;
- State and Local;
- Minority Business;

- U.S. Asia Environmental Partnership;
- Russia, Ukraine, and the Newly Independent States; and
- Small Business.

The TPCC was originally established by executive order of the President of the United States in May 1990. The EXPORT ENHANCEMENT ACT OF (October) 1992 codified the TPCC. *see also* ADVOCACY CENTER.

TRADE PROMOTION EVENTS (TPE) a computerized data base maintained by the INTERNATIONAL TRADE CENTER network throughout Canada, which provides detailed information on domestic and foreign TRADE MISSIONS and TRADE FAIRS. *see also* BUREAU OF SOURCING SUPPLIERS (BOSS); EXPORT TRADE INFORMATION; INTERNATIONAL TRADE DATA BANK (ITDB); WORLD INFORMATION NETWORK (WIN).

TRADE-RELATED ASPECTS OF INTELLECTUAL PROPERTY RIGHTS (TRIP) U.S. intellectual property rights objectives in the Uruguay ROUND. These objectives include achieving a comprehensive GATT agreement that would include
- substantive standards of protection for all areas of intellectual property (patents, trademarks, copyrights, etc.),
- effective enforcement measures (both at the border and internally), and
- effective dispute settlement provisions.

TRADE-RELATED INVESTMENT MEASURES (TRIMs) the use of specified amounts of local inputs rather than imported goods and requirements to EXPORT a certain amount of production. The developed countries (with the exception of Australia) favor prohibiting certain TRIMs. Virtually all developing countries oppose prohibiting any TRIMs.

TRADE ROUNDS a set of MULILATERAL NEGOTIATIONS, held under the auspices of the GENERAL AGREEMENT ON TARIFFS AND TRADE (GATT), in which countries exchanged commitments to reduce TARIFFS and agreed to extensions of the GATT rules. *see also* KENNEDY ROUND and TOKYO ROUND.

TRADE SANCTIONS *see* EMBARGO.

TRADE SHOW a stage-setting event in which firms present their products or services to prospective customers in a preformatted setting (usually a booth of a certain size that is located adjacent to other potential suppliers). The firms are generally in the same industry but not necessarily of the same nationality. A distinguishing factor between TRADE FAIRS and trade shows is size. A trade show is generally viewed as a smaller assembly of participants.

TRADE SURPLUS national trade imbalance where merchandise EXPORTS exceed merchandise IMPORTS. *see also* BALANCE OF PAYMENTS; BALANCE OF TRADE; TRADE DEFICIT.

TRADE TERMS a listing of terms used to establish a basis for carrying out the responsibilities and obligations for buyers and sellers in international transactions. *see also* TERMS OF SALE.

TRADE VISITOR an individual formally invited into a country as a guest with the anticipation that the individual will either invest, purchase, or influence the purchase or investment in goods from the HOST COUNTRY.

TRADE WAR a conflict, usually between two countries, consisting of measures directed at reducing the COMPARATIVE ADVANTAGE one of the countries may have. Some of the tactics that can be used include PREDATORY DUMPING, COUNTERVAILING DUTIES, RETALIATION, REPRISALS, PREDATORY PRICING, and EMBARGO.

TRADE WITH FOREIGN COUNTRIES merchandise trade between a home country and foreign countries. All such trade transactions are normally maintained in official EXPORT and IMPORT statistics.

TRADING AT A DISCOUNT when the FORWARD RATE being quoted for a currency is lower than the quoted SPOT RATE. *see also* TRADING AT A PREMIUM.

TRADING AT A PREMIUM when the FORWARD RATE being quoted for a currency is higher than the quoted SPOT RATE. *see also* TRADING AT A DISCOUNT.

TRADING BLOC a group of countries that are closely associated in international trade. *see also* PREFERENTIAL TRADE AREA (PTA).

TRADING COMPANY *see* TRADING HOUSE.

TRADING HOUSE a business primarily involved in the IMPORT and EXPORT of specific categories of goods from specific countries or regions, for their own account. *see also* CANADIAN COUNCIL OF TRADING HOUSES; DIRECT EXPORT; EXPORT MANAGEMENT COMPANY (EMC); EXPORT TRADING COMPANY.

TRADITIONAL ECONOMY *see* GEMEINSCHAFT.

TRAILER ON FLAT CAR (TOFC) *see* CONTAINER.

TRAMP (TRAMP SHIP, TRAMP STEAMER) ship that carries CARGO and is not operating on regular routes or schedules. *see also* CONFERENCE; NONCONFERENCE LINE; STEAMSHIP CONFERENCE.

TRANCHES *see* CREDIT TRANCHES.

TRANSACTION information collected from other government agencies or calculated from data provided to INTERNATIONAL TRADE DEVELOPMENT CENTERS (ITDC).

TRANSACTION EXPOSURE a FOREIGN EXCHANGE risk that occurs because the firm may have its payables and receivables denominated in a foreign currency. Example: suppose that a U.S. EXPORTER delivered goods to a Japanese IMPORTER for U.S. $10,000 when the rate of exchange of U.S.$1 equals 100 ¥ (Japanese YEN). If the U.S. exporter receives payments in U.S. dollars, then there would be no impact should the exchange rate fluctuate. However, if the payment were to be made in 1,000,000 ¥, the U.S. exporter could be exposed to an exchange rate loss. *see also* HEDGE.

TRANSACTION RISK *see* TRANSACTION EXPOSURE.

TRANSACTION STATEMENT a document that delineates the terms and conditions agreed upon by the IMPORTER and EXPORTER.

TRANSACTION VALUE the price the buyer (IMPORTER) actually pays the seller (EXPORTER). The transaction value is used by the U.S. CUSTOMS SERVICE to determine the DUTIABLE value of merchandise. *see also* COMPUTED VALUE; DEDUCTIVE VALUE.

TRANSACTIONABILITY the ease with which the currency of a country is accepted internationally. A currency with a high degree of transactionability is referred to as a CONVERTIBLE CURRENCY. A currency with a low degree of transactionability is a NONCONVERTIBLE CURRENCY.

TRANSAX DATA a business service offered by the publishers of the JOURNAL OF COMMERCE that provides the following systems and services for the maritime industry:
- electronic TARIFF databases of ocean freight tariffs on file at the U.S. Federal Maritime Commission;
- tariff publishing, pricing, and watching services;
- electronic tariff filing; and
- regulatory counseling.

TRANSBORDER DATA FLOW (TDF) data that are stored and transmitted via computer and telecommunications networks across national borders.

TRANSCEIVER the physical transmitter–receiver device that interfaces a HOST to a LOCAL AREA NETWORK (LAN). Transceivers transmit electronic signals to the LAN cable and sense data collisions.

TRANSFER OF TECHNOLOGY movement of modern or scientific methods of production or distribution from one enterprise to another. *see also* DIRECT INVESTMENT; JOINT VENTURE; OVERSEAS INVESTMENT; TECHNOLOGY TRANSFER.

TRANSFER PAYMENTS transactions that occur between a parent firm and its subsidiaries consisting of payments of ROYALTIES payable to the parent for use of technologies, supplies, operating equipment, etc. *see also* LICENSING.

TRANSFER PRICE (TRANSFER PRICING) the price charged on goods sold between companies that are related through stock ownership, such as parent company to subsidiary or between two subsidiaries owned by the same parent company.

TRANSFERABLE CURRENCY *see* CONVERTIBLE CURRENCY.

TRANSFERABLE ROUBLE *see* INTERNATIONAL BANK FOR ECONOMIC COOPERATION; INTERNATIONAL INVESTMENT BANK.

TRANSIT TARIFF a tax placed on goods simply passing through a country.

TRANSIT ZONE PORT OF ENTRY in a coastal country that is established as a storage and distribution center for the convenience of a neighboring country lacking adequate facilities or access to the sea.

TRANSITIONAL MEASURES short-term actions instituted by governments for a limited duration pending full implementation of a trade agreement. *see also* INJURY; SAFEGUARDS.

TRANSLATION
1. the process of restating financial statements from one currency to another.
2. the process of converting a piece of intellectual property, such as promotional material or company/instruction manuals, from one language to another. *see also* BACK TRANSLATION; CONSOLIDATION.

TRANSLATION EXPOSURE a FOREIGN EXCHANGE risk that results because the subsidiary company must restate its foreign currency financial statements into the reporting currency of the parent company. Example: assume that a subsidiary is operating in a foreign country and that country's currency is weakened by 10% inflation. Then, the other exposed assets held by the company in the foreign country (i.e., foreign bank account) will also be worth 10% less after making allowances for depreciation. *see also* CURRENT RATE METHOD; TEMPORAL METHOD.

TRANSLATION RISK *see* TRANSLATION EXPOSURE.

TRANSMITTAL LETTER a letter from the SHIPPER or the agent transmitting documents relative to a shipment. Usually a list of the documents enclosed and details covering the transportation of the shipment, such as the name of the CARRIER, and date of departure, will be included. *see also* BILL OF LADING (B/L); CERTIFICATE OF INSPECTION; INVOICE; PACKING LIST.

TRANSNATIONAL ENTERPRISES *see* MULTINATIONAL CORPORATIONS.

TRANSPARENT *see* TRANSPARENCY.

TRANSPONDER a device on an airliner that sends out signals allowing air-traffic controllers to track an airplane.

TRANSPORT DOCUMENTS all types of documents evidencing acceptance, receipt, and SHIPMENT of goods. *see also* BILL OF LADING; AIR WAYBILL; CARRIER'S CERTIFICATE.

TRANSPORTATION the physical movement of goods between buyer and seller. *see also* PHYSICAL DISTRIBUTION.

TRANSPORTATION AND EXPORTATION ENTRY a form declaring goods that are entering the United States (for example from Canada) for the purpose of exportation through a U.S. port. Carriers and any warehouse must be bonded.

TRANSPORTATION COSTS all costs associated with the movement of goods from the buyer to the seller. These costs could include charges for freight, loading, unloading, and insurance. The actual transportation costs for the buyer are dependent on the TERMS OF SALE.

TRANSPORTATION TELEPHONE TICKLER a separate service/publication of the JOURNAL OF COMMERCE. It is a complete directory of freight services and facilities in North America. Volume Number I covers the Port of New York, and it lists the companies in alphabetical order, giving addresses, telephone numbers, and names and titles of key personnel. Volumes II, III, and IV cover North American ports other than New York. In addition there are several regional editions including Houston, Tampa, Pacific Coast, Gulf Ports, Boston, Miami, Great Lakes, Baltimore/Washington, Philadelphia, and Ports of Virginia and South Atlantic.

TRANSSHIP
1. to transfer goods from one transportation line to another, from one ship to another, or from one airline to another in order to complete a delivery.
2. to ship to one country and then to RE-EXPORT to another.

TRANSSHIPMENT the process of unloading CARGO at an intermediary port and then reloading it for shipment to its final destination. When the cargo is reloaded, it is possible it can be placed on another mode (i.e., from ocean vessel to truck). *see also* PASS-THROUGH.

TRANSIT ZONES a form of FREE-TRADE ZONE, which are PORTS OF ENTRY in coastal countries that are established as storage and distribution centers for the convenience of a neighboring country lacking adequate port facilities or access to the sea. A transit zone is administered so that goods in transit to and from the neighboring country are not subject to the customs duties, IMPORT controls, or many of the entry and exit formalities of the HOST COUNTRY. Transit zones are more limited facilities then a FOREIGN TRADE ZONE or a FREE PORT.

TRANSMITTAL LETTER a list of the particulars of the shipment and a record of the documents being transmitted together with instructions for disposition of documents. Any special instructions are also included.

TRANSNATIONAL CORPORATION (TNC) a company that operates in a HOME COUNTRY and has an affiliate overseas. Transnational corporation and MULTINATIONAL CORPORATION are now used synonymously. Through the 1970s and 1980s the UNITED NATIONS attempted to assess the impact of TNCs on development and international relations in the world economy. These efforts resulted in considerable complexity in attempting to define a TNC, including associations with impact on developing countries, size, ownership, and other characteristics. Agreement on a specialized definition was never achieved.

TRANSPARENCY the extent to which laws, regulations, agreements, and practices affecting international trade are open, clear, measurable, and verifiable.

TRAVEL ADVISORY PROGRAM the U.S. Department of State manages a travel advisory program that publicizes

- travel warnings that are issued when the State Department decides to recommend that Americans avoid travel to a certain country and
- consular information sheets, issued for every country, that advise travelers of health concerns, immigration and currency regulations, crime and security conditions, areas of unrest or instability, and the location of U.S. embassies or consulates.

   Both travel warnings and consular information sheets are available through the Citizens' Emergency Center's automated answering system.

TRAVEL MISSION a marketing activity carried out in foreign markets. The activity usually involves trade information, presentations, and media activities.

TRAVEL WARNING *see* TRAVEL ADVISORY PROGRAM.

TRAVELER a person who stays for a period of less than 1 year in a country of which he/she is not a resident. Military and other government personnel and their dependents stationed outside their country of residence are not considered travelers, regardless of the length of their stay abroad. They are considered to have remained within the economy of their home country. The definition of travelers also excludes owners or employees of business enterprises who temporarily work abroad in order to further the enterprise's business but intend to return to their country of residence within a reasonable period of time.

TRAVELER'S CHECKS a check designed for business travelers and tourists, issued by a financial institution of sufficient importance that can be readily accepted or cashed by businesses and banks. For safety, many are designed to be countersigned twice by the traveler in order to be valid, once at issuance and once upon being cashed.

TREATIES AND OTHER INTERNATIONAL ACTS SERIES (TIAS) a series of individual pamphlets published by the U.S. Department of State documenting a treaty or an executive agreement when it is first published by the United States. It is assigned a TIAS number and published in slip form in the Treaties and other International Acts Series.

TREATIES IN FORCE a list of all treaties and executive agreements published annually by the U.S. Department of State, both bilateral and multilateral, that are considered to be in force for the United States as of January 1 of the respective year.

TREATY *see* INTERNATIONAL AGREEMENTS.

TREATY OF EUROPEAN UNION *see* MAASTRICHT TREATY.

TREATY OF ROME a European customs union established in March 1957 that requires the elimination of all quantitative restrictions and other measures having an equivalent effect on trade among the European signatory member states. It was intended to create a single market with free movement of goods, persons, services, and capital and envisioned a single internal European market. It became the founding charter for the EUROPEAN ECONOMIC COMMUNITY (EEC), which came into being on January 1, 1958. The treaty had no provisions for monetary arrangements. Accomplishments following the treaty included completion of the CUSTOMS UNION and establishment of the COMMON AGRICULTURAL POLICY (CAP).

TREVI GROUP an international security organization that includes the 12 EUROPEAN ECONOMIC COMMUNITY (EEC) countries. The organization was created to provide a method by which information could be exchanged relating to the control of political terrorism. TREVI is an abbreviation coming from the French words for international terrorism, radicalism, extremism, and violence (Terrorisme, Radicalisme, Extrémisme, Violence Internationale). *see also* INTERNATIONAL MARITIME BUREAU.

TRIAD STRATEGY a plan of action proposing that a Multinational Enterprise should have a presence in Europe, the United States, and Japan.

TRIANGULAR ARBITRAGE the operation of buying and selling FOREIGN EXCHANGE at a profit as a result of price discrepancies where three distinct and separate currencies are involved.

TRIANGULAR TRADE trade among 3 countries in which an attempt is made to create a favorable balance for each. *see also* CONVENTION; INTERNATIONAL TRADE AGREEMENTS; TRILATERAL TRADE; TRILATERAL TRADE AGREEMENTS.

TRIENOS salary increases mandated at 3-year intervals by Spanish law.

TRIGGER PRICE the price of an IMPORTED COMMODITY that is below that charged in the producing country. When the imported good's prices reach or fall under the trigger price, it results in trade restrictions against that particular imported commodity. *see also* TRIGGER PRICE MECHANISM.

TRIGGER PRICE MECHANISM (TPM) an ANTIDUMPING mechanism designed to protect U.S. industries from underpriced IMPORTS. First used in 1978 to protect the steel industry, the TPM is the price of the lowest-cost foreign producer. Imports priced below the trigger price are assessed a DUTY equal to the difference between their price and the trigger price.

TRILATERAL COMMISSION a private organization with offices in New York, London, and Tokyo. The group has been established to represent common interests and foster the cultivation of capitalism in the three major trading areas of North America, Western Europe, and Asia. The organization has achieved a certain amount of notoriety because of the politically well-connected individuals who have been associated with it.

TRILATERAL TRADE commercial transactions among three nations.

TRILATERAL TRADE AGREEMENT a legally binding arrangement among three countries in written form and governed by international law. *see also* CONVENTION; INTERNATIONAL AGREEMENTS.

TRIMs *see* TRADE-RELATED INVESTMENT MEASURES.

TRINIDAD AND TOBAGO DOLLAR unit of currency, Trinidad and Tobago (100 cents equal 1 Trinidad and Tobago dollar).

TRIPARTITE AGREEMENT an agreement relating to or executed by three nations. Example: the NORTH AMERICAN FREE TRADE AGREEMENT (NAFTA) is an agreement executed by three nations—Canada, Mexico, and the United States.

TRIP act of moving cargo from one point to another using CONVEYANCE.

TRIP INITIATION order for transportation services.

TRIPs *see* TRADE-RELATED ASPECTS OF INTELLECTUAL PROPERTY RIGHTS.

TRIP'S AGREEMENT the agreement negotiated in the Uruguary Round that incorporated issues of intellectual property into the WORLD TRADE ORGANIZATION (WTO).

TRI-TEMP CONTAINER that can maintain 3 exact temperature zones in different compartments simultaneously.

TROPICAL PRODUCTS agricultural goods of EXPORT interest to developing countries in the tropical zones of Africa, Latin America, and East Asia (coffee, tea, spices, bananas, and tropical hardwoods).

TRUNK ROOM (TRUNK ROOMING) small lot warehouses located near Tokyo used for storage of nonconsumer goods.

TRUST RECEIPT release of merchandise by a bank to a buyer in which the bank retains title to the merchandise. The buyer, who obtains the goods for manufacturing or sales purposes, is obligated to maintain the goods (or the proceeds from their sale) distinct from the remainder of his/her assets and to hold them ready for repossession by the bank.

TSB *see* TEXTILE SURVEILLANCE BODY.

TSUS *see* TARIFF SCHEDULES OF THE UNITED STATES.

TSUSA *see* TARIFF SCHEDULES OF THE UNITED STATES ANNOTATED.

TT DOLLAR *see* TRINIDAD AND TOBAGO DOLLAR.

TULAREMIA an infectious disease caused by a hardy bacterium, *Francisella tularensis,* found in animals, especially rabbits, hares, and rodents.

TUNA-DOLPHIN CASE cases filed under GENERAL AGREEMENT ON TARIFFS AND TRADE (GATT) in 1991 and 1994 that led to PANEL decisions against the United States resulting from the U.S. ban on IMPORTS of tuna, under the MARINE MAMMAL PROTECTION ACT, from countries that did not effectively prohibit tuna fishers from killing dolphins by catching them together with schools of tuna in large nets.

TUNISIAN DINAR unit of currency, Tunisia (1,000 millim equal 1 Tunisian dinar).

TURKISH LIRA unit of currency, Turkey.

TURNKEY a method of construction whereby the contractor assumes total responsibility from design through completion of the project.

TURNKEY PROJECT *see* TURNKEY.

TWENTY-FOOT EQUIVALENT UNIT (TEU) a measure of a ship's CARGO-carrying capacity. One TEU measures 20 feet by 8 feet by 8 feet—the dimensions of a standard 20-foot container. An FEU (40-foot equivalent unit) equals 2 TEUs.

TWO-TIER MARKET EXCHANGE RATE methodology that normally insulates a country from the BALANCE OF PAYMENTS effects of capital flows while it maintains a stable exchange rate for CURRENT ACCOUNT transactions. *see also* DUAL EXCHANGE RATES; EXCHANGE CONTROLS; IMPORT DEPOSIT REQUIREMENTS; LICENSING.

TYING ARRANGEMENT condition that a seller imposes on a buyer, requiring that if the buyer desires to purchase one product (which is the tying product), the buyer must also agree to purchase another product (which becomes the tied product), which the buyer may or may not want. The laws of some countries prohibit certain tying arrangements.

U

U.A.E. DIRHAM unit of currency, United Arab Emirates (100 fils equal 1 U.A.E. dirham).

UBO *see* ULTIMATE BENEFICIAL OWNER.

UGANDA SHILLING unit of currency, Uganda.

ULTIMATE BENEFICIAL OWNER (UBO) that person, proceeding up a U.S. affiliate's ownership chain beginning with and including the foreign parent, that is not owned more than 50% by another person. The UBO consists of only the ultimate owner; other affiliated persons are excluded. If the foreign parent is not owned more than 50% by another person, the foreign parent and the UBO are the same. A UBO, unlike a foreign parent, may be a U.S. person.

ULTIMATE CONSIGNEE the person located abroad who is the true party in interest, receiving the EXPORT for the designated end use. *see also* CONSIGNEE; CONSIGNOR.

ULTIMATE CONSIGNOR person who is the true party in interest, receiving goods for the designated end use. *see also* CONSIGNEE; CONSIGNOR.

ULTIMO DAY last business day or last stock trading day of a month.

UMA Union du Maghreb Arabe. *see also* ARAB MAGHREB UNION.

UMBRELLA POLICY a special policy designed by the EXPORT-IMPORT BANK OF THE UNITED STATES (EXIMBANK) and the FOREIGN CREDIT INSURANCE ASSOCIATION (FCIA) to assist small businesses. The Umbrella Policy allows commercial lenders, state agencies, finance companies, EXPORT trading and management companies, insurance brokers, and similar agencies to act as intermediaries (administrators) between EXIMBANK and the clients by assisting their clients in obtaining EXPORT credit insurance. The coverage includes 100% political risk protection and 95% commercial risk protection.

UMOA Union Monétaire Ouest-Africaine. *see also* WEST AFRICAN MONETARY UNION.

UMR *see* USUAL MARKETING REQUIREMENTS.

UN *see* UNITED NATIONS.

UNCED *see* UNITED NATIONS CONFERENCE ON ENVIRONMENT AND DEVELOPMENT.

UNCHS *see* UNITED NATIONS COMMISSION ON HUMAN SETTLEMENTS.

UNCITRAL *see* UNITED NATIONS COMMISSION ON INTERNATIONAL TRADE LAW.

UNCJIN *see* UNITED NATIONS CRIMINAL JUSTICE INFORMATION NETWORK.

UNCONFIRMED documentary LETTER OF CREDIT where the advising BANK makes no commitment to pay, accept, or negotiate. *see also* REVOCABLE LETTER OF CREDIT.

UNCONSCIONABLE unreasonable or outrageous. Courts in many countries may refuse to enforce CONTRACTS that they deem to be unconscionable.

UNCOVERED INTEREST ARBITRAGE the transfer from a domestic base to a foreign account of short-term liquid funds on the anticipation of higher earnings. The risk that a downward fluctuation in the EXCHANGE RATE will occur is not covered. *see also* COVERED INTEREST ARBITRAGE.

UNCTAD *see* UNITED NATIONS CONFERENCE ON TRADE AND DEVELOPMENT.

UNDERDEVELOPED COUNTRY nation in which per capita income is proportionately low when contrasted with the per capita real income of nations where industry flourishes. *see also* LESS-DEVELOPED COUNTRY (LDC); LESSER-DEVELOPED COUNTRIES (LLDC); THIRD WORLD; FOURTH WORLD.

UNDERINVOICING the provision of an invoice that states price as less than is actually being paid, possibly to reduce the amount that will be collected by an AD VALOREM TARIFF.

UNDERSELLING the offering of goods being IMPORTED into the United States at prices below those of comparably produced domestic goods. *see also* DUMPING.

UNDERVALUED CURRENCY currency whose value is below market value due to government intervention in an attempt to make its country's EXPORTS less expensive and more competitive. A currency that has been oversold.

UNDP *see* UNITED NATIONS DEVELOPMENT PROGRAM.

UN/ECE *see* UNITED NATIONS ECONOMIC COMMISSION FOR EUROPE.

UNESCO *see* UNITED NATIONS EDUCATIONAL, SCIENTIFIC, AND CULTURAL ORGANIZATION.

UNFAIR TRADE the buying and selling of goods that have been unfairly SUBSIDIZED or DUMPED. Transactions including any of these goods are referred to as unfair trading practices. *see also* U.S. INTERNATIONAL TRADE COMMISSION.

UNFAIR TRADE PRACTICE any act, policy, or practice of a foreign government that
• violates, is inconsistent with, or otherwise denies benefits to the United States under any trade agreement to which the United States is a party;

- is unjustifiable, unreasonable, or discriminatory and burdens or restricts U.S. commerce; or
- is otherwise inconsistent with a favorable SECTION 301 determination by the U.S. TRADE REPRESENTATIVE (USTR).

UNFAIR TRADER an individual or firm engaging in UNFAIR TRADE PRACTICES. *see also* UNFAIR TRADE.

UNFAVORABLE BALANCE OF TRADE the condition when the amount of goods being IMPORTED into a country is greater than that EXPORTED from the country. The balance of trade is favorable when exports are greater than imports. *see also* BALANCE OF PAYMENTS; BALANCE OF TRADE.

UNFPA *see* UNITED NATIONS POPULATION FUND.

UNICEF *see* UNITED NATIONS CHILDREN'S FUND.

UNIDO *see* UNITED NATIONS INDUSTRIAL DEVELOPMENT ORGANIZATION.

UNIFORM COMMERCIAL CODE a U.S. law governing commercial transactions (sales of GOODS, commercial paper, bank deposits and collections, LETTERS OF CREDIT (L/C), bulk transfers, warehouse receipts, BILLS OF LADING (B/L), investment securities, and secured transactions) adopted by all states in the United States except Louisiana.

UNIFORM ORDER BILL OF LADING a negotiable BILL OF LADING made to the order of the shipper. *see also* THROUGH BILL OF LADING; UNIFORM STRAIGHT BILL OF LADING.

UNIFORM STRAIGHT BILL OF LADING a nonnegotiable BILL OF LADING in which the goods are consigned directly to a named CONSIGNEE. *see also* THROUGH BILL OF LADING; UNIFORM ORDER BILL OF LADING.

UNILATERAL TRANSFER a transfer of currency from one country to another for the purchase of goods. However, the country transferring the currency does not sell goods to the transferee in return. Example: one country sends foreign aid to another country that has been devastated by a natural disaster, such as a flood.

UNION DE PAISES EXPORTADORES DE BANANO *see* UNION OF BANANA EXPORTING COUNTRIES.

UNION DOUANIERE ET ECONOMIQUE DE L'AFRIQUE CENTRALE *see* CENTRAL AFRICAN CUSTOMS AND ECONOMIC UNION.

UNION DU MAGHREB ARABE (UMA) *see* ARAB MAGHREB UNION.

UNION INTERNATIONALE DES TELECOMMUNICATIONS *see* INTERNATIONAL TELECOMMUNICATION UNION.

UNION MONETAIRE OUEST-AFRICAINE (UMOE) *see* WEST AFRICAN MONETARY UNION.

UNION OF BANANA EXPORTING COUNTRIES (Spanish: Unión de Países Exportadores de Banano, UPEB) a union of Latin American nations that promotes the banana industry among members. The union was established in 1974, and its headquarters is in Panama. Members include Colombia, Costa Rica, Dominican Republic, Guatemala, Honduras, Nicaragua, Panama, and Venezuela.

UNITAR *see* UNITED NATIONS INSTITUTE FOR TRAINING AND RESEARCH.

UNITARY TAX a method of taxation based on a percentage of a company's worldwide operations instead of basing it on the profits in the area where the taxing authorities are located.

UNITED ARAB REPUBLIC political union (1958–1961) of Egypt and Syria, in an attempt to create an integrated Arab economy. The union was not viewed favorably by other Arab nations. In 1961 Syria withdrew from the union. The union no longer exists. *see also* ARAB UNION.

UNITED NATIONS (UN) an international organization established in 1945 to
- maintain international peace and security;
- develop friendly relations among nations;
- achieve international cooperation in solving economic, social, cultural, and humanitarian problems and in promoting respect for human rights and fundamental freedoms; and
- be a center for harmonizing the actions of nations in attaining these common ends.

United Nations membership includes approximately 170 nations. The UN's headquarters is located in New York City. The United Nations structure includes six principal organs, specialized agencies, major programs, autonomous agencies, committees, subsidiary organs, and approximately a dozen peace-keeping forces. Some of the specialized agencies and other bodies were established before the United Nations was created.

The six principal UN organs are
- The GENERAL ASSEMBLY (composed of all UN member nations),
- SECURITY COUNCIL,
- ECONOMIC AND SOCIAL COUNCIL (ECOSOC),
- Trusteeship Council,
- INTERNATIONAL COURT OF JUSTICE (seated in The Hague, the Netherlands), and
- the Secretariat (which provides studies, information, and facilities for UN bodies).

UNITED NATIONS CHILDREN'S FUND (UNICEF) fund established by the UNITED NATIONS GENERAL ASSEMBLY in 1946, as the United Nations International Children's Emergency Fund. It was an acting body providing emergency assistance to children in war-ravaged countries. In 1953 the fund was given permanent status while changing the name to the United Nations Children's Fund, although it continued to hold the UNICEF symbol. In 1982 the General Assembly increased the membership of UNICEF's Executive Board to 41 states.

UNITED NATIONS COMMISSION ON HUMAN SETTLEMENTS (HABITAT) (UNCHS) a UNITED NATIONS commission established in 1977 that replaced the Committee on Housing, Building, and Planning. Its primary purpose is to help countries and regions manage human settlement problems while promoting greater international cooperation. The United Nations Center for Human Settlements (Habitat) serves as the secretariat to the Commission. The commission meets biennially. It has 58 member nations.

UNITED NATIONS COMMISSION ON INTERNATIONAL TRADE LAW (UNCITRAL) UN commission established in 1966 to aid in harmonizing and unifying international trade law. The commission has focused on four principal international areas:

- sales of goods,
- payments,
- commercial arbitration, and
- legislation pertaining to shipping.

The commission issues publications and sponsors training in international trade law.

UNITED NATIONS CONFERENCE ON ENVIRONMENT AND DEVELOPMENT (UNCED) UN conference that promotes global cooperation between developing and industrialized countries in planning and managing environmentally responsible development in four major areas:

- poverty and the environment;
- growth patterns, consumption standards, demographic pressures and the environment;
- international economic problems; and
- policies, institutions, and sustainable development.

UNCED was established in December 1989, and its headquarters is in Conches, Switzerland.

UNITED NATIONS CONFERENCE ON TRADE AND DEVELOPMENT (UNCTAD) a permanent organ of the UN General Assembly, established in December 1964 as UNCTAD, that promotes international trade and seeks to increase trade between developing countries and countries with different social and economic systems. UNCTAD also examines problems of economic development within the context of principles and policies of international trade and seeks to harmonize trade, development, and regional economic policies. UNCTAD's headquarters is in Geneva, Switzerland.

UNITED NATIONS CRIMINAL JUSTICE INFORMATION NETWORK (UNCJIN) a global crime prevention and criminal justice information network. UNCJIN was established in 1989 and is funded, in part, by the U.S. Bureau of Justice Statistics (BJS). The U.S. BJS has supported UNCJIN since 1990. Other supporters are the United Nations Criminal Justice and Crime Prevention Branch in Vienna, the State University of New York at Albany, and the Research Foundation of the State University of New York.

The Goal of UNCJIN is to establish a worldwide network to enhance dissemination and the exchange of information concerning criminal justice and crime prevention issues.

The objectives of UNCJIN include:
- facilitating information exchange and interlinkages among policy makers, planners, practitioners, scholars and other experts, as well as United Nations national correspondents and research institutions;
- providing gateways permitting the transfer of knowledge, including research results;
- linking criminal justice documentation centers and libraries around the world; and
- supporting the establishment and expansion of computerized national and local criminal justice systems.

The headquarters of UNCJIN is located in Albany, NY.

UNITED NATIONS DEVELOPMENT PROGRAM (UNDP) a voluntary UN development fund that finances the world's largest multilateral program of grant technical cooperation. The UNDP provides multilateral grant technical assistance, including expert advice, training, and limited equipment, to developing countries.

The program was established in 1965, and its headquarters is in New York City. Landmark legislation passed by UNDP's Executive Board in 1994–1995 has given the organization a new substantive mandate and a focused mission responding to the most important development needs and potentials. UNDP's overriding goal is poverty eradication through sustainable human development. UNDP's more than 130 resident representatives normally serve as resident coordinators of the UN system. They report to the UN Secretary-General through the UNDP Administrator. In crisis situations, resident coordinators normally serve as humanitarian coordinators, organizing UN responses to emergencies. Resident coordinators constitute a global network for coherent and cohesive UN action. That network is funded and managed by UNDP at the decision of the UN General Assembly. The Administrator chairs and is advised by the United Nations Development Group (UNDG), a coordinating body reflecting a partnership among UN funds, programs, and other development entities.

UNITED NATIONS EDUCATIONAL, SCIENTIFIC, AND CULTURAL ORGANIZATION (UNESCO) UN organization created in 1945 to promote international cooperation by advancing education, science, and culture for the purpose of achieving justice and human rights and freedom internationally. UNESCO meets biennially, and its board has 51 members. The United States withdrew from membership on December 31, 1984, while the United Kingdom and Singapore withdrew on December 3, 1985. Its offices are in Paris, France.

UNITED NATIONS ENVIRONMENT PROGRAM (UNEP) UN environmental program that assists developing countries in implementing environmentally sound development policies. UNEP produced a worldwide environmental monitoring system to standardize international data. UNEP was established in 1972, and its headquarters is in Nairobi, Kenya.

UNITED NATIONS HIGH COMMISSIONER FOR REFUGEES (UNHCR) UN office created in 1951 to protect the interests of refugees. The High Commissioner can appeal for voluntary funds to enable emergency aid to be given to refugees as well as for their care and feeding. The High Commissioner's office is located in Geneva, Switzerland.

UNITED NATIONS INDUSTRIAL DEVELOPMENT ORGANIZATION (UNIDO) UN development organization that promotes accelerated commercial development in developing countries and encourages industrial cooperation worldwide. As part of its activities, UNIDO brings promising entrepreneurs in the developing world to the attention of potential partners in industrialized countries through a network of INVESTMENT PROMOTION SERVICES (IPS). IPS offices operate in Austria, China, France, Germany, Italy, Japan, Korea, Russia, Switzerland, and the United States (Washington, DC). Established in 1967, UNIDO became a specialized UN agency in 1986. UNIDO's offices are in Vienna, Austria.

UNITED NATIONS INSTITUTE FOR TRAINING AND RESEARCH (UNITAR) institute originally established in 1966 for the primary purpose of offering training programs and research activities usually in multilateral diplomacy as well as economic and social development. Additionally, training efforts have been made for diplomats in the areas of negotiations, conflict resolution and diplomacy. Training programs normally occur in developing countries for the purpose of assisting these nations in developing policies for the purpose of meeting urgent economic and social issues as well as to implement international agreements.

UNITAR's board has up to 30 members, and its offices are located in Geneva, Switzerland.

UNITED NATIONS POPULATION FUND (UNFPA) a UN fund established in 1972 as the United Nations Fund for Population Activities. Its name was changed in 1987, although the acronym was kept, and its headquarters is in New York City. UNFPA assists countries in meeting their family planning and population needs, champions family planning programs, and publicizes population problems.

UNITED NATIONS REGIONAL ECONOMIC COMMISSIONS (ECOSOC) five UN commissions that promote economic development as regional commissions for the EDUCATIONAL, SCIENTIFIC, AND CULTURAL ORGANIZATION (UNESCO):

1. the ECONOMIC COMMISSION FOR AFRICA (ECA), established April 1958, promotes economic and social development among approximately 50 participating nations. The commission's headquarters is in Addis Ababa, Ethiopia.

2. the ECONOMIC COMMISSION FOR EUROPE (ECE), established March 1947, promotes economic cooperation among members. Its headquarters is in Geneva, Switzerland.

3. the ECONOMIC COMMISSION FOR LATIN AMERICA AND THE CARIBBEAN (ECLAC) (Spanish: Comisión Economica para Americana Latina y el Caribe, CEPAL). Originally established as the Economic Commission for Latin America (ECLA) in February 1948, ECLAC promotes economic and social development among approximately 40 member states. Commission headquarters is in Santiago, Chile.

4. the ECONOMIC AND SOCIAL COMMISSION FOR ASIA AND THE PACIFIC (ESCAP), originally established as the Economic Commission for Asia and the Far East (ECAFE) in March 1947. ESCAP promotes economic development planning and related activities among approximately 38 member nations. Commission headquarters is in Bangkok, Thailand.

5. the ECONOMIC AND SOCIAL COMMISSION FOR WESTERN ASIA (ESCWA), originally established as the Economic Commission for Western Asia (ECWA) in August 1973; ESCWA promotes economic reconstruction and development among 14 member nations.

UNITED NATIONS RELIEF AND WORKS AGENCY FOR PALESTINE REFUGEES IN THE NEAR EAST (UNRWA) UN agency established in 1949 originally to provide emergency relief to Palestinian Arab refugees who lost their homes as a result of the Arab–Israeli conflict of 1948. UNRWA's mission was expanded in 1967 to provide humanitarian assistance to Palestinian refugees from the 1967 Middle East hostilities. UNRWA provides preventive and curative, as well as mother-and-child, health care and environmental health services. UNRWA also offers quality education in accordance with the needs, identity, and cultural heritage of the Palestine refugees. UNRWA registers refugees, determines eligibility for agency services, supports families unable to meet their own basic needs, provides temporary direct relief in emergencies, and facilitates longer-term social and economic development for refugees and their communities.

UNRWA has an international staff of about 180 people from more than 30 nations and has almost 19,000 local staff. UNRWA has five fields of operation in Lebanon, Syria, Jordan, the West Bank, and Gaza administered by its headquarters in Vienna, Austria, and in Amman, Jordan. Its Advisory Commission consists of ten nations.

UNITED NATIONS SPECIAL COMMISSION (UNSCOM) was set up to implement the terms and conditions for the formal cease-fire between Iraq and the coalition of Member States cooperating with Kuwait, to implement the nonnuclear provisions of the resolution and to assist the International Atomic Energy Agency (IAEA) in the nuclear areas. The precise terms resolution called for the elimination, under international supervision, of Iraq's weapons of mass destruction and ballistic missiles with a range greater than 150 kilometers, together with related items and production facilities. It also called for measures to ensure that the acquisition and production of prohibited items were not resumed.

UNITED NATIONS UNIVERSITY (UNU) a decentralized system of affiliated academic institutions established in 1972. It is integrated into the world university community dedicated to research into the global problems of human survival, development, and welfare and to postgraduate training of young scholars and research workers.

UNU has established the following research and training centers and programs around the world:
- the World Institute for Development Economics Research (UNU/WIDER), located in Helsinki, Finland;
- the Institute for New Technologies (UNU/INTECH), located in Maastricht, the Netherlands;
- the International Institute for Software Technology (UNU/IIST), located in Macau; and
- the Institute for Natural Resources in Africa (UNU/INRA), tentatively located in Accra, Ghana, with a unit in Lusaka, Zambia.

UNU also has the Program for Biotechnology in Latin America and the Caribbean (UNU/BIOLAC), located in Caracas, Venezuela.

UNU's council has 24 members, and its permanent offices are located in Tokyo, Japan.

UNITED NATIONS VOLUNTEERS (UNV) a multilateral volunteer-sending UN organization created in 1970 to assist the UNITED NATIONS DEVELOPMENT PROGRAM (UNDP) in international development. It has become extremely important in supplying experienced professionals for developing country governments. The UNV has five different programmatic objectives:
- technical cooperation,
- assisting local government developmental and environmental initiatives,
- providing humanitarian relief and rehabilitation,
- assisting in peacemaking including the democratization process, and
- encouraging entrepreneurship in the public and private sectors.

As of 1993 the UNV had more than 2,500 specialists serving in 119 countries of Africa, Asia and the Pacific, the Arab States, Latin America and the Caribbean, Poland, and the CIS Republics. The UNV maintains strong ties with United Nations cooperating organizations and National Focal Points in industrialized and developing countries. UNV's offices are located in the Palais des Nations, Geneva, Switzerland.

UNITED STATES PRICE in the context of DUMPING investigations, the price at which goods are sold in the United States compared to their FOREIGN market value. The comparisons are used in the process of determining whether imported merchandise is sold at less than FAIR VALUE. *see also* CONSTRUCTED VALUE; DOWNSTREAM DUMPING; DUMPING MARGIN; FAIR VALUE; GENERAL AGREEMENTS ON TARIFFS AND TRADE (GATT).

UNITIZATION practice or technique of consolidating many small pieces of FREIGHT into a single unit for easier handling. *see also* PALLETIZATION.

UNIT LOAD strapping or banding together of a number of individual CARGO containers in order to create a single unit. *see also* PALLET; PALLETIZING; PALLETIZATION; UNITIZATION.

UNIT LOAD DEVICE term commonly used when referring to containers and PALLETS. *see also* PALLET TRANSPORTER.

UNIVERSAL COPYRIGHT CONVENTION (UCC) an international agreement adopted in 1954 by some 50 countries, including the United States, providing guidelines relating to the protection of copyrights. UCC countries that do not also adhere to the BERNE CONVENTION often require compliance with certain formalities to maintain copyright protection. Those formalities can be either or both of the following:
- registration and
- the requirement that published copies of a work bear copyright notice, the name of the author, and the date of first publication.

The United States has bilateral copyright agreements with a number of countries, and the laws of these countries may or may not be consistent with either of the copyright conventions. Before first publication of a work anywhere, it is advisable to investigate the scope of and requirements for maintaining copyright protection for those countries in which copyright protection is desired. *see also* UNIVERSAL COPYRIGHT PROTECTION.

UNIVERSAL COPYRIGHT PROTECTION the level and scope of copyright protection available within a country depends on that country's domestic laws and treaty obligations. In most countries, the place of first publication is an important criterion for determining whether foreign works are eligible for copyright protection. Works first published in the United States on or after March 1, 1989 (the date on which U.S. adherence to the BERNE CONVENTION for the Protection of Literary and Artistic Works became effective) are, with few exceptions, automatically protected in the more than 80 countries that belong to the BERNE UNION. Exporters of goods embodying works protected by copyright in the United States should find out how individual Berne Union countries deal with older U.S. works, including those first published (but not first or simultaneously published in a Berne Union country) before March 1, 1989. *see also* UNIVERSAL COPYRIGHT CONVENTION.

UNIVERSAL POSTAL UNION an agency of the UNITED NATIONS that oversees the organization and improvement of international postal services.

UNIVERSAL TIME COORDINATED (UTC) Greenwich Mean Time.

UNLOADING physical removal of CARGO from CARRIER'S CONTAINER. *see also* LOADING.

UNOFFICIAL SERVICE CHARGE *see* BRIBE; MORDIDA.

UNPUBLISHED TECHNICAL DATA technical information generally related to the design, production, or use of a product that is not available to the public. The data are not described in books, magazines, or pamphlets nor are they taught in any college. It is knowhow that an individual will not release without charging for it.

UNRESTRICTED LETTER OF CREDIT a LETTER OF CREDIT (L/C) that may be negotiated through any BANK of the BENEFICIARY'S choice. *see also* CONFIRMED LETTER OF CREDIT.

UNRISD *see* UNITED NATIONS RESEARCH INSTITUTE FOR SOCIAL DEVELOPMENT.

UNRWA *see* UNITED NATIONS RELIEF AND WORKS AGENCY.

UNSTABLE (FOREIGN) EXCHANGE RATE MARKET a market for a country's currency that acts in an unusual manner, possibly going from unsteady to volatile, as a result of political interference or commercial disturbances.

UNTOUCHABLES the lowest caste Indians, referred to by Mahatma Gandhi as children of God.

UNU *see* UNITED NATIONS UNIVERSITY.

UNUSED LICENSE a current available VALIDATED EXPORT LICENSE not having any shipments recorded on it. Any shipments made against the license must be posted on its reverse side. *see also* USED LICENSE.

UPLIFTS additional payments (allowances) provided to an employee for EXPATRIATION, HARDSHIP, DANGER, an EXTENDED WORK WEEK, and ASSIGNMENT COMPLETION, normally expressed as a percentage of base salary.

UPLOAD the transfer of a file from a computer to a HOST system. *see also* DOWNLOAD.

UPSTREAM PRICING the process of determining the market value for COMMODITIES from which other products result or other by-products are created. Marketers controlling upstream pricing do not have as much control of the price of the commodity used in the production of the by-product as those producing the by-product itself. Example: pineapple producers have less control over the prices paid to them for their product than the producers of canned pineapple juice who manufacture and market the canned juice using the pineapples grown by the pineapple farmers. *see also* DOWNSTREAM PRICING.

UPSTREAM SUBSIDIZATION the EXPORT of a GOOD, one of whose inputs has been subsidized. *see also* SUBSIDY.

URBAN LEGENDS controversial stories or rumors that have gone through many transformations and eventually appear on the INTERNET. They cover many different subjects including, for example, stories concerning how various government agencies are spying on NET users as well as various taxes that may be charged to users.

URUGUAY ROUND *see* ROUNDS.

URUGUAYAN PESO (PESO URUGUAYOS) unit of currency, Uruguay.

U.S. ADVISORY COMMITTEE ON TRADE POLICY NEGOTIATIONS (ACTPN) a committee established by the U.S. president under the authority of the OMNIBUS TRADE AND COMPETITIVENESS ACT OF 1988 to provide a forum for advice to be given to the U.S. TRADE REPRESENTATIVE (USTR).

USAEDC *see* U.S. AGRICULTURAL EXPORT DEVELOPMENT COUNCIL.

US-AEP *see* UNITED STATES–ASIA ENVIRONMENTAL PROGRAM.

USANCE the common period fixed for payment by usage, custom, or habit of dealings between the country where a BILL OF EXCHANGE is drawn and that where it is payable. It varies according to the countries involved.

U.S. AFFILIATE a U.S. business enterprise in which there is foreign direct investment—that is, in which a single foreign person owns or controls, directly or indirectly, 10% or more of its voting securities if the enterprise is incorporated or an equivalent interest if the enterprise is unincorporated. The affiliate is called a U.S. affiliate to denote that the affiliate is located in the U.S. (although it is owned by a FOREIGN PERSON).

U.S. AGENCY FOR INTERNATIONAL DEVELOPMENT *see* AGENCY FOR INTERNATIONAL DEVELOPMENT (AID).

U.S. AGRICULTURAL ADJUSTMENT ACT OF 1933 government legislation authorizing the use of QUANTITY RESTRICTIONS on the importation of agricultural products into the United States.

U.S. AGRICULTURAL EXPORT DEVELOPMENT COUNCIL (USAEDC) U.S. council composed predominantly of producer and agribusiness-oriented nonprofit organizations. It represents the interests of COMMODITY organizations participating in the market development program established by the Foreign Agricultural Service. USAEDC was created in 1954.

US&FCS *see* U.S. AND FOREIGN COMMERCIAL SERVICE.

U.S. AND FOREIGN COMMERCIAL SERVICE (US & FCS) the U.S. State Department's Foreign Commercial Service was transferred to U.S. DEPARTMENT OF COMMERCE in April 1980. This group was merged with Commerce's domestic field operations in 1982, creating the U.S. and Foreign Commercial Service.

U.S.–ASIA ENVIRONMENTAL PROGRAM (US-AEP) U.S. program, coordinated by the U.S. Agency for International Development, which helps U.S. companies compete in expanding Asian markets for sales of environmental products, services, technologies, and know-how. US-AEP links the efforts of U.S. government agencies in a one-stop service.

U.S.–CANADA FREE TRADE AGREEMENT an agreement between the United States and Canada that establishes a program leading to the unimpeded exchange and flow of goods and services between the two countries. *see also* FREE-TRADE AGREEMENT (FTA); NORTH AMERICAN FREE TRADE AGREEMENT (NAFTA).

USCIB *see* U.S. COUNCIL FOR INTERNATIONAL BUSINESS.

U.S. CODE two sets of public law reflecting the federal nature of the United States. Public law has been developed reflecting both federal and state legal codes.

U.S. COUNCIL FOR INTERNATIONAL BUSINESS (USCIB) the American affiliate of the INTERNATIONAL CHAMBER OF COMMERCE (ICC), the Business and Advisory Council (BIAC) to the ORGANIZATION FOR ECONOMIC COOPERATION AND DEVELOPMENT, and the International Organization of Employers (IOE). The council advocates U.S. business positions to the U.S. government, to UNITED NATIONS bodies, and to other international organizations. The council administers the ATA CARNET System, which issues and guarantees documents that allow duty-free, temporary importation of merchandise overseas. The council was established in 1945, and its headquarters is in New York City.

U.S. CUSTOMS SERVICE responsible for the administration of the TARIFF ACT OF 1930, as amended. Primary responsibilities include the assessment and collection of all DUTIES, taxes, and fees on IMPORTED merchandise, the enforcement of CUSTOMS and related laws, and the administration of certain navigation laws and TREATIES. U.S. Customs also functions as a major enforcement organization. It combats smuggling and revenue frauds and enforces regulations for other federal agencies at ports of entry and along the land and sea borders of the United States.

U.S. DEPARTMENT OF AGRICULTURE the executive department that serves as the principal adviser to the president on agricultural policy, which works to improve and maintain farm income, implement nutrition programs, and develop and expand markets abroad for U.S. agricultural products. It is also charged with inspecting and grading food products for safe consumption.

U.S. DEPARTMENT OF COMMERCE the principal organization within the Executive Branch of the U.S. government responsible for the promotion of economic growth in the United States. The Department of Commerce plays an active role in advancing U.S. interests in world trade and works to prevent UNFAIR TRADE PRACTICES by foreign competitors. *see also* U.S. INTERNATIONAL TRADE ADMINISTRATION.

U.S. DEPARTMENT OF DEFENSE a civilian executive department providing the military forces needed to deter war and protect the security of the United States.

U.S. DEPARTMENT OF ENERGY an executive department created in 1977 to consolidate all major Federal energy functions into one department. The principal missions are energy programs, weapons and waste cleanup programs, and science and technology programs.

U.S. DEPARTMENT OF LABOR (DOL) the executive department that promotes and develops the welfare of U.S. wage earners, improves working conditions, and advances opportunities for profitable employment. The DOL keeps track of changes in employment, prices, and other national economic measures.

U.S. DEPARTMENT OF STATE the executive department that directs U.S. foreign relations and negotiates treaties and agreements with foreign nations. Activities of the State Department are coordinated with foreign activities of other U.S. departments and agencies.

U.S. DEPARTMENT OF THE INTERIOR the executive department that has responsibility for most federally owned public lands and natural resources; the principal U.S. conservation agency. The office of Territorial and International Affairs oversees activities pertaining to U.S. territorial lands and the Freely Associated States and coordinates the international affairs of the Department.

U.S. DEPARTMENT OF TRANSPORTATION the executive department of the U.S. government that is responsible for developing national transportation policies.

U.S. DIRECT INVESTMENT ABROAD (USDIA) *see* DIRECT INVESTMENTS.

U.S DOLLAR unit of currency, United States (100 cents equal 1 U.S. dollar).

U.S. DOLLAR AREA *see* CURRENCY AREA.

U.S. EXPORT ADMINISTRATION ACT OF 1979 (EAA) act that authorizes the President to control EXPORTS of U.S. goods and technology to all foreign destinations, as necessary, for the purpose of national security, foreign policy, and short supply. As the basic export administration statute, the EAA is the first big revision of export control law since enactment of the Export Control Act of 1949. The EAA is not permanent legislation. It must be reauthorized—usually every 3 years. *see also* BUREAU OF EXPORT ADMINISTRATION (BXA).

U.S. EXPORT ADMINISTRATION REGULATIONS U.S. EXPORT regulations developed as a result of the U.S. EXPORT ADMINISTRATION ACT OF 1979. It provides specific instructions on the use and types of licenses required and controls for various types of COMMODITIES and technical data.

U.S. EXPORT ADMINISTRATION REVIEW BOARD (EARB) a U.S. cabinet-level EXPORT licensing dispute resolution group. The EARB was originally established in June 1970 through a Presidential Executive Order. EARB membership includes the U.S. Departments of Commerce (as chair), State, Defense, and Energy and the Arms Control and Disarmament Agency including the Joint Chiefs of Staff and the Central Intelligence Agency as nonvoting members. The EARB is the final review body to resolve differences among agency views on the granting of an export license.

U.S. FEDERAL REGISTER U.S. publication of federal regulations and legal notices promulgated by the executive department and agencies. It is published daily except Saturdays, Sundays, and holidays. The *Federal Register* is published by the Office of the Federal Register, National Archives and Records Administration, Washington, DC.

U.S. INDUSTRY SECTOR ADVISORY COMMITTEE (USISAC) an organization that is part of the structure advising the U.S. TRADE REPRESENTATIVE (USTR) during trade negotiation. *see also* U.S. ADVISORY COMMITTEE ON TRADE POLICY NEGOTIATIONS.

U.S. INFORMATION AGENCY (USIA) U.S. agency established in 1953 to conduct information and cultural activities abroad. The agency operates the VOICE OF AMERICA, a radio network that carries news and information about the United States in more than forty languages to all parts of the world. In 1978 its functions were assumed by the International Communication Agency. Its name was changed back to the U.S. Information Agency in 1982.

U.S. INTERAGENCY TRADE ORGANIZATION (USITO) an organization established under the authorization of the Omnibus Trade and Competitiveness Act of 1988. It is an executive advisory group established to advise the president and the U.S. TRADE REPRESENTATIVE (USTR) regarding the formation of international trade policy and the coordination and implementation of a worldwide international trade policy. The USITO is chaired by the USTR, and it includes the following executive branch officers: Secretary of Commerce, Secretary of State, Secretary of the Treasury, Secretary of Agriculture, and the Secretary of Labor. *see also* U.S. ADVISORY COMMITTEE ON TRADE POLICY NEGOTIATIONS.

U.S. INTERNATIONAL DEVELOPMENT COOPERATION AGENCY (USIDCA) an independent agency of the U.S. government established in 1979, under the authority of the Foreign Assistance Act of 1961. The principal purpose of the agency is to create policies and coordinate the implementation of programs relating to U.S. economic and developmental relations with DEVELOPING COUNTRIES. The USIDCA includes the following organizations within its structure: AGENCY FOR INTERNATIONAL DEVELOPMENT (AID), TRADE AND DEVELOPMENT PROGRAM (TDP), and OVERSEAS PRIVATE INVESTMENT CORPORATION (OPIC). It is also responsible for U.S. budget setting, policy, and participation within the UNITED NATIONS system. *see also* EXPORT DEVELOPMENT CORPORATION.

U.S. INTERNATIONAL TRADE ADMINISTRATION (ITA) an agency of the U.S. DEPARTMENT OF COMMERCE that has primary responsibility for reviewing and making DUMPING determinations and the amount of any ANTIDUMPING DUTY. The ITA also promotes EXPORTS for U.S. firms, providing exhibitions and staff fluent in local languages to answer questions, and forwards all trade leads to participating firms. The ITA offers guidance and assistance in planning for trade missions and coordinates the support of all relevant offices and the assistance of overseas commercial officers in each foreign city on the itinerary. The ITA's COMMERCIAL LAW DEVELOPMENT PROGRAM helps Central and Eastern Europe and the Baltic States develop a commercial infrastructure consistent with free market principles. The ITA also operates an on-line trade data retrieval system, COMPRO. *see also* CONSORTIA OF AMERICAN BUSINESSES IN THE NEWLY INDEPENDENT STATES (CABNIS); CUSTOMIZED SALES SURVEY (CSS); EXPORTER DATA BASE (EDB); GOLD KEY SERVICE; JAPAN EXPORT INFORMATION CENTER (JEIC); WORLD TRADERS DATA REPORTS (WTDR).

U.S. INTERNATIONAL TRADE COMMISSION (USITC) *see* INTERNATIONAL TRADE COMMISSION.

U.S.–ISRAELI FREE TRADE AGREEMENT a program providing for free or reduced rates of duty for merchandise from Israel to stimulate TRADE between the two countries for specified products. The special treatment includes both preferential DUTY RATES or in some cases DUTY-FREE status. *see also* FREE-TRADE AREA.

U.S.–JAPAN SEMICONDUCTOR TRADE ARRANGEMENT *see* SEMICONDUCTOR TRADE ARRANGEMENT.

U.S. MARITIME ADMINISTRATION (USMA) an operating unit of the U.S. Department of Transportation. The USMA's principal responsibilities include organizing the U.S. merchant marine, and directing emergency merchant ship operations. The USMA offers private carriers insurance against losses caused by hostile acts, under the WAR RISK INSURANCE PROGRAM (WRIP). The WRIP is provided only in the event that the carrier is unable to obtain the coverage from private sources.

U.S. MISSION TO THE EUROPEAN COMMUNITY (USEC) *see* EUROPEAN COMMUNITY; TITLE AND RANK.

U.S. MISSION TO THE UNITED NATIONS (USUN) *see* TITLE AND RANK; UNITED NATIONS.

U.S. MUNITIONS LIST (USML) those items or categories of items considered to be defense articles and defense services subject to EXPORT control. The USML is similar in coverage to the INTERNATIONAL MUNITIONS LIST (IML) but is more restrictive in two ways. First, the USML currently contains some dual-use items that are controlled for national security and foreign policy reasons (such as space-related or encryption-related equipment). Second, the USML contains some nuclear-related items. Under presidential directive, most dual-use items are to be transferred from the USML to the U.S. DEPARTMENT OF COMMERCE's dual-use list. The U.S. Department of State, with the concurrence of the Department of Defense, designates which articles will be controlled under the USML. Items on the Munitions List face a stricter control regime and lack the safeguards to protect commercial competitiveness that apply to dual-use items.

U.S. PERSON any person who is a United States resident or national, including individuals, domestic concerns, and "controlled in fact" FOREIGN SUBSIDIARIES, affiliates, or other permanent foreign establishments of domestic concerns.

U.S. PRICE (USP) the price at which goods are sold in the United States compared to their foreign market value. In the context of DUMPING investigations, the comparisons are used in the process of determining whether imported merchandise is sold at less than FAIR VALUE.

U.S. SOURCE INCOME income or compensation paid within the United States.

U.S. SUPERFUND an account established by the U.S. government for use in cleaning up polluted areas when no other funds existed. The legislation imposed a surtax of 8.2 cents per barrel on domestic petroleum, oil, and lubricants and 11.7 cents per barrel on imported petroleum, oil, and lubricants. In November 1989, 2.5 years from the time the Superfund tax was ruled illegal by the GENERAL AGREEMENT ON TARIFFS AND TRADE (GATT), the legislation was revised by the U.S. Congress, and the tax was withdrawn.

U.S. TRADE AND DEVELOPMENT AGENCY *see* TRADE AND DEVELOPMENT AGENCY (TDA).

U.S. TRADE REPRESENTATIVE (USTR) a U.S. government cabinet-level official with the rank of AMBASSADOR who advises the president on trade policy. The USTR coordinates the development of U.S. trade policy initiatives, leads U.S. international trade negotiations, and seeks to expand U.S. EXPORTS by promoting removal or reduction of foreign trade barriers.

U.S. TRAVEL AND TOURISM ADMINISTRATION (USTTA) an agency in the U.S. DEPARTMENT OF COMMERCE. Its principal mission is to implement broad tourism policy initiatives for the development of international travel to the U.S. as a stimulus for economic stability.

USED LICENSE a VALIDATED EXPORT LICENSE that has expired; also all shipments authorized by the license have been made. Any shipments made against the license must be posted on its reverse side.

USENET a collection of thousands of NEWSGROUPS that are interested in various topics. The USENET is not subscribed to by all INTERNET HOSTS. Many USENET hosts do not appear on the Internet. *see also* NETWORK.

USER NAME a name identifying a computer user. Typically a user name can be any combination of letters and/or numbers.

USER'S FEE assessments collected by the U.S. CUSTOMS SERVICE as part of the ENTRY process to help defray various costs involved in the IMPORTATION of goods to the United States.

USML *see* U.S. MUNITIONS LIST.

USP *see* U.S. PRICE.

USTR *see* U.S. TRADE REPRESENTATIVE.

USUANCE time allowed for payment of an international obligation.

USUAL MARKETING REQUIREMENT (UMR) the amount of a COMMODITY that the U.S. P.L. 480 (Food for Peace) sales agreement requires the recipient country to IMPORT on a commercial basis. This amount is normally based on the country's most recent 5-year average of commercial imports of the commodity from countries friendly to the United States.

UTC *see* UNIVERSAL TIME COORDINATED.

UTILIDATES a special 2-month bonus given to employees in Venezuela.

V

VACATION ALLOWANCE *see* BENEFIT ALLOWANCE.

VAL abbreviation for value.

VALDEZ PRINCIPLES a corporate code of conduct as it relates to the protection of the environment, sponsored and adopted by the U.S. Coalition for Environmentally Responsible Economies on September 17, 1989 after the *Exxon Valdez* oil spill disaster in Alaska. The U.S. Coalition for Environmentally Responsible Economies (CERES) includes groups such as the Sierra Club, the National Audubon Society, and the Humane Society of America. The Valdez Principles submitted to U.S. corporations for signature called for the following:
- eliminate pollutants that damage the air, water, and earth;
- use energy-efficient products and processes;
- use sustainable and renewable natural resources;
- market safe products and services;
- restore any damage to the environment and pay compensation to those who have suffered injury;
- reveal manufacturing hazards and accidents;
- appoint an expert on the environment to the board of directors and create a senior executive position for environmental affairs; and
- conduct and make public an annual audit of worldwide programs.

VALIDATED EXPORT LICENSE a document issued by the U.S. government authorizing the EXPORT of COMMODITIES for which written export authorization is required by law. Two types exist: an Individual Validated License (IVL) and a Special License.

VALIDATED LICENSE *see* VALIDATED EXPORT LICENSE.

VALIDITY time period for which a LETTER OF CREDIT is valid. *see also* EXPIRATION DATE.

VALUATION the method by which dutiable value of merchandise is determined by CUSTOMS for the purpose of determining the amount of DUTY owed by the IMPORTER. The calculation is done using the GATT formula. It is basically the TRANSACTION VALUE, the price the buyer (importer) actually pays the seller (EXPORTER). If the transaction value cannot be used, then certain secondary bases are considered. The secondary bases of value, listed in order of precedence for use, are transaction value of identical merchandise, transaction value of similar merchandise, DEDUCTIVE VALUE, and COMPUTED VALUE. *see also* GATT CUSTOMS VALUATION CODE.

VALUATION CHARGES transportation charges imposed against SHIPPERS who declare a value of goods higher than the carriers' limit of liability.

VALUATION CLAUSE the basis for determining insured value under the open CARGO policy.

VALUE ADDED that part of the total value of produced goods contributed by an individual company's manufacturing process or services. It is determined by subtracting from sales the costs of materials and supplies, energy costs, contract work, and so on, and it includes labor expenses, administrative and sales costs, and other operating profit.

VALUE-ADDED COUNSELING assessing a company's current international business operations and assisting a client in one or more of the following:
- identifying and selecting the most viable markets;
- developing an export market strategy;
- implementing the export market strategy; and
- increasing market presence.

VALUE-ADDED NETWORK (VAN) a telecommunications network that provides services for the medium- to small-sized business, such as protocol conversion, facsimile interfacing, or conference calls.

VALUE-ADDED TAX (VAT)
1. a EUROPEAN COMMUNITY (EC) tax assessed on the increased value of goods as they pass from the raw material stage through the production process to final consumption. The tax on processors or merchants is levied on the amount by which they increase the value of items they purchase. The EC charges a tax equivalent to the value added to imports and rebates value-added taxes on EXPORTS. In most EC countries tourists may obtain a value-added tax refund on their purchases upon leaving the respective country.
2. a tax that is assessed on the increased value of goods at each discrete point in the chain of production and distribution, from the raw material stage to final consumption. The tax on processors or merchants is levied on the amount by which they increase the value of items they purchase and resell. This is achieved by levying the tax at each point en route, as ownership passes from one person to another. At every stage, output tax is charged on the current sales value, but the input tax, which has been charged by those at an earlier stage of the game, can be offset or recovered. Thus the tax liability at each stage is based on the difference between the value of the outputs and the value of the inputs, thus deriving added value.
3. an indirect tax assessed on the increased value of goods at each discrete point in the chain of production and distribution, from the raw material stage to final consumption. The tax on processors or merchants is levied on the amount by which they increase the value of items they purchase and resell.

VALUE CHAIN APPROACH the standard framework used to analyze a firm and its competition in attempting to find ways of developing a competitive advantage, as advocated by Michael Porter.

VALUE FOR CUSTOMS PURPOSES ONLY as defined by the U.S. CUSTOMS SERVICE, the value submitted on the entry documentation by the IMPORTER, which may or may not reflect information from the manufacturer but in no way reflects Customs appraisement of the merchandise.

VALUE QUOTA a QUOTA specifying value (price times quantity) of a GOOD. *see also* ABSOLUTE QUOTA; TARIFF QUOTA.

VARIABLE LEVY (VL) a TARIFF subject to alterations as world market prices change. The alterations are designed to ensure that the IMPORT price after payment of the DUTY will equal a predetermined gate price.

VARIABLE PRICE a selling technique in which buyers and sellers negotiate a final price for goods to be purchased.

VAT *see* VALUE-ADDED TAX.

VATU unit of currency, Vanuatu.

VECTOR an organism that carries germs from one host to another.

VEHICLE CURRENCY a currency used in international trade and investment transactions to make quotes or payments. Because the U.S. DOLLAR is the principal central reserve asset of many countries, it is the most widely used vehicle currency.

VENDOR a company or individual that sells GOODS or SERVICES; a merchant, a retail dealer; a supplier; one who buys to sell. *see also* PURCHASER; PURCHASING AGENT.

VENICE TERMS agreements between representatives of a DEVELOPING COUNTRY wishing to renegotiate its "official" debt (normally excluding debts owed by and to the private sector without official guarantees) and representatives of the PARIS CLUB. It is a request to consolidate all or part of its debt service payments falling due over a specified period and to request longer maturities than the standard 10-year period allowed to reschedule debt by countries not benefiting by the TORONTO TERMS. *see also* DEBT RESCHEDULING; INTERNATIONAL DEBT.

VENTURE CAPITAL monies invested in high-risk projects. These are investments that normally involve a significant investment risk; however, they offer the opportunity for above-average future returns.

VER *see* VOLUNTARY EXPORT RESTRICTION.

VERTICAL EXPORT TRADING COMPANY an EXPORT trading company that integrates a range of functions taking products from suppliers to consumers. In addition to purchasing the materials, it will also market the products, often having retail outlets.

VERTICAL INTEGRATION the control of different stages as a product moves from raw materials to production and then to finished product and distribution.

VERTICAL MOBILITY the opportunity afforded to an individual to move upward in a society to a higher social status. *see also* CASTE SYSTEM.

VES abbreviation for vessel.

VESICLE a blister filled with fluid.

VESSEL TON unit of measurement in the shipping industry assuming that 100 cubic feet of CARGO equals one ton.

VIE *see* VOLUNTARY IMPORT EXPANSION.

VIENNA AGREEMENT formally known as the Vienna Agreement Establishing an International Classification of the Figurative Elements of Marks. It is a MULTILATERAL TREATY administered by the WORLD INTELLECTUAL PROPERTY ORGANIZATION (WIPO) affording the nations signing the agreement protection of intellectual property.

VIENNA CONVENTION ON THE LAW OF TREATIES BE-TWEEN STATES AND INTERNATIONAL ORGANIZATIONS OR BETWEEN INTERNATIONAL ORGANIZATIONS an international agreement that formalized the way in which treaties are negotiated, adopted, and amended.

VISA a stamp in a foreign national's passport issued by an officer of a CONSULATE that creates a legal presumption that there is no apparent reason to deny entry into a country. Regardless of the stamp, the final decision to grant admission is made by an officer of the country at the PORT OF ENTRY. Visas are required by many countries for entry of a foreigner.

VISA WAIVER a program of selected countries to eliminate the VISA requirement on a test basis.

VISEGRAD TRADE association among the European nations of Poland, the Czech Republic, Slovakia, and Hungary. It is somewhat analogous to the EUROPEAN FREE TRADE ASSOCIATION.

VISIBLE TRADE trade in GOODS. *see also* INVISIBLE TRADE.

VISIT USA COMMITTEE a committee of U.S. tourism managers located in foreign markets. Visit USA Committees work with the U.S. AND FOREIGN COMMERCIAL SERVICE (US & FCS) in planning and promoting travel to the United States.

VOICE OF AMERICA (VOA) *see* UNITED STATES INFORMATION AGENCY (USIA).

VOLATILITY measure of the relative deviation of a price from the mean.

VOLUME RATE rate applicable in connection with a specified volume of FREIGHT.

VOLUNTARY EXPORT RESTRAINT a restriction on a country's IMPORTS that is achieved by negotiating with the foreign exporting country for it to restrict its EXPORTS. *see also* TRADE BARRIER; VOLUNTARY EXPORT RESTRICTION (VER); VOLUNTARY RESTRAINT AGREEMENT (VRA).

VOLUNTARY EXPORT RESTRICTION (VER) an understanding between trading partners in which the exporting nation, in order to reduce trade friction, agrees to limit its EXPORTS of a particular good. *see also* VOLUNTARY RESTRAINT AGREEMENT (VRA).

VOLUNTARY IMPORT EXPANSION the use of policies to encourage IMPORTS, in response to pressure from trading partners.

VOLUNTARY RESTRAINT AGREEMENT (VRA) informal bilateral or multilateral understandings in which EXPORTERS voluntarily limit EXPORTS of certain products to a particular country destination in order to avoid economic dislocation in the importing country and the imposition of mandatory IMPORT restrictions. These arrangements do not involve an obligation on the part of the importing country to provide "compensation" to the exporting country, as would be the case if the importing country unilaterally imposed equivalent restraints on imports. *see also* VOLUNTARY EXPORT RESTRICTION (VER).

VRA *see* VOLUNTARY RESTRAINT AGREEMENT.

VT100 a computer terminal formerly manufactured by the Digital Equipment Corporation (DEC). Many COMMUNICATIONS SOFTWARE programs emulate the VT100 by recognizing the same control signals. It is the most common terminal emulation in use on the INTERNET. There are several newer versions.

W

W3 *see* WORLD WIDE WEB.

W.A. *see* WITH AVERAGE.

WACH *see* WEST AFRICAN CLEARINGHOUSE.

WADB *see* WEST AFRICAN DEVELOPMENT BANK.

WAMU *see* WEST AFRICAN MONETARY UNION.

WAOB *see* WORLD AGRICULTURAL OUTLOOK BOARD.

WAIVER an authorized deviation from the terms of a previously negotiated and legally binding agreement. Countries have requested and
received waivers from particular obligations of the GENERAL AGREE-
MENT ON TARIFFS AND TRADE (GATT) and WORLD TRADE ORGANIZATION
(WTO) regulations.

WAR CLAUSE MARINE INSURANCE provision excluding the liability of
an insurer if a loss is caused by war or hostile action. BILLS OF LAD-
ING and CHARTER PARTIES may contain a war clause giving the vessel
options to maintain its safety in case of hostilities. *see also* FREE OF
CAPTURE AND SEIZURE (F.C.&S.); WAR RATES; WAR RISK INSURANCE;
WAR/STRIKE CLAUSE.

WAR RATES additional CARGO insurance charges that will vary
depending upon the current political environments of the geographical region of the shipment's destination. *see also* WAR RISK
INSURANCE.

WAR RISK risk to a vessel, its CARGO, and passengers by aggressive
actions of a hostile nation or group.

WAR RISK INSURANCE separate insurance coverage for loss of
goods in transit that results from any act of war. This insurance is necessary during peacetime due to objects, such as floating mines, left
over from previous wars. War risk insurance in the United States was
underwritten exclusively through the American Cargo War Risk
Reinsurance Exchange, a consortium of private insurers formed to
share the extreme losses possible. Currently, however, the OVERSEAS
PRIVATE INVESTMENT CORPORATION (OPIC) provides for any losses stem-
ming from any act of being at war or being engaged in warlike conflict. *see also* WAR RATES; U.S. INTERNATIONAL DEVELOPMENT COOPERATION
AGENCY; U.S. MARITIME ADMINISTRATION; WAR RISK INSURANCE PROGRAM
(WRIP).

WAR RISK INSURANCE PROGRAM (WRIP) insurance coverage provided by the U.S. MARITIME ADMINISTRATION to protect private
carriers against losses resulting from hostile acts. It is only available
in the event that the insurance from private sources is not available.

WAR/STRIKE CLAUSE an insurance provision that covers loss due to war and/or strike.

WARC *see* WORLD ADMINISTRATIVE RADIO CONFERENCE.

WARDA *see* WEST AFRICA RICE DEVELOPMENT ASSOCIATION.

WAREHOUSE, U.S. CUSTOMS BONDED *see* BONDED WAREHOUSES.

WAREHOUSE ENTRY a form declaring goods imported and placed in a bonded warehouse. Duty payment may not be required until the goods are withdrawn for consumption.

WAREHOUSE RECEIPT a receipt issued by a warehouse listing goods received for storage.

WAREHOUSE TO WAREHOUSE an EXPORT/IMPORT policy clause that provides protection from the shipper's warehouse and during the ordinary course of transit to the CONSIGNEE'S warehouse.

WARRANTY a promise by a contracting party that the other party can rely on certain facts or representations as being true.

WARSAW CONVENTION an international MULTILATERAL TREATY that set the conditions of international transportation by air.

WARSAW PACT formally referred to as the Warsaw Treaty Organization, and originally the Eastern European Mutual Assistance Treaty. It was a mutual defense alliance signed in 1945 by Albania, Czechoslovakia, German Democratic Republic (East Germany), Hungary, Poland, Romania, and the U.S.S.R. It was the COMMUNIST Eastern European equivalent to the NORTH ATLANTIC TREATY ORGANIZATION (NATO). The alliance was dissolved in 1991. *see also* SOUTHEAST ASIA TREATY ORGANIZATION (SEATO).

WATER IN THE TARIFF the extent to which a TARIFF is higher than necessary, so as to reduce imports to zero. *see also* PROHIBITIVE TARIFF.

WAYBILL document prepared by a transportation line at the point of a shipment, showing the POINT OR ORIGIN, destination, route, CONSIGNOR, CONSIGNEE, description of shipment, and amount charged for the transportation service. It is forwarded with the shipment, or by direct mail, to the agent at the transfer point or waybill destination. *see also* AIR WAYBILL; BILL OF LADING.

WCL *see* WORLD CONFEDERATION OF LABOR.

WEAPONS OF MASS DESTRUCTION (WMD) According to the National Defense Authorization Act, any weapon or device that is intended or has the capability to cause death or serious bodily injury to a significant number of people through the release, dissemination, or impact of (A) toxic or poisonous chemicals or their precursors, (B) a disease organism, or (C) radiation or radioactivity.

WEBB-POMERENE ACT OF 1918 federal legislation exempting certain EXPORTERS' associations from certain antitrust regulations. *see also* WEBB-POMERENE ASSOCIATIONS.

WEBB–POMERENE ASSOCIATIONS associations engaged in exporting that combine the products of similar producers for overseas sales. These associations have partial exemption from U.S. antitrust laws but may not engage in IMPORT, domestic, or third-country trade or combine to EXPORT services.

WEEKLY COAL REPORTS TABLE a column appearing each Friday in the JOURNAL OF COMMERCE that compiles a listing of U.S. coal exports for the week arranged by shipper and including port of loading, country of destination, port of discharge, and date of sailing.

WEIGHT BREAK levels at which the FREIGHT rate per 100 pounds (45 kg) decreases because of substantial increases in the weight of the shipment.

WEST AFRICA ECONOMIC COMMUNITY (WAEC) (French: Communauté Economique de l'Afrique de l'Ouest, CEAO) a West African FREE-TRADE AREA (FTA) for agricultural products and raw materials and a preferential trading area for approved industrial products, with a regional cooperation tax (TCR) replacing IMPORT duties and encouraging trade among members. Created in 1974, the WAEC includes Benin, Burkina Faso, Côte d'Ivoire, Mali, Mauritania, Niger, and Senegal. (Togo has observer status.) A community fund (FOSIDEC) promotes private lender community participation in advancement of the community's least developed nations (Burkina Faso, Mali, Mauritania, and Niger). WAEC envisions eventual creation of a CUSTOMS UNION and coordination of fiscal policies. Community headquarters is in Ouagadougou, Burkina Faso.

WEST AFRICA RICE DEVELOPMENT ASSOCIATION (WARDA) one of several centers associated with the Consultative Group on International Agricultural Research. WARDA conducts research on rice improvement in mangrove swamps, inland swamps, upland conditions, and irrigated conditions. WARDA was established in 1970, and its headquarters is in Bouake, Côte d'Ivoire. Members include 17 West African countries: Benin, Burkina Faso, Chad, Côte d'Ivoire, Gambia, Ghana, Guinea, Guinea-Bissau, Liberia, Mali, Mauritania, Niger, Nigeria, Senegal, Sierra Leone, and Togo. *see also* CONSULTATIVE GROUP ON INTERNATIONAL AGRICULTURAL RESEARCH.

WEST AFRICAN CLEARINGHOUSE (WACH) (French: Chambre de Cooperation de l'Afrique de l'Ouest, CCAO) financial authority that provides settlement of payments services among a central bank and other monetary authorities in West Africa. WACH was established in 1975 (began operations in 1976); headquarters is in Freetown, Sierra Leone. Membership includes the CENTRAL BANK OF WEST AFRICAN STATES (representing Benin, Burkina Faso, Côte d'Ivoire, Mali, Niger,

Senegal, and Togo) as well as Gambia, Ghana, Guinea, Guinea-Bissau, Liberia, Mauritania, Nigeria, and Sierra Leone.

WEST AFRICAN DEVELOPMENT BANK (WADB) (French: Banque Ouest-Africaine de Développement, BOAD) bank that promotes regional economic development and integration in West Africa. The bank was established in 1973 (began operations in 1976). Its headquarters is in Lomé, Togo. WADB members include: Benin, Burkina Faso, Côte d'Ivoire, Mali, Niger, Senegal, and Togo.

WEST AFRICAN MONETARY UNION (WAMU) (French: Union Monétaire Ouest Africaine, UMOA) monetary union that began operation in 1963 and was revised in 1973. The union comprises seven French-speaking African countries: Benin, Burkina Faso, Côte d'Ivoire, Mali, Niger, Senegal, and Togo, which share a
- central bank (Banque Centrale des Etats de l'Afrique de l'Ouest), which coordinates the union's monetary and credit policies;
- common currency (CFA franc), which is freely convertible into the French franc at a fixed parity; and
- common regional development bank, the West African Development Bank.
  WAMU's headquarters is in Daka, Senegal.

WESTERN EUROPEAN UNION (WEU) a European union that serves interests between those furthered by the EUROPEAN ECONOMIC COMMUNITY (EEC) and the NORTH ATLANTIC TREATY ORGANIZATION (NATO). It has faced the need to change and has become focused on three missions:
- humanitarian aid,
- peacekeeping and crisis management, and
- some peace enforcement considerations.
  WEU was created in October 1954 to promote mutual defense and progressive political unification of its members. Membership, which included Belgium, France, Germany, Italy, Luxembourg, the Netherlands, Portugal, Spain, and the United Kingdom, has been increasing toward approximately 40 nations as a result of negotiations on membership or associate status with Greece, Turkey, Norway, Iceland, Denmark, and Ireland. WEU headquarters moved from London, England, to Brussels, Belgium, in December 1992.

WESTERN HEMISPHERE TRADE CORPORATION a domestic (U.S.) corporation whose business is done in any country of North, South, or Central America or the West Indies, and which usually receives certain tax advantages.

WEU *see* WESTERN EUROPEAN UNION.

WFC *see* WORLD FOOD COUNCIL.

WFDFI *see* WORLD FEDERATION OF DEVELOPMENT FINANCING INSTITUTIONS.

WFP *see* WORLD FOOD PROGRAM.

WG abbreviation for working group.

WHARF a structure next to which ship's MOOR to load or unload. *see also* DOCK; MOORAGE.

WHARFAGE a charge assessed by a pier or dock owner for handling incoming or outgoing CARGO.

WHO *see* WORLD HEALTH ORGANIZATION.

WHOIS an INTERNET directory program that allows users to search DOMAINS, NETWORKS, and HOSTS for information on users. WHOIS shows a person's name, address, phone number, and E-MAIL address. *see also* DEFENSE DATA NETWORK.

WHOLLY OWNED SUBSIDIARY *see* SUBSIDIARY.

WIPO *see* WORLD INTELLECTUAL PROPERTY ORGANIZATION.

WITH AVERAGE (WA) in MARINE INSURANCE, a shipment is protected from partial damage whenever the damage exceeds 3% (or some other percentage). If the ship is involved in a major catastrophe, such as a collision, fire, or stranding, the minimum percentage requirement is waived and the insurance company pays for all of the damage. *see also* MARINE CARGO INSURANCE.

WITH PARTICULAR AVERAGE (W.P.A.) in MARINE INSURANCE, partial loss or damage to goods is insured. Damage and loss generally must be caused by sea water. Policies may have a minimum percentage of damage before payment, and the insurance may be extended to cover loss by theft, pilferage, delivery, leakage, and breakage.

WITHOUT PENALTY the caveat that IMPORTERS, or any other person liable for the payment of DUTY, shall not be subject to a fine or threat of fine merely because they chose to exercise their right of appeal in the determination of CUSTOMS VALUE. *see also* CUSTOMS VALUATION CODE; GENERAL AGREEMENT ON TARIFFS AND TRADE (GATT).

WITHOUT RECOURSE the acknowledgment that a financial institution purchasing any type of deferred debt relinquishes any right to claim any portion of the instrument's value for any of its previous holders.

WITHOUT RESERVE shipper's agent or representative is empowered to make definitive decisions and adjustments abroad without approval of the group or individual represented.

WMO *see* WORLD METEOROLOGICAL ORGANIZATION.

WON unit of currency, Democratic People's Republic of Korea (100 chon equal 1 won).

WORK PERMIT an authorization by a HOST COUNTRY government that gives an individual the permission to accept paid employment in its country.

WORK VISA a stamp in a foreign national's passport issued by a consular officer. The stamp creates a legal presumption that there are no apparent reasons to deny entry into the country to take up paid employment.

WORKER'S PROTECTION ACT OF 1974 *see* ARBEIDSMILIJØLOVEN.

WORKING CAPITAL GUARANTEE PROGRAM a program of the EXIMBANK that assists small businesses in obtaining working capital to fund their EXPORT activities. The EXIMBANK guarantees 90% of the principal and a limited amount of interest on working capital loans extended by commercial banks to eligible U.S. exporters. The loan may be used for preexport activities such as the purchase of inventory, raw materials, the manufacture of a product, or marketing. The EXIMBANK requires the working capital loan to be fully collateralized using inventory, accounts receivable, or other acceptable collateral. *see also* COMMERCIAL BANK GUARANTEE PROGRAM; DIRECT AND INTERMEDIARY LOAN PROGRAM; LEASE GUARANTEES.

WORLD ADMINISTRATIVE RADIO CONFERENCE (WARC) the conferences convened regularly by the UNITED NATIONS' INTERNATIONAL TELECOMMUNICATIONS UNION (ITU) to allocate and regulate radio frequencies for the purposes of television and radio broadcasting, telephone data communications, navigation, maritime and aeronautical communication, and satellite broadcasting.

WORLD AGRICULTURAL OUTLOOK BOARD (WAOB) the focal point for U.S. economic intelligence related to domestic and international food and agriculture. The board coordinates and clears all COMMODITY and aggregate agricultural and food-related data used to develop outlook and situation material within the U.S. Department of Agriculture. WAOB was established in 1977.

WORLD BANK an integrated group of international institutions that provide financial and technical assistance to developing countries. The World Bank includes the INTERNATIONAL BANK FOR RECONSTRUCTION AND DEVELOPMENT (IBRD) and the INTERNATIONAL DEVELOPMENT ASSOCIATION (IDA). World Bank affiliates, legally and financially separate, include the INTERNATIONAL CENTER FOR THE SETTLEMENT OF INVESTMENT DISPUTES, the INTERNATIONAL FINANCE CORPORATION (IFC), and the MULTILATERAL INVESTMENT GUARANTEE AGENCY. World Bank headquarters is in Washington, DC.

WORLD BANK GROUP a group of four international organizations involved in providing long-term financing to DEVELOPING COUNTRIES. They are the WORLD BANK, the INTERNATIONAL FINANCE CORPORATION (IFC), the INTERNATIONAL DEVELOPMENT ASSOCIATION (IDA), and the MULTILATERAL INVESTMENT GUARANTEE AGENCY. *see also* INTERNATIONAL BANK FOR RECONSTRUCTION AND DEVELOPMENT; MULTILATERAL DEVELOPMENT BANKS.

WORLD BANK INTERNATIONAL CENTER FOR THE SETTLEMENT OF INVESTMENT DISPUTES (ICSID) an independent organization established by the WORLD BANK, under the authorization of the UNITED NATIONS Convention on the Settlement of Investment Disputes between States and Nationals of Other States. The purpose of the ICSID is to act as a conciliator in resolving international disputes involving capital investment, where one of the parties is a SOVEREIGN state or an agency of the state.

WORLD CONFEDERATION OF LABOR (WCL) organization representing the cultural, economic, political, and social interests of millions of workers in Africa, the Americas, Asia, Europe, and the Middle East. The confederation was founded in 1920 as the International Federation of Christian Trade Unions (IFCTU), not to be confused with ICFTU, the International Confederation of Free Trade Unions. WCL headquarters is in Brussels, Belgium.

WORLD FEDERATION OF DEVELOPMENT FINANCING INSTITUTIONS (WFDFI) (Spanish: Federación Mundial de Instituciónes Financieras de Desarollo, WFDFI) world federation that promotes improved technical operations of, and coordination among, worldwide development banking activities. Federation members include development financing institutions. The federation was established in 1979, and its headquarters is in Madrid, Spain.

WORLD FOOD COUNCIL (WFC) a UN body that was created in December 1974 to help eliminate hunger and malnutrition. The council monitors world food production, consumption, and trade patterns. The council provides a forum for international discussion and assistance on ways of improving food production in developing countries and in increasing world food security. WFC headquarters is in Rome, Italy.

WORLD FOOD PROGRAM (WFP) a UN program created in 1963 that administers the International Emergency Food Reserve and supports projects that increase agricultural production, nutrition, and social and economic development in developing countries. Its headquarters is in Rome, Italy.

WORLD HEALTH ORGANIZATION (WHO) (French: Organisation Mondiale de la Santé, OMS) a specialized agency of the United Nations that sets standards for the quality control of drugs, vaccines, and other substances affecting health. WHO was established in July 1946, and its headquarters is in Geneva, Switzerland. *see also* CODEX ALIMENTARIUS COMMISSION.

WORLD INTELLECTUAL PROPERTY ORGANIZATION (WIPO) (French: Organisation Mondiale de la Propriété Intellectuelle, OMPI) organization that promotes protection of intellectual property around the world through cooperation among states and that administers various "unions," each founded on a multilateral treaty and dealing with the legal and administrative aspects of intellectual property. The organization was established in 1967 (came into force in 1970) and became a specialized agency of the UNITED NATIONS in December 1974. Its headquarters is in Geneva, Switzerland.

WORLD METEOROLOGICAL ORGANIZATION (WMO) organization that facilitates worldwide cooperation in establishing a network for meteorological, hydrological, and geophysical observations for exchanging meteorological and related information and for promoting standardization in meteorological measurements. WMO headquarters is in Geneva, Switzerland.

WORLD MONEY FRONT a daily column appearing in the JOURNAL OF COMMERCE that keeps tabs on the U.S. DOLLAR and other key currencies.

WORLD PRICE the price of a GOOD outside of any country's borders and therefore exclusive of any TARIFFS or SUBSIDIES that might apply crossing a border into a country but inclusive of any that might apply crossing out of a country. *see also* MARKET PRICE.

WORLD SHIPPING TIMETABLE a table appearing fortnightly in the second section of the JOURNAL OF COMMERCE. It is a compilation of scheduled ship departures with Estimated Times of Arrival (ETA) listed according to ports of destination, and in alphabetical order. The first date shown is the scheduled sailing date from the loading port. The second date is the estimated date of arrival at the port of destination, followed by the name of the vessel and the carrier's SHIP-CARD number.

WORLD TOURISM ORGANIZATION (WTO) organization associated with the UNITED NATIONS. It is an intergovernmental technical body dealing with all aspects of tourism. The organization promotes and develops tourism as a means of contributing to economic development, international understanding, peace, and prosperity. The WTO provides a world clearinghouse for the collection, analysis, and dissemination of technical tourism information, and it offers national tourism administrations and organizations a means for multilateral approaches to international discussions and negotiations on tourism policy and practice. The organization was established in November 1974, and its headquarters is in Madrid, Spain.

WORLD TRADE CENTER a site, in a city, composed of area business people who represent firms engaged in international trade and shipping, banks, forwarders, customs brokers, government agencies, and other service organizations involved in world trade. These organizations conduct educational programs on international business and organize promotional events to stimulate interest in world trade.

WORLD TRADE CENTER NETWORK *see* NETWORK.

WORLD TRADE CLUBS locally or regionally based organizations in the United States and around the world of IMPORTERS, EXPORTERS, CUSTOMS BROKERS, FREIGHT FORWARDERS, attorneys, bankers, manufacturers, and shippers.

WORLD TRADE ORGANIZATION (WTO) the WTO was established in 1995 as an international organization of comparable stature to the WORLD BANK and the INTERNATIONAL MONETARY FUND (IMF). The organization facilitates implementation of trade agreements reached in the URUGUAY ROUND by bringing them under one institutional umbrella, requiring full participation of all countries in one trading system and providing a permanent forum to discuss new issues facing the international trading system. The WTO system is available only to countries that

- are contracting parties to the GENERAL AGREEMENT ON TARIFFS AND TRADE (GATT),
- agree to adhere to all the Uruguay Round agreements, and
- submit schedules of market access commitments for industrial goods, agricultural goods, and services.

Provisions to establish the WTO were reached in the Uruguay Round of the GATT.

WORLD TRADE ORGANIZATION AGRICULTURE AGREEMENT the agreement within the WORLD TRADE ORGANIZATION (WTO) that commits member governments to improve MARKET ACCESS and reduce trade-distorting SUBSIDIES in agriculture.

WORLD TRADERS DATA REPORTS (WTDR) a U.S. INTERNATIONAL TRADE ADMINISTRATION (ITA) fee-based service that provides a confidential background report on a specific foreign company, prepared by commercial officers overseas. WTDRs provide information about the type of organization, year established, relative size, number of employees, general reputation, territory covered, language preferred, product lines handled, principal owners, financial references, and trade references. WTDRs include narrative information about the reliability of the foreign company.

WORLD WIDE WEB (WWW or W3) a computer-based text retrieval system (hypertext) that enables the user to access or gain information related to a particular text-based, distributed information system. WWW was created by researchers at CERN in Switzerland. Users may create, edit, or browse hypertext documents. The CLIENTS and SERVERS are freely available.

W.P.A. *see* WITH PARTICULAR AVERAGE.

WTDR *see* WORLD TRADERS DATA REPORTS.

WTO *see* WORLD TOURISM ORGANIZATION; WORLD TRADE ORGANIZATION.

WWW *see* WORLD WIDE WEB.

XYZ

XENOPHOBIA irrational fear of strangers or those who are different from oneself.

YEMEN RIAL unit of currency, Yemen (100 fils equal 1 rial).

YEN unit of currency, Japan.

YEN AREA (YEN BLOC) *see* CURRENCY AREA.

YOROSHIKU TANOMU (Japanese) verbal directions given by managers to worker groups to behave appropriately in Japan. Appropriate behavior includes the concepts of initiative and teamwork.

YUAN unit of currency, People's Republic of China (10 jiao equal 100 fen equal 1 yuan).

ZAIBATSU centralized, family-dominated economic groups, which dominated the Japanese economy until the end of World World II, at which time they were dissolved. With the passage of time, many of these groups have come back together, and they now cooperate again, as much as they did at the time they were dissolved. *see also* KEIRETSU.

ZAIKAI the business leaders in Japan who represent the society's "power elite." Zaikai not only represents the leaders in Japan's corporations but also four key groups that personify the totality of the structure of power in Japan. They are Keidanren (Federation of Industrial Organizations), Nikkeiren (Japanese Federation of Employers' Associations), Keizai Doyukai (The Committee for Economic Development), and the Japan Chamber of Commerce.

ZAIRE unit of currency, Zaire.

ZANGGER COMMITTEE a committee of the Nonproliferation Treaty for Exporters that examines controls enacted pursuant to the NUCLEAR NONPROLIFERATION TREATY (NPT) by refining the list of items requiring nuclear safeguards. The Zangger Committee consists of 23 Nuclear Nonproliferation Treaty nuclear supplier nations, which includes all nuclear weapons states except France and China. Through a series of consultations in the early 1970s, the countries of the Zangger Committee compiled a "trigger list" of nuclear materials and equipment. The shipment of any item on the list to a nonnuclear weapons state "triggers" the requirement of INTERNATIONAL ATOMIC ENERGY AGENCY (IAEA) safeguards. Because the Zangger Committee is associated with the NPT, its members are obligated to treat all nonnuclear weapons parties to the treaty alike. For fear of discrediting the NPT, the Zangger countries cannot target strict nuclear controls toward certain nations with questionable proliferation credentials. The NPT binds them to assist nonnuclear weapons states with peaceful atomic energy projects.

ZEP Zone d'Exchanges Préférentiels pour les Etats de l'Afrique de l'Est et de l'Afrique Australe. *see also* PREFERENTIAL TRADE AREA FOR EASTERN AND SOUTHERN AFRICAN STATES.

ZERO COUPON BOND a security that pays no interest, but is sold at a heavy discount from its face value and redeemed at par at some future date.

ZICHTPAPIER (Dutch) *see* SIGHT DRAFT.

ZIONISM a Jewish nationalist movement that came into being during the second half of the nineteenth century in Central and Eastern Europe. Zionists wish to become free to rebuild a Jewish state in Israel.

ZIP CODE numerical code, established by the U.S. Postal Service, used for the purpose of routing and to identify delivery zones. Some U.S. CARRIERS apply this code for FREIGHT in the same manner.

ZLOTY (ZLOTYCH) unit of currency, Poland.

ZOLL (German) *see* CUSTOMS.

ZONE
1. a logical group of computer NETWORK devices.
2. any one of a number of sections or districts in the United States or of the world used for the purpose of establishing proper rates for parcels, mail, pickup, and delivery.

ZONE D'EXCHANGES PREFERENTIELS POUR LES ETATS DE L'AFRIQUE DE L'EST ET DE L'AFRIQUE AUSTRALE (ZEP) *see* PREFERENTIAL TRADE AREA FOR EASTERN AND SOUTHERN AFRICAN STATES.

ZONE FACILITIES areas available in a FOREIGN TRADE ZONE for operations involving storage, testing, distributing, sorting, cleaning, sampling, relabeling, repackaging, repairing, manipulating, mixing, salvaging, destroying, inspecting, exhibiting, assembling, and other processing.

ZONE-RESTRICTED MERCHANDISE a category used by the U.S. CUSTOMS SERVICE when entering IMPORTED goods being forwarded into a FOREIGN TRADE ZONE. Because these goods are considered EXPORTED at the time they are entered into the zone, they cannot be brought back into U.S. Customs territory.

ZONE STATUS legal status of merchandise that has been admitted to a U.S. FOREIGN TRADE ZONE, thereby becoming subject to the provisions of the Foreign Trade Zone Act (FTZA).

ZONE USER corporation, partnership, or party that uses a U.S. FOREIGN TRADE ZONE for storage, handling, processing, or manufacturing merchandise in ZONE status, whether foreign or domestic.

ZPEX special zones set aside as FREE-TRADE AREAS (FTA) in Brazil.

ZYKLON B a form of hydrogen cyanide. Signs and symptoms of inhalation include increased respiratory rate, restlessness, headache, and giddiness, followed later by convulsions, vomiting, respiratory failure, and unconsciousness.

Appendix A
International Abbreviations and Acronyms

A

AADFI Association of African Development Finance Institutions

AAEI American Association of Exporters and Importers

AAIB Arab–African International Bank

AAR Against All Risks

AATPO Association of African Trade Promotion Organizations

ABC American Business Center

ABCA Association des Banques Centrales Africaines

ABEDA Arab Bank for Economic Development in Africa

ABI American Business Initiative; Automated Broker Interface

ABTA Association of British Travel Agents

ACAB Association of Central African Banks

ACC Administration Committee on Coordination; United Nations Administrative Committee on Co-ordination; Arab Cooperation Council

ACCT Agence de Coopération Culturelle et Technique (Agency for Cultural and Technical Cooperation)

ACDA Arms Control and Disarmament Agency

ACEP Advisory Committee on Export Policy

ACH Automated Clearinghouse

ACP African, Caribbean, and Pacific developing countries

ACPC Association of Coffee-Producing Countries

ACS Automated Commercial System

ACT Amazonian Cooperation Treaty

ACTPN Advisory Committee on Trade Policy and Negotiations

ACU Asian Clearing Union

AD Antidumping

ADB Asian Development Bank

ADF African Development Foundation; Asian Development Fund

ADFAED Abu Dhabi Fund for Arab Economic Development

ADRs Advance Determination Rulings; American Depository Receipts

ADS Agent/Distributor Service

Ad Val Ad Valorem

AECA Arms Export Control Act

AEF Africa Enterprise Fund

AEN Administrative Exception Note

AERP Automated Export Reporting Program

AFC African Groundnut Council

AFDB African Development Bank

AFDF African Development Fund

AFESD Arab Fund for Economic and Social Development

AFKN Armed Forces Korea Network

AFREXIMBANK African Export-Import Bank

AFTA ASEAN Free Trade Area

AG Aktiengesellschaft; Australia Group

AGRICOLA Agricultural On-Line Access

AGRIS Agriculture Information System

AIAFD Association of African Development Finance Institutions

AIB Arab International Bank

AIBD Association of International Bond Dealers

AID Agency for International Development

AIES Automated Information Exchange System

AIG Airbus Industries Group

AIOEC Association of Iron Ore Exporting Countries

AIT American Institute in Taiwan

AITS Automated Information Transfer System

AKA Ausfuhrkredit-Gesellschaft

ALADI Asociación Latinoamericana de Integración

ALIDE Associación Latinoamericana de Institutiones Financieras

ALJ Administrative Law Judge

AMB Ambassador

AMF Arab Monetary Fund

AMS Agricultural Marketing Service; Automated Manifest Systems

AMSCO African Management Services Company

AMU Arab Maghreb Union

ANEPC National Accord for Raising Productivity and Quality

ANRPC Association of Natural Rubber Producing Countries

ANS Ansvarlig Selskap

APDF Africa Project Development Facility

APEC Asian–Pacific Economic Cooperation

APO Administrative Protective Order; Army Post Office; Asian Productivity Organization

ARSO African Regional Organization for Standardization

ASDF Asian Development Fund

ASEAN Association of Southeast Asian Nations

ASP American Selling Price

ATFP Arab Trade Financing Program

ATI American Traders Index; Andean Trade Initiative

ATLAS Automated Trade Locator Assistance Network

ATMIC Agricultural Trade and Marketing Information Center

ATO African Timber Organization

ATOs Agricultural Trade Offices

ATP Advanced Technology Products

ATPA Andean Trade Preference Act

ATPI Andean Trade Preference Initiative

AUMA Die Ausstellungs- und Messe-Ausschuss der Deutschen Wirtschaft

AUP Acceptable Use Policy

AVE Ad Valorem Equivalent

AWB Airway Bill

B

BACEN Central Bank of Brazil

BADEA Banque Arabe pour le Développement Economique en Afrique

BAGGAGE General License—BAGGAGE

BANAMEX Banco National de Mexico

BANCOMEXT Banco Nacional de Comercio Exterior

BARs Buy American Restrictions

BCEAO Banque Centrale des Etats de l'Afrique de l'Ouest

BCIE Banco Centroamericano de Integración Económico

BCIU Business Council for International Understanding

BCS Border Cargo Selectivity

BDCI Bank of Documentary Credit Insurance

BDEAC Banque de Développement des Etats de l'Afrique Centrale

BDEGL Banque de Développement des Etats du Grand Lac

BEAC Banque des Etats de l'Afrique Centrale

BECC Border Environment Cooperation Commission

BEET Business Executive Enforcement Team

BENELUX Belgium, Netherlands, and Luxembourg Economic Union

BERI Business Environment Risk Index

BfAi Bundesstelle für Aussenhandelsinformation

BFC Business Facilitation Center

BFCE Banque Française du Commerce Extérieur

BHC Bank Holding Company

BHC British High Commission

BIA Best Information Available

BIC Business Income Coverage

BID Banco Interamericano de Desarrollo

BIE Bureau of International Expositions

BIL Bill of Lading

BIO Business Information Office

BIS Bank for International Settlements

BISNIS Business Information Service for the Newly Independent States

BIT(s) Bilateral Investment Treaty(ies)

B/L Bill of Lading

BLADEX Banco Latinoamericano de Exportaciones

BLEU Belgium–Luxembourg Economic Union

BMWi Bundesministerium für Wirtschaft

BOAD Banque Ouest-Africaine de Développement

BOP Balance of Payments

BOT Balance of Trade

BOTB British Overseas Trade Board

BPI Business Proprietary Information

BRITE Basic Research in Industrial Technologies in Europe

BROU Banco de la Republica Oriental del Uruguay

BSA Bilateral Steel Agreements

BTN Brussels Tariff Nomenclature

BWC Biological Weapons Convention

BXA Bureau of Export Administration

C

C&F Cost and Freight

CABEE Consortia of American Businesses in Eastern Europe

CABEI Central American Bank for Economic Integration

CABNIS Consortia of American Businesses in the Newly Independent States

CAC Codex Alimentarius Commission

CACM Central American Common Market

C.A.D. Cash Against Documents

CAD/CAM Computer Aided Design/Computer Aided Manufacturing

CAEU Council of Economic Arab Unity

CAF Corporación Andina de Fomentó

CAP Common Agricultural Policy

CAR Commercial Activity Report

CARIBCAN Caribbean-Canadian Economic Trade Development Assistance Program

CARICOM Caribbean Common Market

CARIFTA Caribbean Free Trade Association

CASE Council of American States in Europe

CBD Cash Before Delivery; *Commerce Business Daily*

CBERA Caribbean Basin Economic Recovery Act

CBI Caribbean Basin Initiative

CBW Chemical and Biological Weapons

CBWAS Central Bank of West African States

CCAO Chambre de Cooperation de l'Afrique de l'Ouest

CCC Canadian Commercial Corporation; Commodity Credit Corporation; Customs Cooperation Council

CCCE Caisse Centrale de Coopération Economique

CCCN Customs Cooperation Council Nomenclature

CCD Conseil de Coopération Douanière

CCF CoCom Cooperation Forum

CCFF Compensatory and Contingency Financing Facility

CCIR Comité Consultatif International des Radiocommunications

CCITT Consultative Committee for International Telephone and Telegraph; Comité Consultatif International Télégraphique et Téléphonique

CCL Commerce Control List

CCNAA Coordination Council for North American Affairs

CCTH Council of Canadian Trading Houses

CDB Caribbean Development Bank

CDC Commonwealth Development Corporation

CDI Capital Development Initiative

CD-ROM Compact Disc-Read Only Memory

CDT Center for Defense Trade

CE Committee of Experts; Communautés Européenes; Conformité Européene

CEA Chinese Economic Area

CEAO Communauté Economique de l'Afrique de l'Ouest

CEAU Council of Economic Arab Unity

CECA Communauté Européenne du Charbon et de l'Acier

CEE Commission Economique pour l'Europe

CEEAC Communauté Economique des Etats de l'Afrique Centrale

CEEB Customs Electronic Bulletin Board

CEENET Central and East European Networking Association

CEFTA Central Europe Free Trade Association

CEN European Committee for Standardization

CENELEC European Committee for Electrotechnical Standardization

CENTO Central Treaty Organization

CEPAL Comision Económica para America Latina y el Caribe

CEPGL Communauté Economique des Pays des Grands Lacs

CEPT Conference Européenne des Administrations des Postes et Télécommunications

CERN Centre Européen de Recherche Nucleaire

CES Comprehensive Export Schedule

CET Common External Tariff

CFC Common Fund for Commodities

CFCE Centre Français du Commerce Extérieur

CFIS Center for Foreign Investor Services

CFIUS Committee on Foreign Investment in the United States

CFR Code of Federal Regulations

CG Consul General; Consulate Generale

CGIAR Consultative Group on International Agricultural Research

CGT Central Geral dos Trabalhadores

CHB Customhouse Broker

CHG Charge d'Affaires

CIA Cash in Advance; Central Intelligence Agency; Current Insured Amount

CIAT Centro Internacional de Agricultura Tropical

CICA Confederation Internationale du Credit Agricole

CIDA Canadian International Development Agency

CIF Cost, Insurance, and Freight

CILSS Comité Permanent Interétats de Lutte contre la Sécheresse

CIMS Commercial Information Management System

CIPs Commodity Import Programs

CIR Center for International Research

CIS Commonwealth of Independent States

CISG Convention on Contracts for the International Sale of Goods

CIT Court of International Trade

CITA Committee for the Implementation of Textile Agreements

CIV Customs Import Value

CJ Commodity Jurisdiction

CKD Completely Knocked Down

CLDP Commercial Law Development Program

CMA Common Monetary Agreement

CMEA Council for Mutual Economic Assistance
CMN Conselho Monetario Nacional
CNUSA Commercial News USA
COAP Cottonseed Oil Assistance Program
COCOM Coordinating Committee on Multilateral Export Controls
CODEX Codex Alimentarius Commission
COD Cash on Delivery
COE Council of Europe
COFACE Compagnie Française d'Assurance pour le Commerce Extérieur
COFC Container on Flat Car
COM Costs of Manufacture; Chief of Mission
COMECON Council for Mutual Economic Assistance
COMSAT Communications Satellite Corporation
COOC Consultation Office for Overseas Companies
COP Cost of Production
COPAL Cocoa Producers Alliance
COPANT Comision Panamericana de Normas Tecnicas
CORECT Committee on Renewable Energy, Commerce, and Trade
CPCM Comité Permanent Consultatif du Maghreb
CPE Centrally Planned Economy
CPT Carriage Paid To
CSCE Conference on Security and Cooperation in Europe
CSP Common Standard Level of Effective Protection
CSS Customized Sales Survey
CT Countertrade

CTD Committee on Trade and Development
CTF Certified Trade Fair
CTIS Center for Trade and Investment Services
CTL Constructive Total Loss
CTP Composite Theoretical Performance
CV Constructed Value
CVD Countervailing Duty
CUM Brazilian Securities Commission
CWC Chemical Weapons Convention
CWO Cash With Order
CXT Common External Tariff

D

D/A Documents Against Acceptance; Discharged Afloat
DA Development Assistance
DAC Development Assistance Committee
DACON Data on Consulting Firms
DAEs Dynamic Asian Economies
DAF Delivered at Frontier
DANIDA Danish International Development Assistance
DASH Dual Access Storage Handling
DBGLS Development Bank of the Great Lakes States
DBP Development Bank of the Philippines
DCM Deputy Chief of Mission
DCR Domestic Content Requirements
DCS Defense Conversion Subcommittee
DD Double Deck
D/D Date Draft
DDU Delivered Duty Unpaid
DECs District Export Councils

DEG Deutsche Finanzierungsgesellschaft für Beteiligungen in Entwicklungsländern GmbH

DEIP Dairy Export Incentive Program

DEM Deutsche Mark

DEP Department of Export Promotion

DEQ Delivered Ex Quay

DEX Delivered Ex Ship

DFA Development Fund for Africa

DFI Direct Foreign Investment

DFP Duty-Free Port

DFZ Duty-Free Zone

DISC Domestic International Sales Corporation

DL Distribution License

DLO Dispatch Loading Only

DMC Direct Mail Collection

DMs Definitional Missions

DO District Office

DOA Documents on Acceptance

DOL Department of Labor

D/P Documents Against Payment

DP Direct Port

DPA Defense Production Act

DPAS Defense Priorities and Allocation System

D-RAM Dynamic Random Access Memory

DREE Direction des Relations Economiques Extérieures

D/S Days After Sighting

DST Double-Stacked Container Train

DTAG Defense Trade Advisory Group

DTC Defense Trade Controls

DTI Department of Trade and Industry

DTR Defense Trade Regulations

DTSA Defense Technology Security Administration

DTWG Defense Trade Working Group

DV 1 Declaration of Particulars Relating to Customs Value

DVC Delivery Verification Certificate

DW Deadweight

E

E.&O.E. Errors and Omissions Excepted

EAA Export Administration Act

EAC Export Assistance Center

EADB East African Development Bank

EAEC East Asian Economic Caucus

EAI Enterprise for the Americas Initiative

EAITC External Affairs and International Trade Canada

E.A.O.N. Except As Otherwise Noted

EAR Export Administration Regulations

EARB Export Administration Review Board

E.B. Eastbound

EBB Economic Bulletin Board

EBRD European Bank for Reconstruction and Development

EC European Commission; European Community

EC92 Europe 1992

ECA Economic Commission for Africa

ECASS Export Control Automated Support System

ECB European Central Bank

ECCAS Economic Community of Central African States

ECCB East Caribbean Central Bank

ECCN Export Control Classification Number

ECD Exporter Counseling Division

ECE Economic Commission for Europe

ECGD Export Credit Guarantee Department

ECJ European Court of Justice

ECL Export Control List

ECLAC Economic Commission for Latin America and the Caribbean

ECLS Export Contact List Service

ECO Economic Cooperation Organization

ECOSOC Economic and Social Council

ECOWAS Economic Community of West African States

ECRT European Community of Research and Technology

ECSC European Coal and Steel Community

ECU European Currency Unit

EDB Exporter Data Base

EDC Export Development Corporation

EDF European Development Bank

EDIFACT Electronic Data Interchange for Administration, Commerce, and Transportation

EDO Export Development Office

E.E. Errors Excepted

EEA European Economic Area

EEBIC Eastern Europe Business Information Center

EEC European Economic Community

EEP Export Enhancement Program

EES European Economic Space

EEZ Exclusive Economic Zone

EFF Extended Fund Facility; Electronic Frontier Foundation

EFTA European Free Trade Association

EIB European Investment Bank

EIS Export Information System

ELAIN Electronic License Application and Information Network

ELAN Export Legal Assistance Network

ELVIS Electronic Visa Information System; Export License Voice Information System

EMC Export Management Company

EMCF European Monetary and Cooperation Fund

EMI European Monetary Institute

EMS Export Management System; European Monetary System

EMU European Monetary Union

EN European Norm

EOP European Patent Office

EOTC European Organization for Testing and Certification

EP European Parliament

EPC Economic Policy Council; European Patent Convetion

EPCI Enhanced Proliferation Control Initiative

EPIC European Privatization and Investment Corporation

EPO European Patent Office

EPS Export Promotion Services

EPZs Export Processing Zones

ERLC Export Revolving Line of Credit

ERM European Exchange Rate Mechanism; Exchange Rate Mechanism

ERS Economic Research Service

ESA European Space Agency

ESAF Enhanced Structural Adjustment Facility

ESCAP Economic and Social Commission for Asia and the Pacific

ESCB European System of Central Banks

ESCWA Economic and Social Commission for Western Asia

ESF Economic Stabilization Fund; Economic Support Fund

ESP Exporter's Sale Price; Economic Solidarity Pact

EST Estimated

ETA European Technical Approval

ETC Export Trading Company

ETSI European Telecommunications Standards Institute

ETUC European Trade Union Confederation

EU European Union

EUCLID European Cooperation for the Long Term in Defense

EURATOM European Atomic Energy Community

EUREKA European Research Coordination Agency

EURIBOR Euro Interbank Offered Rate

EURL Entreprise Unipersonnelle à Responsabilité Limitée

EUROSTAT Statistical Office of the European Community

EXCEL Export Credit Enhanced Leverage

EXIMBANK Export–Import Bank of the United States

EXPAT Expatriate

EXW Ex Works

F

F/A Free Astray

FAA Free of All Average

FAAS Foreign Affairs Administrative Support

FACET Future Automated Commercial Environment Team

FAK Freight All Kinds

FAO Food and Agricultural Organization

FAS Foreign Agricultural Service; Free Alongside Ship

FASB Financial Accounting Standards Board

FAZ Foreign Access Zone

FBIS Foreign Broadcast Information Service

FBP Foreign Buyer Program

FBSEA Foreign Bank Supervision Enhancement Act

FC&S Free of Capture and Seizure

FCA Free Carrier

FCIA Foreign Credit Insurance Association

FCIB Foreign Credit Interchange Bureau

FCIL Foreign Capital Inducement Law

FCN Friendship, Commerce and Navigation Treaty

FCO Foreign and Commonwealth Office

FCPA Foreign Corrupt Practices Act

FCSC Foreign Claims Settlement Commission

F.D. Free Discharge

FDIUS Foreign Direct Investment in the United States

FECA Foreign Exchange Control Act

FEMA Foreign Extraterritorial Measure Act of 1984

FEMIDE Federacion Mundial de Instituciones Financieras de Desarollo

FEOID Foreign Exchange Operations and Investment Department

FET Foreign Economic Trends

FFU Forty-Foot Units

F.F.A. Free From Average

FFP Food For Progress

FGIS Federal Grain Inspection Service

FI Free In

F.I.A. Full Interest Admitted

FIAS Foreign Investment Advisory Service

FIATA Federation Internationale des Associations de Transitaires

FII Foreign Investment Insurance

F.I.O. Free In and Out

FIRA Foreign Investment Review Agency

FIT Foreign Independent Tour

F.I.W. Free in Wagon

FMC Federal Maritime Commission

FMD Foreign Market Development Program

FMS Foreign Military Sales

FMV Foreign Market Value

FO Free Out

FOB Free on Board

FOGS Functioning of the GATT System

FOMEX Fondo para el Fomentó de las Exportaciones de Productos

FONAPRE Fund for Preventive Assistance

FONATUR National Foundation for Tourism

FONPLATA Fondo Financiero Para el Desarrollo de la Cuenca del Plata

FORDTIS Foreign Disclosure and Technical Information System

FOREX Foreign Exchange

FOR/FOT Free on Rail/Free on Truck

F.O.W. First Open Water

F.P.A. Free of Particular Average

FPAAC Free of Particular Average American Conditions

FPAEC Free of Particular Average English Conditions

FPFS Fines, Penalties, and Forfeitures System

FPG Foreign Parent Group

FPO Fleet Post Office

FR.&C.C. Free of Riot and Civil Commotion

FRA Forward (or Future) Rate Agreement

FSA Freedom Support Act

FSC Foreign Sales Corporation

FSI Foreign Service Institute

FSN Foreign Service National

FSO Foreign Service Officer

FSs Feasibility Studies

FSU Former Soviet Union

FT Foot

FTA Free-Trade Agreement; Free-Trade Area

FTC Federal Trade Commission

FTD Foreign Trade Division

FTI Foreign Traders Index

FTO Foreign Trade Organization

FTSR Foreign Trade Statistical Reporting

FTZs Foreign Trade Zones

F/X Foreign Exchange

G

G-5 Group of Five

G-7 Group of Seven

G-10 Group of Ten

G-11 Group of Eleven

G-15 Group of Fifteen

G-24 Group of Twenty-Four

G-77 Group of Seventy-Seven

GAB General Arrangements to Borrow

GATS General Agreement on Trade-In Services; General License—Aircraft on Temporary Sojourn

GATT General Agreement on Tariffs and Trade
GCC Gulf Cooperation Council
GCCI Global Contract Comprehensive Insurance
GCG General License—Shipments to Agencies of Cooperating Governments
G-COCOM General License—COCOM
GCT General License
G-DEST General License—Destination
GDP Gross Domestic Product
GE General Exception
GEF Global Environmental Facility
GEM Global Export Manager
GEMSU German Economic Monetary and Social Union
GFW General License—Free World
GIE Groupement d'Intérêt Economique
GIFT General License
GIT General License
GL General License
G-NNR General License—Nonnaval Reserve
GLR General License—Return (Replacement)
GLV General License—Shipments of Limited Value
GmbH Gesellschaft mit beschränkter Haftung
G-NGO General License
GNP Gross National Product
GSM General Sales Manager
GSP Generalized System of Preferences
GST Goods and Services Tax
GTDA General License—Technical Data Publicly Available
GTDR General License—Technical Data Restricted by Written Assurance

GTDU General License—Technical Data Restricted Without Written Assurance
G-TEMP General License—Temporary Export
GTF-US General License
GTZ Deutsche Gesellschaft für Technische Zusammenarbeit
GUS General License
GVN General License

H

HC High Commission
HIPC Heavily Indebted Poor Countries
HMHC Her Majesty's High Commission
HS Harmonized System
HT Height
HTS Harmonized Tariff Schedule
HTSUS Harmonized Tariff Schedule of the United States

I

IACAC Inter-American Commercial Arbitration Commission
IACC International Anticounterfeiting Coalition
IACO Inter-African Coffee Organization
IADB Inter-American Development Bank
IAEA International Atomic Energy Agency
IAEL International Atomic Energy List
IAF International Accreditation Forum
IAIGC Inter-Arab Investment Guarantee Corporation
IARCs International Agricultural Research Centers
IASC International Accounting Standards Committee

IATA International Air Transport Association

IAU International Accounting Unit

IBA International Banking Act

IBC International Banking Center

IBEC International Bank for Economic Cooperation

IBEX International Bank for Economic Cooperation

IBF International Banking Facility

IBIS International Business Reply Service

IBOR Interbank Offered Rate

IBOS International Business Opportunities Service

IBRACON Brazilian Institute of Accountants

IBRD International Bank for Reconstruction and Development

IBRS International Business Reply Service

IC Import Certificate

ICA International Cocoa Agreement

ICAC International Confederation of Agricultural Credit

ICAO International Civil Aviation Organization

ICB International Competitive Bidding

ICC International Chamber of Commerce

ICCEC Intergovernmental Council of Copper Exporting Countries

ICE Istituto Nazionale per il Commercio Estero

ICEP Instituto do Comércio de Portugal

ICFTU International Confederation of Free Trade Unions

ICGEB International Center for Genetic Engineering and Biotechnology

ICHCA International Cargo Handling Coordination Association

ICJ International Court of Justice

ICMS Imposto Dobre Circulacão de Mercadorias y Servicos

ICO International Cocoa Organization; International Coffee Organization; International Congress Office

ICON Indexed Currency Option Note

ICS Investment Climate Statement

ICSHT International Center for Science and High Technology

ICSID International Centre for the Settlement for Investment Disputes

ICSU International Council of Scientific Unions

ICTF Intermodal Container Transfer Facility

ICTP International Center for Theoretical Physics

IDA International Development Association

IDB Inter-American Development Bank; International Data Base

IDIN International Development Information Network

IDR International Depository Receipt

IDRC International Development Research Center

IE Infrequent Exporter

IEA International Energy Agency

IEB International Exhibitions Bureau

IEC International Electrotechnical Commission

IEEE Institute of Electrical and Electronics Engineers

IEEPA International Emergency Economic Powers Act

IEP International Economic Policy

IEPG Independent European Program Group

IESC International Executive Service Corps

IFAC Industry Functional Advisory Committee

IFAD International Fund for Agricultural Development

IFC International Finance Corporation

IFE International Fisher Effect

IFRB International Frequency Registration Board

IFS In-Flight Survey

IFU Industrialization Fund for Developing Countries

IGADD Inter-Governmental Authority on Drought and Development

IGC Interagency Group on Countertrade

IIB International Investment Bank

IIC Inter-American Investment Corporation

IINREN Interagency Interim National Research and Education Network

IIPA International Intellectual Property Alliance

IIT Instruments of International Traffic

IJC International Jute Commission

IL Industrial List

ILO International Labor Organization

IMB International Maritime Bureau

IMF International Monetary Fund

IMI International Market Insight

IML International Munitions List

IMO International Maritime Organization

INFONAVIT National Housing Fund

INMARSAT International Maritime Satellite Organization

INPI Instituto Nacional de Propriedade Industrial

INR Initial Negotiating Right

INTELSAT International Telecommunications Satellite Organization

IOGA Industry-Organized, Government-Approved Mission

IOM International Organization for Migration

IPAC Industry Policy Advisory Committee

IPR Intellectual Property Rights

IPS Investment Promotion Services

IRA International Rubber Agreement

ISA Industry Subsector Analysis; International Sugar Agreement

ISAC Industry Sector Advisory Committee

ISDA International Swaps and Derivatives Association

IsDB Islamic Development Bank

ISDN Integrated Services Digital Network

ISLP Investment Sector Loan Program

ISNAR International Service for National Agricultural Research

ISO International Standards Organization

ISO9000 International Standards Organization 9000-9004

ISONET International Standards Organization Information Network

ISS Municipal Service Tax

ISSA International Social Security Association

IST Industry, Science, Technology Canada

ITA International Tin Agreement; International Trade Administration

ITAR International Traffic in Arms Regulations

ITC International Trade Center; International Trade Commission; International Tin Council

ITDB International Trade Data Bank

ITDCs International Trade Development Centers

ITU International Telecommunication Union

IVANS International Value-Added Network Services

IVL Individually Validated License

IWO Interference with Operations

IWC International Wheat Council

J

JCIT Joint Committee for Investment and Trade

JDB Japan Development Bank

JEIC Japan Export Information Center

JETRO Japan External Trade Organization

JEXIM Export–Import Bank of Japan

JI Jemaah Islamiah

JICA Japan International Cooperation Agency

JIT Just in Time

JPRS Joint Publication Research Service

JSF Japan Special Fund

K

KBO Kangera Basin Organization

KCAB Korean Commercial Arbitration Board

KDD Kokusai Denshin Denwa

KFAED Kuwait Fund for Arab Economic Development

KFTA Korea Foreign Trade Association

KfW Kreditanstalt für Wiederaufbau

KG Kommanditgesellschaft

KGAA Kommandit-gesellschaft auf Aktien

KIPO Korean Industrial Property Office

KOBACO Korea Broadcasting Advertising Company

KOTRA Korea Trade Promotion Corporation

L

L&R Lake and Rail Transport

LAES Latin American Economic System

LAFTA Latin American Free Trade Association

LAIA Latin American Integration Association

LAT Latitude

L/C Letter of Credit

LCB Local Competitive Bidding

LCBC Lake Chad Basin Commission

LCL Less Than Carload; Less Than Container Load

L.&D. Loss and Damage

LDC Less-Developed Country

LDG Loading

LIB Limited International Bidding

LIBID London Interbank Bid Rate

LIBOR London Interbank Offered Rate

LIFFE London International Financial Futures and Options Exchange

LIMEAN London Interbank Mean Rate

LLDCs Lesser Developed Countries

LO/LO Lift On/Lift Off

LTD Limited (Liability)

LTL Less Than a Truckload

LTFV Less Than Fair Value

LTGE Lighterage

M

MAI Multilateral Agreement on Investment

MC Minister Counsellor

MCC Mocado Comur Centroamericano

MCCA Mercado Común Centroamericano

MCTL Militarily Critical Technologies List

MDBs Multilateral Development Banks

MDSE Merchandise

MFA Multifiber Arrangement

MFN Most-Favored Nation Treatment

MHW Ministry of Health and Welfare

MIA Maximum Insured Amount

MIF Multilateral Investment Fund

MIGA Multilateral Investment Guarantee Agency

MIME Multipurpose INTERNET Mail Extensions

MIN Manufacture Identification Number

MIPRO Manufactured Imports Promotion Organization

MITI Ministry of International Trade and Industry

MKR Matchmaker Program

MOCP Market-Oriented Cooperation Plan

MOFERT Ministry of Foreign Economic Relations and Trade

MOL Ministry of Labor

MOSS Market-Oriented, Sector-Selective

MOU Memorandum of Understanding

MPP Market Promotion Program

MPT Ministry of Posts and Telecommunications

MRAs Mutual Recognition Agreements

MRU Mano River Union

MSA Multilateral Steel Agreement

MTCR Missile Technology Control Regime

MTEC Missile Technology Export Control Group

MTN Multilateral Trade Negotiations

MTO Multilateral Trade Organization

MTOPS Million Theoretical Operations Per Second

N

NAC National Advisory Council on International Monetary and Financial Policies

NACE North American Commission on the Environment

NADBank North American Development Bank

NAFIN Nacional Financiera

NAFO North Atlantic Fisheries Organization

NAFTA North American Free Trade Agreement

NAL National Agricultural Library

NAM Nonaligned Movement

NASDA National Association of State Departments of Agriculture; National Association of State Development Agencies

NATAP North American Trade Automation Prototype

NATO North Atlantic Treaty Organization

NBA Niger Basin Authority

NBP National Bank of Poland

NCBFAA National Custom Brokers and Forwarders Association of America, Inc.

NCITD National Council on International Trade Documentation

NCTA Northwest Corridor Transit Agreement

NDER National Defense Executive Reserve

NEA Nuclear Energy Agency

NEBS New Exporters to Border States

NEDA National Economic Development Authority

NEXOS New Exporters Overseas

NEXUS New Exports to U.S. South

NGO Nongovernmental Organization

NIB Nordic Investment Bank

NIC National Intelligence Council

NIC Newly Industrializing Countries

NIE Newly Industrializing Economies

NIPA National Income and Product Accounts

NIS Newly Independent States

NIST National Institute of Standards and Technology

NME Nonmarket Economy

NNPA Nuclear Nonproliferation Act

N.O.E. Not Otherwise Enumerated

N.O.H.P. Not Otherwise Herein Provided

N.O.I.B.N. Not Otherwise Indicated by Number; Not Otherwise Indexed by Name

NORAD Norwegian Agency for Development Cooperation

N.O.S. Not Otherwise Specified

NPIS New Product Information Service

NPT Nuclear Nonproliferation Treaty

NRBP Natural Resource-Based Products

NRC Nuclear Regulatory Commission

NSC National Security Council

NSD National Security Directive

NSF National Science Foundation

NSG Nuclear Suppliers Group

NSO National Security Override

N.S.P.F. Not Specifically Provided For

NTBs Nontariff Barriers

NTDB National Trade Data Bank

NTE National Trade Estimates Report

NTF Nigeria Trust Fund

NTM New-To-Market

NTMs Nontariff Measures

NTT Nippon Telegraph and Telephone Corporation

NVOC Nonvessel Owning Carrier

NVOCC Nonvessel Operating Common Carrier

O

O.&R. Ocean and Rail

OAPEC Organization of Arab Petroleum Exporting Countries

OAS Organization of American States

OATUU Organization of African Trade Union Unity

OAU Organization of African Unity

OBL Ocean Bill of Lading

OBR Overseas Business Report

OBU Offshore Banking Unit

OC Operating Committee

ODA Official Development Assistance

ODS Operating Differential Subsidy

OEA Organización de los Estados Americanos (Organization of American States, OAS)

OECD Organization for Economic Cooperation and Development

OECF Overseas Economic Cooperation Fund

OECS Organization of Eastern Caribbean States

OEL Office of Export Licensing

OETCA Office of Export Trading Company Affairs

OFAC Office of Foreign Assets Control

OFD Ocean Freight Differential

OHG Offene Handelsgesellschaft

OIC Organization of the Islamic Conference

OICD Office of International Cooperation and Development

OMA Orderly Marketing Agreement

OMC Office of Munitions Control

OMPI Organisation Mondiale de la Propriété Intellectuelle

OMVG Organisation pour la Mise en Valeur du Fleuve Gambie

OMVS Organisation pour la Mise en Valeur du Fleuve Sénégal

O/N Order Notify

OPEC Organization of Petroleum Exporting Countries

OPIC Overseas Private Investment Corporation

O.S.&D. Over, Short, and Damage

OSROK Office of Supply, Republic of Korea

O.T. On Truck or Railway

OTM Old-To-Market

OVs Orientation Visits

P

P.A. Particular Average

PBAS Polish Business Advisory Service

PBEC Pacific Basin Economic Council

PCT Patent Cooperation Treaty

P.D. Per Diem; Public Domain

PDR Processing Data Rate

PDITI Industrial Development Programs

PEC President's Export Council

PECC Pacific Economic Cooperation Council

PECSEA President's Export Council, Subcommittee on Export Administration

PEFCO Private Export Funding Corporation

PFP Policy Framework Paper

PIERS Port Import/Export Reporting Service

PIP Post-Initiated Promotion

PLC Prelicense Check; Private Limited Company

PNR National Revolutionary Party (Mexico)

PNTR Permanent Normal Trading Relations

PO Principal Officer

PP Purchase Price

PPA Protocol of Provisional Application

PSEG Pact for Stability and Economic Growth

PSV Postshipment Verification

PTA Preferential Trade Area; Preferential Trade Area for Eastern and Southern Africa

PTT Postal Telegraph and Telephone

PVOs Private Voluntary Organizations

P.W. Packed Weight

Q

QRs Quantitative Restrictions

R

R.&.O. Rail and Ocean

R&R Rest and Recreation

RBPs Restrictive Business Practices

R.C.&L. Rail, Canal, and Lake

RCS Regular Catalog Show

RDA Romanian Development Agency

REFG Refrigerating, Refrigeration

RMF Rand Monetary Fund

RPFB Russian Project Finance Bank

RRF Registreate Revisorers Furening

RTT Round-Trip Time

RUIE Russian Union of Industrialists and Entrepreneurs

RWA Returned Without Action

S

S&D Special and Differential Treatment

S.A. Sociedad Anonima; Sociedad Anónima; Société Anonyme

S.A. de CV Sociedad Anónima

SAARC South Asian Association for Regional Cooperation

SABIT Special American Business Internship Training Program

SACU Southern African Customs Union

SADC Southern African Development Community

SAF Structural Adjustment Facility

SARL Société à Responsabilité Limitée

SAS Société par Actions Simplifiée

SASO Saudi Arabian Standards Organization

SBIC Small Business Investment Company Financing

S.C.&S. Strapped, Corded, and Sealed

SCO Senior Commercial Officer

S/D Sight Draft

S.D.D. Store Door Delivery

SDNs Specially Designated Nationals

SDRs Special Drawing Rights

SEA Single European Act

SEATO Southeast Asia Treaty Organization

SECOFI Secretaría de Comercio y Fomentó Industrial

SED Shipper's Export Declaration

SEED Support for East European Democracy

SELA Sistema Económico Latinoamericano

SEM Seminar Mission

SENAC Commercial Trade School Program

SENAI Industrial Training Program

SENC Sociedad en Comandita Simple

SEPD State Export Program Database

SEZ Special Economic Zone

SFO Solo Fair (overseas procured)

SFSC Shared Foreign Sales Corporation

SFW Solo Fair (Washington procured)

SGA Selling, General and Administrative (Expenses)

SIC Standard Industrial Classification

SICE Sistema de Información al Comercio Exterior

SIDA Swedish International Development Authority

SIFIDA Société Internationale Financiére pour les Investissements

SII Structural Impediments Initiative

SIJORI Singapore–Johor–Riau Growth Triangle

SIMIS Single Internal Market Information Service

S/IOGA State/Industry-Organized, Government-Approved Mission

SITC Standard International Tariff Classification

S.L.&C. Shipper's Load and Count

S.L.&T. Shipper's Load and Tally

SLD Ship That Has Sailed

SMART Software for Market Analysis and Restrictions on Trade

SMIPC Small and Medium Industry Promotion Corporation

SMSA Standard Metropolitan Statistical Area

SNAKE European Snake

SNAR International Service for National Agricultural Research

SNC Società in Nome Collettivo

SNDE National Agency for Economic Rights

SNEC Subgroup on Nuclear Export Coordination

S.O. Ship's Options; Shipping Order; Seller's Option

SOAP Sunflower Seed Oil Assistance Program

SOGA/IOGA State/Industry-Organized, Government-Approved Mission

SPA Società Per Azioni

S.P.D. Shipped

SPEC South Pacific Bureau for Economic Cooperation

SPF South Pacific Forum

S.R.&C.C. Strikes, Riots, and Civil Commotions

SRL Società a Responsabilité Limitata

S/S Steamship

S.S. Shipside

SSA Sub-Saharan Africa

S.T. Short Ton

STABEX Stabilisation des Exports

STDS Standards

STEs State Trading Enterprises

STELA System for Tracking Export License Applications

STM State Trade Mission

STR Steamer

SUCL Set Up Carload

SULCL Set Up in Less than a Carload

SV Sailing Vessel

SWEDECORP Swedish International Enterprise Development Corporation

SWIFT Society for Worldwide Interbank Financial Telecommunications

SYSMIN Systéme Mineral des Supports

T

TAA   Trade Adjustment Assistance
TAAC   Trade Adjustment Assistance Centers
TAC   Technical Advisory Committee
TARE   Tare Weight
TARIC   Integrated Tariff of the European Community
TBT   Technical Barrier to Trade
TCI   Third-Country Initiative
TCMD   Third-Country Meat Directive
TCN   Third-Country National
TDA   Trade and Development Agency
TDF   Transborder Data Flow
TDO   Table of Denial Orders
TEA   Targeted Export Assistance Program
TFC   Trade Fair Certification
TIAS   Treaties and Other International Acts Series
TIB   Temporary Importation under Bond
TIC   Trade Information Center
TIEA   Tax Information Exchange Agreement
T.L.O.   Total Loss Only
TM   Trade Mission
TNC   Trade Negotiations Committee; Transnational Corporation
TOFC   Trailer on Flat Car
TOP   Trade Opportunities Program
TOR   Terms of Reference
TPC   Trade Policy Committee
TPCC   Trade Promotion Coordinating Committee
TPE   Trade Promotion Event
TPIS   Trade Policy Information System
TPM   Trigger Price Mechanism
TPRG   Trade Policy Review Group

TPRM   Trade Policy Review Mechanism
TPSC   Trade Policy Staff Committee
TRIMs   Trade-Related Investment Measures
TRIPs   Trade-Related Aspects of Intellectual Property Rights
TRO   Temporary Restraining Order
TS   Trade Specialist
TSB   Textile Surveillance Body
TSUS   Tariff Schedules of the United States
TSUSA   Tariff Schedules of the United States Annotated
TWEA   Trading With the Enemy Act

U

UBO   Ultimate Beneficial Owner
UCC   Universal Copyright Convention
UCP   Uniform Customs and Practices
UDEAC   Union Douanière et Economique de l'Afrique Centrale
UIT   Union Internationale des Télécommunications
UMA   Union du Maghreb Arabe
UMOA   Union Monétaire Ouest-Africaine
UMR   Usual Marketing Requirements
UN   United Nations
UNCDF   United Nations Capital Development Fund
UNCED   United Nations Conference on Environment and Development
UNCHS   United Nations Commission on Human Settlements

UNCITRAL United Nations Commission on International Trade Law

UNCJIN United Nations Criminal Justice Information Network

UNCST United Nations Conference on Science and Technology

UNCTAD United Nations Conference on Trade and Development

UNDP United Nations Development Program

UNDRO United Nations Disaster Relief Organization

UN/ECE United Nations Economic Commission for Europe

UNEP United Nations Environment Program

UNESCO United Nations Educational, Scientific, and Cultural Organization

UNFPA United Nations Fund for Population Activities

UNGA United Nations General Assembly

UNHCR United Nations High Commissioner for Refugees

UNICEF United Nations Children's Fund

UNIDO United Nations Industrial Development Organization

UNIDROIT International Institute for the Unification of Private Law

UNITAR United Nations Institute for Training and Research

UNRISD United Nations Research Institute for Social Development

UNRWA United Nations Relief and Works Agency

UNSCOM United Nations Special Commission

UNU United Nations University

UNV United Nations Volunteers

UPEB Unión de Países Exportadores de Banano

US&FCS U.S. and Foreign Commercial Service

USDA U.S. Department of Agriculture

USAEDC U.S. Agricultural Export Development Council

US-AEP U.S.–Asia Environmental Program

USC U.S. Code

USCIB U.S. Council for International Business

USDIA U.S. Direct Investment Abroad

USEC U.S. Mission to the European Community

USIA U.S. Information Agency

USIDCA U.S. International Development Cooperation Agency

USITC U.S. International Trade Commission

USITO U.S. Interagency Trade Organization

USMA U.S. Maritime Administration

USML U.S. Munitions List

USP U.S. Price

USTR U.S. Trade Representative

USTTA U.S. Travel and Tourism Administration

USUN U.S. Mission to the United Nations

UTC Universal Time Coordinated

V

VAL Value

VAT Value-Added Tax

VER Voluntary Export Restriction
VES Vessel
VIE Voluntary Import Expansion
VL Variable Levy
VOA Voice of America
VRA Voluntary Restraint Agreement

W

W.A. With Average
WACH West African Clearinghouse
WADB West African Development Bank
WAEC West African Economic Community
WAMU West African Monetary Union
WAOB World Agricultural Outlook Board
WARC World Administrative Radio Conference
WARDA West Africa Rice Development Association
WCL World Confederation of Labor

WEU Western European Union
WFC World Food Council
WFDFI World Federation of Development Financing Institutions
WFP World Food Program
WG Working Group
WHO World Health Organization
WIPO World Intellectual Property Organization
WMD Weapons of Mass Destruction
WMO World Meteorological Organization
WPA With Particular Average
WTDR World Traders Data Report
WTO World Tourism Organization; World Trade Organization

Z

ZEP Zone d'Exchanges Préferentiels pour les Etats de l'Afrique de l'Est et de l'Afrique Australe
ZF La Zone Franc

Appendix B
Internet Abbreviations and Acronyms

A
ACK Acknowledgment
ACL Access Control List
AD Administrative Domain
ANSI American National Standards Institute
API Application Program Interface
ARP Address Resolution Protocol
ARPA Defense Advanced Research Projects Agency
ARPANET Advanced Research Projects Agency Network
AS Autonomous System
ASCII American Standard Code for Information Interchange
ASN.1 Abstract Syntax Notation One
ATM Asynchronous Transfer Mode
AUP Acceptable Use Policy

B
BBN INTERNET Network Operations Center at Bolt, Beranek, and Newman
BBS Bulletin Board System
BCNU Be Seein' You
BER Basic Encoding Rules
BGP Border Gateway Protocol
BIND Berkeley INTERNET Name Domain
BOF Birds Of a Feather
BOOTP Bootstrap Protocol

BSD Berkeley Software Distribution
BTW By The Way

C
CCIRN Coordinating Committee for Intercontinental Research Networks
CCITT Comité Consultatif International de Télégraphique et Téléphonique
CERT Computer Emergency Response Team
CNI Coalition for Networked Information
CRC Cyclic Redundancy Check
CREN Corporation for Research and Educational Networking
CWIS Campus-Wide Information System

D
DARPA Defense Advanced Research Projects Agency
DCA Defense Communications Agency
DCE Data Circuit-Terminating Equipment; Distributed Computing Environment
DDN Defense Data Network
DDN NIC Defense Data Network Network Information Center
DEK Data Encryption Key

DES Data Encryption Standard
DISA Defense Information Systems Agency
DNS Domain Name System
DSA Directory System Agent
DTE Data Terminal Equipment
DUA Directory User Agent

E

EARN European Academic and Research Network
EBCDIC Extended Binary Coded Decimal Interchange Code
Ebone Pan-European Backbone Service
EFF Electronic Frontier Foundation
EFLA Extended Four-Letter Acronym
EGP Exterior Gateway Protocol
E-MAIL Electronic Mail

F

F2F Face to Face
FAQ Frequently Asked Question
FDDI Fiber Distributed Data Interface
FIX Federal Information Exchange
FNC Federal Networking Council
FQDN Fully Qualified Domain Name
FTP File Transfer Protocol
FYI For Your Information

G

GIF Graphic Interchange Format
GNU Gnu's Not UNIX
GOSIP Government OSI Profile

H

HIPPI High-Performance Parallel Interface
HPCC High-Performance Computing and Communications

I

IAB INTERNET Architecture Board
IANA INTERNET Assigned Numbers Authority
ICMP INTERNET Control Message Protocol
I-D INTERNET-Draft
IEEE Institute of Electrical and Electronics Engineers
IEN INTERNET Experiment Note
IESG INTERNET Engineering Steering Group
IETF INTERNET Engineering Task Force
IGP Interior Gateway Protocol
IINREN Interagency Interim National Research and Education Network
IMHO In My Humble Opinion
IMR INTERNET Monthly Report
IP INTERNET Protocol
IPX INTERNETwork Packet eXchange
IR INTERNET Registry
IRC INTERNET Relay Chat
IRSG INTERNET Research Steering Group
IRTF INTERNET Research Task Force
IS Intermediate System
IS-IS Intermediate System–Intermediate System
ISDN Integrated Services Digital Network
ISO International Standards Organization

ISOC INTERNET Society
ISODE ISO Development Environment

L

LAN Local Area Network
LLC Logical Link Control

M

MAC Media Access Control
MAN Metropolitan Area Network
MIB Management Information Base
MIME Multipurpose INTERNET Mail Extensions
MOTSS Members of the Same Sex
MTU Maximum Transmission Unit
MUD Multiuser Dungeon
MX Record Mail Exchange Record

N

NAK Negative Acknowledgment
NFS Network File System
NIC Network Information Center
NIS Network Information Services
NIST National Institute of Standards and Technology
NNTP Network News Transfer Protocol
NOC Network Operations Center
NREN National Research and Education Network
NSF National Science Foundation
NSS Nodal Switching System
NTP Network Time Protocol

O

OCLC On-line Computer Library Catalog

OSI Open Systems Interconnection
OSPF Open Shortest-Path First Interior Gateway Protocol

P

PDU Protocol Data Unit
PEM Privacy Enhanced Mail
PING Packet INTERNET Groper
POP Post Office Protocol; Point of Presence
PPP Point-to-Point Protocol
PSN Packet Switch Node
PTT Postal, Telegraph, and Telephone

R

RARE Réseaux Associés pour la Recherche Européenne
RARP Reverse Address Resolution Protocol
RBOC Regional Bell Operating Company
RCP Remote Copy Program
RFC Request For Comments
RIP Routing Information Protocol
RIPE Réseaux IP Européenne
ROTFL Rolling on the Floor Laughing
RPC Remote Procedure Call
RTT Round-Trip Time

S

SLIP Serial Line INTERNET Protocol
SMDS Switched Multimegabit Data Service
SMI Structure of Management Information
SMTP Simple Mail Transfer Protocol
SNA Systems Network Architecture
SNMP Simple Network Management Protocol
SYSOP System Operator

T

TAC   Terminal Access
  Controller (TAC)
TANSTAAFL   There Ain't
  No Such Thing as a Free
  Lunch
TCP   Transmission Control
  Protocol
TCP/IP Protocol Suite
  Transmission Control Protocol
  over INTERNET Protocol
TLA   Three-Letter Acronym
TTFN   Ta-Ta For Now
TTL   Time to Live

U

UDP   User Datagram Protocol
UUCP   UNIX-to-UNIX
  CoPy

W

WAIS   Wide-Area Information
  Servers
WAN   Wide Area Network
WG   Working Group
WRT   With Respect To
WWW   World Wide Web
WYSIWYG   What You See
  is What You Get

X

XDR   External Data
  Representation

Appendix C
United States and Overseas Contacts for Major Foreign Markets

Algeria

American Embassy, Algiers
Street Address:
4 Chemin Cheich Bachir
Brahimi, Algiers
Mailing Address:
U.S. Dept. of State (Algiers),
Washington, DC 20521-6030
Tel: 011-213-2-69-23-17
Fax: 011-213-2-69-18-63

Argentina

American Embassy, Buenos
Aires
Street Address:
4300 Colombia 1425, Buenos
Aires
Mailing Address:
Unit 4334 APO AA 34034
Tel: 011-54-11 4777-4533,
ext. 2226
Fax: 011-54-11-4777 0673

Armenia

American Embassy, Yerevan
Street Address:
18 Gen Bagramian, Yerevan
Mailing Address:
U.S. Dept. of State (Yerevan),
Washington, DC
20521-7020
Tel: 011-3742-151-551
Fax: 011-3742-151-550

Australia

American Consulate General,
Sydney
Street Address:
Level 59, MLC Centre
19-29 Martin Place
Corner King and Castlereagh
Streets
Sydney NSW 2000
Mailing Address:
Unit 11024, APO AP
96554-0002
E-mail Address:
Sydney.Office.Box@
mail.doc.gov
Tel: 011-612-9373-9202
or 9205
Fax: 011-612-9221-0573

American Consulate General,
Melbourne
Street Address:
553 St. Kilda Road,
Melbourne
Mailing Address:
Unit 11011,
APO AP 96551-0002
E-mail Address:
Melbourne.Office.Box@
mail.doc.gov
Tel: 011-613-9526-5925
Fax: 011-613-9510-4660

American Consulate General,
Perth
Street Address:
16 St. George's Terrace,
13th Floor, Perth

Mailing Address:
Unit 11021,
   APO AP 96553-0002
E-mail Address:
Perth.Office.Box@
   mail.doc.gov
Tel: 011-61-8-9231-9410
Fax: 011-61-8-9231-9410

Austria

American Embassy, Vienna
Street Address:
Boltzmanngasse 16,
   A-1091, Vienna
Tel: 011-431-313-39-2296
Fax: 011-431-310-6917

Azerbaijan

American Embassy, Baku
Street Address:
Azadliq Prospetati 83, Baku
Mailing Address:
U.S. Dept. of State (Baku),
Washington, DC 20521-7050
Tel: 011-9-9412-98-03-35
Fax: 011-9-9412-98-61-17

Belarus

American Embassy, Minsk
Street Address:
Starivilenskaya
   No. 46-220002, Minsk
Mailing Address:
U.S. Dept. of State (Minsk),
Washington, DC 20521
Tel: 011-375-172-31-50-00
Fax: 011-375-172-34-78-53

Belgium

American Embassy, Brussels
Street Address:
27 Boulevard du Regent,
Brussels

Mailing Address:
PSC 82, Box 002,
APO AE 09724-1015
Tel: 011-32-2-508-2425
Fax: 011-32-2-512-6653

U.S. Mission to the European
   Community (Brussels)
Street Address:
40 Boulevard du Regent,
Brussels, B-1000
Mailing Address:
PSC 82, Box 002,
APO AE 09724
Tel: 011-32-2-513-2746
Fax: 011-32-2-513-1228

Bosnia

American Embassy, Sarajevo
Street Address:
43 ul. Dure, Dakovica,
   Sarajevo
Mailing Address:
U.S. Dept. of State
(Sarajevo), Washington, DC
   20521-7030
Tel: 011-387-71-445-700
Fax: 011-387-71-659-722

Brazil

American Consulate General,
   Sao Paulo
Street Address:
Rua Estados Unidos 1812,
   Sao Paulo
Mailing Address:
APO AA 34030-0002
Tel: 011-55-11-853-2811
Fax: 011-55-11-853-2744

American Consular Agency, Belo
   Horizonte
Mailing Address:
APO AA 34030-3505
Street Address:
Minas Trade Center,
   Rua Timbiras, 1200,
   7th Floor

Tel: 011-55-31-213-1571
Fax: 011-55-31-213-1575

American Embassy, Brasilia
Street Address:
Avenida das Nocoes,
Lote 3, Brasilia
Mailing Address:
Unit 3500, APO AA 34030
Tel: 011-55-61-321-7272
Fax: 011-55-61-225-3981

American Consualte General,
Rio de Janeiro
Street Address:
Avenida Presidente Wilson,
147 Castelo, Rio de Janeiro
Mailing Address:
APO AA 34030
Tel: 011-55-21-292-7117
Fax: 011-55-21-240-9738

Bulgaria

American Embassy, Sofia
Street Address:
1 Saborna Street, Sofia
Mailing Address:
Unit 1335,
APO AE 09213-1335
Tel: 011-359-2-980-5241
Fax: 011-359-2-980-6850

Canada

American Embassy, Ottawa
Street Address:
World Exchange Plaza,
45 O'Connor, Suite 1140,
Ottawa K1P-1A4
Mailing Address:
P.O. Box 5000,
Ogdensburg, NY
13669-0430
Tel: 1-613-238-5335
Fax: 1-613-238-5999

American Consulate General,
Calgary
Street Address:
615 MacLeod Trail S.E.,
Room 1050, Calgary
Mailing Address:
c/o American Embassy,
Ottawa, P.O. Box 5000,
Ogdensburg, NY 13669
Tel: 1-403-265-2116
Fax: 1-403-264-6630

American Consulate General,
Halifax
Street Address:
Suite 910, Cogswell Tower,
Scotia Square,
Halifax, Nova Scotia
B3J 3K1
Mailing Address:
c/o American Embassy,
Ottawa, P.O. Box 5000,
Ogdensburg, NY 13669
Tel: 1-902-429-2480/2482
Fax: 1-902-429-7690

American Consulate General,
Montreal
Street Address:
455 Rene Levesque
Boulevard,
19th Floor,
Montreal, Quebec, H2Z-1Z2
Mailing Address:
P.O. Box 847,
Champlain, NY 12919-0847
Tel: 1-514-398-9695
Fax: 1-514-398-9430

American Consulate General,
Toronto
Street Address:
360 University Avenue,
Suite 602, Toronto, Ontario,
M5G-1S4
Mailing Address:
P.O. Box 135,
Lewiston, NY 14092
Tel: 1-416-595-5412
Fax: 1-416-595-5419

American Consulate General, Vancouver
Street Address:
1095 West Pender Street,
20th Floor,
Vancouver, British Columbia V6E-2M6
Mailing Address:
P.O. Box 5002,
Point Roberts,
Washington, DC 98281-5002
Tel: 1-604-685-3382
Fax: 1-604-687-6095

Chile

American Embassy, Santiago
Street Address:
Andres Bello 2800,
Los Condes, Santiago
Mailing Address:
Unit 4111,
APO AA 34033
Tel: 011-56-2-330-3316
Fax: 011-56-2-330-3172

China

American Embassy, Beijing
Street Address:
Xiu Shui Bei Jie 3, Beijing
Mailing Address:
PSC 461, Box 50,
FPO AP 96521-0002
E-mail Address:
OBeijing@doc.gov
Tel: 011-86-10-6532-3831 or 6532-6924 through 27
Fax: 011-86-10-6532-3297

American Consulate General, Chengdu
Street Address:
4 Lingshiguan Road,
Chengdu 610041, Sichuan
Mailing Address:
PSC 461, Box 85,
FPO AP 96521-0002
Tel: 011-86-28-558-3992
Fax: 011-86-28-558-9221

American Consulate General, Guangzhou
Street Address:
China Hotel, 14/F Liu Hua Road, Guangzhou
Mailing Address:
PSC 461, Box 100, FPO AP 96521-0002
E-mail Address:
OGuangzh@doc.gov

U.S. Commercial Center, Shanghai
Street Address:
Shanghai Centre
Suite 631, East Tower 1376
Nanjing Xi Lu, Shanghai
E-mail Address:
OShanghai@doc.gov
Tel: 011-86-21-6279-7630
Fax: 011-86-21-6279-7639

American Consulate General, Shenyang
Street Address:
52, 14th Wei Road,
Heping District, Shenyang 110003
Mailing Address:
PSC 461, Box 45,
FPO AP 96521-0002
Tel: 011-86-24-322-1198
Fax: 011-86-24-322-2206

Colombia

American Embassy, Bogota
Street Address:
Calle 22 D bis No. 47-51,
Santa Fe de Bogota
Mailing Address:
Unit 5120,
APO AA 34038
Tel: 011-57-1-315-2126/ 315-0811
Fax: 011-57-1-315-2171/ 315-2190

Costa Rica

American Embassy, San Jose
  Street Address:
  Embajada de los Estados
  Unidos,
  Frente al Centro,
  Commercial del Oeste,
    Unit 2508,
  Pavas, San Jose
  Mailing Address:
  APO AA 34020
  Tel: 011-506-220-2454/3939
  Fax: 011-506-231-4783

Cote d'Ivoire

American Embassy, Abidjan
  Street Address:
  5 Rue Jesse Owens,
  Abidjan 01 B.P. 1712
  Mailing Address:
  U.S. Dept of State (Abidjan),
  Washington, DC 20521-2010
  Tel: 011-225-21-09-79 or
    011-225-21-46-72
  Fax: 011-225-22-32-59

Croatia

American Embassy, Zagreb
  Street Address:
  Andrije Hebranga 2, Zagreb
  Mailing Address:
  Unit 345,
  APO AE 09213-1345
  Tel: 011-385-1-455-5500
  Fax: 011-385-455-3126

Czech Republic

American Embassy, Prague
  Street Address:
  Trziste 15, 11801, Praha 1
  Mailing Address:
  U.S. Dept. of State (Prague),
  Washington, DC 20521-5630
  Tel: 011-420-2-5753-1162
  Fax: 011-420-2-5753-1165

Denmark

American Embassy, Copenhagen
  Street Address:
  Dag Hammarskjold Alle 24,
  Copenhagen
  Mailing Address:
  APO AE 09176
  Tel: 011-45-3555-3144
  Fax: 011-45-3542-0175

Dominican Republic

American Embassy, Santo
    Domingo
  Street Address:
  Corner of Calle Cesar
    Nicolas Penson and Calle
    Leopoldo Navarro,
    Santo Domingo
  Mailing Address:
  Unit 5515,
  APO AA 34041-0008
  Tel: 1-809-221-2171
  Fax: 1-809-688-4838

Ecuador

American Embassy, Quito
  Street Address:
  Avenida 12 de Octubre y
    Avenida Patria, Quito
  Mailing Address:
  Unit 5334,
  APO AA 34039-3420
  Tel: 011-593-2-561-404
  Fax: 011-593-2-504-550

American Consulate General,
    Guayaquil
  Street Address:
  9 de Octubre y Garcia
    Moreno, Guayaquil
  Mailing Address:
  APO AA 34039
  Tel: 011-593-4-530-908
  Fax: 011-593-4-325-286

Egypt

American Embassy, Cairo
Street Address:
8, Kamal el-Din Salah Street,
Garden City, Cairo
Mailing Address:
Unit 64900, Box 11,
APO AE 09839-4900
Tel: 011-20-2-355-7371
Fax: 011-20-2-355-8368

American Consulate General,
Alexandria
Street Address:
110 Avenue Horreya,
Alexandria
Mailing Address:
Unit 64900, Box 24,
FPO AE 09839-4900
Tel: 011-20-3-482-1911
Fax: 011-20-3-482-9199

Finland

American Embassy, Helsinki
Street Address:
Itainen Puistotie,
Helsinki 14ASF
Mailing Address:
APO AE 09723
Tel: 011-358-9-171-931
Fax: 011-358-9-635-332

France

American Embassy, Paris
Street Address:
2 avenue Gabriel, Paris
Mailing Address:
APO AE 09777
Tel: 011-33-1-4312-2370
Fax: 011-33-1-4312-2172

U.S. Mission to the OECD
(Paris)
Street Address:
19, rue de Franqueville,
75016 Paris

Mailing Address:
APO AE 09777
Tel: 011-33-1-4524-7477
Fax: 011-33-1-4524-7480

American Consulate General,
Lyon
Street Address:
Lyon Commerce
International,
69289 Lyon Cedex 02
Mailing Address:
c/o American Embassy, Paris,
APO AE 09777
Tel: 011-33-478-38-05-92
Fax: 011-33-478-38-31-74

American Consulate General,
Marseille
Street Address:
12, boulevard Paul Peytral,
Marseille
Mailing Address:
c/o American Embassy, Paris
APO AE 09777
Tel: 011-33-491-549-623
Fax: 011-33-491-550-947

American Consulate General,
Strasbourg
Street Address:
15, avenue d'Alsace,
Strasbourg
Mailing Address:
c/o American Embassy, Paris,
Unit 21551, APO AE 09777
Tel: 011-33-88-35-31-04
Fax: 011-33-88-24-06-95

Georgia

American Embassy, Tbilisi
Street Address:
25 Atoneli, Tbilisi
Mailing Address:
U.S. Dept. of State (Tbilisi),
Washington, DC 20521-7060
Tel: 011-995-32-933-803
Fax: 011-995-32-933-759

Germany

American Embassy, Bonn
Street Address:
Deichmanns Avenue 29,
Bonn
Mailing Address:
Unit 21701,
Box 53170,
Bonn APO AE
09080 PSC 117
Tel: 011-49-228-339-2063

American Embassy Office,
Berlin
Street Address:
Neustaedtische Kirchstrasse
4-5, Berlin D-10117
Mailing Address:
Unit 10117,
APO AE 09235-5500
Tel: 011-49-30-238-5174
Fax: 011-49-30-238-6296

U.S. Commercial Office,
Dusseldorf
Street Address:
Kennedydamm 15-17,
D-40476 Dusseldorf
Mailing Address:
Unit 21701, Box 30,
APO AE 09080
Tel: 011-49-211-470-6136/
470-6127
Fax: 011-49-211-431-431

American Consulate General,
Frankfurt
Street Address:
Siesmayerstrasse 21,
60323 Frankfurt/Main
Mailing Address:
PSC 115,
APO AE 09213-0115
Tel: 011-49-69-956-2040
Fax: 011-49-69-561-114

American Consulate General,
Hamburg
Street Address:
Alsterufer 27/28,
20354, Hamburg
Mailing Address:
U.S. Dept. of State
(Hamburg),
Washington, DC 20521-5180
Tel: 011-49-40-4117-1304
Fax: 011-49-40-410-6598

American Consulate General,
Leipzig
Street Address:
Wilhelm-Seyfferth-Strasse 4,
04107 Leipzig
Mailing Address:
PSC 120, Box 1000
APO AE 09265
Tel: 011-49-341-213-8421
Fax: 011-49-341-213-8441

American Consulate General,
Munich
Street Address:
Koeniginstrasse 5, Munich
Mailing Address:
APO AE 09178
Tel: 011-49-89-2888-750
Fax: 011-49-89-285-261

Greece

American Embassy, Athens
Street Address:
91 Vasilissis Sophias
Boulevard, Athens
Mailing Address:
PSC 108, APO AE 09482
Tel: 011-30-1-720-2302
Fax: 011-30-1-721-8660

Guatemala

American Embassy, Guatemala
City
Street Address:
7-01 Avenida de la Reforma,
Zona 10, Guatemala City
Mailing Address:
Unit 3306, APO AA 34024
Tel: 011-502-3-31-1541,
X259
Fax: 011-502-3-31-7373

Haiti

American Embassy, Port-au-
Prince
Street Address:
5 Harry Truman Boulevard,
Port-au-Prince
Mailing Address:
U.S. Dept. of State
(Port-au-Prince),
Washington, DC 20521-3400
Tel: 509-22-0345
Fax: 509-23-1641

Honduras

American Embassy, Tegucigalpa
Street Address:
Avenido La Paz, Tegucigalpa
Mailing Address:
APO AA 34022
Tel: 011-504-236-9320/
238-5114
Fax: 011-504-238-2888

Hong Kong

American Consulate General,
Hong Kong
Street Address:
26 Garden Road,
17th Floor,
Hong Kong
Mailing Address:
PSC 464, Box 30, FPO AP
96522-0002
E-mail Address:
OHongKon@doc.gov
Tel: 011-85-22-521-1467
Fax: 011-85-22-845-9800

Hungary

American Embassy, Budapest
Street Address:
Szabadsag Ter 7, H-1054
Budapest
Mailing Address:
U.S. Dept. of State
(Budapest), Washington, DC
20521-5270
Tel: 011-36-1-302-6100
Fax: 011-36-1-302-0089

India

American Embassy, New Delhi
Street Address:
Shanti Path,
Chanakyapuri 110021
New Delhi
Mailing Address:
U.S. Dept. of State
(New Delhi),
Washington, DC 20521-9000
Tel: 011-91-11-611-3033
Fax: 011-91-11-419-0025/
011-91-11-687-2391

Commercial Office, US&FCS,
Ahmedabad
Street Address:
Suite #41/42,
JMC House,
Ambawadi Opp. Parimal
Garden,
Ahmedabad 380 006
Mailing Address:
Same
Tel: 011-91-79-656-5210 and
011-91-79-656-5216
Fax: 011-91-79-565-0763

Commercial Office, US&FCS,
Bangalore
Street Address:
W-202, 2nd Floor,
West Wing,
Sunrise Chambers,
22 Ulsoor Road
Bangalore 560 042
Mailing Address:
Same
Tel: 011-91-80-558-1452
Fax: 011-91-80-558-3630

American Consulate General,
    Calcutta
Street Address:
5/1 Ho Chi Minh Sarani,
Calcutta 700 071
Mailing Address:
U.S. Dept. of State (Calcutta),
Washington, DC 20521-6250
Tel: 011-91-33-282-3611
    through 15
Fax: 011-91-33-282-2335/
    1074

American Consulate General,
    Chennai
Street Address:
220 Anna Salai,
    Chennai 600006
Mailing Address:
U.S. Dept. of State (Chennai),
Washington, DC 20521-6260
Tel: 011-91-44-827-7542
Fax: 011-91-44-827-6580

American Consulate General,
    Mumbai (formerly
    Bombay)
Street Address:
4, New Marine Lines,
Mumbai 400020
Mailing Address:
U.S. Dept. of State (Bombay),
Washington, DC 20521-6240
Tel: 011-91-22-265-2511
Fax: 011-91-22-262-3850

Indonesia

U.S. Commercial Center, Jakarta
Street Address:
World Trade Center,
Wisma Metropolital II,
3rd Floor, Jalan
Jenral Sudirman 29-31,
Jakarta 12920
E-mail Address:
Jakarta.Office.Box@
    mail.doc.gov
Tel: 011-62-21-526-2850
Fax: 011-62-21-526-2855

American Consulate General,
    Surabaya
Street Address:
Jalan Raya Drive, Sutomo 33,
Box 18131, Surabaya
Mailing Address:
APO AP 96520
E-mail Address:
Office.Surabaya@
    mail.doc.gov
Tel: 011-62-31-5619213/
    5676880
Fax: 011-62-31-5677748

Ireland

American Embassy, Dublin
Street Address:
42 Elgin Road,
Ballsbridge, Ireland
Mailing Address:
U.S. Dept. of State (Dublin),
Washington, DC 20521-5290
Tel: 011-353-1-667-4552/
    4553 and 668-2350
Fax: 011-353-1-667-4754

Israel

American Embassy, Tel Aviv
Street Address:
71 Hayarkon Street,
Tel Aviv 63903
Mailing Address:
Unit 7228, Box 0021,
APO AE 09830
Tel: 011-972-3-519-7368
Fax: 011-972-3-510-7215

Italy

American Embassy, Rome
Streeet Address:
Via Veneto 119/A, Rome
Mailing Address:
PSC 59, APO AE 09624
Tel: 011-39-6-46774-2382
Fax: 011-4674-2113

American Consulate General, Florence
Street Address:
Lungarno Amerigo
Vespucci 38, Florence
Mailing Address:
APO AE 09624
Tel: 011-39-55-211-676
Fax: 011-39-55-283-780

American Consulate General, Genoa
Street Address:
Palazzo Borsa, Via Dante 2, Int. 43, Genoa
Mailing Address:
PSC 59, Box G,
APO AE 09624
Tel: 011-39-010-543-877
Fax: 011-39-010-576-1678

American Consulate General, Milan
Street Address:
Via Principe Amerdeo 2/10, 20121, Milan
Mailing Address:
PSC 59, Box M,
APO AE 09624
Tel: 011-39-2-6592-260
Fax: 011-39-2-6592-561

American Consulate General, Naples
Street Address:
Piazza della Repubblica, Naples
Mailing Address:
PSC 810, Box 18,
FPO AE 09619-0002
Tel: 011-39-81-761-1592
Fax: 011-39-81-761-1869

Jamaica

American Embassy, Kingston
Street Address:
Jamaica Mutual Life Center,
2 Oxford Road,
3rd Floor,
Kingston 5

Mailing Address:
U.S. Dept. of State
(Kingston),
Washington DC 20521-3210
Tel: 1-876-926-8115
Fax: 1-809-920-2580

Japan

American Embassy, Tokyo
Street Address:
1-10-5 Akasaka,
1-chrome Minato-ku (107),
Tokyo
Mailing Address:
Unit 45004,
Box 204
APO AP 96337-5004
E-mail Address:
Office.Tokyo@mail.doc.gov
Tel: 011-81-3-3224-5000
Fax: 011-81-3-3589-4235

U.S. Trade Center, Tokyo
Street Address:
7th Floor,
World Import Mart,
1-3 Higoshi Ikebukuro,
3-chome
Toshima-ku, Tokyo 170
Mailing Address:
Unit 45004,
Box 229,
APO AP 96337-5004
E-mail Address:
Office.Tokyotc@
mail.doc.gov
Tel: 011-81-3-3987-2441
Fax: 011-81-3-3987-2447

American Consulate, Fukuoka
Street Address:
5-26 Ohori 2-chome,
Chuo-ku Fukuoka-810
Mailing Address:
Box 10,
FPO AP 98766
Tel: 011-81-92-751-9331
Fax: 011-81-92-713-9222

American Consulate, Nagoya
Street Address:
10-33 Nishiki 3-chome,
Naka-ku, Nagoya 460, Japan
Mailing Address:
c/o American Embassy
Tokyo, Unit 45004, Box 280,
APO AP 96337-0001
E-mail Address:
ONagoya@doc.gov
Tel: 011-81-52-203-4277
Fax: 011-81-52-201-4612

American Consulate General,
Osaka-Kobe
Street Address:
11-5, Nishitenma 2-chome,
Kita-Ku Osaka (530)
Mailing Address:
Unit 45004, Box 239,
APO AP 96337-0002
E-mail Address:
OOsakaKo@doc.gov
Tel: 011-81-6-315-5957
Fax: 011-81-6-315-5963

American Consulate, Sapporo
Street Address:
Kita 1-Jo Nishi 28-chome,
Chuoku Sapporo 064
Mailing Address:
APO AP 96337-0003
Tel: 011-81-11-641-1115
Fax: 011-81-11-643-1283

Kazakhstan

American Embassy, Almaty
Street Address:
99/97 Furmanova Street,
Almaty, 480012
Mailing Address:
U.S. Dept. of State (Almaty),
Washington, DC 20521-7030
Tel: 011-7-3275-81-15-77
Fax: 011-7-3275-81-15-76

Kenya

American Embassy, Nairobi
Street Address:
Moi/Haile Selassie Avenue,
Nairobi
Mailing Address:
P.O. Box 30137, Unit 64100,
APO AE 09831
Tel: 011-254-2-212-354
Fax: 011-254-2-216-648

Korea

American Embassy, Seoul
Street Address:
82 Sejong-Ro Chongro-Ku,
Seoul
Mailing Address:
Unit 15550,
APO AP 96205-0001
E-mail Address:
OSeoul@doc.gov
Tel: 011-82-2-397-4535
Fax: 011-82-2-739-1628

Kuwait

American Embassy, Kuwait
Street Address:
Al Masjeed Al Aqsa,
Street Plot 14, Block 14,
Bayan Plan 3602, Kuwait
Mailing Address:
Unit 6900, Box 10,
APO AE 09880-9000
Tel: 011-965-539-6362/5307
Fax: 011-965-538-0281

Macedonia

American Embassy, Skopje
Street Address:
Bul Linden BB, 9100, Skopje
Mailing Address:
U.S. Dept. of State (Skopje),
Washington, DC 20521-7120
Tel: 011-389-91-116-180
Fax: 011-389-91-117-103

Malaysia

American Embassy, Kuala
    Lumpur
    Street Address:
376 Jalan Tun Razak, Kuala
Lumpur
Mailing Address:
APO AP 96535-5000
Tel: 011-603-457-2724
Fax: 011-603-242-1866

Mexico

American Embassy, Mexico
    Street Address:
Paseo de la Reforma 305,
Colonia Cuauhtemoc, 06500
Mexico, D.F. Mexico
Mailing Address:
P.O. Box 3087,
Laredo, TX 78044-3087
Tel: 011-52-5-209-9100
Fax: 011-52-5-207-8837

U.S. Trade Center, Mexico
    Street Address:
Liverpool 31,
Co. Juarez, 06600 Mexico,
D.F. Mexico
Mailing Address:
P.O. Box 3087,
Laredo, TX 78044-3087
Tel: 011-52-5-591-0155
Fax: 011-52-5-566-1115

American Consulate General,
    Guadalajara
    Street Address:
Jal. Progreso 175,
Guadalajara
Mailing Address:
P.O. Box 3088
Laredo, TX 78044-3098
Tel: 011-52-3-825-2700,
    X371/52-3-827-0258
Fax: 011-52-3-826-3576

American Consulate General,
    Monterrey
    Street Address:
N.L. Avenida Constitucion
411,
Poniente, Monterrey
Mailing Address:
P.O. Box 3098
Laredo, TX 78044-3098
Tel: 011-52-83-45-2120
Fax: 011-52-83-45-5172/
    343-4440

Morocco

American Consulate General,
    Casablanca
    Street Address:
8 Boulevard Moulay Youssef,
Casablanca
Mailing Address:
PSC 74, Box 24,
APO AE 09718
Tel: 011-212-2-26-45-50
Fax: 011-212-2-22-02-59

American Embassy, Rabat
    Street Address:
2 Avenue de Marrakech,
Rabat
Mailing Address:
PSC 74, Box 003,
APO AE 09718
Tel: 011-212-7-622-65
Fax: 011-212-7-656-61

Netherlands

American Embassy, The Hague
    Street Address:
Lange Voorhout 102,
The Hague
Mailing Address:
PSC 71, Box 1000,
APO AE 09715
Tel: 011-31-70-310-9417
Fax: 011-31-70-363-2985

American Consulate General, Amsterdam
Street Address:
Museumplein 19, Amsterdam
Mailing Address:
Box 1000, APO AE 09715
Tel: 011-31-20-575-5351
Fax: 011-31-20-575-5350

New Zealand

American Consulate General, Auckland
Street Address:
4th Floor, Yorkshire General Building, Shortland and O'Connell Streets
Mailing Address:
PSC 467, Box 99, FPO AP 96531-1099
E-mail Address:
OAucklan@doc.gov
Tel: 011-649-303-2038
Fax: 011-649-302-3156

American Embassy, Wellington
Street Address:
29 Fitzherbert Terrace, Thorndon, Wellington
Mailing Address:
PSC 467
Box 1
FPO AP 96531-1001
Tel: 011-644-472-2068
Fax: 011-644-471-2380

Nigeria

American Embassy, Lagos
Street Address:
2 Eleke Crescent, Victoria Island, Lagos
Mailing Address:
U.S. Dept. of State (Lagos), Washington, DC 20521-8300
Tel: 011-234-1-261-0078, X383
Fax: 011-234-1-261-9856

Norway

American Embassy, Oslo
Street Address:
Drammensveien 18, Oslo
Mailing Address:
PSC 69, Box 1000, APO AE 09707
Tel: 011-47-22-44-8550
Fax: 011-47-22-55-8803

Pakistan

American Embassy, Islamabad
Street Address:
Diplomatic Enclave, Ramna 5, Islamabad
Mailing Address:
P.O. Box 1048, Unit 6220, APO AE 09812-2200
Tel: 011-92-51-826-161
Fax: 011-92-51-823-981

American Consulate General, Lahore
Street Address:
50 Shahrah-E-Bin Badees, Lahore
Mailing Address:
Unit 62216, APO AE 09812-2216
Tel: 011-92-42-636-5530
Fax: 011-92-42-636-5177

Panama

American Embassy, Panama City
Street Address:
Avenida Balboa Y Calle 38, Apartado 6959, Panama City
Mailing Address:
Unit 0945, APO AA 34002
Tel: 011-507-227-1777
Fax: 011-507-227-1713

Peru

American Embassy, Lima
Street Address:
Avenida la Encalada,
Cuadro 17, Lima 33
Mailing Address:
Unit 3780, APO AA 34031
Tel: 011-51-1-434-3040
Fax: 011-51-1-434-3041

Philippines

American Embassy, Manila
Street Address:
395 Senator Gil Puyat
Avenue,
Extension Makati, Manila
Mailing Address:
APO AP 96440
E-mail Address:
OManila@doc.gov
Tel: 011-632-890-9362
Fax: 011-632-895-3028

Poland

American Embassy, Warsaw
Street Address:
Aleje Ujazdowskle 29/31,
Warsaw
Mailing Address:
c/o AmConGen (WAW),
Unit 1340,
APO AE 09213-1340
Tel: 011-48-2-628-3041
Fax: 011-48-2-628-8298

U.S. Trade Center, Warsaw
Street Address:
Aleje Jerozolimski 56C,
IKEA Building,
2nd Floor, 00-803
Warsaw
Tel: 011-48-2-621-4515
Fax: 011-48-2-621-6327

Portugal

American Embassy, Lisbon
Street Address:
Avenida das Forcas Armadas,
Lisbon
Mailing Address:
PSC 83, Box FCS,
APO AE 09726
Tel: 011-351-1-727-5086
Fax: 011-351-1-726-8914

American Business Center,
Oporto
Street Address:
Apartado No. 88,
Rua Julio Dinis 826,
3rd Floor, Oporto
Mailing Address:
c/o AmEmbassy Lisbon,
APO AE 09726
Tel: 011-351-2-606-3094
Fax: 011-351-2-600-2737

Romania

American Embassy, Bucharest
Street Address:
Strada Tudor Arghezi 7-9,
Bucharest
Mailing Address:
The Commercial Service,
U.S. Embassy
(Bucharest-5260),
C/O U.S. Dept. of State,
Washington, DC
20521-5260
Tel: 011-40-1-210-4042
Fax: 011-40-1-210-0690

Russia

American Embassy, Moscow
Street Address:
Novinsky Bulvar 19/23,
Moscow
Mailing Address:
APO AE 09721
Tel: 011-7-502-224-1105
Fax: 011-7-402-224-1106

American Consulate General,
St. Petersburg
Street Address:
Furshatskaya 15,
St. Petersburg
Mailing Address:
Box L, APO AE 09723
Tel: 011-7-812-850-1902
Fax: 011-7-812-850-1903

American Consulate General,
Vladivostok
Street Address:
Ulitsa Mordovtseva 12,
Vladivostok
Mailing Address:
APO AE 09721
Tel: 011-7-4232-268-458
Fax: 011-7-4232-268-445

Saudi Arabia

American Embassy, Riyadh
Street Address:
Collector Road M,
Diplomatic Quarter, Riyadh
Mailing Address:
Unit 61307,
APO AE 09803-1307
Tel: 011-966-1-488-3800
Fax: 011-966-1-488-3237

American Consulate General,
Dhahran
Street Address:
Between Aramco
Headquarters and Dhahran
International Airport,
P.O. Box 81,
Dhahran Airport, 31932
Mailing Address:
Unit 66803,
APO AE 09858-6803
Tel: 011-966-3-891-3200
Fax: 011-966-3-891-8332

American Consulate General,
Jeddah
Street Address:
Palestine Road, Ruwais,
P.O. Box 149, Jeddah

Mailing Address:
Unit 62112,
APO AE 09811-2112
Tel: 011-966-2-667-0040
Fax: 011-966-2-665-8106

Singapore

American Embassy, Singapore
Street Address:
27 Napier Road, Singapore
Mailing Address:
FPO AP 96534-0001
E-mail Address:
OSingapo@doc.gov
Tel: 011-65-476-9037
Fax: 011-65-476-9080

Slovak Republic

American Embassy, Bratislava
Street Address:
Hviezdoslavovo Namestie 4,
81102 Bratislava
Mailing Address:
U.S. Dept. of State
(Bratislava),
Washington, DC 20521-5840
Tel: 011-421-7-533-0861
Fax: 011-421-7-335-096

American Business Center,
Bratislava
Street Address:
Grosslingova 35,
81109 Bratislava
Tel: 011-421-7-361-079
Fax: 011-421-7-361-085

South Africa

American Consulate General,
Johannesburg
Street Address:
1 Commercial Service
Office,
15 Chaplin Road,
Illovo 2196, Johannesburg

Mailing Address (Pouch):
U.S. Dept. of State
(Johannesburg),
Washington, DC 20521-2500
Mailing Address
(*International*):
P.O. Box 2155,
Johannesburg 2000,
South Africa
Tel: 011-27-11-442-3571
Fax: 011-27-11-442-3770

American Consulate General,
Cape Town
Street Address:
Broadway Industries Center,
Herrengracht,
Foreshore, Cape Town
Mailing Address:
U.S. Dept. of State
(Cape Town),
Washington, DC 20521-2480
Tel: 011-27-21-214-269
Fax: 011-27-21-254-151

Spain

American Embassy, Madrid
Street Address:
Serrano 75, Madrid
Mailing Address:
PSC 61, Box 0021,
APO AE 09642
Tel: 011-34-91-564-8976
Fax: 011-34-91-563-0859

American Consulate General,
Barcelona
Street Address:
Paseo Leina Elisenda,
23 08034 Barcelona
Mailing Address:
PSC 61, Box 0005,
APO AE 09642
Tel: 011-34-93-280-2227
Fax: 011-34-93-205-7705

Sweden

American Embassy, Stockholm
Street Address:
Strandvagen 101, Stockholm
Mailing Address:
U.S. Dept. of State
(Stockholm),
Washington, DC 20521-5750
Tel: 011-46-8-783-5346
Fax: 011-46-8-660-9181

Switzerland

American Embassy, Bern
Street Address:
Jubilaeumstrasse 93, Bern
Mailing Address:
U.S. Dept. of State (Bern),
Washington, DC 20521-5110
Tel: 011-41-31-357-7270
Fax: 011-41-31-357-7336

U.S. Mission to the GATT
(Geneva)
Street Address:
Botanic Building,
1-3 Avenue de la Paix,
Geneva
Mailing Address:
U.S. Dept. of State (Geneva),
Washington, DC 20521-5130
Tel: 011-41-22-749-5281
Fax: 011-41-22-749-4885

American Consulate General,
Zurich
Street Address:
Zolliikerstrasse 141, Zurich
Mailing Address:
U.S. Dept. of State (Zurich),
Washington, DC 20521-5130
Tel: 011-41-1-552-070
Fax: 011-41-1-382-2655

Taiwan

The American Institute in Taiwan
  Location: Taipei Office
  Street Address:
  600 Min Chuan East Road,
  Taipei
  Mailing Address:
  American Institute in Taiwan,
  Commercial Unit,
  Dept. of State (Taipei),
  Washington, DC 20521
  E-mail Address:
  OTaipei@doc.gov
  Tel: 011-886-2-720-1550
  Fax: 011-886-2-757-7162

Kaohsiung Office
  Street Address:
  3rd Floor,
  #2 Chung Cheng 3rd Road,
  Kaohsiung
  Mailing Address:
  American Institute in Taiwan,
  Commercial Unit,
  Dept. of State
    (Kaohsiung),
  Washington, DC 20521
  E-mail Address:
  OKaohsiu@doc.gov
  Tel: 011-886-7-224-0154
  Fax: 011-886-7-223-8237

Thailand

American Embassy, Bangkok
  Street Address:
  Diethelm 93/1 Wireless Road,
  Towers Building, Bangkok
  Mailing Address:
  APO AP 96546
  E-mail Address:
  OBangkok@doc.gov
  Tel: 011-662-255-4365
  Fax: 011-662-255-2915

Turkey

American Embassy, Ankara
  Street Address:
  110 Ataturk Boulevard,
  Ankara
  Mailing Address:
  PSC 93, Box 5000,
  APO AE 09823
  Tel: 011-90-312-467-0949
  Fax: 011-90-312-467-1366

American Consulate General,
    Istanbul
  Street Address
  104-108 Mesrutiyet Caddesi,
  Tepebasi, Istanbul
  Mailing Address:
  PSC 97, Box 0002,
  APO AE 09827-0002
  Tel: 011-90-1-251-1651
  Fax: 011-90-1-252-2417

American Consulate General,
    Izmir
  Street Address:
  92 Ataturk Caddesi
    (3rd Floor), Izmir
  Mailing Address:
  PSC 88, Box 5000,
  APO AE 09821
  Tel: 011-90-232-421-3643
  Fax: 011-90-232-463-5040

Turkmenistan

American Embassy, Ashgabat
  Street Address:
  9 Pushkin Street, Ashgabat
  Mailing Address:
  U.S. Dept. of State
    (Ashgabat),
  Washington, DC 20521-7070
  Tel: 011-9-7-3632-35-00-45
  Fax: 011-9-7-3632-51-13-05

Ukraine

American Embassy, Kiev
Street Address:
7, Kudriavsky Uzviz, Kiev
Mailing Address:
U.S. Dept. of State (Kiev),
Washington, DC 20521-5850
Tel: 011-380-44-417-2669
Fax: 011-380-44-417-1419

United Arab Emirates

American Consulate General,
  Dubai
Street Address:
Dubai International Trade
Center, 21st Floor,
Dubai
Mailing Address:
U.S. Dept. of State (Dubai),
Washington, DC 20521-6020
Tel: 011-971-4-331-3584
Fax: 011-971-4-331-3121

American Embassy, Abu Dhabi
Street Address:
8th Floor,
Blue Tower Building,
Shaikh Khalifa Bin Zayed
Street,
Abu Dhabi
Mailing Address:
U.S. Dept. of State
  (Abu Dhabi),
Washington, DC 20521-6010
Tel: 011-971-2-273-666
Fax: 011-971-2-271-377

United Kingdom

American Embassy, London
Street Address:
24-31 Grosvenor Square,
London
Mailing Address:
PSC 801, Box 40,
FPO AE 09498-4040
Tel: 011-44-71-408-8019
Fax: 011-44-71-408-8020

Uzbekistan

American Embassy, Tashkent
Street Address:
82 Chelanzanskaya, Tashkent
Mailing Address:
U.S. Dept. of State
  (Tashkent),
Washington, DC 20521-7110
Tel: 011-7-3712-771-407
Fax: 011-7-3712-776-953

Venezuela

American Embassy, Caracas
Street Address:
Calle F con Calle Suapure
Colinas de Valle Arriba
Codigo
Postal 1060, Caracas
Mailing Address:
Unit 4958, APO AA 34037
Tel: 011-58-2-977-2792
Fax: 011-58-2-977-2177

Vietnam

Commercial Service, Hanoi
Street Address:
U.S. Commercial Center,
31 Hai Ba Trung, 4th Floor,
Hanoi
E-mail Address:
10312.3220@
compuserve.com
Tel: 011-844-824-2422
Fax: 011-844-824-2421

Appendix D
International Trade Commission Offices

Argentina

1600 New Hampshire Ave., NW
Washington, DC 20009
Tel: 202-939-6416
Fax: 202-775-4388

12 West 56th Street
4th Floor
New York, NY 10019
Tel: 212-603-0401
Fax: 212-541-7746

Australia

2049 Century Park East
19th Floor
Los Angeles, CA 90067
Tel: 310-229-4800
Fax: 310-277-2258

636 Fifth Avenue
New York, NY 10111
Tel: 212-408-8400
Fax: 212-265-2768

1601 Massachusetts Avenue, NW
Washington, DC 20036
Tel: 202-797-3000
Fax: 202-797-3362

Austria

11601 Wilshire Boulevard
Suite 2420
Los Angeles, CA 90025
Tel: 310-477-9988
Fax: 310-477-1643

150 East 52nd Street
New York, NY 10022
Tel: 212-421-5250
Fax: 212-751-4765

500 North Michigan Avenue
Suite 1950
Chicago, IL 60611
Tel: 312-644-5556

Bangladesh

821 United Nations Plaza,
  8th Floor
New York, NY 10017
Tel: 212-867-3434

Belgium

1330 Avenue of the Americas
New York, NY 10019-5422
Tel: 212-664-0930
Fax: 212-664-0944

3330 Garfield Street, NW
Washington, DC 20008
Tel: 202-625-5822
Fax: 202-342-2358

333 North Michigan Avenue
Suite 2017
Chicago, IL 60601
Tel: 312-251-0622
Fax: 312-251-0624

Botswana

3400 International Drive, NW
Suite 7M
Washington, DC 20008
Tel: 202-244-4990
Fax: 202-244-4164

Brazil

300 Montgomery Street
Suite 900
San Francisco, CA 94109
Tel: 415-981-8170
Fax: 415-981-3628

3006 Massachusetts Avenue,
  NW
Washington, DC 20008
Tel: 202-745-2700
Fax: 202-745-2827

551 Fifth Avenue, Room 210
New York, NY 10176
Tel: 212-916-3211
Fax: 212-573-9406

Burma

10 East 77th Street
New York, NY 10021
Tel: 212-535-1310

Cameroon

22 East 73rd Street
New York, NY 10021
Tel: 212-794-2295
Fax: 212-249-0533

Canada

300 South Grand Avenue
10th Floor
Los Angeles, CA 90071
Tel: 213-687-7432
Fax: 213-620-0533

310 South Michigan Avenue
12th Floor
Chicago, IL 60604
Tel: 312-427-1031

750 North St. Paul Street
Suite 1700
Dallas, TX 75201
Tel: 214-922-9806
Fax: 214-922-9815

Chile

1900 Avenue of the Stars
Suite 2470
Los Angeles, CA 90067
Tel: 310-553-4541

866 United Nations Plaza
Suite 302
New York, NY 10017
Tel: 212-207-3266
Fax: 212-207-3649

Colombia

1001 South Bayshore Drive
Suite 1904
Miami, FL 33130
Tel: 305-374-3144

6100 Wilshire Boulevard
Suite 1170
Los Angeles, CA 90048
Tel: 213-965-9760
Fax: 213-965-5029

Banco Bilbao Vizcava Plaza
Piso 11 A-2
Avenida Franklin D. Roosevelt,
   No. 1510
Caparra, Puerto Rico 00968
Tel: 809-766-0495
Fax: 809-766-0494

1 Canadian Place
Suite 5801
Toronto, Ontario
Canada M5X 1E2
Tel: 416-363-9225
Fax: 416-363-0808

277 Park Avenue
47th Floor
New York, NY 10172
Tel: 212-223-1120
Fax: 212-223-1325

Costa Rica

108 East 66th Street
Suite 6A
New York, NY 10021
Tel: 212-988-5190

Cyprus

13 East 40th Street
New York, NY 10016
Tel: 212-213-9100
Fax: 212-213-2918

Ecuador

3785 N. W. 82nd Avenue
Suite 317
Miami, FL 33166-6631
Tel: 305-716-5252
Fax: 305-716-9296

Finland

1900 Avenue of the Stars
Suite 1025
Los Angeles, CA 90067
Tel: 310-203-9903
Fax: 310-203-0301

1300 Post Oak Boulevard
Suite 1990
Houston, TX 77056
Tel: 713-627-9700
Fax: 713-629-5052

866 United Nations Plaza
Suite 250
New York, NY 10017-1822
Tel: 212-808-9721
Fax: 212-370-2863

France

1801 Avenue of the Stars
Suite 921
Los Angeles, CA 90067
Tel: 310-843-1700
Fax: 310-843-1701

810 7th Avenue, 38th Floor
New York, NY 10019
Tel: 212-307-8800
Fax: 212-315-1017

285 Peachtree Center Avenue
Suite 921
Atlanta, GA 30303
Tel: 404-522-4843
Fax: 404-522-3039

1 E. Wacker Street
Chicago, IL 60601
Tel: 312-661-1880
Fax: 312- 661-0976

5847 San Felipe Street
Suite 1600
Houston, TX 77057
Tel: 713-307-8800
Fax: 713-266-3424

Germany

5220 Pacific Concourse Drive
Suite 280
Los Angeles, CA 90045
Tel: 310-297-7979
Fax: 310-297-7966

Greece

2211 Massachusetts Avenue, NW
Washington, DC 20008
Tel: 202-332-2844
Fax: 202-328-3105

168 North Michigan Avenue
Suite 500
Chicago, IL 60601
Tel: 312-332-1716
Fax: 312-236-5127

150 East 58th Street
Suite 1701
New York, NY 10022
Tel: 212-592-2278
Fax: 212-592-2278

Honduras

3007 Tilden Street, NW
Washington, DC 20008
Tel: 202-966-7702
Fax: 202-966-9751

80 Wall Street
9th Floor
New York, NY 10005
Tel: 212-269-3611

Hong Kong Trade Development Council

347 Bay Street
Suite 1100
Toronto, Ontario
CANADA M5H 2R7
Tel: 905-366-3594
Fax: 905-366-1569

350 South Figueroa Street
Suite 202
Los Angeles, CA 90071
Tel: 213-622-3194
Fax: 213-613-1490

333 North Michigan Avenue
Suite 2028
Chicago, IL 60601
Tel: 312-726-4515

219 East 46th Street
New York, NY 10017
Tel: 800-TDC-HKTE
Fax: 212-838-8688

501 Brickell Key Drive
Couvoiser Center
Miami, FL 33131
Tel: 305-577-0414
Fax: 305-372-9142

904A-938 Howe Street
Vancouver, BC
CANADA V6Z 1N9
Tel: 604-685-0883
Fax: 604-331-4418

Hungary

150 East 58th Street
33rd Floor
New York, NY 10022
Tel: 212-752-3060
Fax: 212-486-2968

2401 Calvert Street, NW
Suite 1021
Washington, DC 20008
Tel: 202-387-3191
Fax: 202-387-3140

130 East Randolph Street
1 Prudential Plaza
Suite 1130
Chicago, IL 60601
Tel: 312-856-0274
Fax: 312-856-1080

Iceland

P.O. Box 4649
Grand Central Station
New York, NY 10163-4649
Tel: 212-949-2333
Fax: 212-983-5260

India

445 Park Avenue
New York, NY 10022
Tel: 212-753-6655
Fax: 212-319-6914

Ireland

50 West San Fernando Street
Fairmont Plaza
San Jose, CA 95113
Tel: 408-294-9903

Israel

350 Fifth Avenue
19th Floor
New York, NY 10118
Tel: 212-560-0600 Ext 3
Fax: 212-564-8964

6380 Wilshire Boulevard
Suite 1700
Los Angeles, CA 90048
Tel: 213-658-7924
Fax: 213-651-0572

230 North Michigan Avenue
Suite 1620
Chicago, IL 60601
Tel: 312-332-2160
Fax: 312-332-2163

110 Spring Street, NW
Suite 330
Atlanta, GA 30309
Tel: 404-724-0830
Fax: 404-724-9030

Italy

499 Park Avenue
New York, NY 10022
Tel: 212-980-1500
Fax: 212-758-1050

Jamaica

214 King Street West
Suite 214
Toronto, Ontario
CANADA M5H 3S6
Tel: 905-598-3393
Fax: 905-593-4821

Japan
(External Trade Office)

1221 Avenue of the Americas
New York, NY 10020
Tel: 212-997-0400
Fax: 212-997-0464

Jordan

3504 International Drive, NW
Washington, DC 20008
Tel: 202-966-2664
Fax: 202-966-3110

Korea

4801 Wilshire Boulevard
Suite 104
Los Angeles, CA 90010
Tel: 800-KOTRA-4-U
Fax: 213-954-1707

460 Park Avenue
Suite 402
New York, NY 10022
Tel: 212-826-0900
Fax: 212-888-4930

Malaysia

550 South Hope Street
Suite 400
Los Angeles, CA 90071
Tel: 213-892-9034
Fax: 213-892-9142

313 East 43rd Street
3rd Floor
New York, NY 10017
Tel: 212-682-0232
Fax: 212-983-1987

Mexico

66 Wellington Street
Suite 2712
P.O. Box 32
Toronto, Ontario
CANADA M5K 1A1
Tel: 905-867-9292
Fax: 905-867-1847

350 South Figueroa Street
Suite 296
World Trade Center
Los Angeles, CA 90071
Tel: 213-628-1220
Fax: 213-628-8466

100 North Biscayne Boulevard
Suite 1601
New World Tower
Miami, FL 33132
Tel: 305-372-9929
Fax: 305-374-1238

229 Peachtree Street, NE
Suite 917
Cain Tower
Atlanta, GA 30303
Tel: 404-522-5373
Fax: 404-681-3361

225 North Michigan Avenue
Suite 708
Chicago, IL 60601
Tel: 312-856-0316
Fax: 312-856-1834

375 Park Avenue
19th Floor, Suite 1905
New York, NY 10152-0002
Tel: 212-826-2916
Fax: 212-826-2979

2777 Stemmons Freeway
Suite 1622
Dallas, TX 75207
Tel: 214-688-4095
Fax: 214-905-3831

1100 NW Loop 410
Suite 409
San Antonio, TX 78213
Tel: 210-525-9748
Fax: 210-525-8355

New Zealand

12400 Wilshire Boulevard
Suite 1120
Los Angeles, CA 90025
Tel: 310-207-1145
Fax: 310-207-4645

780 Third Avenue
New York, NY 10017
Tel: 212-832-4038

Nigeria

828 Second Avenue
New York, NY 10017-4301
Tel: 212-715-7200

Norway

20 California Street
6th Floor
San Francisco, CA 94111
Tel: 415-986-0770
Fax: 415-986-6025

800 Third Avenue
New York, NY 10022
Tel: 212-421-9210
Fax: 212-838-0374

Panama

2862 McGill Terrace, NW
Washington, DC 20008
Tel: 202-483-1407
Fax: 202-483-8416

1477 South Miami Avenue
Miami, FL 33130
Tel: 305-374-8435

Philippines

447 Sutter Street
Suite 514
San Francisco, CA 94108
Tel: 415-981-3303
Fax: 415-981-6022

556 Fifth Avenue
New York, NY 10036
Tel: 212-575-7925
Fax: 212-575-7759

Poland

c/o Commerical Counselor's
  Office
100 Park Avenue
19th Floor
New York, NY 10017
Tel: 212-370-5300
Fax: 212-818-9623

3000 Bloor Street W.
Suite 1660
Toronto, ON
CANADA M8X 2W8
Tel: 416-233-6671
Fax: 416-233-9678

Portugal

590 5th Avenue
New York, NY 10036
Tel: 212-354-4810
Tel: 800-PORTUGAL
Fax: 212-575-4737

Singapore

55 East 59th Street
21st Floor
New York, NY 10022
Fax: 212-888-2897

South Africa

2 First Canadian Place
P.O. Box 424
Toronto, Ontario
CANADA M6X 1E3
Tel: 916-364-0314
Fax: 916-364-8761

Spain

350 South Figueroa Street
Suite 498
Los Angeles, CA 90071
Tel: 213-628-1406
Fax: 213-628-1504

2558 Massachusetts Avenue,
 NW
Washington, DC 20008
Tel: 202-265-8600
Fax: 202-265-9478

406 Lexington Avenue
44th Floor
New York, NY 10017
Tel: 212-661-4959
Fax: 212- 972-2494
Fax: 212-876-6055

Sweden

150 North Michigan Avenue
Suite 1200
Chicago, IL 60601
Tel: 312-486-8699

599 Lexington Avenue
New York, NY 10022
Tel: 212-486-8699

Syria

2215 Wyoming Avenue, NW
Washington, DC 20008
Tel: 202-232-6313

Tanzania

2139 R Street, NW
Washington, DC 20008
Tel: 202-939-6125
Fax: 202-797-7408

Thailand

5 World Trade Center
New York, NY 10048
Tel: 212-466-1777
Fax: 212-524-0972

Turkey

821 United Nations Plaza
4th Floor
New York, NY 10017
Tel: 212-687-1530
Fax: 212-687-2078

United Kingdom

245 Peachtree Center Avenue
Atlanta, GA 30303
Tel: 404-524-8823
Fax: 404-524-3153

600 Atlantic Avenue
25th Floor
Boston, MA 02210
Tel: 617-248-9555
Fax: 617-248-9578

33 North Dearborn Street
Chicago, IL 60602
Tel: 312-346-1810
Fax: 312-346-7021

55 Public Square
Suite 1650
Cleveland, OH 44113
Tel: 216-621-7675
Fax: 216-621-2615

2730 Stemmons Freeway
813 Stemmons Tower West
Dallas, TX 75207
Tel: 214-637-3600
Fax: 214-634-9408

1000 Louisana
Suite 1900
Houston, TX 77002
Tel: 713-659-6270
Fax: 713-659-7094

11766 Wilshire Boulevard
Suite 400
Los Angeles, CA 90025
Tel: 310-477-3322
Fax: 310-575-1450

1001 South Bayshore Drive
Brickell Bay Office Tower
Suite 2110
Miami, FL 33131
Tel: 305-374-1522
Fax: 305-374-8196

845 Third Avenue
11th Floor
New York, NY 10022
Tel: 212-745-0495
Fax: 212-745-9456

1509 Lopez Landrum Street
Santurce, PR 00911
Tel: 809-721-5193
Fax: 809-728-6366

1 Sansome Street
Suite 850
San Francisco, CA 94104
Tel: 415-981-3030
Fax: 415-434-2018

999 Third Avenue
820 Interstate Center
Seattle, WA 98104
Tel: 206-622-9255
Fax: 206-622-4728

Uruguay

747 Third Avenue
21st Floor
New York, NY 10017
Tel: 212-751-7137
Fax: 212-758-4126

Venezuela

7 East 51st Street
New York, NY 10022
Tel: 212-826-1660
Fax: 212-644-7471

Appendix E
U.S. Customs Officers in Foreign Countries

Austria
Customs Attaché
American Embassy
Boltzmanngasse 16, A-1091
Vienna, AUSTRIA
Tel: 315-5511 Ext. 2112

Belgium
Customs Attaché
U.S. Mission to the European
   Communities
PSC 82 Box 002
APO AE 09724
Tel: 502-3300

Canada
Customs Attaché
American Embassy
100 Wellington Street
Ottawa, Ontario
CANADA, KIP 5TI
Tel: (613) 238-5335 Ext. 322

France
Customs Attaché
American Embassy
58 bis Rue la Boetie
Room 317
76008 Paris, FRANCE
Tel: 4296-1202 Ext. 2392-2393

Germany
Customs Attaché
American Embassy
Deichmanns Aue. 29
5300 Bonn 2, GERMANY
Tel: 228/3392207
   228/3312853

Hong Kong
Senior Cuistoms Representative
American Consulate General
St. John's Building, 11th Floor
33 Garden Road
HONG KONG
Tel: 5-239011 Ext. 244

Italy
Customs Attaché
American Embassy
Via Veneto 119
Rome, ITALY
Tel: 6-467-42475

Senior Customs Representative
American Consulate General
Via Principe Amedeo
2/10-20121 Milano, ITALY
Tel: 2-655-4973

Japan
Customs Attaché
American Embassy
10-5 Akasaka 1-Chome
Minato-ku, Tokyo 107
JAPAN
Tel: 81-3-3224-5433

Korea
Customs Attaché
82 Sejong Ro
Chongro-Ku
Seoul 110-050, KOREA
Tel: 732-2601, Ext. 4563

Mexico
Customs Attaché
American Embassy
Paseo De La Reforma 305
Colonia Cuahtemoc
Mexico City, MEXICO
Tel: 211-042, Ext. 3687

Sr. Customs Representative
American Consulate General
No. 139 Morelia
Hermosillo, Son., MEXICO
Tel: 621-7-5258

Sr. Customs Representative
American Consulate
Paseo Montejo 453
Merida, Yucatan
   MEXICO 97000
Tel: 99-25-8235

Sr. Customs Representative
American Consulate General
Avenida Constitucion
411 Poniente
Monterrey, N.L., MEXICO
Tel: 45-21-20

The Netherlands
Customs Attaché
American Embassy
Lange Voorhout 102
2514EJ The Hague,
   THE NETHERLANDS
Tel: 703-924-651

Panama
Customs Attaché
Calle 38 & Avenida Balboa
Panama City, R.P.
Tel: 507271777, Ext. 2440

Singapore
Customs Attaché
American Embassy
30 Hill Road
SINGAPORE 0617
Tel: 621-7-5258

Thailand
Customs Attaché
American Embassy
95 Wireless Road
Bangkok, THAILAND
Tel: 252-5040 Ext. 2539

United Kingdom
Customs Attaché
American Embassy
24/31 Grosvenor Square
London, W. 1A 1AE
   ENGLAND
Tel: 71/493-4599

Uruguay
Customs Attaché
American Embassy
APO Miami, FL 34035
Tel: 598-223-6061

Appendix F
U.S. Customs Regions and Districts

Headquarters
  U.S. Customs Service
  1301 Constitution Avenue,
    NW
  Washington, DC 20229

Northeast Region
Boston, Massachusetts
  02222-1056

Districts:
  Baltimore, Maryland 21202
  Boston, Massachusetts
    02222-1056
  Buffalo, New York 14202
  Norfolk, Virginia 23510
  Ogdensburg, New York
    13669
  Philadelphia, Pennsylvania
    19106
  Portland, Maine 04112
  Providence, Rhode Island
    02905
  St. Albans, Vermont 05478
  Washington, DC 20041

New York Region
New York, New York 10048

Kennedy Airport Area
  Jamaica, NY 11430

Newark Area
  Newark, NJ 07102

New York Seaport Area
  New York, NY 10048

Southeast Region
Miami, Florida 33131

Districts:
  Charleston, South Carolina
    29402
  Miami, Florida 33131
  St. Thomas, Virgin Islands
    00801
  San Juan, Puerto Rico 00901
  Savannah, Georgia 31401
  Tampa, Florida 33605
  Wilmington, North Carolina
    28401

South Central Region
New Orleans, Louisiana 70130

Districts:
  Mobile, Alabama 36602
  New Orleans, Louisiana
    70130

Southwest Region
Houston, Texas 77057

Districts:
  Dallas/Fort Worth 75261
  El Paso, Texas 79985
  Houston/Galveston, Texas
    77029
  Laredo, Texas 78041-3130
  Port Arthur, Texas 77642

Pacific Region
Los Angeles, California
90831-0700

Districts:
Anchorage. Alaska 99501
Great Falls, Montana 59405
Honolulu, Hawaii 96806
Los Angeles/Long Beach,
  California 90731
Nogales, Arizona 85261
Portland, Oregon 97209
San Diego, California 92188
San Francisco, California
  94126
Seattle, Washington 98104

North Central Region
Chicago, Illinois 60603-5790

Districts:
Chicago, Illinois 60607
Cleveland, Ohio 44114
Detroit, Michigan
  48226-2568
Duluth, Minnesota
  55802-1390
Milwaukee, Wisconsin
  53237-0260
Minneapolis-St.Paul,
  Minnesota 55401
Pembina, North Dakota
  58271
St. Louis, Missouri 63105

Appendix G
Multilingual Reference Table

English	German	Spanish
ad valorem (*according to value*)	Ad Valorem	ad valorem (sobre el valor)
agent	Agent	agente
agreement	Zustimmung	acuerdo, convenio
airway bill	Luftfrachtbrief	guia aérea, conocimiento (de transporte) aéreo
arrival	Ankunft	llegada
balance sheet	Bilanz	balance
bank	Bank	banco
beneficiary	Begunstigter	beneficiario
bill of lading	Konnossement	conocimiento (de embarque)
broker	Makler	corredor
certificate	Bescheinigung, Zertifikat, Zeugnis	certificado
commodity	Ware, Artikel, Rohstoff	mercancia, producto
consignee	Empfänger	consignatario, destinatario
consignment	Sendung	expedición, envio
consignor	Absender	expedidor, consignador, remitente

French	Italian	Japanese
ad valorem	ad valorem	juka no
agent, commissionaire	agente	dairi nin
accord	accordo	goi
lettre de transport aérien (LTA)	lettera di trasport aereo (LTA)	koku kamotsu uketori sho
arrivée	arrivo	tochaku/chaku ni
bilan	bilancio	taishaku taisho hyo
banque	banca	ginko
bénéficiaire	beneficiario	uketori nin
connaissement	polizza di carico (P/C)	funani shoken
courtier	mediatore, intermediario	nakagai nin
certificat	certificato	shomei sho
marchandise, denrée, produit	merce, derrata, prodotto	shohin
consignataire, destinataire	consegnatario, destinatario	jutaku sha
expédition, envoi	spedizione, invio	hanbai itaku
expéditeur, consignateur	mittente, speditore	itakusha/ninushi

English	German	Spanish
consolidator (*groupage agent*)	Sammelladungs-spediteur	consolidador, agrupador
cost and freight	Kosten und Fracht	costo y flete
cost, insurance, freight	Kosten, Versicherung, Fracht	costo, seguro, flete
currency	Währung	moneda
customer	Kunde	cliente
customs	Zoll	aduana
date	Datum	fecha
delivered duty paid	geliefert verzollt	entregado libre de derechos
demurrage (*charges*)	Überliegegeld	(gastos de) sobreestadias, demoras
departure	Abfahrt, Abgang	salida, partida
discount (*on goods*)	Preisnachlass, Diskont	descuento (sobre la mercancia)
discrepancies	Abweichungen	discrepancias
dock	Dock, Hafenbecken	muelle
documents	Dokumente	documentos
documents against acceptance	Dokumente gegen Akzept	(entrega de) documentos contra aceplación
documents against payment	Dokumente gegen Zahlung	(entrega de) documentos contra pago
draft	Tratte, Wechsel	giro, letra

French	Italian	Japanese
groupeur	consolidatore (operatore di "groupage")	togo seirisha
coût et fret	costo e nolo	unchin komi nedan
CAF—coût, assurance, fret	costo, assicurazione e nolo	hokenryo unchin komi nedan
monnaie	moneta	tsuka
client	cliente	kokyaku
douane	dogana	zeikan
date	data	hizuke
rendu droits acquittés	reso sdoganato	kanzei shiharaizumi watashi
(idemnités de) surestaries	controstallie (indennitá)	teitai ryo
départ	partenza	shuppatsu/haihan
rabais, excompte	sconto (sul prezzo delle merci)	waribiki
irrégularités	discrepanze, divergenze	soi
bassin, dock	"dock," calata, bacino	dokku
documents	documenti	shorui
(remise des) documents contre acceptation	documenti contro accettazione (D/A)	hikiuke watashi
(remise des) documents contre paiement	documenti contro pagamento (D/P)	shiharai watashi
traite	tratta	tegata furidashi shita gaki (document)

English	German	Spanish
drawee	Bezogener	girado, librado (= persona)
drawer	Aussteller	girador, librador
duty, duties (*customs*)	Abgabe, (pl) Abgaben	derecho, impuesto (pl) derechos, impuestos
estimated time of arrival	voraussichtlicher Ankunftstermin	tiempo estimado de llegada
estimated time of departure	voraussichtlicher Abfahrtstermin	tiempo estimado de partida
ex ship	ab Schiff	ex, sobre buque
ex works	ab Werk	ex, en fábrica
excise	Verbrauchssteuer	derechos de consumo, impuesto sobre consumos
expiration	Ablauf	vencimiento
expiry date	Verfalldatum	fecha de vencimiento
foreign currency	Devisen	divisas
forwarder	Spediteur	transportista embarcador, expedidor de carga
forwarding	Spedition, Beförderung	expedición, despacho
free alongside ship	frei Längsseite Seeschiff	libre/franco al costado del buque
free on board	frei an Bord	libre/franco a bordo
import(ation)	Einfuhr	importación
invoice	Rechnung	factura
less than container load	Teil Containerladung	menos de contenedor completo

French	Italian	Japanese
liré (= personne)	trassato	tegata naate nin
tireur	traente	tegata furidashi nin
droit, (pl) droits	diritto/i doganale/i	kanzei
horaire d'arrivée prévu	tempo d'arrivo previsto	tochaku yotei jikoku
horaire de départ prévu	tempo di partenza previsto	shuppatsu yotei jikoku
ex ship, ex navire	ex ship	chakusen watashi
à l'usine	franco fabbrica	kojo watashi
accise	accisa, imposta di consumo	kokunai shohi zei
expiration	scadenza	kikan manryo/manki
date de validité	data di scadenza	tegata kaitori saishu bi
devises	divisa	gaika
transporteur, chargeur, expéditeur	spedizioniere	unso gyosha
expédition	spedizione	unso/kurikoshi
franco le long du navire	franco sottobordo	sensoku watashi
franco bord	franco a bordo	honsen watashi
importation	importazione	yunyu suru
facture	fattura	okurijo
charge incomplète du conteneur	carico incompleto del contenitore (di "groupage")	ichi knotena miman sekisai ryo

English	German	Spanish
letter of credit	Akkreditiv, Kreditbrief	carta de crédito
maturity	Fälligkeit	vencimiento
payee	Wechselnehmer	beneficiario, tomadór de una letra
permitted no/menkyo	gestattet	permitido
premium	Aufgeld, Agio	prima
rate	Deviserkurs	tasa
seller	Verkäufer	vendedor
sender	Absender	expedidor, remitente
shipment	Sendung	expedición, despacho
shipper (*consignor*)	Verlader	embarcador, cargador
shipper (*one who delivers goods to carrier*)	Absender	expedidor, remitente
trade	Handel	comercio
transfer (*money*)	Überweisung	giro

French	Italian	Japanese
lettre de crédit	lettera di credito (L/C)	shin-yo jo
échéance	scadenza	manki
preneur d'un effet, bénéficiaire	beneficiario	uketori nin
permis	consentito	kyokazumi no/menkyo sho o uketa
prime	premio	hoken ryo
cour	tasso, aliquota	wariai
vendeur	vendiatore	urite
expéditeur	speditore, caricatore	okurinushi
expédition, envoi	spedizione, invio	shukka
chargeur	caricatore	ni nushi
expéditeur	speditore	funagaisha dairi ten
commerce	commercio	torihiki
virement	trasferimento, rimessa	joto

Appendix H
Weights and Measures Conversion Table

U.S. Unit	Metric Equivalent
mile	1.609 kilometers
yard	0.914 meters
foot	30.480 centimeters
inch	2.540 centimeters
square mile	2.590 square kilometers
acre	0.405 hectares
square yard	0.836 square meters
square foot	0.093 square meters
square inch	6.451 square cenitmeters
cubic yard	0.765 cubic meters
cubic foot	0.028 cubic meters
cubic inch	16.387 cubic centimeters
short ton	0.907 metric tons
long ton	1.016 metric tons
short hundredweight	45.359 kilograms
long hundredweight	50.802 kilograms
pound	0.453 kilograms
ounce	28.349 grams
gallon	3.785 liters
quart	0.946 liters
pint	0.473 liters
fluid ounce	29.573 milliliters
bushel	35.238 liters
peck	8.809 liters
quart (dry)	1.101 liters
pint (dry)	0.550 liters

Appendix I
Currency Index

Currency*	Country
Afghani(s)	Afghanistan
Agoro/agorot	Israel
Ariary	Madagascar
Aurar	Iceland
Avo(s)	Macao
Baht	Thailand
Baisa	Oman, Pakistan
Balboa(s)	Panama
Ban(i)	Romania
Birr	Ethiopia
Bolivar(es)	Venezuela
Boliviano(s)	Bolivia
Butut	The Gambia
Cedi	Ghana
Cent(s)	Aruba, Australia, the Bahamas, Barbados, Belize, Bermuda, Brunei, Canada, Cayman Islands, Cook Island, Cyprus, East Caribbean, Ethiopia, Fiji Islands, Hong Kong, Jamaica, Kenya, Liberia, Malta, Mauritius, The Netherlands, New Zealand, Seychelles, Singapore, Soloman Islands, South Africa, Sri Lanka, Suriname, Swaziland, Trinidad and Tobago, United States of America, Zimbabwe
Centas (centai or centy)	Lithuania

---

*Italics indicate fractions (100 *cents* equal 1 dollar)

Escudo(s)	Cape Verde, Portugal
EURO	Austria, Belgium, Finland, France, Germany, Ireland, Italy, Luxembourg, Netherlands, Portugal, Spain
Eyrir	Iceland
Fen	People's Republic of China
Filler	Hungary
Fils	Bahrain, Iraq, Jordan, Kuwait, United Arab Emirates, Yemen
Florin	Aruba
Florint	Hungary
Franc(s)	Belgium, Burundi, Comoro Island, Djibouti, France, Guinea (Conarky), Liechtenstein, Luxembourg, Monaco, Rwanda, Switzerland
Franc(s) CFA Central	Cameroon, Central African Republic, Chad, Congo, Equatorial Guinea, Gabon
Franc(s) CFA West	Benin, Burkina Faso, Côte d'Ivoire, Mali, Niger, Senegal, Togo, West African States
Franc(s) CFP	French Polynesia, New Caledonia
Girsh	Sudan
Gourde(s)	Haiti
Grosch(en)	Austria
Gulden	The Netherlands, Netherlands Antilles, Suriname
Halala(s)	Saudi Arabia
Haler(u)	Czech Republic, Slovakia
Jiao	China, People's Republic
Kapeik	Belarus
Karbovanetz	Ukraine
Kina	Papua New Guinea
Kip(s)	Laos
Kobo	Nigeria
Korun(a)	Czech Republic, Slovakia
Krone(r)	Denmark, Norway
Krona(or)	Sweden

Króna(ur)	Faroe Islands, Iceland
Kroon(i)	Estonia
Kwacha	Malawi, Zambia
Kwanza(s)	Angola
Kyat	Myanmar
Laari	Maldives
Lat	Latvia
Lek(ë)	Albania
Lempira(s)	Honduras
Leone(s)	Sierra Leone
Leu(i)	Moldava, Romania
Lev(a)	Bulgaria
Lira(e)	Cyprus, Italy, Malta, Turkey, San Marino, Vatican City
Lisente	Lesotho
Litas (Litai or Lity)	Lithuania
Livre(s)	Lebanon
Loti	Lesotho
Luma	Armenia
Maloti	Lesotho
Manat	Azerbaijan
Mark	Germany
Markka(a)	Finland
Metica/Meticais	Mozambique
Millim	Tunisia
Naira	Nigeria
New Dong	Vietnam
Ngultrum	Nepal
Novo Kwanza	Angola
Nuevo(s) Peso(s)	Mexico, Uruguay
Øre	Denmark, Faroe Islands, Norway, Sweden
Ougiya	Mauritania
Pa'anga	Tonga
Paisa/paise	India, Nepal

Pataca(s)	Macao
Penni(ä)	Finland
Penny (pence)	England, Falkland/Malvinas Islands, Gibraltar, Guernsey, Ireland, Scotland, St. Helena
Peseta(s)	Spain
Peso(s)	Argentina, Chile, Colombia, Cuba, Dominican Republic, Guinea-Bissau, Mexico, Uruguay
Peso Uruguayo	Uruguay
Pfennig	Germany
Piaster(s)	Egypt, Syria
Piso	The Philippines
Poisha	Bangladesh
Pound(s)	Cyprus, Egypt, England, Falkland/Malvinas Islands, Gibraltar, Guernsey, Ireland, Isle of Man, Jersey, Northern Ireland, Scotland, St. Helena, Sudan, Syria
Pul	Afghanistan
Pula	Botswana
Punt	Ireland
Pya(s)	Myanmar
Qindar	Albania
Quetzal(es)	Guatemala
Rand	South Africa
Real	Brazil
Renminbi	China, People's Republic
Rial(s)	Iran
Rial(s)	Oman, Yemen
Riel(s)	Cambodia
Ringgit	Brunei, Malaysia
Rubel	Belarus
Ruble(s)	Georgia, Kazakhstan, Kirgiz Republic, Russia, Tajikistan, Turkmenistan, Uzbekistan
Rublis/Rubli/Rublu	Latvia
Rufiya(a)	Maldive Islands

Rupee(s)	India, Mauritius, Nepal, Pakistan, Seychelles, Sri Lanka
Rupiah	Indonesia
Satang	Thailand
Schilling	Austria
Sen	Malaysia
Sene	Western Samoa
Seniti	Tonga
Sent(i)	Estonia
Sente	Lesotho
Sentimo(s)	Philippines
Sheqel (sheqalim)	Israel
Shilin	Somalia
Shilling(s)	Kenya, Tanzania, Uganda
Sol(es)	Peru
Som	Kirgiz Republic, Tajikistan
Stotinka/stotinki	Bulgaria
Sucre	Ecuador
Taka	Bangladesh
Tambala	Malawi
Tanga	Kazakhstan
Thebe	Botswana
Toea	Papua New Guinea
Tolar(jev)	Slovenia
Toman	Iran
Tugrik	Mongolia
Tyyn	Kirgiz Republic
Vatu	Vanuatu
Won	DPR Korea, Republic of Korea
Yen	Japan
Yuan	China, People's Republic, Taiwan—Republic of China
Zaire(s)	Zaire
Zlote (zlotych)	Poland

Appendix J
International Business Resources on the World Wide Web

Gobal Economy: Background and News

ELECTRONIC EMBASSY
http://www.embassy.org a guide to all of the foreign embassies in Washington, DC. It is an excellent source for conducting country-specific business research.

EMERGING MARKETS COMPANION
http://www.emgmkts.com provides an on-line source of financial intelligence for investors in the Emerging Markets.

THE INTERNATIONAL LIST
http://www.internationalist.com a preferred site for various sources of information of interest for firms doing business internationally. It offers products, information, and web links of interest to international businesspersons.

WNC: WORLD NEWS CONNECTION
http://wnc.fedworld.gov an on-line news service from the various intelligence sources of the United States government. The site provides extensive news and information from around the world.

Import and Export Trade Information Sources

CIBERWEB
http://www3mgmt.purdue.edu/ciber the federal government of the United States supports the study of international business by funding 27 Centers for International Business Education and Research around the country. This site provides links to each individual CIBER's web site, also providing links to a large variety of other web sites of interest to the international businessperson.

INTERNATIONAL TRADE ADMINISTRATION, U.S. DEPARTMENT OF COMMERCE
http://www.ita.doc.gov the trade area of the U.S. Department of Commerce. The ITA provides support to U.S. businesses seeking to export their products or services through a variety of programs and information resources.

STAT-USA/INTERNET INFORMATION SYSTEM
http://www.stat-usa-gov subscription-based service operated by a division of the Department of Commerce; it is an excellent source of information for international marketers. It is a collection of business information from more than five federal agencies.

International Business Organizations and Directories

GLOBAL NETWORK OF CHAMBERS OF COMMERCE AND INDUSTRY
http://www.worldchambers.com/chamber.html a collection of links to Chambers of Commerce around the world. The site also hosts the Global Business Exchange, a limited collection of trade leads and business opportunities submitted by member organizations and their member companies.

INTERNATIONAL BUSINESS RESOURCES OF THE WWW
http://ciber.bus.msu.edu/busres/htm a site of international business resources maintained by Michigan State University. The links are divided into categories, providing a sizeable collection of country-specific information.

THE INTERNATIONAL CHAMBER OF COMMERCE
http://www.iccwbo.org introduces the organization and its members, but also provides a number of research and marketing tools useful to international businesspersons.

U.S. COUNCIL FOR INTERNATIONAL BUSINESS
http://www.uscob.org the site of the American affiliate of the International Chamber of Commerce; its role is to advance U.S. businesses in international markets.

WORLD TRADE ORGANIZATION
http://www.wto.org home page located on its server in Geneva, Switzerland. The site offers a variety of resources for those involved in international trade.

Reference Resources

AGRI MARKETING
http://www.agrimark.com worldwide agricultural information resource on-line. The site is divided by subject: markets, weather, news groups, newspapers and news sources, crops, and livestock. The site also covers each world region separately.

CHINESE LIBRARIES ON-LINE
http://online.anu.edu.au/Asia/Chi/ChiLib.html for on-line research at libraries in China, Hong Kong, Macau, Taiwan, and Singapore.

COLLEGENET
http://www.collegenet.com/ searchable database of 2,500 universities in the United States and Canada.

CURRENCY CONVERSIONS
http://www.dna.lth.se/cgi-bin/kurt/rates converts currencies of 40 countries.

GALAXY REFERENCE
http://galaxy.einet.net/galaxy/Reference.html a comprehensive listing of useful reference tools, including foreign dictionaries, thesauruses, grant information, books, documents, and other publications.

INTERNATIONAL DATABASE (IDB)
http://www.census.gov/ftp/pub/ipc/www/idbnew.html a computerized database containing statistical tables of demographic, socioeconomic data for all countries of the world.

INTERNATIONAL EXCELLENCE ON-LINE
http://www.tmisnet.com/~engholm/group.htm business information resource site that contains: Emerging Market News, Business Toolbox of Internet business search links to locate businesses worldwide, major business periodicals, U.S. economic data, market research and demographics, career development / job search, personal finance, and international entertainment reviews.

LOCAL TIMES AROUND THE WORLD
http://www.hilink.com.au/times/ on-line guide providing a list of local times in all of the world's countries and many of its islands. Times quoted as UTC offset do not consider Daylight Savings Time. Except for the Pacific and Caribbean Islands, islands are often included with the corresponding country listing, or with the nearest continent.

NATIONAL LIBRARY CATALOGS WORLDWIDE
http://www.uq.edu.au/~mljeast/ an on-line guide of national library catalogs alphabetically by country; provides information necessary to connect to the catalog.

RELOCATION SALARY CONVERTER
http://homefair.com/home/ the Relocation Wizard calculates in the local currency what you would need to earn, based on your present salary, if you were to relocate to any U.S. or major international location. The site also provides useful information about relocation expenses and how to prepare for and calculate them.

STATISTICAL DATA LOCATORS
http://www.ntu.edu.sg/library/statdata.htm a guide to locating sources of statistics for a country. Links to sources of statistics available from the Internet (economics, trade, demographics, and so on). Categories: Asia, Oceania, United States, Europe, Africa, and Global Metasites for statistics.

STATISTICS LINKS
http://www.cbs.nl/eng/link/index.htm links to foreign statistical agencies in Europe, the Americas, Africa, Asia, and Oceania.

THOMAS REGISTER
http://www.thomasregister.com the largest on-line industrial buying source; a database of American manufacturers with an internal search engine. Covers 155,000 companies and 55,000 product and service headings; 3,100 on-line supplier catalogs give 42,000 pages of detailed buying and specifying information.

U.S. LIBRARY OF CONGRESS
http://www.loc.gov/ access to the Library of Congress resources and links on the Internet.

VIRTUAL INTERNATIONAL BUSINESS AND ECONOMIC SOURCES (VIBES)
http://www.uncc.edu/lis/library/reference/intbus/vibehome.htm provides a list of links to sources of international business information. These include links to full-text files, statistical tables, and graphs on topics related to international business. Excellent reference source for country/industry/other international subject research.

THE WEB OF CULTURE
http://webofculture.com people exchanging insights into their native culture.

News and Periodicals On-line

ACCESS INDIA
http://www.india-times.com/accessindia/ daily business news from India.

ARAB NEWS ON-LINE
http://www.arab.net/arabnews/welcome.html daily international business and economic news, as well as sports and entertainment from the Middle East.

ARGUMENTY I FAKTY
http://www.russianstory.com/infcoll/aif/aif.htm weekly Russian newspaper providing in-depth analysis of Russian political and economic events and published interviews with key people in Russia.

ASIA PACIFIC ECONOMIC REVIEW
http://www.moshix2.net/APER/ a U.S.-based international business magazine focused on the Asia Pacific region.

ASIAN NEWS BOOKMARK
http://www.asiatown.com/news/news.htm comprehensive list of on-line Asian newspapers and magazines.

ATHENS NEWS AGENCY ARCHIVE
http://www.hri.org/ana/ daily news releases from the Athens News Agency focusing on business and political news.

THE AUSTRALIAN FINANCIAL REVIEW
http://www.afr.com.au/index.html review of markets, industries, and companies, in Australia.

BRAZIL SPECIAL REPORT
http://www.usbrazil.com/report/ monthly magazine, covering news, trends, trade, and calendar of events in Brazil.

BUSINESS LINE INDIA
http://www.indiaserver.com/news/bline/bline.html India's business newspaper.

CANADA NEWSWIRE
http://www.newswire.ca/ real-time Canadian news release database searchable by industry, company name, category, subject, or key words.

CANADIAN CORPORATE NEWS
http://www.cdn-news.com on-line database of Canadian companies, including archives and the ability to search.

CENTRAL EUROPE ON-LINE
http://www.centraleurope.com/ daily business and political news source for Central European countries.

CHANNEL A—ASIAN BUSINESS
http://www.channela.com/business/index.html on-line news site providing a large variety of information on Asian business, from news to commentaries, to information articles and "how-to" guides.

CHINA BUSINESS AND INVESTMENT UPDATE
http://www.china-invest.com/cbiu/cbiu.html on-line newsletter designed to assist readers in understanding Chinese laws and regulations related to business and investments.

DAILY TELEGRAPH
http://www.telegraph.co.uk on-line version of the *Daily Telegraph* of London.

THE ECONOMIST
http://www.economist.com/ the on-line home for a limited selection of articles from the current issue of the *Economist Review*, a monthly books and multimedia supplement to *The Economist*, and several surveys.

FAR EASTERN ECONOMIC REVIEW
http://www.feer.com/ covers Asian current affairs, business, economies, and investing. The site includes many of the magazine's key stories, as well as live market information from Dow Jones Telerate, the FEER's many other products and services, and other useful information resources. Includes search and archival facilities. Registration is required, but free.

FINANCIAL TIMES
http://www.ft.com/ world financial and economic news reported by the U.K.'s best business newspaper. Free registration.

GLOBES
http://www.globes.co.il Israel's largest business newspaper, continuously updated.

HONG KONG TRADER
http://www.tdc.org.hk trade and economic news from the Hong Kong Trade Development Center.

THE HUNGARY REPORT
http://www.isys.hu/hrep weekly e-mail newsletter about Hungary, providing information on current events, business news, and other features.

INTERNATIONAL NEWSPAPERS ON-LINE
http://inkpot.com/news/ links to over 400 international newspapers, categorized by country.

THE IRISH TIMES
http://www.irish-times.ie Ireland's daily national newspaper with coverage and analysis of politics, finance, foreign news, sports, and the arts.

THE JERUSALEM POST INTERNET EDITION—BUSINESS SECTION
http://www.jpost.co.il/Business business headlines, stock market reports, and company news from Israel.

LONDON TIMES and SUNDAY TIMES
http://www.the-times.co.uk on-line version of the British newspaper.

NIKKEI NET
http://www.nikkei.co.jp/enews primary business information source for top corporate executives and decision makers in Japan. This site is an on-line version of five newspapers covering business news and financial markets in Japan.

THE PRESS
http://www.press.co.nz business and financial news from New Zealand.

SCANDANAVIA ON-LINE
http://www.elfco.se/scandnow/ business, financial, and industry news for Sweden, Norway, Finland, and Denmark.

THE SCOTSMAN
http://www.scotsman.com/index.html an on-line newspaper from Scotland.

SINGAPORE TRADE NEWS
http://www.tdb.gov.sg/stn/stn_main.html bimonthly publication of the Singapore Trade Development Board.

TURKISH DAILY NEWS CONNECTIONS
http://www/turkey/org/turkey/current.htm a collection of political, economic, and business news from Turkey, compiled by the Turkish Embassy in Washington, DC.

UN NEWS
http://www/un.org/News/ daily coverage of events at the United Nations.

THE WARSAW VOICE
http://www.warsawvoice.com Poland and Central European business review, English-language weekly newspaper.

International Law Resources

CHINA: LAW ON-LINE
http://www.lawhk.hku.hk Chinese-oriented law and business information, in English and Chinese.

FEDWORLD
http://www.fedworld.gov/ government information, documents, and files; access to more than 14,000 files including information on business, health and safety, and the environment.

NAFTA COMMISSION FOR ENVIRONMENTAL COOPERATION (CEC)
http://www.cec.org research site for laws, treaties, and agreements for NAFTA regarding the environment; provides a database for answering environmental questions, supplies books and reports, periodicals, and related environmental and NAFTA Internet links.

SOUTH AFRICA—DENEYS REITZ ATTORNEYS
http://www.deneysreitz.co.za/ on-line site providing a summary of the law in South Africa.

THE U.S. HOUSE OF REPRESENTATIVES INTERNET LAW LIBRARY
http://law.house.gov on-line site providing the complete text of public regulations issued by the agencies of the federal government.

UNITED NATIONS COMMISSION ON INTERNATIONAL TRADE LAW
http://www.un.or.at/uncitral/ home page of the International Trade Law Branch of the United Nations Office of Legal Affairs servicing the United Nations Commission on International Trade Law (UNCITRAL).

THE WORLD LIST
http://www.law.osaka-u.ac.jp/legal-info/worldlist.html non U.S. law-related on-line resources, covering more than 50 countries.

WORLDWIDE LEGAL INFORMATION ASSOCIATION (WWLIA) LEGAL DICTIONARY
http://wwlia.org/diction.htm alphabetical index listing and dictionary of legal terms in an international context; includes links to law information sites in the Pacific, United Kingdom, Canada, and the United States. On-line international law magazine, and comprehensive directory of law firm home pages on the Internet.

Entrepreneur and Small Business On-line

THE BUSINESS HOTLINE ON-LINE (Hawaii)
http://www.bizhotline.com a free business publication covering important topics facing small and home-based businesses. Topics include marketing tips, MLM, franchising, business opportunities, legal issues, accounting, finance, marketing on the Internet, advertising, and international trade.

INTERNATIONAL SMALL BUSINESS CONSORTIUM (ISBC)
http://www.isbc.com/ a volunteer organization that assists small businesses worldwide in competing in international markets; also a small business directory with a search engine that enables businesses to locate and match product/service needs. The directory search engine can help small businesses locate distributors, agents, and representatives.

NAFTANET: NEW WEB SITE FOR SMALL BUSINESS
http://www.nafta.net the first electronic commerce port of trade geared to small and medium-sized business enterprises interested in international trade. NAFTANet potentially reduces trading costs and turnaround time using EC/EDI.

THE SMALL BUSINESS JOURNAL
http://www.tsbj.com an on-line magazine for small business owners and entrepreneurs; includes information on finance, sales and marketing, taxation, management, technology, business ethics, software reviews, and so on.

SMALL BUSINESS NEWS ON-LINE
http://www.hotspots.hawaii.com/SBH_on_H4/SBNews896.html provides year-round business information and legislative services through the Legislative Action Committee (LAC) and Biz Fax Net.

SMALL BUSINESS RESOURCE CENTER
http://www.retailadvz.com provides entrepreneurs with a comprehensive list of interactive on-line management resources, and "how-to" management guides for small businesses.

Foreign Language Resources

ARABIC AND MIDDLE EAST DISTANCE LEARNING
http://www.eigc.com/mamdouh/mamdouh.htm information concerning Arab-language, Middle East information, magazines, and newspapers for Arab organizations.

CHINESE-LANGUAGE-RELATED INFORMATION PAGE
http://www.webcom.com/~bamboo/chinese/chinese.html a comprehensive navigational tool that aids in accessing Chinese language-related resources.

CULTURAL ITALIAN AMERICAN ORGANIZATION (CIAO)
http://www.umich.edu/~newitclu links to Italy-related web sites.

ERGANE
http://www.travlang.com/Ergane/erganeen.htm a program that can be downloaded and that can translate words and short expressions from one language to another.

FOREIGN LANGUAGE LEARNING CENTER
http://fllc.smu.edu an extensive list of web sites related to the Spanish language as it is spoken in Spain, Mexico, and South America.

FOREIGN LANGUAGES FOR TRAVELERS
http://llwww.travlang.com/languages site for learning the basics of a foreign language; also provides access to the pronunciation of many popular phrases.

FOREIGN LANGUAGES LEARNING CENTER
http://fllc.smu.edu/languages/japanese.html provides access to all types of Japanese-language web sites.

THE HUMAN LANGUAGES PAGE
http://www.june29.com/HLP/ a comprehensive catalog of language-related Internet resources. Over 1,400 HLP databases; an extensive list of the best language links the Web has to offer.

INTRODUCTION TO JAPANESE
http://www.j-world.com/jp/lang/japanese.html comprehensive list of web sites concerning Japanese language, Japanese learning, and Japanese computing.

ITALIAN LANGUAGE AND CULTURE
http://www.tcom.ohiou.edu/OU_Language/italian/ an extensive list of Italian language and culture sites.

JAPANESE CHARACTERS ON SCREEN
http://central.itp.berkeley.edu/~eal/jpchar.html access to different methods of displaying Japanese characters on screen.

LANGUAGES LINK
http://webpages.marshall.edu/~jmullens/lang.html comprehensive list of sites pertaining to various Chinese languages, including access to magazines, books, and so on.

MY FAVORITE MULTIMEDIA INSIDE CHINESE LANGUAGE LAB
http://peijean.ficnet.net.tw an exciting way to learn the Chinese language on-line; requires sound downloading and playing capability.

Regional/Country Specific Information

North America
DEPARTMENT OF FOREIGN AFFAIRS
AND INTERNATIONAL TRADE (CANADA)
http://www.dfait-maeci.gc.ca combines the functions of the U.S. Department of State and the Department of Commerce's International Trade Administration into a single ministry; answers a wide variety of frequently posed questions regarding trade with Canada.

Latin America
LATINOLINK
http://www.latinolink.com a web resource for business and general users of Latino descent. The business section provides coverage of border business events as well as the business climate in Central and Latin America.

MEXICAN CONSULATE IN NEW YORK CITY
http://www.quicklink.com/mexico offers a smart and user-friendly, English-language web site for businesspersons interested in Mexico; provides information of investment opportunities, trade regulations, and current state of the Mexican business climate.

MEXICO TRADE
http://www.mexico-trade.com brought by the Trade Commission of Mexico in Los Angeles; a handy and comprehensive set of links to business sites pertaining to Mexico. From this site one can link directly to Mexican exporters, secure information of NAFTA, a trade show calendar, government agencies in Mexico, and many other web sites related to commercial activity in Mexico.

SIMPEX
http://mexico.businessline.gob.mx an extensive on-line database maintained by BancoMex, the Mexican Bank for Foreign Trade. It offers information on foreign trade with Mexico, including import/export regulations and financing options. This is also a directory of over 4,000 Mexican firms seeking foreign trading or investment partners.

U.S. COMMERCIAL SERVICE IN MEXICO
http:www.uscommerce.org.mx maintained by the office of the U.S. foreign commercial service at the American Embassy in Mexico City. It provides direct contact to country officers who work in Mexico promoting U.S. business interests and trade between the two countries.

Specialized Resources for
Latin American Countries

AMERICAN CHAMBER OF COMMERCE—BRAZIL
http:www.amcham.com.br provides a summary of current business conditions and a directory of the Chamber's members, including foreign-owned companies, Brazilian business, and joint venture partnerships.

ARGENTINA: EL SUR DEL SUR
http://www.surdelsur.com provides general information about the Argentine Republic (in English and Spanish).

BRAZILIAN WEB RESOURCES
http://www.brazilnuts.com a collection of links to Internet resources related to Brazil, accompanied by a description of each site.

CHILEAN-AMERICAN CHAMBER OF COMMERCE
http://www.business1.com/cacc/english/welcome.htm a San Francisco-based trade organization that offers advice on doing business in Chile; provides updates on current business conditions and a list of contacts looking to do business with the United States.

DOING BUSINESS IN BRAZIL
http://www.brazilbiz.com.br/english/ an on-line database of Brazilian businesses that can be searched by product category from agriculture to travel agencies, or the search engine can be used to find a company name.

Asia and Japan (including India)
ASIA'S BUSINESS CONNECTION
http://asiabiz.com a large compilation of links to business information about, and business entities in, the Asia Pacific region. Importers and exporters will find hundreds of links to Asia-oriented manufacturers, trading companies, business services, and so on. Links can be browsed by country, industry, or business service category, or a search can be conducted by company name.

ASIA BUSINESS NEWS
http://www.asia-online.com/index1.html offers headlines and breaking news for Asia and Pacific Rim countries.

ASIA NET
http://asiapacific.com provides business channels, on-line country information, current trade updates, and more for all Asian countries.

ASIA ONE
http://asia1.com.sg/ provides extensive information on Asia.

ASIAN DEVELOPMENT BANK
http://www.asiandevbank.org/index/html extensive amount of information of the 56-member, development financial institution.

FOCUS ASIA—ASIA DIRECTORY AND USER SERVICE
http:www.focusasia.com company names, trade names, and product services from the Asia Directory. Information is categorized by business, leisure, government, education, and region.

HONG KONG EXPORTERS ON-LINE
http://www.exp.com.hk/ for international traders interested in sourcing products from manufacturers and brokers in Hong Kong.

HONG KONG PRODUCT CATALOGUE
http://www.hkstar.com/~rado/hkpc/product.html a directory of Hong Kong manufacturers and product brokers, organized by product category. Individuals can review available products, preview upcoming trade shows, or post a trade inquiry. Available product categories include electronic products, industrial supplies, and most consumer goods.

INDIA ON-LINE
http://www.IndiaOnline.com provides international marketers with current information regarding India's business climate and actual trade leads; a useful site for businesspeople seeking interaction with Indian counterparts.

INTERNET GUIDE TO JAPAN INFORMATION RESOURCES
http://fuju.stanford.edu/XGUIDE an extensive menu of Japanese sites offered by the U.S.-Japan Technology Management Center at Stanford University.

JAPAN ECONOMIC TRENDS, INDUSTRY, MARKETS, AND BUSINESS PRACTICES
http://www.jetro/go/jp/japan/index.html only one of the several Internet resources offered by the Japan External Trade Organization (JETRO); provides the most focused coverage of conducting business with Japan, and combines market research information with a step-by-step guide to exporting to Japan.

JAPAN WINDOW (AT STANFORD)
http://www/jwindow.net a collaborative effort between Stanford University and Nippon Telegraph and Telephone Corporation; an excellent source of information for learning about and doing business with Japan.

KOREA.COM
http://www.korea.com of value to travelers and businesspeople, where they can find out about Korean culture and events, as well as read selected articles of Internet technologies for doing business on the Web.

SINGAPORE ON-LINE
http://www.singapore.com/cgibin/var/online/var.htm provides users with an extensive variety of quality information on doing business with Singapore.

The Middle East
INTERACTIVE BUSINESS DIRECTORY OF ISRAEL
http://www.Chamber/org/il the Federation of Israeli Chambers of Commerce provides this interactive business directory for foreign companies seeking business partners in Israel.

ISRAEL'S INFOMEDIA
http://www.ibc.co.il provides a collection of links to web sites in Israel organized by business and subject categories.

Europe
BIZ*NET INFORSERVICES (GREECE)
http://www.biznet.com/gr/ provides a variety of information on Greece and Greek businesses.

EUROLINK
http:www.syselog.com/eurolink an excellent guide to finding information on the World Wide Web for specific European countries. Through Eurolink one can access an index of web sites from more than 16 different European nations.

EUROPA (THE EUROPEAN UNION)
http:wwweurops.eu.int/index.htm a World Wide Web server run by the member institutions of the European Union; disseminates information about the EU's policies and endeavors to the Internet community. Researchers seeking a specific topic regarding the European Union can run a key word search on the entire site's contents.

EUROPA'S CONSUMER GUIDE TO THE EUROPEAN SINGLE MARKET
http://www.europa.eu.int/en/comm/spc/cg/index/htm a guide where individuals can find information on legislation relating to the European Union; provides an overview of how consumers are treated under the European Union regime.

GENEVA GUIDE
http://isoft.ch/GenevaGuide/ an on-line directory of businesses in Switzerland, indexed by region and industry.

SWEDEN ON-LINE
http://www.swedentrade.com a collection of information resources and links related to Sweden. Visitors to the site can get updated information on business news, search for a Swedish company, or post a business inquiry.

UK DEPARTMENT OF TRADE AND INDUSTRY
http://www.dti.gov.uk the Department of Trade and Industry (DTI) is the British equivalent of the U.S. Department of Commerce. One of the functions of the DTI web site is to provide assistance to foreign companies seeking to do business in Great Britain.

Eastern Europe
CHAMBER OF COMMERCE & INDUSTRY OF ROMANIA
http://www.G77TIN.org/Romcchip.html the site of the national economic and trade organization of Romania; it disseminates financial and economic data on Romania.

CROATIAN CHAMBER OF ECONOMY
http://www1.usa1.com/~ibnet/hrccehp.html based in Zagreb, Croatia; offers an overview of CCE services and an index of books, reports, and other publications available pertaining to the Croatian economy and business climate.

CZECH INFO CENTER
http://www.muselik.com of interest to anyone interested in the Czech Republic's history, culture, and so on; one can also access a wide variety of business information by visiting the Information Resource Center and pressing on Business and Commerce. A number of useful links will come up, including those for a directory of companies, a government directory, and information on exporting and importing.

THE HUNGARIAN HOME PAGE
http://www.fsz/bme.hu/hungary/homepage/html provides a collection of links to non-web resources related to Hungary on the Internet; there is also a group of foreign web sources on Hungary that may be useful to the business researcher.

ROMANIA: ROMANIAN CYBERSPACE
http://www.yi.com/home/MiroiuAlex/romania.html a large directory of links with access to news, information, company directories, telephone directories (including e-mail addresses), and a list of professionals involved in economic and business development in Romania and Moldava.

Russia and the Newly Independent States
THE BALTICS ON-LINE
http://www.viabalt.ee/ a review of politics, economics, and culture in the Baltics, as provided by a server in Estonia. A separate section provides commercial news and lists business opportunities.

BISNIS
http://www.itaiep.doc.gov.bisnis/bisnis/html BISNIS stands for the Business Information Service for the Newly Independent States, created and maintained by the U.S. Department of Commerce. The site has been categorized as the "one-stop shop" for doing business in Russia and the other states of the former Soviet Union.

UKRAINE: UkraiNET
http://www.ukrainet.org a virtual directory of Ukrainian resources on the Internet; directory of business links, economic interests, investments, industries, news, politics, maps, literature, and history.

UZBEKISTAN: CYBER UZBEKISTAN
http://www.cu-online-com/~k a/uzbekistan contains all of the links and resources needed to research and do business with Uzbekistan.

Africa
AFRICA DATA DISSEMINATION SERVICE
http://wdcintl.cr.usgs.gov/adds/adds/html information by geographic area, region/country/data for the African continent.

AFRICA DOT.COM
http://africa.com provides travel and business information on South Africa in addition to links to South African businesses, property listings, and a list of trade leads.

AFRICA INTELLIGENCE
http://www.indigo-net.com/africa.html the first professional web on Africa; offers exclusive news on political and economic events in Africa. Updated almost daily.

SOUTH AFRICA SEARCH ENGINE
http://www.anazi.co.za South Africa's official web site directory. "Ananzi," for Internet links to businesses and industry, government, and research organizations.

More selected BARRON'S titles:

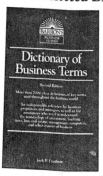